Last of the Empires

In this book, John Keep gives a narrative history of the USSR from the last years of Stalin's despotic rule to the eventual collapse of the empire in 1991. During these years living standards slowly improved as various attempts were made to reform Communist rule. Although material prosperity rose under Khrushchev and Breshnev, the Communist system began to erode as official ideology grew less relevant to people's everyday concerns; the Party lost its moral authority. The early 1980s saw a growing black market economy, incompetent management, and agricultural waste. When control passed to pragmatic, younger leaders like Gorbachev, their attempts to reinvigorate the economy by appealing to the intelligentsia opened a Pandora's box of conflicting opinions. The Party surrendered its monopoly of power, central institutions crumbled, and the centrifugal forces emanating from national minorities culminated in the empire's downfall.

OPUS General Editors
Christopher Butler
Robert Evans
John Skorupski

OPUS books provide concise, original, and authoritative introductions to a wide range of subjects in the humanities and sciences. They are written by experts for the general reader as well as for students.

John Keep has studied and lectured in Russian History for many years. He was a research assistant with the Foreign Office from 1953–4, a lecturer in Modern Russian History at the University of London between 1954 and 1966, and Reader in Russian Studies there from 1966 to 1970. In 1964 he became a Visiting Associate Professor at the University of Washington, Seattle, and he was Professor of Russian History at the University of Toronto between 1970 and 1988. He has now retired. His previous publications include *The Rise of Social Democracy in Russia* (Clarendon Press, 1963), *Contemporary History in the Soviet Mirror* (edited with L. Brisby in 1964), *The Russian Revolution: A Study in Mass Mobilization* (1976), and *Soldiers of the Tsar: Army and Society in Russia, 1462–1874* (Clarendon Press, 1985).

Last of the Empires

A History of the Soviet Union

1945–1991

John L. H. Keep

Oxford   New York

OXFORD UNIVERSITY PRESS

1996

Oxford University Press, Walton Street, Oxford OX2 6DP

Oxford New York
Athens Auckland Bangkok Bombay
Calcutta Cape Town Dar es Salaam Delhi
Florence Hong Kong Istanbul Karachi
Kuala Lumpur Madras Madrid Melbourne
Mexico City Nairobi Paris Singapore
Taipei Tokyo Toronto
and associated companies in
Berlin Ibadan

Oxford is a trade mark of Oxford University Press

First published by Oxford University Press 1995
First issued as an Oxford University Press paperback 1996

British Library Cataloguing in Publication Data
Data available

Library of Congress Cataloging in Publication Data
Keep, John L. H.
Last of the empires: a history of the Soviet Union, 1945–1991 /
John L. H. Keep
p. cm.
Includes bibliographical references and index.
1. Soviet Union—History. I. Title.
DK267.K38 1995 947.084—dc20 94-37237
ISBN 0-19-289237-1

10 9 8 7 6 5 4 3 2 1

Printed in Great Britain

Acknowledgements

Several friends and colleagues kindly read parts of the manuscript of this book before publication and made helpful suggestions. Special thanks are due to the following: Jane Ellis, Raymond Hutchings, Alexei Litvin, Alastair McAuley, Martin McCauley, Peter Reddaway, John Massey Stewart, Harry Rigby, Alfred Steinegger, and Boris Thomson. None of them are to blame for its shortcomings, for which responsibility is mine alone. My final privilege is to pay tribute to the support and encouragement given by my wife Ann, who did more to make this book possible than I had any right to expect.

Contents

viii   *Contents*

List of Tables

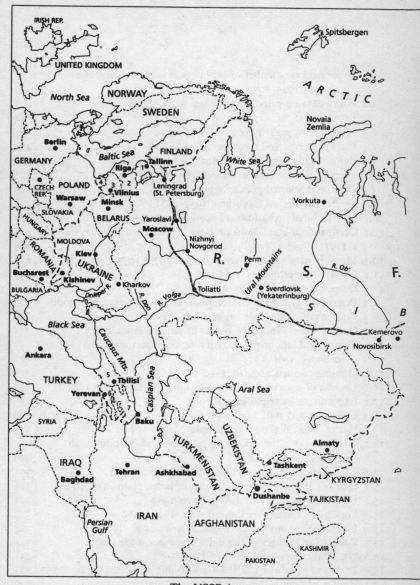

The USSR in 1991

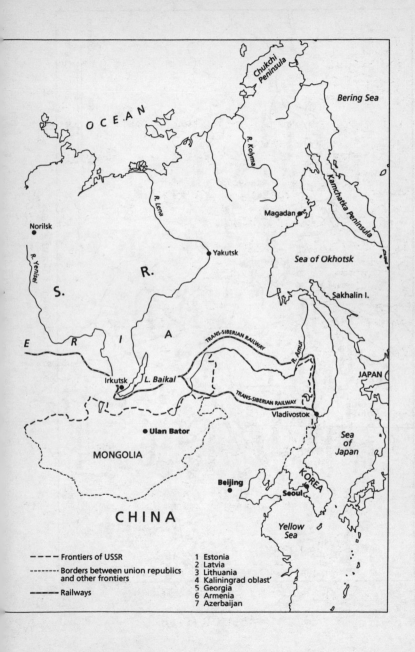

O C E A N

Chukchi
Peninsula

Bering Sea

R. Kolyma

Kamchatka Peninsula

Norilsk

R. Lena

S. R.

Magadan

R. Yenisei

Yakutsk

Sea of Okhotsk

S.

E R I A

Sakhalin I.

TRANS-SIBERIAN RAILWAY

R. Amur

JAPAN

Irkutsk   L. Baikal

TRANS-SIBERIAN RAILWAY

Vladivostok

Ulan Bator

Sea
of
Japan

MONGOLIA

Beijing

KOREA

Seoul

CHINA

Yellow
Sea

- - - - Frontiers of USSR

- - - - - Borders between union republics
and other frontiers

——— Railways

1 Estonia
2 Latvia
3 Lithuania
4 Kaliningrad oblast'
5 Georgia
6 Armenia
7 Azerbaijan

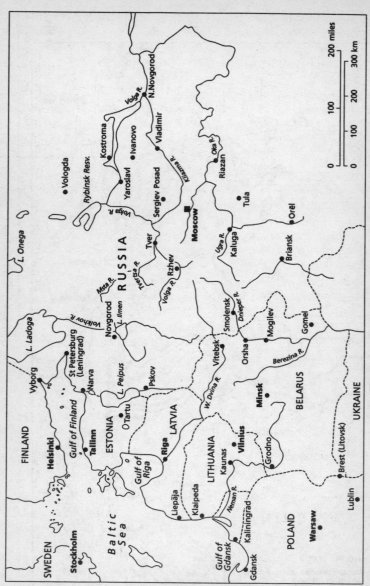

The Baltic States and adjoining lands

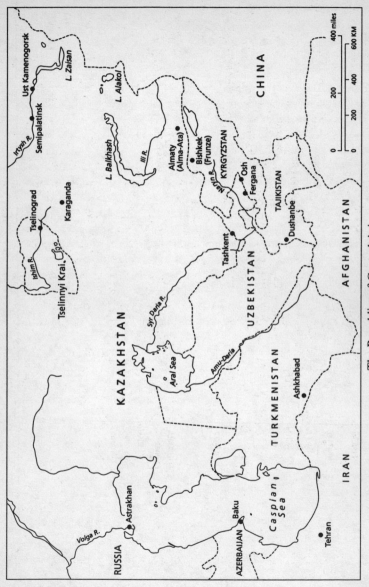

The Republics of Central Asia

Introduction

This is a narrative history of the USSR from the end of World War II to its collapse in 1991. It has been designed with the general reader in mind and does not set out to be comprehensive; foreign affairs and defence issues have been excluded. The emphasis is on the central themes of political, economic, social, and cultural development, with a good deal of attention being paid to the key problem of inter-ethnic relations. For whatever else the Soviet Union may have been, it was certainly an empire—although one of a peculiar kind, since it cost Russians dear as well as non-Russians. There were more than one hundred nationalities in the USSR: we deal here only with those that held union-republic status, especially the Baltic peoples and those of Central Asia. Whether the USSR was indeed the *last* empire, as our title suggests, only the future will show, but at least any future multinational state in this region will be based on intellectual and institutional foundations different from those of the Soviet era.

The state ideology of Marxism-Leninism, the Communist Party's organizational practices, the workings of the governmental system and the 'planned' or command economy—all these topics are the subject of a vast literature by Western specialists. We have made use of this 'sovietological' expertise, complementing it wherever possible by new information that has become available since 1988, when the mantle of Soviet secrecy began to lift. Historians and publicists in what is now the Commonwealth of Independent States are currently hard at work exploring the vast archival resources that have recently become accessible. It will take decades before their labours, and those of scholars from other lands, bear monographic fruit. We are at the beginning of a new era of independent historical inquiry. But that is no excuse for not trying to sum up what is now generally known, even if we are still too close to events to be able to judge them with proper objectivity. In the mid-1990s the defects of the Stalinist and post-Stalinist regimes loom larger than their successes. The perspective may change in the decades to come. This survey can be no more than a provisional one.

In Part I we consider briefly the last years of Josef Stalin's despotic rule. No attempt is made here to explore the origins of Stalinism or its links with Lenin's revolutionary bolshevism. There are many other works which examine these matters with great sophistication. This chapter serves as an introduction to the examination in Part II of Nikita Khrushchev's abortive attempts to reform (but not necessarily to liberalize) Communist rule. In some ways the period 1953–64 was an optimistic era, marked by a relaxation of police terror and an improvement in living standards, especially for townspeople. The peasants, organized in a rigidly controlled network of state and collective farms, were the object of much concern on the authorities' part, but in the last resort all their efforts produced little in the way of concrete results. In intellectual and cultural life, too, the record was mixed.

Under Khrushchev educated society was just beginning to recover from the ravages of Stalinism. In the late 1960s, after his fall from power, it became an active participant in public life. The so-called 'dissidents' in the human rights movement, though few in number, expressed the yearnings of millions for a greater measure of individual autonomy and emancipation from tutelage by an omnipresent state. Accordingly in Part III (1964–85) our attention shifts downward from the élite to the lower reaches of Soviet society. Leonid Brezhnev's long tenure of power (1964–82) brought greater material prosperity but marked a setback to popular aspirations for change in other respects. Censorship and police controls were reinforced. Yet subtly the system was being eroded. The official ideology became less relevant than ever to people's everyday concerns. The Party lost moral authority as corruption spread through its ranks. Thousands of illicit entrepreneurs learned how to by-pass the centrally regulated 'socialist' sector of the economy, which could not satisfy consumers' growing demands. Management was often incompetent and waste rife, especially in the agricultural sector. Politicians and planners continued to give priority to investment in heavy industry, not least in order to enhance the USSR's vast military buildup. It gradually dawned on Soviet citizens that this lopsided development was exacting a heavy cost on the environment as well as on consumers. Public concern at the destruction of non-renewable resources, such as Lake Baikal or the Aral Sea, fuelled the appetite for radical change, especially among non-Russians. For these peoples had now acquired, or re-acquired, élites whose members were increasingly conscious of their lost national heritage. They often managed to press their interests behind the scenes, and where their efforts were blocked this added to their frustration.

In 1985 a younger and more pragmatic group of Soviet leaders, symbolized by Mikhail Gorbachev, took over. The chequered fate of their reform policies is the subject of Part IV. In the hope of reinvigorating the economy and undercutting hard-liners in the Party apparatus, Gorbachev turned for support to the intelligentsia. But relaxation of thought control released pent-up popular demand for freedom of opinion. A Pandora's box had been opened. Reflective Soviet citizens wanted to learn the truth about the regime's past abuses and present shortcomings. In 1989 the USSR forfeited its 'external empire' in Eastern Europe. Under pressure from below the Party surrendered its monopoly of power and moved hesitantly towards pluralism and constitutional government. But even the most skilful political manœuvring could not save Gorbachev and his cause of a reformed, 'democratic' Communism. As the central institutions crumbled, the national minorities vociferously claimed their rights and in 1991 centrifugal pressures brought about the empire's collapse.

Such in outline is the story told here. Running through it like a red thread is the legacy of Stalin's terror—the regime's guilty secret, as it were. Some nineteen million persons perished, perhaps even more, at the state's hands during his ascendancy. Khrushchev began to make amends by releasing the surviving prisoners. But the process of 'rehabilitation' was conducted in secret and was not taken to its logical conclusion lest it destabilize the regime. The secret police machinery remained in being, as did some of the forced-labour camps in what Solzhenitsyn so memorably christened the 'Gulag Archipelago'. During the Brezhnev era the Committee for State Security (KGB), under its stern and wily master Yurii Andropov, refined its repressive apparatus. There was no return to mass terror on the scale of the 1930s, but the security establishment kept close watch on the population and bent the law to serve its own purposes. It was potentially stronger than the Party it served. If Andropov had sought to advance his political ambitions earlier than he did, we contend, Soviet and world history would have run a very

different course. As it was, the KGB initially backed Gorbachev—
and managed to survive his fall more easily than the CPSU did. The
new, constitutional Russia of Boris Yeltsin would still face problems in ensuring that officials observed the law or that prisoners were
treated humanely. In Russia respect for the rights of the individual
has seldom rested on firm foundations. It will take generations
before the country can shake off the legacy of seven decades of
arbitrary rule. Over much of this period the regime can, in our view,
properly be characterized as 'totalitarian'.

This term is still controversial. It was bitterly rejected by the
generation of 'sovietologists' that came to the fore in the late 1960s,
particularly in the United States. (It was far less of an issue among
their peers in continental Europe.) The reasons for this have to do
in part with changing intellectual fashions. Scholarship on the
Communist countries could not remain indifferent to such agoniz-
ing contemporary issues as the Vietnam war or the 'events of '68'.
As in so many other spheres of life, established authorities were
called in question and there was a search for new values. Historians
were urged to pay more heed to developments in sociology and
other social sciences. 'Revisionism' in Soviet studies was a healthy
reaction to an excessively political emphasis in some earlier work.
It showed that broad elements in Soviet society participated actively
in implementing the regime's policies. But it failed to consider who
bore moral responsibility for activities that were by any standards
unethical and even criminal. Sometimes revisionism took an extreme
form, as when scholars who took an interest in law, religion,
military studies or diplomacy were held up to ridicule as 'cold
warriors'. Responding to these attacks, some political scientists
came up with alternatives to the term 'totalitarianism', with its
negative associations, and suggested 'mono-organizational society'
(T. H. Rigby) or 'mobilized society' (R. Orr)—or else offered more
sophisticated definitions than earlier scholars had provided of the
salient characteristics of such a system.

By the mid-1980s the controversy seemed to be losing its emotional force as a more balanced approach gained ground. To the
embarrassment of the revisionists, once Soviet (and other East
European) historians and publicists were free to contemplate the
recent past, many of them adopted the approach and terminology
of the so-called 'totalitarian school' (which, let it be said, never
existed as such!). This support is not in itself evidence in favour of

the correctness of any particular interpretation, but it helped to push back the pendulum of Western opinion, a movement already launched by the public reaction to Solzhenitsyn's work and other developments. A. J. Motyl (1992) lists this support as one of three reasons why the term should be retained—not as a *model*, for which it is insufficiently grounded in social theory, but as a *concept* or 'typological construct', which is useful when drawing international analogies. The other reasons he gives are that: (*a*) it suggests total control of society as at least an aspiration on the regime's part, if not an actuality; and (*b*) it has moral overtones which ought not to be a matter of indifference to social scientists. R. Karklins (1994) argues that the concept has a 'dynamic side' wrongly denied by its critics, and that resort to it can help to explain why the regime collapsed. Yu. I. Igritsky (1993) offers Russian readers a fresh definition of the term and argues that 'Bolshevik Russia was distinguished by the practical incorporation of intentions that were totalitarian in aim and scope'. The debate continues.

Labels can confuse as much as they clarify. Historians should avoid the temptation to fit their material into any preordained theoretical categories, which can at best serve as guideposts. In these pages we are concerned with the history not of Communism but of the Soviet Union. We shall avoid abstractions as far as possible and try to depict concrete reality, which is always complex and contradictory. In doing so one cannot but be aware that one is merely scraping the surface of one of the most tragic experiences in human history, to which only a moral philosopher or theologian could do justice.

Note.

The terms 'minority', 'native', 'empire', and 'patriot' are used here in a neutral sense and have no positive or negative implications. The pronoun 'he' and its other forms, when not used in a gender-specific sense, refer to persons of both sexes. Transliteration follows a simplifed Library of Congress system, except for initial Ya, Ye, and Yu. Republic and place names (except Leningrad) follow current (post-Soviet) usage. To save space, references are given in abbreviated form. For additional data see Bibliography. For an explanation of Russian and other specialized terms, see Glossary. For initials or first names, see Index. 'Milliard' (md.) means one thousand million (US: billion). 1 hectare = 2.47 acres. Tons are metric (tonnes).

PART I

The Dark Ages

1 Stalin's Last Years

When cannon fired salutes across the land to celebrate VE-Day in May 1945, Soviet citizens had every ground for pride in their achievement and relief that the epic four-year struggle was at an end. Their armies had driven back the Nazi invaders and gone on to liberate most of eastern and central Europe. Internationally the USSR was at the zenith of its power and prestige. It seemed reasonable to hope that, with fears of 'capitalist encirclement' laid to rest, the populace would be permitted some respite from the inhuman pressures to which it had been subjected ever since the Bolshevik revolution, and more particularly since Stalin had launched his 'revolution from above' in 1929. Surely the Soviet state would now treat its long-suffering subjects with greater consideration? Alas, this optimism was misplaced. It left out of account the lethal logic of the Stalinist regime, which could maintain itself only by mobilizing its subjects in an unceasing struggle against external and internal foes. Where such enemies did not exist, they had to be invented.

Over forty years later, in the first flush of *perestroika*, the Soviet philosopher Yurii Levada would write that the 'emancipatory messianism' characteristic of the final phase of the Soviet–German war gave way to a 'hysterical isolationism', a mood that had nothing to do with any genuine threat to the country's security but was 'a product designed purely for domestic use, to make it easier to divide and rule'. Paradoxically, one effect of the victory of the Grand Alliance was to consolidate the dominion over the Soviet peoples of a tyrant whose murderous record was on a par with Hitler's. Although the exact toll of human life is not known, it must have risen by several million during the eight years that elapsed between May 1945 and the dictator's death in March 1953.

The slave class

Among the first to experience the effects of Stalin's fear of external contagion were the unfortunate soldiers and civilians who had been either taken prisoner by the Germans or deported for war work in the Reich. Many of them had endured genocidal conditions in Nazi concentration camps; some had fought in resistance movements in various parts of occupied Europe. But these sufferings and services in the common cause were disregarded. For Stalin looked on prisoners as traitors and interpreted the concept of 'collaboration' with the enemy very widely—despite (or more probably, because of) his own dubious record as Hitler's ally between 1939 and 1941. Those who had seen too much of life in foreign lands were perceived as a security risk and therefore slated for annihilation. When freed by advancing Soviet troops, or handed over by the Western Allies, they were subjected to 'filtering' (*fil'tratsiia*) by the security services (NKVD, NKGB, SMERSH). The work of these agencies was enshrouded in secrecy until 1990, and even now the curtain has been only partially lifted.

According to data from police sources that have yet to be independently verified, by October 1945 about 4.1 million Soviet citizens, including 2.6 million civilians, had been repatriated from abroad.[1] Of these over half (58 per cent) were allowed to go home—where, however, they were liable to discriminatory treatment by local officials or over-zealous fellow-citizens. Another fifth (19 per cent) were returned to the armed forces. Of the others 14.5 per cent (608,000) were despatched to labour battalions under the supervision of the Defence ministry, and 6.5 per cent (273,000), among whom were practically all captured officers, formed what was called a 'special contingent' of prisoners. Placed under the NKVD's control, they were shipped off to various islands in the 'Gulag Archipelago'. They formed one of the principal 'streams' of new arrivals in these years, along with alleged 'collaborators' from former enemy-occupied territory—although a higher proportion of persons in this category will have been summarily shot.

It is only fitting to begin a sketch of the condition of Soviet society in Stalin's last years with such macabre matters, for the machinery of repression was the core of his political system and its victims made up a sizeable segment of the population. We might call this the 'slave class'. The prisoners' status was regulated by a host of secret administrative provisions. Their very existence was not publicly recognized: they were 'unpersons'. In this they differed from slaves in earlier centuries of Russian history.[2] Their forced labour made a significant contribution to the economy, notably in such fields as logging and gold-mining. Some more favoured prisoners were farmed out to enterprises or government agencies and put to work in industrial, agricultural, or construction jobs. For example, the grandiose skyscraper built in 1948–54 for Moscow State University on the Vorob'ev (Lenin) Hills just outside the city was erected in part by prison labour. Barbed wire separated these *zeks* (as prisoners were called) from students performing their 'voluntary' labour tasks nearby. 'We were not embarrassed or frightened, for we took the conventional view that they were undergoing re-education through labour, the very foundation of human dignity', writes A. Ajubei (1989), at that time a conformist student of journalism (and later Khrushchev's son-in-law).

Readers of Solzhenitsyn's epic 'literary investigation' of the prison system will need no reminder how the Stalinist repressive apparatus functioned. A few of its more striking features may, however, be mentioned here (see also below, Chapter 9). Suspects would be arrested at dead of night. Investigators applied various physical and psychological means of pressure (i.e. torture) to extract confessions to fanciful crimes that they themselves knew to be false. Many cases were framed on the basis of false allegations by delators, and informers (*stukachi*) were also recruited among prisoners (they formed 8 per cent of the total in 1947: Zemskov 1991*b*). The accused were kept in total isolation from the outside world. Relatives were often given false information as to their whereabouts—and might then in turn be arrested, simply on grounds of affinity. Prisoners were detained in overcrowded cells lacking basic sanitary facilities and had inadequate food or exercise. Alleged misconduct or failure to co-operate in the investigation might bring solitary confinement in a 'punishment cell' no larger than a box. Sentence would often be pronounced by quasi-judicial 'trios' (*troikas*) which scarcely bothered to glance at the 'evidence', for the penalty had in fact been determined in advance. The norm at this time was twenty-five years' camp—'for nothing you get ten years', said a guard at Novosibirsk transit prison in 1945—and was virtually equivalent to a suspended death sentence.

For those spared VMN ('the supreme measure of punishment', i.e. execution) there followed the long journey eastward to an unknown and inhospitable destination. Escape from a camp in the Gulag was virtually impossible. Food, clothing, and accommodation were inadequate for an extreme climate. Each prisoner wore a jacket inscribed with his identification number. Sadistic and arbitrary acts were commonly committed by camp authorities, guards, and the ordinary criminals employed as overseers. When marching to their daily work assignment, prisoners would be warned by their escort that a single step to the right or left of the file could mean instant death. Labour norms were impossibly high, especially for convicts enfeebled by near-starvation rations, but food supply and other 'privileges' depended on their fulfilment. Those who fell sick were penalized and generally fated to succumb. Prisoners with the best chances of survival were the hardiest and luckiest (e.g. those who secured indoor jobs in a cookhouse, dispensary, etc.). Solzhenitsyn himself survived by being assigned to 'special' work in a scientific laboratory manned mainly by prisoners. There were separate installations for women prisoners and even for children. A prisoner's sentence might be arbitrarily extended when his term expired. The fortunate were reclassified as exiles with a slightly less onerous regime. It was, however, the central authorities' express intention that no prisoner should ever taste freedom again. A recently published *ukaz* of 21 February 1948 ordered that when their sentence ended political offenders 'and individuals presenting a danger on account of their anti-Soviet [i.e. foreign] ties' should be exiled indefinitely to remote regions of eastern Siberia or Kazakhstan (*Ist.* 2/1994).

Ordinary citizens knew of the existence of the camps but avoided talking about them lest they be denounced and fall into the clutches of the dreaded 'organs'. Those brave or careless enough to engage in loose talk of this kind committed an offence informally categorized as 'ASA' (anti-Soviet agitation)—one of several such labels that were the operative reality behind the celebrated catch-all Article 58 of the criminal code. Other code-words included 'KRD' (counter-revolutionary activity), 'SOE' (socially dangerous element) or—a post-war innovation—'VAD' (admirer of American democracy), i.e. someone deemed to have spoken favourably of the United States. In practice the 'organs' wielded absolute power. They defined the charge, decided the sentence, and carried it out. A number of ex-*zeks* who had served their term or had been released during the war were re-arrested in 1947–9 on the *former* charges (Vakser 1992). By the last months of Stalin's rule people were being taken into custody and 'repressed' simply on racial grounds, i.e. for being Jewish.

As regards the number held in captivity, some information has recently come to light from police sources (Bugai 1991; Zemskov 1991; Dugin 1990). Confidence in its reliability is not enhanced by the authors' clear propagandist intent (Ahlberg 1992). These data should be regarded as provisional until they can be checked independently.

TABLE 1.1. *Police data on number of prisoners in labour camps and colonies, 1945–1953* [a]

Year	Camps (ITL)	Colonies (ITK)	Total
1945	715,505[b]	745,171	1,460,676
1946	746,871	956,224	1,703,095
1947	808,839	912,704	1,721,543
1948	1,108,057	1,091,478	2,199,535[c]
1949	1,216,361	1,140,324	2,356,685
1950	1,416,300	1,145,051	2,561,351
1951	1,533,767[d]	994,379	2,528,146
1952	1,711,202	793,312	2,504,514
1953	1,727,970	740,554	2,468,524

[a] 1 Jan.
[b] Variously given as 715,515 or 715,506.
[c] Reported by Interior minister Kruglov to Stalin.
[d] *Source*: Zemskov 1991*a*, Table 2; other data from Ahlberg 1992, citing A. N. Dugin 1990.

To the figures given in Table 1.1 should be added those held in prisons, who in 1947 numbered *c.*300,000, and, far more important, the exiles or 'special settlers'. These numbered 2,464,000 in October 1946 and 2,753,000 in January 1953.[3] They were predominantly non-Russians. Among them were the 'punished peoples' (Volga Germans, Crimean Tatars, Kalmyks, and various groups from the north Caucasus) which Stalin had deported from their homelands, at great human cost, during the war. In the late Stalin era their numbers were swollen by the addition of the principal categories set out in Table 1.2.

These 'settlements' were located mainly in Central Asia and Siberia. In October 1946 33.7 per cent of the inmates were women and 39.7 per cent children aged under sixteen (Bugai 1991).

We also have a breakdown by sex for the inmates of camps and colonies. In 1945 women comprised 24.0 per cent in the former category and 38.0 per cent in the latter; thereafter their share fell.

The annual mortality rate in the camps, which had risen to 175 per thousand at the height of the war (January 1942), was officially reckoned at 61 per thousand in January 1945 and 44 per thousand in January 1947; later figures are not yet available. Mortality in prisons (1947) has been put at approximately 14 per thousand (4,142 deaths). These figures are probably all underestimates.

Data have also been published recently on the number of sentences passed by the security organs (Table 1.3), which show that relatively few were sent directly into exile.

At this time sentences by ordinary courts were running at around one million a year. They reached a peak in 1947 (1,391,786 offenders); by 1952 the figure had fallen to 969,943. These data exclude workers and peasants sentenced for absenteeism or laziness (e.g. failing to perform the requisite number of labour-days). They numbered 1,207,808 in 1946 and then slowly declined to 47,492 in 1952. Writing before *glasnost'*, a Western researcher estimated the total number of sentences by the criminal courts at 2.76 million in 1947, falling to 1.9 million in 1952 (Van den Berg 1987). If one may

TABLE 1.2.   *Police data on principal additions to exile population, 1945–1952*

Ukrainian anti-Communists ('Banderites', 'Melnikovites'), 1944–52	175,063
Baltic peoples, 1945–51 (139,957 + 18,104)	158,061[a]
Greeks, Armenians, and others from Black Sea coast, Georgia, 1949, 1951–2 (57,142 + 11,685)	68,827
Former members of Russian Liberation Army ('Vlasovites')	56,746
Residents of Moldova (Moldavia),1949	35,838
Jehovah's Witnesses (1951)	9,363
So-called 'parasites', idlers (1948, 1951)	33,266[b]
Others (incl. estimate for family members)	[?]
TOTAL:	c.600,000

Sources: Zemskov 1989; V. P. Popov 1992.

[a] The number of Balts in ITL and ITK respectively rose from 8,129 + 878 in Jan. 1945 to 75,647 + 20,507 in Jan. 1951. In Jan. 1953 172,362 Balts were detained in special settlements and another 6,192 had the status of 'permanent exiles' (see n. 4).

[b] According to a decree of 2 June 1948, for which Khrushchev was partially responsible (Popov 1993), from that date until March 1953 a total of 33,266 persons were exiled under this provision. Apart from this, several thousand peasant families were deported from Belarus and the western Ukraine in addition to those from the Baltic states included above.

trust the new data, this calculation was somewhat on the high side. On the other hand, Popov's figures do not appear to account for the increase in the number of inmates of camps and exile settlements. One difficulty here is that a number of offenders were sentenced to terms of labour service 'without deprivation of liberty', i.e. at their workplace. It should be pointed out that many of those commonly categorized as 'ordinary' convicts, who were sentenced by the regular courts, ought really to be counted as political offenders, in so far as their delinquency was motivated by national or religious loyalties, or else sheer resentment at the harshness of the system.

The peasantry

Only a little better off than the slaves was the bulk of the peasantry, whose legal status had some affinities with that of serfs before 1861: they did not, for instance, qualify for internal passports and so were in practice bound to the farms where they lived. These were of two types: the more privileged state farms (*sovkhozy*), envisaged as large-scale industrial concerns and therefore further advanced towards socialism, and collective farms (*kolkhozy*), which allowed

TABLE 1.3. *Sentences by security organs, 1945–1953* [a]

Year	Total	Of which sentenced to			
		Death	Camps prisons	Exile[b]	Other penalties
1945	123,248	4,252	116,681	1,647	668
1946	123,294	2,896	117,943	1,498	957
1947	78,810	1,105	76,581	666	458
1948	73,269	[-][c]	72,552	419	298
1949	75,133	8	64,509	10,316	300
1950	60,641	475	54,466	5,225	475
1951	54,775	1,609	49,142	3,425	599
1952	28,800	1,612	25,824	773	591
1953[d]	8,403	198	7,894	38	273
TOTALS	626,373	12,155	585,592	24,007	4,619

Source: V. P. Popov 1992.
[a] Collegium of NKVD/MVD and MGB, Special Council.
[b] *ssylka* and *vysylka*.
[c] The death penalty was abolished in May 1947 but reimposed in Jan. 1950.
[d] Jan.–June.

some temporary concessions to private enterprise. This system, imposed on the countryside in the 1930s, was irrational and left farmers precious little incentive to better their lot. On *sovkhozy* they were viewed as agricultural employees and at least received a regular wage, but *kolkhozniki* were remunerated for their obligatory work in the collective fields by a share of the farm's profits, distributed at the year's end—after all its other obligations to the state had been met—in cash and/or kind, according to the number of 'labour days' (*trudodni*) each household had worked. These rewards were often trivial, perhaps no more than a sack of potatoes, so that in practice collective farmers subsisted as best they could on the produce from their private plots. Yet this activity was looked on with suspicion by the authorities and subjected to all manner of restrictions.

The tenacity of the past was also evident in the famine that afflicted a wide swathe of territory in the south of the country, from Moldova to the middle Volga, in 1946–7. Its prime cause was an unusually severe drought: in some areas no rain fell for seventy days. But matters were made worse by war-time losses—the amount of rural labour available was only one-third as great as in 1940 and most farm machinery had been destroyed—as well as by the insensitive bureaucratic approach taken by the central authorities. Although in many areas yields were down to less than 3 centners per hectare, the state procurement organs took 60 to 70 per cent of the grain harvested. Taxes were levied on farms according to their acreage, even though much land remained unseeded. Norms for livestock deliveries also remained unchanged, and the prices for cattle were 'essentially symbolic' (Volkov, 1991).

Volkov's article is the first historical study of the tragedy, for like the great famine of 1932–3 it was kept secret at the time. As on the earlier occasion, Stalin and his associates pretended to themselves that nothing amiss had occurred. The Politburo fired off threatening telegrams to local officials ordering them to speed up deliveries. High-level dignitaries were then despatched to key areas. For instance, Malenkov went to the Siberian Altai region, Mikoian to Kazakhstan. Both regions duly fulfilled their plan targets, but overall the achievement rate was only 77 per cent and the human cost was high. In Belarus one-third of collective farmers received no payment at all for their work in the 'socialist sector', and it was the same story on 600 farms in Smolensk province. Here the blame was put on local farm chairmen, 420 of whom were sacked as scapegoats. In Moldova 389,000 people were afflicted by malnutrition and dystrophy in the winter of 1946–7. Less than a third received hospital treatment; between 70,000 and 80,000 died. In 1947 the mortality rate in Ukraine was 1.7 times greater than it had been in the previous year.

Aid was sent to the afflicted regions, but belatedly and on an inadequate scale. A peasant woman in Ukraine, driven mad by hunger, killed and ate two of her children. This became known to Khrushchev, first secretary of the Ukrainian CP, who reported on the situation in his republic to Stalin. The Boss (as he was known to his intimates) charged him with softness: 'they are deceiving you by trying to appeal to your emotions . . . and make you distribute all the reserves.' In his memoirs Khrushchev claims to have pressed, at some personal risk, for a more flexible line to be taken on sowing cereal crops in different regions. He failed to carry the point and was punished by the loss of his Party fiefdom, Kaganovich being sent down to replace him. He spent nine months in limbo before regaining favour.

The problem was not choosing between different policy options but changing the system, which was fundamentally hostile to peasant farmers. They were regarded with suspicion as prone to 'petty-bourgeois' individualist leanings. According to the official ideology the key to the future was industrial development. Agriculture was therefore treated as a Cinderella by the planners, who looked on it as a limitless 'reserve' of money and manpower that could be drawn on to foster 'socialist construction'. Stalin was only half joking when he told the Finance minister, Zverev, when he objected to a rise in rural taxation, that 'it's enough for a peasant to sell a chicken for him to keep the Finance ministry happy.' Such attitudes were common throughout the bureaucracy. It was the reason why most country-dwellers ceased to be eligible for food rations from October 1946: overnight the number fell from 27 to 4.5 million. In practice only the rural élite qualified, the rest had to fend for themselves. Yet officials considered it their duty to combat the allegedly 'egoistic' behaviour of farmers who toiled on their plots primarily to keep themselves alive and sold any surplus produce on so-called collective-farm markets, at prices generally higher than those in state stores. This trade was obstructed in manifold ways, e.g. by denying peasants the use of farm vehicles on the pretext that they were needed elsewhere. The most serious blow to private farming came in September 1946 with a decree confiscating the collective land which peasants (and some institutions) had taken over and farmed on their own account during the war. About 14 million hectares were returned along with 140,000 head of cattle. However, 'much of the recovered land lay fallow since the *kolkhozy* had neither the labour nor the machinery to work it' (McCauley 1981). In these years the rural labour force consisted largely of women because the casualty rate among young males had been so catastrophic.

At the same time efforts were made to thin down rural officialdom, which in some areas accounted for up to a quarter of the labour force. 'Inquiries . . . revealed the existence on *kolkhozy* of numerous individuals, often completely unknown, whom the peasants had tolerated because they assured them a real measure of independence' (Carrère d'Encausse 1981). Some of these were classed as 'parasites' and dealt with appropriately. Nearly half a million people are said to have been transferred from administrative to productive work. Yet the abuses continued. A collective farm in Penza province in 1948 reportedly employed eight guards for a mere sixty-five active members. Inflated staffs were inherent in socialized agriculture.

A drive was undertaken to increase the number of Party activists on the farms and to strengthen the machine-tractor stations (MTS). Many of the former were soldiers who, having joined the Party during the war, returned to their villages on demobilization. They made up in zeal for what they lacked in knowledge and few were properly trained to assume administrative responsibilities. This was one reason why many Party members preferred to stay in their villages rather than move out to the farms and actively implement policies that they knew would be unpopular. Pressure was brought to bear from above to overcome this tendency. In Orel province over the fifteen-month period January 1945 to April 1946 the number of Party members in villages rose from 2,000 to 7,500, but in *kolkhozy* from 300 to 1,600.

The MTS, set up in 1933, were state agencies that looked after heavy equipment and performed much of the farm work, such as ploughing, seeding, and harvesting. As payment for their services members of these brigades received (in addition to their wages) payments from the farms. These were a heavy burden on all but the richest. In practice the MTS held a whip hand over all farms within their purview, for by giving any of them a low priority in the queue for assistance they could prevent them from fulfilling their quota of deliveries to the state procurement agencies. Moreover, each MTS had a political department, normally four men strong, one of whom was a security police operative, so that defaulters ran the risk of being punished as counter-revolutionary saboteurs.

From 1947 onwards the leadership stiffened its attitude towards collective farmers. Instead of raising procurement prices to make agriculture profitable, delivery quotas were increased and other burdens imposed. *Kolkhozy* were obliged to maintain seed reserves of their own instead of being able to obtain them from the Procurements ministry. They were prohibited from setting up their own stalls in town markets. In August 1948 taxes were increased on both the farms themselves and on individual peasants. The latter's private income was assessed in an arbitrary fashion, according to a price scale unrelated to what they could actually earn from the sale of stock or produce. The object of these measures was to encourage a proper 'socialist' attitude to collective labour by making it less profitable for peasants to work their plots, and especially to keep cattle. By 1952 the numbers of cows, sheep, goats, and pigs owned by *kolkhozniki* were all considerably below what they had been before the war. Only just over half such householders now possessed a cow. Yet all of them had to deliver, on average, 210 to 250 litres of milk a year, as well as specified amounts of meat, vegetables, eggs, and so on. Those who had no cow 'had to beg, borrow or buy this milk' (Nove 1990). There were cases of people chopping down fruit-trees to avoid having to pay the tax on them.

Farmers' incomes in 1949 were only 50 per cent of what they had been in 1928, before collectivization; by 1952 the proportion had risen to 60 per cent. In the latter year the average peasant household had a cash income from collective work of only 623 roubles, which in real terms was less than in a 'good' pre-war year. Although the farms now earned more, their financial obligations had risen so steeply that they could afford to distribute less than 29 per cent of their income, as against nearly half in 1937, to their members in payment for their labour. (To the recipients payments in kind mattered more, especially because they could be resold.) In the late 1940s a year's cash wages were less than sufficient to buy a poor-quality suit; twenty days' work (twenty-eight *trudodni*) were required for a bottle of vodka (Nove 1990). According to recent calculations, this income accounted for only 15 to 20 per cent of total earnings by collective farmers in 1946–51 (Verbitskaia 1992).

The corollary of these restrictive measures was a policy of forcing farms to amalgamate. In principle this had some merit, since many *kolkhozy*, especially in central Russia, were below optimum size and so one could hope for economies of scale. But the real reason was that larger farms would be easier to control. Typically such mergers were pushed through by dictation from above without regard for local specifics, so that the new enlarged units were artificial creations, lacking in cohesion, and the real focus of agricultural operations continued to be the village. Thus not too much should be made of statistics showing that the number of *kolkhozy* declined rapidly, from 254,000 in January 1950 to 97,000 by October 1952.

The heart of the problem was that the state did not have the wherewithal to make such mergers beneficial to the rural population. Khrushchev, who was the main proponent of this drive, put forward a fanciful scheme for the construction in rural areas of 'agricultural towns' (*agrogoroda*), i.e. large urban-type settlements with modern amenities (but without kitchen gardens!) to which peasants would be compelled to move, leaving their old huts and hamlets to rot away. It was a typically 'revolutionary', utopian idea which ignored financial or social realities, to say nothing of people's feelings. The day after a speech advocating it was belatedly published in *Pravda* (4 March 1951), an editorial note appeared to the effect that it was for discussion only, which was tantamount to disavowal. Khrushchev's rivals, notably Malenkov, criticized the scheme, but for the wrong reasons: it did not, as was alleged, reflect an excessively 'consumerist' approach, but rather an unduly administrative one.

This difference of opinion was linked to another debate on the best way labour tasks should be organized on the farms' collective fields. Stalin's agricultural supremo in the first post-war years, Andreev, took a relatively flexible line. He advocated, and permitted, the so-called 'link' (*zveno*) system, whereby a small group of six to ten collective farmers was given a particular area of land to cultivate or jobs to perform, payment being made according to results. This method had affinities with the traditional way Russian peasants, organized in the *dvor* (patriarchal household) and *artel'* (artisans' co-operative), had coped with complex tasks. Precisely this made it objectionable to the ideologues. They favoured 'brigades'—much larger units of several dozen workers, based on the industrial prototype. Such groups, organized on hierarchical rather than co-operative lines, could not be suspected of partiality for the family farm or private enterprise. In practice the 'link' did sometimes quietly survive as a sub-unit within a brigade, but deprived of its natural, spontaneous character. As for Andreev, his career went into decline after 1950 and he was not re-elected to the top policy-making body at the Nineteenth Party congress in October 1952.

By this time Stalin's agrarian policy had become less realistic than ever. In October 1948 he had launched a grandiose twenty-year campaign for the 'transformation of nature'. This involved planting belts of trees across the southern steppe to prevent soil erosion and constructing a network of irrigation canals. No less than 5.7 million hectares were to be forested, the lion's share (3.6 million hectares) being maintained and paid for by the farms themselves. The scheme owed much to the pseudo-scientific enthusiasm of Lysenko (see below, p. 33), and most of the effort was wasted. As Nove writes, 'the trees refused to obey Stalin and did not grow; very few canals were built.' One that was, between the Volga and the Don—by prison labour, naturally—was suitably embellished by a giant bronze statue of the Leader. His last work, *Economic Problems of Socialism*, was hailed as a masterpiece. It consisted mostly of abstruse logic-chopping and abounded in banal, hackneyed phrases. Stalin rejected the idea that the MTS bureaucracy should be eliminated by selling off agricultural machinery to the collective farms. On the contrary, *kolkhozy* were to lose the last shadow of their autonomy by being 'raised' to the level of state farms. 'Commodity circulation', i.e. buying and selling goods for money, was to give way to the direct exchange of products, in accordance with the Marxist blueprint for a fully Communist society. This in a land where even basic foodstuffs were lacking! The actual grain harvest in 1952—as distinct from the fraudulent one hailed by the propagandists—was less than that in 1940, when there had been fewer mouths to feed; the same was true even of potatoes. Agricultural producers were worse off than consumers in the towns. Many of them sought to flee from a countryside which, according to no less an authority than Khrushchev, looked as though the Tatar hordes had just passed through.

The industrial scene

The purpose behind these exactions was to reconstruct and expand the industrial sector of the economy, particularly the 'Group A' (producers' goods) industries that provided the sinews of war—for Stalin was convinced that further struggles with 'imperialism' were in the offing. The armed forces' equipment was modernized and the country's military preparedness reinforced: there was to be no repeat of 1941. The details of this buildup cannot concern us here, and are in any case well concealed in official statistics.

The Fourth Five-Year Plan (1946–50) was modelled on its pre-war forerunners. Capital investment took a very large slice of available resources. By 1950 gross industrial production was said to have exceeded the 1940 figure by 73 per cent, although the use of index numbers calculated in obsolete 1926–7 prices, which gave excessive weight to 'new' products such as machinery, distorts the picture. Taking 1940 as 100, the ratio between the output of 'Group A' goods (205) and of consumers' goods in 'Group B' (123) is perhaps rather more meaningful. In the first year of peace industrial reconstruction was slow—the sudden termination of Lend-Lease caused problems, as did the shortage of trained labour—but from 1946 onward recovery was impressively rapid. Thousands of factories and mines that had been destroyed or damaged were rebuilt, often being modernized in the process. High on the priority list was the Dnepropetrovsk hydro-electric power station, a symbol of 'socialist industrialization', which was repaired and brought back on stream by 1947. The coal-mines of the Donets basin, which had been flooded, surpassed pre-war output levels by 1950. By 1953 total coal output, at 320 million tons, was nearly double the figure for 1940 (166 million tons); for natural gas the growth rate was even faster (from 3.3 to 6.9 milliard cubic metres). Before the war the USSR had produced 18.3 million tons of steel. By 1945 output was down by a third, but three years later the 1940 level had been exceeded and by 1953 the figure was 38.1 million tons. The defects of centralized planning, which would loom so large in later years, were less evident in the reconstruction period, when all attention was focused on achieving a relatively limited number of priority targets.

For managers and workpeople meeting their factory's allotted goals involved a great deal of stress. There was also a certain amount of partnership between them as they sought to defend routine practices against upheavals caused by zealots for 'socialist emulation'. It was common practice for enterprises, industrial branches or whole regions to pledge to reach certain targets within a stated time period and to challenge others to emulate their 'feats of labour heroism', which were played up in the media. The degree of spontaneous enthusiasm in such officially sponsored campaigns was slight. People had learned from experience that they were manipulated and in the long run led to a general raising of norms. On the other hand it was dangerous to resist such pressures too openly. Everyone knew of the harsh fate that awaited slackers, who (if they avoided prison and exile) might find themselves sentenced to a term of corrective labour in the factory at reduced wages. In the initial post-war years there seems to have been a genuine feeling that another spell of hard work and self-sacrifice was necessary to get the country back on its feet and improve living standards. However, this mood evaporated as it became clear that the prospect facing ordinary folk was one of endless hardship. 'By 1947 people in the cities had again lost heart. The stress laid on reconstructing heavy industry and continuing difficulties in daily life obscured the effects of Victory' (Carrère d'Encausse 1981). This in turn led to a reinforcement of controls.

One particular source of grievance was the currency reform decreed in December 1947, whereby all cash in private hands had to be exchanged at the rate of ten to one. This wiped out nine-tenths of the savings that many people, especially peasants, had accumulated during the war and had kept under their mattresses. Those with modest accounts in savings banks did not lose, but holders of state bonds suddenly found them worth two-thirds less and carrying a lower rate of interest (2 per cent). From the state's viewpoint the measure could be justified as a way of mopping up the excessive amount of money in circulation and so keeping down inflation. Only a dictatorial regime could have afforded to take such a drastic step instead of trying to solve the problem by boosting the supply of consumer goods. The output of footwear, for example, did not exceed the pre-war level until 1951. Until that year fewer pairs of shoes were produced per annum than there were inhabitants. Much the same was true of knitted garments, production of which totalled only 198 million items in 1950 (1940: 183 million, but compare 1953: 341 million). There was a relative abundance of radio receivers (over a million produced in 1950), whereas a refrigerator or television set remained an almost unattainable luxury until the later 1950s. Even humdrum domestic objects were expensive. Many of them could be obtained only on the 'free' market, where prices were roughly 30 per cent above the official level—although the gap narrowed as output in the public sector picked up.

Each spring from 1948 to 1954 the prices fixed for certain commodities were reduced. Bread cost less than half as much in 1950 as it had at the end of 1947. After one such reduction, in March 1952, the State Security minister, Ignat'ev, sent Stalin a secret report, based on intercepted correspondence, about popular reactions in the capital. 'Moscow is really celebrating', wrote a certain Bagaeva to a friend in Riazan' province. 'Comrade Stalin always keeps his promises', commented another. M. Kaldobskaia was less circumspect: 'the whole thing is pure fiction', she complained. Goods were scarce, and the state would surely offset the loss by extracting savings from the people in some other way. One such device was obligatory subscriptions to state bonds. These took the equivalent of several weeks' wages annually and drew critical comment from several letter-writers (Kraiushkin and Teptsov 1992). Such grumbling did not necessarily imply any fundamental objection to the state socialist order. People had little information as to its workings, for economics and sociology were among the disciplines that, along with genetics, were virtually prohibited in the late Stalin era. There were no opinion polls—and precious few statistics. This was a country of the blind, in which all but the most foolhardy citizens regurgitated meaningless chunks of jargon and refrained from raising awkward questions.

Stalinist political culture

The post-war cultural freeze is often referred to as the *Zhdanovsh-china*, although it reached its peak only after the death in August 1948 of Andrei Zhdanov, a Stalin associate who in the first years after the war seemed to be earmarked as heir apparent. In 1946, as a member of the Politburo and Secretariat, where his functions included oversight of Party administration and ideology, Zhdanov sharply criticized alleged errors and deviations from the 'Party line' in Ukraine and Leningrad. It has been argued (Hahn 1982) that this campaign may have been part of an intrigue against Malenkov and his supporters rather than the beginning of a general onslaught on nonconformity in every sphere of life, which was what eventually came about.

Whatever the truth of this argument, it is clear that all members of Stalin's entourage, irrespective of their personal preferences, were prepared to pander to their leader's paranoid suspiciousness and to execute his will. Their motives can be attributed partly to careerist calculations but, above all, to sheer terror. For Stalin's 'court' was not a milieu where politicians could afford to have an honest disagreement or even discuss policy issues in a frank, comradely fashion. Rather it was the scene of constant manœuvring for advantage between senior functionaries, while Stalin remained in the background and pulled the strings. A dissonant opinion, even on some academic problem seemingly remote from high politics, might cost a man his job or even his life. It is true that only one Politburo member—Voznesensky, a deputy premier and head of Gosplan—was put to death during these years. But memories of the Great Terror were still fresh and no one knew whether the Boss might not decide to repeat the experience.

The atmosphere in the Kremlin had incalculable effects on the country's intellectual and cultural life. Writers and artists, scientists and scholars were closely supervised by relatively junior officials who shaped their conduct according to the whims of those at the top. To protect themselves they tended to over-react, since they seldom received explicit instructions. Instead they were expected to 'read the signs'. This demanded skill in understanding the esoteric code whereby decision-makers communicated their preferences or orders. A major shift of policy might be heralded by some recondite allusion in *Pravda*. Nowhere was the late Stalinist regime's guiding idea set out unambiguously. To have done so would have revealed how far Stalin had departed from what was commonly considered to be the Marxist-Leninist heritage.

At a victory celebration in May 1945 he referred to the Russian people as 'the most outstanding nation of all the nations within the Soviet Union'. This would become a *leitmotif* of propaganda in the years that followed. One should not, however, conclude that Russian nationalism had replaced Leninist revolutionary internationalism as the core of official doctrine. Far from it: Marxism-Leninism was a malleable creed that could be manipulated almost at will by the country's successive leaders. Already before the war Stalin had realized that it was expedient to tap the patriotic emotions engendered by the construction of 'socialism in one country'. The war gave a fillip to national sentiment—not only among Russians. This made it all the more necessary to beat the chauvinist drum, but the beat was muffled, lest too much offence be given to non-Russians. Accordingly emphasis was laid on the *Soviet* character of all achievements, past and present, that were adjudged worthy of acclaim. In short, the regime took the credit for them. It was less a matter of Stalin making concessions to Russian nationalism than of his skilfully harnessing its emotional force and exploiting it towards a greater end. The same was true of religious beliefs, especially among Orthodox Christians. He was willing to tolerate them within narrow limits so long as their expression was kept under close administrative control. Orthodoxy, too, could be subsumed into the state ideology. The aim of this ideology was, quite simply: *to exalt the Soviet order, epitomized by the dictator himself.*

The Stalin cult was an integral part of this pseudo-intellectual edifice which, along with Russian/Soviet nationalism, was designed to buttress the power of the regime. It did so by catering to the monarchist and paternalist sentiments common among the populace. Millions of people, uprooted by violent social change and the destruction of familiar landmarks, were reassured by the thought that their destinies were guided by a father figure—a substitute deity, as it were, for a materialistic age. In public Stalin deprecated this adulation. Whether he really enjoyed it, or stimulated it, is beside the point. Probably his attitude was ambivalent. What matters is that he valued its *utility* in consolidating mass support and so in a sense legitimizing his rule.

The actual fashioning of the cult was done by minions whose labours reached a climax in grandiose celebrations of the Leader's seventieth birthday in December 1949. It was then that his image appeared in the night sky above the Kremlin, suspended from a balloon and illuminated by searchlights. Poets and scholars vied with one another in the quest for appropriate metaphors with which to hail his greatness: 'Father of the Toiling World' (Sholokhov), for example, 'Coryphaeus of the Sciences' and the like. Gifts poured in to the Kremlin from many lands. Portraits and busts of the Leader were ubiquitous in these years. Each day newspapers gave pride of place to stylized messages addressed to him by humble folk. All of this served to convey the impression that Party and people were unbreakably united in a mortal struggle against wily foes at home and abroad, but that the Cause was inexorably bound to triumph.

Literature and the arts

This then was the message. It took some time to impose it on the cultural and scientific establishment. This was done in haphazard fashion. The first victims were the writers. The so-called 'Zhdanov decrees' of August 1946 condemned two Leningrad literary journals (*Zvezda, Leningrad*) for publishing 'ideologically harmful' work. Singled out for public humiliation were Anna Akhmatova, Russia's greatest living poet, and the humorous writer Mikhail Zoshchenko, who had recently been appointed to *Zvezda*'s editorial board.[5] This periodical was placed under the chief editorship of an Agitprop official, while the other journal was simply suppressed. Both writers were subsequently expelled from the Union of Soviet Writers (USW), which meant that their work could not appear and they were deprived of their livelihood. Boris Pasternak was treated a little less harshly, being allowed to publish translations but not his verse. In March 1947 he, too, came under attack at a literary conference for being out of step with his times.

One of his critics was a senior literary functionary, Alexander Fadeev, who achieved the feat of rewriting his novel *The Young Guard* (1945) in such a way as to satisfy the censors. In the second version (1951), which won a Stalin prize, he emphasized the *Party's* role in organizing the partisan movement behind German lines. This was 'a profoundly conservative, hierarchical and patriarchal work' which combined praise for heroic revolutionary traditions with 'the supreme values of mother love and dedication to the Russian soil' (Hosking 1985). Superficially, these values had much in common with those of the nineteenth-century middle class—virtuous toil, respect for the family, patriotism, and so on—but they were intrinsically false. We should not be deceived by appearances. They were imposed artificially from above and ignored elementary truths about man's contemporary experience. One effect of the *Zhdanovsh-china* was to enhance the didactic character of Soviet 'socialist realist' literature. It existed in isolation from modernist trends in the West, which were dutifully execrated by the critics.

The 'socialist realist' canon was less fully articulated in regard to the visual arts. Scholarly discussions in this field were trite and reductionist, in the sense that an artist's output was seen wholly in terms of his personal and public behaviour. Those who 'heeded the Party's advice' were well regarded, whereas those influenced by Impressionism, and especially by 'formalist' genres, were discountenanced. Photographic realism was the supreme objective. The work of A. Gerasimov, Stalin's 'court painter', became more elaborately detailed and iconographic. In *The Oath* (1949) he depicted members of the Politburo lined up hierarchically. Another artist, Z. Volkonskaia, portrayed Stalin as a boy teaching his comrades. They hang on his words attentively, while his mother pauses in her domestic tasks to hearken to his words of wisdom, in a scene with pseudo-Christian overtones (Goldberg 1990). In 1952 the celebrated sculptor V. I. Mukhina complained to Stalin that cultural officials found her statue of Tchaikovsky 'insufficiently popular' and refused to authorize its erection in front of the Moscow Conservatory, which bore the composer's name. Both Stalin and the artist had died before the monument was duly put up in 1954 (*Ist.* 1/1994).

In January 1948 it was the composers' turn to be lectured, at a conference called by the CC, on the need to reflect Russian folk themes in their music. An edict singled out V. Muradeli's opera *The Great Friendship* for ideological errors. Both Prokof'ev and Shostakovich came under fire, as did countless lesser figures. In this earnest world light entertainment was suspect. Jazz was banned as alien and decadent. In 1949 saxophones were actually confiscated by the cultural bosses, who saw to it that instead balalaikas were produced in profusion (Stites 1992). So it was, too, in the milieu of stage and screen. Stalin liked simple tales which gave a fallacious picture of the happy life enjoyed by country folk, as in *Kuban Cossacks* (1949); there was no place for a serious, balanced, and truthful picture of reality. The number of Soviet films produced, which had regained the pre-war level by 1947, fell to seventeen in 1948 and to a mere five in 1952.

The spirit of the times was expressed most vividly in the monumental edifices constructed in the capital. When he travelled by road from the Kremlin to his suburban dacha at Kuntsevo the dictator could behold a succession of vast skyscrapers: apartment buildings for the privileged few, offices, and hotels. He supervised each design personally. In case he should prefer to travel by underground railway (Metro), construction was begun of a special line, doubling the one used by ordinary mortals. (It was still unfinished at his death.) The aim of these projects was to erect prestigious monuments worthy of the age of socialism triumphant. This would have been less questionable had the population's basic housing needs been taken care of. As it was, some people still had to live in dug-outs—in Belarus this was the lot of 34,000 families in 1947, although a quarter of a million units had been built since 1944—or else in overcrowded communal apartments, often with more than one family to a room.

The emphasis laid on public buildings accorded well with Stalinist ideological priorities. Ambitious plans were drawn up for the total reconstruction of Moscow, whose privileged, sacramental character was underlined by lavish celebrations in 1947 of the (somewhat spurious) eight-hundredth anniversary of its foundation. It was to become a model city for the whole country, which would thereby acquire a homogeneous appearance (Groys 1990). Vast squares were intended to accommodate parades, with hundreds of thousands of participants, on festive occasions. Such public rituals were a central element in what I. Golomstock (1990) calls the 'political liturgy' of Stalinism. Its purpose was to celebrate and symbolize the supposedly harmonious nature of Soviet society, purged of social or ethnic 'contradictions'. There was nothing spontaneous about these gatherings. They were carefully regulated, right down to such details as the size and order of the leaders' portraits that the marchers carried or the wording of the official slogans so prominently displayed. These slogans, the content of which changed slightly from year to year, were scrutinized by the non-initiated for possible hints as to the direction of policy. Other clues were offered by the order in which the leaders stood when taking the salute from the tribune atop the Lenin mausoleum in Red Square.

Stalinist society was hieratic and rank-conscious. Not only officers but many civilian officials, too, wore uniforms embellished with gold braid, decorations, badges of merit, and the like. Shock workers in industry, performing artists, scientists, and even prolific mothers qualified for medals and marks of distinction. They served to mark off those most zealous in the cause from the common throng. It was certainly a far cry from the iconoclastic informality of Lenin's day. But one should not misconstrue the nature of this élitism or the seemingly archaic features in late Stalinist official culture (e.g. the subordinate roles allotted to women). Soviet society had indeed become conservative, but not in the conventional sense of the word. A more appropriate term is 'left-conservative'. The privileges enjoyed by members of the élite were accorded to them as individuals in return for specific achievements or services. What the state had given it could take away—and frequently did. Office-holders had no security of tenure; property could not be inherited. To be sure, one can see in the Stalinist era the makings of a new 'ruling class'. But the process of social stabilization was a slow, long-term phenomenon. Only later did members of the *nomenkla-tura* acquire a consciousness of their collective interests and begin to exercise informal pressure on the shaping of public policy (see below, p. 203). This could not happen until they had been freed from the political terror that was the Stalinist regime's hallmark.

The world of learning

History

Historians played a fateful role in developing the Stalin cult and a veritable mythology capable of buttressing the regime's pretensions. Their profession had long since been purged of dissonant voices. In the 1930s archives had been closed, original research discountenanced and historians turned into little more than propagandists with academic credentials. Like other scholars, they were required to lace their work with references to the Marxist-Leninist classics (i.e. to Stalin), whether these were appropriate or not. The emphasis now placed on Russia's achievements necessitated a revaluation of the imperial legacy. One aspect of this was a positive appreciation of certain rulers (e.g. Ivan IV, Peter I) or military leaders (Suvorov, Kutuzov), deemed 'progressive', whose deeds of prowess had prefigured Stalin's own. One might well wonder how this 'personalist' interpretation could be reconciled with continued adherence to a revolutionary line that stressed the virtues of class struggle, from Muscovite peasant rebels through the Decembrists (but omitting Populists and Social Democrats!) to the Bolsheviks. Somehow historians, by skilfully juggling facts and concepts, managed to accomplish this feat. They also dutifully falsified the record by presenting the Russian people, from antiquity onward, as the source of 'progressive' influences on other peoples presently in the USSR, but never as their recipient. In her international relations, too, Russia was depicted as having consistently triumphed over foreign aggressors. Charles XII, Napoleon, and Hitler were joined in the rogues' gallery by President Woodrow Wilson, portrayed as the real inspirer of Allied intervention in Soviet Russia during the civil war. In this way present concerns were simply retrojected into the past. Political correctness mattered more than historical truth.

Other social sciences

The other social sciences fared little better in Stalin's final years. 'Dogmatism, rote learning, stagnation and inertia prevailed. There was no room for free discussion or the contest of various opinions ... Truth was not what corresponded to the facts, to empirical research, but what Comrade Stalin had declared to be true' (R. A. Medvedev 1989). In economics, quotation-mongering replaced independent thought. This was because the discipline was so closely bound up with high policy. In 1947 the eminent Hungarian-born scholar E. Varga got into trouble for holding that the advanced capitalist economies had been so transformed by the war as to make revolutionary upheavals unlikely; it followed that the USSR could afford to seek a rapprochement with reformist (Social Democratic) Western governments. Among critics of this 'soft' approach was Voznesensky, author of a book on the Soviet wartime economy (1946) which became very popular, especially because scholarly works were so rare at the time. It was this popularity, rather than the content, that seems to have aroused Stalin's suspicions, for he fancied himself as supreme authority in this domain. A recent study (Kutuzov 1989) suggests that Voznesensky fell into disfavour over a disagreement about the allocation of resources. A Zhdanov protégé, he was implicated in the so-called 'Leningrad case' (see below, p. 34). Varga escaped disgrace but suffered the loss of his institute. In his *Economic Problems of Socialism* (1952) Stalin indirectly replied to both men. He argued that international capitalism, far from becoming modernized, faced a major crisis in the near future, and so was in a dangerously aggressive mood. The USSR might be granted a temporary respite while the 'imperialists' fought each other (as in 1939–41), but it should use this interval to build up its defences, promote heavy industry, and strengthen the socialist state; there was to be no internal relaxation—least of all, as we have seen, for the peasants. This highly charged atmosphere, together with the lack of reliable statistics, prevented economists from doing serious professional work.

Philosophy likewise degenerated into an adjunct of ideological wrangles. In 1946 Alexandrov, head of Agitprop and a Zhdanov associate, produced a history of Western European philosophy that aroused Stalin's objections. Their precise nature is still unclear, but the subsequent 'discussion' concentrated on the author's failure to consider native Russian thought. Such neglect was perfectly comprehensible, given the derivative character of (secular) Russian philosophy in the eighteenth and nineteenth centuries. This charge was probably just a smoke-screen concealing a faction fight between two groups of ideologists. The critics, who held to a more dogmatic line, were taking revenge for defeat in an earlier (1944) debate, when they had been accused of being too kind to Hegel. Unfortunately no one could deal frankly with the underlying issue, Lenin's 'russification' of Marxist thought and Stalin's subsequent elevation to the rank of Communism's chief theorist.

The Leader's lack of qualifications for such a role became painfully clear in 1950, when he came out with a pretentious statement condemning the eccentric philological teachings of the long-deceased Academician Marr. He had held that all languages derived from common roots and would one day amalgamate into a universal proletarian idiom. This notion was indeed unscientific, as Stalin pointed out. Unfortunately his own position 'was scarcely any more Marxist, since he asserted that language was a permanent feature of a nation's culture and implied that it was impervious to social change' (Hosking 1985). 'Stalin's idiotic ramblings', writes one Western biographer, 'were acclaimed by no fewer than eight professors of linguistics who published panegyrics in the same edition of *Pravda*—a miserable indication of his regime's reduction of every field of human endeavour to the crudest thuggery' (De Jonge 1986). The pronouncement served to encourage chauvinistic claims on behalf of the natural beauties of Russian ('the language of Pushkin and Lenin') and to foster its use by other Soviet nationalities. As in tsarist times, the teaching of Russian was seen as an integrating device.

To encourage respect and admiration for their 'elder brother', non-Russians were also subjected to a bombastic propaganda campaign lauding Russian achievements, past and present. 'It was suddenly found that Russians had discovered everything worth discovering. Anything their geniuses had not hit upon was either not worth knowing or simply false' (McCauley 1981). The claims ranged from the discovery of radio waves (by Popov, not Marconi!) to voyages of exploration in the Pacific. The functionaries responsible for such extravagances were often junior men who exploited the hysterical atmosphere in order to advance their careers or play off old scores. Ajubei (1989) likens his experiences to living in the theatre of the absurd. He recalls that, when he once stood up for a fellow-student accused of some ideological fault, he was not allowed to march on parade with his colleagues but had to mount guard in his faculty instead. This was the least onerous of penalties. Countless others active in the country's intellectual life paid for their sins with dismissal, imprisonment, or worse. In the academic world spies and delators were everywhere, ready to pounce on their fellows at the slightest sign of deviant thought or conduct.

Science

Long before the war the agrobiologist Trofim Lysenko had put forward unsubstantiated claims on behalf of a process, called 'vernalization', that he claimed could increase dramatically the yields of cereal crops. Although inadequately demonstrated by practical experiments (which he sometimes falsified), it won the favour of ignorant Party officials eager for quick results, but encountered opposition within the scientific establishment. As director of the Academy of Agricultural Sciences, Lysenko denounced his critics, among them the eminent Academician N. I. Vavilov, as 'wreckers' and 'Trotskyites'. Vavilov was arrested in 1940 and later died in the Gulag. After the war Lysenko was able to turn the xenophobic mood at the top to his own account by posing as an authentic man of the people who was defending 'socialist' biology against its 'bourgeois' enemies. He pronounced 'Michurinist' genetics, named after an earlier Russian scientist, inherently superior to the 'reactionary' theories of such Western geneticists as Weissmann, Mendel, and Morgan. Lysenko continued to meet with resistance from scientists, organized notably by the Belarusian Academician A. A. Zherbak. Even within his own academy his views were termed 'metaphysical'. But Stalin was entranced by the idea that man could remake nature. As is now known, he personally edited the text of Lysenko's celebrated address to the Agricultural Academy in July–August 1948, sharpening his criticisms of Western authorities in the field (Yesakov *et al.* 1991; Rossianov 1994). As a result Lysenko was able to force through the election of his own protégés. He was aided by the sudden death shortly afterwards of Zhdanov, who seems to have been lukewarm towards Lysenko—although he did not back his opponents whole-heartedly either, leaving it to his son Yurii, head of Agitprop's scientific department, to try to limit his power. As a result of these manœuvres the quack biologist was able to remain in the saddle for many more years (see below, p. 109).

The damage done to physics was of a different character, in that this scientific discipline was promoted energetically—to serve military ends. Already in 1946 the USSR started up its first atomic reactor. This success was followed in August 1949 by the explosion of an atomic bomb, so ending the Americans' monopoly of the nuclear weapon. This topic will not be examined further here. Suffice it to note that the Soviet counterpart to the Manhattan project absorbed the lion's share of the country's scientific resources. It was directed by an eight-man committee under the ultimate authority of Beria, the security police chief, who contributed to it a vast force of prison labour (Knight 1993).

Politics, 1948–53

Zhdanov's sudden (and possibly unnatural) death had political repercussions. His principal rival, Malenkov, with the assistance of Beria and undoubtedly also Stalin's tacit assent, engineered a plot against the late leader's adherents in Leningrad which resulted ultimately in the imprisonment or liquidation of at least two hundred senior officials. It was the most serious case ('affair')[6] in post-war Soviet politics. Much about it remains obscure even after recent publication of studies based on archival evidence. One motive was certainly Stalin's fear of Peter the Great's capital as a source of contagious Western influence: as we know, he was eager to accord Moscow privileged status. He had never trusted Russia's second metropolis: it was there that Kirov had been murdered at his instigation in 1934, setting in motion the machinery of the Great

Terror, and during the war he had been slow to help relieve the agony of its nine-hundred-day siege. In 1948 his foreign enemies included Titoist 'revisionists', and an official delegation from Yugoslavia had been received in Leningrad with what to his suspicious mind may well have seemed undue cordiality.[7] According to Kutuzov (1989), the immediate pretext for action was an anonymous denunciation alleging irregularity in counting the votes at a Party conference held in December 1948. Two months later Malenkov arrived in the city for a meeting of the regional committee (*obkom*) bureau and denounced three local politicians—Popkov, Kapustin, and Badaev—for alleged 'anti-Party activities'. Popkov admitted, no doubt under physical pressure, that he had wanted to set up a *Russian* Communist Party. Further expulsions and personnel changes followed in the city committee (*gorkom*), which was assured by Leningrad's new boss, Andrianov, of Stalin's 'fatherly concern'. Works mentioning those repressed were ordered to be withdrawn from circulation. In September 1950, after a secret trial in familiar style, six of the accused, including Voznesensky and a CC secretary, Kuznetsov, were condemned to be shot. The execution of five more known individuals, and an unknown number of 'responsible workers', followed soon afterwards. Among them were two of Voznesensky's kin—a characteristically Stalinist touch. Other accused were sent to the Gulag. All were eventually rehabilitated and the Party members reinstated (but not until 1988!).

By 1948 Stalin's latent anti-Semitism had been fully aroused. Malenkov again acted as his handyman in the so-called 'anti-Zionist case'. This involved members of a wartime organization of Soviet Jews, the Jewish Anti-Fascist Committee. In January its chairman, the famous actor Solomon Mikhoels, was killed by police (on Stalin's orders, naturally) in what was falsely represented as a motor accident; he was buried with honours. Two Jewish academics, an economist and a literary scholar, were coerced into providing false testimony that members of the committee had acted improperly, but some time passed before the case was concocted (*ICC* 12/1989). The most prominent victim was the 'old Bolshevik' trade-union leader S. A. Lozovsky, who in 1944 had suggested, in a memorandum to Stalin, setting up a Jewish autonomous republic in the Crimea. This was now represented as a treasonable idea. In January 1949 Malenkov made Lozovsky confess to criminal activity. He was expelled from the CC and arrested, as were eleven other men. The Supreme Court's Military Collegium heard the case in August 1952. The judges did not believe the evidence (which had been obtained by torture), but when told that the Politburo had decided what should be done duly sentenced thirteen of the accused to death and six others to prison and exile. Of 110 other Jews caught up in the ramifications of this case, ten were shot. This was only the tip of the iceberg. Jewish cultural institutions were closed down. Thousands were dismissed from their jobs and harassed simply because of their national allegiance. (One wretched individual had to endure several years in a camp for praising Charlie Chaplin!)

Stalin had previously had Molotov's wife, who was Jewish, arrested, and later he replaced his faithful acolyte at the Foreign ministry by the infamous Vyshinsky. He apparently suspected Beria, too, of partiality for Jewish interests and of neglecting his duties as security overlord. In 1951 he ordered MGB chief Abakumov (who was not a Beria client) to put together a case involving alleged conspiracy by several of Beria's associates in his native Mingrelia, a region in the west of Georgia. Thereupon Abakumov was himself sacked and arrested, but in eight months of 1952 over four hundred Georgian officials lost their jobs. Beria's position was clearly at risk. He managed to fend off a purge of his supporters but at the end of 1952 two senior police officials, one of whom (Eitingon) was Jewish, were arrested. Meanwhile in Czechoslovakia the former Party leader Slanský and his associates were facing trial for alleged 'cosmopolitanism'; most of the defendants were Jews.

'The Prague trial can be seen as a forerunner of the subsequent doctors' plot trial in Moscow' (Knight 1993), for the charge of political murder by doctors was common to both. Early in January 1953 the Party's theoretical journal *Kommunist* published an ominous article urging vigilance against internal enemies. It was clear that Jews were meant. Then, on the thirteenth, came the sensational announcement that a group of 'terrorist doctors' had been uncovered and arrested. They had allegedly caused the deaths of Zhdanov and another Party leader (Shcherbakov) by deliberate maltreatment and tried to damage the health of several senior officers. Large segments of the populace were willing to believe these fantastic charges, and there was a frenzied wave of anti-Semitic attacks. The scene was clearly being set for a massive purge. Rumours spread that all Jews were to be rounded up and deported to the east. The security services had given ample proof that they were capable of organizing such an operation.

It became known later that the so-called 'doctors' plot' case was set in motion by a delator, a police informer named Dr Lydia Timashuk. She was presumably put up to it by Ignat'ev, who had replaced Abakumov at the MGB, and his deputy Riumin—acting at the Boss's behest.[8] Stalin had been in ill health for some time. Earlier in 1952 his personal physician, the eminent V. N. Vinogradov, had incautiously suggested that the Leader should reduce his activities. Stalin, furious, cried 'put him in irons!' Such tantrums are characteristic of those suffering from cerebral arteriosclerosis (Rapoport 1991). He was afraid of death and saw plotters everywhere. Much like Ivan IV four centuries earlier, he had lost his zest for life yet clung to power. Alone but for an occasional visit by trembling cronies, he stalked the Kremlin or his suburban *dacha*, a prey to melancholic musings.

One of his rare public appearances was at the long-delayed Nineteenth Party congress, in October 1952, the first such gathering since 1939. But he said little, leaving it to Malenkov to deliver the keynote address. This suggested that he was now the heir apparent. Yet no one in the inner circle could be sure of the Leader's favour. At a CC meeting held directly after the congress Stalin singled out Molotov and Mikoian for criticism. He may have planned to destroy the entire Politburo in the purge. For at his suggestion the CC elected a large Presidium (twenty-five members and eleven candidates), within which was an unpublicized nine-man 'bureau' of senior officials. The latter were apparently to be replaced by newcomers drawn from the former body. This at any rate was the view of Khrushchev, who would have been among the victims.

But human mortality intervened. On 1 March 1953, after one of his customary night-long drinking parties, Stalin suffered a burst blood vessel in the brain. He was found, by a maid or his guards, on the floor of his *dacha*, where he had evidently lain for some hours.[9] The staff demanded that doctors be called but the leaders who arrived (Malenkov, Beria, and, later, Khrushchev) failed to act promptly. Not until after 8.30 a.m. on 2 March did the dying man receive medical treatment. The delay may have been deliberate. Beria, who had the most to gain, is the prime suspect, but there is no hard evidence against him, nor is it likely that he conspired with other leaders, since they were riven by mutual suspicion. More plausibly, the delay was due to fear that, if Stalin recovered, he would hold them responsible for whatever doctors had done or not done. If this was so, then Stalin indirectly owed the manner of his death to his homicidal attitude towards the medical profession. Probably doctors could not have saved him anyway. He suffered what his daughter, S. Allilueva, calls 'a difficult and terrible death', lingering on in agony as his comrades held vigil. At 9.50 p.m. on 5 March his life ended. The system he had created would survive him for over thirty years.

PART II

Hope Frustrated

2 A Reformer in the Kremlin

The succession struggle

Unlike Lenin, Stalin left no 'last testament'. This meant that the succession would be settled simply by bargaining between his closest associates rather than by any legal means. On 5 March 1953, when Stalin died at his *dacha* outside Moscow, those who gathered at his bedside had mixed emotions. On one hand they were relieved of anxiety lest they become victims of the new purge that Stalin had been preparing. On the other hand they had good reason to be afraid, both of each other and of the popular reaction to their takeover. No one could be sure of the extent to which Soviet society had been 'Stalinized'. In the event there was little of the 'disarray and panic' of which they warned in the official announcement of his death. That casualties occurred during the funeral ceremony was due to the authorities' own nervousness. The streets of Moscow were filled with police. The crowd stampeded and several dozen people were trampled to death. Rumour promptly inflated the figure to hundreds or even thousands. Yet the country remained quiet. Only in the Gulag did some *zeks* shout with joy at the news that the old ogre was no more. Elsewhere the public mood was one of cautious anticipation. On hearing of the Leader's fatal illness a soldier said: 'Stalin won't last long and that's all to the good. You'll see how everything will change at once.' He was overheard and his offence investigated (Lazarev 1992).

Nikita Khrushchev was not the only functionary to shed tears—sincerely, as he relates in his memoirs—at Stalin's passing. The writer Konstantin Simonov's initial sentiment was 'that we had lost a great man'; later he came to feel 'that it might have been better to have lost him earlier'. The sobering-up process was assisted in his case by a reprimand, passed down from on high, for writing too eloquent a tribute to 'the great genius of all ages and all peoples'. This style of adulation, deprecated as 'cult of the individual', was now swiftly going out of fashion. The new watchword was 'collective leadership'.

Stalin's heirs did their best to present a united front to the world, sometimes going to ridiculous lengths by simultaneously opening all doors of their car when alighting. To be sure, there was a degree of consensus among them, notably on the need to adopt a more benign attitude towards popular aspirations for greater prosperity. But this was outweighed by the element of personal rivalry that was present from the start. Malenkov and Beria first moved to concentrate power in their own hands. By a decision published on 7 March the former assumed the role of head of government (chairman of the Council of Ministers), while retaining his post as a Party secretary; the latter became one of four first deputy chairmen and minister of Internal Affairs. This agency absorbed the hitherto independent State Security ministry. They thus controlled the three chief instruments of rule. Among the losers in this reshuffle was Khrushchev. He held no government appointment and forfeited his post as head of the Party committee in Moscow. However, he was the only Party secretary who had a seat on the Presidium (as the Politburo was now known) and the Secretariat. This gave him a political base which he lost no time in exploiting. Within days he had engineered a redistribution of offices which elevated the Party's position *vis-à-vis* that of the state organs. The Central Committee met on 14 March. Malenkov gave up his post on the Secretariat, and Khrushchev's name now headed the list of its five members. In effect he now became Party chief, a position regularized a few months later by the award of the title of First Secretary. Colloquially he was referred to by intimates simply as 'First' (*pervyi*), a politer form of Stalin's appellation 'Boss' (*khoziain*). But much remained to be done before his power would approach that of his forerunner—if indeed it ever did so.

The first task facing members of the new ruling collective was to rid themselves of the fearsome Beria. According to Khrushchev's account, he was the prime mover in the affair. There seems no reason to doubt his claim, although the details have yet to be corroborated. He secured the reluctant support first of Malenkov, Voroshilov—'I had a job persuading him', he once remarked in his presence, 'as he was very afraid it would all go wrong'—and Kaganovich, who needed reassurance that a majority of Presidium members was in favour. Khrushchev had probably already obtained the support of Mikoian, who likewise took some persuading, since he hoped Beria might reform his ways, and of the Defence minister, Bulganin. Even more important was the backing, in this case given enthusiastically, of Marshal Zhukov, although Khrushchev chose to downplay his role in most later versions of his story.

Beria seems to have underestimated his adversaries' willingness to take such a grave risk. He was in any case at a disadvantage in that he had no firm base of political support in the Party's upper echelons. That was why he sought to curry favour by assuming an implausible 'liberal' guise. At the end of March an amnesty was announced, which however did not extend to political offenders. On 4 April the 'doctors' plot' was formally declared to have been based on fraudulent testimony extracted from the accused 'by the use of impermissible means of investigation strictly forbidden under Soviet law', i.e. by torture. The surviving victims were freed and their torturers arrested in their place. Dr Timashuk, whose denunciation of her colleagues had launched the affair, was deprived of the Order of Lenin she had earlier been awarded. The previous security chief, Ignat'ev, lost his position as a Party secretary. The purge that had been carried out in Georgia in 1951–2, popularly known as the 'Mingrelian case', which at the time had threatened Beria's position, was likewise reversed. In this republic, as in several others, new leaders were appointed who belonged to the titular nationality. The most important of these changes was in Ukraine, where Kirichenko replaced Mel'nikov as Party boss. The latter was criticized for 'gross errors in the selection of cadres', with the implication that in future local men should be appointed to leadership posts at republican and regional level. A Presidium decision of 20 May 1953, published forty years later, made the latter point in regard to Lithuania, from where officials ignorant of the native language were to be recalled. The order was countermanded after Beria's fall and actually removed from the Presidium's minutes (*IA* 6/1993). This idea clearly went too far for Khrushchev and others at the centre. After his fall Beria would be attacked for 'attempting to sow discord and enmity between the nations of the USSR . . . under the false pretext of struggling against distortions of the Party's nationality policy'. Other charges against him included deviations over agricultural policy—he is thought to have advocated giving peasants internal passports, so making them equal in status to other citizens—and foreign relations. But the real reason, of course, was that he had accumulated too much power for his colleagues' comfort: they felt they must unseat him before he turned his mighty police machine against them. Malenkov later complained that Beria had spied on his Presidium colleagues through their bodyguards and had their phones tapped—the normal duty of a security police chief in Stalin's Russia. Khrushchev added that Beria had sought to downgrade the Party to a propaganda agency and that he had 'boasted he could get anyone [under investigation] to confess they were linked to the king or queen of England'. (These details became known in 1991.) The charges against Beria by his erstwhile associates were clearly exaggerated by partisanship. It is not yet clear how far his 'liberalism' was sincere (or realistic) and how far it was just a political ploy. His conduct is given the benefit of the doubt by his knowledgeable Western biographer (Knight 1993), but the police chief's earlier bloody record speaks in favour of the conventional view.

The *coup*, for such it was, of 26 June was carried out at a Presidium meeting by senior military officers at Khrushchev's and his fellow plotters' behest. It was a dangerous business. Beria, caught off guard when arraigned by Khrushchev, reached for his briefcase, which others present feared might well contain a weapon. Fortunately it did not, and he was led away unresistingly to face his investigators. No public announcement was made until 10 July. According to Andrei Sakharov, who saw it, a secret document was circulated through Party channels detailing some of the sadistic acts of which Beria was culpable. There can be no doubt that he amply deserved the death sentence, which may have been carried out before December 1953, when the verdict was announced. Six senior collaborators likewise faced the supreme penalty. But justice was manifestly *not* done: the trial was held in secret, in Stalinist style, and the brief public announcement clearly mendacious. Moreover, only a limited purge was carried out of the secret police apparatus.

The struggle was now fought out principally between Khrushchev and Malenkov, whose source of support lay respectively in the Party and state machinery. Since the two apparatuses were interlocked, this is an over-simplified way of looking at matters, but there is enough truth in the cliché to make it serviceable. The dispute was not just about style of leadership or the placing of cadres. It inevitably involved policy differences as well, which became more marked as the months passed. In a nutshell,

Malenkov sought to increase the production of consumer goods by switching investment and resources away from the heavy industrial sector, including defence, while Khrushchev argued that refrigerators were of no use without sufficient food to put in them. His emphasis was therefore on raising agricultural output by an assortment of fairly radical measures to be examined shortly, for which he took an unusual amount of personal responsibility. To achieve his ends he formed a coalition with the heavy industry and defence lobby, and this in turn affected the shape of the USSR's 'new course' in foreign policy, stiffening conditions for détente with the West.

The First Secretary, whose control over the Party was reinforced by a massive replacement of Stalinist 'has-beens' by men of a new generation loyal to himself, clearly held the stronger cards. Within a year and a half Malenkov had been worsted. Before the Supreme Soviet on 8 February 1955 he was obliged to confess his errors over agricultural policy (which had been in his charge under Stalin) and to resign as head of government in favour of Khrushchev's ally Bulganin. Another useful ally during this period was Molotov, with whom Khrushchev's relations were then good, as the latter has since revealed; but later in 1955 they parted ways. Molotov opposed Khrushchev's unconventional foreign policy moves and in October of that year was forced to make a humiliating acknowledgement of an elementary doctrinal error, by seeming to question the formula that 'socialism' had already been achieved in the USSR. This ideological tenet remained unchallenged in public until the Gorbachev era, when it was exposed as a fallacy.

Molotov remained a Stalinist until his death in 1986 at the venerable age of ninety-six. 'After Lenin no individual was greater, more consistent or talented than Stalin', he told an interviewer in 1972 (Chuev 1991). His association with the dictator dated from 1917. Of the Kremlin leadership in the early 1920s, Molotov alone survived the purges, in the organization of which he took a prominent part: together with Stalin he authorized the elimination of nearly a quarter of a million individuals whose names figured on the notorious lists submitted to them by the NKVD (on orders from above). As the mouthpiece of Soviet foreign policy after the war he earned the sobriquet 'stone-bottom' for his intransigent attitude towards the Western powers. Regardless of the dangers of war in a nuclear age, he persisted in seeing the world as divided into irrevocably hostile ideological blocs. With equal stubbornness he opposed change at home, treating Khrushchev as a mere school-boy, intelligent but uncultured and lacking proper Bolshevik steadfastness.

Malenkov, born in 1902, belonged to a later generation of men whose careers took off at the time of the Great Terror. He rose to prominence during the war, when he organized the supply of aircraft and other military goods to the front. As we know, in 1948 he helped Beria organize the 'Leningrad case' and at the end of Stalin's life occupied the number two position. A flabby-faced, unsociable man of mediocre talent, Malenkov in a sense typified the entire Stalinist clique; Roi Medvedev calls him 'squalid and evil'. After his enforced resignation as premier he remained in the Party Presidium, where with other members of the old guard he continued to intrigue against Khrushchev, while cultivating good relations with him on the surface.

Khrushchev

Nikita Khrushchev differed from his comrades less in his career profile than in certain traits of character. He too had risen to high office in the 1930s, as a client of Kaganovich, and had demonstrated the requisite degree of toughness in the struggle against alleged 'deviationists'. 'At times the tone of his reports was no different from that of Vyshinsky, [the prosecutor] at the show trials' (Pomer-antsev 1993). He cannot escape a share of responsibility for the purges. But he operated at a relatively subordinate level. Whereas Kaganovich is thought to have personally signed the death war-rants of 36,000 people, Khrushchev's victims were probably num-bered in thousands. When he took over as Ukrainian Party boss in January 1938, several thousand people under investigation, includ-ing 1,200 security men, were taken out of jail and summarily shot. Yet it is not clear how far this wave of terror was due to his personal initiative (for Yezhov also came to Kiev around this time). In his memoirs Khrushchev claims to have exposed the activities of a notorious local delator, and says that he once found himself denounced by a man under investigation. Summoned to Stalin and confronted with the 'evidence', he denied the accusation as the dictator closely studied his facial expression. It was a near escape. For some reason his explanation was accepted, but things could easily have gone the other way. In this atmosphere of general suspicion Khrushchev, like countless others, helped to stoke the infernal machine in the hope of saving his own skin, while keeping his doubts to himself. He knew how dangerous it was to know too much and did not ask awkward questions.

Almost miraculously, he seems to have preserved some sense of moral values, of conscience, to which he later gave expression by dissociating himself, at least partially, from the darkest aspects of Stalin's legacy. Strangely, the older man seems to have trusted him more than he did such devoted cronies as Beria or Molotov. Was he perhaps taken in by Khrushchev's readiness to play the jester at his macabre court? For Khrushchev often affected an air of simple joviality. Later, once he had taken charge of Russia's destiny, this would delude many foreign observers.

In truth Nikita Sergeevich was a complex and contradictory individual. In appearance he had the rough earthiness of his peasant origins, which he liked to emphasize: rotund and rubicund, with several warts on his face, irregular teeth and sharp, alert brown eyes. His speech too was full of folksy aphorisms, proverbs, and metaphors. He would discourse volubly on agricultural or other matters close to his heart, interspersing the cascade of jargon with shafts of wit or telling informal asides. At congresses and the like, when subordinates were addressing the throng with Khrushchev in the chair, they might find themselves rudely interrupted with some abrasive remark. If they failed to respond in the manner expected of them, deferentially but with a display of expertise, they faced public humiliation, perhaps dismissal. The 'First' was temperamental and irascible, prone to fits of anger. He judged people capriciously, just as he decided complicated problems on impulse, without having made a thorough preliminary study of the pros and cons. For him it was results that counted—and yet this pragmatism was allied to a burning ideological zeal.

Khrushchev was a true believer in the Communist cause, a man whose youthful romantic vision of a future utopia had been less tarnished by the exercise of power than was the case with any of his comrades. But this idealism had a down-to-earth materialistic flavour. He once said that 'it was no use everyone having the correct ideology if they had to walk around without any trousers on'. Not being an intellectual, he cared little for abstractions unless their practical worth could be tangibly demonstrated in terms comprehensible to the common man. Thus the bright Soviet paradise once full Communism had been attained was something that he visualized concretely as an abundance of food and consumer goods, a society in which labour had lost its harsh, obligatory character and become a natural leisure activity, a pastime. This dream world, he held, was a feasible objective that could be reached in the course of a few generations by the exercise of will-power and organizational drive.

To those more aware of realities this optimism seemed at best naïve, at worst a harmful delusion; but it was dangerous to utter such sentiments in public. For Khrushchev was no liberal, no 'pluralist' as we might say today, ready to debate and qualify, or to acknowledge that there might be many ways to the truth. Here his education, or rather the lack of it, showed to his disadvantage. He was intolerant of any opinion he deemed subversive or 'incorrect', and considered it his right and duty to censure those who held them. At such moments, as his son-in-law Ajubei says, he 'wouldn't listen to anyone who objected'. The obverse of this was that he trusted advisers who told him what he wanted to hear, whether they were pseudo-scientific charlatans like Lysenko or simply aspiring *apparatchiki* given to flattery. This weakness grew more dangerous the longer he held power. On the other hand, Khrushchev could learn from his mistakes and even acknowledge them—but by then, as likely as not, the damage had been done. The basic fault, of course, lay not in his character but in the system he headed, which set narrow limits on what any leader, however gifted, could achieve.

'De-Stalinization'

Could one really, as Khrushchev hoped, rid the Party, and Soviet society generally, of the 'deformations' of socialism associated with Stalin and return to a 'truly Leninist' path? Some time in 1954–5 Khrushchev became aware of the full extent of the crimes that had been committed under his predecessor, and seems to have been genuinely shocked. As a shrewd politician he also realized that this information was political dynamite. Whoever released it, even to a limited number of Party functionaries, would gain considerably in stature *vis-à-vis* his comrades whose hands were more deeply stained with blood. They would be morally and politically discredited. To be sure, a Stalinist might ask: 'where were you when these crimes were committed?' The story goes that, at a gathering which Khrushchev addressed, someone in the audience actually put this question. 'Who said that?', the leader demanded. Silence. 'There's your answer: then, too, we were all scared.' Though probably apocryphal, the exchange reflects a grim reality.

Far graver was the objection that the Party would be exposed to ridicule, and its hold on power jeopardized, if the truth about Stalin were revealed. To this Khrushchev responded with practical considerations. First, with Gulag survivors returning *en masse*, the facts could no longer be kept secret anyhow. Unless the Party tried to come to terms honestly with its past it could make no progress towards a better future, which required it to 'strengthen its ties with the masses'. Second, only a partial, limited revision of the historical record was to be made. No general purge was contemplated of Stalinist cadres, who would keep their jobs and privileges. Arguments such as these, advanced in private, helped to overcome the scruples of his Presidium colleagues, who strove first to prevent and then to delay delivery of an official report to the next Party congress summarizing the findings of the investigating commission that had meanwhile been set up. They agreed on condition that the report be given in a secret (closed) session. The text was then to be made known to Party members at restricted meetings, but not to the population as a whole. This compromise was not, however, adhered to.

On the evening of 24 February 1956 delegates to the Twentieth Party congress were unexpectedly summoned back to the chamber. They listened in stunned silence, punctuated by outbursts of indignation, as Khrushchev, using unusually straightforward language, exposed the hero they had once deified as a criminal who had inflicted untold damage on the Party and the people. He quoted from Lenin's 'Testament', in which the founder of the Soviet state had warned of Stalin's character defects and urged his removal as Secretary-General. (People had been shot for mere possession of this document.) The assassination of Kirov in 1934, he strongly implied, had been Stalin's own handiwork, as had been the totally unjustified 'mass repressions' that followed. Leading Party officials had been treated with 'brutal wilfulness', expelled from its ranks in contravention of the statutes and forced to confess to imaginary crimes by 'cruel and inhuman tortures'. Appeals for mercy by the innocent victims had gone unheeded. There had been 383 blacklists, each containing the names of hundreds if not thousands of Party, soviet, Komsomol, military, and economic workers, all of whom had been shot. These cases were now being reviewed and many of them declared void because the evidence had been falsified: 'since 1954 the Military Collegium of the Supreme Court has rehabilitated 7,679 individuals, many of them posthumously.'

Khrushchev was equally scathing about Stalin's vaunted reputation as war leader and also as an authority on scientific, economic, and ideological matters. He told his audience that Stalin had personally edited his official biography to augment praise for his accomplishments, and had caused costly monuments to be erected to his glory at a time when people were living in log cabins. Towards the end of his life he had become suspicious of even his closest associates and had planned to annihilate them. 'You are blind kittens,' he had told members of the Politburo, 'what will happen without me? The country will perish because you cannot recognize enemies.' Khrushchev concluded by observing that in eliminating the 'cult of the individual' one had to proceed cautiously: 'we should not give ammunition to the enemy [or] wash our dirty linen before their eyes.' The Party would surely emerge from its self-examination strengthened both morally and politically, poised 'to lead the Soviet people along the Leninist path to new successes, new victories'.

His final peroration was greeted with tumultuous applause—and no wonder. Psychologically, his listeners were immensely relieved that all the excesses and errors could be so conveniently blamed on the dead leader, while the system of rule he had established was to continue more or less unchanged. Judged politically, the speech was astute. It had incidentally thrown discredit on Malenkov, Voroshilov, and his other opponents in the Kremlin. Judged as historical analysis, it was highly deficient. Khrushchev was selective in his indictment of Stalin. He made no reference to any wrongdoing prior to 1934, or to the sufferings endured by non-Party people during the Terror. Only some of the deported national minorities rated a mention. Moreover, he offered no convincing explanation how 'Leninist' rule, purportedly so progressive, could have degenerated into such an odious tyranny. In effect he substituted new myths for old ones as a way of legitimizing the Party's continuing monopoly on power and information. It was far from clear how the 'cult of the individual'—an inadequate and misleading term—could really be overcome. Even so, for all its faults the 'secret speech' was an act of considerable political courage. Khrushchev had grasped the nettle. He also exhibited a characteristic recklessness. The road ahead would be rockier than he expected, for he overestimated ordinary people's gullibility. In a sense the whole of later Soviet history may be seen as a reaction to his revelations.

Khrushchev may not have been too concerned when, despite the security precautions, the text of his speech became public knowledge worldwide. (In the USSR it would not be published until 1988.) Copies circulated on the Moscow black market and in the Academy of Sciences some Party members demanded that all the guilty be brought to justice: their primary organization (cell) had to be disbanded. Others were confused and disoriented. Over a period of four and a half months to May 1957, 128 cases of alleged 'anti-Soviet' activity were submitted to the RSFSR Supreme Court (Barsukov 1994). In Tbilisi Georgian nationalist students misguidedly demonstrated in Stalin's defence; the police opened fire and there were many casualties. Abroad the reaction was far more serious. Riots broke out in East Germany and Poland; later in 1956 Hungary would rise in revolution. Some Western Communists resigned in disillusion. All this shook Khrushchev's position at home, and he had to engage in a damage limitation exercise. On 30 June 1956 the Central Committee published a resolution which attempted unconvincingly to provide a Marxist analysis of the reasons for the Stalin cult and reiterated the Party's claims to sole leadership: only 'enemies and slanderers' could allege that the system itself was at fault. Clearly, 'de-Stalinization' did not signal abandonment of the dictatorship or a move towards multi-party rule.

The media played down criticism of Stalin, preferring to attribute past violations of legality to Beria. In October the ideological journal *Kommunist* censured 'immature' Party members for comparing the leadership unfavourably to that in (unnamed) 'fraternal' countries, where problems were being solved in a different spirit: presumably Yugoslavia was meant. Addressing the crowds on the anniversary of the October revolution, Suslov took a tough line on East European affairs and coupled this with explicit positive mention of the former Soviet leader.

Earlier, in June, Molotov and Kaganovich had lost their senior government appointments. They were rewarded some months later by new jobs as ministers of state control and building-materials production. This indicated that they still wielded considerable influence behind the scenes. Presumably owing to differences within the leadership, a Central Committee (CC) plenum planned for September was postponed until the year's end. When it met it administered a rebuff to Khrushchev's plans for a reform of economic decision-making which would weaken the central industrial ministries and give more authority to the local Party cadres. Instead the talk was of revising current output targets, a task entrusted not to the regular agency Gosplan, as one would have expected, but to the relatively obscure State Economic Commission, which was turned into a high-powered cabinet of technocrats under Pervukhin. At a New Year's Eve reception Khrushchev ostentatiously praised Stalin as 'a great Marxist', adding that 'when it comes to combating imperialism we are all Stalinists'. During the following weeks he made several more statements in the same sense. When he went to Hungary early in January Malenkov accompanied him as a top-level watchdog.

By February 1957 the First Secretary was on the rebound. The reasons for this are still unclear. One theory is that he managed to regain a majority on the Presidium (and the CC) as a result of pressure from below by those who saw themselves as potential beneficiaries of his industrial reform. In any case the February 1957 meeting of the Party's 'parliament' agreed to publish his proposals on the subject. They received wide publicity and aroused a good deal of controversy. The State Economic Commission suffered a decline in status and was subsequently disbanded, Pervukhin being given an ordinary ministerial job. Gosplan regained its former pre-eminence and the bureaucratic system of industrial management came in for harsh criticism. The appointment to the Secretariat of Kozlov and Shepilov also seems to have strengthened Khrushchev's hand, although neither man could be termed his whole-hearted supporter—like, for instance, Brezhnev, who had joined that body one year earlier. In short, the political balance in the Kremlin was still shaky.

The 'anti-Party group'

From 5 to 14 June Khrushchev was away from Moscow, paying an official visit to Finland. His absence gave his opponents a chance to concert plans to unseat the mercurial First Secretary and turn back the clock. Malenkov seems to have been the prime mover, with Molotov, Voroshilov, and Kaganovich as his willing accomplices. Bulganin, Pervukhin, and Saburov joined in later. This gave them a 7 : 4 majority in the Presidium. Only Suslov, Mikoian, and Kirichenko were left as Khrushchev's allies—along with most of the six candidate members, who had no voting rights (Shepilov initially backed Khrushchev, but then changed sides), as well as of the secretaries. On 18 June a stormy four-day meeting began. The majority group demanded that the First Secretary resign and that a rotating chairmanship be instituted—which they evidently saw as the first step to his ouster, to be followed by sanctions against him and other reformers. Among those they wished to dismiss was the police chief, Serov, for he held compromising materials on the plotters' criminal activities under Stalin, which they no doubt wanted to destroy. In 1993, when the minutes were published of the ensuing meeting of the CC, it became clear that for the previous two years or so the Presidium had been deeply divided over most questions of current policy. For instance, the majority objected to Khrushchev's unilateral decision to reduce taxes on peasants' private plots.

Although the Presidium voted a resolution in the sense desired by the left-conservative faction, the conspirators reckoned without the army, the KGB, and the mass of Party functionaries, who were favourable to reform. Marshal Zhukov (a candidate member of the Presidium) and the security police chief Serov passed word to one of the secretaries, Kozlov, who was then visiting his home base in Leningrad. He arrived with a delegation from that city and requested admission to the conclave, but in vain. A larger delegation, headed by Serov, demanded that the discussion be transferred to a plenary meeting of the Central Committee. Bulganin, representing the Presidium majority, came out to respond, as did for their part Khrushchev and Mikoian. During the confrontation Serov grabbed Voroshilov by the collar and threatened that if necessary a plenum would be called without the Presidium's approval. In terms of Party discipline ('democratic centralism') this was an act of insubordination.

By this time Zhukov had arranged for a fleet of military aircraft to transport Central Committee members from the provinces *en masse*, and on 22 June this body went into a week-long session.

Gradually the Presidium majority melted away as one member after another made repentant speeches. Molotov held out most stubbornly, as one would expect, but defended himself with a certain dignity. The proceedings were unruly, with serious and trivial charges mixed up together, and the 'deviationists' continually barracked. The crisis was brought to an end by a political bargain. Molotov, Malenkov, and Kaganovich were to lose their ministerial appointments and Presidium membership, but no disciplinary measures were to be taken against them. The first-named was sent, as if in jest, to serve as ambassador to Mongolia, while Malenkov became manager of a power-station in scarcely less remote Kazakhstan. Kaganovich, true to character, pleaded with Khrushchev to spare his life, and was told sternly that times had changed. He ended up in charge of a cement works in Sverdlovsk.

When the crisis was revealed to the public on 4 July—until then it had been a well-kept secret—the victors pinned on the defeated faction the epithet 'anti-Party group'. This is misleading, for under the old dispensation they *were* 'the Party': a majority in its topmost gremium was all that counted. But the fiction of a united leadership had to be upheld. That the reactionary faction had initially been in the majority became apparent later, as its other members were subjected to criticism and dismissed. In March 1958 Bulganin surrendered office as Prime Minister to none other than Khrushchev and went off to a management position at Stavropol' in the north Caucasus. In the circumstances they were all treated with remarkable leniency. Times had indeed changed.

Khrushchev's supremacy

On the new Presidium, expanded to fifteen members, at least twelve were Khrushchev supporters.[1] On the surface his position looked impregnable. By combining the top Party and government jobs he held, on paper, as much power as Stalin had enjoyed during the war. But Khrushchev was not another Stalin. He appreciated the homage that was increasingly paid to him at Party meetings and in the press—another leader cult in embryo—but did not seek to rule as an infallible tyrant. Whatever his intentions, in practice his power was limited by the weight of opinion in the leading strata of the Party and in society generally. He had to earn the authority he wielded by winning successes in domestic and foreign policy. In the international arena this compulsion led to rash or adventuristic actions over Berlin, at the UN, and above all in the Cuban crisis of 1962, which brought the world to the verge of nuclear war. At home his policy was often erratic, especially in agrarian matters; he would interfere in details better left to experts and jump from one expedient to another, making others the scapegoats for setbacks. By his autocratic demeanour Nikita Sergeevich irritated and alienated several groups of important potential supporters within the establishment. Until 1958 he had shown skill in building coalitions; this facility seemed to desert him as he accumulated power that he was unable to exercise with sufficient responsibility.

The first indication of this came already in October 1957, when Marshal Zhukov, the Defence minister, was summarily dismissed from his Party and government offices. He was accused *inter alia* of having sponsored a personality cult of his own and obstructed the work of Party organs in the military. Rumours circulated that he harboured 'Bonapartist aspirations'. At the time Western observers were inclined to think that the charges must have some substance, and that elements in the armed forces stood behind Zhukov in challenging Party pre-eminence. Closer analysis (Colton 1977) shows that the explanation must be sought rather in the personal antagonism that developed between two proud, ebullient leaders rather than in institutional rivalries. We now know that this conflict had much to do with the rehabilitation of the 40,000 or so officers who had fallen victim to the Terror, in which Voroshilov in particular was deeply implicated. Zhukov, in common with other army leaders, was keener to see justice done than Khrushchev, who was bound by the terms of the unwritten deal with his erstwhile Presidium colleagues. This provided *inter alia* that such matters should not be mentioned in public references to the June 1957 crisis.

One reason for Zhukov's dismissal may have been that at the CC meeting in June Bulganin alleged that Zhukov had agreed with him (Bulganin) that the question of Khrushchev's removal was worthy of discussion. Such ambivalence would not have gone unpunished, even though in the debate Zhukov had taken the lead in attacking the reactionaries. According to the unexpurgated version of Khrushchev's memoirs he was told by another general, Moskalenko, that Zhukov was planning to seize power, and he (Khrushchev) suspected that Malinovsky was involved in a plot. However, in view of the role played by the military in Beria's arrest, the incident was papered over. Malinovsky succeeded Zhukov at the Defence ministry. Along with many others in the military establishment, he objected to Khrushchev's subsequent efforts to reduce the armed forces and to concentrate on missiles carrying nuclear warheads. But this controversy will not be explored here.

Among civilians Khrushchev faced passive opposition among middle-level functionaries who felt that the anti-Stalin campaign had gone far enough and yearned for political stability. This sentiment could have been overcome if the First Secretary had been assisted by a capable team of committed reformers, but this was not the case. The men appointed to the Presidium after the defeat of the so-called 'anti-Party group' were in the main either middle-aged mediocrities (Aristov, Beliaev, Ignatov) or 'old warhorses' (A. Nove) like Kuusinen (born 1881), Shvernik—and Mikoian, a perennial survivor. 'The ship of state', write two reflective Soviet historians, 'was manned by people who had no marked profile as individuals, let alone a political one' (Volobuev and Kuleshov 1988). This was due less to Khrushchev's 'blindness', as they suggest, than to the dearth of talent within the Party apparatus. All these men (and the lone woman, Yekaterina Furtseva) disappeared from the Presidium over the next few years, as did rather more effective, if brutal, leaders like Kirichenko and his successor Kozlov. The last-named seemed for a time to be marked out as possible heir apparent, but he took a hard line on foreign policy issues and then suffered a heart attack. Kosygin, Podgorny, and Poliansky, who in May 1960 were promoted to full membership of the Presidium, were less beholden to Khrushchev than their predecessors. The latter would pay the price for his inability to build up a reliable phalanx of political clients, as Stalin had done in the 1920s and Brezhnev would do later.

In September 1958 the First Secretary won the Central Committee's acceptance for his plan to hold an 'extraordinary' Party congress—that is, one convoked ahead of schedule—in the following January. To replace the current Five-Year Plan, which was facing failure due to the unrealistically high targets imposed on certain branches of industry, the delegates adopted one to cover the seven years until 1965, which was relatively consumer-friendly (see below, p. 85). Several speakers vehemently condemned the 'anti-Party group': Khrushchev evidently now felt less compunction about observing the terms of the 1957 'armistice' with his old foes but lacked the will, or the strength, to have them punished further. Over the next years the Stalin issue would resurface periodically as a convenient stick with which to belabour those who questioned his innovations.

These upset some ideological conventions. At the congress Khrushchev proclaimed that the Soviet Union, having achieved 'full socialism', was now entering upon 'the era of the extensive construction of a Communist society' and that it was therefore time to take steps towards the ultimate goal of the 'withering away of the state' by transferring powers from official agencies to 'public organizations'. Given the Party's political privilege—*it* was definitely *not* to wither away!—such ideas were easier to enunciate than to implement, but to many they seemed threatening. A commission was set up under the veteran Kuusinen to elaborate a new Party programme, which was formally adopted at the next (regular) congress, held in October 1961.

According to some of his collaborators, Kuusinen, although in his late seventies, showed himself to be a tolerant and even creative interpreter of Communist doctrine; he evidently had preserved something of the idealism of his early years as a young revolutionary and so found common language with Khrushchev. Whether their ideas were at all practicable, or even sensible, is another matter. When shown a report on 'the transition to an all-people's state', most Party leaders were aghast at its utopian, visionary character. 'People looked at each other in confusion: hadn't he gone too far?' (Nosov 1988). They complained that the citations from Lenin employed in the document were unfamiliar to ordinary mortals. Suslov, the most erudite Marxist-Leninist theoretician, was among the sceptics; another was Ilyichev, Khrushchev's ideological factotum (and a personal foe of Suslov), who admitted privately that in his view it would take forty to fifty years to build Communism, rather than the ten to twenty years envisaged in the new Party programme. The timetable was far more specific than was usual in such documents. It fairly bristled with projections for the output of fuel, machinery, and consumer durables, all expressed in quantitative terms, without consideration of the structural changes that such an expansion would require. Khrushchev was not just being cynical. The programme reflected his simple faith in the inherent superiority of the Soviet socio-economic system over its capitalist rivals, supposedly prey to inescapable and fatal 'contradictions'. Curiously enough, even some normally sober-minded Americans began to worry about the 'threat' of being overtaken by the Soviets in the race for material abundance: the fairy-tale atmosphere in Kuusinen's *dacha* was surprisingly infectious!

Of still greater concern to conservatives, at least in the USSR, were the changes made in 1961 to the CPSU's 'rules' or statute, which provided for automatic rotation of office-holders and a maximum of three regular terms of service in any job. This egalitarian notion dated back to the early nineteenth-century utopian socialists. Khrushchev took to it enthusiastically, but despite his authority he was obliged to tone down its revolutionary implications.

On the eve of the Twenty-second congress Molotov, who had meanwhile exchanged the delights of Ulan-Bator for those of Vienna, wrote a letter to the Central Committee criticizing the draft programme. This was equivalent to a declaration of war. Khrushchev responded by launching a new wave of attacks on the 'anti-Party group', linking their recent misdeeds with the crimes they had committed under Stalin. A congress called to endorse Khrushchev's exalted vision of the future degenerated into a reckoning with the horrors of the past. Many new facts about the Terror were revealed for the first time to the general public, which shocked those unacquainted with his 1956 'secret speech'. All members of the Presidium were obliged to give their opinion. It soon became clear that they were seriously divided, and that a majority had no wish to apply sanctions against the defeated leaders. Mikoian, Suslov, and Kosygin were among those who hinted at the need for restraint. Out of a total of seventy-seven prominent delegates twenty-three were sympathetic to Khrushchev's anti-Stalinist line, whereas ten took an ambiguous stand and forty-four were opposed; there were differences of emphasis within each group (Tatu 1969).

On 30 October, in a highly symbolic gesture, the congress resolved to remove Stalin's mummified corpse from the Lenin mausoleum in Red Square, where it had lain since 1953. Dora Lazurkina, a delegate who had spent seventeen years in the Gulag, created a stir by declaring that it was her pious habit to commune with Lenin daily, and he had told her that 'it is unpleasant for me to lie next to Stalin, who brought so much misfortune to the Party.' Subsequently Stalingrad was renamed Volgograd (it has since reverted to its pre-revolutionary name, Tsaritsyn) and the same fate was meted out to Molotov (Perm') and Voroshilovgrad (Lugansk), along with sundry other places. The purifying effect of these acts was somewhat impaired by the fact that Novogeorgievsk, a locality in the Ukraine, now appeared on maps as Khrushchev. Moreover, none of the defeated leaders was allowed to give his version of events to the congress or in the press. This showed that the Party had not become any more tolerant of dissenting opinions. Two years or so later it was revealed that the three principal culprits had lost their Party membership, but no judicial proceedings were taken against them, as Khrushchev evidently had wanted.

Nor did the First Secretary have everything his own way over the Party programme, which despite its utopian features was actually a very conservative document. The Communist order of the future was envisaged simply as a more efficient version of the 'socialist' one now allegedly built, and was to be attained by continuing present policies. Ideological training was to be intensified to elimi-nate all 'survivals of bourgeois views and morals'. There was to be no room for individual freedom as commonly understood. Instead, the future society would be 'highly organized', with the Party and planning agencies, as ostensibly civic associations, controlling citizens' 'needs' to ensure that they received no more goods than they were entitled to. The quantitative targets (e.g. for a quadrup-ling of national income and a five-fold increase in industrial output) over the next twenty years, by when the 'basis' of Communism was to have been built, clearly had little substance. They were designed essentially as a device for social mobilization. This function was epitomized by the programme's concluding phrase, 'the present generation of Soviet people shall live under Communism!' Within a few years the embarrassing document would be consigned to limbo by Khrushchev's more prosaic successors.

The elections to the Party's leading bodies at the congress did not strengthen Khrushchev politically. It seemed that his colleagues wanted to set limits to his power, but as yet they went no further than this. There was still a consensus on the general direction of policy, but considerable disagreement over the priority to be given to specific projects or the manner in which they should be tackled. Over the next three years Khrushchev's fortunes oscillated marked-ly. In March 1962 the Central Committee did not agree to boost agricultural investment, at the expense of defence and heavy industry, to the extent he had suggested in his opening speech to the gathering. Instead funds had to be found by cutting the subsidies that kept down food prices for urban consumers. The increases were unpopular and led to a serious riot at Novocherkassk in the Ukraine (see below, Chapter 4).

Far more serious were the setbacks in foreign policy. Installing offensive missiles in Cuba was a typically Khrushchevian gamble which, followed by their enforced withdrawal, cost the USSR dearly in international prestige. The conflict with China sharpened, and in the eyes of senior officials in Moscow came to look more and more like a personal vendetta by the First Secretary.

Meanwhile at home Khrushchev launched a wide-ranging plan for restructuring the Party apparatus that threatened the job security of thousands of regional officials. The leader antagonized intellectuals, too, by peremptorily deciding what they might or might not publish. In October 1962 he personally authorized the appearance in *Pravda* of a poem by the controversial Yevtushenko entitled 'Stalin's Heirs', which underlined the need for vigilance against a possible resurgence of Stalinism: 'double or treble the guard at his grave lest his spirit escape.' Also approved for publication, in the teeth of obstruction by his Presidium colleagues, was 'A Day in the Life of Ivan Denisovich', by the still little-known Solzhenitsyn, which broke the taboo on mentioning the Gulag. The whole issue of Stalin and Stalinism served as a talisman by which one could judge the attitude towards reform of particular individuals. In March 1963, in a speech to intellectuals, Khrushchev appeared to retreat on this issue. As in early 1957, he claimed that Stalin's merits as leader outweighed his shortcomings and blamed Beria for his excesses. This was obviously a tactical move and did not represent his real opinion. In July 1963, at a rally for the visiting Hungarian leader Kádár, he delivered an impromptu diatribe against the dictator's 'black deeds' along with a justification of his own welfare-oriented policies. The offending remarks were excised from the text of his speech as carried in *Pravda*—a fate that not infrequently befell the record of his endless harangues to gatherings of local officials whenever he toured the provinces.

The disappearance from the political scene of Kozlov in April 1963, and his replacement as secretary two months later by Brezhnev and Podgorny, seemed to fortify Khrushchev's position. At a more fundamental level, however, his strength was being steadily eroded by the disappointing performance of the economy. The 1962 grain harvest had been excellent, but next year yields were the lowest since 1954: 108 as against 142 million tons. To improve matters Khrushchev reverted to an idea he had long been mooting, but to little effect: a massive increase in the output of chemical fertilizer. In typical Bolshevik fashion this was boosted as a panacea and financial and human resources mobilized in a well-publicized campaign that inevitably led to confusion. The officials whose work was cast into disarray joined the ranks of the disgruntled, and further surprise reorganizations of the rural apparatus had the same effect. Khrushchev was having to run ever faster to stay in the same place. His weakness stemmed as much from his own inconsistencies as it did from intrigues by enemies in high places. He failed to stem public adulation of his own person, which reached a peak in April 1964 when he celebrated his seventieth birthday. People both resented the cult and felt ashamed of their own insincere participation in it. There is no reason to believe, as has been contended, that it was deliberately fostered by his enemies, but it was certainly a contributory factor in his growing unpopularity.

Khrushchev's fall

A conspiracy against Khrushchev's rule began to take shape in February or March 1964. The initiator was long thought to be Suslov, but that bespectacled doctrinaire—in his office he kept a card index of Lenin citations for ready reference—was not fond of taking risks. In 1988–9, when Gorbachev's *glasnost'* opened up Soviet history to the public, several memoirists, including Khrushchev's son and son-in-law (Ajubei), suggested that the initiator had been Shelepin. The former (1958–61) security chief, now a Party secretary, had a powerful network of clients and entertained good relations with his successor at the KGB, Semichastny. After Khrushchev's fall Shelepin became one of the most powerful men in the land, until he was dropped from the top leadership in 1967. A generation later he emerged from obscurity to give his own version of the affair (Barsukov 1992). This attributed the key roles to Brezhnev and Podgorny, who were distrustful of Suslov and brought him in only later. Much the same picture was given by Semichastny, who however did acknowledge his own initiating role, and by Shelest (in 1964 a candidate member of the Presidium).

Ajubei then privately concurred in identifying Podgorny as principal plotter. Most sources (Voronov is an exception) portray Brezhnev as acting at the instigation of others and showing extreme nervousness—as well he might.

Khrushchev's son Sergei, a rocket engineer uninvolved in politics, learned of the plot in dramatic circumstances from an ex-bodyguard of Ignatov, a former Party secretary who bore Khrushchev a grudge because he had not been re-elected to the Party's top policy-making bodies in 1962. His role in the conspiracy was to recruit support among leading regional Party officials. When Sergei Khrushchev told his father he was remarkably unconcerned, evidently believing that the men named as principal conspirators (Brezhnev, Podgorny, and Shelepin) were too far apart from each other to co-operate in such a hazardous venture. Khrushchev then told both Mikoian and Podgorny about the story. The latter, as Khrushchev says, 'simply laughed at me: "how can you think such a thing, Nikita Sergeevich?" Those were his very words.'

He had in truth lost the will to govern. On several occasions he had spoken publicly of his advanced age and possible retirement. On 13 October 1964, when summoned from his holiday home in the Crimea to attend a Presidium meeting, he seems to have recognized what was afoot. His suspicions were confirmed when at the airport he was met, not by all his colleagues as protocol required, but by Semichastny, who had taken elaborate security precautions. At the meeting he was confronted by a hail of accusations, some justified, others trifling or contrived. He rejected them all categorically, adding that 'none of you told me openly and honestly about my shortcomings: you were all yes men.' What rankled most was that the conspirators were not members of the old guard but close associates whose careers he had himself furthered. Mikoian alone stood by him, but in a half-hearted way. The Central Committee met on 14 October. Khrushchev sat silently as Suslov pedantically catalogued no less than fifteen errors, among them 'hare-brained scheming', slighting his colleagues, exacerbating international tension, and even undermining the workers' welfare. The resolution depriving him of his posts was, needless to say, unanimous.

The fallen leader was treated in reasonably civilized fashion. He was awarded a pension and allowed to live in Moscow—under constant surveillance, to be sure, which became oppressive when he began to dictate his invaluable memoirs. That he was not just quietly done away with, as would have happened under Stalin, showed the political progress achieved during the decade or so in which he wielded supreme power. His greatest accomplishment was to end the reign of fear and to bring the security police under Party control. Millions owed him release from the camps. But he stopped short of dismantling the Stalinist system of which police and Party were the principal bulwarks. The dictatorship, instead of being eased, was actually strengthened in so far as the CPSU became more efficient in performing its allotted task of acting as the 'guiding force' in Soviet society. For all his anti-Stalinism Khrushchev was himself a prisoner of Stalinist concepts, of his own past. 'In his very genes', writes one recent Soviet critic, 'he bore those attributes of power in which he had been brought up for decades' (Kozyrev 1988). He remained a militant atheist, hostile to political pluralism or market economics. He looked on intellectuals as propagandists for the Communist way of life. Writers, scholars and scientists, officials, managers—all were in the last resort seen as mere cogs in a machine whose function it was to impose on the people a grand design elaborated from above.

Khrushchev's populism was a matter of style, not substance. With hindsight it can be argued that he missed an opportunity to democratize the Party, so preparing the ground for a transition to multiparty rule. But apart from the fact that this was not his aim, Soviet society was still almost wholly in thrall to Stalinist patterns of thought and conduct. There did not as yet exist any realistic alternative to the existing bureaucratic structure, which proved so resistant to efforts at reform. Later Khrushchev would blame himself for not having been more resolute. 'My leadership was sometimes more administrative than creative. I was too concerned with restricting or prohibiting. I admit my responsibility for the years I was in power, but today I am opposed to this form of government. I would have opened all the doors and windows if I could.' In September 1971, shortly after uttering these words, he died at the age of 76. They are a fitting epitaph.

3 Civilizing Soviet Government

The Party

To understand why the Party bureaucracy proved such a hard nut for any reformist leader to crack we need to examine the way this 'peculiar institution' functioned. On close inspection it emerges that, contrary to appearances, beneath the façade of monolithic unity and ideological conformism a slow metamorphosis had begun which, within the space of another generation or so, would undermine the CPSU's *raison d'être*. Ultimately this process was the result of the maturation of Soviet society. More immediately it was an unintended consequence of the post-Stalin leadership's drive to reinvigorate a body which until 1953 had been a mere adjunct of the despot's rule, to enhance its authority in the eyes of the people by restoring, as the jargon phrase went, 'Leninist norms of Party life'.

This was associated with a general move away from a tyrannical mode of government towards an oligarchic one with a democratic camouflage. Under Khrushchev the Party maintained its monopoly on political power while abandoning mass terror. It sought to rule more by persuasion than by coercion, to reduce the level of domestic tension, and to build up mass support by appealing to people's material interests as well as to their idealism. It also attempted to reduce somewhat the role that Marxist-Leninist doctrine played in so many domains of practical policy.

Some commentators (such as G. Gill) hold that during this period Soviet government became more institutionalized. Certainly there were pressures in this direction. Officials endeavoured to gain more security by ensuring that existing informal rules and conventions were observed. But progress was slow at best. The leader's personality—or, to be precise, that of the ruling oligarchs—was of much the same import in 1964 as it had been in 1953. At a lower level many functionaries emulated the style, habits, and even language of those on high, just as had been the case under the autocracy of old.

The Soviet system might even be termed 'neo-feudal', in so far as the relationship between clients and patrons vaguely resembles that between knights, barons, and overlords—although of course the historical parallel should not be pressed too far.

Although the CPSU's institutional structure scarcely changed over the Khrushchev decade, two important things happened. First, Party membership grew apace. Second, the physiognomy of the apparatus men (*apparatchiki*) underwent a subtle change. 'The new generation . . . ', noted one Western authority (Fainsod) in 1963, 'is increasingly technical-minded, involved intimately in problems of production, organization and administration; and it is educated with these responsibilities in mind'. The changed outlook was partly a generational phenomenon: the younger and better educated men who rose to positions of authority in the years 1953–65 (whose numbers were, however, thinned by wartime casualties) had different backgrounds and experiences than the first and second post-revlutionary cohorts. This did not by any means make them automatically more innovative, let alone more tolerant: many unthinkingly adopted the simplistic views of their patrons or predecessors. Nevertheless the passing of time did make it more likely that some individuals of a more sophisticated cast of mind would enter the ranks of officialdom.

Such functionaries were more likely to recognize that the problems facing them were as a rule complex, and that they could be solved in several different ways; or that people could be managed more effectively by dialogue and consultation than by wielding a big stick. There were two extreme character profiles—rough-hewn 'trouble-shooters' and specialized 'professionals', as one might call them. Somewhere between these two poles stood the mass of decision-makers, torn this way and that by contradictory pressures, who tempered their conduct according to the prevailing wind. In a 'liberal' phase they veered towards more civilized standards of behaviour, whereas in a reactionary one they reverted to type, as it were. By and large they rejected both radical reform and reversion to terrorist methods of government, since either course imperilled their security, their quiet enjoyment of the fruits of office.

They seldom made their views known by criticizing Party policy out loud at meetings, as was their statutory right, still less by infringing Party discipline: rather they applied techniques of passive resistance or simply gave way to natural inertia—slacking on the job, abstaining from civic activities, and putting personal interests first. If enough Party members (and especially officials) acted in this way, they could make it virtually impossible for the leadership to implement policies of which they disapproved. It was easy to foul up the bureaucratic mechanism in a mass of red tape. Time and again Khrushchev would inveigh against those who 'replace live organizing of the masses with mere talk' or 'lock themselves in their offices issuing resolutions while life passes them by', but to little avail. Although the Party was structured on hierachical lines, it could not have operated if there had not been an element of flexibility and an information feedback from below. Indeed, the constant flow of such data upwards, largely through informal channels of communication, might matter as much as the orders and directives that rained down non-stop on humble executants of policy, whether in the form of Central Committee decisions, *Pravda* editorials, or visits by stern agents of the centre with the power to reprimand, discipline and purge the Party's ranks of disloyal or dubious elements.

The Party nearly doubled in size during the Khrushchev decade, from 6.8 million members in 1952 to 11.8 million in 1965 (figures for 1 January). Related to total population, the rise was less significant, from 3.6 to 5.1 per cent (higher if set against the number of adults). Between 1957 and 1964 the annual increases ranged from 4.5 to 6.6 per cent, reaching a post-war peak in the latter year. Losses from death or expulsion were generally around 1.3 per cent: in 1962–4 attrition was running at about 30,000 a year. The age of Party members remained considerably below that of the adult population as a whole, with an over-representation of men in their thirties. The proportion of women members remained stable at around 20 per cent.

Party members' educational levels registered a steady upward trend. Those who had completed higher education accounted for 11.2 per cent in 1956 and 15.0 per cent by 1965, while another 3 per cent or so had had some exposure to post-secondary education (i.e. had dropped out) and several hundred thousand others had a specialized secondary education. Those with no more than primary schooling dropped from 29.6 to 24.4 per cent over the period. This led to the presence of 'a large undigested body of members . . . [with] a pragmatic or technical outlook and a higher level of education than their superiors' (Mickiewicz 1971), which naturally bred a sense of frustration.

The recruitment drive was aimed predominantly at workers and peasants. It seems to have been successful, for the proportion of members from these two groups combined rose during the decade by nearly five percentage points, to 53.8 per cent. But Soviet statisticians employed a misleading method of categorizing people by social class. Many of these recruits, while perhaps of humble origin, will have been in non-manual managerial or technical occupations at the time of joining. The real point to bear in mind is that the white-collar members were, quite naturally, those most likely to rise to the upper levels of the Party hierarchy and to exercise political influence, whether in the Party's own *apparat* of full-time officials, believed to have numbered some 200,000 to 250,000, as officers in the armed forces and security services, government officials, lawyers, judges, scientists, or in other occupational groups with a high degree of Party 'penetration'. Of particular significance are those classified as engineers, technologists, or agricultural specialists, who could be expected to have a more pragmatic outlook than, say, administrators or teachers. They grew from 20 per cent of all white-collar Party members in 1956 to 32.5 per cent in 1965; as a proportion of total membership their share rose from 10.2 to 15.1 per cent. There was thus 'a trend from bureaucrats to specialists', or in our terminology from trouble-shooters to professionals. In 1959 about one-fifth of people classified as 'persons of mental labour' were in the Party. Unless the social élite had been preferentially represented in the CPSU, it could scarcely have ruled the country. It was natural for such persons to seek to perpetuate their authority as far as they could. But members of this 'power élite' did not enjoy the security of their counterparts elsewhere in the world. Lacking property, and exposed to the whims of those at the top, they were impelled to compensate for this by building patronage (cliency) systems and making the most of the uncertain authority they wielded over the population at large.

The temptation to nepotism and other forms of corruption was immense, and more will be said of this below (see Chapter 10). Senior officials in charge of personnel matters were constantly warning against 'errors in cadre policy', especially the tendency to form 'family circles' of like-minded comrades. Such associates would do one another favours, for instance by arranging accelerated promotion to better-paid jobs regardless of merit. The Party Control Commission, the chief disciplinary authority, would take vigorous measures against such groups, but no sooner were they suppressed in one place than they appeared in another.

Efforts at reform

The limited purge of the apparatus that followed Stalin's death had a more overtly political character, being directed against actual or potential 'left-conservative' opponents of Khrushchev. Between September 1953 and the convocation of the Twentieth congress in February 1956 'some 45 out of 84 secretaries of republic and regional Party committees were replaced; both the new appointees as well as those left undisturbed had special reason to rally to Khrushchev's support' (Fainsod 1963)—which they did, as we have seen, in dramatic fashion in the June 1957 crisis. In 1956 over one-third of the full members and over half the candidate members of the Central Committee were fresh to the job. Another shock wave struck the regional secretaries in 1960–1, when within a year 55 out of 114 were replaced. As a rule these men received other appointments, but the sense of dissatisfaction and alarm was palpable.

No less than ten drafts had to be prepared of the scheme approved in 1961 for compulsory rotation of jobs. This was aimed primarily at the lower tiers of the Party bureaucracy. At least half the members of urban and district Party committees, and of bureaux in primary organizations ('cells') at the lowest level of all, were to be renewed at each regular election. Higher up, at regional and republic level, the proportion was one-third, and at the top (Central Committee and its organs) only one-quarter. Special provision was made for 'outstanding individuals' to serve more than three successive terms. This escape clause was designed to allow Khrushchev and others of his persuasion to manipulate the lower levels of the apparatus in the direction they desired. The whole idea was dropped in 1966 in the interest of granting officials greater security of tenure, a policy which became a hallmark of the Brezhnev regime.

Khrushchev's scheme was in effect, if not in intention, a pseudo-reform—a move towards centralism rather than democracy within the Party. As such it went against the spirit of earlier measures designed to devolve power from the centre to regional officials. In May 1957 rules had been issued which limited the number of paid secretarial posts at the 'cell' level. It was claimed in 1961 that as a result of this and other such ordinances well over one thousand committees had been abolished and the number of 'responsible officials' reduced by over a quarter (25.2 per cent—a suspiciously precise figure, in view of official silence as to the total size of the *apparat!*). This measure needs to be seen in the context of Khrushchev's efforts to 'deconcentrate' power in the state bureaucracy, which were also none too successful.

What did he really mean by 'democratization' of the Party? As one commentator put it, 'Khrushchev quite clearly wished to upgrade the role and influence of the laity in relation to the apparatus [priesthood?!]' (Jowitt 1990). This meant that the 300,000 or so lower organizations got more discretion in dealing with such matters as assigning staff or publishing journals. Although they still had to submit regular detailed reports to higher authority, there was rather more freedom of discussion and a fresh, dynamic spirit. Ideological concerns and the exposure of suspected subversives mattered less than they had done in the late Stalin era, and junior Party committees were almost wholly absorbed in practical tasks of industrial and agricultural management. This certainly involved much meddling in other people's business, and was not necessarily conducive to enhanced efficiency, but it did at least accord with the Party's statutory function within the governmental system as laid down in 1919. It was an activity that had a genuine appeal for the ambitious, and explains why the recruitment drive was a success.

At a higher level 'democratization' meant enhancing the role of the Party congress and the Central Committee (CC). Under Stalin the Party's 'highest body' was supposed by statute to meet every three years, but no less than thirteen years elapsed between the Eighteenth congress (1939) and the Nineteenth (1952), when a four-year term was instituted. This was kept to thereafter. The epochal Twentieth congress was followed by an 'extraordinary' one in 1959 and a regular one in 1961. However, their proceedings continued to be largely ritualistic. They began with an exhausting jargon-ridden report by the First Secretary on all aspects of the present 'historical conjuncture'. This offered guidelines for the future that concealed as much as they revealed about the leaders' real intentions. The delegates' role was to applaud (in carefully measured doses) and to ratify decisions that had been made elsewhere. Those given the chance to speak had their scripts vetted beforehand, which explains why their utterances were so uniform. Only by close examination could one detect here and there a slight shading of emphasis that reflected some particular local or occupational interest. All decisions were of course unanimous.

It was the same scenario at meetings of the CC, which formally had charge of the Party's affairs between congresses and so was of greater account. Its meetings became more frequent, reaching a peak of six in 1958, and its size swelled from 125 members and 111 alternates in 1952 to 175 and 155 respectively in 1961. This made it more unwieldy as a decision-making agency, but then this was not its purpose. Like the congress its role was to confer legitimacy on decisions taken elsewhere. The exception proves the rule. In 1957 the CC came into its own by intervening to resolve the crisis in the divided Presidium. Yet the initiative was taken, not by the delegates themselves, but by the reformist minority in the Presidium and its allies, who in effect utilized the deliberative body as their instrument. Subsequently the CC's role declined, not least because Khrushchev introduced the practice, later abandoned, of expanding the attendance at its sessions to include various experts on the matter under discussion. But at least its proceedings were now published—a timid step in the direction of *glasnost'* (transparency, freedom of information), which likewise proved temporary.

The Party's real nerve centre was the Secretariat which Khrushchev, like Stalin before him, used to circumvent his foes on the Presidium. This body determined the Presidium's agenda and implemented its decisions. Its activities were—and still are—enshrouded in secrecy. Each secretary normally had charge of one or more subordinate departments, which had a combined staff of several thousand. These departments varied in number, as did the number of secretaries. There were apparently sixteen of them in 1958 (and twenty-four in 1984). In 1956 a parallel set of departments was created for the RSFSR, which acquired its own Bureau under the Secretariat. This served Khrushchev as yet another institutional base; it was also in part designed to further decentralization.

Each department was responsible for a certain subject area, an arrangement that conveniently fitted in with that of the *government* departments (ministries etc.) whose activities they controlled. But some departments of the Party Secretariat had no governmental counterparts. Among them were the Party Organs department, the Administrative Organs department, responsible for the security police, judiciary, etc., and the General department, which prepared business for the Politburo and Secretariat and also ran the CC apparatus. This latter was the successor to Stalin's personal secretariat and had charge of Party archives, files on members and so on. In practice their functions probably overlapped.

Of more general interest is the department of agitation and propaganda, or 'Agitprop' as it was familiarly known. It supervised the media and cultural activities generally, and also ran a vast apparatus of Party schools and institutes, as well as the 'Knowledge' (*Znanie*) society which arranged lectures for the general public. During the Khrushchev years this kind of activity received much attention, for the aim was to give the entire adult population some form of 'political education'. The number of persons enrolled in such schools rose from 6.2 million in 1957/8 to no less than 36 million in 1964/5, over three times the Party's total effectives. Some 200,000 students were enlisted in 'evening universities of Marxism-Leninism', designed *inter alia* to train propagandists to carry on this vast enterprise. The content of the instruction was reformed. Abstract themes such as dialectical materialism or Party history were de-emphasized and the focus shifted to practical subjects, especially those helpful in boosting economic growth. Lectures gave way to less formal seminars and group activities.

How effective all this preaching was it is difficult to say. Sociological studies conducted some years later suggest that nearly half those attending thought that it had not modified their conduct. There is ample anecdotal evidence that people resented having to attend such sessions after a long working day, and found the material repetitious or irrelevant. On the other hand, the million-strong army of propagandists had a captive audience still largely isolated from alternative sources of information. The indoctrination system was well calibrated to suit varying levels of sophistication. Propagandists were taught how to respond to unsolicited awkward questions from the floor. Moreover, the ubiquitous street posters, slogans, monuments, and so forth may have influenced passers-by subliminally.

The real problem for Party propagandists was to justify its *raison d'être* in terms meaningful to ordinary folk now that memories of the early revolutionary struggles, and even of war against the Nazi invader, were fading. If today the task was simply to improve people's living standards, why not leave this to the experts? Khrushchev tried to answer this question in his own way. In November 1962 he pushed through his scheme for the bifurcation of all Party organs, from republican level downwards, into separate agencies for industrial and agricultural matters; for good measure the Komsomol (youth organization), soviets, and trade unions were divided on similar lines. This downgraded the Party's non-economic functions, since ideological work was left to commissions that clearly lacked the authority of the two mainstream bodies. The measure was poorly thought-out and not properly debated. (Reportedly the other leaders agreed to it at a casual meeting by the swimming pool at Khrushchev's Crimean *dacha*!) Quite apart from the practical problem of deciding who was to do what—for example, training teachers for rural schools was rated an 'industrial' activity—it threatened to undermine the Party's cohesion and its universalistic pretensions. It favoured the 'professional' element at the expense of the generalists, who were left with little to do except safeguard the ideological verities. This was the conservatives' main objection to it. They realized that in the long run it would render the Party superfluous. In the short term it would cause career disruption and the very bureaucratic proliferation that the reformers inveighed against.

Thus at the end of his years in office the First Secretary was indirectly encouraging a recentralization of authority within the Party. His well-meaning but clumsy efforts at democratization brought the very idea into disrepute among those who had to implement it. They reacted against the confusion and chaos that it seemed likely to bring in its wake. Far wiser, they felt, to play safe.

Government

The drive to reform the governmental structure was scarcely more effective, although it may have had unexpectedly positive long-term consequences. This was because the thinking behind it was seriously defective. It was not enough to devolve power from central (all-Union) ministries to union-republican ones, or even to give more weight in decision-making to the soviets, the local authorities in town and country. What was needed was a firm commitment to a legal order, a *Rechtsstaat*. Neither Khrushchev nor any of his colleagues or advisers in the reformist camp were prepared to go so far. On the contrary, they held fast to outdated class-based Marxian notions of government. They sought to recapture the authentic spirit of revolutionary Leninism while preserving the Stalinist command economy and the bureaucratic apparatus that went with it. This meant that they tried to encourage 'mass participation' in administrative tasks at a lower level without weakening the control exercised by superior organs in the government (soviet) hierarchy or by the Party. Moreover, despite Khrushchev's achievement in reducing the size of the Gulag, the security police remained in being. Law was still seen as an instrument for upholding Party rule. The 'dictatorship of the proletariat' might be discarded as an ideological concept: the dictatorship of the Party continued to exist as a concrete, coercive reality.

Perhaps the most telling sign of this was the fact that the CPSU's funds were augmented from the state treasury. Party membership dues and the profits from its publishing ventures were far from adequate to support its manifold activities. But such subsidies were never referred to in public and their size at this time can still only be guessed at.

Changes were least marked in the upper reaches of the governmental system. For instance, the role of the USSR Supreme Soviet, the topmost legislative body, continued to be a purely formal one. It would normally meet twice a year for a few days to adopt the budget, by a unanimous vote, and ratify decrees or other acts promulgated in the interim by its Presidium and in most cases already in force. The deputies to the two chambers were invariably elected by resounding majorities at uncontested polls. Thus in 1962 no less than 99.95 per cent of electors voted, of whom all but 0.53 per cent and 0.40 per cent respectively cast their ballots in favour of the 'Party and non-Party bloc'. Not all deputies were Party members, yet all were subject to Party discipline. Their presence in the chambers served to demonstrate the 'monolithic unity' that supposedly bound together Party and people, and in more practical terms to test the ability of the organizers in each constituency to bring several thousand people from home or workplace to the polling station. It took considerable courage for an individual not to drop his ballot paper into the box under the eyes of representatives of the local electoral commission but to go into a polling-booth and strike out the name of the single candidate. The latter had of course been pre-selected at a meeting of the appropriate Party organization, perhaps after informally canvassing local opinion and receiving 'advice' from above. In their choice the selectors were guided by a concern to ensure a rough and ready 'representation' of various segments both of the population at large and of the governing élite (to call them 'interest groups' would go too far). Thus in 1962 45 per cent of those chosen were manual workers, as opposed to only 19 per cent in 1954. This reflected the reformists' concern to give the Supreme Soviet a more 'popular' image. The other deputies comprised carefully controlled dosages of Party and government officials, factory managers, army officers, writers, and so on.

None of these men and women, if called on to speak, could express the specific wishes of their electors, in so far as these went against current Party policy. But could they influence the shaping of policy behind the scenes? The two chambers of the Supreme Soviet had several standing commissions, of which some dealt with budgetary or economic matters. Since these deliberations took place in private, deputies had a better opportunity here to ventilate their own or their electors' aspirations (or grievances) without incurring sanctions for infringing Party discipline. They might, for example, cautiously suggest that higher budgetary appropriations or resource allocations be made to their republic or region. How often they did so, in this period at least, is unclear. Perhaps the chief benefits were indirect: such deputies might acquire detailed advance information about the planners' intentions, and, if they dared, leak it informally to certain 'constituents' when they reported back, as they were obliged to do. This information might help local lobbies, especially in union republics where some officials harboured 'national communist' inclinations (see Chapter 7). But one can hardly call this a significant advance towards parliamentarianism, an idea that would have shocked even the most committed reformers in the leadership. In their eyes the legislature was no more than a sounding board for Party policies.

At the local level the picture is slightly less bleak. 'Khrushchev, while no democratic liberal, most certainly had a stronger feeling for Lenin's anti-state and anti-bureaucratic [ideas] than did either his predecessor or his successors. He saw mass activism and enthusiasm as keys to reviving the revolution' (Friedgut 1979). This meant encouraging popular participation in the work of local soviets, trade unions, and other such bodies while avoiding the cardinal sin of 'localism'—that is, placing the interests of the local collective before those of the larger community. A resolution in this sense adopted by the Central Committee in January 1957 condemned interference by Party bodies in matters properly within the competence of the soviets, especially the arbitrary appointment and dismissal of their personnel. Instead Party members were exhorted to influence local government work from within by moral suasion and by setting an example. Soviets were encouraged to hold sessions regularly—in 1955 35 per cent of those in the RSFSR had lagged in this regard—and to diversify their activities. They were given more power over local industry, although in this respect they soon lost out to the regional economic councils and ultimately to the central bodies.

In 1961 Khrushchev, then in utopian mood, declared that 'every Soviet person must become an active participant in the administration of community affairs.' This meant transferring functions from the soviets to self-help groups of unpaid volunteers—who would, of course, take their cue from local Party officials. Many thousands of such groups were set up, often based on 'housing operations offices' responsible for an area smaller than that run by an urban soviet, the 'mini-district' or *mikroraion*. Housing problems were in the forefront of city-residents' concerns, along with the provision of kindergartens, parks, cultural facilities, and the like. In one Moscow district (1961) the soviet had only two paid staff members but twenty-nine volunteers, who together ran fifteen libraries, twelve clubs, ten cinemas and six bookstores—as well as sixty-five small propaganda outlets ('Red corners') which displayed approved political literature. In rural areas of Krasnodar region, in the Kuban', in the single year 1963 volunteer neighbourhood committees planted over one and a half million trees and shrubs—and installed extensive loudspeaker systems so that the inhabitants could hear the voice of Authority over the ether. These examples illustrate the ambiguous implications of this development. So long as the Party remained at the core of all Soviet social organizations, popular participation in government was bound to have an artificial, 'other-directed' character, however useful the results might be. Inevitably there was a slackening of motivation on the part of the volunteers involved, many of whom were pensioners. In Sverdlovsk it was reported (1961) that participation in 'public activities' was often merely formal and had 'an insignificant influence on life in the city'. Activists came to feel that their goodwill was being exploited. They had to make up for the negligence of the regular soviet authorities, which lacked sufficient funding to hire trained employees and do the job more efficiently. The trouble was that local soviets were not autonomous bodies. Their budgets were centrally determined and came low in the queue for state appropriations.

Nor were their competence and rights clearly defined, still less guaranteed by law. Senior bodies would gratuitously interfere in the affairs of those below them, in addition to the constant meddling through Party channels. Had 'democratization' of government been seriously attempted, this should have been the first task to tackle. But the reformers' objective was not to establish stable, regularly functioning institutions on the 'bourgeois' pattern. As Marxist-Leninists their ideal was to replace regular government altogether by the 'self-administration' of a populace thoroughly indoctrinated in Communist principles. The result was predictable: increased bureaucracy. Between 1958 and 1964 the staff of the central soviet organs increased by 60,000. At republic level the apparatus grew by 18 per cent, at the all-Union level by 26 per cent. Many of these officials had previously served in junior bodies, where they gave way to volunteers. Others were newcomers who chose to make a career in government because it was less risky than service in, say, the Party or the armed forces, even though the rewards might not be spectacular.

'Socialist legality'

For the same reasons the USSR registered only modest progress towards the rule of law in the Khrushchev era. This was not the regime's aim, after all: it sought to return to 'socialist legality', a vague term which meant, if anything, dictatorship without mass terror. In the legal field the reformist leadership did two things. First, it took steps to release the bulk of those incarcerated in the Gulag and to rehabilitate them (in many cases only posthumously) and to curb the security police's arbitrary powers. Second, it improved the status of the legal profession, issued new law codes, and reduced the penalties imposed on offenders. None of these policies was carried through consistently, for fear of encouraging autonomous forces that might endanger the dictatorship.

It is not certain how many people were held in the NKVD's empire at Stalin's death, since research in the relevant archives has barely begun. In his memoirs Khrushchev put the number at 'up to ten million, . . . more than an English pirate could have dreamed of', as he added gratuitously. This was probably not meant to be an accurate figure, and he had no access to documents when writing his memoirs. While in office he received information on the matter from the Procurator-General, Rudenko, and other officials; the writer Yulian Semenov states that a figure of twelve million was reported to Stalin early in 1953 by the then State Security minister, Ignat'ev. In 1987 a Dutch legal scholar, proceeding from published data on the labour-force, arrived at a 'rough estimate' of four million forced labourers, of whom 3.3 million were in camps; to them should be added those unable to work and prisoners (Van den Berg). Next year the Soviet archives began to yield their secrets. Zemskov and others provide the following data for 1 January 1953:

Camps	1,727,970[a]
Colonies	740,554
'Special settlements'	2,753,356
TOTAL	5,221,880

[a] '30 per cent political'.

There will also have been several hundred thousand prisoners in jails. Adding them in, one comes to a total of some five and a half million. In 1990 the Western specialist S. G. Wheatcroft arrived at a total of 5.35 million. Some scholars adhere to higher figures, arguing that the KGB falsified data in its possession. There is evidence that it did so. In the late 1980s Shatunovskaia, a member of an investigation commission set up in 1960, found that files she had seen then had since been tampered with or had disappeared. The scale of any such error cannot be estimated until detailed studies of particular camp complexes are undertaken.

Whatever the number of Gulag inmates may have been, there can be no doubt that the situation in the camps forced the leadership to yield. Already in 1952 there had been acts of insubordination by prisoners in Kazakhstan and at Vorkuta, in the north-east of European Russia. Informers were liquidated and rudimentary clandestine organizations formed, notably by Ukrainians, Balts, Chechens, and other national minority *zeks*. By the summer of 1953 the atmosphere at Noril'sk, in the Siberian high north, was electric. After guards killed four inmates a strike was declared. Commissioners from Moscow offered to end abuses and pay standard wages if the prisoners returned to work. They refused. In July and August troops stormed two rebel camps in this complex, killing seventy-nine and injuring 280. At Vorkuta, where an outbreak began shortly afterwards, events took a broadly similar course. Some four thousand men struck work in four of the thirteen camps; sixty fatal casualties were incurred. Here, too, the insurgents showed considerable organizational and tactical skill, whereas the authorities were nervous and indecisive. Their morale was shaken by Beria's downfall and the East Berlin uprising, news of which inspired the strikers to redouble their resistance. Many men were transferred to other camps, which spread the contagion. There was further violence at Kengir, Kazakhstan, in June 1954. Insurgent prisoners held out for forty days before they were bloodily suppressed. Throughout the Gulag *zeks* took heart from these experiences, which led not only to important material concessions, such as the removal of numbers from prison uniforms, but also to the speeding up of releases (Graziosi 1992, Kokurin 1994).

Among the first prisoners to be freed were relatives of the current leaders, such as Molotov's wife Polina. In 1953 the pace was slow. The dissident historian Roi Medvedev offers an estimate of one thousand, to which should be added, from recently revealed data, 8,042 settlers in one special category ('exiles'). According to Zemskov, in 1954–5 88,278 'politicals' were released, 55,480 of them on the basis of an amnesty for alleged wartime collaborators and 32,798 'because their cases were reviewed', i.e. their sentences had been voided. Elsewhere he states that the March 1953 amnesty affected over 40 per cent of the Gulag's population. Most inmates appear to have been simply let go *before* the judicial authorities could deal with their cases individually. The volume of work was overwhelming, and the hundred or so teams that toured the camps disbursed a rough and ready form of justice. Zemskov puts the number of 'politicals' released in 1955 at 195,353, leaving 113,735 of whom all but 11,027 had been freed by April 1959. The total Gulag population at that date was still nigh on one million (948,447), and some of those classified as 'non-political' ought really to be recategorized. 'Special settlers' numbered 146,000 in 1958 (Bugai 1992). If both these figures and our estimate for 1953 are correct, then some four and a half million people in all will have been liberated. Writing before the era of *glasnost'*, another Dutch scholar, in a study of the de-Stalinization process, noted that 2.3 million persons were added to the electoral lists between 1954 and 1958, over and above the natural increase due to demographic growth (Van Goudoever 1986).

The ex-inmates were generally in poor physical state and many died within a few years of their release. 'In railway trains and stations', writes a contemporary, 'there appeared survivors of the camps, with leaden grey hair, sunken eyes and a faded look; they choked and dragged their feet like old men' (Nosov 1988). It was hard to adjust to 'normal' conditions. There were poignant scenes when families were reunited. Some men's wives had given them up for lost and remarried. To their children they were strangers, ghosts returned from a world that was not supposed to exist. The editor of a leading Party journal was so devastated when his wife returned that he committed suicide. Returnees received compensation worth two months' salary—a mere pittance, help in finding accommodation, and a job if they could manage one. But at their old place of work they were viewed by Party loyalists as 'anti-social elements' who probably deserved their fate. They might even be confronted by the very delator responsible for it. Former Party members could apply for reinstatement. Less than 6,000 survivors' applications had been granted before the Twentieth congress speeded up the process, whereupon a further 47,000 were readmitted by 1962. This was about 6 per cent of all the Party members who had fallen victim to Stalin's terror. In the circumstances it was surprising that so many retained their faith.

More important in our context, survivors had to apply to the procuracy for a document confirming their rehabilitation. This was a brief, bald statement which contained no hint of an apology for the wrongs that had been done. As for non-survivors, rehabilitation was granted only if there were relatives to apply on their behalf. In such cases the document often contained a fraudulent statement as to the date and circumstances of the victim's death.

Clearly, rehabilitation in the post-Stalin years had a superficial, grudging character. It was less a legal than a political matter, subject to the vagaries of the struggle in the Kremlin and the

interests of the Party as interpreted by the victors. There was no
suggestion in official quarters that justice should be pursued for its
own sake. In April 1954 the old State Security ministry publicly
resurfaced—it had never expired—as the State Security Committee
(KGB). The change of title reflected a slight loss of status, but the
personnel were largely the same. Its new chief, Serov, had engineered the purge in the Baltic in 1940–1. Kruglov, who in 1953 had
replaced Beria as Interior minister and bore much responsibility for
the wartime deportations, was among 347 secret police operatives
who (according to data released in 1989) were expelled from the
Party. Among them were ten former ministers and their deputies,
seventy-seven NKVD or MGB officers at all-Union or republic
level, and seventy-two at local level; forty others received lesser
sanctions but kept their Party cards. Beria and twenty-three other
senior officials are known to have been tried[1] and executed (Knight
1993). But no regular *judicial* action was taken against those
implicated in the Terror. The reason for this lies ready to hand. The
law was the Party's servant, and public exposure of these crimes
would have raised questions about the responsibility of the current
leaders. It would have put in doubt the Party's 'leading role'
in society, past and present. So long as it remained in power,
there could be no Soviet counterpart to the Nuremberg trials. As
Khrushchev said privately, 'we do not want a St. Bartholomew's
Day massacre'—a remark which tells us a lot about his view of legal
process.

What then was achieved? Essentially, the KGB could no longer
threaten the Party, but it continued to threaten popular rights and
liberties to the extent that the Party leaders wished. The former
NKVD's fearsome three-man Special Board (*soveshchanie*), dating
from 1924, was abolished in September 1953, as were the special
tribunals (*troiki*) established in 1929—although this was not announced until April 1956. The Procurator-General's office, which
was formally responsible for ensuring observance of the law, and
its subordinate agencies throughout the land, underwent personnel
changes designed to foster legal professionalism. They now pulled
greater weight in the investigation of cases. Likewise the Supreme
Court was reformed, six of its judges who had compromised
themselves being replaced (1955). Its hierarchy of special divisions
(*kollegii*), which enforced labour discipline on the railways or in the
Gulag, were abolished, but not the military one, which had passed

sentence at the 1930s show trials (and the major post-war cases). In 1957 the Supreme Court was granted the right, in certain circumstances, to decide whether verdicts of republic-level Supreme Courts infringed all-Union law—but it could *not*, however, pronounce on the constitutionality of acts passed by republic *governments*, or that of the Union, since under the Soviet system it had no independent authority: separation of powers was regarded as a 'bourgeois' notion. Its judges, like those throughout the system, were theoretically subject only to the law, but as Party members they were pledged to pursue other objectives. Where the two came into conflict, duty to the law almost invariably took second place.

The Justice ministry was one of those affected by Khrushchev's effort to devolve power within the state bureaucracy from all-Union to republic level. The move benefited the more nationally-conscious Party officials in minority regions, at least for a time. It also affected the legal codes according to which the law was, in theory, administered. In December 1958 the Supreme Soviet adopted 'fundamental principles' for the civil and criminal codes that the sixteen republics were scheduled to adopt. These differed only in minor details from those of the RSFSR, but did make some important improvements. It was now formally stated that no one could be punished except by sentence of a court. The nature of offences was defined more precisely than before, as were the circumstances diminishing an accused's liability. The principle of criminal analogy, much valued by the infamous Vyshinsky, and the punishment of an accused's kinsmen on the specious grounds that they must have known of his offence, were explicitly disavowed. Confession was no longer held to be the 'queen of proof'. Penalties were reduced: the maximum term of imprisonment ('deprivation of liberty') was reduced from twenty-five years to fifteen and the minimum from one year to three months. The age of criminal responsibility was raised from fourteen years to sixteen and provision made for milder treatment of minors.

Other reforms restricted the occasions when a court could meet in secret, laid down that an accused was to be presumed innocent until found guilty, and guaranteed the rights of defence advocates. Yet these rights, like all others in Soviet law, were subject to interpretation by officialdom according to considerations of political expediency. For example, although defence advocates were now allowed to be present *during* the preliminary investigation of their client, and not only at his trial, they had no right to be there *from the start of* the investigation or to see the relevant papers at a sufficiently early stage in the proceedings. Progressive lawyers like M. S. Strogovich pressed for such concessions, and the equivalent of *habeas corpus*, but without success. Many officials in the judicial apparatus took the view that 'if the accused weren't guilty he wouldn't be here.' Legal culture was spread alarmingly thinly.

Moreover, there was nothing in the codes to prevent new offences or penalties being introduced if the Party authorities thought fit. Already in 1961 judges found themselves under intensified political pressure and a trend set in towards harsher sentencing. In May an edict sanctioned the death penalty—which the 1958 reform had restricted to a few exceptionally grave crimes—for large-scale embezzlement of state property, forgery, and serious offences against labour camp regulations (which were rewritten at this time). In July its scope was extended to professional currency speculators. A number of offenders were thereupon promptly executed, some of them for crimes committed *before* the new law had been passed. Two Jewish black-marketeers previously sentenced to fifteen years' imprisonment for corruption suffered the supreme penalty instead after Khrushchev personally intervened, overruling a protest by the Procurator-General. According to Sakharov, the leader feared that if the pair were left alive they would talk about high-ranking customers whom they had supplied with jewellery. Even more sinister than the 'retroactive justice' in this case was the fact that news of the executions was generally welcomed by the public. One Western authority calculates that in 1962 alone about ninety people were put to death (Van den Berg 1983).

Another decree of May 1961 specified that so-called 'parasites' might be condemned to exile in 'specially assigned localities' for terms of two to five years. 'Parasites' were loosely defined as persons who 'do not work honestly according to their abilities' or 'gain unearned income'. Another group consisted of those holding jobs in the public sector *pro forma* while earning their livelihood by unauthorized private enterprise. Culprits in the latter category might not even have the privilege of a court hearing, but could be sentenced by a 'workers' collective', which in practice meant by local Party officials. Such 'comrades' courts', as they were known— Western critics called them 'kangaroo courts'—were officially seen as means of 'building Communism' by transferring power from state to 'public' organs. They handled minor cases such as non-payment of rent, hooliganism, embezzlement and so on. In Moscow by 1965 there were 5,580 such courts, involving 52,000 people (Friedgut 1979). Each had up to twelve members, none of whom necessarily had legal training, and generally met after hours on factory premises. They could impose fines and other sanctions, for example recommending that nonconformists be evicted from their state-owned apartments. Their operations recalled the arbitrariness of an earlier age, which is why they lost their more 'revolutionary' characteristics once Khrushchev fell from power.

Fortunately the First Secretary envisaged the 'transition to Communism' as a fairly gradual, if finite, process. The principal means employed to make people conform were education and peer pressure rather than outright coercion. Some of the fears expressed by Western critics at the time proved exaggerated: there was no general reversion to 'terror from below'. However, the regime's approach to legal reform was half-hearted and vacillating. It shrank from de-politicizing the administration of justice. Government did become a bit more civilized than it had been under Stalin, but in the legal field the chance for radical reform had been missed.

4 Reorienting the Economy

Industrial growth

In the post-Stalin era the command ('planned') economy, for all its built-in defects, still had reserves of strength that could be tapped to obtain a high rate of growth. Fundamentally this was a natural process of recovery from the ravages of war, as in Western countries at this time, but government policy also had much to do with it. In Stalin's last years the interests of consumers, and peasants in particular, had been deliberately neglected in favour of investment of resources in producers' goods—in Soviet parlance, 'Group A' industries as distinct from those in 'Group B' that catered to citizens' current needs. As we have seen, there was general agreement among his successors that the disproportion should be corrected. If Malenkov's 'new course' had been carried through, rewards for the consumer might have been greater than they were, since this policy was aimed at a long-term expansion of the 'Group B' sector, whereas under Khrushchev economic priorities varied according to the temporary exigencies of high politics. A dissident Soviet economist, who lost his job in 1972 for challenging the veracity of official statistics, has recently estimated the annual growth of national income from 1950 to 1960 at 7.2 per cent, but only 4.4 per cent from 1960 to 1965, with a much steeper decline over the next twenty years (Harrison citing G. I. Khanin 1993). Some contemporary American experts put the annual growth rate at respectively 5.2 and 4.8 per cent—or, in another calculation, at 7.1 per cent for 1951–7 and 5.3 per cent for 1959–64. On a per capita basis the growth rate declined from 5.7 per cent in the 1950s to 3.5 per cent in 1960–5 (Buck and Cole 1987). Inflation, the existence of which was never publicly admitted, is thought to have been kept down to around 1.6 to 1.8 per cent.

The growth rate fell off after 1958, not least because resources were diverted to military use, notably for the space and missile programme. In 1958 industrial investment was 16 per cent greater than it had been in the previous year, but over the next two years the figure fell successively to 13 and 8 per cent, and over the next three years to between 4 and 5 per cent. Yet in 1963 the proportion of Soviet GNP devoted to total (gross) investment was said to be the third highest in the world, exceeded only by Japan and Norway (Kaser 1970). In 1958 consumption in all forms accounted for about 60 per cent of GNP (Campbell 1967, citing N. Nimitz).

Khrushchev was not really the consumers' advocate he sometimes pretended to be. In 1955 he described the idea of giving priority to light industry as 'alien to the Marxist-Leninist spirit'. This polemical outburst was partly tactical, designed to discredit Malenkov; but neither the Seven-Year Plan, launched with great fanfare in 1959, nor the new Party programme contained a commitment to favour 'Group B'. The rates of annual increase for the two sectors were targeted by the plan at 9.3 and 7.7 per cent respectively, which was less 'consumer-friendly' even than the now abandoned Sixth Five-Year Plan. By May 1961 Khrushchev was talking of equalizing the two, but his remarks did not appear in print. The same fate awaited his formal proposal to the Presidium a few weeks before his fall to give priority to consumer goods: this proved to be his swan-song. By this time some of the more thoughtful economists had come to see that the traditional division of industries into sectors no longer made much sense, and that sustained growth required a radically new approach.

The Seven-Year Plan, more realistic than its predecessor, did achieve its basic objectives (except in agriculture), but consumers fared less well than they had been led to expect. The output of consumer goods grew by 60 per cent, that of producers' goods by 96 per cent. The figures for individual items are still more eloquent, as may be seen from Table 4.1. Plan fulfilment was much higher in respect of the first group of commodities than of the second.

The most important development to be noted concerns the country's energy supplies, its greatest natural resource. Coal-fired power-stations were giving way to hydroelectric ones. But in August 1958, when Khrushchev opened the world's largest hydroelectric power-station near Samara (then Kuibyshev) on the Volga, he astonished his listeners by stressing the advantages of thermal power. Its higher running costs, he argued, were more than offset by the fact that such stations were quicker and cheaper to build. 'The Soviet leader was calling for introduction of the time

TABLE 4.1.   *Output of selected goods, 1955–1965*

Product	1955 (actual)	1958 (actual)	1965 (plan)	1965 (actual)
Group A				
Iron ore (million tons)	71.9	88.8	150–160	153.4
Pig iron (million tons)	33.3	39.6	65–70	66.2
Steel (million tons)	45.3	54.9	86–91	91.0
Coal (million tons)	391.3	496.1	600–612	577.7
Oil (million tons)	70.8	113.2	230–240	242.9
Electricity (milliard kWh)	170.2	235.4	500–520	506.7
Tractors (000)[a]	314	415.3	—	803.8
Mineral fertilizer (million tons)	9.7	12.4	35	31.3
Metal-cutting lathes (000)	117.1	138.3	190–200	186.1
Cement (million tons)	22.5	33.3	75–81	72.4
Automobiles (000)[b]	445	511.1	—	616.3
Group B				
Cotton fabrics (million sq. metres)	4.2	4.3	7.7–8.0	5.5
Woollen fabrics (million sq. metres)	316	385	500	466
Leather footwear (million pairs)[c]	271	356	515	486
Housing (million sq. metres)[d]	48.1	94.8	—	98.1
TV sets (000)	495	979	—	3655
Refrigerators (000)	151	360	—	1675
Motor-cycles and scooters (000)[e]	245	400	—	721
Sewing-machines (000)	1611	2686	—	800
Watches and clocks (millions)	19.7	24.8	—	30.6
Retail-trade turnover[f]	50.2	67.2	—	104.8
Food-trade turnover	5.9	6.4	—	10.1

[a] converted to 15 h.p. units.
[b] includes trucks.
[c] includes fabric footwear, an example of statistical falsification (Jasny 1962).
[d] state, co-operative, collective farm and public; useful (communal) space; averages 1950–5, 1956–60, 1961–5.
[e] excludes mopeds.
[f] state and co-operative, incl. food, million new roubles.

Sources: *Narodnoe Khoziaistvo SSSR v 1959, 1968*; Clarke 1972; Nove 1969/1990.

factor into cost calculations' (Schwartz 1965), and moving towards the 'capitalist' concept of an interest charge on investment funds, lack of which was a major defect of the 'planned' economy. This further step towards rationality would be taken by his successors.

More immediately it meant that hydroelectric power, which in 1960 contributed 17.4 per cent of all electricity generated, thereafter accounted for a declining share although its output more than doubled (from 51 to 124 milliard kWh.) over the next decade. Plans for a massive development of nuclear power-stations were postponed. Instead use was made of recently discovered coal deposits in central Siberia, where a new industrial base was now arising, and of reserves of oil and natural gas in the northern Caucasus and Ukraine, which were gradually linked by a network of pipelines to major centres in European Russia. As these reserves waned their place would be taken by deposits in the Volga–Urals area and western Siberia. Natural gas accounted for only 2.3 per cent of fuel supplies in 1950 but 15.6 per cent by 1965; oil doubled from 17.4 to 35.9 per cent, whereas coal sank from 66.1 to 42.9 per cent. Total energy supplies grew apace during the Khrushchev era (see Table 4.1), but on a per capita basis were still below those of advanced Western countries.

Several other developments during the Seven-Year Plan were of more immediate concern to consumers. One was the shift from natural to synthetic fibres for clothing and other domestic items. Several high-level resolutions on the matter were passed in 1957–8, *inter alia* ordering a 4.6-fold increase in the output of such fibres and an eightfold rise in plastics and synthetic resins. This drive was a belated response to Western technological progress, of which Soviet officials were more aware now that the ban on international travel and exchanges had been relaxed. The 'iron curtain' was thinnest in the Baltic republics, which led the way in developing stylish articles of clothing, furniture, and so on, but for most Soviet consumers fashion mattered less than price, as we shall see in a moment.

The 'command economy'

As the plan neared completion the structural defects of the 'command economy' became ever more evident. Although officials (and the general public) now had access to much statistical data previously treated as secret, there were no fundamental changes in the techniques by which planners arrived at the targets for each industrial branch, region, or enterprise, and verified the results reported. Khrushchev's predilection for campaign methods wrought havoc with many of their projections, which had to be continually revised. 'Storming' was a fact of life at enterprise level, too. Supply bottlenecks frequently disrupted production, so that factories operated in fits and starts, with periods of enforced idleness punctuated by mad rushes at month's end to complete the allotted target on time. Paradoxically, successful plan fulfilment often owed much to *shortcomings* in the administrative set-up, which allowed—indeed, compelled—factory managers to take illicit action in order to obtain the supplies of raw materials and labour they needed to attain the goals set. Penalties for non-fulfilment were severe. Yet despite constant exhortations and threats they found ways to evade compliance with orders from above and were none too eager to introduce technical innovations that seemed to them likely to disturb the rhythm of the production process. Nor did they respond well to the multiplicity of bonus schemes that were in operation. Their example was emulated by workers on the shop-floor, who had long since developed techniques of passive disobedience and avoidance of responsibility. According to a recent critic (Wegren 1994) the principal difference between the Soviet enterprise and its Western counterpart was not the existence of a plan or endemic supply shortages but the 'authoritarian, paternalistic' attitude of management to the work-force. Control over the production process actually lay with 'cadre workers' who took the initiative in overcoming dislocations that threatened plan fulfilment; in return managers made informal, discretionary concessions to this 'labour aristocracy' that its members came to regard as a right.

Economic decision-makers had every reason to be concerned at the declining rate of increase of labour productivity: from 7.6 per cent in 1951–5 to 4.8 per cent in 1961–5, according to official figures. The Soviet rate was about 40 to 50 per cent of that in the United States. In 1963 Soviet miners produced 2.1 tons of coal per day, their American counterparts 14 tons, although the level of mechanization was roughly the same. Full employment policies meant that pits employed far more people than was necessary for efficiency—and this was the pattern throughout the economy. But the plentiful reserves of rural labour that had existed in the early stages of industrialization were now approaching exhaustion, and the falling birth rate made it essential to move on from extensive to intensive methods of operation. This meant exercising the utmost economy in the use of manpower, energy, and materials. Alas, waste of resources was one of the most telling characteristics of the centralized 'planned' economy. For example, large amounts of capital were tied up in grandiose projects that might have to be left incomplete for years because the money for them had run out.

If the 'cult of bigness' was one residue of Stalinism, another was the pursuit of industrial expansion at any cost, with output goals expressed in quantitative figures. Fulfilment of these goals was the criterion by which managers were in practice judged, even though they were also expected to meet others for quality, costs of production, profit, and so on. The system had been designed to get results quickly in certain favoured sectors, regardless of consequences elsewhere, as if disaster were just around the corner. It was effective up to a point as a means of mobilizing resources in an overwhelming emergency, but ill-fitted for more normal circumstances, especially in a complex world where the number of commodities that had to be produced was growing exponentially. The problem was in part one of information flow, of obtaining and absorbing the vast amount of detailed data required to run the great machine, in which each cog was interlocked with dozens of others. 'The more inter-dependence there is among economic decisions, the more difficult it becomes to give decision-makers the kind of information . . . that will guide them in taking rational decisions' (Campbell 1967).

The most serious hindrance to optimal resource allocation was the inflexibility of the centrally determined price system. Since prices were not arrived at through operation of the laws of supply and demand, they did not reflect the real cost of production but planners' (or politicians') preferences. Some items were too expensive, others too cheap—i.e. they were subsidized, at a growing cost to the budget. Not only were prices fixed arbitrarily, but they remained virtually unaltered for years, despite (unacknowledged) inflation, changes in consumer taste, and improvements in technology. Above all, for ideological reasons prices did not allow for an interest charge on the use of capital. In practice administrators *did* try to 'cost out' the various options that confronted them, by calculating the recoupment ('pay-off') period of each, but this was inevitably a hit-or-miss affair.

Of greater consequence was the fact that the more progressive-minded economists were beginning to grapple seriously with the problem of reconciling interest charges and other features of the market economy with the principles of 'socialist planning' as hitherto understood. This was perhaps the most significant development of the period so far as the economy was concerned. Under Stalin, as we have seen, economics as a scientific discipline had barely existed. Now senior scholars (e.g. Nemchinov and Novozhilov) reappeared from obscurity—some of them from the camps—and a vigorous debate began. While conservatives held to the established 'direct methods' of counting and controlling, viewing the economy as a single vast factory, younger and brighter men came round to the idea that the dysfunctions in the system were due precisely to over-centralization. They understood that the control exercised needed to be flexible and determined by objective factors rather than by bureaucratic whim.

None of them, be it noted, dared to challenge openly the idea of planning as such. They were better at discerning the faults of the existing system than at devising alternatives to it. Some put their trust in mathematical techniques like linear programming, which had been developed in 1939 by Kantorovich but subsequently neglected, and hoped that the development of cybernetics (computerization) would make possible a sophisticated and rational method of regulating the economy's performance; they would allow the price of non-essentials to fluctuate, if only within a limited range. Others urged the merits of decentralizing decision-making to factory level, dismantling the central supply mechanism and replacing it by a wholesale trade network that functioned more or less according to market criteria. Yet even these brave spirits did not go as far as their colleagues in the East European 'people's democracies'. It is indicative of the spirit of public life in Khrushchev's Russia that they could not even refer openly to a 'socialist market economy' but had to use convoluted euphemisms such as 'money–commodity relations'. It was heresy to say, for example, that there was a discordance ('contradiction') between the interests of the state and those of producers or consumers.

In September 1962 the economists' debate reached a wider

audience when Professor Liberman of Khar'kov was allowed to suggest in *Pravda* that incentive payments to managers be based on a single indicator, the rate of profit earned on the capital invested by the state in their enterprise. Officials should no longer issue detailed targets but only those for the amount of output and dates for its delivery. This meant that managers should be free to decide how much raw material to buy and how to dispose of their goods. To critics in the establishment this looked too much like 'capitalism' at a 'micro' level, although Liberman did not propose a wide-ranging liberalization of prices, and unless this were done it was hard to see how the amount of profit earned could be evaluated. Would enterprises be allowed to sack surplus workers, so raising the spectre of unemployment?

Decentralization

Until 1964 at least, Khrushchev was near the conservative end of the spectrum of official opinion. As we know, in 1957 he had recouped his political fortunes with a scheme for deconcentration of industrial management. This looked more radical than it was. It might be termed 'horizontal centralization at the local level' (Breslauer 1982). The gainers were not enterprise managers but regional and district Party officials. True to his neo-Leninist principles, Khrushchev looked on them as the key decision-makers. The underlying assumption was that they would not be just 'troubleshooters' of the Stalinist type but technically well-educated professionals, who could give wise advice to the managers within their purview (who were, of course, Party members in the main) and use objectively valid criteria when checking on their efficiency. That this notion was utopian goes without saying.

The heart of the measure was the introduction in July 1957 of 105 regional councils of national economy (*sovnarkhozy*, or SNKhs: the term went back to Lenin). Each was to be responsible (to the union-republic government) for all but the smallest industrial plants in their locality. Meanwhile the central economic ministries were phased out, their officials abandoning their comfortable Moscow armchairs for the bracing provincial air. By 1962 there were only two such ministries left. However, at the same time Gosplan's competence was extended. It was empowered to 'co-ordinate', i.e. to amend and reject, each SNKh's plans and to maintain control over wages, prices and the supply of raw materials. As predicted by many observers at the time, this reform merely perpetuated the old evils in new guise and led to a proliferation of bureaucracy at the provincial level. 'The cure was worse than the disease' (Nove). It was not long before complaints appeared in the press of 'localism' (*mestnichestvo*), i.e. that officials were placing local interests ahead of those of the economy as a whole, or that enterprises were failing to meet orders placed by trading partners situated outside their own region. The quality of the councils' personnel left much to be desired. Of seventy-six chairmen whose background is known, sixty-two did have some technical competence—but they and the other council members were within the *nomenklatura* of the local Party organization. Not unexpectedly, its chief ensured that jobs went primarily to local boys: in Penza, for instance, no less than 352 out of 390, although five of the top officials here were outsiders (Barker 1973).

With attention focused on pleasing their immediate bosses, it was natural for such officials, and the managers they supervised, not just to neglect their wider obligations but to behave in a corrupt manner. In Karaganda, Kazakhstan, the SNKh chairman was alleged in 1958 to have 'taken funds away from a major iron and steel combine project and employed them to build a circus, a theatre, rest homes, two swimming pools and similar non-productive installations' (Schwartz 1965). It does not necessarily follow that such activities were more prevalent now than they had been before, but they certainly served as ammunition for conservative critics. One official complained that an order for ball-bearings for tractors had to go through six to eight instances before it could be fulfilled, and no less than fifteen instances if they were for cars.

In June 1960 the RSFSR and two Central Asian republics which had more than one SNKh each were ordered to set up co-ordinating agencies. This only made confusion worse. Next year virtually the whole Union was divided into seventeen 'major economic regions', each of which as a rule had six SNKhs under its authority. In 1963 the number of regional councils was reduced to forty-seven, the contraction being particularly evident in the RSFSR (from sixty-seven to twenty-four). Finally, a powerful new agency appeared at the centre, the Supreme Economic Council. Its head, Ustinov, had made his career in the arms industry and would go on to become Defence minister under Brezhnev. Below it there were now no less than four central bodies for planning, construction, supply and scientific-technical co-ordination as well as about thirty 'state committees' (equivalent to ministries) for specific branches of industry. Khrushchev's reform was effectively dead, although the SNKhs were not formally abolished until after his overthrow.

The labour scene

Despite these false starts and setbacks, in the post-Stalin decade most Soviet citizens' living standards improved. This was an early phase in a 'revolution of rising expectations'—to use a term then in vogue in the West—when it seemed as though people's material well-being could be bettered almost indefinitely. The regime profited politically from this rather naïve sentiment, acquiring a greater measure of acceptance on the part of the bulk of the population, but for mundane reasons that had little to do with the lofty aim of 'building Communism'. There was of course a danger here, in that sooner or later the underlying structural problems of the command economy would make themselves felt in 'supply difficulties', a euphemism for reduced consumption. This, together with other factors, would eventually help to 'de-legitimize' the Soviet regime.

An early indication of what lay ahead was the riot at Novocherkassk in 1962. The unexpected announcement of a sharp rise in the price of meat and dairy products from 1 June coincided with a decision by the management of a major local employer, the Budennyi locomotive construction works, to cut workers' wages. Several thousand men came out on strike. A senior local official who tried to calm the crowd was showered with sticks and bottles. There followed what an official report (made public in 1991) describes as 'hooligan acts'. Some of the soldiers that were hastily summoned fraternized with the protesters; others were injured. On 2 June a high-level delegation of Presidium members arrived. Mikoian and Kozlov authorized the troops to fire if necessary in self-defence. Some rioters entered and damaged the city-soviet building, whereupon several salvos killed twenty-four and wounded thirty-nine. The facts were hushed up for nearly thirty years, when under *perestroika* ninety-one of the 114 individuals who had been convicted of banditry, vandalism, and other offences had their sentences quashed or reduced—some of them posthumously (Trubin 1991). The affair had curiously archaic features: some protesters carried portraits of Lenin and banners with loyalist slogans, as if re-enacting 'Bloody Sunday' in 1905.

It must be stressed that such violent incidents were a rarity. Elsewhere in the country, as is clear from police reports that have since been published, opposition was limited to protest notices or graffiti in public places. One ironical notice in Tallinn read: 'Eat grass. You don't need meat.' KGB informers reported grumbling in Tbilisi, Leningrad, and elsewhere (Lebedev 1992). As a rule labour discontent was nipped in the bud by the ubiquitous agents of authority: Party organizations in the factories and trade-union officials.

The trade unions were a key component of the bureaucratic apparatus. In December 1957 they were criticized at a Central Committee plenum for failing to represent and defend workers' interests adequately. The powers of factory trade-union committees were redefined and extended (July 1958). They had to give their consent before a worker could be dismissed, and were to be consulted over new managerial appointments, the distribution of bonuses and establishing wage categories for different jobs. But these rights were not really new and have to be seen in context. The union officials' chief task was still to assist management in fulfilling the plan, notably at production conferences, held monthly or quarterly, to which workers in each plant chose representatives—under the Party's watchful eye. These measures did not signify a genuine advance to industrial democracy with free bargaining between the parties. Nevertheless they may have helped to ease tension on the shop-floor.

So too did the abandonment in April 1956 of government powers to direct people to certain jobs, a residue of wartime regimentation. In theory the existence of a labour market within an otherwise 'planned' economy was an anomaly; in practice it was a necessary concession to social realities. Workers were still required to carry 'labour books' recording jobs held (and any misconduct), which had to be shown when seeking employment. But prospective employers often disregarded such negative remarks when hiring workers. The authorities were concerned at what they regarded as an unduly high rate of labour turnover: no less than 38 per cent of all jobs in 1956, when people took advantage of their new freedom, falling to 20 per cent in 1961–2. This mobility had an adverse effect on production, notably in certain areas of Siberia (Kuzbas), where in 1962 as many workers left jobs in the construction industry as took them on, so that no growth occurred in the labour-force. People generally moved in search of better living conditions, rather than simply to earn higher wages, or else in order to escape from enterprises where work norms were excessively high (Filtzer 1987). Norm-setting was a matter of conflict on the shop-floor in many factories. Failure to fulfil one's allotted task could lead to loss of wages and other disabilities, so there was a continual struggle between more and less privileged groups as to how the burden should be distributed. Decisions on such matters were taken at a low level, by foremen and other 'cadre workers', who often abused their authority.

Wages and pensions

The same was true of wages, although probably to a lesser extent since these were of course centrally determined. In the late Stalin years the various branches of industry each had their own tariff scales, which led to 'a dizzying array of local anomalies' (Filtzer 1989). Miners and steelworkers earned twice as much as textile-workers; an accountant in a metallurgical works earned 72 roubles a month, while his counterpart in a meat-packing plant got only 38 roubles (Kaser 1970). A reform initiated in 1956 set out to make the system more uniform. It abolished some of the worst distortions, instituted a new bonus system, and reduced the extent of piece-rate payments, e.g. for workers doing jobs that demanded precision. As might be expected, it led to new anomalies—for instance, precision workers lost money and had to be compensated by over-generous bonuses—and managers continued to resort to all manner of dubious stratagems when pay-day came round. From the standpoint of industrial efficiency the problem was the lack of a stable and predictable system of incentives. From the standpoint of the more skilled and fortunately placed wage-earners, things were easier than they had been. Others, however, resented piecework as inequitable because it took inadequate account of the variability of conditions on the shop floor, e.g. differences in the quality of materials or equipment. The same resentment exists in other countries, too.

Another step taken in 1956 was to introduce a minimum wage of 270–350 roubles a month, which by 1962 had increased to 400–450 roubles (40–45 roubles in the new 'heavy' currency introduced in January 1961).[1] This was what a doorman or street-sweeper could expect to earn, but in December 1963, 60 per cent of manual workers received between 50 and 120 roubles, and 20–25 per cent of wage-earners more than this (Sorlin 1964). A skilled worker might well get higher wages than an engineer without high qualifications, and some very proficient miners or mechanics belonged to the social élite. The general tendency was towards a reduction of differentials, but policy on the matter was neither well thought-out nor consistent (McAuley 1979). The difference between those in the top and bottom decile (10 per cent) of wage-earners was put at 5.8 : 1 in 1959, as against 8 : 1 in 1934 (Yanowitch 1963).

Considerable efforts have been made by Western specialists to establish the extent of income inequality and privilege in the USSR, a topic to which we shall return (see p. 212). Early studies (J. Chapman and R. E. Golden) estimated that real personal consumption per capita grew by 6 to 7 per cent per annum between 1950 and 1958 (in 1937 prices), but more slowly thereafter. A more thorough analysis was undertaken by A. McAuley for the years 1960–74. He points out that wages are an inadequate measure of welfare. One needs to take household rather than individual income as a basis and allow for (a) other personal income, both monetary and non-monetary (e.g. produce from a private plot of land), and (b) the value of subsidized housing, transport, schooling and other public services. For ideological reasons the Soviet authorities preferred the increase in popular well-being to take the form of improved social facilities ('social consumption') rather than additional disposable personal income (which would also be inflationary, given the shortage of goods). The latter is estimated to have risen between 1960 and 1965 by 22.4 per cent, an annual average of 4.1 per cent, after allowing for inflation, or in cash terms from 419 to 550 roubles. This refers to the population as a whole; for state employees, i.e. everyone except collective farmers, the figures were 500 and 624 roubles respectively, a rise of 24.8 per cent. In 1960 an industrial worker's household comprised on average 3.6 members. Its total disposable personal income is estimated to have risen from 2,140 roubles in that year to

2,504 roubles five years later, or by an average of 3.16 per cent annually.

Pensioners also made material gains at this time, but many of them remained close to the poverty line or below it. Hitherto nearly all old-age and disability pensioners had received derisory amounts since they were liable to a 'maximum reckonable earnings rule' that restricted their entitlement. This was dropped in July 1956 and pensions calculated according to actual earnings on a sliding scale basis, with the lowest paid receiving 100 per cent, and those at the top of the scale 50 per cent, of their previous wage, with a ceiling of 1,200 (old) roubles and a minimum of 300 roubles per annum. Men qualified at age 60, women at 55. Benefits were tied to length of service (25 or 20 years) at a particular enterprise, but this restriction was lifted four years later.

Those suffering physical disabilities also had their pensions increased in 1956, but fared less well. Collective farmers were not included in the pension scheme until 1964–5. Since pensions were still very low in terms of purchasing power, many retired people preferred to go on working for as long as they could, a practice encouraged by the authorities. The official attitude to welfare stressed the social value of labour rather than entitlement to benefits as an individual right, in the manner of contemporary Western 'welfare states'. For the same reason the poverty level was not seen as a sacrosanct figure which needed to be constantly updated to allow for inflation (which supposedly did not exist anyway) or as a determinant of policy. Consequently a sizeable segment of the urban population continued to live in conditions which by Western standards were close to destitution.

Housing

One reason for this was the continuing migration into the towns of people from the countryside—13 million between 1956 and 1959 alone—anxious to improve their career prospects and, as they hoped, enjoy better amenities. This put enormous pressure on urban housing, which had scarcely recovered from wartime destruction. In 1957 the total area of actual living space per person (excluding 'communal space') was only 54 square feet, little more than half of the 97 square feet (9 square metres) laid down as the norm in the 1920s. The Seven-Year Plan provided for the construction of 15 million apartments, as much as all urban housing built since the revolution. Even so experts reckoned that the increase would barely keep pace with the influx, although the country's total stock of accommodation nearly doubled during the period.

The construction of state- and co-operative-owned urban housing rose from 25 million square metres total space in 1955 to 55.8 million in 1960 and 62.4 million square metres in 1965. To this may be added privately built housing, which initially received some financial and material support from the state. This rose from 8.4 million square metres in 1955 to a peak of 27.2 million in 1959, but then declined steadily until by 1965 it reached 15.5 million square metres, less than double the 1955 figure. The reasons for this were ideological. Khrushchev even launched a campaign to confiscate suburban cottages (*dachas*), for he suspected their proprietors of entertaining a 'bourgeois' desire for private ownership. They had to be circumspect about trying to make them more comfortable. In the case of the newly authorized co-operative apartments, as a rule built by enterprises rather than associations of individuals, the minimum down payment (40 per cent) was high by Western standards but the interest rate attractively low, a mere 0.5 per cent per annum. This was an option available primarily to the relatively well-off.

The communal apartments (*kommunalki*) shared by several families were gradually being phased out. By 1964 the total amount of floor space per person was on average 9.7 square metres, of which about two-thirds will have been 'effective' living area. There were approximately 1.5 occupants to a room. This was high by Western standards—but that was not necessarily the criterion whereby the residents judged them. They were more likely to contrast their new habitat with the overcrowded hut or barrack in which they had lived before, and to take pride in the huge cranes that dotted the skyline on the outskirts of many cities. Young couples in particular appreciated gaining independence from their parents, with whom they had been obliged to spend the first years of married life.

The principal architectural feature of the urban landscape now became the rows of twelve-floor apartment blocks, built of prefabricated sections by industrial techniques. Graceless and monotonous, they often lacked such 'frills' as balconies or even elevators. 'A large proportion have no main water supply or drainage' (Hanson 1968). Between 1959 and 1962 12 per cent of newly constructed accommodation had to be (temporarily?) evacuated or abandoned because of shoddy workmanship (Sorlin 1964).

Consumer affairs

Similar objections could be raised—and were—about the quality of many household objects. The supply of 'consumer durables' increased markedly, but was often irregular. One had to put one's name down for some of them in advance. By 1968 almost 50 per cent of Soviet households had television sets and washing machines, nearly 25 per cent refrigerators and 10 per cent vacuum cleaners—not all of them, we may assume, in working order (Matthews 1972). Spare parts and repair facilities were notoriously short.

One curious feature of the consumer scene was that it was much more difficult to obtain a telephone connection than a radio or television set. Critics alleged that this was because the authorities were keener to facilitate downward vertical communications than horizontal ones which it was harder to control. Another anomaly, at least to Western observers, was the low priority accorded to private motor vehicles. 'During the entire period 1953–64 . . . total Soviet production of passenger cars was little more than 1 million, or less than two months' average US automobile output in 1963' (Schwartz 1965). Again one must beware of misleading comparisons. It would have made no sense to build a 'Soviet Detroit' unless there were enough paved roads for the cars to run on, garages, and so forth. The 1,400-kilometre road from Moscow to the Crimea had only thirteen filling stations along its course, and of these two alone could repair vehicles (Kaser 1970). The Soviet automobile industry preferred to concentrate on producing heavy vehicles that served the needs of factory or farm rather than the rare private motorist, and the industry's price structure was geared accordingly. Here, too, there was an ideological element. Khrushchev said on more than one occasion that the collectivist 'new Soviet man' of the future would choose to take a taxi rather than drive his own car—on grounds of principle, not just to economize, and still less to keep down atmospheric pollution, something that few people as yet worried about.

The Soviet traveller was reasonably well served by rail, which in

1960 accounted for 69 per cent of all passenger movements (254 milliard kilometres); air travel accounted for 4.7 per cent (12.1 milliard kilometres): and buses and cars for less than a quarter. Muscovites were legitimately proud of their underground railway (Metro) system, which was extended and also emulated in other cities, although on a less lavish scale. Few paused to contemplate either the human cost of its construction (in part by *zeks*) in the 1930s or the fiscal cost of the heavy subsidies that enabled fares to be kept at an uneconomically low level.

Transport accounted for a mere 2 per cent of the average family budget, a trivial amount compared with clothing and food. Studies of such matters were still in their infancy, but one survey conducted in Moscow in the early 1960s showed that expenditure on clothing took 12.4 per cent of that of a poor household (monthly income 44 roubles), rising to 15.4 and 15.9 per cent of intermediate and well-off ones (income 82 and 113 roubles per month). For food-stuffs the proportions were respectively 55, 45.9 and 40.2 per cent (Matthews 1972)—according to another calculation (Hanson 1968), 43 per cent for all groups. The rest went on furniture and other 'cultural goods', rent, and amenities—or else was saved, at a low rate of interest. In general these goods were prohibitively expensive. A visitor in 1964 noted that for his monthly wage of 60 roubles an unskilled worker could buy two pairs of shoes—but nothing else! (Mihajlov 1964). The price of clothing and footwear (except that for children) was deliberately kept high relative to that of books, rented accommodation, and public utilities—all of which were relatively much cheaper than in the West.

As more goods became available consumers naturally grew more selective as to what they purchased. This was particularly true of clothing and footwear. Surplus stocks of out-of-date or inferior models began to accumulate in shops and warehouses. This presented the officials responsible with a problem, since bargain sales were considered a dubious 'capitalist' practice and needed high-level authorization. Characteristically, rather than change over to new models they preferred to reduce production of existing ones to create a scarcity and so boost sales of old-design clocks, watches, and sewing-machines. Another device was to permit short-term hire-purchase (instalment credit) arrangements, but this innovation did not become widespread: only 11 per cent of clothing was sold on this basis in 1963. Soviet officialdom looked askance at the 'consumer culture' of the West. Advertising, packaging, the layout of shops, the training and remuneration of staff in retail trade: all these were deliberately neglected sectors of the 'planned' economy. The interests of producers were paramount. Consumers had no lobby. They could complain about hygienic standards in a shop or other incidentals, but not about the price charged for the goods sold there. In a 'non-competitive market' (a contradiction in terms, to be sure) those in charge were free to take items out of circulation, raise the price or lower the quality without having to fear any organized response by shoppers.

A visitor to Moscow who returned in the late 1950s after a lapse of over twenty years remarked: 'Today [people] can buy things at GUM [the large department store in Red Square] which they never even dreamed of in 1936. But if you mingle with the customers now, you will hear quite a lot of criticism—prices are too high, quality is poor, service is not all it should be and so on. In other words, people are becoming more discriminating and exacting' (Mehnert 1962). He deduced that this would lead to articulate criticism among younger members of the social élite. This was correct—but only in the long run; it was also true that the bulk of the populace did not go beyond 'passive resistance' in refusing to purchase certain items. Proverbially patient, they had been accustomed to austerity for so long that the increased supply of consumer goods served its intended purpose of reconciling them to the *status quo*.

Was this equally true of foodstuffs? The Novocherkassk riot would suggest the contrary. As we have just seen, food was the chief item of expenditure. Town-dwellers' diet improved. It was nutritionally adequate but unbalanced, with an excess of carbohydrates. In 1965 urban families consumed 62.3 kilograms of meat annually, well above the national average of 41 kilograms. The figures for milk and dairy products were 334 and 251 kilograms; for eggs 177 and 124 units (Wegren 1992). A study of purchasing habits in 1959 showed that bread, potatoes, and flour products accounted for 18 per cent of the total, a considerable decrease since 1951 (29 per cent); dairy products and fats rose from 14 to 21 per cent, meat from 11 to 14 per cent. Only 7.6 per cent of the total went on fruit and vegetables, partly for cultural reasons but largely because they were often in short supply. Usually they had to be bought on a collective-farm market, where prices were considerably higher than in state stores. I recall visiting one such market in 1959, which had a stall prominently marked 'Fruit'. It was attended by a buxom peasant woman whose only offering was—a single large cabbage. Was it perhaps the sole relic of a lively day's trading? Apparently not. Rather it epitomized the primitive conditions under which collective farmers were obliged to ply their trade. To understand why this was so, we need to look at the all-important agricultural sector of the economy, the branch that was the principal focus of the Khrushchev regime's efforts to improve the Soviet people's living standards.

5 Priority for the Village

When Stalin died Soviet agriculture was in a parlous state. 'Nearly everything was wrong: planning, organization, management, the price system, taxation, physical equipment and facilities, the composition of the labour-force, the distribution system and, above all, incentives' (Grossman 1963). The list could be extended. One of the most glaring deficiencies was the lack of statistics. These had been deliberately falsified, to the point that even the country's leaders were ignorant of the actual state of the countryside.

It was announced [by Malenkov in October 1952] at the Nineteenth Party congress that the gross grain harvest amounted to 8 milliard poods [130 million tons] and that the grain problem had supposedly been solved. But it had been 'solved' only on paper, by estimating the 'biological yield', i.e. by looking at how much was growing in the fields. In fact the amount collected was only 5.6 milliard poods [92.2 million tons], of which only 2.1 milliards [34.6 million tons] were actually procured by state agencies, although in some cases farmers had to surrender their seed grain. (Valovoi 1988)

Moreover, 1952 was a 'good year'. In 1953 there were actually fewer head of cattle than there had been in Russia during World War I. Total traction power (mechanical and animal) per hectare of sown area was one-fifth less than it had been in 1928 (Grossman 1956).

Clearly, some allowance must be made for the effects of World War II, and the figures for such non-edible crops as cotton were relatively encouraging. It is also true that in most areas of the USSR soil and climatic factors made farming a risky business. Even the famous black soil (*chernozem*) of the steppe, the world's richest, crumbles into fine powder when too dry and turns into paste when too wet. Rural poverty had long-term roots. Nevertheless the basic reasons for poor performance were ideological and structural: doctrinal prejudice against the peasant, the tendency to ignore scientific advice where it conflicted with Party policy, the failure to use prices as an instrument of policy, and the belief that detailed regulation was the best way to get things done. Farm managers were often ignorant bullies, as were the umpteen officials set in authority above them. Their work ethos was satirized by the Ukrainian playwright Alexander Korneichuk in his play *Wings* (1956), where the local boss, one Dremliuga ('Sleepy'), plans to hold a meeting at which thirty-six speakers will praise his leadership, while output falls until the cows, fed only on straw, give as much milk as goats and 'potatoes cost more than bananas'. Korneichuk was no foe of the regime but simply echoed the criticisms uttered by Stalin's successors.

Khrushchev had grown up on a farm and fancied himself an authority on agricultural problems. As an autodidact without formal qualifications in this domain (unlike Gorbachev later), he looked with suspicion on those with agronomic expertise. He did, however, gain considerable bureaucratic experience while Party boss in Ukraine from 1938 to 1949 (apart from the brief spell in 1947 when he was blamed for the famine there). His approach was, however, a supremely administrative one, as exemplified by the 'agro-town' scheme, and it would remain the keynote of Soviet agrarian policy during the decade that Khrushchev held power. This explains why, at the end of the day, his many initiatives had such meagre results, for all the attention lavished on them.

These policies may be grouped under several heads, which we shall consider here in their order of importance to the regime. This, arguably, was the reverse of their order of importance as regards a truly beneficial reform of the rural economy. These measures were designed to strengthen 'socialist agriculture' by making it more efficient and productive without changing either its structure or its underlying philosophy. In turn they were as follows: (i) organizational changes to decentralize decision-making and professionalize farm management; (ii) increased inputs of money, scientific know-how, skilled manpower, machinery, and fertilizer; (iii) expansion of the area sown to grain by cultivating virgin and fallow land, mainly in eastern parts of the country; and (iv) provision of better incentives, notably by raising the procurement prices paid by the state.

Administration

It was no fun to be Agriculture minister with Nikita Sergeevich indulging in his favourite ploy of making this official and his staff the butt of his sarcasm, the scapegoat for all rural Russia's ills. In March 1955 Benediktov, the holder of this office, was demoted to replace the minister for state farms, Kozlov, who was sacked for inefficiency. After a seven-month interlude during which agricultural affairs were in practice run largely by the First Secretary himself, he was replaced by Matskevich, an animal-husbandry specialist whom Khrushchev had known since his days in Ukraine. But by 1961 he too had fallen into disfavour and lost his job. No fewer than nine republic-level agricultural ministers along with a host of minor officials were dismissed at this time. The Agriculture ministry lost its direct supervisory functions, being reduced to an agency to promote scientific farming methods. Many of its officials found themselves transferred to rural areas, perhaps as members of a 12,000-strong corps of inspectors under a new State Procurement Committee. Their main job was to negotiate with farm chairmen contracts whereby they pledged to deliver certain amounts and types of produce. They were in fact charged with supervising all Soviet agriculture at the local level, and could bring pressure to bear, through Party and government channels, against any farm management whose activities they found unsatisfactory.

This devolution of authority did not lead to a real increase in autonomy for the farms, which were still subjected to niggling controls over what kind of crops might be planted and countless other matters. But at least they now owned the heavy equipment (tractors, combine harvesters, etc.) they needed. Until 1958 management of these items had been vested in so-called machine-tractor stations (MTS). The post of 'deputy director for political affairs' was abolished in September 1953, but simultaneously the powers of the MTS over the farms were *enhanced*. They were assigned a Party secretary and a group of instructors. The intention was to make them an effective agency through which the Party's district (*raion*) organization could rule the countryside.

This measure limited the effect of a decree issued earlier, in March 1955, which denounced detailed planning of farm activities from the centre and tried to encourage greater initiative by farm administrations, which were called on to take decisions in the light of local experience and conditions. The MTS were now officially seen less as controllers than as partners which would give farm chairmen the benefit of their advice (many MTS directors were trained agronomists). But all too often the message did not get through, and Party officials in rural organizations, including the MTS, instead of interacting creatively with producers, continued to meddle in farms' affairs and to impose their own ideas. They could scarcely do otherwise so long as they were empowered to verify each farm's plan fulfilment. Seven signatures, it has been said, were needed before a peasant could slaughter a cow (Nove 1984).

In March–April 1958 Khrushchev took the unexpected and controversial step of abolishing the MTS, and by the end of that year most of the machinery had been sold off to the farms. In their place there appeared repair and service stations, which could exercise at most only an indirect control in so far as they were sole suppliers of fuel and spare parts.[1] Unfortunately the reform, introduced hastily in the teeth of bureaucratic resistance, was not well thought through. The price of the equipment was fixed too high, much of it was substandard, and farms were given niggardly credits with which to buy machines and build appropriate shelters for them. Many of the poorer farms were bankrupted by the operation, which in Roi Medvedev's view caused 'irreparable damage' to Soviet agriculture. They now found themselves saddled with the obligation of paying the former MTS technicians the equivalent of that part of their wages which they had previously received from the state. The total burden has been estimated at 1.8 to 2 milliard roubles. Moreover, to compensate for the abolition of the compulsory payments in kind for MTS services, which had been an important source of state procurements, farms had their delivery quotas increased—although at least the system whereby they were assessed was made more flexible.

In stepping into the unknown, as it appeared to Soviet officials, Khrushchev took heart from the continuing amalgamation of collective farms—their number dropped to 38,000 by 1964—and the conversion of many of them into ideologically more respectable *sovkhozy*. By 1965 the latter had more than doubled their number, to over 10,000, and had increased their sown area to 97.4 million hectares, as against 18.2 million in 1953. (By 1970 they would overtake the *kolkhozy* in this respect). Khrushchev also calculated that the Party's rural structure was now strong enough to prevent farmers from putting their own interests ahead of those of the state. The number of Party members working in the agricultural sector rose from 1.2 million in September 1953 to about 1.5 million in 1958; by January 1964 it would exceed 2 million. Of these men about 60 per cent worked on collective farms. When Khrushchev took over approximately one-fifth of these farms had no Party organization, but by 1958 there were hardly any that did not (the figure for 1962 was below 200)—the process being assisted by the transfer to them of machinery operators from the former MTS. Already by April 1956 the share of collective-farm chairmen who were Party members exceeded 90 per cent, and the rise continued thereafter. Traditionally Party members were more strongly represented among supervisory personnel, as was only to be expected, but the general tendency was 'away from the office and into the fields', and by 1965 five out of six were said to be 'directly engaged in production' (Rigby 1968). It was therefore relatively safe politically, as well as more rational, to eliminate a situation in which, as Khrushchev put it in 1958, 'we have two masters on the same land, the collective-farm chairman and the MTS director, and where there are two masters there can be no good management.'

Unfortunately this insight did not prevent a multiplication of supervisory authorities in the countryside during the last years of his rule. In March 1962 new bodies called farm territorial production associations (TPAs) were set up. They were made responsible to an all-Union Agricultural Committee under Ignatov, which however never met. Their staffs were drawn from existing local Party and government officials. The TPA office was situated symbolically on the most efficient farm in the region, with the idea that its experience would be diffused among its more backward neighbours by a mobile force of 'inspector-organizers'. The latter were to report any refusal by a farm management to heed their advice. This 'reform' was clearly a step back towards centralized control. It did not work well: there were boundary disputes between these new plenipotentiaries and the regular Party and soviet officials. It did not solve the problem of improving the quality of local officialdom, the low standard of which had been amply revealed by an episode in Riazan' province in 1959.

The Party secretary here was an enterprising individual named Larionov. Responding to pressure from above, he promised to double the province's deliveries of meat and other livestock products. The easiest way of doing so was to slaughter more animals, including breeding stock, but this had the disadvantage of reducing output in subsequent years. Why not, therefore, he reasoned, buy animals from farms in neighbouring provinces, and even send out agents at night to steal them? Another ruse was to buy animals from the peasants, record them as deliveries to the state, sell them back again and repurchase them, in an endless succession of bogus deals, until the plan had been fulfilled—on paper, at least. In 1959 Riazan' sold the state 150,000 tons of meat, three times as much as in 1958, but in 1960 it could deliver only 30,000 tons. The authorities soon got wind of the fraud. Larionov 'went the way of his animals: he shot himself' (McCauley 1991).

This was but the most spectacular of countless deceptions that seldom came to light. One such episode occurred in the Pavlodar province of Kazakhstan in 1959. When a zealous official reported it to the CC, he was reprimanded. 'Iron discipline in the Party apparatus', he reminisced many years later, 'prevented people from displaying initiative and creativity' (Smirnov 1993). 'Many officials, taught under Stalin not to contradict [authority]', wrote another, 'went along with the manipulation of figures and prevaricated in their reports, pretending that what those at the top wanted was what really existed' (Nosov 1988). In January 1961 Khrushchev publicly rebuked the Kyrgyz Party leader, Razzakov, for covering up malfeasance by a subordinate who had encouraged farmers to fulfil their delivery quotas for butter by buying up supplies in shops. A few months later a decree was issued on 'measures to prevent deception of the state and to strengthen supervision of the reliability of plan fulfilment reports'. The wordy title concealed its inner emptiness. Corruption was inseparable from the centralized planning system, which encouraged officials to curry favour with their superiors even if this meant behaving irrationally.

Agronomics

The bureaucratic approach got in the way of the regime's efforts to make farming more scientific. Khrushchev's view was that the agronomists' function was to help boost output: nothing else counted. 'Science existed . . . to serve the interests of the people and the state. If it became divorced from life it became false science . . . He saw science as an instrument of government policy' (McCauley 1976). It was a very Stalinist attitude, and explains why Khrushchev, like Stalin, was captivated by the quack biologist Lysenko's fraudulent theories and gave him the political support that enabled him to remain in the Academy of Sciences, despite growing opposition, until shortly after Khrushchev's fall (see below p. 136). Lysenko was one of those who, following the theories of Viliams (1863–1939), championed *travopol'e*, the name given to a system of crop rotation that left much of the land under grass for long periods. It was not the principle that was at fault but its application on a universal scale, regardless of local conditions. Khrushchev made the same mistake in reverse, so to speak. He strongly criticized excessive use of grasses, as well as of fallow, which he saw simply as land lying waste that could otherwise be sown to crop, especially maize (US: corn). 'In academic institutions Viliams's portraits were taken down and copies of his works removed from their libraries' (Nosov 1988). Khrushchev argued that *travopol'e* was suited only to the central non-black-earth zone of European Russia, where there was sufficient rainfall, and should not be extended to the dry steppe lands of Ukraine or Kazakhstan. During his rule the area under grass and fallow sank appreciably. The reduction of fallow had serious consequences in the drier zones of the country, and in the more humid zones it was detrimental to plough up so much grassland.

Maize was a crop that had become familiar to Khrushchev in Ukraine, where it grew well. A good case could be made out for sowing more of it, especially as cattle fodder. But the 'First' treated the drive as if it were a military campaign on which the nation's life depended. In 1955 he set a target of 30 million hectares by 1960, from an existing (1954) level of 4.2 million hectares. Party and people were lectured on the advantages of the 'square-cluster method' of planting—a pet idea of the leader's—and the need to harvest the crop in the 'milky-wax stage', when it was still immature and could be ensilaged. In his view unripened maize was the key to increasing the country's livestock herd, since its nutritive value was much higher than that of hay (a point some contested). Under pressure from above farmers across the land joined in the campaign with apparent gusto. By 1956 24 million, and by 1962 no less than 36 million hectares had been sown to this crop. Entertainers did their bit to raise public consciousness, dancing in costumes adorned with corn cobs, 'but when in accord with fashion maize was sown in places where it had never grown and could not grow, destroying the traditional crop cycle, it was not so funny' (Voskresensky 1987). The yields achieved were disappointing and much was wasted. By 1965 the campaign had been abandoned. In that year only

3.2 million hectares were sown to this crop. The underlying idea was sound enough: 'where Khrushchev went wrong was to take everything to excess' (McCauley 1976).

It was the same story with the campaign to increase radically the supply of mineral fertilizer, which necessitated a vast expansion of the chemical industry. There was opposition to this among the scientific partisans of *travopol'e* as well as among planners and industrial managers (popularly tagged 'steel-eaters'), who objected to the extra capital expenditure involved and won political support in the Party Presidium. (There were also valid ecological grounds for concern at excessive use of pesticides and fertilizers, but these had yet to make themselves heard.) In 1953 the USSR produced 7.0 million tons of fertilizers. At the Central Committee plenum in September, when he launched his great agricultural offensive, Khrushchev called for output to rise to 16.5–17.5 million tons by 1959 and 28–30 million tons by 1964, but the initial spurt was not sustained and by 1958 the figure reached was only 12.4 million tons. Most of this went to improve the yields of technical (non-food) crops. Another drive was instituted, and by the end of 1963 the figure had gone up to nearly 20 million tons. This was a 15 per cent rise on the previous year, and in part a response to yet a *third* drive which the premier launched with great fanfare in July. The 1970 target was then fixed, with characteristic excess of zeal, at 100 million tons and had to be scaled down later. Pesticide output was to rise no less than 7.5 times, the total cost being put at 42 milliard roubles.

In all this, as with the maize campaign, the leader had in mind the example of the United States, which he visited in 1959, and where fertilizer output and application, for good or ill, far exceeded Soviet rates. Credits to finance the development were obtained from Britain, France, and Japan. Yet this was not a rational way of employing scarce resources. It would have made more sense to ensure that farms made proper use of what was currently available. For instance, fertilizer was supplied in bulk instead of in bags, and farms had to pay for transporting it from the unloading point. Not surprisingly, much went to waste. Khrushchev himself spoke of piles of fertilizer left unprotected until they froze solid and, covered with snow, made a splendid sleigh-run for local children. Moreover, the price that farm managers had to pay was disproportionately high, which acted as a disincentive—although that did not stop some of them applying excessive amounts to cover up other shortcomings.

Among these malpractices was the inefficient way they used machines. In part this was a by-product of the transfer of responsibility for their care to the farms once the MTS had been liquidated. In December 1960 the government made such negligence a criminal offence. But it was also partly the result of faults by designers and planners. Output of agricultural machinery was cut back in the late 1950s, partly to meet the needs of defence. Only a limited range of standardized items was available, and these did not take due account of farmers' actual needs, which varied regionally. The most striking lack was of small machine tools suitable for use on the peasants' private plots, which obliged them to adhere to techniques that had scarcely changed since the Middle Ages. Another failing was a 'product mix' that gave pride of place to the combine harvester and tractor, veritable symbols of collectivization, while neglecting trucks. Farm vehicles were unduly heavy, because much metal was used in their construction and they frequently came to grief on rural Russia's notoriously rough roads.

Last but not least, the over-centralization of machinery supply led to an endemic lack of repair facilities. Mechanics could work wonders 'cannibalizing' vehicles, and these therefore had an unduly brief life-span. 'The rate of scrapping in 1957–62,' noted one Western specialist, 'was at the level of 7 to 11 per cent per year . . ., which meant that a year's scrapping was equivalent to a considerable part of . . . new acquisitions, varying from 43 to 64 per cent' (Dovring 1966). In plain words, one or two of every three tractors supplied ended up on the scrap heap within twelve months of delivery. Rusting piles of old iron were, and still are, a typical feature of the Russian farmyard. On the positive side, basic agricultural operations were now almost entirely mechanized: ploughing by 1953, harvesting by 1957. Since rural labour was still comparatively abundant, this did not lead to the spectacular decline in the farm work-force one might have expected. This fell by a mere 1.1 million between 1959 and 1964, and costs of production remained high (Volin 1970). It would be unfair to put *all* the blame for this on the system, since rural over-population was a legacy of Russia's historic development lag. This took generations to overcome, and in the process gave rise to new problems. In the meantime 'socialist agriculture' at least gave every villager a job, or the appearance of one—albeit at a high cost in economic efficiency.

The 'virgin lands' drive

The most ambitious project associated with Khrushchev's name was the campaign to bring under cultivation vast expanses of steppe, the so-called 'virgin and idle lands', situated mainly in northern Kazakhstan and western Siberia. The term 'virgin' is misleading, in so far as much of this territory had hitherto been used for cattle-grazing, particularly by Kazakh herdsmen, who could hardly be expected to welcome an invasion of their republic by hundreds of thousands of Slavs. These were in the main young volunteers, but the Komsomol and other official agencies 'assisted' them in making their choice. Some military units 'adopted' farms which they undertook to keep supplied with demobilized conscripts. Conditions in the new lands were initially very harsh. No proper preparations were made to receive the migrants, some of whom had to live in tents until hutted camps could be built. A number gave up the struggle and returned as soon as they could to more agreeable regions.

The strategic calculation behind the scheme was that wheat grown here would help feed the burgeoning cities, allowing the non-black-earth lands of European Russia to provide animal fodder, but this regional diversification was not conceived rigidly. Development of the steppe had precedents dating back to tsarist times. It was seen first as a stopgap measure but soon came to be viewed as permanent. Introducing the idea to a Central Committee plenum in February 1954, Khrushchev put forward a target of 13 million hectares to be ploughed, and 2.3 million sown, over the next two years. Characteristically, the goals were repeatedly raised until by October 1961 a total of 50 million hectares of land were set to be sown. By 1960 a total of 41.8 million hectares had been ploughed up, of which 25.5 million lay in Kazakhstan, where a new administrative region named for the virgin lands (Tselinnyi *krai*) made its appearance. During this period the total sown area increased by 36 million hectares. Not much was added during the next four years and some marginal land dropped out of cultivation, partly because of lack of capital and partly because of climatic considerations (lack of rainfall!). Scientists had warned at the outset that there was a high risk of soil erosion on the steppe, which was subject to a dry wind (*sukhovei*) from Central Asia, and that harvests were bound to be uncertain. But they had not been listened to.

A bumper crop in 1956 seemed to justify the venture and helped Khrushchev to worst his political opponents. In that year the basic virgin land areas contributed 50.8 per cent of the total grain harvest. The next best years were 1959 and 1960 (45.8 and 46.8 per cent). Taking the eight years 1957 to 1964 together, the virgin lands' share averages out at 41.4 per cent. In terms of state procurements the best results were recorded in 1956 (68 per cent) and 1960 (62.2 per cent). In the early 1960s output tended to level off. It should be added that much of the grain was heavily weed-infested, and that over half a million tons of soil were washed away annually. In 1960 alone dust storms damaged over 13,000 square miles of land. Yields per hectare in the Tselinnyi *krai* were about half those of Ukraine or north Caucasus, and only western Siberia reached its target of 10 centners per hectare. Over the period grain cost about 20 per cent more to produce in Kazakhstan than the national average, but in 1961–4 the figure was twice as high. All in all, most specialists take the view that the effort was economically worthwhile. Extending the sown area gave the government the extra produce it needed in the short term. But it did not constitute a long-term solution to the grain problem. This required an intensification of effort in the traditional farming areas, which could come about only by abandoning collectivism and effecting a painful transition to a market economy.

Incentives

Needless to say, this was not a prospect entertained by Khrushchev or his colleagues. They recognized that material incentives were essential to stimulate improved performance, but did not want these to foster 'petty-bourgeois' proprietorial tendencies. Policy was accordingly contradictory, and moral exhortation continued to play a major role. The first concessions came in August 1953, when farmers' taxes were drastically reduced and arrears cancelled. Shortly afterwards compulsory delivery quotas were reduced for a variety of products and prices raised significantly: by 25 to 40 per cent for vegetables, 100 per cent for milk and butter, and 550 per cent for livestock. Those delivering produce above their quota benefited

from a two- to threefold price increase. Further reforms followed
in 1958, when compulsory deliveries ceased altogether. The system
of procurements, or purchases as they were now called, was
homogenized, a single price being established for each commodity
on a regional basis. Quotas were fixed in advance for five to seven
years, subject to an annual review (which characteristically could
raise but not lower them!). Farms were reimbursed the cost
of transporting their produce beyond a 25-kilometre radius. Up to
one-quarter of the purchase price might be paid in advance of
delivery. By 1959 the prices paid for agricultural produce were
on average three times what they had been in 1952, and for grain
seven times more—whereas cotton-growers hardly benefited at all.

None of this represented 'marketization'. Quotas had not been
abolished and prices were still fixed according to official estimates
of average production costs, which might be seriously in error. For
example, farms in remoter locations had higher costs, but these
were frequently disregarded. The work of the various purchasing
agencies was poorly co-ordinated. In 1958 the prices paid to
farmers were *reduced* across the board on the grounds that the
harvest was so bountiful (31 per cent up on the previous year), but
they were not increased in the following year when it fell by 12 per
cent! And in 1961, as we have seen, the State Procurement Committee with its regional inspectorates was set up, which increased
the opportunities for arbitrary action—such as denying cash advances to farms which allegedly lagged in their deliveries, or even
taking grain which they needed as seed. It is only fair to add that
farm managers played the same sort of tricks on officials, or with
their tacit connivance—as in the case of Larionov, cited above.

One of the problems here was that storage facilities (e.g. grain
elevators) were notoriously poor. They were managed, not by the
farms themselves, but by official agencies. When they were full,
their managers would refuse to accept delivery of perishable produce, which rotted away. There is ample anecdotal evidence of
roads lined with vegetables that had fallen from rickety farm
vehicles. In a word, the system for marketing agricultural produce
was both archaic and coercive. Farms had insufficient incentive to
garner and sell as much foodstuffs as they could. Although by 1964
the state was paying out three times as much as it had in 1955 (19
milliard as against 6.4 milliard roubles), in 1960 the prices still
covered only two-thirds the cost of producing beef and eggs. In

1963–5 the price received for grain, cotton, and potatoes was well above cost, whereas on cattle, milk, or eggs the farm had no hope of turning a profit. Indeed, sometimes the greater the output the greater the loss. For the farm manager and accountant it was a nightmare situation.

Private plots

The same applies with even greater force to the *kolkhoznik* anxious to earn extra cash by selling produce from his household plot on the collective-farm market in a nearby town. This was still an important source of income: as much as 28 per cent, contemporary sample rural budget surveys suggest (1966: De Pauw 1969). According to one Western calculation private activity in general accounted for 52.2 per cent of collective farmers' total personal income in 1960, but fell to 42.3 per cent in 1965 (McAuley 1979). The downward trend continued thereafter as work in the 'socialist' sector (i.e. on land run by the farm) became more remunerative and living standards rose. If one could buy milk in the local shop, why go to the bother of keeping a cow?

Khrushchev declared in September 1953 that privately owned livestock did not threaten socialist agriculture, and in 1954 the arbitrary tax levied on those possessing animals was lifted. Encouraged by this more tolerant attitude in high places, collective farmers boosted their private livestock holdings. But soon the country's leaders were having second thoughts. For ideological reasons they could not accept the idea that peasant incomes might increase more rapidly than those of workers. In 1956 private owners were prohibited, on pain of heavy fines, from buying grain to feed their stock. To prevent a mass slaughter of animals, local authorities were encouraged to buy them. Farms were also 'recommended' to alter their statutes to ensure that private plots be reduced in size. Their area was to be determined by the amount of labour that each household put in on collective land. It seems that these measures were largely ignored, at least in the countryside (some town-dwellers had plots and even kept cattle!). In January 1958 private owners were freed from the requirement to deliver part of their produce to the procurement agencies, and peasant incomes benefited in consequence. But the authorities had by no means moderated their negative attitude. In December of that year Khrushchev declared ominously: 'we must examine the question whether workers and employees should keep their own livestock and have large private gardens.' He added that coercion should not be used, and what followed was less a grandiose offensive in Stalinist style than a series of minor restrictions spread over a five-year period, backed up by a great deal of propaganda, targeted primarily at town-dwellers. Workers on state farms, who also had plots, were pressed to get rid of their cattle. Collective-farm managers took the hint and reduced the amount of feed for privately owned animals or curtailed their access to pasture. Simultaneously, municipal authorities regulated the prices which peasants could charge for their produce at *kolkhoz* markets.

Despite the uncongenial atmosphere, and the fact that most work on private plots was done by female and elderly members of peasant families, the private sector, with about 3 per cent of the sown area, yielded about one-third of the country's agricultural produce. This was possible because the land was cultivated intensively and the produce was of high value. Over the eight years 1958–65 no less than 77.3 per cent of eggs, 64.4 per cent of potatoes, 45.8 per cent of milk, 44.2 per cent of meat, and 42.9 per cent of vegetables were produced privately. Taking 1958 as the base year (= 100), in 1965 the index figures for these privately produced food items were respectively 100, 98, 92, 100, and 107 (De Pauw 1969). This suggests that private farmers successfully resisted the government's restrictive measures. Had farmers received consistent encouragement from officialdom, they might well have been able to keep town-dwellers plentifully supplied from their gardens and poultry yards.

Rural life

As it was, rural Russia was condemned to squalor and misery. Leonid Pliushch recalls in his memoirs that in 1959, when he took up a post as a village teacher, he was astonished to find one-third of the inhabitants suffering from tuberculosis: all the milk they produced had to be surrendered to the collective. An equally depressing picture is drawn by another dissident, Andrei Amalrik, who in the mid-1960s was exiled to a village near Tomsk in Siberia. Here at least there was no lack of fodder, but cows gave only four to six quarts of milk a day. The peasants' material condition was precarious and their mood apathetic. No one, for example, would take the initiative to mend a rotting barn. They used no fertilizer and no food could be bought in the local shop. The villagers spent their leisure hours drinking and quarrelling. They would complain at the hard life they led but could not visualize any alternative to it. 'They haven't the slightest idea how much an egg, a quart of milk, or a pound of pork costs them to produce. Since they don't pay any money for them, they are under the illusion that they get them for nothing. They rate the value of their own work just as low as does the *kolkhoz* or the state' (Amalrik 1970).

Western Siberia may have been a particularly backward region. But everywhere collective farmers were socially disadvantaged as compared with town-dwellers (and also state-farm employees). Although they did not qualify for an internal passport until 1975, this restriction did not hinder the flight from the land of many of the younger and brighter members of rural society (see Chapter 12). In 1965 a Komsomol source lamented the fact that on many collective farms members' average age had risen to 50.

This exodus was scarcely slowed down by the rise in wages, from an average of 164 roubles a year in 1953 to 445 roubles in 1964, or the introduction of a minimum wage (27 roubles a month in 1957, 40 roubles in 1965). Wages paid in kind, instead of cash, declined in importance but still accounted for 32 per cent of the total in 1963–4. The old system of calculation by 'labour days' gradually gave way to payment of regular monthly wages, which were treated as advances against the anticipated sum due at year's end. (Not until 1966 did collective farmers get a guaranteed wage.) In comparative terms wage rates were on average very low: 40 per cent of industrial workers' earnings in 1958, 50 per cent in 1964 (Matthews 1972). The picture is less bleak when private-sector earnings are included. Opinion is divided as to whether the gap narrowed between collective farmers' *total* income and that of state employees.[2] The differential between collective farmers and state-farm employees did narrow, and people in collectives that were transferred to *sovkhoz* status could expect to earn more. One should add that there were also significant wage and income differentials *within* each collective farm. An élite of managerial and office personnel, including brigade leaders—some 3 per cent of the farm labour-force—earned more than tractor-drivers or construction workers, while those who looked after animals did better than humble tillers of the soil. Since women had more household duties to perform, they worked fewer hours in the collective fields and so generally earned less than men. Of all groups in Soviet society (excluding prisoners) rural women had the hardest lot. Data for 1963 show that collective farmers (of both sexes) spent 15 per cent more of their income on food than industrial workers did. They consumed less meat, fish, or sugar, but more bread, potatoes, and eggs.

Increased output of food was crucial if the post-Stalin leaders were to achieve their principal domestic goal, to raise people's living standards and so strengthen the regime's legitimacy. Results fell far short of expectations. The proud boast at the Twenty-first Party congress that within a few years the USSR would overtake the United States in the production of meat and butter was soon exposed as a mirage. The Seven-Year Plan called for a 56 per cent rise in agricultural output per capita: in the event it barely increased. The poor harvest in 1963 dramatized the Khrushchev government's dilemma. It was unwilling to risk further popular commotion by raising procurement prices. Nor was it ideologically possible to contemplate radical concessions to the private sector. So Khrushchev abandoned his scruples and decided to import grain from the 'capitalist' West to tide the country over the crisis, while continuing existing policies in the hope of eventual success. Alas, the road taken was the wrong one and prosperity never came.

Nevertheless it would be unfair to write off the leader's efforts at reform as a complete failure. For one thing he had kept peasant affairs at the centre of attention for an entire decade. No other Russian ruler had ever done this, or would do so. For another, he presided over a substantial increase in agricultural output. As the figures in Table 5.1 suggest, for grain the rise was greatest in the years 1954–8 and then tapered off, while for livestock the reverse was the case.

TABLE 5.1. *Output of selected foodstuffs, 1952–1964* (million tons)

	1952	1953–6	1957–60	1961–4
Cereals (excl. maize)	82.0[a]	98.8	120.3	132.1
Meat	5.2	6.3	8.2	9.1
Milk	35.7	41.7	59.2	62.7

[a] 1949–52 average.

Sources: Smith 1987; Nove 1970; Clarke 1972.

This was partly the result of over-confidence, which in 1958–9 led the government to back-pedal on agricultural investment and machinery supply, while toughening its line on private plots. Taken by themselves, these figures were not so bad. But they need to be looked at in the light of the enormous inputs of money and manpower that it took to achieve them. Agriculture accounted for 19.8 per cent of gross investment in the economy from 1956 to 1960, and 18.0 per cent from 1961 to 1965. This was less than half as much as was invested in industry, and was insufficient to meet rural Russia's needs. For decades agriculture had been starved of funds and even treated as a resource for more favoured sectors of the economy. This was the heart of the problem. The country was bleeding itself white to accumulate capital resources but then spending them unwisely. Or, to put it differently, by subsidizing socialized agriculture the state was ensuring that it remained inefficient. The backwardness of the private sector adversely affected the health of the whole. But those who toppled Khrushchev in October 1964 did not see things this way, and another quarter-century would pass before structural reform would be attempted.

6 The Rebirth of Conscience

The literary revival

In retrospect it seems quite logical that, once Stalinist controls over the Soviet cultural scene were relaxed, writers and artists should have gradually resumed the role they had played before the revolution as 'conscience of the nation'. Then they had spoken up on behalf of the oppressed *narod* (people) and encouraged Russia's intellectuals to view opposition to tsarism as a sacred cause. A similar moral fervour would characterize the movement of open dissent from state-imposed values that began, in far more difficult circumstances, in the mid-1960s. The first post-Stalin decade was a time of preparation, when a growing number of courageous intellectuals challenged the censors by ventilating their pent-up thoughts and feelings. In doing so they broke free from the confines of 'socialist realism', the Stalinist literary doctrine, and became spokesmen for the mute millions: for all those in Soviet society who doubted the veracity of official slogans and felt uneasy about many aspects of current reality, yet did not dare voice such sentiments openly.

Once Khrushchev had lifted the curtain, even if only partially, on the crimes of the Stalin era, bland propaganda about Soviet achievements and the bright Communist future lost its appeal for thinking people. But many citizens were ambivalent or confused. Political opposition was still rare, at least among members of the majority nation. Even so it was in these years that a movement of cultural dissent took shape. It was informal and unstructured. Its leaders were poets, dramatists, critics, and novelists, some of them well-known figures in the literary establishment, while others belonged to a new generation who rebelled against the conformism of their elders. These pioneers broke many long-standing taboos on the treatment of politically sensitive topics. They also experimented with new styles and genres, often inspired by modern Western literary works, to which it was now easier to gain access. Others looked back to the Russian classical tradition. The writings of Dostoevsky were reissued, although in a selected edition; so too were those of the emigré Bunin. In this cultural ferment a particularly important role was played by the literary monthlies, with *Novyi mir* ('New World') in the vanguard. The fluctuating fortunes of its editor, the poet Alexander Tvardovsky—dismissed in 1954 but reinstated four years later—served as a barometer of the country's intellectual climate.

It is admittedly an over-simplification to view the creative intelligentsia as locked in perpetual battle with the politico-literary establishment. First, as members of the official Union of Soviet Writers (USW) authors were, so to speak, an integral part of the system. They enjoyed important privileges, but in exchange were dependent on the favour of journal editors and officials in the state publishing houses. The appearance in print of a work on a sensitive theme was the result of a complex bargaining process in which there were no hard and fast rules. The situation was such that few writers could avoid compromising themselves or, indeed, acting as their own censors. It was this that made the Soviet pattern of literary controls so insidious. Secondly, the Writers' Union had a large number of conservative members who were content to adhere to the official canon. Thirdly, the boundaries of 'socialist realism' were never fixed with clarity. It was rather a matter of writers being required to follow certain model narratives with a simple linear plot and a 'positive hero' who finally triumphed over every adversity—a mythical version of the Stalinist perception of Soviet historical development (K. Clark 1981). This left authors a good deal of leeway to interpret the formula as they thought fit. It explains why already in Stalin's last years some writers were apparently able to go beyond the bounds of the canon, so anticipating events after March 1953.

The first sign of movement on the literary scene was an article in *Literaturnaia gazeta* (16 April 1953) by the frail but stout-hearted poetess Olga Berggol'ts, a heroine of the Leningrad blockade whose husband had been shot. She called for more lyricism and personal feeling in verse. The theme was taken up by several other writers, among them Vladimir Pomerantsev. In November 1953 he published an essay in *Novyi mir*, 'On Sincerity in Literature', which created a sensation with its daring attack on the habit of 'varnishing' reality. He urged writers to abandon the often subtle devices they had adopted to avoid dealing in depth with controversial topics. Pomerantsev was a man of sterling character who had used his legal knowledge to help innocent persons condemned to terms in the Gulag.

A rather more controversial figure was Il'ia Ehrenburg, a Stalin prize-winner (1952) best known for his role as wartime propagandist. In 1953 he redeemed himself from the slur of excessive willingness to compromise by publishing, in *Znamia* ('The Banner'), an article critical of censorship. 'A writer cannot correct his heroes' lives', he wrote, 'in the way a sub-editor corrects proofs'; instead it was his duty to explore the inner life of his characters. Later Ehrenburg would give a name to this period of Soviet cultural history with his novella *The Thaw* (1954). It contrasted the fates of two writers, one of whom conformed and enjoyed success while the other refused to bend the knee and lived in poverty—until Stalin's death, whereupon the roles were reversed. The optimistic conclusion was typical of a 'socialist realist' novel. Judged as literature *The Thaw* was undistinguished; yet it summed up nicely the current situation in the arts, and this lent it significance.

Over the next decade there would be several successive 'thaws' and 'freezes'. With each turn of the screw writers would retreat, only to return with redoubled vigour as the pressures eased, until the Russian literary world produced artistic giants of international stature comparable with those of the nineteenth century. This development had much to do with a religious renaissance which in part was a response to Khrushchev's onslaught on the churches (see Chapter 8).

The chief battleground in the struggle was literary criticism. While some courageous critics praised writers who revealed the ills of Soviet society, others acted as cultural policemen. A harsh review of some 'heretical' writer's work in a specialized journal might be followed by, say, an article in *Pravda*. This would serve as a signal for a general propaganda onslaught, as likely as not backed by administrative measures: a ban on publishing, or even mentioning, the offender's works, threats by 'orthodox' colleagues, a summons to confession and public condemnation, and in the last instance expulsion from the USW—for a writer tantamount to a death sentence. Pomerantsev was one author who suffered a fatal heart attack when told that printing of his work had been discontinued. Others might survive materially by taking prosaic jobs, relying for moral support on their families and circles of faithful friends, and writing occasional pieces 'for the drawer' until the wheel turned.

The first wave of repression climaxed in the summer of 1954, when the Moscow and Leningrad Party organizations held meetings with writers in an attempt to bring them into line. Among those criticized was Tvardovsky. He refused to make the abject apology demanded of him, but had to yield his editorial post in favour of Simonov, who showed less resilience under pressure. The change did not signal a full turn towards reaction, for Khrushchev needed the writers' support and sought a *modus vivendi* with them. December 1954 saw the convocation of the Second congress of the USW. Of the 738 delegates only 123 had attended the First congress twenty years earlier. The purges, along with the war and natural causes, had taken their toll. Several of those who had perished or disappeared were rehabilitated. New editions of their works were promised, an undertaking honoured only in part. The union's newly appointed first secretary, Alexander Surkov, who had an unenviable reputation as a bully, and other official spokesmen distanced themselves from the *Zhdanovshchina* of the late Stalin era but made it clear that tolerance of discordant views would be confined within narrow limits. They expressly condemned 'naturalism', i.e. the truthful representation of reality. In responding to these strictures the delegates were sharply divided. Optimists hoped that a new creative golden age had dawned, while others sounded a more sceptical note. Afterwards many of the more liberal writers demonstrated their independence of spirit by remaining silent.

The latent tensions within the literary community burst forth in 1956, which contemporaries termed (with some exaggeration) 'the year of protest'. Shaken by the 'secret speech', the novelist Alexander Fadeev, who had headed the USW after the war, committed suicide, apparently in shame at the perfidious role he had played. The intelligentsia took heart. Although this second 'thaw' lasted for only a few months, it left its mark on Soviet fiction. The writers' ranks were swelled by returnees from the camps, to whose grim testimony few could remain indifferent. At a meeting of the all-Union theatrical society Ehrenburg revealed Vsevolod Meierhold's (1874–1940) final speech to the closed tribunal that had sentenced him to death, in which he repudiated evidence that he had given under duress. The belletrist Sergei Zalygin made a cautious reference to the Terror in the pages of *Novyi mir*, which also published a moving poem, 'That Year', by Berggol'ts honouring the survivors: 'that year when | from the bottom of the seas, | from the canals, | suddenly friends began to return. | Why hide it? Few returned | Seventeen years is seventeen after all . . .' She hinted that the welcome given to the victims informally mattered more than their defective official rehabilitation (Frankel 1981). In the same spirit Margarita Aliger, in 'The Real Truth', voiced her anguish at having 'raised my hand and voted for calumny' instead of speaking out to defend an accused friend who had subsequently been sentenced to an identically long term of imprisonment. But, in general, references to the Terror or the Gulag were rare. It was safer to criticize bureaucracy, past and present—a target that up to a point had official sanction, especially if the offenders were incompetent rural bosses.

This gave an impetus to practitioners of the 'rural prose' school in Soviet fiction, which later would take off in a more nationalistic direction (see below, p. 294). Its roots lay in the late Stalin era, with Valentin Ovechkin's *Sketches of Rural Daily Life* (1952), which contrasted the complacency of one Party official with the intelligent attitude of another. This was villain versus hero, in conventional style, to be sure, but the picture drawn of conditions in the countryside was more truthful than had been usual hitherto. In 1954 Fedor Abramov roundly condemned earlier Soviet fiction on peasant themes and hinted that all was not well with current Party policy either. This fitted in with Khrushchev's reformist line, but in some points went beyond it. Brought up in Archangel province, Abramov understood well the mental world of the country-dwellers whose ways he portrayed. So too did Yefim Dorosh, whose *Village Diary*, written in leisurely style over a sixteen-year span from 1954, describes life in 'Raigorod',[1] in which a collective-farm chairman, Ivan Fedoseevich, battles with local officials who seek to make him the scapegoat for their own errors. Dorosh evinced a deep sympathy for peasant women and deplored the loss of village traditions, particularly the disappearance of the churches that had once given cohesion to the rural community. He saw clearly, long before this became a commonplace, that cultural progress in the countryside depended on restoring the sundered link between the tiller and the soil.

Less elegiac was the mood of Vladimir Dudintsev's *Not by Bread*

Alone (1956). This was a *succès de scandale*. Published in *Novyi mir*, the novel dealt with the inventor Lopatkin's struggle to patent a useful discovery in the teeth of obstruction by a petty bureaucrat, Drozdov, an arrogant careerist whose wife leaves him for the hero—but not before he has been despatched to a camp on a trumped-up charge. 'A peculiar mixture of conventional socialist realism and relatively penetrating criticism' (Shatz 1980), it was in form a typical production novel, with neatly paired chief characters, but the critical note was sustained and bitter. Moreover, the ending was deliberately ambiguous, since the anti-hero Drozdov goes unpunished and prepares to counter-attack: 'the real battle had only just begun'. As Konstantin Paustovsky boldly pointed out at a USW meeting called to discuss the book, 'the Drozdovs' were a sociological phenomenon, a stratum of privileged philistines embedded in Soviet society whose function was to suppress all creativity. Dudintsev had implied that the problem lay in the *system*, not just in its executants, and that Stalinism was still very much alive. This was seen as an unpardonable offence. For some years he published little, surviving on the generosity of friends, but the term 'Drozdov' entered the language.

Two short stories of 1956 dealt more profoundly with the problem of bureaucracy. In 'Potholes' Vladimir Tendriakov contrasted the conduct of a routine-minded rural official, who refuses to take steps that could have saved the life of a man injured in an accident, with that of a humane, simple peasant woman. The moral of the tale was underlined by a reviewer in *Novyi mir* who suggested that socialism actually enhanced the threat posed by bureaucracy to individual rights. The title of Alexander Yashin's 'Levers' referred to the Stalinist metaphor of Soviet citizens as cogs in a machine that is set in motion when Party members, the levers, turn on the current. Five rural Communists, jammed together in a smoke-filled office, are discussing their problems: lack of sugar and soap, constant amendments to the farm's plan. 'They don't trust us, that's the truth,' laments one. But what is Truth? 'Is that how it is: truth is needed only at meetings and on holidays, like criticism and self-criticism, and doesn't apply to specifics?' suggests another. A third relates that he has been told by the local boss: 'your job is to persuade the others and push through the Party line. After all, you're our levers in the village.' The conversation lingers on until the lamp goes out. 'Oh, damn it, it's going out for want of air. A lamp needs air too.' So long as they are in this informal setting, the men discuss matters frankly, but once a meeting is called they undergo a magic transformation: 'as though an invisible hand had raised an invisible lever, these intelligent people become soulless cogs in the machine and accept word for word everything they had criticized mercilessly a moment earlier. In short, Truth was powerless before the official lie' (Heller 1975).

Even more worrying for the authorities was the emergence of a school of writers who reflected the concerns of youth. Among poets Yevtushenko was the best-known figure. His verse echoed current popular fashions, many of them imports from the supposedly 'decadent' West, and often referred to foreign places his listeners would have loved to visit. Uninhibitedly extrovert, he would give poetry recitals that attracted thousands and were dramatic events in themselves. To his admirers he was a spokesman for their generation. Many others thought him naïve, or too self-centred and condescending. He took care to offset his more daring utterances with politically safe verses, and when pressed by authority would compromise and even recant.

Before long Yevtushenko shared his fame with Andrei Voznesensky, a 'poet of sound' (D. Brown 1978) whose enigmatic verse 'combined the normal with the grotesque', and popular balladeers like Bulat Okudzhava. The latter's lyrics, sung to guitar accompaniment, were emotional and often ironic. They parodied bureaucratic jargon and put into words what ordinary people instinctively felt. By blowing away the atmosphere of pious respect for authority these genuine artefacts of popular culture were perhaps even more important than literary works with higher aesthetic pretensions that appealed largely to members of the élite (Stites 1992). In metropolitan centres an informal youth sub-culture developed. Girls sported short skirts and wore bright lipstick, while boys donned broadshouldered 'zoot suits' and went around in gangs. This perturbed staid Komsomol officials, who called them *stiliagi*, or (foreign) 'style-chasers', but found it hard to bring them into line.

It was easier to harass the literary intelligentsia. The almanac *Literary Moscow*, edited by Paustovsky, was suppressed after two issues. The first volume caused a sensation by printing, along with work by new writers, some verse by Anna Akhmatova, who had been silenced under Stalin, and an essay by Boris Pasternak. The second, which contained Yashin's story alluded to above, was still more adventurous. As seen by the USW leadership, a coterie of intellectuals was trying to challenge its monopoly at a time when the system was being called in question by the Hungarian revolution. If left unchecked, Moscow's example might be emulated in other cities. At a plenary meeting of the union's board in May 1957 the editors were lambasted but they refused to recant. Khrushchev summoned a bevy of writers in secret to a government villa outside Moscow and lectured them on 'the close connection between literature, art, and the life of the people'—the title given to his address when it was published some months later. His intervention strengthened the position of conservatives within the USW, which in 1958 acquired a separate 'bureau' for the RSFSR, designed to tighten control in that republic.

But a few months later a scandal erupted that totally discredited the entire politico-literary establishment. Pasternak, ostracized during the Stalin era, had survived by publishing occasional verse and translations while working quietly on a major novel. *Dr Zhivago* was completed in 1955 and copies of the manuscript submitted to two journals. Receiving no reply, the author handed a copy to a representative of an Italian publisher. In doing so he lit a fuse that produced an explosion two years later, in October 1958 (Hingley 1983). He won the coveted Nobel Prize for Literature—although his work had been published abroad without official permission.

Yurii Zhivago is part Pasternak himself: a poet (and doctor) who, like so many Russian intellectuals, initially sympathizes with the revolution but soon realizes that it threatens his most cherished ideals: beauty, love, even Life itself (to which the hero's name refers), the individual's right to devote himself to art as a means of overcoming death. As a character Yurii is weak and indecisive; but on a symbolic plane he is a martyr whose experience replicates Christ's Passion. The work closes with several religious poems, ostensibly by Zhivago, in one of which Christ Himself speaks from the garden of Gethsemane: 'The centuries will float toward me out of the darkness | And I shall judge them.' Pasternak professed a mystical, aestheticized form of Christianity which saw the divine spirit as present in nature and the flow of life itself. As Yurii puts it in an oft-cited passage: 'Reshaping life? People who can say that have never understood a thing about life . . . They look on it as a lump of raw material which needs to be processed . . . But life is never a material . . . [it] is the principle of self-renewal, it is constantly . . . changing and transfiguring itself, it is infinitely beyond your or my theories about it.'

What offended the conventionally minded was Pasternak's aloofness from mundane political concerns. He was indifferent to the protest literature of his contemporaries. The novel focuses on its characters' personal experiences, on the romance of Yurii and Lara, caught up in the destructive fury of civil war. Revolutionary ideologues, with their platitudinous language, are dismissed as an irrelevance, even as 'a comical remnant of the past'. They had destroyed the established order but left 'the bare, shivering human soul, stripped to the last shred', for whom salvation could come only through the New Testament. If *Dr Zhivago* was an attack on anything, it was on modern secular civilization, not just on things Soviet. However, even in the West many critics failed to see this. In the USSR Pasternak was condemned for his irreverent treatment of 'glorious October' and its sequel.

No sooner had he signalled his acceptance of the Nobel Prize—awarded for his total *œuvre*, not specifically for *Dr Zhivago*—than a hate campaign was launched against him. The USW presidium obediently resolved to expel the writer from the union's ranks. No one leaped to his defence, although to their credit some members of the Moscow writers' organization did at least stay away when the vote was taken. As he did not want to risk being sent into foreign exile, Pasternak renounced the prize and in the columns of *Pravda* acknowledged that he had been wrong to accept it. He was 69 and seriously ill. The affair accelerated his death, which came in May 1960. For years thereafter his simple grave at Peredelkino, a writers' colony outside Moscow, would attract countless pilgrims. He was widely seen as a *muchenik*, a sufferer for the truth. Even his persecutors had second thoughts. In his memoirs Khrushchev admits that he had not read *Dr Zhivago* before ordering Pasternak's humiliation, and expresses 'sincere regret' for what he had done. This did not, however, imply any sympathy for the ethical values that informed the writer's masterpiece, which placed the enforced dialogue between creative intellectuals and the regime on a far more elevated plane than hitherto.

Soon another bright star appeared in the firmament of Russian letters: Alexander Solzhenitsyn. His experience of Stalinism had been harsher than Pasternak's. In 1945, as a Red Army officer, he had been arrested and sentenced to eight years behind bars for criticizing the leader in private correspondence, which the censors had intercepted. He would later describe memorably, in *The First Circle*, his years as a 'special assignment prisoner' in an institute for scientific research (*sharashka*). Other impressions would serve as the basis of his monumental *The Gulag Archipelago* (1973–5). In 1953 came exile 'in perpetuity' to Kazakhstan. While there he contracted cancer, but miraculously survived to tell this story, too, in *Cancer Ward*. (None of these books, on which his literary reputation largely rests, appeared in the USSR until the late 1980s.) Three years thereafter he was among the millions released from the Gulag, and in 1957 secured a job teaching physics at a school in Riazan'. This gave him enough leisure to write. In six weeks of 1959 he penned the short story that would bring him to the world's attention. 'One Day in the Life of Ivan Denisovich', as he came to call it, was on the surface a deceptively simple narrative. Shukhov, a peasant convict, leaps from his bunk when reveille sounds, swabs out the guardhouse, attends roll-call, goes through the body-search ritual, marches off to the work site, and starts to lay bricks. The men in his brigade are so carried away by their task that they disregard the order to stop and are almost punished for their zeal. After marching back to camp, Shukhov does a favour for an intellectual fellow inmate, who lets him have his own supper. The pleasure that a half-starved man derives from food is described in precise detail. Shukhov buys some tobacco, chats with his comrades (among them a stout-hearted Baptist), and falls asleep content. 'The day was over, a day without a cloud, almost a happy day.'

In this story, as later in *The First Circle*, Solzhenitsyn makes 'a universal statement about the human condition' that invites comparison with Tolstoi or Dostoevsky. He gives the reader 'a sense that the whole of Soviet society, including the inmates of the camps, was bound together in an indissoluble symbiosis . . . that those in the labour camps were freer than those allegedly and formally "at liberty". Paradoxically, the land of Gulag was the only place where a Soviet citizen had nothing further to fear' (Scammell 1984). He spoke for all the silent millions. Many survivors wrote to him to express their gratitude once the story was published.

Its appearance (in *Novyi mir* in November 1962) was a lucky fluke. It owed much to the determination of Tvardovsky and certain members of his staff, as well as to the political predicament in which Khrushchev currently found himself. Told that it was a masterpiece by a hitherto unknown writer, he asked his personal assistant, Lebedev, to read out extracts. These evidently left him under the impression that the story celebrated 'honest toil' by prisoners who remained loyal to the system, and concluded that it would be useful ammunition against high-placed Stalinists. With the concurrence of Mikoian he had copies prepared for all Central Committee members, and in his address to the gathering mentioned it favourably (22 November). Within weeks his mood had changed, but by then hundreds of thousands of copies had gone on sale. Solzhenitsyn was 'catapulted to fame virtually overnight'.

The Gulag theme was picked up by dozens of other writers, some of them former inmates, but relatively few of these works saw the light of day.[2] If they did, the text was mutilated by the censors. The incident that swung the pendulum back to 'freeze' was the Soviet leader's visit to an art exhibition at Moscow's Manège gallery on 1 December. On seeing works by some modernist and abstract painters, he exploded with indignation. Solzhenitsyn was able to publish only three more stories in *Novyi mir* before being silenced. Among others forcefully criticized were Yevtushenko, both for his poem 'Babyi iar' (which broke the taboo on mentioning the Holocaust) and for publishing his autobiography abroad without permission, and Vasilii Aksionov, author of the popular *Ticket to the Stars* (1961), which seemed to exalt rebellious youth. *Novyi mir* came under attack for printing Ehrenburg's memoirs, *People, Years, Life*, which, although superficial, offered a wistful picture of literary life in Russia and abroad before the Stalin era. Recently published documents reveal that at a meeting of the Party's Ideological Commission, held shortly after the Manège affair, several artists stood up for creative freedom. 'Since the Twentieth congress', said one, 'we are no longer afraid' (Nikiforov 1993).

By mid-1963 the atmosphere had cleared again, but in the interim Khrushchev gave the country's intellectuals a nasty shock. Summoning some six hundred of them to the Kremlin for the second such meeting in four months, he virulently attacked Andrei Voznesensky. Many years later the poet recalled: 'He yelled: "Get out of the country, comrade Shelepin [the KGB chief] will make out your passport." I thought it was the end . . . I said I would read out some of my verse . . . When I came to the lines "An ashen chill has gripped my motherland! My tortured Muse, what would you have sung in the camps?", the hall was silent, rejoicing at my misfortune. "Agent of imperialism!", the premier cried out. Well, I thought, they'll surely come for me now . . . In a fog I listened to his address, in which he praised Stalin . . . An empty space formed around me and friends averted their gaze.' A year later Khrushchev apologized, but the incident exemplifies the Soviet cultural climate under his rule—which a few years later writers would look back on as an age of relative freedom.

Scholarship

The humanities

In their championing of human values creative intellectuals enjoyed at least passive support from a growing number of professional people—scholars and scientists, teachers, doctors, engineers, and so on—who might be termed ideological agnostics. Their attitude to the regime was ambivalent. On one hand they were irritated by niggling controls, but on the other hand they appreciated the material support they received in furthering their professional objectives. In this group there were as yet few individual 'heroes' ready to articulate critical opinions, but the latent disaffection of a broad segment of the élite was important. It engendered scepticism about the Supreme Purpose that was the ruling Party's *raison d'être*, and so gradually eroded the foundations on which its power rested. Educated people often started out by privately questioning some detail of Party teaching or policy that adversely affected them and then, finding their complaints disregarded by authority, moved towards a more general rejection of the *status quo*. It was but a step from seeking greater professional autonomy to harbouring dissident opinions. But people might also be pulled in the reverse direction, for example by opportunities to travel abroad, or even to influence the policy-making process as members of unpublicized academic think-tanks, which came into fashion at this time.

This temptation was strongest among the 18,000 research workers employed by the Academy of Sciences, with its two hundred or so institutes, which controlled research throughout the country in virtually every sphere of knowledge. In 1958 it had 167 full and 361 corresponding members, heavily concentrated in technology and the natural sciences. The full members had the right to choose the Academy's governing body (and to admit new members). The electoral process was of course subject to political controls, particularly where the humanities were concerned; nevertheless a small margin of freedom remained which some members at least valued and were eager to expand.

One by-product of this extreme centralization was the lack of horizontal contact between people in various subject areas, each of which had its own bureaucratic niche. Interdisciplinary councils were set up to counteract this tendency, but to little effect, for the Party's agents in each institute, university faculty, and so on, whose scholarly credentials often left much to be desired, found their task of surveillance easier if their charges' movements were restricted. Attendance at scholarly conferences, for example, was closely regulated, especially if they involved contact with foreigners. By Western standards such gatherings were formal, ritualistic affairs. Some disciplines, banned under Stalin, were now taking only the first steps toward recovery. Economics and law were kept under particularly close watch—which did not prevent individual scholars of reformist bent from doing useful work, as we have seen.

It was much harder for philosophers and historians to escape ideological constraints. Dialectical and historical materialism were foundation stones of Marxism-Leninism, at least in the form this doctrine was given by Stalin and his successors. Accordingly historians had a political function to perform: to help legitimize the Party's power monopoly by showing, in their detailed research, that it was fulfilling its founders' behests and acting in conformity with the supposed 'laws' or 'regularities' (*zakonomernosti*) of the historical process. In doing so one had to demonstrate 'Party-mindedness' (*partiinost'*), which by a dialectical sleight of hand was deemed to be not partisan bias but 'true' objectivity, the polar opposite of 'bourgeois objectivism', with its respect for the facts (decried as 'factology'). Historians were expected to be militant fighters for Communism. Moreover, since the building of a Communist society in the USSR was officially regarded as the culmination of mankind's struggle for progress throughout the ages, historians of other societies and earlier eras were required to evaluate the contribution made by 'progressive' individuals, groups, popular movements, social classes—and even nations, for, as we have seen, Stalin had given the doctrine a Russian nationalist twist. This bias was only slightly moderated. In consequence a historian writing on, say, seventeenth-century Russo-Polish relations had to show that the Muscovite diplomats had had the better case. The growth of the Russian empire continued to be represented as a 'progressive' development for the subject peoples concerned. In general, the further back one went in time the safer the ground on which a Soviet historian stood. But Andrei Amalrik, later a prominent dissident, first got into trouble for writing a thesis on the Rus' lands in the early Middle Ages, in which he gave undue prominence to the role of foreigners in creating the country's first 'state'.

Although it was dangerous to transgress the canon in any respect, this did not prevent a number of historians, especially younger men, from extending its limits in a number of subtle ways. In doing so they took advantage of the situation created by the Twentieth Party congress, when the existing state of the discipline had been strongly criticized. Improved professional standards required wider access to archival sources, hitherto a closely guarded preserve of the security police, better publication facilities, and freer contact with Western colleagues. In all these areas there was progress. The state of scholarship in 1953 is exemplified by recently published correspondence (Chernev 1992), in which no less a figure than the president of the Academy of Sciences asked Khrushchev to decide the length of articles on the USSR and the RSFSR in the *Large Soviet Encyclopedia*. Shortly afterwards its editor submitted to Suslov a list of 'negative persons', whereupon it was solemnly resolved at highest level to include Lord Curzon and (Sir) Stafford Cripps but to exclude Duff Cooper and Cardinal Spellman. (This was the moment when subscribers were told to cut out a page containing an entry on the deposed Beria and replace it by one featuring the Bering Strait!) Later such matters were handled more discreetly, though with no greater respect for historical truth.

In 1955 the country's leading historical journal, *Voprosy istorii* ('Problems of History'), came under fire behind the scenes for articles on Plekhanov, the founder of Russian Marxism, and the 1917 revolution which to left-conservative stalwarts seemed to jeopardize Lenin's iconic status and the Party's infallibility. The chief editor, A. M. Pankratova, certainly no liberal, offered a spirited defence. She and her colleagues were vindicated by the subsequent revelations at the Twentieth congress. These shook the profession to its roots. The dispute became public. One of the journal's editors, Burdzhalov, published an article showing that the Bolshevik leaders had been badly divided over tactics in the spring of 1917, while another historian took up the defence of the imam Shamil (1797–1871), leader of the Caucasian Muslim peoples' resistance to tsarist aggression. After a press campaign warning historians of the dangers of 'bourgeois ideological subversion', in March 1957 the Central Committee formally censured the journal and purged its editorial board.

Two years later an authoritative textbook on Party history appeared to replace Stalin's now discredited *Short Course*. Fifty million copies of the latter were quietly pulped. The new version was less strident than the old, with its paranoid denunciations of 'enemies of the people', but scarcely less mendacious. It contained no positive reference to Trotsky or Bukharin, neither of whom had been rehabilitated.[3] Stalin, too, underwent a partial eclipse, and only passing mention was made of the excesses of collectivization or the Terror. In effect the faithful were presented with a new mythology that left numerous 'blank spots'.

After the Twenty-second congress it seemed for a moment as though there would be a break with Stalinist tradition. At a nation-wide conference in December 1962 Ponomarev, the leading Party historian (these historians formed a separate professional category and had their own institutes, journals, etc.) inveighed against the consequences of the 'cult of the individual'; many of those present spoke out boldly. But when the political constellation changed so did the official line. Several historians began to work on such problems as collectivization (Moshkov, Zelenin) or Nazi-Soviet relations before 1941 (Nekrich), but they soon ran into trouble with the censors. Another development was the appearance of a number of valuable memoirs, notably by senior officers of the armed forces, who for a time enjoyed a liberty in this respect denied to civilians. Roi Medvedev started to write a critical biography of Stalin, but despite the improved intellectual climate this could not be published in the USSR. The upshot was that people did not believe the official version of their history yet were denied access to any alternative. Psychologically the result was disastrous: to truncate and falsify the nation's memory. As Nekrich put it later: 'the Party pursued the aim, never stated directly in public, of creating a new collective memory . . . an artificial memory, so to speak . . . If someone were suddenly to clap his hands and exclaim: "but for heaven's sake, it didn't happen like that!", he was regarded as extremely dangerous. Authority at once demanded that he renounce and recant his opinions. If he did not do so, it took revenge on him' (Nekrich 1979).

Science

The impact of totalitarian controls on the natural sciences was on the whole less catastrophic, except in the fields of biology and agronomics. The harm done here by Lysenko was to some extent offset by successes in nuclear physics, mathematics, metallurgy, and other areas with a defence application. The unevenness of Soviet scientific performance was insufficiently appreciated by Western public opinion at the time. On hearing the beeps from Sputnik I (4 October 1957), the first artificial earth satellite, many people leaped to the conclusion that the USSR had acquired a definitive lead over the West, not only in exploration of the cosmos but in science and technology generally. Actually the Sputnik programme was 'an enormous stroke of luck for Khrushchev' (Berry 1987), who exploited its propagandist impact masterfully. Succeeded within a month by Sputnik II, a larger craft carrying a dog (for experimental purposes), the launchings acted as a glorious backdrop to the celebrations of the fortieth anniversary of the 1917 revolution. Few paused to consider that there was no logical connection between scientific prowess of this kind and Lenin's dream of world-wide proletarian revolution, unless the world were to be 'revolutionized' by military force, in the shape of intercontinental missiles! There followed the Lunik series, which landed a red pennant on the Moon and took the first photographs of its dark side (1959), the launching of heavier vehicles designed to carry human beings, and then, on 12 April 1961, the flight of Yurii Gagarin, the first man in space. He returned to a symbolic welcome on Lenin's mausoleum. More than seven thousand medals were distributed, two of them to Khrushchev himself. This feat was soon superseded: the astronaut G. Titov spent more than twenty-four hours in space, and larger spacecraft permitted group flights, each lasting several days. Valentina Tereshkova became the first woman to leave and return to Earth.

As in the United States, the military connotations of these endeavours were deliberately played down and attention focused on the astronauts' (incontestable) bravery and the alleged 'spin-off' benefits. In fact the 'space race' was a concomitant of the Cold War and the drive for ever more powerful missiles. Participation in it made little sense for a developing country like the USSR. The only gainer was its powerful military-industrial complex, which continued to absorb a vast proportion of the nation's resources, not least of scientific manpower. Above all heavy arms expenditure kept down the living standards of the mass of citizens, for many of whom, however, the space-suited heroes symbolized the USSR's supposed international scientific pre-eminence and were a source of pride.

The development of Soviet rocket technology owed much to Korolev, who had been rescued from the depths of the Gulag by a fellow engineer, the aircraft designer Tupolev, and to the physicist Igor Kurchatov. The last-named became unofficial scientific adviser to Khrushchev. Despite his considerable influence he was unable to overcome the leader's naïve infatuation with Lysenko's theories, which, although totally fraudulent (and based on manipulation of the evidence), held out the illusion of achieving striking practical advances in agriculture on the cheap. The scientific community was deeply divided over Lysenko. As early as 1955 several hundred biologists signed a letter to the Central Committee protesting at his activities. He lost his position as president of the Timiriazev Agricultural Academy, but won the job back five years later after regaining political support. A further campaign against him got under way in 1962, when an inspection of his genetics institute, the first in twenty years, revealed his malpractices. Lysenko parried the blow by inviting Khrushchev to carry out his own inspection. The 'First' duly praised 'the achievements of Michurinist biology', ordered the inspection commission dissolved, and set up in its place another one headed by Lysenko's partisans. A temporary stalemate ensued. But knowledge of Western discoveries in the field of genetics (DNA) could not be ignored indefinitely, for 'by now our scientific community had grown up' (Zh. Medvedev 1969).

The last round in the struggle was epic. In 1964 Khrushchev ordered the creation of five new seats in the Academy of Sciences, to which Lysenko's followers were to be 'elected'. At the meeting two members protested, one of them the as yet little-known Sakharov. When the ballot was taken, twenty-two (or twenty-four) members voted for the leader's nominees, but 126 opposed them. Furious, Khrushchev ordered measures that would bring about dissolution of the prestigious body—'a crude political mistake', as Suslov would term it some months later, in his indictment of the fallen leader ('Materialy . . .' 1993). Khrushchev also tried to liquidate the Agricultural Academy because most of its staff did not share his (or Lysenko's) views: he complained on one occasion that the students could not tell hemp from nettles. But within a few months of Khrushchev's deposition the by now discredited biologist followed him into limbo.

Although the academicians showed courage on this occasion, they failed to give adequate support to Sakharov. When only thirty-two he had been admitted, by a rare unanimous vote, in recognition of his work on the Soviet hydrogen bomb, first tested in August 1953. Two years later the Stalin prize-winner experienced pangs of conscience at the accidental death of over ninety people during atmospheric testing of a new nuclear device. He soon came to realize that such weapon tests had incalculable harmful genetic effects, and in 1957 expressed his concerns in print. Each roentgen of radioactivity emitted reduced by one week the life expectancy of those exposed to fall-out, he wrote, and each device currently being tested could cost half a million lives. To his credit Khrushchev personally authorized publication of Sakharov's article, but probably from tactical calculation rather than for humanitarian reasons. The physicist continued his work and received further honours. His status was such that in 1962 he succeeded in persuading the leader to negotiate the partial (atmospheric) test-ban treaty signed the following July, which represented a breakthrough in arms control. This signal achievement went unremarked by the USSR's scientific community. Had it been generally known, one may doubt whether it would have been appreciated, for the vast majority of Soviet scientists were wedded to the politico-military establishment, from which they derived their lofty status and handsome privileges. (Many of them lived in 'closed cities' designated by numbers, the very existence of which was unknown to the general public.) It was one thing for scientists to protest arbitrary political interference in professional matters, but another to challenge the Party line, whether on military policy or—Sakharov's main concern later—human rights.

Educational reform

Passive resistance to Party policy by members of the social élite was more evident at lower levels in the country's educational system. Many parents, teachers, and pupils took what one specialist calls a 'personally instrumental' view of schooling, regarding it as a means of acquiring social status and culture, while looking down on vocational training as something inferior (Lane 1985). Such an attitude was antithetical to that of Party ideologues, especially Khrushchev himself, who had once been a part-time student in a so-called *rabfak* or 'workers' faculty'. He was a partisan of polytechnical education. This had been in vogue in his youth and once again made headway in the 1950s. As he saw it, the school system was excessively academic and 'divorced from life'. It served to prepare pupils for admission to higher educational institutions (in Soviet parlance, *VUZy*), while neglecting the need for technicians who could keep the factories running. There was also a practical side to the issue. Universities and technical colleges could not provide enough places for the rapidly growing number of qualified school-leavers. In 1954 there were 1,114,000 applicants for only 276,000 places, and over the four years to 1956 a total of 2.2 million would-be entrants failed to secure admission. The leadership concluded that the goal, adopted at the Nineteenth Party congress in 1952, of extending the duration of secondary schooling from seven to ten years by 1960 was too ambitious. Between 1956 and 1958 some six hundred schools introduced polytechnical studies into the curriculum on an experimental basis, while others added an extra year in which pupils worked for two to three days a week in a nearby industrial plant or farm. This was in addition to the normal practice whereby schools despatched 'brigades' of children to help bring in the harvest.

On 18 April 1958, addressing a congress of the Komsomol, Khrushchev called for a 'fundamental reorganization' of the school system. All pupils should be trained to perform 'useful labour', irrespective of their parents' social position, and after spending *eight* years in school should be required to gain practical experience in production before entering a VUZ. While working, they were to be encouraged to enrol in night school or correspondence courses (a prominent feature of the Soviet educational system). Alternatively, youngsters might spend three to four years in a vocational school or study part-time in a 'school of working youth' attached to a factory.[4] This would end the situation, 'intolerable' under socialism, in which well-to-do parents frightened their offspring with the prospect of having to do manual labour, and 60 to 70 per cent of those enrolling in universities were children of intellectuals.

It took five months before these radical ideas were endorsed by the Central Committee—evidently with some reluctance, for the scheme was modified in such a way that, although obligatory secondary instruction would last eight years, the total duration of schooling might be ten or eleven years, and not more than one-third of the last three years would be spent on practical tasks. Khrushchev claimed that the overall amount of tuition would not be reduced and, to gild the pill, promised that the several thousand élite schools for children specially gifted in the arts or mathematics would continue to exist. Moreover, the reform was to be introduced *gradually*, over a five-year term. Another three months passed before legislation was issued. It laid down that four-fifths of VUZ entrants, and ultimately all of them, were to be drawn from those who had completed labour assignments (or military service).

It was easier to draft such regulations than to enforce them. Enterprise managers objected that having to train unmotivated youngsters interfered with plan fulfilment; all the hours spent toiling at the work-bench added little to production and did not noticeably improve the trainees' competence. The RSFSR Education minister eventually pronounced the scheme 'a useless waste of time', while scientists complained that incoming students had lower levels of achievement than before. Few students, on completing higher education, returned to the mundane jobs for which they had been initially trained. In opting for a softer life they were abetted by their parents, who were naturally eager for their offspring to get ahead. Members of the *nomenklatura* had a myriad informal ways of avoiding compliance with the regulations, and exemptions were continually being granted in favour of one group of students or another. By the autumn of 1964 only 62 per cent of regular VUZ entrants had the required practical background.

When Khrushchev fell a commission was promptly set up to re-examine school curricula. The upshot was a decision that not more than two hours a week should be spent on labour tasks. In effect the whole idea of polytechnical education was side-lined, and in 1966 the old goal of ten years of schooling for all was reinstated (with 1970 as the new target date). These moves brought increased regimentation. Hitherto republic-level Education ministries had enjoyed a certain leeway in applying Party policy. Now an all-Union ministry was set up to ensure tighter control.

Although the bureaucracy was the ultimate winner, the

intelligentsia (in the Soviet sense of the term) had shown that there were limits beyond which it was no longer willing to be pushed. This was a lesson Khrushchev's successors would have to live with. To be sure, this victory was one for vested interests, and one has to see it in context. By and large educated people were satisfied with the school system, which served as a potent instrument of socio-political integration. It was expanding fast, at all levels. Between 1956/7 and 1970/1 the number of pupils in general schools rose by 61 per cent and in specialized schools by 107 per cent, of students in higher education by 81 per cent. Teachers, backed by the youth organizations, instilled strict discipline in the classroom. Regimentation and indoctrination were seen by many parents and pupils as the price that had to be paid for academic excellence and the hope of a well-paid job. In the short term this instrumental view of education was compatible with official values, but in the long run it would help to undermine them.

7 The National Mosaic

Nationality policies under Khrushchev

Nowhere were hopes of change after Stalin's death more bitterly disappointed than among the country's non-Russian peoples. In nationality policy, too, this was a preparatory period, during which decisions were taken (or not taken) that would lead to the USSR's collapse a generation or so later. At the time the gravity of this problem was not readily apparent. There was little open dissent, at least among the other fourteen nations who shared union-republic status with the Russians—and it is with them that for reasons of space we shall be mainly concerned. Opposition mainly took the form of cultural protest and was expressed with exemplary restraint. Many minority intellectuals were willing to give the regime the benefit of the doubt. Heartened by the development of national Communism elsewhere within the Soviet bloc, they shared the aspirations of Dubček and fellow within-system reformers for 'socialism with a human face'. The crushing of the Prague spring and the swing back to more hard-line policies in the USSR made this moderate position seem unrealistic.

In discussing the nationalities problem we must take the twenty-year span that followed Stalin's death, for Khrushchev's removal had no immediate impact on policy in this field and in order to draw conclusions about long-term social trends one needs to compare data from the 1959 and 1970 censuses. These data testify to the emergence (or re-emergence) of a sense of national identity among many of these ethnic groups. Most Western observers see this development as a response to 'modernization', but this term, developed by political scientists in search of an explanatory model, needs careful handling in a historical context.[1] It was also an unintended consequence of what might be termed the Soviet regime's 'pseudo-liberalism' in nationality affairs. Since Lenin's day it had carved up its territory for administrative purposes on ethnic lines, granted minorities representation in Party and state bodies at all levels, and encouraged the development of minority languages and literatures. Yet the Leninist 'dialectic' ensured that all the 'rights' so granted were conditional and purely formal. Their implementation depended on current Party policy, which was often unclear and could not be challenged, in the courts or elsewhere, by citizens who felt that their rights were being denied in practice. Thus union republics (and also national regions, districts, etc.) had scarcely more autonomy than any Russian province (*oblast'*); use of national languages in schools, publications, etc. was restricted in favour of Russian, as the lingua franca of the empire; all-Union symbols took precedence over national ones; and minorities were hindered from expressing their own cultural values in literature, scholarship, or religious observance wherever Party *apparatchiki* deemed that by doing so they were displaying unhealthy 'bourgeois nationalist' tendencies.

This devious policy bred the very phenomenon so dreaded by zealous advocates of 'proletarian internationalism'—a concept which in practice meant no more than uncritical endorsement of Moscow's line on all questions. People in minority groups were bound to resent the gulf between promise and reality. Yet this did not automatically make them active opponents of the regime. Their attitude was likely to be ambivalent, especially as the price paid for dissent was so high. Moreover, bureaucratic controls were not as absolute as outsiders often assumed. In practice, as we have noted in the context of literature, there was a good deal of 'slack' or flux within the system which allowed informal bargaining with local bosses, for it was they who interpreted central policy. Accordingly the situation varied greatly from one area to another. Indeed, in regard to the cultural questions that 'marked' or defined national identity—and this is what patriots were mainly concerned with at this time—the situation was anomalous. As one Western scholar (of Estonian extraction) writes, although the authorities pursued the goal of total homogeneity, 'the Soviet Union is in many ways one of the most culturally pluralistic societies in the world, in its institutional structure and momentum' (Parming 1977).

Many other observers took a harsher view. They saw the CPSU as having embarked on a deliberate policy of 'russification' of the minority cultures, which were said to face assimilation and extinction. But one has to distinguish between russification and sovietization. Russians, too, were victimized by the regime's repressive policies. One may agree that the USSR was an empire and that its leaders pursued an imperialistic policy. But theirs was a 'neo-imperialism' of an unconventional type. It was designed to bring about a utopian supranational order based on Marxist-Leninist ideology, not just to ensure Russian hegemony over 'lesser breeds'. What was objectionable about it was not its 'Russian-ness' but its totalitarian features: fanaticism, manipulation of the law, censorship, secret-police surveillance, and so forth. It was to combat such evils that there took shape in the late 1960s a Union-wide human rights movement which brought together representatives of many minorities who renounced the narrow nationalism of an earlier age and pursued broader objectives in co-operation with like-minded Russians and other fellow citizens.

One has to add some qualifications here. Although Russians enjoyed no privileges by virtue of their nationality, they were often favoured in appointments or in other informal ways because they were seen as politically more reliable. Moreover, some members of the 'hegemonic' or 'imperial' nation harboured chauvinistic sentiments. If they occupied official positions (especially in the armed forces), they might on occasion think and act like old-fashioned imperialists, while to many of those over whom they ruled what mattered most was precisely their masters' 'Russian-ness'. These reciprocal misperceptions mattered. They may indeed have been even more significant than the reality. One should add that some minority peoples, like the Armenians and Azerbaijanis, identified 'the enemy' with members of a neighbouring ethnic group rather than with Russians.

These simmering tensions went largely unremarked by the Soviet leadership, which exhibited a remarkable degree of complacency. Stalin's successors convinced themselves that the nationality problem had been solved. It followed that any trouble must be the work of foreign agents and best dealt with by police measures. Even the academic study of ethnic relations was neglected until the 1970 census results suggested that all was not well in this domain. Khrushchev was a native of the Russo-Ukrainian borderland (Kursk province), and seems to have assumed that the relatively conflict-free situation here was typical of the whole country. In 1954 he made a bid for Ukrainian national support by transferring the Crimea from the RSFSR to the Ukrainian SSR and staging elaborate celebrations of the tercentenary of the two peoples' 'unification' (historically, a misleading term). This move would cause unexpected problems forty years later.

As has since become clear (*Ist.* 3/1994), he also shared the anti-Semitic prejudices current among members of the ruling élite—and considerable segments of the Slavic population as well. Jews continued to be discriminated against during the post-Stalin era in regard to employment opportunities, access to higher education and so on. This eventually led to a strong current of opinion in favour of emigration, to which the authorities responded with further repressive measures. However, this aspect of the nationality question will not be examined closely here: suffice it to note that Jews, along with Germans and Crimean Tatars—none of whom enjoyed union-republic status—played a signal role in crystallizing dissent among the Soviet Union's national minorities.

Khrushchev was actually more of a centralist than Beria, whose fall from power in June 1953 owed much to a 'gamble on the national-minority cadres' (Fairbanks 1978) that went too far for his Politburo rivals (see Chapter 2). Khrushchev stood for the principle of 'internationalization of cadres', which in practice meant that outside the RSFSR the second Party secretary was usually a Russian with more power than his nominal superior, a native. This informal rule served to give citizens the impression that they were governed by fellow-nationals. From 1954 to 1976 over 86 per cent of republic first secretaries were non-Russians (Gitelman 1990). Some other important posts, such as the head of the KGB organization in each republic, were also tacitly reserved for Russians, or at any rate Slavs, and few officers of national-minority background reached general's rank.

Minorities were more than adequately represented in senior legislative bodies. The Supreme Soviet's Council of Nationalities, or 'upper house', had twenty-five deputies from each union republic, eleven from each autonomous republic and five from each autonomous region; but as we know these men had precious little power. Far more important was minority representation in senior Party bodies. In the CC the proportion of Russians declined from 71.5 per cent in 1952 to 55.0 per cent in 1966; particularly marked was the increase of Ukrainians (from 6.8 to 15.8 per cent, reaching nearly 18 per cent in 1961). This was partly because many of Khrushchev's clients (notably Podgorny and Kirichenko) were of Ukrainian extraction and had their own patronage systems.

This did not in itself signal any greater laxity toward 'bourgeois nationalism' in Ukraine or elsewhere.

At the Twenty-second Party congress there were apparently more non-Russian delegates than there had been at its immediate predecessors, a development that reflected changes taking place in the CPSU's ethnic composition. Between July 1961 and January 1965 the Russian proportion of its total membership declined by 1.15 per cent, but increased representation of Ukrainians and Belarusians meant that the combined Slav element remained stable at 81 per cent. In 1965 for every thousand Russians 58 were Party members; for Ukrainians and Belarusians the figure was 44. Among Balts, as one would expect, it was far lower (Estonians 31, Latvians 29, Lithuanians 24 per thousand), while for Central Asians it ranged from 29 (Uzbeks, Turkmens, Tajiks) to 45 per thousand for Kazakhs. All these groups had increased their representation since 1961, as had the Georgians (65 per thousand), the champions in this respect (Rigby 1968).[2] In other words a growing proportion of the native élite was being co-opted into the ruling Party. This can be taken to indicate a greater measure of support for its policies, although of course careerist motives were also present. Despite this shift the non-Slav share of total membership was smaller than it had been in 1927, although in the interim the demographic balance had tilted in favour of these peoples.

In the Baltic states many Party cadres were russified natives who had lived for years in the RSFSR. The local organizations also contained many Russian immigrants. In Lithuania, for example, Party membership more than doubled between 1954 and 1965 (from 34,500 to 86,400), but only some of the newcomers were ethnic Lithuanians. These comprised 38 per cent of the total in 1954 but 61.5 per cent in 1965 (Misiunas and Taagepera 1983). Likewise in Ukraine the native share of membership grew from 60.3 to 65.1 per cent over the decade 1958–68, but was still less than the Ukrainian share of that republic's population (1970: 74.9 per cent). Russian residents here were over-represented—especially, it seems, at upper levels of the apparatus.

Moscow was worried at 'national-Communist' tendencies throughout the western borderlands. In 1959 a major purge in Latvia cost over two thousand officials their jobs. The deputy chairman of the Council of Ministers, Berklāvs, was accused of favouring the development of industries that used local labour and materials, and putting the republic's economic interests ahead of those of the Union as a whole. Thereafter extensive personnel changes were also carried out in Moldova, Armenia, Azerbaijan, and three Central Asian republics. In the latter instances the reasons given were nepotism and corruption, but these offences often masked political dissidence.

Around 1958 there was an undeclared shift to the right in Party nationality policy. At the Twentieth congress Khrushchev had laid weight on the 'efflorescence' of nations in the present rather than their subsequent 'approximation' or ultimate 'merger' under full Communism. But at the Twenty-second congress the emphasis was on the later stages in this supposedly ineluctable process. Nothing was said about the dangers of Great Russian chauvinism; instead there was talk of 'an international culture common to all Soviet nations' and of boundaries 'losing their former significance'. The development of national languages should not accentuate ethnic differences but encourage a closer relationship based on Russian, which 'has become in fact the second native language for the peoples of the Soviet Union'. Somewhat paradoxically the role of Russian was thrust into the foreground by a 'democratic' provision of the 1958 education reform, which made tuition of native languages in general (Russian-language) schools optional. The problem here was that in Soviet conditions the choice would be made, not freely by parents, but by local bosses. There was a good deal of opposition to the change, especially in Latvia and Ukraine—even Supreme Soviet deputies from several republics joined in—but in the end it became law.

Economic aspects

Another straw in the wind was the gradual shift back to centralized administration of industry (see Chapter 4), which took away powers recently granted to republic-level officials, who had, however, seldom been able to use them in the best interests of the local population. In the Stalinist command economy all major decisions on investment and other inputs were taken according to all-Union needs as determined by Moscow. Strategic factors and technical efficiency were what counted when deciding where new industrial plants should be located, what they should produce, or how fast they should expand. The aim of equalizing living standards between different national groups, which had been taken seriously in the 1920s, held a very low priority rating. Nor did the economic regions (whose boundaries did not necessarily match those of the republics) have any effective institutional mechanism for communicating horizontally. Their officials' job was to implement directives from above in the interests of the economy as a whole. They could lobby behind the scenes for additional inputs but had 'no independent control over resource flows or uses' (Ericson 1992). As we have seen, the administrative deconcentration that took place under Khrushchev did not prevent the Party from launching massive campaigns whose implementation was binding on officials throughout the country. After 1958 the Chinese threat caused a shift of resources to eastern Siberia and the Far East, but the main focus of attention remained on what geographers term the 'economic core region'. This covered central European Russia, Ukraine, and the Baltic states, whose peoples accordingly 'benefited'—if that is the right term—from this development. Leaving aside the ecological impact (largely disregarded by contemporaries), it brought increased employment possibilities and the prospect of higher incomes, but also the likelihood of more immigration by Russians (or, in the Baltic case, Slavs generally), to the detriment of their republic's ethnic homogeneity. This was a major concern for nationally conscious minority leaders, who saw economic growth as a mixed blessing—although there were also some who complained that their republics were being neglected when appropriations for development were being made.

Were the national minorities 'exploited', as their more intransigent spokesmen claimed? This is not an easy question to answer, since so many imponderables are involved. In principle, one may agree, any decision taken elsewhere which affects a people's wellbeing is discriminatory. But national autarky is scarcely a realistic proposition in the modern world, with its multiple interdependent relationships. In any state there are bound to be disparities between regions, which central governments (especially federal ones) attempt to alleviate with varied success. One authority estimates that in the USSR *c.*1970 these regional inequalities were two-thirds as great as in the United States, half those of France or Japan, and less marked than in the United Kingdom (McAuley 1979). It is when they are set against the lofty aims of the regime's founders that they appear inordinate, but that may not be the right criterion to apply.

It is safe to conclude that those peoples did best that had good starting points in the race for modernity: more plentiful natural resources, better communications, a more urbanized population and a skilled labour force. But this does not take us very far and needs refinement in regard to specific occupations and subregions, for which data are lacking. We cannot estimate accurately the value of belonging to a rouble zone with an unusually stable currency, or that of defence expenditure by the centre on the constituent republics' behalf; nor can we know what prices goods exported from a non-Russian republic would have fetched if inter-republican trade had been conducted on free-market principles. It seems that Ukraine, given the scale of its resources, did less well out of the 'imperial' economy than the Baltic lands, for example. Soviet data on per capita national income by republic (*not* ethnic groups!) for 1960 and 1970 (Katz *et al.* 1975) show Ukraine standing at the all-Union average (76 per cent growth), whereas the RSFSR showed 81 per cent, Estonia 82 per cent, Latvia 84 per cent, and Lithuania 110 per cent growth; the Central Asian republics fared much worse (Tajikistan 52 per cent, Uzbekistan 44 per cent). But the reliability of these figures is not very great. The three Baltic states did best in terms of increased trade turnover, and were also high on the list as regards money kept in savings accounts.

Data on personal per capita income in 1960 and 1970 confirm the trend. Taking the USSR average as 100, Estonia was well ahead, rising over the decade from 129 to 133, and Lithuania from 108 to 118. The Central Asian republics remained stable or registered a drop (Kazakhstan 95 to 88, Uzbekistan 77 to 74, Tajikistan 66 to 63) (McAuley 1979). Collective farmers did better in the Baltic—but so too did farmers in Central Asia. This was due to intensive exploitation of household plots and the growth of a lively 'second economy'. In Central Asia in the 1960s over 15 per cent of the total population of working age was privately employed (Lubin 1984). As Muslims they preferred traditional occupations to work in the industrial plants set up, and usually run, by Slav immigrants. This would create serious problems later (see Chapter 15). Likewise the Baltic peoples were not inwardly reconciled to the Soviet regime by the fact that living standards were rising: they compared them adversely with what they had known before 1940. These two examples show that one cannot assume, as might seem plausible at first sight, any necessary correspondence between improved material wellbeing and conformist political attitudes.

Cultural aspects

In the shaping of national consciousness socio-economic realities mattered less than subjective perceptions. These were the product of a myriad uncontrollable influences, among them memories of old injustices. In the Baltic states, as in western Belarus and (more especially) Ukraine, there was nostalgia for the days of independence or Polish rule respectively. In the late Stalin era all these regions had suffered disproportionately from barbaric measures of repression and forced collectivization. Large elements of their population saw their homelands as being under foreign occupation. An especially important role was played by the return of surviving *zeks*. According to recently published figures for the Baltic states, at least 172,500 such individuals were in the Gulag in January 1954 (half of them women, one quarter children), but 'only' 7,300 five years later; in 1957 alone 18,900 Lithuanians were released (Zemskov 1993). The impact which such individuals had on their compatriots must have been immense. One of the first writers to break the taboo on mentioning the prison-camp system was H. Heislers, a young Latvian poet and former *zek*, in 'The Unfinished Song' (1956). He told of innocents languishing 'behind swamps and gullies of bluish hills' and, in the spirit of Pomerantsev, called for greater 'sincerity' (i.e. truthfulness) and humanity in literature. The poem had a sensational effect in Latvia. The author was condemned in *Pravda*, together with two other writers, for displaying a 'lack of Party spirit'. Two of those criticized partially recanted their 'errors' (Ekmanis 1975). In Estonia R. Sirge's novel *The Land and the People* (1956) mentioned the 1941 deportations (Kirby 1994).

National-minority writers had much in common with their Russian contemporaries (for example, Dudintsev), as regards both style and subject matter. Although less well known, especially abroad, they played an equally dynamic role in awakening a sense of social conscience. Almost any reference to a sensitive theme could be interpreted as an act of national defiance, whether it was intended as such or not. In Ukraine the young poets of the 'sixties' group looked back to the 1860s, which had likewise been an era of national cultural renaissance. Using language vibrant with new images, they explored the frailty of human relationships, never allowing their basic humanism to be obscured by their political commitment (Luckyj 1975). The poet V. Symonenko, who died of cancer in 1963 at the age of twenty-nine, was revered by other Ukrainian intellectuals for his civic courage. 'My nation exists! In its hot veins | Cossack blood pulsates and hums', he wrote in a work that could not be published. Ivan Drach's long poem 'Knife in the Sun' (1961), which did get through the censor, was a meditation on Ukrainian history that evoked the devastation caused by Stalin but ended with a (forced) tribute to the present regime. Among those Ukrainians released from the camps was the novelist Zinaida Tulub, who shortly before her death in 1964 wrote about the sufferings in exile of the national hero Taras Shevchenko. His memorial in Kiev was the scene of unauthorized commemorations by dissidents each year from 1964 (the one hundred and fiftieth anniversary of his birth) to 1972. Wreaths would be laid and patriotic songs sung. This was done on the day when the poet's ashes had been brought back from Russia, to distinguish the occasion from the official celebrations, held on his birthday in March.

Bohdan Hmelnyckyj was another historical figure who was pressed into service in the ideological tug-of-war between Communists and patriots over the correct interpretation of the nation's past. Had he been a social rebel or the leader of a broad-based movement for independence? One young historian, Braichevsky, got into trouble for writing an essay on the treaty of 1654 which the censor deemed too nationalistic; it was subsequently circulated in *samizdat*. A strong patriotic motif ran through the novel *The Cathedral* by Oles Honchar (1968), a senior official in the cultural establishment. It portrayed a conflict between an idealistic student and a Party functionary over the fate of an old Cossack church—a dual symbol of Ukrainian religious and national identity. It was criticized for its 'dubious subtext'. Virtually anything with historical associations could carry symbolic references: collections of ethnographic artefacts, for example, or traditional folk songs. One folklorist, Leopold Yashchenko, was dismissed from the musicians' union and harassed by the authorities because the programme his choral troupe presented was thought too nationalistic. Records of the offending songs were removed from shops and members of the choir forced to quit.

In the Baltic states the authorities showed greater tact. Some historic buildings with national associations could be restored. A song festival held in Tallinn in 1969 attracted no less than a quarter of a million people, for many of whom the event struck a powerful emotional chord. (These events had been a feature of the nineteenth-century national awakening.) Religious beliefs were a major factor in sustaining national consciousness, particularly among Latin-rite Uniates in western Ukraine and Catholics in Lithuania (see Chapter 8)—and of course in the Muslim republics as well. Here a cultural renaissance got under way in 1956. It was most marked in Uzbekistan. The dramatist Uyghun, in *Friends* (1961), dealt cautiously with the problems facing a returning *zek* who encountered both well-wishers and enemies. The motif, conveyed by recondite allusions, was that victims of injustice should show manliness but not be vengeful (Allworth 1990). In Kazakhstan nationally conscious historians and other intellectuals, aware of their weakness *vis-à-vis* the strong Russian presence in their republic, adopted a 'rearguard strategy' which involved treating their nation's history in a more objective spirit and winning rehabilitation for past writers. Original literary work also highlighted traditional themes (Olcott 1985).

The language issue

Patriotic activists everywhere saw themselves as defending their national culture from alien influences which threatened to destroy traditional values and impose a soulless materialistic homogeneity. Since the most important 'marker' of an individual's ethnicity was the language he spoke, they naturally gave such matters a great deal of attention. There were two main aspects to the question. The first was the scale of native language tuition in schools and colleges, as well as its use in the press, publications, and among the population generally—those living within the eponymous republic as well as those in the diaspora. (A subordinate feature was philological: the extent of borrowings from Russian in the vocabulary or syntax of the local language.) The second was the amount of immigration by Russians (or other Slavs) into the other republics relative to native outmigration, the corresponding rates of population growth, and the demographic balance that resulted. Let us examine these issues in turn.

Every empire needs a lingua franca, and no one doubted that in the USSR this language should be Russian. The central authorities no longer so brazenly exalted its merits, but made no secret of their desire to maximize its role. In practice this meant encouraging minority peoples to become bilingual, as the necessary preliminary to any eventual 'language shift', which clearly would require several generations. Since the educational system and the media were under tight control, this seemed to policy-makers a feasible goal. Like other objectives, it was never stated unambiguously, lest this add to nationalist resentment. Official statements invariably endorsed the principle of linguistic equality. Propagandists never tired of pointing to the large number of books and periodicals published in languages other than Russian. But reality often belied these claims. The principle of linguistic equality implied an acceptance of *reciprocity*, yet no one spoke of the 'enrichment' of Russian by external influences, only of the reverse! A great many bilingual dictionaries were published, but of the two languages one was always the 'imperial' one. Works by minority writers might be translated into Russian, but not into other minority languages, and were in any case less common than translations from Russian. For the controllers' aim was to create a uniform 'Soviet literature', to which all peoples were expected to make a contribution, but one devoid of ethnic distinctiveness.

In the non-Russian areas there were usually two types of general school, distinguished by the language in which instruction was given. Most pupils attended those where this was the native language, while the others catered not only for Russian residents but also for a segment of the indigenous population. The proportion of the latter in these schools varied greatly. The highest figures were registered in Kazakhstan (35 per cent), the lowest in the Baltic (Estonia 2 per cent), Ukraine falling in the middle (14 per cent) (Pool 1978).[3] Balts, Armenians, and Georgians put up stout resistance to the penetration of Russian as the medium of tuition. To counter the resulting physical segregation of Russian and native pupils, bilingual schools with parallel classes were set up in some places, but these did not prosper. Nationalists contended that Russian-language schools were favoured in the provision of funds, and so were larger and better equipped. But this 'discrimination' was partly due to the fact that they tended to be located in urban environments with an ethnically mixed population. There was more substance to complaints that no native-language schooling was provided for minority nationals who lived in Russian (or other) cities that had large concentrations of non-Russians. The reason for this was not just a practical one (additional expense) but reflected the central authorities' view that children of such migrants were prime candidates for assimilation into the multi-ethnic Soviet culture and so did not need separate schools.

Other valid objections related to Russian immigrants' reluctance to learn the native language and to the nature of the school curriculum generally. In 1970 13 per cent of Russians in Estonia could speak Estonian; the figure for Latvia was 18 per cent (Parming 1980). They had fewer difficulties, naturally, in the 'fraternal' Slav republics, but more in Central Asia where the cultural divide was wider than anywhere else. Teaching of subjects in the humanities such as history or literature was geared to the inculcation of Soviet values and displayed an obvious bias against national cultural traditions. Children in the Baltic, for example, were given a mendacious picture of life in their republics during the independence period, while Central Asian pupils were lectured on the 'reactionary' nature of Islam. To some extent these influences could be counteracted in the home, but parents could do nothing about school textbooks, which teachers were obliged to adhere to closely. A particular problem was the availability of manuals in non-Russian languages. In republics that had fewer native-language schools, pupils in them had only 35 per cent as many such textbooks as did their Russian-language counterparts (Connor 1992). The higher one went up the educational ladder, the greater was the proportion of texts in Russian. At VUZ level they were ten times as numerous—and entrance examinations were held in Russian, too. The authorities denied that this amounted to discrimination, and defended themselves with economic or pedagogical arguments. But these lacked credibility, and were belied by official claims that bilingualism (in Russian, of course) was spreading rapidly.

The data on language use provided by the 1970 census were apparently considered unsatisfactory by the 'fusionist' lobby in Moscow and led to increased russifying pressures (see Chapter 15). They showed that a very high proportion of respondents still spoke their native language 'first', i.e. generally (the question posed was ambiguous, perhaps deliberately so). The non-Slavic nations of the

Baltic all recorded scores of over 95 per cent, and a slightly *higher* proportion than in 1959 (0.3 per cent for Estonians, 0.1 per cent for Latvians and Lithuanians). The percentage claiming to speak Russian as their first language was higher among Latvians (4.5 per cent) and Estonians (4.4 per cent) than it was among Lithuanians (1.6 per cent). In Georgia and Azerbaijan the proportion of native-language speakers was over 98 per cent, and except in Georgia (down 0.2 per cent) the trend was upwards. The same was true of Central Asia, apart from Kazakhstan. The Kyrgyz held the record for linguistic resistance with 98.8 per cent, 0.1 higher than in 1959. This phenomenon was largely due to differential birth rates, for native children were of course brought up in the republic's titular language. The linguistic russification tendency was marked only among other Slav peoples (as well as Jews and Germans). The proportion of Ukrainian respondents who spoke Russian as their 'first' language went up by over two percentage points (from 12.2 to 14.3 per cent), and of Belarusians by nearly four (15.3 to 19.0 per cent).

No comparable data were available on the growth of bilingualism, since this question had not been asked in the 1959 census. The figures for 1970 were generally high, with Belarusians scoring highest at 49.0 per cent, Ukrainians 36.3 per cent, and even Estonians claiming (falsely, as it later turned out) an encouraging 29.0 per cent. In the southern and eastern republics the ratio was lower, especially in Central Asia (Turkmens and Tajiks 15.4, Uzbeks 14.5 per cent). When looked at more closely, the figures were much less comforting to officialdom. In the first place, they were not accurate, for census-takers could not verify the 'fluency' claimed by respondents, and when actual levels of competence in Russian were tested later they were found to be deplorably low. Secondly, knowledge of Russian was more widespread among those non-Russians who lived outside their titular republic, and was concentrated among adolescents and young adults. The inescapable conclusion was that at current rates it would take aeons even for bilingualism, let alone linguistic assimilation, to become generalized. It depended mainly on natural factors like migration or the ageing of the population. The temptation for officials was therefore to try to force the process by improving tuition methods, limiting the circulation of non-Russian periodicals, and so on, even at the cost of antagonizing non-Russians and stiffening their resistance to what increasingly looked like 'russification'.

Migration patterns

Theoretically the CPSU leaders could have adopted draconian measures to enforce their will. But population transfers and genocide in the Stalin manner were no longer a realistic option. The deportations of the 1940s had been disowned and even direction of labour had been abandoned (in 1956). What followed was therefore a largely spontaneous movement of people who were attracted by better employment opportunities and living conditions. No central agency existed to promote the 'merger' of nations, which was not even rated a high-priority objective. Minority nationalists suspected that the authorities had a hidden political agenda, but although this cannot be ruled out no evidence of it has yet come to light. One Soviet scholar reckoned that overall 10 to 12 per cent of migrants moved on an 'organized basis' (cited by Rywkin 1982). Nor was it simply a matter of Slavs 'colonizing' the Baltic or Kazakhstan. There was also a large movement in the reverse direction, notably by Ukrainians, Belarusians, and Moldavians. Transcaucasia was less affected by Slav immigration, and in Central Asia it was offset by the high native birth rate.

Most Russian migrants went to live in towns and industrial centres. The influx was concentrated in the capital cities and certain regions of the minority republics, notably northern Estonia and eastern and southern Ukraine (Donets, Crimea). The more northerly Baltic republics, along with Moldova, registered a great increase in the Russian share of total population between 1959 and 1970. Latvia received 146,000 Russian immigrants between 1961 and 1970. Their share of the republic's population growth was 42 per cent to 1966, and 36 per cent over the next four years (Besemeres 1980); the native share of the total population fell from 62.0 to 56.8 per cent between the two censuses. In Estonia the Russian element grew ten times faster than the natives, by 39.6 as against 3.6 per cent. The indigenous share of Estonia's population fell from 74.6 to 68.2 per cent over the eleven years. The Lithuanians, however, managed to increase their share of the total population of their republic slightly to 80.1 per cent; here only 12 per cent of the increase (50,000 out of 417,000) was due to immigration. The reasons for this were less political, as some Baltic nationalists believed, than socio-demographic. In the non-Catholic Baltic lands birth rates were naturally low and, because of the age structure, mortality rates high. The preference here was for small families. Divorce and abortion were commonplace. Even in rustic (and Catholic) Lithuania the divorce rate tripled during the 1960s. Yet enough surplus skilled labour was available here to man the burgeoning industries, which was apparently not the case further north. Estonia experienced an acute demographic crisis in the mid-1960s, but thereafter reproduction rates recovered. A similar recovery occurred in Latvia, where by 1970 the birth rate was only 0.1 per thousand below that in the RSFSR; more children were being born to Latvian mothers than to Slav immigrant ones.

Kazakhstan was swamped by Slav immigrants during the 'virgin lands' drive of the 1950s, but between the two censuses the balance shifted back towards the natives by 1.8 per cent. Russians accounted for 43.2 per cent in 1959 and declined by a mere 0.4 per cent by 1970, when they numbered 5.5 million as against 4 million eleven years earlier. The proportion of Muslims rose from 34 to 37 per cent (3.6 to 5.3 million). (Over one-tenth of the population were Germans and other deportees.) In Kyrgyzstan the corresponding figures for Muslims were 56 and 60 per cent; elsewhere in Central Asia they accounted for four-fifths or more of the population in 1970. Everywhere they were reproducing faster than the Slavs. During the intercensal period the Muslim nations of the USSR grew from 24.7 to 35.1 million, or from 11.8 to 14.5 per cent of total population. Over the next two decades the trend would gather strength, drastically changing the Soviet Union's demographic balance (see Chapter 15).

Assimilation?

Nationalists sometimes worried that their peoples might lose their 'genetic identity' and be physically wiped off the map. These fears, it is now clear, were exaggerated. Even in the Baltic republics, where the threat of 'denationalization' (Remeikis 1977) was most acute, immigrants tended to live apart. Relatively few of them married Estonians: a 1968 study showed that only 6 to 7 per cent of marriages in that republic were exogamous. Rates were higher in Latvia and Ukraine (around 30 per cent in 1969), but much lower in the Muslim lands, ranging from 20.1 per cent in Tajikistan to 6.3 per cent in Azerbaijan. Moreover, most of these matches were with fellow Muslims. Islamic custom forbade marriage by Muslim women to non-Muslims, and this rule was strictly kept to. Exogamy was more frequent among the urbanized, educated, and bilingually competent groups. Its frequency or infrequency can be explained by socio-demographic factors that have little to do with nationalism (Fisher 1977). Nor were there grounds for assuming that children of mixed marriages would automatically opt for Russian nationality on reaching the age of sixteen. A nine-year study of Latvia in the 1960s showed that 57 per cent did so. Such decisions were far more likely to be made within the family for personal reasons than in compliance with whatever the authorities desired. By and large young people's career prospects (outside politics and the military) were not noticeably improved if they chose to declare themselves Russian.

In short, the threat of assimilation was a long-term one and most minority nations had enough demographic and cultural resources to ward it off. Those most exposed were peoples that lacked union-republic status, such as Jews, Bashkirs, or Karelians. (Some smaller ethnic groups were becoming assimilated to larger non-Slav neighbours like the Uzbeks or Yakuts.) The fact that many non-Russians spoke the lingua franca did not signify any willingness to abandon their own tongue, or suggest that this would be degraded to a mere 'kitchen language', as alarmists thought. It might make non-Russians more multi-cultural in outlook, but it did not mean that they, or even their children, would experience a metamorphosis of their national identity. On the contrary, the boot was on the other foot. The 'new Soviet man' dear to the propagandists was a myth. What was under threat by 1970 was the 'neo-imperialist' order itself, the entire Soviet pseudo-federal system, whose inadequacies were increasingly clear to the élites of the several dozen nations that this very system had unwittingly allowed to develop. It was already evident that the road ahead led not to homogenization but to an increased awareness of national differences, to conflict rather than co-operation.

Western analysts, as we know, related this to deep-rooted socio-economic processes. 'Modernization,' wrote one, 'far from opening the way to integration, engenders a nationalism that is asserting itself more consciously than ever before' (Carrère d'Encausse, *L'empire éclaté* 1978)—although it was harder to predict at what point 'the empire' would actually 'burst asunder' (*éclater*). Another observer put the point rather less euphorically: 'as societies grow more sophisticated socially and economically, ethnic tensions and chauvinistic excesses, far from abating, actually tend to increase' (Besemeres 1980). This left open the possibility that they could be checked by timely action, an option that by the early 1970s had not yet been entirely foreclosed. However, the likelihood of the central authorities displaying such wisdom was not high.

Political opposition; national Communism

Instead, Moscow did two things that made the situation worse. First, the regime adopted a repressive line towards manifestations of cultural nationalism that led its exponents to become more active politically, which in turn called forth even tougher police reprisals. Second, they permitted, and to some extent encouraged, limited expressions of *Russian* national consciousness, which in the long run would also help to undermine the system. We may look at the first of these here and the second in Chapter 14.

Under Khrushchev overt political protest was sporadic and unorganized. In 1956 there were manifestations of sympathy in the Baltic states and elsewhere on behalf of the Hungarian revolutionaries. On Remembrance Day (no longer officially celebrated) candles were lit before a national monument in Riga. Several students in Tartu were arrested and sentenced to terms of imprisonment. In 1960 a number of Lithuanians were killed when protesting against a visit by Serov, the KGB chief who had played an infamous role in 'pacifying' their republic after the war. Between 1958 and 1962 the security police broke up four clandestine groups in the Baltic and a dozen in western Ukraine. At least three activists were shot. The death sentence, later commuted, was also passed on the lawyer Levko Luk'ianenko, who in the late 1980s would become a notable figure in Ukrainian politics. Together with eight colleagues he planned to set up a body, the Workers' and Peasants' Union, to campaign for the republic to secede from the USSR—a goal formally permitted by the Constitution. As these instances show, conditions were such as to render organized underground activity all but fruitless. In Kiev even literary evenings held under Komsomol auspices at a 'club of creative youth' were prohibited for 'nationalist deviations'.

Nevertheless from the mid-1960s onwards several clandestine political organizations did come into existence in Ukraine,

Armenia, and Russia itself. The Odessa Democratic Union of Socialists (1964) claimed six members, the Ukrainian National Front (1967) nine. In Ukraine the turning point came in August 1965, when the KGB launched its first major operation against dissenters since Stalin's death. Twenty-six individuals were arrested, of whom eighteen refused to recant their errors and were put on trial. The journalist Viacheslav Chornovil—who like Luk'ianenko would eventually rise to prominence in post-Soviet Ukraine—compiled a dossier on these arbitrary acts and was in turn arrested (August 1966). At his trial three months later he cited Lenin's criticisms of 'Great-Power chauvinism' and his relatively benign attitude towards the national minorities. This embarrassed the authorities, who made such strident claims for their Leninist orthodoxy. Up to a point this was a tactical manœuvre—the leading Ukrainian dissidents of this era (Chornovil, Dziuba, Karavanskyj, Moroz) ultimately wanted national independence, which was *not* compatible with Leninism!—but it also implied that *if* the regime lived up to its principles and permitted a measure of 'national Communism' there was room for at least a temporary compromise.

The point to stress here is that the Party first secretary in the republic, Petro Shelest, was a 'reform Communist' not wholly unsympathetic to Ukrainian national aspirations. He had started his career in the republic, followed in Khrushchev's 'tail' to Moscow, and returned in 1963 as local boss, to the discomfiture of his more hard-line rival, the prime minister Shcherbitsky. The arch-conservative Suslov distrusted him, too. Shelest protected certain regional officials who were in trouble for their national leanings and pushed the republic's economic interests at Party forums. He called for more textbooks to be published in Ukrainian and in 1965 authorized (or tolerated) an address to university rectors by the republic's Higher Education minister, Dadenkov, in which he urged greater use of that language in teaching and administration. In response to an official invitation, Ivan Dziuba compiled a detailed memorandum of Ukrainian grievances and aspirations that highlighted language use, immigration, and the judicial persecution of nationally conscious intellectuals. The text was subsequently leaked abroad and caused a sensation. Shelest appears to have protected Dziuba from his orthodox critics: he was not dismissed until 1972, shortly before Shelest himself fell from power. One of the reasons given for his ouster was his authorship of a popular propagandist work entitled *O Our Soviet Ukraine* (1970), which went too far for Moscow's taste in lauding Ukrainian historical achievements.[4] There was thus for a time an ambiguous relationship between elements in the Ukrainian Party leadership and nationalist dissenters. So long as Moscow 'called the shots', however, the potential for a compromise, such as it was, could not develop.

The situation was somewhat similar in two of the Baltic republics. Lithuania was for thirty years virtually the fiefdom of Anastas Sniečkus, whose skilful manœuvring enabled him to get away with more than Shelest could. His legions were fewer and his position less exposed. Astute and influential, Sniečkus 'knew [his] limits and managed to contain nationalistic tendencies through a combination of threats, bargaining for concessions in the Kremlin, and safeguarding his cadres' (Remeikis 1980). In Estonia Johannes (Ivan) Käbin, the Party boss from 1950 to 1978, faced a somewhat easier task since until 1970 at least (when the 'Tallinn Four' tried to form a clandestine national party) the population was more acquiescent—'lulled by the fleshpots of consumerism', in the view of some zealous nationalist emigrés. Käbin was a 'Russian Estonian' who had difficulty speaking his native language correctly, but over the years he underwent a process of 'reculturation' that turned him into a buffer between Moscow and the local *nomenklatura*.

This did not happen in the recently purged parties of Latvia—or Azerbaijan. On the other hand, in Georgia and Armenia, where kinship ties counted for so much, the Party leaders developed a network of informal ties to native entrepreneurial elements. The dismissal of Mzhavanadze, the Georgian boss, in 1972 was followed by no less than 25,000 arrests. What began here as a primarily socio-economic movement would increasingly acquire a nationalist tinge.

Summing up, one may say that functionaries in the union-republic parties often enjoyed a certain leeway in implementing the centre's directives. Caught between countervailing pressures, they attempted to bolster their standing with the native élite while convincing their superiors that such tactical flexibility was all for the good of the cause. This was a dangerous game with many players and no fixed rules. It led to the arrest, trial, and imprisonment of hundreds of individuals. From 1958 onward an increasing number of people in the camps (or 'colonies', as they were now officially called) were members of national-minority groups. A few desperate men were driven to public suicide. The first such case occurred in Kiev in December 1968, and the most celebrated, by the student R. Kalanta, in Kaunas (Lithuania) in May 1972. Yet the patriots' efforts were not in vain. Together with changes in society at large, they prepared the way for the empire's ultimate collapse. In the short term they helped to strengthen the Democratic movement, whose members took up the cause of human rights in an unequal struggle that captured the world's imagination.

PART III

Civil Society Resurgent

8 For Faith and Freedom

Religious repression and dissent

The cultural renaissance led to a renewed concern with spiritual values. In Solzhenitsyn's story 'Matriona's House' the central character is a simple, saintly peasant woman: demanding nothing of her fellow men and giving all, 'she was that Righteous One without whom, as the proverb says, no village can stand. Nor any city. Nor our whole land.' Josef Brodsky's 'Christmas Poem' (1965) ends with a tribute to God's gift to man of the miracle of life. Perhaps some intellectuals turned to religion out of faddishness or a superficial revulsion against the technological bias of Soviet society. But the movement had an inner core of earnest seeking after ultimate truths that recalled developments at the beginning of the century. Marxism-Leninism had been tried but had clearly failed to offer an answer to the basic problems of human existence.

Moreover, in 1959 the protagonists of this secular faith had reverted to the pre-war pattern by launching a major offensive against organized religion. The fragile compromise established in Stalin's last years, whereby the churches were tolerated within narrowly circumscribed limits in return for support of the regime's foreign policy objectives, was unilaterally rescinded in the name of anti-Stalinism. A hard-liner, Kuroedov, was appointed to head the Council for Russian Orthodox Church Affairs, one of two government agencies set up to 'supervise' (actually to infiltrate and control) the Christian churches. Atheistic propaganda was stepped up, especially among the young, and administrative measures taken to foster secular rituals as alternatives to baptism, confirmation, and marriage. Churches were forcibly closed, even razed to the ground before the eyes of parishioners, and clergy arrested on fabricated charges. At least forty-four trials were held of Orthodox ecclesiastics alone. According to recently published archival data, over the seven years 1958–65 inclusive the number of Orthodox priests fell from 11,123 to 6,800, and that of registered churches from 13,413 to 7,501 (Davis 1991, Odintsov 1994).[1]

Over 60 per cent of those that survived were in Ukraine. Over half those in the north-eastern region of Viatka (Kirov) were closed, and 40 per cent in the north-western region of Tver' (Kalinin); some other areas, especially in the south-east, were less affected. The Orthodox Church lost five of its eight seminaries and over three-quarters of its monastic institutions, which had numbered sixty-seven in the late 1950s. At the Uspensky monastery (Pochaev, Ternopol' province) the buildings were confiscated, the monks dispersed (some to hard labour), novices beaten to death, nuns robbed and raped. These atrocities became known abroad and international protests helped to end the persecution, but not before 'many monks passed on to eternal life before their time' (Levitin). Frequently the anti-parasite laws (see Chapter 3) were invoked against members of religious congregations. In 1962 new legislation was brought in which made their leaders criminally responsible for accepting minors into them. In practice this meant that it was no longer safe to give children religious instruction, even in the home.

Protestants

The first to protest against this onslaught were the Evangelical Christians and Baptists, the official name taken by the Protestant churches whose administrations had been forcibly amalgamated in 1944. Scattered throughout the country, but especially strong in the Baltic, the Baptists (as we may call them for short) claimed some three million members in the mid-1950s (not all of whom were necessarily baptized), and were more dynamic than other denominations. Their teachings were attractive to many working people and also to the young. Khrushchev's campaign led to the closure of about half the Protestant churches. In 1960, under pressure from the secular authorities, the Baptists' All-Union Council adopted a new statute and a letter instructing senior presbyters to restrict mission-ary work, infant baptism, and children's attendance at divine service. This provoked demands by churchmen for the documents to be discussed at an extraordinary congress, but the council refused to hold one. Two leaders of an Action Group formed in May 1961, Prokof'ev (an ex-prisoner of conscience) and Kriuchkov, roundly denounced the council as 'servants of Satan' for accepting orders that 'openly contradict God's commandments'. A considerable number of parishes followed the lead of the rebels, popularly known as *initsiativniki*. In February 1962 they secretly convoked a representative conference. This set up an Organizing Committee, under Kriuchkov and Vins, to call an extraordinary congress, the purpose of which was to reprimand the council for 'its conscious deviation from the truth and . . . persistent work against the Church'. Four months later the committee went on to excommunicate seven members of the council and took over management of the Church's affairs in the interim. It then transformed itself into a rival council, so finalizing the schism.

This was not to the taste of the state controllers, who allowed the 'official' council to hold two congresses (1963, 1966) and to show flexibility towards the dissidents. At the first congress the offending documents were repealed. A new statute made significant concessions that led several thousand believers to rejoin the parent Church. The schism, however, was not healed, since persecution continued. Prokof'ev had been rearrested in 1962 and sentenced to ten years' deprivation of liberty. By the end of the decade over 500 Baptists had been sent to jail. A number of children were taken away from their families, allegedly to protect them from 'religious fanaticism'. These repressive acts stimulated active resistance as well as readiness for martyrdom. In 1965 and 1966 Protestants held several well-attended services in public places. Five hundred delegates from 130 towns staged a demonstration before the Party Central Committee building, demanding an end to arbitrariness and recognition of the right to give religious instruction. The dissident leaders took care to emphasize their political loyalty. They merely wanted the state to observe its own laws: the Stalinist restrictive legislation of 1929 should be repealed and the new Constitution, then under discussion, should guarantee freedom of both religious and anti-religious propaganda, as had been the case in the early years of Soviet rule.

In September 1965 Mikoian received a Baptist delegation and promised to investigate the Church's grievances. But the post-Khrushchev regime did not adhere to its initially more forthcoming attitude. The church closure campaign abated, but other restrictions remained in force or were intensified. In 1966 the RSFSR penal code was amended to make it an offence to prepare or distribute 'documents calling for infringement of the laws on religious cults', to hold 'ceremonies prejudicial to social order', or to teach religion to minors 'contrary to regulations'—regulations that were nowhere clearly laid down and so were open to interpretation by local KGB officials and those of the Council for Religious Affairs (CRA), whom they directed.[2] Private prayer meetings were disrupted, the apartments where they were held ransacked, and Baptist children encouraged to denounce their parents. Kriuchkov, Vins, and other dissident leaders were among those arrested. In a case that won international attention the five children of Nadezhda Sloboda, a peasant in one of the western provinces, were removed to public care. After they had repeatedly fled, they were arrested at home, together with their mother, who in 1968 was sentenced to four years' imprisonment for organizing an 'illegal religious community'. In the camps religious prisoners earned the respect of fellow *zeks* for their honesty and fortitude. M. I. Khorev went blind during a three-year spell in captivity (1966–9), resumed church activities on his release, and was promptly rearrested.

Even more impressive was the fact that Baptist protesters remained strictly within the limits of the law, which put their persecutors in the embarrassing position of acting illegally. Although the appeals that circulated in the later 1960s often focused on particular injustices, rather than suggesting an alternative pattern of Church–State relations (Fletcher 1971), in 1969 one petition, signed by as many as 1,453 mothers, duly invoked the International Declaration on Human Rights (to which the USSR was a party) and relevant Soviet legislation. In this way the Baptists' struggle became part of a wider movement of opinion that sought to persuade the Soviet authorities to observe more civilized standards of conduct.

Orthodox

More immediately, their example inspired emulation, albeit in a minor key, among the Orthodox. Although much stronger numerically, and so of greater potential weight in bringing about change, the Russian Orthodox Church was hampered by its hierarchical structure, which exposed it more readily to state control and police infiltration. Moreover, the tradition of compromise, exemplified by Metropolitan Sergei's pledge of loyalty to 'the Soviet Union as our civil motherland' (1927), hampered any effort to resist illegal actions by the secular power. Time and again Patriarch Alexii (Simansky) and other dignitaries would publicly declare that no repressive measures were being taken, although they knew the contrary to be true, and even assist the secular authorities to close churches and punish clergy who stepped out of line.

A particularly unsavoury offender in this respect was Metropolitan Nikodim (Rotov), who in 1961 became head of the patriarchate's foreign relations department (and *de facto* deputy Patriarch) in lieu of Metropolitan Nikolai (Yarushevich), who had been unceremoniously deposed and is thought to have met an unnatural death. When Nikodim, aged only thirty, was consecrated bishop the Patriarch warned against 'certain persons trying especially hard to penetrate the Church's precincts with self-interested, evil and even perfidious motives'—a remark which many took as referring to the incumbent. Alexii dared go no further. The degree to which the Church was subject to atheist control is evident from the episcopal council (Synod) convoked irregularly in July 1961. In contravention of Church canons it endorsed regulations that made each priest an employee of the parish council. These lay bodies were often penetrated by 'dubious persons', i.e. CRA and KGB agents. The hierarchs' decision was taken reluctantly, in the presence of 'three well-dressed, well-known figures' seated at a small table behind the assembled bishops. 'The holders of [real] power had arranged everything and there could be no objections' (Levitin).

The results were disastrous for the Church, as we have seen. Boris Talantov, the layman son of a priest who perished in the Gulag, later revealed the methods that had been used to close parish churches in his diocese (Viatka). For example, in March 1963 a gang of workers, after fortifying themselves by drinking communion wine, entered SS. Zosima and Sara, Korshik, hacked out the iconostasis, smashed sacred vessels, burned liturgical books, and made off with whatever of value was left. The building, scheduled to become a club, was totally wrecked. Talantov held the ecclesiastical hierarchy responsible for the destruction: 'it could have opposed these arbitrary acts on legal grounds ... yet with few exceptions the bishops completely dissociated themselves from any struggle for believers' rights.' One local dignitary, Ioann, 'replaced strong Christian priests with drunkards and often behaved outrageously himself'; he once threatened a churchwarden who resisted the forcible closure of consecrated buildings that he would hand him over to the KGB. Talantov pointed out that collaboration between prelates and security officials violated the law on separation of Church and State, and concluded that to regenerate Orthodoxy morally 'the faithful must cleanse the Church from false brothers and false pastors'. For this he was dismissed from his post and sent to a monastery. Another protest against ecclesiastical appeasement came from two Moscow priests, Nikolai Eshliman (a former camp inmate) and Gleb Yakunin. They too were sanctioned, the Patriarch calling their actions 'illegal and depraved'. Far from meekly accepting this censure, which they held was uncanonical, they appealed against it and distributed copies of their statement to all bishops. Reduced to essentials, their argument was that the Church administration's subservience to the secular authorities infringed the rights of millions of believers.

Another scourge of ecclesiastical double-dealing was Anatolii Levitin, a layman and fervent Christian publicist. Dismissed from a teaching appointment in 1966, he took a job as a humble church watchman. In measured terms, and with considerable erudition, he defended the two priests and exposed the uncanonical behaviour of the hierarchs. Eloquently he warned the ageing Patriarch (then 89) that, unless he hearkened to his 'unquiet conscience', he would soon face 'a righteous Judge who attaches no significance to pompous titles', while on earth he would stand condemned by 'the court of history'. Levitin's political leanings were towards democratic socialism. He became the chief link between the religious dissidents and the human rights movement, which led to his arrest in 1969. He, too, had previously served time in Stalin's camps and would suffer yet another arrest in 1971.[3]

By then Patriarch Alexii had passed away. Another synod was held, which elected as his successor Pimen' (Izvekov 1971–90), who followed the same policies. The gathering confirmed the controversial decisions on parish administration taken ten years earlier. This left many churchmen and believers dissatisfied. Their concerns were forthrightly expressed by Solzhenitsyn in a *Lenten Letter* to the Patriarch (1972), in which he called on Pimen' to emulate the martyrs of the early Church by taking the road of self-sacrifice. But his clarion call was too radical for men brought up in the kenotic mainstream of Orthodox thought (Ellis 1986).

The Orthodox dissidents were less successful than the Baptists in acquiring an institutional base. One effort to do so by forming a clandestine organization, the 'All-Russian Social Christian Union', soon ran foul of the police. Betrayed from within in 1965, it was allowed to continue under surveillance for a time before being broken up. In 1968 seventeen of its leaders, among them Igor Ogurtsov, were sentenced to long prison terms. The group's political programme contained the interesting (if impractical) idea that in a future democratic Russia the upper chamber of parliament should consist of clergy with a right of veto on ethically complex matters. Given the enormous obstacles they faced, the Orthodox dissenters' achievements were remarkable. They put the ecclesiastical establishment on the defensive morally and showed that there was an alternative to their supine conduct. Their ideas helped to stimulate the Russian national revival of the 1970s, which became an important current in the broad stream of opposition thought.

Other churches

The autocephalous Georgian and Armenian Orthodox churches were more successful in resisting state control, for reasons that have to do with local nationalism and foreign policy we cannot examine here. In 1956 the diplomatic skills of Vazgen I, Catholicos (head) of the Armenian Church, led to an informal concordat with Moscow which benefited the hierarchy—and indirectly believers as well. Nationalism was also a key factor among Lithuanian Catholics and Uniates in Ukraine, as we know. In the former republic the movement began in 1968, partly under the influence of events in Czechoslovakia, when two priests protested at the lack of seminary places and liturgical books. They were reprimanded and transferred to other parishes. Next year forty clergymen submitted a more extensive catalogue of grievances. This time the authorities reacted more harshly and the movement snowballed. At least two dozen petitions circulated which attracted hundreds and even thousands of signatures. The record in this respect was achieved in December 1971, when despite police obstruction no less than 17,054 people endorsed a memorandum to Brezhnev (through the United Nations) protesting at the authorities' infringements of the Constitution and demanding 'rights equal to those of other Soviet citizens'. Several other petitions attracted support on the same scale, notably among young people who objected to compulsory classes in atheism at school. In 1972 the movement acquired its own clandestine journal, the *Chronicle of the Lithuanian Catholic Church*. Each issue contained editorials and documents detailing the struggle against administrative arbitrariness. The line taken was politically loyal, in the sense that no explicit demand was put forward for national independence, although this goal was in the minds of many Catholic activists. In neighbouring Latvia, where Catholics formed a sizeable minority of the population (c.300,000 believers) and the hierarchy had responsibility for fellow-believers elsewhere in the USSR, 'churchmen never challenged the government over religious instruction or other matters' (Vardys 1990)—a matter of some concern to Lithuanian activists.

In western Ukraine (Galicia, Transcarpathia) the Greek Catholics or Uniates managed to sustain a vigorous underground or 'catacomb' church organization. These believers bitterly resented the forced takeover of their church by the Russian Orthodox in 1946. Some so-called 'penitents' (*pokutnyky*), mainly peasant women, repudiated *all* contact with the regime and adhered to an apocalyptic ultra-nationalist world-view. Less extreme were those who recognized the primacy of Cardinal Slipyi, who in 1963 was allowed to leave for Rome after eighteen years in prison. He secretly installed three bishops, who had under them about three hundred priests, many of whom had also spent time behind bars. Although frequently harassed by the police, they managed to hold services, sometimes in woods or private homes. In 1968 they became more active, for in neighbouring Slovakia during the reform period a large majority of Orthodox parishes reverted to the Uniates, who also won state recognition of their own hierarchy. This led Uniates in Ukraine to take over some Orthodox churches that had been closed and to request that their Church, too, be granted legal status. One such petition (1973) amassed 12,000 signatures. These demands were ignored and leaders of the movement, including two 'underground' bishops, arrested.

In this repression the secular authorities were energetically abetted by Russian Orthodox prelates, notably Filaret (Denysenko), exarch of Ukraine. Lavish celebrations were held to mark the twenty-fifth anniversary of the forced 'reunion' of the two churches, and propagandists in Moscow denounced the Uniates as 'schismatics' serving the interests of the Vatican. In a parallel move the Russian hierarchy made concessions to the Orthodox in Ukraine over ritual matters and appointed more native Ukrainians, some of them former Uniates, to episcopal office. However, such measures could not overcome suspicion of the 'Muscovites' among nationally conscious believers, especially as Orthodox converts were also liable to persecution if they became too sympathetic to Ukrainian national aspirations. Furthermore, the Uniate cause won the support of secular intellectuals such as Moroz and Luk'ianenko. Thus here religious and national dissent blended into a force of considerable explosive potential.

Mainstream dissent

It is not surprising that 'national democrats' in the non-Russian republics and members of certain religious groups should have been in the van of what became known as the Democratic movement, for they had greater hopes of securing at least passive mass support than did progressive Russian intellectuals, who were more isolated from their potential popular 'base'. For writers, dramatists and other cultural figures their audience or readership was restricted essentially to the educated élite—a substantial group of 25 million by 1970 (from which one has to deduct Party functionaries and other *nomenklatura* appointees naturally unsympathetic to critical ideas). One should not of course generalize: Andrei Sakharov was a highly privileged scientist, Petro Grigorenko an army general. Initially the movement was 'carried' by members of the cultural and scientific intelligentsia, although with time it became more differentiated socially. Using data on 738 individuals, Amalrik arrived at the following percentage breakdown (*c.*1968): academics, 45; in the arts, 22; engineers and technicians, 13; publishing, medicine, law, 9; workers, 6; and students, 5. But in 1976 40 per cent of those arrested are said to have been workers (Alexeyeva 1985). This may be an overestimate, but recent research confirms that the trend existed. A study of 385 former oppositionists (1956–85) shows that when first arrested 29.1 per cent belonged to the cohort aged 16–20 in 1956 and that over 71 per cent had some higher education; the proportion of 'intellectuals in the humanities' is put at 29.4 per cent (Voronkov 1993).

Statistics are of limited help in coming to terms with dissent. It can best be understood through the psychological development of the individuals concerned. Most underwent some traumatic early experience: arrest or punishment for some minor fault, loss of a close relative in Stalin's camps, or sudden confrontation with unpleasant socio-political realities (e.g. loss of élite privileges) after a 'cocooned' upbringing. The revelations at the Twentieth congress led many to formulate doubts they had previously entertained in private, perhaps for years. For one woman questions first arose when, as a law student in 1940, she had to help confiscate the possessions of peasants convicted for trifling offences; they were fortified in 1948 when official policy became anti-Semitic (Kaminskaya 1982). Grigorenko's friend Sergei Pisarev, although subjected to thirty-eight bouts of torture under Stalin, wrote to the dictator in 1953 contesting the accusations against the Kremlin doctors. Grigorenko himself dated his opposition from 1961, when he publicly criticized the new Party programme for its half-hearted condemnation of Stalin. Leonid Pliushch lost his Communist faith in 1956 and five years later took part in a university *fronde*. Others came to the movement because as writers they were frustrated by censorship, or found that the system made it impossible for them to perform their professional duties properly. Of great importance was the role of circles (*kruzhki*) of friends and colleagues, which would meet informally to listen to camp songs or ballads by Okudzhava or Vysotsky—and exchange the latest political gossip.[4] Potentially these groups, which might be forty to fifty strong, were nuclei of clandestine political parties, but it was far harder for such organizations to form than it had been a century earlier owing to the ubiquity of police informers and listening devices. It must be stressed that under Khrushchev members of the cultural opposition were still basically loyal to the system and objected only to certain features, which they hoped would be corrected by timely reform from above.

The turning point came in 1965. The Brezhnev–Kosygin regime (see Chapter 9), after some months of vacillation, embarked on a reactionary course. Criticism of the 'cult of the individual' ceased and it became harder to publish controversial literary works. In April 1965 a group of young writers, who took the name SMOG (in Russian, the initials stood for courage, thought, image, and profundity) held a demonstration before the USW building in Moscow—the first since 1927. Some two hundred people took part. A collection of short stories and poems called *Sphinxes*, edited by Valerii Tarsis, was published without having been submitted to the censorship. Although not the first volume of its kind—it had been preceded in 1958–61 by *Syntax* and *Phoenix*—its appearance marked the beginning of *samizdat*, which was to become the 'trade-mark' of the Democratic movement.

The term was an acronym modelled ironically on Gosizdat (State Publishing House) and meant literally 'self-publishing'. The idea caught on quickly. Petitions, appeals, accounts of trials, philosophical treatises, fictional works, and political manifestos were reproduced in multiple copies by skilled women typists and distributed by hand (the spying activities of the postal service made this too dangerous to use), further copies being made in the process. Photographers also helped. But until the mid-1970s such documents were rarely duplicated or photocopied, since such equipment was not allowed to be sold to private individuals (some machines were constructed by do-it-yourself methods). Initially at least most of those involved in this variant of the 'chain-mail' system worked without payment. Expenses were sometimes met by selling the 'product', at a price usually determined by its bulk. The operation was always risky, liable to interruption at any moment when premises were searched. It became still more difficult once the KGB began to check the typefaces of all typewriters (details of which were centrally registered). Although *samizdat* publications reached thousands, recipients could not ensure that a response on their part would reach the original author, which naturally inhibited the free exchange of ideas. However, *samizdat* was the only possible way of evading tight censorship controls and certainly a great advance on the previous practice of 'writing for the drawer'.

Thanks to the aid given by certain foreign correspondents, some material was smuggled out of the country. By 1971 about seven hundred such items had reached the West—a small fraction of the total produced. An archive was established in Amsterdam which by the mid-1980s contained over four thousand documents. Several works were published abroad, in what was called *tamizdat* (= 'published over there'), and their content reported back by foreign broadcasting stations, so that they reached a mass audience. On the debit side of the ledger it should be added that some Western journalists or their employers occasionally treated information obtained through unofficial channels in an irresponsible manner, for instance by reproducing fraudulent material that had been circulated by the KGB in order to discredit the movement.

In the autumn of 1965 the police arrested two well-known writers, Andrei Siniavsky and Yulii Daniel. Under the pseudonym 'A. Terts' Siniavsky had written a devastating critique of socialist realism. Daniel was the author of a chilling satire on Stalin's terror.

Alexander Yesenin-Volpin, son of the poet Sergei Yesenin, circulated a 'civic appeal' warning that to treat literary activity as anti-state conduct was to revert to Stalinist methods. He called on the public to exercise vigilance. On Constitution Day (5 December) over one hundred students from the literary institute where Siniavsky had taught rallied in Moscow's Maiakovsky Square and demanded that the writers should receive a fair and open trial. The militia had been tipped off. The demonstrators' banners were seized and twenty persons briefly detained. The trial itself was a surrealistic judicial farce. Applying 'a dogged literalism' (Alexeyeva), the prosecution attributed to the two authors the views of their fictional characters, as if the latter were in the dock. The writers were sentenced to seven and five years' imprisonment respectively.[5]

The government followed up this move, clearly designed to intimidate the intelligentsia, by amending the RSFSR criminal code to make it an offence to engage in 'propaganda or agitation designed to weaken or subvert Soviet power' or to 'disseminate false fabrications' with such intent.[6] Curiously, *samizdat* itself was not mentioned, presumably because it was embarrassing to admit its existence. The outcome of the trial was to discredit the regime and touch off a wave of petitions. One was signed by thirteen luminaries from various professional backgrounds, among them the scientists Kapitsa and Sakharov, the writer Paustovsky, the cinematographer Romm, the historian and diplomat Maisky, and the ballerina Plisetskaia. Alexander Ginzburg, Yurii Galanskov, and two others compiled a *White Book* containing the transcript of the Siniavsky–Daniel trial and some of the letters of protest circulating on their behalf, and were in turn arrested. In January 1967 another protest demonstration was held, again before Pushkin's statue on Maiakovsky Square. According to Sakharov, who was present, the scene was photographed by the KGB with infra-red cameras and the film shown to Party leaders. The demonstrators demanded freedom for 'the Four' and repeal of the new repressive decrees.

In May 1967 Solzhenitsyn entered the fray with an open letter to the USW's fourth all-Union congress. He had of course not been invited to attend, but in the corridors the writers talked of nothing else, for his letter was the first direct challenge to the censorship in forty years. Solzhenitsyn pointed out that its very existence was illegal; its 'intolerable oppression', he argued, was prejudicial to Russia's best interests, since it deprived world literature of 'the fruits . . . of our spiritual experience'. All censorship should be abolished and publishers freed from state control. The writers' union's task, he added, was to defend its members, not to help persecute them. Although his charges were scrupulously ignored at public sessions of the congress, eighty writers responded to his move by signing letters of protest.

The Maiakovsky Square demonstrators were dealt with in separate trials in February and August 1967. The sentences were relatively mild: three years' imprisonment for the two principal accused, one of whom was the writer Vladimir Bukovsky. Then in his mid-twenties, Bukovsky's career had been cut short by arrest and two years' confinement in a special psychiatric hospital (see below, p. 191) for his deviant political views. He stood four-square for democracy, civil rights, and the rule of law. In the preliminary investigation and later in court he showed remarkable composure and determination; even one of the KGB officers came to admire his courage. The woman judge allowed the accused considerable latitude to state their case, perhaps because she knew the indictment was absurd. The proceedings were supposed to be in public, but the court was packed with policemen and their stooges in plain clothes. Despite this someone succeeded in noting down or recording the proceedings, which then circulated in *samizdat*. The verdict had been predetermined by the Party authorities. In his final address Bukovsky argued that without freedom of opinion the civil rights provisions in the Constitution were meaningless; citizens were under an obligation to display civic courage and to behave honourably. It was 'a momentous event, . . . the first time that such merciless criticism of the Soviet system had been uttered at an open court hearing' (Kaminskaya 1982). Bukovsky remained behind bars after his sentence expired—another continuing feature of Soviet quasi-judicial practice—and was not released until December 1976, when he was exchanged for a Chilean political prisoner.

In January 1968 came another political trial, that of 'the Four'. They received severer sentences which cost one defendant his life: the writer Galanskov died in the Gulag four years later. The proceedings had an even greater public impact than their forerunners. Partly under the influence of the 'Prague spring', the next few months saw a wave of protest. Appeals attracted dozens and even hundreds of signatures. Two events stand out. One was the courageous response of seven Moscow dissidents to news of the Warsaw

Pact troops' entry into Czechoslovakia at Soviet behest. On 25 August they assembled in Red Square. Hardly had they unfurled their banners than they were set upon by KGB agents. From a practical viewpoint their action was foolhardy, but as one of them said later, 'for ten minutes I was a citizen'. Larisa Daniel, wife of the jailed writer, thought that 'to have remained silent would have been to lie'. The seven saved their country's honour at a moment when the USSR faced world-wide condemnation.

The *Chronicle*; Sakharov and others

The other development was the appearance in April of the first issue of the *Chronicle of Current Events*. This was a bulletin, patterned on one put out by the Crimean Tatars but more ambitious in scope, which sought to provide regular, accurate information about the activities of a steadily widening variety of opposition groups (Reddaway 1972). It became the unofficial organ of the Democratic movement, the principal means of holding its multifarious strands together. By July 1972 twenty-six, and by mid-1983 no less than sixty-four issues had been produced, all by elementary *samizdat* methods. When one editor was arrested, another soon took over,[7] although there were moments when it seemed as though the slender thread had been cut; between late 1972 and spring 1974 four issues were compiled that could not be circulated until later. The *Chronicle* relied on the services of hundreds of anonymous correspondents across the land. The geographical spread of the network was impressive, as was the breadth of editorial coverage. Space was accorded to individuals or groups of very divergent views, with a minimum of editorial comment. The aim was not to guide the movement but to reflect it. The *Chronicle* was not the organ of any party or ideological tendency. In this it differed from underground publications in pre-revolutionary days, which had been highly partisan. This was testimony to the democrats' intellectual maturity. Ideology had become discredited by its abuse under the Soviet regime. Few people still believed that there must be a single 'correct' way to a bright future, or that a single group held the key to its discovery. Instead, the watchwords were tolerance and pragmatism. The *Chronicle*'s 'platform' was defence of legality, *glasnost'* (freedom of information) and basic human rights. It was, so to speak, a minimalist position—the lowest common denominator of all competing tendencies. On its cover each issue cited Article 190 of the Universal Declaration of Human Rights: every individual may hold or express his opinion and obtain and spread information or ideas through any medium, regardless of frontiers.

Legalistic tactics were dictated by circumstances. They cannot be attributed with assurance to any one individual. As we have seen, they were common to Protestant and Ukrainian activists. Among Russian intellectuals priority has been claimed for Yesenin-Volpin who distinguished between obedience to the law, which was binding on all citizens, and subservience to ideology, which was not. This was a valid distinction which soon secured general acceptance. For the dissidents were 'disloyal' only in the eyes of a government that itself scorned the law. At least some of them were still beholden to Marxist ideas, which were thought to be compatible with liberal and democratic principles. Gradually their thinking moved to the right, mainly because the regime turned a deaf ear to all pleas for dialogue.

In 1969 the activists began to 'internationalize' their struggle. Fifteen sent the United Nations a letter detailing human rights violations in the USSR, which was signed by an 'Action Group for the Defence of Human Rights'. Neither this nor four subsequent letters received a reply. Yet the move was fundamental in ensuring the movement's future. Sakharov and two fellow physicists, who were behind it, were more pragmatic (and perhaps more experienced politically) than some of their literary forerunners. They appreciated the international force of the argument that a nuclear superpower which repressed its own citizens could not be a reliable partner in détente with foreign states, and that progress in both spheres had to be complementary. This novel idea ultimately found expression in the 1975 Helsinki accords. It made Soviet internal policies a legitimate matter of concern to a wide swathe of international opinion. The three-man Moscow Human Rights Committee (HRC), formed in November 1970, obtained affiliation with one of the non-governmental agencies recognized by the UN. This did not protect it from repression, but at least ensured that this received media coverage abroad. The focus of its activities became more academic: studying and publicizing Soviet human rights violations and helping victims with legal advice, instead of protests and demonstrations. These would have been counter-productive in the harsher political climate that prevailed after 1971–2, when the KGB launched a wave of arrests of oppositionists.

The effectiveness of the new tactics owed much to Sakharov's immense prestige, which in 1975 won him the Nobel Peace Prize. If Solzhenitsyn was the 'prophet' of dissent, Sakharov was the movement's 'saint'. Alarmed at the direction the country's leaders were taking, he became ever more closely associated with political and civic causes. In 1966 he protested against the new repressive laws and then wrote to Brezhnev in support of 'the Four'. His *Thoughts on Progress, Peaceful Co-existence, and Intellectual Freedom* (1968) urged democratization of Soviet society as an essential step to avert world-wide nuclear catastrophe. The pamphlet sold eighteen million copies in the West, but in the USSR people were punished for distributing it. Sakharov lost his security clearance and came to realize that his aim of 'convergence' between the superpowers was too sanguine. With characteristic idealism he donated his entire savings to charity after his wife died of cancer, and in 1970 organized a campaign to rescue the scientist Zhores Medvedev from a psychiatric prison. Its success led him to intervene on behalf of many other victims of repression, including Jews and Crimean Tatars. In 1972 Sakharov marked the fiftieth anniversary of the formation of the USSR with a collective letter demanding an amnesty for all political prisoners. He also published a memorandum he had previously sent to Brezhnev developing his earlier arguments for a reorientation of Soviet domestic and foreign policies. Here he anticipated Gorbachev's *perestroika*, but at the time his ideas seemed utopian. Although under constant surveillance, his moral stature was so colossal that the KGB hesitated to move directly against him.

With other dissidents they were less circumspect. The historian Andrei Amalrik, on securing release from Siberian exile (see Chapter 5), was kept under surveillance; it soon became clear that a new 'case' was being prepared against him. Before his rearrest and sentence to another three years' hard labour (November 1970) Amalrik wrote a mordant essay, 'Will the USSR Survive until 1984?', in which he analysed the strengths and weaknesses of the regime and its critics. The Orwellian allusion in the title was deliberate, for Amalrik saw the country's educated élite as having 'the psychology of officials'. Lacking sincerely held values, they were willing to adjust their views as required and 'look[ed] on the regime as a lesser evil compared with the painful process of changing it'. Only an external shock, he argued, could cause the system to crumble. Amalrik also criticized the dissidents for being so fragmented, and for this was gently taken to task by his friend Petr Yakir.[8]

Yakir was the author of a bold letter to *Kommunist* (1969) demanding that Stalin be posthumously tried for his crimes. An honest, trusting soul who had spent seventeen years in the Gulag, he was one of the few dissidents who, under intense police pressure, agreed to recant his 'errors' in public (1973). Grigorenko writes charitably that this act of weakness should not be held against him. Not everyone was able to emulate the former general's moral stamina. In 1964–5 he spent a year in various prisons and psycho-prisons which gave him invaluable insight into the sinister purpose of the latter institutions. In 1968 he took up the cause of the deported Crimean Tatars and was again briefly arrested; later he was assaulted in the street by drunken police agents. Despite such harassment he frequently attended trials of citizens indicted for defending their constitutional rights, and in May 1969 again found himself placed in a mental asylum. He resisted every illegal move taken against him, so that it took twelve men to force him into a strait-jacket. He went on hunger strike, wrote letters protesting at the cruelties perpetrated on his fellow inmates, and told the invest-igating 'doctor': 'if you recognize as normal only citizens who bow obediently before every arbitrary act, then I am abnormal. I am not capable of such obedience, however often you beat me.'[9]

Such courage inspired a whole generation. We may mention here only two other individuals: Pavel Litvinov, grandson of Soviet Russia's pre-war foreign commissar, and Anatolii Marchenko. Unlike most fellow dissidents, Marchenko first earned his living by manual work. In 1960 he escaped from the Gulag and tried to cross the frontier illegally, but was caught and sentenced to six years in jail. In *My Testimony* (1968) he gives an accomplished literary account of his camp experiences. 'Honest to the point of obstinacy', as Sakharov puts it, while in the camp bath-house Marchenko was asked by a guard why he was so thin. His reply—'because the Communists drank my blood'—earned him two additional years. Rearrested in 1975, he received yet another sentence of fifteen years in 1981 which cost him his life. He died just before the dictatorial system that killed him itself received its death warrant.

Before turning to examine this system, let us note the Democratic movement's signal achievement in bringing together spokesmen for a variety of national groups—Russians, Ukrainians, Jews, Tatars, Balts—each of which had grounds for suspicion of the others. Shared experience in the camps often helped to overcome such prejudice. The civil rights activists realized that 'without national liberation there can be no individual freedom or genuine democratization', as one early writer put it—in other words, that the Soviet empire should be allowed to break up if its constituent nations wanted independence. Amalrik correctly predicted that the Baltic peoples would lead the way. Even Solzhenitsyn, who propagated a revival of Russian national traditions, in his *Letter to the Soviet Leaders* (1973) was prepared to let the non-Slav peoples go their own way if they insisted. It is also true that the human rights movement was an unstable coalition that was bound to break apart once its goals had been achieved, and that these men, prone to think in universal categories, did not sufficiently appreciate the destructive force of nationalism. But this was a defect these leaders shared with contemporary Western politicians who had infinitely greater resources of information at their disposal.

9 The Lubianka and the Kremlin

The KGB

As the Committee for State Security (KGB) managed to preserve its secrets once the USSR collapsed, much remains obscure about the history of the organization that played such a cardinal role in sustaining the Party's dictatorship. The relationship between the Lubianka and the Kremlin (more correctly, Old Square, the location of the CPSU CC and its apparatus) was complex. It fluctuated over the years. Although Khrushchev had managed to bring the security police under Party control, from 1961 onward it began to regain something of its former autonomy. Shelepin and his successor, Semichastny, played a part in engineering Khrushchev's downfall. The resurgence of the KGB was accelerated in May 1967 by the appointment of Andropov as its chief, evidently with the assignment of cracking down on dissent. Six years later he was elevated to full membership of the Politburo, an honour shared by the Defence and Foreign ministers, Grechko and Gromyko. Contemporaries thought that the trio acted as a kind of supportive 'inner cabinet' (Berner *et al.* 1975). In 1978 a minor change in the KGB's official designation made its head a member of the Council of Ministers. Several security officials, notably Aliev and Pugo, rose to senior rank in the Party. By 1981 no less than four full members of the Politburo had police affiliations, whereas twenty years earlier this had been true of only a single candidate member (Hauslohner 1990). The security organs' 'representation' on the CC likewise increased.

The KGB's effectives have been put at nearly half a million in 1973 and 700,000 in 1986. These figures exclude the border troops, who numbered around a quarter of a million by the latter date, as well as an unquantifiable 'active reserve' (mainly veterans) and an army of secret informers (*seksoty*). The recruitment, disposition and remuneration of all these agents could be decided 'in house'. Formally, the KGB came under the Party CC's Administrative

Organs department, which had to approve appointments, and as if to symbolize its subordinate status it submitted an annual report to the CC. Andropov also had to put up with three deputies who apparently reported directly to Brezhnev. But in reality the control system was reciprocal. The two hierarchies were interlocked in a power-sharing arrangement that by and large suited those involved in it. The security police maintained files on individuals at every level of the Party and state apparatus, and could use this information (colloquially called *kompromat*) to compromise those it wished to harm.

By the mid-1970s it had the physical wherewithal to substitute itself for the Party. However, this option does not seem to have been entertained, even though the General Secretary was clearly no longer up to the mark and the regime showed signs of degeneration. How can one explain such restraint? Andropov was not another Beria. He shared his forerunner's cold-blooded cynicism but had a sharp analytical intellect—perhaps the best in the ruling group—and even some pretensions to culture. He probably reckoned that any overt move to rock the boat would provoke resistance among the more professionally minded Party cadres, and that it was enough to maintain the existing thorough police penetration of the *nomenklatura*—or else simply thought that the time was not yet ripe for action. In any case the stalemate, which lasted nigh on a decade, was symptomatic of the latent crisis in the entire political system. The regime could not revert to Stalin-type terror without condemning itself to isolation and backwardness, yet by embarking on reform it risked unleashing forces that could not readily be contained.

Among the general public the KGB cultivated an impression of omnipotence, but in fact its controls were selective. Technical and financial constraints made universal surveillance a utopian goal. In the last resort the organization's power rested on the willingness of so many Soviet citizens to denounce one another for deviant thought or conduct. Such delators were motivated in part by the hope of securing material advantages (e.g. better accommodation) and in part by ideological zeal; another factor was fear of the victims' revenge should their activity ever become known (Marie-Schwartzenberg 1993). Their paymasters understood well the frailties of the human psyche. Indeed, psychology was among the scientific disciplines in which officers were coached as the service became more 'professional' under Andropov's guidance. The objective was to bring about political conformity by the use of sophisticated manipulative methods rather than by coercion and physical violence, as before. From this standpoint every arrest was a setback, since it recognized the existence of an 'incorrigible' internal enemy.

The controls which the KGB exercised over the media, and the flow of information generally, allowed it to engage in a variety of propaganda and psychological warfare operations. Among them was a major public relations drive, designed to improve its tarnished image at home and abroad. By 1977, when the centennial of Dzerzhinsky's birth was celebrated on a lavish scale, some two thousand books had been published extolling the security services' accomplishments over the years (Knight 1986). This campaign seems to have had some effect. In any event not everyone lived in constant dread of 'the organs' (as they were popularly called). According to an opinion poll taken in 1991–2, 29 per cent of respondents in the RSFSR admitted to having feared the police to some degree. In Ukraine the figure was lower (23 per cent), in Kazakhstan higher (36 per cent); the data doubtless understate reality and none were recorded from the Baltic states (White and Kryshtanovskaya 1993).

Administratively the KGB was divided into sixteen chief directorates, divisions and sections, whose areas of responsibility to some extent overlapped. The bureaucratic refinements of this vast hierarchy need not detain us. Of particular relevance in controlling Soviet society was the Fourth division, which watched over communications, the Sixth, for surveillance of industrial employees, and the Fifth, whose functions included supervision of the churches and 'ideological defence'. Created in the late 1960s, its head for many years was reputedly General Bobkov, and initially at any rate it had a relatively small staff.

Repression of dissent

From dissident sources one can build up a rough picture of its *modus operandi*. Routine surveillance of suspects, known in police jargon as '*pk*' (*postoiannyi kontrol'*), might be personal (i.e. through agents or informers) and/or by electronic eavesdropping ('Operation M'). By the 1960s technology had reached the point where a pin-sized 'bug' could be fastened to a person's coat, for example in a crowded bus, and his subsequent conversations overheard within a 500-metre radius (Savitsky 1991). More usually such devices were inserted in telephones or the walls of buildings, so that citizens anxious to preserve their privacy preferred to use street call boxes. (Since there were no conventional public phone-directories, one had to memorize one's friends' numbers!) In apartment blocks concierges kept watch on residents' movements, as did 'floor ladies' in hotels, where the surveillance system was perforce more elaborate. The methods used in the late Stalin era for spying into people's correspondence were subsequently revealed by an operative who emigrated (Avzeger 1991): they involved a secret bureau installed in the post office and extremely thorough procedures; any incautious expression might lead to the letter-writer's summary arrest and disappearance.

By the 1960s disloyal utterances of this or any other kind were more likely to lead to the offender being warned to mend his ways—initially perhaps by the secretary of the Party 'cell' at his workplace and then, in the case of persistent 'error', at local KGB headquarters. If the suspect's attitude was uncooperative, such 'friendly chats' might well lead to loss of one's job. Other employers, once forewarned, would be reluctant to engage such an individual, and if they did so would offer him work beneath his qualifications. Refusal to accept it could lead to exile on a charge of 'parasitism', the regulations on which were tightened up (1975). Thus Grigorenko was successively refused permission to work as an engineer (his former profession), carpenter, and chauffeur; after a brief spell as a concierge, in which capacity his superior intelligence attracted unfavourable notice, he ended up selling fruit and vegetables—until he was put behind bars again.

The day-to-day struggle against police harassment of this kind absorbed the energies of countless citizens who happened to hold independent views. For many the next unpleasantness was a search of their apartment for 'dubious' books, *samizdat* material and other *kompromat*. This might be carried out by the regular police (militia), which formally came under the Interior ministry (MVD) but had many KGB agents on its staff and operated under the latter's supervision. To comply with the letter of the law, investigators would normally be accompanied by an 'independent' witness, such as the concierge, who on occasion would show his or her true colours by enthusiastically joining in the search. If a suspect could alert his friends in time, they might be able to rush to his premises and lend moral support. When Grigorenko's apartment was searched in November 1968 no fewer than fifty persons assembled, for to the police officers' amazement they had heard an instant report by a foreign broadcasting station. But their presence could not prevent confiscation of material that had nothing to do with any alleged 'anti-Soviet' activity. Such items had in theory to be returned to the offender on expiry of his sentence, but all too often they languished in the KGB's voluminous archive (administered by the Tenth section). Some have since been returned to their rightful owners.

Similarly, the rights of persons under arrest were liable to gross infringement, since the security organs had much influence over the procuracy and the courts. The criminal code gave them the right to investigate 'especially dangerous crimes against the state' (EDCS); these powers were enlarged in December 1965 to cover theft of state property, and in practice were interpreted elastically. As noted above, it was common for the public to be denied access to a supposedly 'open' trial by filling the courtroom with police agents. These people might afterwards be entertained to vodka and *zakuski* as a reward for their pains. Another ruse was to hold the proceedings in a provincial town remote from the eyes of relatives, friends, or foreign correspondents. In such localities the police were in any case less likely to be particular about legal formalities. In 1975 Sergei Kovalev, a prominent Moscow human rights activist, was taken to Vilnius for trial and given a heavy sentence. It is now known that from 1967 to 1975 the number of people prosecuted annually under Articles 70 (or its predecessor) and 190–1 of the criminal code averaged 176, as against 254 in 1959–66 and 89 in 1977–86 (Reddaway 1993).[1]

The Stalinist 'show trial' was no longer characteristic of this era, but this does not mean that proceedings were fair or the verdict properly founded in law. On the contrary, the judicial system was manipulated by the political authorities in a host of ways. 'I never encountered a truly independent judge,' remarks Kaminskaya. One of them said privately that political nonconformists deserved to have their eyes gouged out. The court performance of judges, assessors, and procurators was regularly vetted by the local Party organization, which detailed a functionary for the purpose. In Moscow microphones hidden in the courtroom transmitted the proceedings directly to those who 'needed to know'. Records of political cases bore a particular coded designation and were registered separately; such cases were also dealt with by a special bench. Trials were brief. Much time was taken up by formalities and little spent on actual examination of the evidence.

Defence lawyers laboured under many disadvantages. In political cases they had to be chosen from a special panel of advocates granted 'access', a limitation that had no basis in law; in Moscow such persons comprised only one-tenth of bar members. They were normally allowed to see their client in pre-trial detention (*after* the preliminary investigation had been completed, as noted in Chapter 3) and to consult the records of the case; but no proper accommodation was provided for this, and conversations between lawyer and client might well be 'bugged'. In court witnesses for the defence were sometimes not called and valid objections overruled. There were cases of such witnesses being taunted and the judge cheerfully joining in the mockery. In 1968, when sentences of up to seven years' imprisonment were pronounced on 'the Four', there were shouts of 'too little!' by police agents in disguise. In political cases acquittals were unknown. Transcripts of the proceedings were not provided and appeals for judicial review usually rejected. Very few prisoners of conscience benefited from any of the four amnesties granted during the 1970s.

Khrushchev's enthusiasm for the death penalty was tempered by his successors. About thirty cases were reported in the press annually. Not all of these were necessarily carried out, but neither were all such sentences reported. The Supreme Court, to its credit, proposed marking the fiftieth anniversary of the revolution by eliminating the death penalty for certain economic crimes, but the idea did not find favour (Hazard 1971). For political offenders the usual sentence was a term in a prison camp (officially now called a 'colony'), followed by one of exile. First and minor offenders were supposed to serve their term in the republic where they resided; others were despatched to a remote region. Camps were located throughout the country, but the main complexes were now in the Mordovian autonomous republic and Perm' province, respectively south-east and north-east of Moscow. In 1969 the Mordovian complex, Dubrovlag, had one central prison and eighteen known camps, designated by numbers, and an estimated 15,000 inmates of whom 2,000 were 'politicals' (Reddaway 1972). There are now thought to have been about 1,200 camps in all, with a population of over one million.[2] In addition there were 656 regular and 'investigatory' prisons. One of the most notorious, at Vladimir, harboured a number of political offenders. They were crammed ten to a cell, with the most rudimentary hygienic and exercise facilities.

Similar overcrowding was the rule when prisoners were transported to their camp, first in vans (*voronki*) and then in 'Stolypin' rail wagons (named after the pre-revolutionary prime minister) with compartments that might hold up to thirty people rather than the regulation eight, for a journey taking as long as one month. While in transit windows were kept closed, even in the summer heat. Warm food was provided once every four days. Camps were enclosed by barbed wire and watch-towers, as in the 'good old days' recalled by 'faithful Ruslan', the guard dog in Vladimov's story of that name. Each had its allotted regime—'ordinary', 'hard', 'intensified', and 'strict' (or 'special')—which determined prisoners' work norms, food rations, privileges (correspondence, visits etc.), and general chance of survival. The camp authorities were empowered to punish prisoners by transferring them to a harsher regime and had much leeway in interpreting the 'regulations on internal order'. These regulations were revised twice (1969, 1972) in a more restrictive sense. They were not published until 1986, but their content had previously been reconstructed by Western scholars on the basis of dissidents' reports. They laid down, for instance, that prisoners had to wear distinctive marks on their outer clothing and were not allowed to receive parcels until they had completed half their sentence. The content of such parcels was also rigidly prescribed.

According to regulations the food ration should suffice to maintain 'normal vital activity', but norms could be reduced for those in punishment cells or under a strict regime. This meant an intake of 1,300 calories in lieu of 2,500—far from adequate to maintain health, especially where the obligation to work remained in effect. Moreover, the food supplied was often rotten, so that prisoners were reduced to eating grass or nettles to compensate for its deficiency. Medical facilities were primitive and sick prisoners often treated as malingerers. Tuberculosis was widespread. (No information is yet available about death rates in this period.) A complaints procedure existed, but was a mere formality since it gave vast powers to officers at the most subordinate levels in the hierarchy. Although the camps were run by regular police, the last word remained with the KGB.

How far, one might innocently ask, did the security authorities respect the law? The question cannot really be posed in such terms, for in a very real sense the KGB's will *was* the law. We should speak rather of a system of 'legalized arbitrariness', in that 'legality may give way to arbitrariness whenever political interests demand it' (Ioffe 1985). The key terms here are *expediency* and *discretion*. By and large, the extent to which laws and regulations were observed diminished as one went down the hierarchical ladder. Junior officials were under pressure to obtain results, and their superiors left them discretion as to how far it was expedient to go in abrogating rules that, although formally binding on all, were essentially decorative in purpose. Or, as one Western legal scholar puts it neatly, 'rule violation is part of the rule system itself' (Feldbrugge 1977).

Physical abuse of prisoners was 'not routine', or so the careful compilers of an Amnesty International report (1975/1980) concluded. However, there were cases of beatings and even murder at Vladimir, in Uzbekistan and elsewhere—usually by criminal prisoners (*blatnye*) at the behest of guards or with their sanction. In 1972 prisoners in one Karelian camp rioted after a *zek* was 'accidentally' killed by a guard. Several prisoners who had co-operated with the administration in the so-called 'internal order section' were in turn put to death. Violence of this kind seems to have been infrequent. Far more prevalent were hunger-strikes and acts of passive resistance. Indeed, the camps were the scene of a continual struggle between prisoners and officials in which the former learned to fight for their legal rights. By the 1980s women's camps in Mordovia had reputedly become 'a veritable protest centre' (Karklins 1989). As early as 1969 there was a wave of hunger strikes in the Dubrovlag complex linked to International Human Rights Day, details of which were reported in the *Chronicle of Current Events*. Such action was fraught with hazard, since the authorities responded by forcefeeding participants, using clumsy and violent methods. Where hunger-strikes were undertaken to protest maltreatment of other prisoners, especially if the victims came from other ethnic groups, they were an effective way of demonstrating solidarity that helped to sustain the inmates' morale.

The lot of exiles was only slightly easier. They had to live in an assigned area (normally in the east) under surveillance, and to perform manual labour in state enterprises. They were subject to much administrative harassment and sometimes had their terms extended for arbitrary reasons. Even after release they faced discrimination, being obliged to live in rural regions (or at least not in cities or the border zone), and to report every so often to the local police for as many years as authority thought fit. From 1972 onward some well-known prisoners of conscience were made to emigrate against their will, on pain of further incarceration if they refused. Among those so treated were the historian Amalrik and the writers Brodsky, Siniavsky, Maksimov—and, most notably of all, Solzhenitsyn (February 1974). They were then as a rule deprived of Soviet citizenship. This repugnant (and illegal) tactic did not achieve its aim of beheading the Democratic movement, since new leaders emerged. Such actions attracted adverse publicity abroad. This embarrassed the Soviet government and harmed its propaganda image. When Western governments gingerly took up the cause of human rights in the USSR, they often managed to win concessions for individual activists. To some extent the severity of the KGB's treatment of dissidents increased or diminished in proportion to the strength of foreign pressure.

Psychiatric abuse

The most vicious weapon in the security police's armoury was the abuse of psychiatry for political ends. The practice of putting healthy people in mental asylums seems to have begun under Stalin, when victims regarded it as preferable to slow death in a labour camp. When the Gulag was dismantled the KGB found this a useful alternative way of dealing with people whom it was inconvenient to 'frame' and put on trial. Some victims were indeed sent to an asylum after quasi-legal proceedings, but most were committed under civil procedure, for this required no more than a single psychiatrist's opinion in the first instance. Several medical 'experts' were willing to prostitute their knowledge for non-professional ends.[3] Their diagnoses abounded in vague expressions such as 'psychomotor excitement', 'sluggish schizophrenia', or even 'reformist delusions'. Individuals so remanded were detained in one of eleven 'special psychiatric hospitals' (SPH) run under KGB auspices

('Dr' Lunts was once spotted wearing a KGB colonel's uniform!). The situation was grotesque: 'the dissenter is immersed in a highly disturbed environment, surrounded . . . by genuine patients with severe mental illnesses, many of whom have committed violent crimes such as rape, assault, and murder' (Reddaway 1984). He could not contact defence counsel and was dependent on the little that relatives or friends could do on his behalf. The 'treatment' administered was punitive and had no therapeutic value. The drug sulphazin in particular was most painful and produced a high fever, tremors, and loss of memory. Some five hundred cases have been authenticated of persons subjected to psychiatric abuse of this kind between 1962 and 1983. About half of them were human rights activists, the others religious believers, would-be emigrants, and national minority representatives. The Serbsky Institute alone examined, in the course of some thirty years from 1961, 370 individuals referred to it for deviant political behaviour (Kondrat'ev 1994).

Even the use of such extreme methods did not bring the KGB the flood of recantations it expected. Some patients, encouraged by an informal guide to behaviour compiled by Bukovsky, followed Grigorenko's lead in resisting assault on their persons. Outside the SPHs Alexander Podrabinek and others set up a 'working commission' on psychiatric abuse (1977) which accumulated and published a mass of data and built up a 'resourceful, flexible infra-structure' (Bloch and Reddaway 1984). Of particular value were the independent examinations of former SPH inmates conducted by a few genuine psychiatric consultants, which showed that there had been no medical reason for their incarceration. The commission members were arrested and given heavy sentences. Anatolii Koriagin, the best known of these courageous doctors, was himself subjected to physical torture. Such obviously unethical conduct served to mobilize international professional opinion. In 1977 the World Psychiatric Association belatedly condemned Soviet malpractices and set up a committee to monitor them. When it became clear that its report would be critical, the USSR chose to withdraw from the organization (1983) rather than face overwhelming censure. The move was widely seen as an admission of guilt. The KGB had lost its battle to establish its international credibility—and the principal culprit was clearly identified as the political regime from which it took orders.

Brezhnev

The chief characteristic of this regime was the monopoly on power exercised by the CPSU. Over the twenty years that followed the fall of Khrushchev the Party's leaders did nothing intentionally to weaken the Party's pre-eminence in government. On the contrary, they sought to reinforce the apparatus of social control and to preserve the secrecy in which the decision-making process was enshrouded. As we shall see presently, the Party's real authority was gradually becoming eroded. This threat did not go unobserved by some of the more percipient members of the apparatus, but timid efforts on their part to avert trouble by timely reform ran up against the inertia of the bulk of Party cadres, who had an interest in keeping things as they were. It was sufficient for them to dub proposed innovations as 'revisionist' for them to be quietly pigeon-holed.

The *immobilisme* of the political establishment found its physical embodiment in Leonid Ilyich Brezhnev. When chosen by his comrades to succeed Khrushchev as Party leader, he was 58 years old. His age was one factor in their decision. He was younger than Suslov or Kosygin (neither of whom aspired to the chief office) as well as Podgorny, but older and more experienced than Shelepin (46), Poliansky (47), or other ambitious members of the 'post-war generation' of Party leaders. Shelepin, a former KGB chief who had built up a powerful band of clients from his Komsomol days and made no secret of his ambitions, evoked apprehension among his Politburo colleagues. Brezhnev seemed a safe choice. Sturdily built, beetle-browed, he was—until his health gave way—a cheerful and sociable man who treated others courteously and had considerable charm. There was also a darker, more devious side to his character. In early life, before becoming an engineer and then entering politics, he had wanted to be an actor, and could still play a part to perfection. 'He was a fine artist,' remarked Shelepin ruefully many years later.

Another of his aides called Brezhnev 'a typical regional *apparat-chik*'. Intellectually he was a mediocrity, but this was not necessarily a disadvantage in the jockeying for power. He derived no pleasure from literature or the arts, and allegedly came to Politburo meetings carrying under his arm a copy of the satirical magazine *Krokodil*. He would have assistants prepare several drafts of a speech and then choose between them, for unlike Khrushchev he was incapable of drafting one himself. Burlatsky says that 'he never uttered an original idea'. Naturally rather indolent, he felt most at ease on hunting expeditions and favoured a self-indulgent life-style that others were quick to copy. Long before his accession to power officials noticed his inordinate fondness for parades and ceremonies—a weakness that later would be taken to ridiculous lengths as his vanity came to the fore. This defect of character, coupled with the temptations of near-absolute power, made him susceptible to flattery. Before many years had passed he would sponsor or tolerate a 'cult' of his own person that had even less justification than the self-adulation fostered by his predecessors Khrushchev and Stalin. To both men Brezhnev was indebted for his rise to high office, but his attitude towards them differed. He treated Khrushchev ungenerously, suppressing all public mention of his name, but sanctioned a positive re-evaluation of the great tyrant's historical 'achievements'.

Brezhnev's rule is often referred to as 'neo-Stalinist'. This is an exaggeration in that he did not revert to mass terror or genocide, although in other respects the system did indeed remain essentially unchanged. Under Gorbachev the entire period 1964–85 was written off as 'an era of stagnation'. This, too, was unfair, for although Brezhnev was a conservative who undertook no striking initiatives in any policy area, it was only after 1976, the year when he reached the zenith of his power, that his physical and mental abilities seriously degenerated. Even then he managed to preserve his patronage network. It has been calculated that this comprised 18.6 per cent of Central Committee members in 1976 and 17.4 per cent in 1981, although as the leader aged he had to rely more on the judgement of subordinates when making appointments (Willerton 1992).

At least from 1971 onward, the watchword of his administration was 'stability of cadres'. Frequently Brezhnev would urge Party officials 'to be sensitive to people, to their needs and desires, to set an example at work and in general conduct', as he put it in his address to the Twenty-fifth Party congress (February 1976). 'A solicitous attitude' in personnel policy, he claimed, had 'become firmly established': this meant avoiding unnecessary transfers and taking due account both of candidates' professional competence and their 'Party-mindedness'. The trouble was, of course, that these attributes were incompatible. The general tendency was for ministers and others to remain in office for lengthy periods—the record in this respect was held by Ishkov, minister of the Fishing Industry for no less than thirty-nine years (1940–79)—and to treat their jobs as sinecures, as a source of privilege and even private gain, while paying lip service to an ideology in which they no longer believed and which stood in crass contradiction to their careers and lifestyle. If the history of the Soviet leadership is regarded as having alternated between periods of dynamism and consolidation, then the Brezhnev era saw the latter principle taken to excess: 'motivated largely by an effort to restore the political security of officialdom, th[e] conservative reaction ultimately led the country back to stagnation' (Breslauer 1989).

Politics, 1964–76

In his first years the new leader sought to rule by consensus. Aware of his own limitations, and perhaps that he owed his primacy to a stroke of fortune, he made it a practice to consult his colleagues. His style was undramatic and strove to give an impression of normalcy. Party gatherings were held at regular intervals; institutional continuity was assured and there was none of the populist campaigning associated with Khrushchev, whose innovations were swiftly countermanded. The struggle for power at the top continued, but in a muted form. Brezhnev was fortunate in having Kosygin as a *de facto* junior partner. Entrusted with running the government, Kosygin was generally regarded as a competent technician. Although they differed over certain policy priorities, and Brezhnev seems to have seen Kosygin as a potential rival, there was less tension between the two men than between Khrushchev and Malenkov in 1953–5. Less smooth were Brezhnev's relations with Podgorny and Shelepin. In May 1965 the former lost out against Suslov in a butter-before-guns exchange and for several weeks suffered an illness that 'had all the marks of a political disease' (Tatu 1969). Later that year the Party organization in Khar'kov, with which Podgorny had been associated, was singled out for 'serious shortcomings' in its recruitment policies. In December he was chosen as head of state, a largely honorary position which Brezhnev himself had once occupied in rather similar circumstances. 'The spectacular formal promotion marked eviction from the Secretariat, the true centre of power.'

At the same time Shelepin suffered a blow with the liquidation of the joint Party-State control committee, which he had headed, and was demoted from the post of deputy prime minister 'to concentrate on his work in the Central Committee'. Semichastny, a Shelepin client, recalled later: 'Frequently Brezhnev would tell Shelepin irritatedly, "You have a different opinion from mine on every issue".' In 1967, when Shelepin opposed him over agricultural policy at an 'expanded' meeting of the Politburo⁴ attended by republic and regional leaders, he was summoned to Brezhnev's office and reprimanded. 'You have come out against me personally, although you know agriculture is my preserve. Don't try to teach me what to do!' (Barsukov 1992). Shortly afterwards he was sent to head the trade unions. He lost his secretaryship (September) but— in a typically Brezhnevian move—was allowed to remain in the Politburo until April 1975. A few months before his demotion in 1967 the same fate befell Semichastny, who was held responsible for the growth of dissent, and particularly for the defection abroad of Svetlana Allilueva, Stalin's daughter. He received a senior post in Ukraine. Another associate ended up as ambassador to Norway.

These bloodless victories helped Brezhnev to consolidate his personal power. By December 1965 he had already won majority support in both the Presidium and the Secretariat. The Twenty-third Party congress (March–April 1966) accorded him the title of 'General Secretary', redolent of Stalin. Between this congress and the next in 1971 well over half the senior officials were replaced. At Politburo level the proportion was 45 per cent (9 out of 20), in the Secretariat 60 per cent (6 out of 10), among heads of CC departments 67 per cent (14 out of 21), and in the Council of Ministers 75 per cent (67 out of 85). Among republican and provincial Party chiefs the figure was 72 per cent, the changes being particularly marked in the non-Slavic republics (Willerton 1992). But this was a 'gentle purge' in which those who lost their jobs generally made 'soft landings' in other positions of responsibility. They were not criticized, threatened, or abused, as had been the practice hitherto. For Brezhnev, while promoting his own clients from the so-called 'Dnepropetrovsk mafia' and elsewhere, took care to build coalitions with leaders in other networks than his own. In this way the ruling élite represented a wide range of institutional and regional interests.

This was a sensible strategy, althoug[...]
political scientist compares Brezhnev to [...]
'led from the middle' rather than the fr[...]
Important matters were shelved, awkward issues[...]
in the inner sanctum. Brezhnev sought to be 'all thi[...]
He stood for higher defence expenditure, which appea[...]
marshals, but also for détente; for more investment in light in[...]
and agriculture, but without renouncing priority for 'Group[...]
industries. (There was some vacillation on this latter point in the
Ninth Five-Year Plan (1971-5), launched in the wake of the Polish
troubles, but it did not last for long.)

The first real challenge he faced came in the foreign-policy field.
The Czech Communist reformers threatened the Soviet hold over
the East European satellites. For some months Brezhnev hesitated,
but when he took the decision to send in troops, under pressure
from 'hawks' in his entourage, he acted harshly and duplicitously.
'Normalization' under Husák was accompanied by the so-called
'Brezhnev doctrine', which asserted the USSR's right to intervene
in the internal affairs of any 'socialist' country whenever it considered the bloc's security in jeopardy. What was new was not the
principle but its crude manner of expression. Subsequently Brezhnev
devoted much energy to an effort to mend fences with the West, and
used his 'successes' in this field to bolster his position domestically.
From 1974 onwards détente gave way to confrontational policies
and to an arms build-up which reinforced the leader's close connections with the military-industrial complex, represented in the highest circles by the Defence minister, Ustinov, a candidate member of
the Politburo and an intimate associate of Brezhnev's.

In 1970 a 'mini-crisis', whose precise nature remains obscure,
forced the leadership to postpone the Twenty-fourth Party congress
for a year or so. When it met (April 1971) it was 'business as usual':
Brezhnev had weathered the storm and was able to promote to full
membership of the Politburo, now expanded to fifteen, his supporters Grishin, Kulakov, and Kunaev, while dropping several men
associated with his rivals. Henceforward the congress was to meet
at five-year rather than four-year intervals, which made for greater
stability. In the union-republics the replacement of Mzhavanadze
by Shevardnadze (Georgia) in 1972, and Shelest by Shcherbitsky in
Ukraine in the following year also strengthened Brezhnev's position. In Azerbaijan the changeover from Akhundov, a Shelepin

It was followed, as in ... ...ny of whom were put on

...ebates Soviet public life ...pty ceremonies. The one-...th (1970) was followed two ...ry of the formation of the ...ns were called on to commem-... of 1905 and 1917. All these ...st propaganda effort. Museums ...litary and labour heroes, monu-...ed. By the mid-1970s the 'Znanie' s... ...lion lectures annually, attended by 775 mill... people (nearly three times the total adult population!). The army of prop... ...mbered 1.3 million (Mickiewicz 1981). Forests of timber were ... down to print massive editions of the Marxist-Leninist classics: 2 million copies for the founders of the faith, 18 million for Lenin (1973: White 1979). Brezhnev claimed at the Twenty-fifth congress that 20 million people were enrolled in Party schools, including 7 million who were not Party members. About a quarter of a million men and women graduated from these schools between 1971 and 1975, of whom some 20,000 received higher degrees.

Brezhnev in decline

By this time Leonid Ilyich had become one of the most bemedalled of Soviet citizens. He had twice been made a Hero of the Soviet Union and received no less than five Lenin orders (his final total was four and seven respectively). In 1973 he won the Lenin Peace Prize, which was no obstacle to his acting simultaneously as commander-in-chief of the armed forces. Three years later he rose to the rank of marshal, and in 1978 won the highest military honour, the Order of Victory. From 1973 onwards his name was placed first, outside alphabetical order, in lists of Politburo members, one of whom suggested that they should all stand up when he entered the room. By 1976 he was being described as *Vozhd'*, a term that had been used of Stalin. In his memoirs, apparently ghost-written, Brezhnev extolled his service in a relatively minor campaign during World War II. The work, printed in millions of

This was a sensible strategy, although it exacted its price. A British political scientist compares Brezhnev to Stanley Baldwin in that he 'led from the middle' rather than the front (A. Brown 1980). Important matters were shelved, awkward issues not discussed even in the inner sanctum. Brezhnev sought to be 'all things to all men'. He stood for higher defence expenditure, which appealed to the marshals, but also for détente; for more investment in light industry and agriculture, but without renouncing priority for 'Group A' industries. (There was some vacillation on this latter point in the Ninth Five-Year Plan (1971–5), launched in the wake of the Polish troubles, but it did not last for long.)

The first real challenge he faced came in the foreign-policy field. The Czech Communist reformers threatened the Soviet hold over the East European satellites. For some months Brezhnev hesitated, but when he took the decision to send in troops, under pressure from 'hawks' in his entourage, he acted harshly and duplicitously. 'Normalization' under Husák was accompanied by the so-called 'Brezhnev doctrine', which asserted the USSR's right to intervene in the internal affairs of any 'socialist' country whenever it considered the bloc's security in jeopardy. What was new was not the principle but its crude manner of expression. Subsequently Brezhnev devoted much energy to an effort to mend fences with the West, and used his 'successes' in this field to bolster his position domestically. From 1974 onwards détente gave way to confrontational policies and to an arms build-up which reinforced the leader's close connections with the military-industrial complex, represented in the highest circles by the Defence minister, Ustinov, a candidate member of the Politburo and an intimate associate of Brezhnev's.

In 1970 a 'mini-crisis', whose precise nature remains obscure, forced the leadership to postpone the Twenty-fourth Party congress for a year or so. When it met (April 1971) it was 'business as usual': Brezhnev had weathered the storm and was able to promote to full membership of the Politburo, now expanded to fifteen, his supporters Grishin, Kulakov, and Kunaev, while dropping several men associated with his rivals. Henceforward the congress was to meet at five-year rather than four-year intervals, which made for greater stability. In the union-republics the replacement of Mzhavanadze by Shevardnadze (Georgia) in 1972, and Shelest by Shcherbitsky in Ukraine in the following year also strengthened Brezhnev's position. In Azerbaijan the changeover from Akhundov, a Shelepin protégé, to Aliev had occurred in 1969. It was followed, as in Georgia, by a blitz on corrupt officials, many of whom were put on trial (Hegaard 1977).

In the absence of genuine policy debates Soviet public life now revolved increasingly around empty ceremonies. The one-hundredth anniversary of Lenin's birth (1970) was followed two years later by the sixtieth anniversary of the formation of the USSR. In 1975 and 1977 Soviet citizens were called on to commemorate the revolutionary upheavals of 1905 and 1917. All these non-events were the focus of a vast propaganda effort. Museums were opened in the homes of military and labour heroes, monuments erected and streets renamed. By the mid-1970s the 'Znanie' society was giving over 15 million lectures annually, attended by 775 million people (nearly three times the total adult population!). The army of propagandists numbered 1.3 million (Mickiewicz 1981). Forests of timber were cut down to print massive editions of the Marxist-Leninist classics: 2 million copies for the founders of the faith, 18 million for Lenin (1973: White 1979). Brezhnev claimed at the Twenty-fifth congress that 20 million people were enrolled in Party schools, including 7 million who were not Party members. About a quarter of a million men and women graduated from these schools between 1971 and 1975, of whom some 20,000 received higher degrees.

Brezhnev in decline

By this time Leonid Ilyich had become one of the most bemedalled of Soviet citizens. He had twice been made a Hero of the Soviet Union and received no less than five Lenin orders (his final total was four and seven respectively). In 1973 he won the Lenin Peace Prize, which was no obstacle to his acting simultaneously as commander-in-chief of the armed forces. Three years later he rose to the rank of marshal, and in 1978 won the highest military honour, the Order of Victory. From 1973 onwards his name was placed first, outside alphabetical order, in lists of Politburo members, one of whom suggested that they should all stand up when he entered the room. By 1976 he was being described as *Vozhd'*, a term that had been used of Stalin. In his memoirs, apparently ghost-written, Brezhnev extolled his service in a relatively minor campaign during World War II. The work, printed in millions of copies, was deemed obligatory reading. This was bad enough, but quite inexcusably this run-of-the-mill opuscule earned the author the Lenin Prize for Literature (1979).[5] The most important step of all came during the celebrations of the sixtieth anniversary of the revolution, when Brezhnev replaced Podgorny, whose position he had previously weakened, as head of state, an elevation which even Stalin had not sought.

Alas, 'pride goeth before destruction, and an haughty spirit before a fall.' The Leader's failing health did not allow him to enjoy the powers and honours he had accumulated. Already in August 1968, during the top-level negotiations with the Czech reformers, he had suffered a sudden heart attack that scared his colleagues. Five years later arteriosclerosis set in which began to affect his nervous system. Gradually he turned against his doctors. Refusing to follow their advice, he sought the care of a woman healer whose remedies, according to orthodox medical opinion, 'had a pernicious influence . . . and hastened his degradation: this is a concrete objective fact which contributed more to the collapse of the country's leadership than dozens of dissident groups' (Chazov 1992). In a sense this was History's revenge: there was a curious parallel here with the Rasputin scandal which had undermined the Romanov monarchy before the 1917 revolution—although Brezhnev was more determined to cling to power than Nicholas II had been, and also more successful in concealing the gravity of the affliction.[6]

The cover-up was arranged by Andropov. According to Dr Chazov, an 'Andropov man' and confidant, the police chief was against raising the matter in the Politburo because he did not want to 'reactivate the struggle for power' and feared that, if Brezhnev resigned on health grounds, the beneficiaries would be Shelepin, Suslov, Podgorny, or Kirilenko. 'You see,' he told Chazov, 'there's no lack of pretenders. For the tranquillity of the country and the Party, and the well-being of the people, we have to keep quiet now and try to conceal Brezhnev's deficiencies.' Chazov comments that 'Andropov, having reached the heights of power, . . . did not want to risk it', for he knew that it depended on Brezhnev remaining in office, even if, after 1976, 'he did not in fact do any work'. This explanation is acceptable so far as it goes, but further evidence is needed as to Andropov's motives: after 1982 he would behave differently. Presumably he feared that a premature bid for supreme power on his part would bring about a coalition against him. It is not clear why none of the other leaders acted. Perhaps they were too distrustful of each other. Alternatively, they may have reckoned that the existing situation was advantageous to them, since it enabled them to enjoy the fruits of office and to distribute patronage liberally. In the latter case we would have empirical confirmation of an American political scientist's hypothesis of 'a post-Stalin consensus within the political establishment, ... a broadly shared élite concern to manage ... conflicting imperatives and ... to keep conflict within bounds by removing the most divisive issues from the policy agenda' (Breslauer 1989).

The 'Brezhnev' Constitution

Another factor that risks being overlooked is the significance which the ailing but incorrigibly vain leader seems to have attached to the Constitution that for long bore his name. Adopted on 7 November 1977, sixty years to the day since Lenin took power, it replaced the so-called Stalin Constitution of 1936. Leonid Ilyich, who (nominally at least) chaired the drafting commission,[7] doubtless expected that this document would remain in force for at least as long as its predecessor. His aim was to place the conservative bureaucratic regime he embodied on the foundations of 'socialist legality'. That he was well aware of the Stalinist precedent is clear from the manner in which the Constitution was prepared. The commission's draft was submitted to the general public for discussion, amidst a flurry of propaganda, as in 1936. That year 43,000 suggestions for amendment had been received, which eventuated in 48 corrections being made to the draft. Brezhnev, naturally, did better: 400,000 suggestions yielded 150 amendments! Among them were some that at first glance might seem substantial. For example, officials who penalized citizens for uttering criticisms were themselves to be held legally responsible for the offence (Art. 49). Article 52 guaranteed Soviet citizens 'freedom of conscience, that is, the right to profess any religion or none ...' Article 108 introduced the principle of popular referendum.

But no provision in the new Constitution did anything to limit the Party's monopoly of power, which on the contrary was explicitly reaffirmed in Article 6: 'the CPSU is the force which directs and guides Soviet society, the nucleus of its political system ... and of social organizations.' (A similar declaration had featured in the

1936 Constitution, but less prominently as Article 126.) Under the Party's guidance the USSR was said (in the preamble) to have built a 'mature socialist society', as a stage on the road to full Communism; indeed, 'the entire Soviet people' was allegedly guided by 'the ideas of scientific Communism'. This was pure Leninism and left no room for autonomous action by individuals or groups. Party organizations were 'to act within the framework of the Constitution'—but the Constitution itself was tailored to the Party's ideological and political requirements.

This meant that citizens could expect no genuine improvement in their juridical situation. Article 49 did not make any innovation, since it was Party officials who decided what the limits of acceptable criticism were. Article 52 stated that 'the incitement of hostility and hatred in connection with religious beliefs is prohibited', a formula that the CRA could interpret broadly as allowing it to continue to interfere in church affairs whenever expedient. Seen in this light, it was quite 'constitutional' for Yakunin, who founded a committee to defend believers' rights, to be arrested and tried for 'anti-Soviet propaganda' in 1979. For all the rights and freedoms which the Constitution conferred were conditional, not absolute. They were granted 'in conformity with the interests of the people and in order to strengthen and develop the socialist system' (Art. 50); their exercise was not to 'harm the interests of society and the state' and was 'inseparable from the performance by the citizen of his obligations' (Arts. 39, 59).

These obligations were spelled out in greater detail than before. They included service as conscripts in the armed forces, where their duty was 'to defend stoutly the socialist Fatherland and to be able to give an instant rebuff to any aggressor' (Art. 31). This at first sight reasonable requirement has to be read in conjunction with Article 28, which declared that Soviet foreign policy 'shall be directed toward . . . strengthening the positions of world socialism [and] supporting the struggle of peoples for national liberation . . .' Two years later the USSR would send its conscript soldiers into Afghanistan with this aim in view—in conformity with the Brezhnev Constitution! The ten principles governing international relations agreed on in the 1975 Helsinki Declaration were written into this document (Art. 29), but no provision was made to ensure their observance.

A progressive lawyer, Savitsky, suggested including a provision to define the purpose of law as 'to defend the legal rights and interests of citizens' as well as those of the state and social order. It was rejected. So were his proposals to 'constitutionalize' the presumption of an accused's innocence, or to state that 'no one has the right to interfere in the exercise of justice or to influence judges'. No better success attended similar efforts to ensure that defence advocates should have a constitutional right to be present during the preliminary investigation of their clients, or to ensure more independence for the procuracy (Lesage 1978). Needless to say, the legislators took no notice of a letter from two leading dissidents (Grigorenko, Turchin) calling for constitutional recognition of an absolute right to freedom of speech.

Some kindly-disposed Western commentators found in the document evidence of an advance towards *Rechtsstaatlichkeit* (roughly, subordination of the state to objective laws), for instance in the greater precision of certain formulations. Certainly it made some innovations in the governmental structure, preserved the principle of federalism (which some zealots wanted to abandon) and sanctioned continuation of the private agricultural plot. But first and foremost it was a propaganda exercise, designed to delude Soviet citizens as to the degree to which their rulers were prepared to heed the law and to encourage conformist thinking, discipline and respect for those in authority. It conferred on the regime a spurious image of modernity and dynamism. Yet the preamble stated quite correctly that the new Constitution 'maintained a continuity of ideas and principles' with its predecessors. It updated the form and language of these documents to take some account of changed conditions, while using Leninist dialectical sleight of hand to subvert the very meaning of such key terms as legality or 'socialist democracy'.

Brezhnev's Constitution did have one saving grace: it could be amended. A few years after his death a new leader would breathe life into it by introducing the notion of separation of powers, so taking a major step forward to democracy and the rule of law. This could not of itself create constitutional government, but it did at least reduce the weight of the fictitious element in the political order, which Brezhnev and his epigones had accentuated.

10 The Party in Disarray

The CPSU under Brezhnev

To the outward eye Brezhnev's eighteen-year rule saw the Party reinforce its position as motor of the political process. It maintained intact both its institutional structure and its mechanism for supervising government and society. The *nomenklatura* system of appointment to positions of authority was backed up by a host of controllers, who kept constant watch on officials' performance. Party membership expanded to keep pace with population growth. An increasing proportion of those entering its ranks possessed good educational qualifications, and many had practical experience in running the economy that apparently equipped them for effective leadership. Yet what occurred in practice was precisely the reverse: the Party's proudly acclaimed 'leading role' was eroded, its grip on society grew shaky, and its ideology lost credibility. Unable to accommodate autonomous political forces or social action, the CPSU's absolute power was gradually whittled away. Eventually it would become an empty shell, a refuge for nostalgics unable to accept the challenge facing all organizations in a changing world: adapt or perish.

Already in the 1960s a percipient observer noted that the Party was forfeiting 'its mystique . . . as an order of men set apart from and above the masses' in so far as the act of joining it became 'a normal expectation for an ever larger proportion of young adults' (Rigby 1968). The next twenty years would prove the point. The most striking development was the spread of corruption. This was of course no new phenomenon—Lenin and Trotsky had inveighed against it in the 1920s—but half a century after their harangues it had become more pervasive than ever. The leaders were aware of the problem. The KGB had an organization of its own for social research and reported its findings quite frankly to the Politburo. But an effective response necessitated abandonment of the secrecy that enshrouded Soviet government and a profound shake-up of the political system. Before such a prospect the country's ageing leaders quailed—not just because they had become set in their ways or feared for their privileges, but because they knew that most Soviet citizens shared their apprehensions. Ordinary folk might complain about shortages and individual abuses, but by and large they accepted the existing order as a fact of life. It provided them with steady employment and a measure of social security in exchange for a modest work load and civic obligations that could in practice often be evaded. Rulers and ruled were bound by an unwritten social compact that encouraged them to leave things as they were.

There was some pressure for change from within the CPSU, but it was unfocused and could not be articulated openly. No 'reform movement' developed comparable to that within the Czechoslovak CP in the mid-1960s or later in its Polish counterpart. It was rather a matter of the Soviet Party, while preserving an appearance of 'monolithic unity', becoming internally fragmented into groupings differentiated by age, experience, and function. These groupings reflected larger divisions within the élite as a whole. Admittedly, it is misleading to speak of 'the élite' in the Soviet context—in any case Soviet writers rejected the term, clinging to the equally misleading term 'intelligentsia'. There were actually *several* coexisting élites, one of which consisted of Party and government officials. Another appellation for it would be the 'political class' (Bialer). Within this group it would be wrong to distinguish Party from government officials, since the two hierarchies were so thoroughly interpenetrated, but in the ruling *apparat* one may legitimately discern differences of approach that can be explained by the life-situation of the individuals concerned.

All these groupings were 'represented', in varying degrees, in the Central Committee. This body expanded in size, from 360 members in 1966 to 470 in 1981, as if to accommodate the growing diversity within the political class. It met seventeen times in 1966–70 but only twelve times over the next quinquennium, a frequency sustained in later years—each time for only a few days. As an institution the CC had only a formal role in policy formation, but its members were politically active throughout the year. Along with senior officials in the Secretariat apparatus, they might be consulted on their regional or professional specialities, serve on commissions, and attend seminars at the now fashionable think tanks. Such officials were engaged in a non-stop informal bargaining process. This revolved less around policy orientations, a matter reserved to the political leadership, than around resource allocations (as indeed it did in other administrations where the political process was more open) and especially appointments. Such bargaining did not lead to the formation of clearly demarcated factions. This would have infringed the rules, which put such a high premium on unity. Instead on either side of an issue there were alignments of people who belonged to the same functional grouping and/or patronage network—these did not necessarily coincide. The complexity of most issues made such groupings even more impermanent. Individuals might simultaneously form part of several shifting alliances or 'coalitions'. It must be admitted that our knowledge of the way the political system operated is still limited, for participants in these disputes and bargains have so far preferred to keep silent. Nor have surviving archival records yet been tapped.

Contemporary Western observers discerned a 'post-Stalin generation' of *apparatchiki* who gained their initial political experience in the main during the 1950s. Whether intellectually disposed towards reform or not, they were likely to be less 'proletarian' in family background, better educated, and more professionally or technically oriented. Some had reached responsible positions in the economy before being 'co-opted' into the ranks of Party officialdom, where it was thought that their expertise would be of use when taking decisions and vetting performance. However, such a career pattern was the exception rather than the rule. The main avenue to the top was via the regional Party apparatus, which these men would enter after serving only a brief (four years or so) apprenticeship as engineers, enterprise managers, or the like. They were not, as had so often been the case under Stalin and Khrushchev, 'generalists' who moved frequently from one post to the next (the type we characterized in Chapter 3 as 'trouble-shooters') but men who stayed in a single province for most of their careers and were 'highly specialized . . . in one type of job geared to [its] profile'. These qualifications enabled them to advance rapidly to positions of political responsibility at provincial level and below. Data on seven non-Slavic republics for 1975–6 show that exactly two-thirds (66.6 per cent) of the first secretaries of city and district committees were of this generation; at provincial level they comprised 38.5 per cent, and at union-republic level over one-quarter (Bialer 1980). In the cities of Moscow and Leningrad they comprised no less than three-quarters of the local leadership. But it was much harder for these ambitious men, then in their forties or early fifties, to enter the Party's central decision-making bodies. In 1978 they constituted only 5.8 per cent of Secretariat department heads; in the Secretariat itself they numbered three out of eleven but in the holy of holies, the Politburo, two out of twenty-three. This promotion block made for 'a great deal of pent-up frustration and impatience among younger members of the élite'—an age cohort larger, and thus more of a threat, than its immediate predecessor, which had suffered so heavily from wartime depletion that it has been referred to as 'the lost generation'.

The promotion block resulted from the Brezhnevian policy of 'stability of cadres'. It seemed as though he had made 'an informal promise . . . to forswear the massive replacements of personnel so characteristic of previous Soviet regimes' (Beissinger 1983). The figures are suggestive: in the Central Committee members' average age rose from 56 in 1966 to 63 in 1982, and in the Council of Ministers from 58 to 65; for the Politburo the figures were 55 and 68. Of the CC members elected at the Twenty-third congress (1966) 44 per cent were still there after the Twenty-sixth congress in 1981.

For the younger generation it was of course more than just a matter of unsatisfied ambition. The older men in the Party's ranks were 'Stalin's heirs', identified with conservative policies, especially on economic matters, where they held fast to well-tried formulas, whereas the deficiencies of centralized planning were apparent to at least some of the younger men. Their attitudes were managerial rather than ideological. It has been estimated that in 1977 three-quarters of Party secretaries at district and city level had received a higher education; for those at provincial or union-republic level the figure is put at 85 per cent. Of these 60 and 70 per cent respectively were 'specialist professionals in the national economy'. Among government officials the proportion was similar. Higher figures are encountered in Soviet sources—it was claimed that 90 per cent of CC members and 63 per cent of its departmental staff had higher education—but one must bear in mind that many of these men graduated from one of two Party-run establishments where the tuition was heavily ideologized (although some might have previously earned a degree from a regular VUZ).

'Party education' at all levels was changing its emphasis towards practical subjects, including 'scientific management'. This was seen as a way of accelerating social promotion for youngsters of worker and peasant background. For it was now more likely that those entering the political class would be from the 'intelligentsia' (in the Soviet sense of the term) than children of men who had spent their working life in the fields or at a factory bench. A 1976 Soviet study of the apparatus in twenty-nine cities and districts showed that 56.3 per cent fell into the former category. For ideological reasons many Party members claimed to be of worker or peasant origin, and the authorities did their best to encourage people with the 'correct' background to join. It was probably easier for the humbly-born to rise to high political office in the USSR than in Western industrialized countries.

It was also easier for them to climb up through the Party–government apparatus than to become a doctor, engineer, or scientist, because the competition here was more intense. The children of élite families were disinclined to choose a political career and sought rather to enter the professions, which had higher prestige. Indeed, many intellectuals looked down on the Party precisely because of its carefully cultivated 'lower class' image, and were reinforced in their negative perceptions when they encountered 'vulgar upstarts' (cultural officials, for example) who restricted their creative endeavours and adopted pretentious manners. Intellectuals and Party officials may be regarded as rival élites, between which there was the least common ground. Officers of the USW and other cultural bodies belonged to the *nomenklatura*, and the rank-and-file members were as a rule in the Party, but this did not prevent tensions arising. To a lesser extent the same was true of the managerial élite, which occupied an intermediate position in this respect. It comprised the bulk of appointments in the *nomenklatura*.

The *nomenklatura*

This term is often used loosely to mean everyone in authority or enjoying privileges. In a narrower, more technical sense it denotes state employees, at the level of section head or higher (or their equivalents),[1] whose appointments were decided by a Party organ of appropriate seniority, from district committee up to the Politburo and Secretariat (in practice, the General Secretary himself). Thus

a provincial committee (*obkom*) would appoint the manager of a
small factory, the deputy director of a medium-sized one, a techno-
logist in a large one, and a section chief in a corporation (*kombinat*)—in each case either approving a suggestion by the enterprise
or choosing a candidate from a card index which it kept itself.
It actually maintained *two* such indexes, one of suitably qualified
personnel and the other called colloquially the 'reserve' (Barker
1973). Some of these individuals might already hold an official
position, say at junior level. The actual selection would be done by
a 'department for Party organizational work', normally headed by
the relevant committee's second secretary, and then be approved by
the committee proper (Hill 1990), each appointment or promotion
being previously cleared with the KGB. All this, needless to say,
was done in deepest secrecy, for even the existence of the *nomenklatura* system could not be mentioned in print.

How large was it? One Western estimate of five million (including
families) is probably on the high side. M. Voslensky, the emigré
dissident whose book on the subject (1980) made the term generally
familiar, arrives at three million, adding ironically that 'this 1.5 per
cent of the population proclaims itself to be . . . the force directing
and guiding our country, the organizer and inspirer of all the
people's victories'. For actual office-holders (the *nomenklatura*
proper) he offers the rough breakdown (for 1970) set out in Table
10.1.

TABLE 10.1. *Occupational breakdown of* nomenklatura
proper (1970)

Party and government	
Centre	100,000
Periphery	150,000[2]
Industrial and agricultural managers	300,000
Science and education	150,000
Others	50,000
TOTAL	750,000

This estimate may be set against two other sets of data: (*a*) those
officially defined as 'having positions of responsibility and leadership'; and (*b*) the total number of specialists (cadres). The former
may be broken down (for 1970) as set out in Table 10.2.

TABLE 10.2. *Occupational breakdown of those in 'positions of responsibility' (1970)*

Party and government officials (incl. 'social organizations')	406,000
Planning and finance	86,000
Economic managers (industry, agriculture)	1,570,000
Engineering and technology	282,000
Trade, supply, and catering	463,000
Education, publishing, the arts	693,000
Health	58,000
TOTAL	3,558,000

The total number of specialists was 16.8 million, or 18.7 per cent of the total labour-force. Of these 40 per cent (6.8 million) had higher education. By 1977 the figures had risen to 25.2 million (23.7 per cent) and 10.5 million. Two years later the percentage of people in employment who had completed higher education was 10 per cent, as against 6.5 per cent in 1970; adding in those who did not complete their studies, we arrive at 7.8 and 11 per cent (1970, 1979; 12.2 per cent in 1986). Therefore, if Voslensky's estimate is correct, in 1970 the *nomenklatura* embraced 11 per cent of cadres with (complete) higher education and 4.5 per cent of the total. The rest held jobs that were evidently not thought important enough to merit close political screening. They were subject to the same general controls through Party and police agencies as the rest of the population.

If we take the most inclusive measure of social differentiation, by 1986 about one in three of those employed was doing non-manual work; 161 million had had at least seven years' schooling and 20.1 million had completed higher education—a considerable advance on 1970, when the comparable figures had been 95 and 8.3 million. It is clear that a scholastically mature, occupationally complex society such as this could no longer be governed by traditional Bolshevik methods of mass mobilization and coercion. With each year that passed it became harder for the Party to achieve its stated aim of co-ordinating the activities of a myriad groups and directing them towards a single goal. Its power to make decisions was not matched by its power to implement them. Scientific advances in management posed the risk that officials would approach their tasks in a technocratic spirit and disregard the Party's injunctions as irrelevant and time-wasting. The multitude of administrative units and the overlapping of responsibilities created a phenomenon aptly described as 'bureaucratic pluralism' (Nove), in which various agencies sought to defend their own interests, neglecting the common task. The Party came to see itself as 'the sole centripetal force in a society consisting of increasingly powerful centrifugal forces' (Hoffmann 1980): these forces included ethnic loyalties and political indifference among the young. It strove to avoid the dissipation of its power amidst a welter of competing pressure groups.

The very multiplicity of control instruments made them easy to evade. Apart from the two police forces (KGB, militia), the procuracy, Gosplan, and the State Bank, there was a Party Control Committee (KPK), a People's Control Committee (KNK), and a body for the protection of state property (OBKhSS). Brezhnev approved of all this: 'public inspectors have become ubiquitous in Soviet society,' he remarked in 1965. 'Their pervasiveness has impressively strengthened [its] participatory character' (Christian 1982.) To take the KNK, by January 1976 it claimed 9.5 million inspectors, double as many as ten years earlier, organized into 1,277 'groups' and 'points' located in enterprises, schools, local soviets and so forth. Over half the members belonged to either the Party or the Komsomol (Adams 1978). They were supervised by an impressive bureaucratic superstructure of fourteen departments and a central committee—and all this with the ostensible aim of eliminating waste and inefficiency! Is it any wonder that corruption was rife?

Patronage

Patronage networks constituted an informal 'second polity', a substitute for a legitimate opposition, restraining the hegemony of those in power and 'providing coherence to the political process' (Willerton 1992). This explains why they persisted in the teeth of official censure. Yet at the same time they subverted the goals and interests of the ruling group and were a central element in what K. Jowitt (1983) calls the 'neo-traditionalization of the Leninist party regime', i.e. its degradation from a 'proletarian dictatorship' with universalist pretensions into a run-of-the-mill authoritarian order concerned above all to preserve its own power and privileges.

Functionaries could arrange for kinsmen to obtain government jobs and other favours. Khrushchev's journalist son-in-law Ajubei became editor of *Izvestiia*—and paid the penalty, when his father-in-law fell from power, of exclusion from the CC and years of ostracism. This was nothing new: Stalin had made his son Vasilii an air force lieutenant-general; for that matter Lenin had entrusted high office to both his wife and his brother-in-law. But Brezhnev went further. His son Yurii became a senior official of the Foreign Trade ministry and a candidate member of the CC. His daughter Galina, who behaved in an eccentric and scandalous manner, eventually married an unscrupulous official in the Interior ministry, Churbanov. He was promoted rapidly from lieutenant to colonel-general and became first deputy minister, a candidate member of the CC and a Supreme Soviet deputy. With the protection of his superior, Shchelokov, he used his official position to embezzle large sums and maintained links with the criminal underworld. When Churbanov was eventually brought to trial (1988) he received a heavy sentence of twelve years' imprisonment in a strict-regime labour camp. The affair discredited both General Secretary Brezhnev personally and the regime he embodied. On his behalf it may be said that he was by then physically incapacitated—but this points up the lack of effective institutional checks upon high-level malfeasance.

The children of several other leaders (Mikoian, Kosygin, Gromyko) made more respectable careers in research or journalism. Whether one can legitimately deduce from this that nepotism 'was the rule rather than the exception', as Voslensky claims, must remain a matter of opinion. It was partly a consequence of the fact that the state was the sole employer: there was no private sector to accommodate well-connected young people. Certainly earnest efforts were made to prevent *junior* officials from acting similarly.

What were often called 'family circles' normally consisted, not of relatives, but of friends or associates. They had a long tradition. It became increasingly necessary for a would-be official to obtain the protection of a patron already ensconced in the system. A study of 886 emigrés of various age groups and backgrounds shows that this had been true of 265 of them (29.9 per cent). For those appointed before 1930 the figure was only 6.9 per cent; it then rose steadily to 25.8 per cent of appointees in the late Stalin era (1951–5), and after stabilizing for a while reached 43.6 per cent and 50.9 per cent respectively of those appointed in 1971–5 and 1976–81 (Zimmerman 1987). Evidently clientelism was on the increase and extending downwards to the lower ranks in the system—incidentally, much as place-seeking (*mestnichestvo*) had done in the seventeenth century. An earlier study of persons appointed to leading posts in Moscow showed that between 1953 and 1971, 78 per cent were recruited from within the city and only 4 per cent from outside (the background of the remainder is unknown). 'Long years of service in the city . . . resulted in the interweaving of career lines and the formation of a close network of personal contacts' (J. H. Oliver 1973). Data on twelve cities for 1965–70 show that 'insiders' accounted for 74 per cent of Party first secretaries and 94 per cent of local government chiefs (chairmen of soviet executive committees). The rapid turnover of personnel characteristic of those years, far from disrupting 'family circles', actually broadened the scope of such informal local networks.

Further research would be necessary to ascertain how far personal links counted, as against professional expertise, in promoting officials within particular organizational hierarchies. Each of them will have had its own ethos in the matter, depending on the personality of successive chiefs and the type of work done. During the Brezhnev era many Party *apparatchiki* endeavoured to improve their qualifications by obtaining somewhat spurious academic degrees. One favoured institution was the Academy of Social Sciences attached to the Central Committee. The higher school that prepared budding diplomats had a reputation as a closed, caste-ridden institution; much the same was true of colleges run by the military, the KGB, the Interior ministry and the Komsomol. Candidates were admitted on recommendation by the CC Secretariat and enjoyed living standards far superior to those of ordinary university students.

Privileges

Members of the *nomenklatura*, and more particularly of the Party *apparat*, had access to relatively luxurious dining facilities, graded according to rank. The 'Kremlin canteen' (*Kremlevka*) and that of the CC obtained food supplies through a depot referred to anonymously as 'base 208' (Peskov 1992–3), served by specially designated state farms. Attached to the former was a shop that sold imported luxury items at prices lower than those in state stores. Some of these stores had 'special sections' to which only pass-holders had access. There were also facilities known as 'closed distributors', such as a Moscow pharmacy reserved for members of the militia, or a health-food shop that catered for Gosplan officials. Some of these emporia bore name-plates designed to mislead the public, but canny Muscovites soon learned their real nature. 'You'll find everything there except birds' milk', ran a popular saying. In 1984 a manager of a leading food store was executed in connection with the Churbanov scandal. Chauffeurs in official limousines would collect supplies from these outlets for the well-to-do, who could also order meals for consumption at home. In this way 'a few tens of thousand' officials and their families surreptitiously benefited (Matthews 1978). At provincial level and below officials had greater power to make their own arrangements and were less dependent on official channels for the supply of material goods (Simis 1982).

Citizens who had acquired foreign currency, legally or otherwise, could purchase food and luxury goods in shops of the 'Berezka' (Birch-tree) chain, whose business greatly expanded from the mid-1960s onward: by 1975 there were no less than fifteen of them in Moscow alone. They also accepted the so-called 'certificate roubles' which some officials received; these came in three varieties, but the details need not concern us. From the authorities' viewpoint they were a useful means of mopping up foreign currency holdings and maintaining the value of the rouble, a goal which took precedence over adherence to egalitarian principles.

The state likewise turned a blind eye to crass inequalities in the provision of housing. At a time when the average citizen had only 6 square metres of space (rising to 8.6 square metres in 1980), and tens of thousands of families were on the waiting list for apartments, those fortunate enough to be allotted additional space already had the 'sanitary minimum' (fixed in 1922!) of 9 square metres a head. About 10 per cent of new housing was of 'improved design', as the official euphemism had it (Peskov 1992–3). Important agencies like the KGB or the Academy of Sciences maintained their own housing stock, as did large industrial enterprises. The officials who allocated such accommodation discriminated in favour of applicants with money or influence. Those unable to secure an apartment through official channels were well placed to acquire a co-operative one, for these inevitably tended to be bought by members of the various élites.

Possession of a country cottage, or *dacha*, was by now something of a status symbol for the fortunate. Ordinary mortals had to be content with what were often little better than allotment huts—regulations forbade their owners from putting in stoves, toilets, etc. so that they could live in them all the year round—whereas privileged officials could hope to spend their holidays in a villa-type state *dacha*, paying only a nominal rent. These were generally located in suburban complexes, 'situated in pleasant scenery, easily accessible, surrounded by a tall hedge to protect them from indiscreet eyes' (Voslensky)—but were also equipped with concealed microphones! Tenants would neither plant flowers nor do the least repair, lest they arouse suspicion of proprietorial instincts. Instead they would spend their leisure reading or playing games, 'in striking contrast to ordinary *dacha* owners, who were digging, nailing, and plastering from morning to night'.

When travelling to the country for the weekend, or to work in the morning, a senior official would as likely as not ride in a government limousine, its size and availability determined by his rank. The poll of emigrés alluded to earlier disclosed that 7.5 per cent of senior-level professionals had this privilege; for managers the figure was 17.3 per cent, for 'political leaders' 26.8 per cent (Zimmerman 1987). These proportions are not high by Western standards, but then the USSR was not yet a 'motorized' society. The provision of such vehicles was important in several ways. It isolated the occupants from the real world outside—literally so, since a passenger in a ZIL could draw curtains across the windows—and gave the driver a chance to trade illegally in state-supplied petrol, spare parts, etc.; some chauffeurs also provided a casual taxi service between official jobs. In the case of top-level leaders the elaborate security arrangements were taken to ridiculous lengths. On major Moscow boulevards the central lane was reserved for their traffic, and militiamen worked out an intricate system of whistles and lights to ensure that their limousines moved without impediment.

Similar arrangements enabled members of the political class to avoid mixing with ordinary folk at airports or railway stations, where they could use comfortable lounges supposedly earmarked for Supreme Soviet deputies. When holidaying in a recreation area, for example on the Black Sea coast, they enjoyed privileged treatment in spacious villas and health spas, far from the bustle of overcrowded beaches. Khrushchev, not content with palaces from the tsarist era, built a luxurious mansion at Pitsunda in the Crimea, which he had to leave hurriedly in October 1964. Countless other functionaries might likewise find themselves suddenly deprived of these baubles. For, as mentioned above, no one had a *right* to any of them. All such privileges depended on one's current status in an informal network of power relationships.

In a sense life itself was such a privilege, since invalids cared for in the 'Kremlin hospital' had a better chance of survival than other citizens. This 'hospital' was a shorthand designation for a complex of medical establishments administered by two powerful secret agencies: the KGB's Ninth and the Health ministry's Fourth main directorates. It included a rehabilitation centre at Zhiguli on the Volga, an architectural and medical showplace where politically congenial foreigners were sometimes treated as well (Chazov 1992). Unfortunately Chazov reveals no details about any of the facilities he helped to run. According to Voslensky, the 'health *kombinat*' in Moscow was furnished with the latest Western equipment and drugs. 'The food and care are beyond praise, the staff abundant, competent and smiling.' As the ruling group aged, we may assume that expenditure on its health increased—at a time when the share of the state budget assigned to health care was actually falling, from 6.6 per cent in 1960 to 4.6 per cent in 1985, and the system's failings were leading to a 'veritable crisis' (Powell 1991).

Was the divide between élite and mass greater in the USSR than in advanced Western countries? There are no data as yet on the cost of these various facilities for the privileged. In 1990 it was revealed (by Yu. A. Peskov) that subsidies for *dachas* in the Moscow area alone had lately been running at 1.6–1.8 million roubles a year, and that even after abolition of the Fourth main directorate the CPSU still had 23 sanatoria with 7,100 beds (0.28 per cent of the total). Even if we had figures for all official agencies and enterprises, it would hardly be possible to distinguish their expenditure on privileged individuals from their general outlays. According to one estimate (1984) the top 1.5 per cent of the population enjoyed benefits and extra income worth 100 per cent of their basic monetary earnings (Buck and Cole 1987). D. Lane (1985) offers a theoretical defence of inequalities under Soviet socialism and points to some of the complexities in measuring it (for instance, the relation-ween income and status differentials, or the relative oppor- r social mobility). Although 'perks and privileges . . . are obviously important facts,' he argues, 'one must not ignore the equally important point that the general tendency has been towards the reduction of income differentials.' Fashions change, and ten years later researchers would probably be more likely to ask whether income differentials gave members of the élite *enough* motivation to do their best. From this viewpoint the Soviet system looks archaic, since officially sanctioned rewards probably went in the main to administrators with political or security functions, rather than to economic leaders. The latter were therefore likelier, and had better opportunities, to seek other ways of satisfying their wants.

The earnings differential between an enterprise manager or medium-level official and an industrial worker was somewhere in the range 4 : 1 to 8 : 1,[3] which cannot be considered excessive. Doctors, teachers, and many other professional people had low incomes that did not reflect their high qualifications.

The 'second economy'

Let us now look at the ways in which citizens of *all* social strata tried to better their condition by engaging in economic activities beyond or on the margin of the law. The 'second economy' is not easy to pin down, since it involved operations of so many different kinds. The best definition is 'activities that escape control by the state' (Feldbrugge 1984), which sets aside the question of their legality or illegality. Nor can one draw a clear dividing line between them and the official corruption examined above. K. Simis (1982) tells a story that might have come straight out of the seventeenth century. Large amounts of food were seen arriving at the office of a functionary near Archangel, who distributed most of it among the population, thereby winning their respect and support. They were pleased because his 'take' was unusually modest. Periodically he would hold a feast, to which leading citizens were invited for a modest fee (the food being supplied gratuitously by local farms). Those outside the charmed circle did not consider this practice illegal but took such tribute for granted.

Rulers and ruled acted in collusion, partly because they shared common cultural traits, partly because they had the same needs. The basic reason for these activities (and attitudes) was the shortage of essential consumer goods, which itself resulted from the over-centralized system of economic management and distribution. Entrepreneurial elements who could not find enough scope for their talents within the command economy naturally turned to unauthorized activities. These did not play an entirely negative (dysfunctional) role. By 'oiling the machine' they enabled it to function. This helps to explain the feebleness of the authorities' response. 'Speculation' expressed, albeit in a perverted form, the vitality of a society striving to break free from the strait-jacket of a control system that had outlived its *raison d'être*. The criminal mafia arose in symbiosis with the political mafia that had run the country for so long. Each fed on the other in an uneasy relationship, fraught with tension and marked by sporadic acts of violence on either side.

In the West, study of the second economy began in earnest with A. Katsenelinboigen's stimulating proposition (1977) that there existed a range of markets in the USSR which could be designated by colours. These categories repay close examination. First, the official ('red') distribution system had some market elements, e.g. in employment and consumption. Closely allied to it were two other authorized markets: 'pink', for the sale by private individuals through so-called 'commission shops' of articles in their possession they no longer needed; and 'white', the markets where collective farmers sold produce from their plots. 'Grey', semi-licit markets were of two types, for consumer and producers' goods. Examples of the former included workers doing minor repairs, teachers tutoring pupils, or doctors visiting patients at home. An instance of the latter type was the bartering of materials between enterprises to help each other fulfil the Plan. In both cases the *source* of the commodity was legal but the *mode* of transaction was not.

Such semi-licit deals were popularly referred to as *nalevo*, literally 'on the left' in the sense of 'on the side'. For J. R. Millar (1985) these 'reciprocity exchanges' were evidence that the Brezhnev regime had struck a bargain with the population, which he called ironically 'the little deal'.[4] He noted that 'petty trade, petty middleman activities, petty private enterprise, even petty theft . . . of government property have for the most part been winked at by the [authorities].' Such informal transactions often amounted to an exchange of favours, with or without payment, between those with access to scarce commodities or services. If one wanted theatre ts or restaurant seats—even a place at university or in a hospital—it was helpful to know the relevant official (usually called the *administrator*), who expected reciprocal treatment.

Returning to Katsenelinboigen's 'coloured' markets, the next types to be considered were wholly illegal. They comprised 'brown' operations, in which the partners pursued a public interest as well as their own, and the 'black' market proper, in which they did not. Practitioners of the former usually faced administrative penalties, while those in the latter category were treated as criminals. 'Brown' trading, too, might be carried on either in consumer or in producers' goods. A shop assistant might reserve scarce goods for a favoured customer in return for an additional payment, which would then be shared with senior staff, or an official chauffeur might give a pedestrian a lift for payment. These deals were not wholly detrimental to the state because they made it possible to keep such employees' wages low, while supply of spare parts from state stocks helped to maintain tractors in working order during the ploughing season.

Finally, the 'black' market proper was carried on both in legally obtained goods in short supply and in illegally produced, imported (i.e. smuggled) or stolen commodities. People involved in this trade were officially called 'speculators' and may have numbered in the hundreds of thousands. Among them were the so-called *fartsovsh-chiki*, who dealt in foreign currency. This was a hazardous activity, sometimes conducted with the knowledge of the KGB. The security police needed such funds for its undercover operations abroad, but would summarily dispose of its unsavoury contacts when they ceased to be useful (e.g. by sending them to a labour camp as informers). Another lucrative trade in which the KGB co-operated with the criminal underworld was in stolen and forged antiques, above all icons.

Particularly important was the black market in alcoholic beverages. Illicitly distilled vodka (*samogon*) is estimated to have accounted for 44 per cent of total consumption in the late 1950s, declining to 35 per cent by the late 1970s, with annual output rising from 1.0 to 1.6 milliard litres (Treml 1985). In the late 1970s average annual consumption of spirits was put at 15 litres a head; total consumption almost quadrupled during Brezhnev's rule (Walker 1986). *Samogon* was easy to produce and extremely profitable, even after allowing for payment of 'protection money'. Sold at 4.50 to 5 roubles a litre (in the mid-1970s), it could bring a full-time 'speculator' an income ten to fifteen times the average wage. Much liquor was also stolen from state depots, where security was lax, or in transit. Excessive drinking became one of the USSR's gravest social problems, especially in the Slav republics (see Chapter 13).

The 'second economy' in alcoholic beverages was related to the first (regular) economy only in indirect fashion, for one could not really complain about a shortage of the product in state stores. With the black market in motor vehicles matters were rather different, since under the plan potential purchasers were deliberately disadvantaged. Cars were to be only one-tenth as plentiful as television sets (O'Hearn 1980). 'To be a private motorist in the Soviet Union', noted one Western journalist, 'is to live permanently on the fringe of the black market' (Walker 1986). Many vehicles were sold through unauthorized channels. *Izvestiia* complained that in 1972–3 more than a third of private cars were running on state petrol, which drivers would siphon out of the tanks of official vehicles. Workmen at the Gor'ky motor works smuggled out vehicle parts, which were then painstakingly reassembled until they made up a complete unit (Simis 1982).

Pilfering of state property was not generally regarded as a serious offence. 'The state is too vast, too impersonal to be seen as a victim' (Binyon 1983). Workers would take material home from the factory where they were employed—evading the inspectors posted at its gates—and make it up into garments and other useful articles for sale to neighbours. Repair jobs, too, as we have noted, were frequently done by private individuals, who provided quicker and more reliable service than the few state agencies that existed for the purpose, each of which had its own designated 'speciality' (shoes, watches, musical instruments, etc.). So extensive was this trade that some publicists suggested that it should be privatized, as in Eastern Europe. But Soviet ideologists feared 'capitalist' contamination: 'if entrepreneurs started repairing umbrellas themselves, they might end up manufacturing and selling new ones'.

The scale of the 'second economy' cannot be estimated precisely, but is generally thought to have accounted for at least 10 per cent, and perhaps as much as 20–5 per cent, of GNP—and as much as 30 to 40 per cent of total personal income (Goldman 1983; 1987 as cited by Åslund 1991). Another recent estimate, by A. Vaksberg, puts it at 400 milliard roubles a year, more than double semi-official ates of 150–200 milliard roubles (W. A. Clark 1993), but since in 1985 GNP was officially put at 569 milliard roubles, the lower figures are probably nearer the truth.[5] D. Lane points out that if the shadow economy were only 10 per cent of GNP it would be 'smaller than those of industrial Western societies', and adds that since 'its existence is probably inevitable in any society' Westerners should not moralize about it. The point is well taken, yet historically it mattered because it discredited and subverted the 'planned' economy, to whose defects it largely owed its existence.

Official reactions

The real question is why the authorities were slow to curb it, either by taking timely steps towards 'market socialism' or by repressing illicit activities through the police and the courts. Reforms were indeed attempted, but they were too modest in scope and ran into the sand (see Chapter 11). As for repression, the purges in Azerbaijan and Georgia in the early 1970s showed what the KGB could do when given its head. In 1976 *all* thirty inspectors of the Azerbaijani Trade ministry were put on trial. But the security organs were hampered by their own ties to the mafia: they were part of the problem, not the solution.

This applied particularly to the Interior ministry (MVD) under Brezhnev's crony Shchelokov. From 1979 onward there was increasingly frequent press criticism of this ministry, and of the procuracy, for their laxity in combating economic crime. The laws were tightened and penalties increased (1979, 1981). The Central Committee circulated a 'closed' letter to Party organizations ordering them to be more vigilant. In this campaign an increasingly high profile was taken by the KGB, although its hands, as we know, were by no means clean. It claimed credit for catching a large group of diamond smugglers. In another sensational case, involving the export of caviar disguised as herring, two hundred officials were arraigned, among them a deputy minister who was executed.

Politically this further expansion of the KGB's role came as grist to Andropov's mill. He could not only strengthen his agency's hold over the MVD but also unseat Brezhnev's men. For reasons yet to be clarified he moved prudently—perhaps too slowly for the good of the system he sought to preserve. In January 1982 his deputy Tsvigun, one of Brezhnev's 'watchdogs' in the KGB, committed suicide. He is thought to have tried, and failed, to obstruct a KGB investigation into the scandal involving Brezhnev's daughter, Churbanov, and Shchelokov. One week later Suslov died of natural causes. Andropov, who succeeded him as the Party's second most senior figure, felt free to arrest Churbanov and banish Shchelokov, whom he referred to privately as 'a crook and a rogue' (Chazov 1992). As soon as Brezhnev died in November 1982, Shchelokov was replaced by a senior KGB man. Two years later he was stripped of his military rank and in turn committed suicide, apparently after first killing his wife. Not until 1988 did the public learn the extent of the ex-minister's abuse of power. According to the prosecution he imported luxury cars for use by members of his family, stole art works valued at a quarter of a million roubles, and bought several apartments (including one used for sexual orgies); he also had his son appointed a leading official of the Komsomol.

Shchelokov was incriminated in the exotic misdeeds of the long-time Party boss in Uzbekistan, Rashidov, who likewise died in mysterious circumstances in 1983. Rashidov headed a patronage network of several thousand clients, one of whom was a *sovkhoz* chairman, Adylov. He ran his farm like a medieval Oriental sheikhdom. It had its own police force, harem, and prison where opponents were tortured and murdered. Rashidov's gang is alleged to have embezzled 50 million roubles over fifteen years, much of it through falsification of statistics on cotton output. The recipient of no less than ten Orders of Lenin, Rashidov kept in with Brezhnev by presenting him with lavish gifts, including several of the limousines he was so fond of.

Andropov's brief tenure of power (November 1982–February 1984) was accompanied by a drive to reinforce order and discipline. It involved *inter alia* a purge of the MVD and of Brezhnev clients in the Central Committee. But the rot had gone too deep and the new leader, 68 years old on his accession, was too sick to stay the course. In any case a change of personnel was no longer enough to root out the evil of corruption. This required a change of system—and even then the evil would resurface in new forms.

11　An Economy in Trouble

Economic growth

The 'first' economy would not undergo the radical transformation it needed for some twenty years after Brezhnev took over. Under his regime only patchwork repairs were attempted to the centralized system of planning and resource allocation. They were thwarted by powerful vested interests and had little practical impact. Not only the country's leaders and managerial élite but also many professional economists with advanced views underestimated the gravity of the problems they faced. By the mid-1980s the USSR was in what Gorbachev would call a 'pre-crisis situation'. The most obvious symptom was the diminishing rate of return on the massive investments of capital, which meant that GNP and industrial output, although continuing to rise each year, did so at a slackening pace. A 1982 American study showed that in the economy as a whole capital productivity fell by 1.9 per cent annually in 1966–70, 3.8 per cent in 1971–5, and 2.9 per cent in 1976–9. The corresponding figures for labour productivity showed an increase, but one that was likewise slowing down: from 3.4 to 2.3 per cent in the first two quinquennia, and then to 1.3 per cent. Poor performance in lagging sectors of the economy, notably agriculture, dragged down the overall rates.[1]

The GNP grew more rapidly in the late 1960s than it had done in the previous quinquennium. Expressed in 1970 prices (and excluding arms expenditure), the annual increase was 5.3 as against 4.9 per cent, but thereafter the rate fell to 3.7 per cent (Wright 1980). The CIA's estimate for the Ninth Five-Year Plan (1971–5) is in agreement, but for the next five years puts the annual increase at only 2.7 per cent. Reckoned on a per capita basis, the figures are lower: in 1979, a particularly bad year, there was actually a *decrease* of 0.4 per cent (Buck and Cole 1987), and this situation probably continued into the early 1980s (Ellman 1986). It is only fair to add that falling growth rates were characteristic of many other industrialized countries at this time, not to mention developing ones.

An increasing share of Soviet GNP was allocated to investment: by 1980 this had reached 33 per cent, although the annual rate of increase was slower now than it had been earlier: less than 3 per cent as against 7.6 per cent in 1965–70. Much of it went on defence. Estimating this expenditure is a contentious matter, which at one time led to a 'cold war' between Western intelligence experts as well as between the superpowers. In 1976 the CIA revised its estimate upwards to 12–13 per cent of GNP (1970) and put the annual increase at 4–5 per cent (Hanson 1978). Its figure for 1982 was also 13 per cent. In real terms Western estimates for expenditure in 1975 ranged from 42 to 76 milliard roubles (Bater 1989, citing R. E. Leggett and S. T. Rabin 1978), in percentage terms from 10 to 20 per cent of GNP; most were in the middle of this range. More recent calculations put expenditure on arms production alone at 86 to 95 milliard roubles out of a total of 804 milliard roubles, or 10.7–11.8 per cent (1985: Kushnirsky 1993). No one doubts that this was a very heavy burden indeed.

It is hardly necessary to add that all these estimates need to be verified against the documentary evidence, should this ever become available. From 1987 onward several Soviet economists openly questioned official statistics. Seliunin and Khanin caused a sensation by stating that since 1928 the national income had grown by a factor of only 6.9, not 89.5 as had been claimed. They showed how officials had wilfully manipulated and falsified data, creating a 'veil of illusion' to conceal disagreeable realities. Serious Western observers had, of course, always adjusted published Soviet figures to allow for such malpractices, as well as for hidden inflation ('price drift'). Thus their estimate of national income growth since 1928 was 10.9-fold, and that for the annual increase since 1950 was 3.8 per cent, the same as Khanin's. More relevant in the present context are the comparative data for growth rates since 1965 shown in Table 11.1.

TABLE 11.1.   *Growth rate estimates, 1965–1985*

	1965–70	1970–5	1975–80	1980–5
Western[a]	4.9	3.0	1.9	1.8
Khanin	4.1	3.2	1.0	0.6

[a] *CIA/Moorsteen and Powell.*

Source: Harrison 1993.

TABLE 11.2. *Output of selected goods, 1965–1985*

Product	1965	1970	1975	1980	1985
Iron ore (million tons)	153.4	197	235	245	248
Pig iron (million tons)	66.2	85.9	103	107	110
Steel (million tons)	91.0	116	141	148	155
Coal (million tons)	577.7	624.1	701.3	716	726
Oil (million tons)[a]	242.9	353.0	490.8	603	595
Gas (milliard cu. metres)	128	197.9	289.3	435	643
Electricity (milliard kWh)	506.7	740.9	1038.6	1294	1545
Tractors (units, 000)	355	459	550	555	585
Mineral fertilizer (million tons)	31.3	55	90.2	104	112
Metal-cutting lathes (000)	186.1	202.2	231.4	216	182
Cement (million tons)	72.4	95.2	122	125	131
Automobiles (000)[b]	201.2	344.2	1201	1327	1332
Cotton fabrics (milliard sq. metres)	5.5	6.2	6.6	7.1	7.7
Woollen fabrics (milliard sq. metres)	466	643	740	762	700-99[d]
Synthetic resins and plastics (000 tons)	803	1670	2838	3637	5020
Chemical fibres and threads (000 tons)	407	623	955	1176	1394
Leather footwear (million pairs)	486	679	698	743	787
Housing (million sq. metres)[c]	97.6	106.0	109.9	105.0	113.0
TV sets (000)	3655	6682	6960	7528	9371
of which coloured	—	46	584	2262	4024
Refrigerators (000)	1675	4140	5579	5925	5859
Motor cycles and scooters (000)	711	833	1029	1090	1148
Sewing machines (000)	800	1400	1360	1323	1503
Watches and clocks (million)	30.6	40.2	55.1	66.7	67.2
Cameras (000)	1053	2045	3031	4255	2090

[a] Includes gas condensate.
[b] Excludes trucks.
[c] Includes state, co-operative and private (with state credits), collective farms, and public.
[d] Estimated.

Khanin puts the annual rate of inflation at 2.6, 2.3, and 2.9 per cent for the three post-1965 quinquennia, considerably higher than in the Khrushchev era (roughly twice as much for investment goods).[2] According to another Soviet economist, Bogomolov, by 1987 the cost of living had more than doubled over the previous thirty years, whereas the official price index showed an increase of less than 10 per cent. Another estimate was 43 per cent for the twelve-year period 1971–83 (Nove 1988, 1989; Rumer 1989).

Gross industrial production expanded at a relatively steady rate until the mid-1970s: by 50 per cent in 1965–70, and 43 per cent in 1970–5; in the next quinquennium the figure fell to 24 per cent, and in 1980–5 to 20 per cent (Nove 1990). These official data obscure the fact that so much of this growth occurred in the defence sector. More illuminating were the data for specific branches of industry or products (see Table 11.2). Output of consumer goods, taken in the aggregate, exceeded the planned figure by 4.5 per cent in 1965–70 (149 as against 144.5), but in the next three quinquennia fell short by 11.5, 10, and 7 percentage points respectively. The slackening rate of increase in the production of such staples as iron ore or steel can be explained only in part by a switch to more modern materials. It also reflected the exhaustion of physical plant and the use of outdated technologies. In the 1980s robots were utilized for certain industrial processes but, like automated production lines, were much rarer than in Japan or other advanced countries. Turbine generators produced in 1985 had considerably less power potential than those made ten years earlier. The picture was similar in regard to several other types of machinery. The data-processing industry expanded tenfold from 1970 to 1981— measured in *monetary* terms, which statisticians preferred, for obvious reasons. Wits joked that Soviet computers might be less numerous than in the West, but at least had the advantage of weight! The first home-produced personal (micro-) computer, the Agat, could not be mass-produced because of a shortage of floppy disks, and was ten times the price of a comparable Western machine (Walker 1986).

Fuels, transport

Far more successful were the extractive industries, other than coal, the output of which was deliberately levelled down in favour of oil and more especially natural gas from the Volga–Urals area and western Siberia. These regions were linked by pipelines to European

Russia and central Europe. The total length of gas pipeline was eventually four times greater than the Earth's circumference at the Equator. Exports of oil and gas to the West were a major factor in Soviet foreign trade and a source of much-needed hard currency. Although not a member of OPEC, the USSR benefited from the general rise in world oil prices between 1973 and 1986. In the early 1980s nine thousand new oil-wells were being sunk each year. One problem here was that most oil rigs used non-rotating turbo-drills, which could not reach depths below three thousand metres, rather than high-pressure drills made of high-quality steel, which domestic industry could not supply (Bater 1989). Breakdowns were frequent and much expensive equipment lay idle.

Until 1980 oil output grew rapidly but then stabilized, whereas that of natural gas continued to expand. By 1985 the amount produced was fourteen and a half times greater than it had been twenty years earlier and the pipelines transported 1,131 milliard ton-kilometres of gas. Over half came from the great fields recently discovered in western Siberia, where a 'gold-rush' atmosphere prevailed. Workers were flown in for two-week stints, their high earnings compensating for the hardships of life in hutted camps. All the emphasis was on short-term gain and little attention paid to the environmental effects, which were catastrophic. By 1985 natural gas accounted for 35.5 per cent of the country's fuel balance, over twice as much as twenty years earlier (15.6 per cent). Oil's share rose from 35.9 per cent in 1965 to 45.3 per cent in 1980, but then dropped 5.5 percentage points over the next five years, while coal sank from 42.9 to 22.8 per cent (1965–85).

The amount of electricity generated tripled over the twenty-year period, with nuclear power contributing a rapidly increasing share: 10.8 per cent of the total by 1985. Development in this field began in earnest in the 1970s. The graphite-moderated (RBMK) reactors initially favoured had serious design flaws. Campaign methods led to neglect of elementary safety precautions. The USSR was 'on the road to Chernobyl', the world's first major nuclear disaster (see Chapter 12). Even from a strictly economic viewpoint, the cost-effectiveness of developing nuclear power was questionable, given the plentifulness of other sources of energy. There was a lot to be said for investing in new pits in the Donets coal-mining basin, where old seams were becoming exhausted and—despite the relatively high wages that miners received—labour morale sinking. In the Siberian Kuzbas, too, absenteeism was rife and productivity low—but management jobs on the increase. Here as elsewhere in the east much coal was mined by cheap but ecologically harmful opencast techniques. Development of Siberia's resources made sense in a long-term perspective (and also strategically), but too much of the country's fuel needs were met from regions remote from the chief manufacturing areas in European Russia and Ukraine. This made for excessively high transport costs—indeed, that was precisely the argument used by those who advocated siting nuclear facilities at Chernobyl and elsewhere in Ukraine.

The rail network was expanded, both by double-tracking existing lines and by the construction of new ones. Much effort went into completing the 3,500-kilometre long BAM (Baikal–Amur *magistral'*) through the eastern Siberian taiga. Designed to relieve pressure on the Trans-Siberian and to open up a new region to settlement (as well as to deepen defences against China), it was a technological feat that required the construction of over three thousand bridges and thirty kilometres of tunnels (Mote 1992). The engineers initially underestimated the problems that would be created by permafrost, and the schedule for completion of the project had to be repeatedly extended. By the mid-1980s about one-third of the USSR's rail network had been electrified. The total amount of goods transported by rail almost doubled over the twenty-year period, from 1,950 to 3,719 milliard ton-kilometres, but it was another question whether all these journeys were strictly necessary.

Air freight increased more rapidly, from 1.3 to 3.4 milliard ton-kilometres, and road traffic faster still (121 to 477 ton-kilometres); passenger traffic grew at roughly the same pace. Yet haulage vehicles covered an average distance of only 18 kilometres, as against 940 kilometres for rail wagons, since the state of Soviet roads continued to be one of benign neglect. The Brezhnev regime was, however, more favourable to the private automobile than its predecessor. Production expanded five-fold, helped by the construction in 1967–72 of a large plant at Tol'iatti on the Volga by the Italian car-maker Fiat. Another foreign venture was the construction of a fine new airport at Sheremetevo outside Moscow. Aeroflot was justly proud of its second-generation jet aircraft, especially the giant TU-154M. By 1980 this state enterprise was carrying over a hundred million passengers a year and making regular flights to cities all over the globe—a development that, to be sure, was of advantage mainly to the favoured few, for whom fares were relatively cheap. Ordinary citizens wishing to leave the country, even as tourists, continued to face administrative hurdles—to say nothing of the harassment encountered by would-be emigrants. As in the developing world generally, travel was a luxury; for most people it was confined to the daily journey to and from work.

Consumer goods

As the figures in Table 11.2 suggest, consumers now had more goods available, although if one takes population growth into account the increases are less striking. According to Western estimates annual consumption grew on average by 2.9 per cent per annum during the 1950s and 1960s (with an upward 'blip' in the late 1960s), but fell to 2.2 per cent in the 1970s and to about 1 per cent by 1982 (Lane 1985). By sectors the annual rates of growth during the Eighth and Tenth Plan periods are as shown in Table 11.3.

TABLE 11.3. *Percentage growth in consumption of selected consumer goods*

Sector	1966–70	1976–80
Food	4.3	1.3
Soft goods	7.1	3.1
Durables	9.1	5.4
Personal	5.8	3.4

If one were to take the following quinquennium, the drop would be more marked—but at least supplies were still increasing, however slowly. Goods were harder to find in the shops—but when tracked down their fixed price might well not reflect their scarcity value. Moreover, rents, light, and power continued to be heavily subsidized, as were staple foodstuffs. Many items were of poor quality and indifferently styled.

Consumer resistance to their purchase, noted above in Chapter 4, was one factor in the buildup of savings deposits (which was deliberately encouraged for budgetary reasons). These deposits grew by an annual average of 19.9 per cent in 1966–70 and 14.3 per cent in 1971–5. In 1965 the total accumulated in state savings bank branches was 18.7 milliard roubles; by 1975 it had leaped to 91, and ten years later to 221 milliard roubles. As much as 100 milliard roubles more may have been 'buried under the mattress' by those engaged in the second economy. This 'overhang' of purchasing power would eventually be mopped up after 1988, when owners of these savings had to draw on them to ensure their physical survival. The problems ahead were apparent already a decade earlier. 'The pent-up distortions caused by the failure to make incremental changes', noted M. I. Goldman in 1983, 'could unleash uncontrollable forces, even if a fundamental reform of the economy were gradual . . . A sudden decontrol would . . . generate immense inflationary and import pressures.' The basic reason was that for half a century the economic managers had made so little effort to serve consumers' needs.

In 1970 61 per cent of urban households and 32 per cent of rural ones owned a television set. Sixteen years later a few 'two-TV families' had arrived (reputedly, in Armenia!), for the figures had leaped to 102 and 94 respectively. Clearly, country-dwellers were no longer at a serious disadvantage in this respect at least. A comparable increase occurred in the possession of other consumer durables: 43 per cent of urban households had a refrigerator in 1970, 101 per cent had one in 1986; in rural areas the figures were 13 and 78 per cent. The official statisticians do not tell us how many of these machines were in working order. Repair of items of domestic hardware was a problem generally solved by private entrepreneurs *nalevo*, as we know. Even by 1986 relatively few households had vacuum cleaners: 50 per cent in the towns, 21 per cent in the villages. The official figures for the stock of various items presumably include those piling up in warehouses, which may or may not have been sold later, as well as worn-out machines in private hands. Actual sales did rise over the two decades: for every thousand inhabitants 14 television sets were sold in 1965 and 29 twenty years later, and respectively 6 and 16 refrigerators. But how many purchasers bought them only because the machines they already owned had expired after too brief a life?

Household budget data show that the proportion of expenditure that went on durables increased (1970: 5.7 per cent; 1986: 7.8 per cent), while that on clothing and foodstuffs declined. The latter took 34.7 per cent of the average household budget in 1970 and 27.9 per cent in 1986.[3] Annual per capita meat consumption (including fat and offal) is said to have risen from 41 kilograms in 1965 to 61.4 kilograms in 1985, and that of potatoes to have fallen from 142 to

104 kilograms. Figures for some other products are given in Table 11.4. (Five-year averages, which would give a more accurate picture, are not available.) The big improvements came in the late 1960s; subsequently the rise for most non-carbohydrate items was slower. The citizens' diet was 'far from balanced'; for example, bread and potatoes supplied nearly half the calorie intake, whereas the scientifically recommended norm was 37 per cent (Jones and Smogorzewska 1982).

TABLE 11.4. *Food consumption per capita, 1965–1985*

	1965	1970	%+/–	1975	%+/–	1980	%+/–	1985	%+/–
Milk and dairy products[a]	251	307	22.3	316	2.9	314	–0.6	323	2.9
Eggs (units)	124	159	28.2	216	35.8	239	10.6	260	8.8
Fish and fish products	12.6	15.4	22.2	16.8	9.1	17.6	4.8	17.7	0.6
Sugar	34.2	38.8	13.5	40.9	5.4	44.4	8.6	42.0	–5.6
Oil (vegetable)	7.1	6.8	–4.2	7.6	11.8	8.8	15.8	9.7	10.2
Vegetables (incl. melons)	72	82	13.9	89	8.5	97	9.0	102	5.2
Fruit, berries	28	35	25.0	39	11.4	38	–2.6	46	21.1
Bakery products[b]	156	149	–4.7	141	–5.4	138	–2.1	133	–3.6

[a] In terms of milk.
[b] Bread, bakeries, flour, careals, pulses.

Note: All items are in kg. unless otherwise stated.

Source: Hedlund 1984.

Such statistics can give no impression of the difficulties encountered in finding the items listed, the loss of time spent queuing for them, or their relative availability in state stores as against higher-priced collective-farm markets. Nor do they take account of the vast differences between a privileged centre like Moscow and provincial towns, where even at the best of times supplies were irregular. The capital city attracted customers from a wide swathe of surrounding territory, and supplies there were usually increased on the eve of public holidays or during special events (e.g. the 1980 Olympic Games). Foreigners were astonished that traders should fly to Moscow from Transcaucasia to sell a few kilograms of fruit or berries, yet return with a handsome profit.

Internationally, Soviet living standards were low, but comparisons are necessarily hazardous. It would be less misleading to take as the foreign reference point an Asian country rather than a Western one, as is generally done. However, a 1979 survey of the price of a 'weekly shopping basket' for four persons is of interest. It is calculated in 'work-time units', i.e. the number of minutes that a factory worker earning average wages would need to work in order to buy the item listed.

TABLE 11.5 *Cost of weekly shopping basket in selected cities, March 1979* (in 'work-time' units)

	Moscow	London	Washington
Bread (6 kg.)	272	72	48
Beef (1 kg.)	132	123	63
Sausages (1 kg.)	145	43	31
Milk (10 litres)	180	90	70
Eggs (17)	100	26	14
Potatoes (9 kg.)	63	36	18
Cabbage (2 kg.)	18	18	10
Apples (1 kg.)	40	15	11
Tea (1/10 kg.)	50	6	11
Beer (3 litres)	60	66	24
Weekly 'shopping basket' (hours)	42.3	21.4	12.5

Note: Deduction made for income tax and social security contributions or equivalents (in Western countries); no adjustment for variations in number of wage-earners per household or in dietary habits.

Source: Bush 1981.

Housing

The calculation was much more favourable to the Moscow wage-earner in regard to rental payments. For a (subsidized) unfurnished apartment of 50 square metres he worked 12 hours, his British and American counterparts 23 and 53 hours respectively. Rent accounted for only 3 to 5 per cent of a household's budget, and of this modest sum most went to pay for heating and water supply. Only one-third of maintenance costs were met from this source, the rest being covered by subsidies. There was some flexibility in fixing rents, with space in excess of the local norm being paid for at a higher rate. But the 'market element' here was slight, and public funds were spent on assisting many who could have afforded to pay more. Those hardest hit were individuals living in communal apartments shared by several families—still 20 per cent of the total in 1980—or in dormitories. The latter were occupied mainly by young men who had recently arrived in an urban environment from the countryside. Isolated and subject to barrack-like discipline, they formed a 'cultural fringe group' (Mickiewicz 1981) and lacked adequate leisure facilities. Many swiftly became alienated, took to drink or drugs, and entered the criminal underworld. Migrants might have to endure such conditions for ten years or so before securing a room of their own.

These realities were obscured in official statistics, which present a picture of a massive growth of housing construction. During the Eighth Five-Year Plan the total built was 518.5 million square metres, 5.7 per cent more than in 1961–5. One key to this success was the development of co-operative housing, which more than doubled (from 13.4 to 33.6 million square metres of total space) and accounted for 6.5 per cent of the total as against 2.8 per cent in the previous quinquennium. Even more important was construction by 'the population' (mainly enterprises) with the aid of state credits, which accounted for 29.7 per cent of the total. But neither of these systems was considered ideologically sound, and their proportion declined during the 1970s and early 1980s, with adverse effects on the overall growth rate.[4] The 'dip' in the graph during the later 1970s could not be made good, and the 1960 rate of 109.6 million square metres was not significantly exceeded until 1983.

By 1970 the average amount of 'living space' per capita in urban areas had reached 6 square metres (9 if total 'useful' space is measured). Ten years later it had climbed to 8.6, and by 1987 to 9.4 square metres. There was considerable variation between republics. The RSFSR was just on the average (9.4), Ukraine higher (10.1) and the Baltic republics higher still, with Estonia the champion at 11.7 square metres. At the bottom of the scale was Turkmenistan, with an average of only 6.6 square metres per inhabitant. But these figures are deceptive in that all the Central Asian republics (except Kazakhstan) had proportionately more privately owned living space: over half the total housing stock, in some cases, as against a mere 13 per cent in the RSFSR (1979: Rywkin 1982). Their buildings were also better adapted to climatic conditions and the native life-style.

The accommodation built elsewhere was often of substandard quality. This was particularly true of the new towns springing up in Siberia. *Pravda* complained in 1974 that 'it often happens that in a freshly built apartment block the corners freeze through, so that heaters have to be added and third panes of glass put into the windows.' Some residents would hang rugs over their windows to reduce the icy blasts, for no extra insulation had been put in on the windy side of the buildings, which were badly sited (Seeger 1981). Even in the fashionable Moscow suburb of Cheremushki in 1984 the owners of a top-floor flat proudly showed the present writer a heating rail running around the living-room wall at ceiling height, which had been added to compensate for faulty design. The reason for such shoddy work was that the same prefabricated units were used all over the country—itself a result of the over-centralized system of manufacture and supply, coupled with excessive haste by the builders. They were concerned above all else with fulfilling their plan targets, which were expressed in crude quantitative units.

The 'Kosygin reform'

Such irrational behaviour ought by rights to have been a thing of the past, for in 1965 the Brezhnev regime embarked on an overhaul of the economic administration. The 'Kosygin reform', as it was popularly known in the West after the prime minister of the day, was much talked about but its implementation was half-hearted and inconsistent. It did not challenge any of the fundamental principles of the Stalinist 'command economy' and fell short of the proposals earlier advanced by Yevsei Liberman (see Chapter 4). Even its official designation reflected the doubts felt about it by politicians and officials: a 'new system of planning and economic stimulation' was not likely to induce many decision-makers to change their set ways. Moreover, Kosygin himself did not take a particularly prominent part in promoting it, perhaps because the new ruling team was anxious not to repeat Khrushchev's mistakes.

Essentially the reform did at least eight things. First, it reduced the number of indicators binding on an enterprise and shifted their emphasis from quantitative targets to 'economic levers' such as the amount of goods sold and of profit made. Second, it linked bonuses paid to managers and workers to their enterprise's record in this respect. Third, it gave enterprises greater leeway to enter into relationships with one another. Fourth, it introduced a charge (usually 6 per cent) for capital funds issued through the State Bank (1967) and made enterprises pay for the use of certain natural resources such as water (1970). Fifth, it raised wholesale prices (July 1967). Sixth, it fostered the formation of industrial associations ('firms', *firmy*) or 'corporations' (*kombinaty*) which co-ordinated the activities of several enterprises, the largest or most efficient assuming a directing role, in the hope of achieving economies of scale. Seventh, it encouraged planners to use mathematical techniques, especially electronic data-processing, and managers to approach their tasks in a more scientific spirit, learning from the West. Eighth, it relaxed the stringency of ideological criticism of such 'capitalist' practices as profit-seeking or marketing.

An equally long list could be compiled of what the Kosygin reform did *not* do, but its limitations are best indicated by looking at the way it was put into practice. No single edict set out its objectives clearly. Instead it was introduced piecemeal. Prices were not liberalized. Far from attempting to remodel the administrative machinery comprehensively, Kosygin and his colleagues simply resurrected the system that had existed before Khrushchev had begun to tinker with it. The *sovnarkhozy* disappeared, the central economic ministries resurfaced. They even expanded their powers somewhat at the expense of those at union-republic level. Gosplan, the chief planning agency, was expanded—it had about forty departments for different branches of the economy—and its authority reinforced. It shared with Gossnab, the central agency for material supplies, responsibility for balancing inputs and outputs. Beneath the various economic ministries, whose number increased from sixteen to twenty-seven between 1966 and 1975, came twenty to thirty main administrations (*glavki*), each concerned with certain types of product. These did not, however, control all the enterprises in their respective domain. Instead, the various constituent units of a *firma* might come under different *glavki* as well as under different local government bodies, according to their geographical location.

This cumbersome arrangement gave officials, anxious not to lose any of their power, ample scope for meddling and bureaucratic empire-building. Despite a 1969 decree transferring certain enterprises to what was termed 'non-allocational supply', the purchase of raw materials was in practice regulated by a quota system, so that there was no genuine trade in producers' goods. Nor could enterprises freely decide for themselves how much money to borrow, how much labour to employ, or what assortment of goods to produce. In practice targets for output, productivity, and so on continued to be set, even though such directives contradicted the letter and spirit of the reform. The director of the Rosa Luxemburg knitwear factory in Kiev complained that he had to submit reports on the fulfilment of fifteen different indicators, and at the Red October plant in Tsaritsyn (then Volgograd) an economist said that their number was approaching twenty: 'for some reason we're looked after as though we were babies: even if we spend a mere thousand roubles on capital repairs we have to make out an application form.'

Managers had every reason to play safe and comply with such orders, especially since they soon learned through the grape-vine that senior politicians were having second thoughts about the new measures. The impetus behind them weakened as Brezhnev's powers grew *vis-à-vis* Kosygin's. The Party leader is said to have grumbled privately: 'reforms, reforms! . . . people ought to work better, that's the problem.' This reactionary attitude was reinforced by events in Czechoslovakia. Hard-liners lost no time in pointing to the dangerous similarities between East European 'market socialism' and the home-grown variety. 'The maximization of profit', ran one such critical article, 'is not the best local criterion of optimization; to make profits an absolute yardstick, the basis of market equilibrium, betrays an exaggerated notion of the role of market relations under socialism' (Kaser 1975, citing D. Allakhverdian 1970). Others warned that loosening price controls was leading to inflation, although the (modest) price rises that occurred actually stemmed from lack of competition and the accumulation of so much unsatisfied demand.

The trend to monopoly (or, more properly, oligopoly) was accentuated. By 1965 the number of 'firms' had reached 592. Over the next four years only 180 new ones were formed—but 240 of those already in existence were liquidated. This was the result partly of interference by ministries and *glavki*, which prevented them from functioning effectively, and partly of collusion by managers, for whom such mergers threatened salary cuts and loss of influence (Gorlin 1974). By 1971 the 650 'firms' comprised 2,700 enterprises and employed 8.5 per cent of the labour-force. They were concentrated in light industries (e.g. food-processing), where they accounted for 22 per cent of goods sold and 25 per cent of employees, and had on average about 4,000 individuals on their payroll. Geographically, they were most prevalent in Ukraine, the Baltic states, and the two main Russian metropolises. In Leningrad they produced 90 per cent of all clothing manufactured. Each 'firm' was supposed to have its own unit for R & D (research and development). But instead of this information improving the association's competitive position, it had to be shared, since planners wanted the experience of 'leading' enterprises to be spread as widely as possible, so rationalizing performance throughout the economy. As 'firms' grew in size, they became almost indistinguishable from *glavki* and more remote from the concerns of ordinary workpeople. Meanwhile their constituent enterprises were tempted to engage in 'selfish' practices on the margin of the law. This in turn led to demands for closer control from above. Despite these problems amalgamations continued. By 1985 the number of 'firms' is said to have reached 4,400. Comprising 8,600 enterprises and 10,200 'production units', they were responsible for just over half the country's industrial output.

Trying to motivate all these managers was a major preoccupation of the reformers. Their main instrument was the enterprise bonus fund, whose size depended not just on the amount of profit (as Liberman had suggested) but on its ratio to the amount of capital invested and the size of the wage bill. Under the original dispensation any deviation from 100 per cent fulfilment of the allotted target brought a penalty. In exchange the authorities undertook not to boost an enterprise's norms each year, as had often been the practice; instead norms were to run for five years. The new system was not popular and helped to slow down productivity growth. Accordingly in 1971 came a return to more traditional methods. The absolute size of the fund was again fixed by central agencies, and managers were encouraged to overfulfil the norms set. Simultaneously, though, bonuses were also awarded for producing fresh lines of goods or those of superior quality. Unhappily, inspectors discovered that many managers were submitting fraudulent claims on behalf of certain 'improved' products. There were also complaints by workers that too large a share of the bonus fund was going to administrative, engineering, or technical staff. Senior men did indeed receive a much greater proportion of their total earnings—in excess of the legal maximum of 60 per cent in some cases—in the form of bonus payments than bench workers did. Efforts were made to stop this discrimination by ordering the bonus to be distributed between each group according to its relative share of the wage bill, but this measure does not appear to have been successful (Adam 1980). Nor did it help much when, in 1979, bonuses were made dependent on performance in three areas: productivity growth, the proportion of high-quality goods produced, and accurate fulfilment of contracts. A new vogue word came in, 'normative net output', but few were quite sure what this meant. Not many enterprises adopted this complicated method of evaluation, and efforts to implement it increased the 'information overload' on central officials (Hanson 1983).

'Scientific management'

These officials were almost as dissatisfied with the practices of industrial management as workers were—and their discontents were politically more significant, at least in the short term. Professional economists and other 'establishment intellectuals' became increasingly concerned at the evident unresponsiveness of the centralized administrative system to efforts at reform. Some of these men were now familiar with advanced Western thought, particularly on questions of scientific management. 'Systems analysis' seemed to them a promising way of rationalizing the direction of complex organizations. Naïvely, they assumed that it could be taken over simply as a technical device, divorced from the cultural milieu in which it had been developed. Nemchinov's Central Economico-Mathematical Institute (CEMI) played a key role in devising a new planning system christened SOFE (System of Optimal Functioning of the Economy). It proceeded from scientifically determined estimates of long-term goals and available resources rather than, as at present, from data on existing capacity and potential—data which were then adjusted incrementally on the 'ratchet' principle. Instead of having to rely on information arrived at arbitrarily, or even fraudulently, by managers and subordinate officials, planners would be able to make accurate computer projections for national requirements and then break these down between various industrial branches, regions, and, ultimately, enterprises, as operational targets for a series of shorter time-spans.

This seductive notion required creation of a giant national computer grid, nicknamed OGAS,[5] 'a total informational processing system with an analytical function' (Conyngham 1982). The scheme was presented to the public at the Twenty-fourth Party congress in 1971. It was to comprise fifteen republic and 200 regional computer centres, and below them about 25,000 automated management systems (ASUs) at the level of 'firms' or enterprises. Ultimately it was to be integrated with the national networks in other East European countries that belonged to the CMEA ('Comecon').

The Orwellian monster was never born. Although treated as a priority project by the leadership, the task proved too much for Soviet resources and cybernetic skills. Nearly ten years were spent trying to construct it. There were problems in developing the necessary hardware and jurisdictional conflicts. For instance, the military resisted control over their information network by the State Committee for Science and Technology (GKNT), which was slated to be the project's 'general staff'. This committee was never able to exercise its allotted powers to the full. The various 'subsystems' jealously guarded their autonomy and impeded efforts to co-ordinate their respective programmes. Computers were indeed widely used in distributing electricity and agricultural implements, but by and large enterprise managers did not take kindly to the scientific 'boffins' and young enthusiasts who tried to convert them to their fashionable modern ideas. For example, the supply agency Gossnab increased the amount of data it processed between 1970 and 1975 by almost two-thirds (65.8 per cent), and claimed that thereby it had saved the work of 62,000 employees. Yet an investigation showed that 'managers implemented only four of fifty-seven optimal plans without correction [and these] corrections ... were so extensive that the adjusted plans had greater losses than if they had been computed manually' (Conyngham 1982). Fearing that without control over information they would lose status, managers complained that 'making a fetish of technology [is] pushing human problems to the rear.' Printouts would often lie around factory workshops unutilized because foremen considered the computer's recommendations misleading or false. They complained of stress and disorientation.

According to a poll taken in L'viv (mid-1970s) managers did not think computers promoted innovation, but rather that they increased the amount of regimentation and led to inequities in the wage structure.

By the early 1980s the drive for scientific management seems to have slowed down. Officials at all levels went back to the familiar routine, according to which they spent the bulk of their time sorting out current crises in order to keep production flowing at all costs. They preferred to rely on informal links to obtain scarce supplies and to keep their superiors well-disposed by padding statistical reports and performing other old tricks. Hoarding stocks, 'storming' at month's end, and a reluctance to innovate would remain characteristic of the Soviet industrial scene until the era of *perestroika*. It then became painfully apparent that the limited training these functionaries had received rendered them woefully unfit for the managerial role they were expected to perform.

However, they are not the only ones to merit censure. The economists and mathematicians who sought to perfect the system of total planning were out of touch with socio-political reality. They were trying to push the Soviet economy in the wrong direction, away from market relationships or humanization of conditions in the workplace. To be fair, the behaviourists among them did seek to give the reform movement an orientation in this sense, but theirs was a minority school of thought. In practice it led simply to increased pressure on workers to raise productivity by reverting to the long-since discredited ideas of F. W. Taylor,[6] which Lenin had endorsed, and Gastev's 'scientific labour organization' school of the 1920s, which amounted to 'treatment of men as machines' (Wiles 1981).

The world of labour

That conditions in the workplace needed improvement goes without saying, but the right approach would have been to allow trade unions more power to defend their members' interests. Instead they remained part of the managerial bureaucracy. Their role was to help integrate workers into the existing system—or, to use Soviet 'wooden language', 'to enhance the material and spiritual position of labour in building Communism'. This meant encouraging initiatives from below to introduce technical innovations or promote 'socialist emulation' drives, administering training and social insurance schemes, verifying observance of safety regulations, and running sanatoria, sports clubs, etc. Ideologists claimed that under Brezhnevian 'mature socialism' the trade unions had taken over many functions previously performed by state organs, and that AUCCTU (the central trade-union body) was regularly consulted when framing labour legislation, as well as on planning problems generally. Such consultation likewise went on at lower levels in the hierarchy. In 1982 there were nearly one million (914,000) trade-union officials at town or district level or above, and another seven million at factory level (Lane 1985). In larger factories a trade-union branch would have several commissions for wages, safety, housing, cultural activities, and so on, as well as 'shop committees' mainly concerned with production matters.

In all their work these officials liaised closely with Party and management. Their most important function was to take part in drawing up collective agreements defining output levels and the way the part of the bonus fund accruing to the workers (but *not*, of course, wages!) should be distributed. Nothing a trade-union branch did could go against official policy. Even so, although they were not autonomous bodies, there was in practice a certain 'grey area' that allowed informal bargaining. Managers who exhibited 'bureaucratic tendencies' might find themselves called to account. In 1980 two hundred managers were reportedly dismissed from their posts at the unions' behest. Two years later the same fate allegedly befell no less than 9,800 of them for infringing health and safety regulations alone (Lane 1985). It is probable, however, that most such dismissals were previously agreed on with Party and government organs and that they should be considered part of normal turnover. On the other hand, the illusion that unions *did* have such power may have helped to keep some of their members docile.

Not all of them were taken in. In 1979 workers at a dairy-products *kombinat* in Tol'iatti wrote an open letter, which was published abroad, complaining that their trade-union branch chair-woman had been imposed by the factory's director. The pair were accomplices in a swindle which, when exposed, led to the director's dismissal but left the chairwoman in place. 'We, who "elected" her, do not have the right to demand from [her] an account of how she worked in her trade-union job. We have only the right to be silent' (Godson 1981).

The state of workers' morale depended in large degree on immediate material factors (nature of work done, wage rates, hygienic conditions, availability of food and housing, etc.), as well as on the general 'climate' in the enterprise, so that any generalization on the subject is likely to be misleading. Some information can be derived indirectly from rates of absenteeism and labour mobility, although such behaviour had many causes and cannot automatically be attributed to disaffection. The prevalence of absenteeism was a frequent topic of complaint in the media. The official 'allowance' was three days a year, but in 1978 one Soviet researcher estimated it at more than 10 per cent. Combined with other reasons for absence (sickness, 'intra-shift down time', etc.), total loss of labour time amounted to 51 per cent (1974: Pietsch 1987, citing A. McAuley and A. Helgeson). Absenteeism was often connected with drinking bouts. Offenders would be reprimanded and disciplined but rarely suffered serious penalties.

Total annual labour turnover was about 30 per cent[7] but many enterprises reported rates of 70 per cent or more. In part this efflux was due to lack of adequate public information about alternative employment opportunities, which meant that the only way to find a better job was to quit. But a 1977 poll in one small Belarusian town reported that over half those who left did so because they were dissatisfied with the nature of their work or pay rates (Dyker 1981). Turnover tended to be higher in less industrialized regions (e.g. Tajikistan), low-priority industries such as food-processing, and small plants. Many of those who left also changed occupations, which meant that the money spent on training them was largely wasted (Powell 1983). There developed something of an underclass of 'rolling stones' who stayed nowhere for long and performed poorly wherever they found employment. Especially worrying for the authorities was the high proportion of young workers who changed jobs. They were likely to be less satisfied with the system than their elders.

On the other hand, a certain level of mobility was clearly desirable, *inter alia* to fill the new job vacancies opening up in the Siberian oil and gas fields. (Persons employed in areas with a severe climate qualified for supplementary pay, which gave them a strong incentive to move there, at least for a brief spell.) The authorities recognized that many enterprises were overstaffed. Already in 1967 a campaign was launched to persuade them to shed unneeded workers. The 'Shchekino experiment' was named for a place in Tula province where a chemical combine was the first to adopt the plan. It involved setting fixed limits to output targets and the wages fund in order to give management an incentive to cut down on excess staff. By 1970 1,039 jobs out of 7,000 at Shchekino had been cut, output had surged by 87 per cent, and labour productivity by even more (114 per cent). Accordingly another 126 plants were converted to the system. Thereafter the figure constantly rose, particularly in the oil and petro-chemical industries, reaching 1,200 enterprises in 1977 and 3,300 in 1982. Nearly a million jobs were said to have been saved (1983). But the more widely the scheme was practised the lower the proportionate savings. As a rule those dismissed found jobs elsewhere—often indeed in the same factory. The rest included a fair number of 'dead souls' who had contributed little anyway. Above all, the law obliged managers, in conjunction with local government agencies, to find alternative jobs for men sacked (Rutland 1984). The principle of full employment was still considered sacred—indeed unemployment would be kept artificially low for years even after the USSR had collapsed. Powerful ideological and institutional constraints militated against any move towards a free labour market. Moreover, the authorities would intervene to prevent the wage fund increasing 'unduly' in factories involved in the scheme, so that pay rates and bonuses were adversely affected and workers grew distrustful. 'Those marked for dismissal began to protest, and morale, even among those who ultimately stayed, suffered' (Goldman 1983).

Social psychologists pointed out, in Aesopian language, that the lack of democracy in the workplace was engendering a feeling of powerlessness. They pleaded for a return to the values of the early revolutionary era, when efforts had been made to introduce 'workers' control'. Such ideas, however laudable, were scarcely realistic. Experience in Eastern Europe reinforced the determination of those in power to maintain existing controls over the labour-force. There was little likelihood of Russian workers emulating Polish 'Solidarity'. In 1981 scattered demonstrations did occur in a number of outlying provincial cities (Tobol'sk, Krasnodar, Odessa). Strikes were also reported from Kiev, Nizhnii Novgorod (then Gor'ky), and Tol'iatti. The motives were purely economic: local food shortages and cuts in piece-work rates.

In 1978 V. Klebanov, an unemployed worker, and others set up a 'free trade union' in Moscow. The organizers were arrested and sent to an SPH, but the idea gained some ground. A 'Free Inter-professional Workers' Association' (SMOT) took shape, under the leadership of three engineers and technicians, which strove to defend workers' socio-economic rights. It secured three hundred adherents, of whom about half were workers—and half women (Novak 1990)—and published thirty-five issues of a *samizdat* information bulletin. Its failure to attract broader support was due only in part to the pervasiveness of police, Party, and trade-union controls. The mass of Russian workers, although often critical of their masters, were not hostile to the system. It offered them, after all, job security and a modest wage in return for a relatively easy life.

The popular East European saying 'you pretend to pay us, we pretend to work' applies with even greater force to the USSR. Worker apathy or inertia was as fundamental an obstacle to the reformers' efforts as the suspiciousness of ideologists and the vested interests of managers. As if this opposition were not enough, the reformers were themselves divided and lacked a firm institutional base outside the academic world. Moreover, their ideas were, in the last resort, inconsistent. For how could one get people in industry, whether managers or workers, to become profit- and efficiency-oriented unless prices were freed and the market economy made respectable?

12 Agrarian and Environmental Dilemmas

Khrushchev's successors took over his basic strategy for ensuring a rapid growth of agricultural output but applied it in a more consistent manner. There was less 'campaigning' and bureaucratic interference in farm management, but no major change of the organizational pattern inherited from Stalin. Investment allocations were increased and agricultural prices raised, but farms still found it hard to cover their costs. Only in two years (1976, 1978) did the grain harvest exceed the target under the plan, and in the early 1980s the situation in this respect was so bad that statisticians were forbidden to publish the actual figures. Deficiencies repeatedly had to be made good by imports, especially of fodder grains, from the West. By 1985 these amounted to 24 per cent of domestic cereals production. Nevertheless output of agricultural goods did increase significantly. In the Tenth Five-Year Plan (1976–80) it was greater by half than in 1961–5. The problem was less one of production than of productivity, of 'a drastic fall in the return to capital invested' (Hedlund 1984): whereas capital stock in agriculture rose by 160 per cent between 1965 and 1980, gross output increased by less than 20 per cent.

The most obvious symptom of rural Russia's profound malaise was the exodus from the villages of skilled young men. Those left behind, increasingly the aged and infirm, lacked their peasant ancestors' emotional bond to the land. Apathetic and disheartened, they eked out a living from their private household plots and neglected their responsibilities towards the 'socialist collective'. Although monetary incomes rose and the rural population was no longer at such a material disadvantage *vis-à-vis* industrial workers, social conditions in the countryside remained primitive. Even more serious was the degradation of the environment in so many areas, the outcome of half a century's hectic forced development.

Agricultural policy after 1964

Agriculture was the focus of the first Central Committee plenum to be held after the new leadership had firmly established itself, in March 1965. It ended the administrative confusion of Khrushchev's last years, eased restrictions on private plots, promised farm managers greater autonomy, reduced delivery quotas, and raised prices for agricultural deliveries. The taxes that *kolkhozy* had to pay were revised downwards and their debts to the state written off. Above all, investment in 1966–70 was to be more than double what it had been in the previous quinquennium. To optimists it seemed as though the regime had at last learned from its earlier mistakes and that a new age had dawned for farmers.

But not all the promised investment materialized. In 1970 the figure was 58 per cent greater than it had been in 1965, but not double. Over the next fifteen years agriculture's proportion of total state investment stabilized at 26 to 27 per cent—more if industries servicing rural needs are included. Altogether this was more than double the share set aside under Stalin; the total from 1966 to 1982 was 500 milliard roubles. It was a very heavy burden for the state, especially if food subsidies are taken into account. In the mid-1970s beef, on sale to the consumer at 2 roubles per kilogram, cost 3.50 roubles to produce. In 1980 subsidies for livestock alone were running at 25 milliard roubles, or 37 per cent of the value of all livestock produced, and state agricultural investment that year was put at 36 milliard roubles.

This situation was of concern to officials trying to balance the budget yet did not please farm managers either. Only a favoured few succeeded in keeping their books straight. Most farms, faced with uncertain or declining incomes and rising wage costs, again fell into debt. The (regionally differentiated) prices they received for their produce were fixed centrally, without regard to the vagaries of the harvest, so that revenues fluctuated considerably. Technical crops paid well, whereas livestock was generally raised at a loss. Yet farms lacked the freedom to choose activities that would earn the maximum profit. Instead, 'the most inefficient farms with the highest costs would be paid the highest prices' (Hedlund 1984), and differentials between rich and poor widened.

A particular problem was that collective farms were not allowed to hold financial reserves large enough to meet their varying seasonal needs. These had to be met largely from their own resources, especially on the weaker farms, which did not readily qualify for bank credits—whereas *sovkhozy* were treated far more liberally and could retain more of their income (Millar 1973). Collective-farm debts rose from 4 milliard roubles in 1965 to 60 milliard roubles in 1980, equivalent to 55 per cent of their capital funds, and in 1982 one-tenth of them again had to be written off. Half of all farms (of both types) were unprofitable.

Another source of discontent was that supplies of equipment and fertilizer were frequently inadequate or delayed. In Poltava province in 1968 farmers received only 58 per cent of the tractors they had put in for, 28 per cent of the trucks, and 18 per cent of the milking machines. The quality of the latter left much to be desired. From western Siberia, for example, it was reported that only 15 per cent of them worked properly, and 'on some farms the apparatus goes wrong sixty to a hundred times a month' (Nove 1970). Such breakdowns might well be due as much to faulty maintenance by unskilled hands as to poor design by the supplier. But there was often a shortage of ploughs and other implements for attachment to tractors for various tasks in the field. In 1981, according to *Pravda*, the Agricultural Machinery ministry produced a new model that could accommodate thirty-three such implements, but only four of them were actually available. Much equipment was said to be obsolete and hard to maintain. The widely used combine harvester SK-4 had 200 lubricating points, fifty-five of which had to be oiled daily (Karcz 1970).

The lack of spare parts continued to be a major problem for farmers. Factories did not find it worth while to produce them, for the plan could be fulfilled more easily by manufacturing large, heavy pieces of equipment. Farms had to have their own repair workshops, since the state agency responsible could not cope with the demand. There was a thriving black market in stolen items and scrap. Livestock-raising and vegetable cultivation had low ratios of mechanization. Despite a campaign to build grain elevators, storage facilities remained notoriously inadequate. Much waste ensued from the lack of refrigerated equipment to handle perishable goods on the way to market. Rural roads, rutted and uneven, were more than a match even for stoutly built Soviet-made haulage vehicles. A farm truck had a life expectancy of less than six years. Many of them were open to the elements, with predictable results. No less than 620,000 tons of fertilizer were lost in transit annually, or so *Sovetskaia Rossiia* reported in 1981. But this was only one-third of the amount lost in storage and handling, and only one-tenth of what was lost through negligence on the farm. Overall, such wastage accounted for over 9 million tons, or 10 per cent of total fertilizer output.

Farmers frequently complained that the type of fertilizer delivered did not accord with local requirements. This was because they could not deal directly with the producers, for all supplies were channelled through the state agency Selkhozkhimiia. In terms of nutrient content, mineral fertilizer output more than quadrupled between 1965 and 1985 (from 7.4 to 33.2 million tons), and that of insecticides almost tripled (from 201,000 to 595,000 tons). Some of this was exported. The share 'supplied to agriculture' (a term not necessarily identical with 'being spread on the land'!) declined from 84.7 per cent in 1965 to 76.5 per cent in 1985. The great expansion occurred in nitrogenous and phosphate-bearing chemicals, which were notoriously polluting. Yet the USSR was behind many other European countries in its use of fertilizer per hectare.[1] The 1981 figure was 66 kilograms, as against 274 kilograms in Hungary (Wädekin 1988). A similar lag can be shown in many other respects, for example in the amount of electrical power used per farm worker (or per hectare).

Output and yields

A healthy dose of scepticism is in order when considering official statistics on agricultural output. In 1988 Soviet writers admitted that, as Western experts had long argued, an allowance had to be made for the 'non-usable content' of grain, sugar beet, potatoes, and cotton delivered to procurement agencies, because they contained weeds, soil, and other impurities. According to Hedlund, a deduction of 5 to 10 per cent should be made for this from the published figures, depending on how wet the weather was during the harvest. The practice of calculating crops' 'bunker yield' failed to make allowance for moisture and foreign matter. In 1988 L. Ivanov put the difference between this estimate and actual barn yield at 25 per cent or more. However, if one assumes that the degree of such falsification was probably constant over time, official data on output growth rates over the twenty-year period can be

TABLE 12.1. *Growth of agricultural output by quinquennia, 1966–1985*

	1966–70	1971–5	1976–80	1981–5
Gross agricultural output (milliard roubles)[a]	100.4	113.7	123.9	131
Cereals (million tons)	167.6	181.6	205	181[b]
Meat (million tons)[c]	11.6	14.0	14.8	16.2
Milk (million tons)	80.6	87.4	2.6	94.5
Eggs (milliard)	35.8	51.4	63.1	4.4
Vegetables (million tons)	19.5	23.0	26.3	29.2
Potatoes (million tons)	94.8	89.8	82.6	78.4
Sugar beet (million tons)	81.1	6.0	88.7	76.3
Cotton (million tons)	6.1	7.7	8.9	9.1

[a] 1973 prices.
[b] A. Nove 1990.
[c] Slaughter weight.

accepted as indicative of the trend. We should take five-year averages to allow for annual fluctuations due to bad weather. The vagaries of the Russian climate struck hard in 1967, 1972, and 1975. In 1978 the grain harvest was a record 237 million tons, but in 1981 only 160 million tons, and 46 million more had to be imported.

Gross agricultural output rose by 3.9 per cent per annum in the late 1960s, but by only 1.2 per cent in the 1970s (Johnson 1983). The yield of vegetables, in centners per hectare, rose from 132 to 161, whereas that of potatoes remained the same. The number of head of cattle rose from 93.4 million on 1 January 1966 to 120.8 million twenty years later, an increase of 29 per cent. Since the number of cows rose by only 9 per cent, the expansion was most marked in beef cattle. Pigs increased by 30.4 per cent to 77.7 million, sheep by only 8.2 per cent to 140.5 million; poultry quadrupled. Dairy cattle took a lot of looking after: 8 to 9 hours for 100 kilograms of milk, about half as much as in 1965 but still far more than in the West. Yields were below target and after the mid-1970s remained stable at an average (1981–5) of 2,220 kilograms. This was lower than anywhere else in Eastern Europe except Romania (data for 1979: Jones and Smogorzewska 1982).

Moreover, cows on private plots were less productive than those belonging to the state. The major reason for this was the poor quality of locally produced fodder, which was lacking in protein but had a harmful surfeit of nitrates. Yields of silage and hay were half what they should have been, given the amount of wheat and maize produced. In drought years hay was often in short supply, and concentrates accounted for only one-third of the 'fodder balance'. Since no animal feed was on sale publicly, private producers had to obtain it, legally or otherwise, from the farm's stocks. When there was none to spare, they would use bread and potatoes, and when these stocks ran out would have to slaughter their animals. One such massacre took place in 1975/6, for which drought was blamed. The situation was as a rule less grim in the Baltic provinces, where consumption of dairy products was far above the all-Union average.

Private plots; contract brigades

The same regional differences can be observed in regard to private plots. In the Baltic they were double the average size, but in Kazakhstan only one-third of the all-Union figure (1970: Wädekin 1975). They were particularly important in Georgia, where they accounted for one-fifth of that republic's total cultivated area, as against a mere 3 per cent in the USSR as a whole. Yet they supplied over one-quarter of the country's needs of meat and dairy products. In 1981–5 the figures were 25.3 per cent of all milk produced, 28.9 per cent of meat, 29.8 per cent of eggs—and (1979) 42 per cent of fruit and berries. All fruit and vegetables consumed by the rural population and three-quarters of their milk and meat were privately produced. The plots' share of total agricultural output was declining slowly—according to official figures from 32.5 per cent in 1965 to 26.5 per cent in 1979—as the socialist sector's performance improved and staple foodstuffs became more regularly available. But state trading agencies continued to show little interest in such products. If it was too troublesome for farmers to take them to the nearest collective-farm market, they were eaten, exchanged, or sold locally.

The regulations on private farming were scarcely affected by revisions made in 1969 to the 1936 collective-farm charter. The maximum permitted size for a plot remained at half a hectare. Not until 1980, when there was an abnormally severe meat shortage, were farm managements encouraged to take a more co-operative attitude towards private producers. They could, for example, allow publicly owned animals (especially pigs) to be taken over by individual peasant households to be fattened up and eventually slaughtered, the profits being split evenly between the partners to the deal. Peasants could also obtain bank loans to purchase livestock. However, rural officials looked askance at such practices and most farmers, reasonably enough, continued to see the two sectors of the agricultural economy as rival claimants on their time and resources.

The rural bureaucracy wrecked promising schemes to encourage the formation of 'links' (*zven'ia*) or 'contract brigades'—that is, labour teams—which would draw up contracts with the farm management to perform certain tasks and receive pay according to results. The notion was not new, having been adopted already in 1939, but had fallen victim to the post-war ideological freeze (see p. 20). In the early 1960s the idea revived. Experiments were conducted, notably in Siberia, which showed that applying such working methods could raise yields and lower production costs appreciably. For example, one could obtain 11 to 13 centners of soya beans per hectare in lieu of the customary 2 to 3 centners.

One noted activist in these experiments was Khudenko, a *sovkhoz* chairman in Kazakhstan. On a model farm in that republic he demonstrated that a centner of grain could be produced for 1.66 instead of 6.38 roubles, with team members' incomes tripling. He calculated that state farms had twelve times as many operatives as they neded. But what was to be done with the surplus manpower? Farm chairmen and other officials rallied to suppress what they saw as a threat to their vital interests and as a concession to the 'capitalistic' practices of the small family farm. Khudenko was denounced and arrested. Convicted on false charges, he died in jail in 1974. Journalists and academics kept the idea alive. In 1982–3 it resurfaced, this time with Gorbachev as its principal protagonist. As Party first secretary in Stavropol' region (1970–8) he authorized its application on a modest scale. When appointed CC secretary with responsibility for agriculture, he took the idea up at top level but ran into heavy opposition. Not until after Brezhnev's death did the scheme go forward.

By October 1985 30 per cent of farm workers were said to have been enrolled in 'contract brigades' and yields to have risen. But appearances were, as usual, deceptive. Many of these teams existed only on paper, for the campaign to introduce them was conducted in typical bureaucratic fashion, by order from above. One eighteen-man team had nine male 'mechanizers' and nine female subordinates who did the hard work! (Nove 1984.) It was found that to achieve good results a contract had to be concluded on a long-term basis and be linked to a specific plot of land (Gagnon 1987). But this meant resuscitating proprietorial instincts, and in effect abandoning collective farming. Neither Gorbachev nor the CPSU was yet ready for such a step. Furthermore, industry could not provide the regular flow of supplies which the teams needed if their members' incomes and morale were to be sustained. Where these supplies were lacking, brigades quickly broke up, as their members chose to go back to receiving a regular wage.

Other policy initiatives

Nor did the rural population benefit much from the few other initiatives taken during Brezhnev's rule. In April 1974 an edict was issued on the development of the northern parts of the RSFSR (the 'non-black-earth zone', as it was tactfully called in order not to upset non-Russians!). Much money was sunk into swamp drainage and other melioration schemes, some of which did more harm than good. There was talk of setting up 'agro-industrial complexes' for manufacturing agricultural by-products and turning small villages into urban-type settlements—a notion which echoed the ill-fated *agrogoroda* (see p. 20). No less than 15 million people in 143,000 so-called 'futureless' (*besperspektivnye*) villages were to be 'concentrated' in 29,000 new-fangled agglomerations, each of them with a minimum population of one thousand and equipped with all the latest amenities. In one district of Tver' province 423 out of 527 villages were officially declared to be 'non-viable' (Agursky 1982). The scheme aroused fierce opposition, not least from writers of the national school. A start was made on it by building five-storey blocks to accommodate villagers slated for relocation, but lack of funds prevented the plan from being implemented on the scale intended. According to the writer V. Belov (1987) tens of thousands of places did disappear from the map—but this seems to have been a spontaneous phenomenon rather than a 'restructuring' carried out by administrative fiat.

The so-called 'food programme', announced with loud fanfares in May 1982, was a sequel to this drive, and also in part

Gorbachev's handiwork. He came up against the opposition of Prime Minister Tikhonov, who was determined not to allot more resources to agriculture. This explains why contemporaries dismissed it as 'shockingly unimaginative' (Johnson 1983). It created new bureaucratic bodies called 'agricultural industrial associations' and increased yet again the procurement prices paid to the farms which, since prices to the consumer remained unaffected, caused agricultural subsidies to leap by nearly 50 per cent.[2]

Rural outmigration; social conditions

The object of all these measures was to make life in the villages more attractive and to stem the outflow of migrants to the towns. According to a decree of February 1975 peasants were granted the right to hold internal passports. This made them in principle the legal equals of townspeople. But the wording was ambiguous, and in practice, it seems, few received them. In 1985 G. Hosking noted in this context that 'the "second serfdom" remains in force, at least in the sense that the *kolkhoznik* is fixed to the land'. Passports were not issued to all adult Soviet citizens until 1981. The system of residential registration prevented any sudden efflux. Nevertheless one should not exaggerate the force of the administrative restrictions on mobility. The demand for labour was such that enterprise managers often colluded with prospective employees to evade the law. Conscript soldiers were not in practice forced to return to their native village when their term of service ended. Urban girls, especially if they lived in Moscow, were favoured marriage partners for rural youths, who could hope thereby to receive the coveted permit (*propiska*). These documents were as a rule issued for a limited period only, hence the popular term for those who held them, *limitchiki*. Many cities also had sizeable numbers of unregistered residents. Migrants in both categories, as we have noted, generally had to put up with inferior housing—and harsher working conditions, too. These dismal prospects did not stop the drift, although it fluctuated considerably from one year to another.

Up to a point the movement to the towns had the authorities' sanction, although they became increasingly concerned at the effect it was having on rural birth rates and at the loss of manpower in strategic or labour-short regions such as eastern Siberia. Especially harmful was the fact that migrants tended to be ' "the best and brightest", young people with energy, ambition and skills, . . . tractor and truck drivers, combine operators, as well as members of the rural intelligentsia' (Powell 1983). As to the causes, there was general agreement that migrants were attracted by the hope of securing more interesting and better-paid jobs, as well as educational advancement and improved services. A 1970 study in Smolensk province found that 40 per cent of migrants cited boredom as one reason for quitting the village, as against 17 per cent six years earlier. The number of migrants between 1959 and 1970 was put at 16 million. Over the period 1965–85 the annual average net loss to the countryside was 630,000, and the rural share of total population sank from 46.7 to 34.4 per cent.[3] It was largely a Slavic (and Baltic) phenomenon. Over the twenty-year intercensal period 1959–79 the all-Union rate of urbanization was 14 per cent. Each of the three Slav republics had higher rates, Belarus leading the field at 24 per cent, compared with a mere 2 per cent in Turkmenistan and Tajikistan.

Collective farmers who remained on the land now enjoyed a guaranteed wage (at least 70 to 80 per cent of the sum due at year's end), a chance of bonus payments, and a pension on reaching retirement age. These reforms, introduced in 1965–6, were the outcome of Khrushchev's policies. Initially rural pensions were tiny, only about half as large as the minimum paid to (urban) employees or *sovkhoz* workers, but they rose later. The system discriminated in favour of tractor-drivers and other machine operators, which was galling to ordinary farm labourers. The unspoken assumption was that elderly peasants would go on working their allotments until they dropped, and that they would meet their basic needs from this source.

Such income did indeed retain its importance for country folk of all ages—and for many urban-dwellers as well. In 1965 *kolkhoznik* households obtained over one-third (36.5 per cent) of their total income from the sale of produce. According to official budget surveys (admittedly error-prone), by 1980 the proportion had fallen to 27.5 per cent, and five years later to 26.2 per cent. Pension income and family members' wages each accounted for about 10 per cent of total household income, and *kolkhoz* pay for half. (It should be noted that *kolkhozniki* were paid only for the actual days they worked, and that some were unemployed for part of the year.) A tractor-driver could hope to receive 60 per cent more than a labourer and was also more likely to earn a bonus. This might bring his income up to the level of an agronomist or other specialist. The earnings of such qualified personnel (e.g. veterinarians) fell *vis-à-vis* those of manual labourers—but farm chairmen continued to do much better than either group. Their 'take-home pay' might be three to four times that of a labourer. Both the total wage bill and differential pay rates varied greatly according to a farm's location and its relative success. In general the trend was upwards—as indeed was only to be expected, given the scale of agricultural investment. Farmers improved their position *vis-à-vis* industrial workers and employees. If in 1966 they were only half as well off as the latter, by 1970 the ratio had climbed to two-thirds, and by 1985 to 81 per cent.[4] Rural old-age pensioners actually did slightly (5.4 per cent) better than their counterparts in the towns because of the greater availability of foodstuffs. To most *kolkhozniki* the comparison that mattered most was that between their earnings and those of their privileged neighbours on state farms. Here as in other respects the gap narrowed. By 1980 they were only 3 roubles per month behind, and by 1985 had overtaken them—according to official data, at least.

Such figures should not be taken as indicating an approximation of the urban and rural worlds. Socially and culturally, the gulf remained wide. It was accentuated by the *embourgeoisement* of the working-class élite and by the fact that migrants to the cities tried to dissociate themselves from their rural background. As several foreign travellers noted, peasants who came to market in the towns *looked* different from their customers. Soviet budgetary data show that the two residential groups had different spending habits (see Table 12.2). It is remarkable that *kolkhozniki*, despite the greater availability of 'free' home-grown produce, should have spent more on food than workers and employees did.

Buying and preparing food, caring for livestock and poultry: these were only some of the duties that fell to Russia's rural womenfolk. They comprised 52 per cent of the labour-force on collectives and 45 per cent overall (1974). Unless they had succeeded when in their teens in joining the efflux from the villages—and surveys showed that two-thirds of country girls aspired to join what was officially called the intelligentsia—this meant leaving home to acquire a higher education. Those who stayed behind married local lads and found themselves bound for life to their husband's household. On collective farms women put in four-fifths as much labour time (184 days) as men did, and even those of pensionable age worked for 83 days (1971: Dunn 1977). On top of this they spent another one-third of their time on the household plot, as against only one-eighth by their menfolk. Not surprisingly, four out of five rural women polled complained about their lot.

Rural officials were insensitive to such problems. Nor could women hope to displace them. 'Women . . . occupied a minuscule portion of top management positions', concluded one Western specialist. Female farm chairmen comprised 1.6 per cent of the total on state, 1.9 per cent on collective farms (1976). Successful women ended up mainly as zootechnicians or 'brigadiers' in charge of livestock. This was due less to 'male chauvinist' prejudice than to the fact that relatively few women possessed the right educational qualifications or career profile when senior appointments were made (Stuart 1979).

TABLE 12.2. *Expenditure by social group, 1989 (per cent)*

Type of expenditure	Workers and employees	Collective farmers
Food	33.7	36.3
Clothing, footwear	15.7	13.1
Furnishings	4.2	3.4
Cultural goods	2.9	1.6
Medical	4.4	4.7
Vehicles, fuel	1.9	4.1
Alcohol	3.0	4.2
Housing (rent, services)	3.0	2.1
Taxes	9.4	1.8
Savings	7.8	11.2
Other	14.0	17.5
TOTALS	100.0	100.0

Source: [TsSU], *Sots. razvitie,* 1991.

Environmental pollution

In the traditional agrarian economy, in Russia as elsewhere, peasants lived close to the soil and by and large respected their natural environment. The damage they did to it at least remained within tolerable limits. Collectivization of agriculture sundered this psychological bond to the land. The apostles of progress were townsmen who scorned rural values and dreamed of transforming not just the economy but man himself. The beneficiaries of Stalin's 'cultural revolution' prided themselves on their rational, mechanistic world outlook. They looked on nature as a foe to be conquered. Maxim Gor'ky spoke of 'organized scientific reason' waging total war on the elements, of constructing a 'second Nature' on the relics of the first, deemed 'unorganized and even hostile to the interests of working people' (Lemeshev 1991). For doctrinaire Marxists land, air, and water had no intrinsic value; they were a 'free' resource for society to appropriate and acquired value only once human labour was applied. It followed that under socialism enterprises should not have to pay rent for them. This principle was not breached until the 1970s, when a charge was introduced for the industrial use of water and penalties imposed for excessive consumption.

The command economy was geared to military and industrial expansion and favoured large-scale organization. Planners, managers, and other decision-makers, under pressure to meet production targets, could not afford to observe strictly the laws on protection of the environment or regulations on safety in the workplace. Ironically, the USSR was initially ahead of many other countries in enacting such legislation. But the laws were couched in general terms and made inadequate provision for enforcement. By 1963 all the union republics had followed Estonia's example in passing statutes on environmental protection. All-Union legislation followed on land use (1968), water pollution (1970), and forest conservation (1975). Decrees were also issued to preserve specific threatened stretches of water such as Lake Baikal or the Caspian Sea. But when proceedings were taken under these acts against polluters, the enterprises responsible had to pay only a derisory fine, instead of being closed down, for emitting hazardous waste. Much of the money allocated to environmental protection was spent on land melioration and other tangentially related projects (Kramer 1983), and budgetary appropriations under this head were actually reduced under the 1981–5 plan. Too many rival agencies were involved in these programmes, which lacked co-ordination. Where scientific advice encroached on ministerial prerogatives it might be disregarded. In any case the experts were themselves often divided.

Policy battles had to be fought out behind closed doors, for no genuine public debate could take place. The authorities tried to keep decisions secret and were loath to admit mistakes. They often took refuge in bombastic claims about the USSR's alleged superiority over other industrialized countries in ecological matters—while keeping compliance with international accords on pollution control to a minimum. A 'Green' lobby did emerge, but the political establishment treated it as potentially subversive. The nature conservation agency, ostensibly a civic body, actually functioned as an integral part of the bureaucracy. It was too weak to make itself heard when powerful vested interests were at stake.

On landing at Moscow airport travellers saw a brown haze covering the city at a height of about five hundred metres. Carbon monoxide levels in the capital were ten to thirteen times the maximum permissible daily concentration (1 mg. per cubic metre), according to a scientist who circulated in *samizdat* the first unofficial account, *The Destruction of Nature in the Soviet Union* ('B. Komarov' [Vol'fson] 1980)—although this limit was set very low. Along major traffic arteries the level was twice as high. Although there were fewer vehicles than in Western metropolises, they ran on fuel with a high sulphur content and—initially at least—lacked catalytic converters. Another source of pollution were the city's factories, especially chemical plants. The smoking chimneys that had once been symbols of progress emitted seven to eight times the permitted level of hydrogen sulphide. The situation was worst during the long winter months, when there was an air inversion effect. The same phenomenon occurred in many other towns across the land, from Yerevan in Armenia to Noril'sk in the Siberian Arctic, which alone produced two-thirds of the country's nickel and emitted 2.5 million tons of sulphur dioxide annually (as much as all of Italy). The record for atmospheric pollution was held by Leninogorsk (eastern Kazakhstan), where concentrations of lead reached thirty to forty times the permitted level. In Bashkiria (Bashkortostan) the population risked mercury poisoning, while in the Black Sea port of Novorossiisk cement works were responsible for invisible nitrogen and sulphur oxides bound in ash particles.

Trees withered, the incidence of disease increased. At Cheliabinsk the cancer rate was over twice the national average by the late 1980s. At Novokuznetsk (central Siberia), where nearly one million tons of noxious substances were emitted in 1988, a study showed that among people living close to the metallurgical plant eye diseases were 72 per cent and bronchial asthma seven and a half times more frequent than in the countryside nearby; a rapidly growing proportion of new-born infants suffered from respiratory problems and 7 to 8 per cent were born with genetic defects (Lemeshev 1991). In 1985 68.3 million tons of noxious substances were emitted into the atmosphere, or 0.36 tons per head of population. In Estonia the rate was nearly double (0.67 tons), while Azerbaijan claimed the purest air with 'only' 0.17 tons (Massey Stewart 1992; Bater 1989). The peak rate for emission of air-borne pollutants was reached in 1983 (108 million tons: Golitsyn 1993). In most places rates improved in the later 1980s, in part because of government action. More factory chimneys were fitted with filters, although these did not work well, letting through on average 23 per cent of the noxious gases they were supposed to contain. The switch to natural gas as a fuel also helped. But in 1988 sixty-eight cities were declared dangerous to live in. A real improvement would come only when industrial production fell off drastically after 1989.

Still more serious was the pollution of the country's waterways (which was responsible for some of the adverse health effects mentioned above). In many less-favoured urban areas untreated sewage was discharged into river systems. In 1970 only two-thirds of 1,800 towns had sewers. Even in Leningrad only 68 per cent of the sewage was treated mechanically or biologically (1968: Goldman 1972). The overall figure for purified sewage reached 63 per cent in 1979 and 77 per cent in 1990, but only one-third of that treated was really clean. A particular culprit in regard to PCBs (polychlorinated biphenyls) was a military plant at Dzerzhinsk near Nizhnii Novgorod. As much as 80 per cent of the fertilizer used in agriculture is said to have drained off the fields, and the same was true of pesticides, which were often applied in excess or incorrectly (Vol'fson 1980). Leaks from oil-wells sunk into the bed of the Caspian Sea created a black film on the surface. Pollution levels on the coast near Baku were twenty times the norm—and even more on the Lithuanian shore near Klaipeda.

Each year the rivers brought down tens of thousands of tons of oil spillage. Much more remained in the soil, especially near leaky pipelines and depots. In June 1993 scientists discovered an underground lake beneath the central Siberian city of Abakan containing 25,000 tons of oil, which had leaked from the local depot over several decades. About 200 metres away was the river that served as the source of the town's drinking water, putting at risk the health of some 150,000 people. The Volga had once been rich in stur-geon—the source of caviar—and other fish. But the water-level sank, partly because so many industrial enterprises along its banks still used fresh water from the river instead of recycling it. In common with many other southern watercourses, the Volga was losing its ability to cleanse itself from pollutants. The sturgeon catch (over 20,000 tons annually before the war) dwindled to insignificance, and efforts to breed the fish in artificial basins could not make up for the loss. According to Lemeshev the river flowed at only one-twelfth its previous speed; 'stagnation, entropization and rotting organic waste pose a catastrophic threat to human health . . . in the entire catchment area, extending over one-quarter of European Russia.'

Particularly tragic was the fate of the land-locked Aral Sea, fed by the Amu-dar'ia and Syr-dar'ia rivers with water from the Pamirs. Their flow was diverted by irrigation projects, mainly to grow cotton and rice. By 1968 thirty-seven such canals had been dug, the most famous the Kara-kum, designed to bring the 'Hungry Steppe' under cultivation. The result was that between 1960 and 1990 the water-level sank by 14 metres and the Sea's area was reduced by 40 per cent. The water that remained and the surrounding desert (28,000 square kilometres by 1989) had three times as much salt as before, and wind carried the salt to places 400 kilometres distant. Not only did this put paid to the fishing industry that had been the inhabitants' main source of livelihood, but it also led to a high incidence of disease: cancer, tuberculosis, hepatitis, and anaemia, the latter particularly evident among children. Cancer of the oeso-phagus in the Amu-dar'ia delta was fifteen times the national average (Micklin 1992; Siegl 1991).

During the early 1980s the average amount of water withdrawn per hectare of irrigated land was reduced by over one-quarter. Efforts were made to lessen water evaporation from the canals, e.g. by lining them with plastic sheets, and irrigation methods were also modernized by introducing sprinklers and drip-feed systems. The aim was to halve the loss of water in transit to 20 per cent of the total. But this programme was expensive and could not be carried out in full. A visitor to Aral'sk in 1991 found the drinking water 'milky yellow, contaminated with nitrates and other chemicals from pesticides entering the groundwater', and the inhabitants demora-lized. The town, once on the lake's shore, was now nearly 100 kilometres distant from it. The advancing desert also threatened Ashkhabad, the Turkmen capital, as well as several other places in Central Asia. In earlier years local politicians had strongly backed a plan to refill the Aral Sea by constructing yet another giant canal, 2,500 kilometres long, to convey water from the rivers Ob' and Irtysh in Siberia. Although feasible technically, the scheme would have had incalculable adverse ecological effects. It was also prohibitively expensive. In August 1986 design and construction work on the first section was halted, as much for economic as ecological reasons. The decision came as a disappointment to the Uzbek leadership, already dissatisfied with Moscow for imposing on that republic an excessive dependence on cotton, and helped to fuel local nationalism.

The Green lobby first made its presence felt over the conservation of Lake Baikal, the Earth's largest (and oldest!) natural reservoir of fresh water, generally recognized as an unparalleled resource. In 1960, when work began on building two pulp and paper mills on its shore, a local writer, Buiantsev, published a pamphlet outlining the threat to marine life and the lake's exceptional purity. It was several years, however, before the issue attracted national media attention. In the absence of a forum for public debate the controversy soon became bogged down in inter-ministerial squabbles. Although a law laid down that the plants should not be opened until their purification systems were working, its provisions were simply ignored by local functionaries. They had the support of the military, which wanted the cellulose cord for aircraft tyres. Since alternative materials were available, the development at Baikal'sk was 'harmful and absurd from the start', as Sakharov commented; he tried to mobilize support among academicians but to little avail. Administrative pressure was brought to bear on the safety inspectors and in 1966-7 the first plant opened before its waste could be properly dealt with. Within eighteen months islands of sewage, one of them several miles long, formed on the lake's surface. Despite some improvement over the years, by the late 1980s Baikal'sk had discharged 1.5 milliard cubic metres of effluent, which affected an area 30 square kilometres in extent. Toxic waste was also emitted into the lake from Severobaikal'sk, a new town of 30,000 inhabitants built to house workers on the BAM rail project. The upshot was a victory for the establishment, achieved at fearful environmental cost, for the objectors' dire warnings were proved correct. The

Greens could at least take comfort from the fact that they had established their credibility (Goldman 1972, 1992; Massey Stewart 1992).

Rather than continue the catalogue of woe in regard to deforestation, the effects of opencast mining, erosion of the soil through man-made dust storms and so on, all of which cost the country a large proportion of its arable land, we may close with a brief glimpse at the damage done by careless handling of radioactive materials. The Chernobyl nuclear catastrophe (26 April 1986) was the result of earlier policy errors and design faults, as noted above. By that date fourteen plants of the same type were functioning in the USSR. They were built to technical specifications worked out in the 1950s, when the object was to produce, not electric power, but plutonium for military purposes (Zh. A. Medvedev 1990). As the world soon learned to its cost, RBMK reactors had no protective container; their thousands of pipes and welded joints were vulnerable to leaks; and the rods used to control the intensity of the chain reaction were too short. The experiment that led to the meltdown of the core in Chernobyl's reactor No. 4 ought to have been carried out two years earlier, but was postponed in order to complete the plant and bring its current on stream as soon as possible.

Excessive haste and neglect of elementary safety precautions were typical of the Soviet nuclear programme throughout, as were the reluctance to divulge full information after the accident, the shortage of Geiger counters, and delays in evacuating nearby residents. Unofficial sources state that five to ten thousand of the 210,000 workers (many of them servicemen) involved in cleaning up the site had died by 1991 (Marples 1991, 1993). Not only were the 116,000 evacuees from the 30-kilometre zone around the plant exposed to a harmful dose of radioactivity; so too were the 4.3 million people who lived in the heavily contaminated provinces of Ukraine and Belarus.[5] The frequency of 'minor' accidents in several other Soviet (or ex-Soviet) reactors since 1986 strengthens the case of those who hold that Chernobyl was less an accident than a *predictable* catastrophe, the result of 'systemic' factors.

Official complacency about the risks involved was characteristic not just of the nuclear-power industry but of the entire military-industrial complex. In 1992–3 it became known that from 1960 onward the Soviet navy had regularly sunk unserviceable reactors from atomic-powered vessels (indeed, entire submarines!) in Arctic waters, along with thousands of containers holding nuclear waste. The total volume has been put at 223,000 cubic metres. No less than twenty-two radioactive accidents occurred at sea, including two meltdowns of reactor cores (1979, 1985) and one explosion (1985). On land large areas of Kazakhstan were rendered unfit for agricultural use by the deposit of radioactive materials during the years when the region was used as a nuclear-test site. The worst nuclear accident before Chernobyl occurred in 1957 at a secret plutonium plant, 'Cheliabinsk-40', at Kyshtym in the Urals. It affected an area of some one thousand square kilometres, the population of which was secretly evacuated. The number of casualties is unknown, as is the exact cause of the explosion: it is thought that leakage from an accumulation of nuclear waste was responsible (Zh. Medvedev 1979). It later became known that at Sverdlovsk, in the same region, at least forty-two people died in a major accident (1979) connected with the manufacture of biological weapons, and hundreds of thousands of tons of these were disposed of in Arctic waters.

Other secrets are slowly emerging. The chief ecological adviser to the Russian government, Yablokov, has revealed that in some badly polluted cities life expectancy had dropped to 44 years. The environmental crisis was the most dramatic aspect of a calamitous situation that affected the very fabric of society.

13 Social Breakdown, Cultural Renovation

The term 'crisis' is contested by some Western scholars, who would prefer the less value-laden term 'disequilibrium'. Likewise, the vast majority of Soviet citizens (outside minority areas, at least) failed to appreciate the seriousness of the country's situation by the mid-1980s. Though few accepted at face value the official line that the people's well-being was in the forefront of the authorities' concern, many considered themselves fortunate in enjoying blessings supposedly denied to ordinary folk in the West and attributed shortcomings to the pressing needs of defence against the 'imperialist' menace. Nevertheless a sizeable proportion of educated people—not just intellectuals but functionaries, too—did realize that Soviet society was seriously sick. They were uncertain what the remedy should be. Some were for imposing stricter discipline, others for reform. When Gorbachev took over in March 1985 he could tap into both constituencies and mobilize considerable support for what came to be called *perestroika* (see Chapter 16). The ideas behind this programme took shape in the previous period, which may be considered one of cultural renovation beneath a veneer of ideological conformity. They were articulated by social scientists like Tatiana Zaslavskaia, as well as by writers of various schools, whether individualists (liberals) or patriots (nationalists). Leaving the Russian national revival until the next chapter, we shall consider here some other aspects of the cultural scene, after first taking a look at the social background to these developments.

Population and public health

Between 1965 and 1985 the Soviet population increased from 232.2 to 276.3 million (end-of-year figures). The overall growth rate was declining. In the 1950s the annual rate of natural increase had been 1.8 per cent, but by the early 1980s it had fallen to 0.8 per cent. This general trend was attributable to long-term social processes: the phasing out of the post-war 'baby boom', an increase in mortality rates due to the higher proportion of elderly people, and especially to the impact of 'modernization': the growing proportion of town-dwellers (65.6 per cent in 1985 as against 53.3 per cent twenty years earlier), educational advances, and the rise of white-collar groups. As elsewhere in the developed world, couples chose to have fewer children than had been usual in their parents' generation. In the RSFSR the average number was now two, as against four or more prior to World War II (Ben-Barak 1990). The slowdown in population growth was more marked among Slavic (and Baltic) peoples than it was in Transcaucasia or Central Asia. The Russians grew by 13.1 per cent between 1959 and 1970, but by only 6.5 per cent during the next intercensal period; in the years 1979–89 the rate fell to 5.7 per cent. Ukrainians fell from 9.4 to 3.9 per cent, but then recovered slightly to 4.3 per cent. This record stood in stark contrast to that of, say, the Tajiks, who increased by 52.9 per cent in 1959–70, 35.7 per cent in 1970–9, and 45.5 per cent in 1979–89.[1] What this differential implied for inter-ethnic relations will be considered further in Chapter 15. Confining ourselves for the moment to the Russians, the figures showed that there were grounds for concern. For it was common knowledge that the declining rate of population growth was due in part to poor social conditions: urban poverty, the housing shortage, deteriorating health care, alcoholism, drug abuse, and so on.

According to official figures average life expectancy for both sexes across the Union *fell* from 69.3 years in 1969/70 to 67.7 years in 1979/80; by 1989 it had recovered to 69.5 years. The decline in the 1970s was steeper for men than for women (1.6 as against 0.9 years). Western experts consider these data too generous; the 1980 figure for males should be 61.9 years, not 62.2 as stated (Buck and Cole 1987, citing J.-C. Chesnais). Certainly the sex differential was very wide by international standards (officially 10.3 years in 1980, 9.4 years in 1989) and reflects the high proportion of stress-related deaths among men, who were more likely to be involved in accidents—or to die from alcohol poisoning. Regional differences were important. According to official figures in 1969/70 inhabitants of the Baltic states lived 1.4 to 2.3 years longer than RSFSR residents, and Armenians 4.1 years longer. Ten years later the gap was the same for Baltic residents but had widened to 5.3 years for

Armenians. Over the next decade the best results in the longevity stakes were scored by residents of Tajikistan and Moldova. In this respect the situation in the Baltic did not recover to the extent that it did in the RSFSR, while the Armenians, stricken by war and earthquake, were the only group to decline.

Soviet infant mortality statistics are untrustworthy, since deaths within the first week after birth were not registered, necessitating an adjustment of 15 per cent or more. According to official figures there was a drop during the 1960s, from 35 to 22.6 deaths per thousand births (1971). Thereafter poor nutrition and the deterioration of medical services in maternity clinics caused the rate to jump to 27.9 by 1974, and to hold steady for the rest of the decade (Field 1987). So bad was the situation that official information on the topic dried up. Subsequently there seems to have been an improvement. In 1986 the rate was officially put at 25.4, but 'unofficially was said to be nearer 30' (Bater 1989). Here, too, regional disparities mattered a lot: in Turkmenistan the rate was over five times as high as it was in Latvia (Juviler 1992). Infections and parasite-borne diseases killed fourteen times more infants in Central Asia than they did in the Baltic (TsSU 1991). However, in general such inter-republican differentials were gradually being reduced. In the decade 1975–85 the number of beds for sick children rose by only 1.1 per cent in the RSFSR, but by 15.5 per cent in Tajikistan.

A similar trend, but less marked, can be seen in the ratio of doctors or hospital beds to the size of the local population. It has been claimed that human resources in health care were more evenly distributed in the USSR in 1981 than they were in a comparable mix of seventeen other (industrialized and developing) countries (Buck and Cole 1987). However, such statistical exercises tell us little about the quality of the care provided, and we have to beware of falsification of data. 'Apparently there are quotas for all types of [surgical] operations, and these quotas are always met, at least on paper. If the number of operations actually performed falls below expectations, more cases are invented to fill the quota. The same applies to hospital occupancy rates' (Field 1987). The standard of training at medical schools left much to be desired, especially as these institutions were outside the university system. Doctors' and nurses' pay was notoriously low, so that they lacked motivation, changed jobs frequently, took bribes, and were insensitive to their patients' needs. The 'neglect of the human factor' so criticized by reformers in the late 1980s applied with particular force to the public-health system.

Hospitals were underequipped and lacked even elementary amenities such as proper sanitation. It was later revealed that in 1986 one-quarter of the 3,900 district-level hospitals depended on septic tanks for the evacuation of waste and 17 per cent did not even have running water (only 35 per cent had a supply of *hot* water!). In Uzbekistan 46 per cent failed to meet minimum hygienic requirements. 'Time and again complaints are voiced that pharmaceuticals are unavailable, and even the simplest items—bandages, aspirin, thermometers, and iodine—are difficult to procure' (Field 1987). Patients were forced to turn to the shadow economy to obtain them, and even to gain admission to hospital. In Azerbaijan in 1979 there was a scandal involving misappropriation by medical staff of food brought by relatives to supplement the meagre fare that was the patients' normal lot. Elderly patients with incurable diseases were sometimes refused admission because the officials in charge feared that this would raise their hospital's 'death quota' above the norm. A lack of effective administrative control went hand in hand with an excess of bureaucratic regimentation. Until the late 1980s the operation of the health system was enshrouded in secrecy. When the veil was lifted it became clear that the incidence of many serious diseases had been increasing during the period 1980–5. The cancer rate, for example, went up by 13 per cent, hepatitis by 16 per cent, and scarlet fever by 21 per cent, while cases of whooping-cough and diphtheria rose roughly fourfold. (For all, except cancer, rates were lower in 1989.)

Alcoholism

Newly reported cases of alcohol morbidity rose by 10 per cent over the quinquennium 1980–5, and the total number of alcoholics who received medical treatment by 37 per cent, to nearly 4.5 million. This figure does not include those who simply passed through 'sobering-up stations' (*vytrezviteli*) run by the militia, which in 1979 processed no less than 16 to 18 million drunks (including 'repeaters'). In Leningrad alone 11.6 per cent of the adult population was arrested for this reason in 1979 (Treml 1987; equivalent data for other places or years are not available). Still more evocative are figures released later for alcohol-related *deaths*. In 1980 19.0 went to their graves for every 100,000 of population, which gives a total of over 50,000; by 1985 the figure had fallen below 40,000. This reflected the effects of the temperance campaign initiated by Andropov and taken further by Gorbachev. By 1989 the number is said to have been brought down to 23,000. In the pre-reform period the figures are staggering. If one includes accidental deaths, murders, and suicides related to drunkenness, the total number of fatalities may have been as high as 200,000 per annum, four times the 'official' figure (Treml 1987). 'The consumption of all alcoholic beverages converted to pure alcohol was over seventeen litres for every person fifteen years or older.' Of this some 4.5 litres was home-distilled brew, mostly *samogon*, and stolen alcohol may have accounted for an additional litre. The rate of consumption of state-produced alcoholic beverages was increasing at about 6.9 per cent per annum, largely because more women and adolescents were taking to the bottle. Sales decreased temporarily in 1981–2, when the price was put up, but this led to increased purchases of sugar for home-brewing.

Alcohol abuse was very much a regional (or ethnic) problem. In 1985 the RSFSR registered a number of deaths from this source over one-third higher than the all-Union average (19.3 as against 14.4 per 100,000 population). Ukraine was slightly above the average, Belarus below it—as was Latvia, whereas Estonia and Lithuania were in the same category as the RSFSR. The Muslim republics of Central Asia, by contrast, had no problem at all. Uzbekistan's rate was a mere 1.5 per 100,000, falling to 0.6 in 1987. If official statistics can be credited, the same was true of Azerbaijan and even Armenia, famed for its strong brandy—but not of Georgia, which recorded a mortality rate from this cause of 2.5 per 100,000. Here, as in Moldova, home-made wine was mainly responsible. It was less harmful to the drinker's health than the traditional Great Russian habit of *napoi*, or rapid ingestion of vodka to the point of total inebriation.

It has been estimated that the total social cost of alcohol abuse was equivalent to 7 to 8 per cent of the USSR's national income in the early 1970s, and 8 to 9 per cent in 1980. But it cannot be measured in mere monetary terms. It is reflected in the link between heavy drinking and crime (in 1972 62 per cent of thefts were alcohol-related), in high rates of absenteeism at the workplace, and particularly in domestic violence leading to the breakdown of family life.

Family matters

Already in 1969 a Moscow lawyer noted that 40 per cent of all divorces were caused by drunkenness of one spouse, usually the husband. Habitual drunks maltreated their children; their 'prolonged impotence . . . [was] cited as a source of marital tensions'; and over 90 per cent of those who contracted venereal disease did so 'under the influence' (Connor 1971). A 1978 survey showed that drunkenness was a cause of divorce in 59.5 per cent of cases among 'couples of manual-class background', whereas among the élite it took second place to psychological motives. In the USSR, as elsewhere in the 'developed' world, the divorce rate showed an upward trend. In 1978 there was one divorce for every three marriages concluded—in urban areas of European Russia, one in two. Per thousand of population, the rate was 1.6 in 1965, 3.1 in 1975, and 3.4 in 1985. Since divorce was expensive (up to 250 roubles), many couples preferred to separate. The real rate of family disintegration was therefore around 5 per thousand, comparable with the US figure (Lane 1985).

Also comparable was the age of marriage, which was falling. Despite the passage of time since the war, which had cost so many male lives, there was still an imbalance between the sexes, particularly in the countryside. A woman's chances of finding a husband 'drop[ped] sharply after twenty-five and [were] negligible after thirty' (Madison 1977). By 1989, however, there were 139 men in Russian villages to 100 women, and therefore a high proportion of bachelors. This was because so many young girls left home at an early age; there was no such problem, though, in Uzbekistan (Perevedentsev 1993).

Single parents and unmarried couples with children became an ubiquitous phenomenon, especially in towns. According to one Western commentator on such matters, half the young brides were pregnant (Juviler 1991). Illegitimate children were particularly common in Estonia (by 1989 25 per cent of the total born, and in rural areas 34 per cent!), whereas in Azerbaijan the rate was only 2.5 per cent—*less* than it had been in 1980. The RSFSR registered an increase over the decade, to arrive at 13.5 per cent in 1989. Those who reared them suffered social ostracism and received limited financial support; once again, the human factor was neglected. So, too, with birth control: contraceptives were in short supply and family planning advice clinics even rarer,[2] with the result that the USSR had one of the world's highest abortion rates. In 1980 there were 7 million registered abortions to 4.9 million births, more than one for every ten women aged between 15 and 49; thereafter the ratio declined. But in the RSFSR the number of abortions carried out was 23 per cent above the all-Union average (1985). They were performed least frequently in Armenia (38 per cent of the all-Union average); the figures were low in all the Transcaucasian and Central Asian republics, as well as in Catholic Lithuania. However, official statistics give only an inadequate picture, for in some areas as many as four-fifths of all abortions were performed illegally (Juviler 1991)—as a rule in conditions even less hygienic than those in officially recognized clinics. A Soviet doctor estimated the 'unofficial' share at one-third of the total and claimed that upwards of 70 per cent of women in towns, and 90 per cent in the countryside, had had abortions (A. Popov 1988).

It will come as no surprise to learn that the large 'extended' family was a thing of the past. The average size fell from 3.7 to 3.5 between 1970 and 1979. Baltic residents tended to have smaller families than Russian ones (in Estonia the rate remained constant at 3.1), whereas in Central Asia households of 4 to 5 were usual; in Tajikistan family size actually *increased*, to 6.1 in 1989. In the RSFSR the proportion of families with 5 or more members fell from 21 per cent in 1970 to 13 per cent in 1979; a drop of no more than 1 per cent over the next decade may reflect a greater degree of cohesion among that republic's non-Russian residents.

The state, generally so interventionist, adopted a policy of benevolent (or complacent?) neglect in this domain until the first results of the 1970 census showed that something had to be done. One reason for inaction was that the old (1947) system of minimal child allowances, paid to all who qualified regardless of their income, was amended in 1974 to restrict payments to the poorest (those earning less than 50 roubles a month). This benefited Muslim families in the main, or so it was alleged, but not until 1981 were experts' pleas for a more differentiated approach, to even out regional disparities in family size, heeded. The new pro-natalist measures were sensible enough. They provided for larger lump-sum grants at the birth of the first and second child than for children born subsequently, quadrupled the monthly allowance paid to unwed mothers (and extended its duration), and adopted a more generous policy on maternity leave for working mothers, who could now stay away for up to eighteen months, under flexible pay arrangements, without suffering loss of seniority. Nearly all women who qualified opted for this scheme, which helps to explain why the birth rate recovered in the years that followed.

Gender

None of this indicated that the Soviet authorities had modified their old-fashioned attitude to what the Bolsheviks used to call 'the Woman Question'. In the late 1970s feminist protest groups emerged in Leningrad, influenced in part by Western ideas. T. Mamonova and others published in *samizdat* exposés of deficiencies in health care and discrimination over pay rates. But the movement did not strike deep root and soon developed in a more spiritual direction. A 'Maria Club' was formed, and in 1981 four editors of its journal, *Maria*, were expelled abroad. Undeniably, they had good grounds for concern.

Four out of five women of working age held jobs. They comprised about 45 per cent of the total industrial labour-force. The metallurgical (or metal-working) and chemical branches employed 12 per cent of all working women, while another 10 per cent were in the textile branch (1970). Throughout industry they were disproportionately clustered in less skilled jobs, and consequently their earnings were lower than men's, although their educational qualifications were higher. In the economy as a whole the rate was 70 per cent of men's (1979: Anderson 1987). Women workers were frequently allotted physically demanding tasks that strained their health, despite elaborate laws on labour protection laying down maximum loads that could be carried and the like. Even as late as 1989, when data on such matters were again published, 43 per cent of women in industry, as against 26 per cent of men, were engaged in manual tasks ('attending machines or not', as the statisticians curiously put it).[3] In construction the figures were even more unfavourable: 74 per cent of female workers, as against 44 per cent of males!

Not surprisingly, one-quarter registered dissatisfaction to official pollsters and many tried to secure professional or semi-professional jobs. Women made up 99 per cent of the USSR's nurses and typists, 85 per cent of laboratory technicians, 74 per cent of physicians, and 72 per cent of school-teachers (1970). Among engineers they were most prominent (74 per cent) in the foodstuffs and consumer goods sectors, where earnings were four-fifths of those in construction. In education and health it was harder for women than for men to rise to the top of the profession. In 1974/5 the proportion of women who served as heads of primary schools was the same as the proportion of female teachers, but directors of eight-year or secondary schools were nearly three times as likely to be men (Dodge 1977). Despite this the general trend was towards a 'feminization' of the profession, which led to male complaints. The proportion of women with doctorates employed in research institutes or universities rose from 10 per cent in 1960 to 14 per cent in 1974; but there were only 14 women among 749 members of the Academy of Sciences (1977). In 1975 women comprised 10 per cent of full professors and 22 per cent of associates. Here too the tendency was upward.

Overall, Soviet women were 'concentrated in sectors with lower prestige and financial reward', and in political positions, too, 'the proportion of women varie[d] inversely with the power of the office or legislative body [concerned]' (Fischer 1983). Yet one should not lose sight of the fact that this discrimination, along with imbalances in the distribution of jobs by gender, to some extent reflected women's preferences. For example, the fact that 68 per cent of linguists but only 13 per cent of legal scholars were female does not necessarily indicate a greater degree of 'male chauvinism' in law faculties. Moreover, teachers worked shorter hours than engineers, which was one reason why the job was attractive to women, especially if they had children of their own to look after (Chapman 1977). As elsewhere in the world, women with family responsibilities were less mobile than men, and most couples' place of residence was determined by the husband's occupation. The wife's earnings were generally seen as a supplementary source of family income. Nevertheless an element of hidden bias undoubtedly did exist. Had the bulk of Soviet dentists been men, their pay rates would probably not have remained unchanged throughout this twenty-year period! A certain 'feminization of poverty' was occurring, but the authorities preferred to close their eyes to it, as they did to so many uncongenial developments on the social scene.

The harshest aspect of urban women's lot was their dual burden of combining a job with looking after a home and family. Sociologists spoke of 'uneven role distribution' between the sexes. What this meant in practice was that the wife was not just mother and auxiliary breadwinner but also did all or most of the shopping, cooking, cleaning, and so forth. In 1970 it was officially estimated that Soviet citizens spent 30 milliard hours a year chasing supplies in the stores, the equivalent of 21 eight-hour working days for each individual—and three-quarters of the shoppers were women! (Mickiewicz 1981.) In the early 1970s women were said to spend over 27 hours a week on housework, as against less than 12 hours for men; for 'cultural activities' the figures were respectively less than 12 hours for women and nearly 20 hours for men. Women had one hour a day less time for sleeping, eating, and so on. Looking ahead to 1990, when more elaborate calculations were made, there was little to choose between the sexes in the latter regard but men had much the same proportion of 'free time' as before. Urban women worked almost as long as their menfolk did, yet spent nearly three times as much of their lives on domestic pursuits: 27 as against 10 hours. Of this shopping took up 5 hours for women, 2 for men. Their respective use of leisure time is apparent from Table 13.1. To put it differently, while Ivan Petrovich watched television, Maria Sergeevna washed the dishes and looked after the children.

Leisure use; popular culture

Visits to the theatre and to museums increased between 1980 and 1985; the cinema was less well frequented, although it remained a popular medium. Attendance declined from 4.7 to 4.1 million visits between 1975 and 1985. This was due not just to the superior appeal of television but also to the nature of the films shown. Three-quarters of them were serious dramas (and of these 12 per cent dealt with World War II themes!), whereas audiences preferred light comedies. The censors were nervous about realistic cinematic portrayals of everyday life, although they did allow some films in this genre to be imported from approved Third-World countries.

TABLE 13.1.   *Use of 'free time' by townspeople, March 1990* (average in hours-minutes per employed person)

Total 'free time'	Men		Women	
	Working day	Holiday	Working day	Holiday
Watching TV, listening to radio	1–47	3–00	0–50	1–55
Reading	0–35	1–04	0–14	0–30
Public entertainment[a]	0–07	0–26	0–05	0–23
Sport[b]	0–12	0–48	0–06	0–33
Study, civic activities	0–03	0–02	0–03	0–02
Hobbies	0–04	0–13	0–01	0–05
Time spent with children	0–27	0–47	0–30	0–47
Entertainment, visiting, miscellaneous	0–13	1–48	0–08	1–17
Total 'free time'	3–28	8–08	1–57	5–32

[a] Including attendance at sports events.
[b] Including walking (except with children).

Source: [TsSU], *Sots. razvitie*, 1991.

During the Brezhnev years young people increasingly demon-strated disinterest in officially approved cultural artefacts. The authorities were obliged to liberalize their policy slightly in order to prevent youngsters from becoming totally alienated. In the mid-1970s the first discothèques appeared. By then Moscow already had several hundred bands playing popular music of Western inspiration. By the early 1980s there were 1,500 of them in Moscow province alone. 'Rock-and-rollers' wore flamboyant costumes and sang lyrics that 'punctured official pieties' (Stites 1992). Cultural bureaucrats looked askance at such developments. Unofficial clubs were sometimes closed down and performing groups broken up. But a policy of outright repression was no longer practicable in an age of tape-recorders and (eventually) video-cassettes. There were simply too many devotees of such idols as the crooner Alla

Pugacheva, known as much for her luxuriant red hair and stormy love affairs as for her voice. The popular balladeers A. Galich (Ginzburg) and V. Vysotsky, both Jewish, sang of the dispossessed (soldiers, prisoners, alcoholics) and poked fun at established customs or official hypocrisy. Galich, who emigrated in 1974 (to be killed three years later in an accident in suspicious circumstances) developed a 'caustic, socially conscious black humour' in his verse (D. Brown 1978). Vysotsky introduced into his lyrics the rich, outspoken language of the underworld and the Gulag. His death, at the age of 42, in 1980, although unmentioned in the controlled press, was an occasion for nation-wide mourning. 'He was our bard, the keeper of the nation's spirit, of our pain and all our joys', declared the theatre director Yurii Liubimov in his funeral oration. Tens of thousands attended the ceremony.

The Composers' Union, a body of men with conservative tastes, condemned popular musical culture for its vulgarity and 'decadence'. Under Andropov there was a crackdown: it was ruled that 80 per cent of offerings should be by Soviet composers. Once again, as in the 1960s, patrols of Komsomol vigilantes toured places of entertainment and disciplined those who misbehaved. But the reaction did not last long. The appeal of the consumer-oriented, hedonistic international youth culture was too strong. *Glasnost'* led to suspension of the jamming of foreign radio broadcasts (1987). A lively trade developed in imported gadgets, jeans, and T-shirts. Some informal associations of young people, initially formed to support a sports team or to play forbidden music, turned into gangs that gained a powerful hold over their members. A few became hippies or punks. More ominously, there were the 'heavy metal boys' (*metallisty*) and the *liubery* (named for the Moscow suburb of Liubertsy where they congregated), who cultivated their physique and adopted an aggressive, quasi-Fascist demeanour. The first open gathering of some fifty young blackshirts in Moscow took place on 20 April 1982 (Hitler's birthday). At the time few paid much attention: it seemed an untypical hyper-reaction to official sermonizing, a mere gesture designed to shock the elderly and conventionally minded (Riordan 1988). Yet it was a way of expressing the deep psychological malaise that afflicted the younger generation. They had lost their fathers' faith in socialist values and were desperately searching for alternatives. Particularly exposed to the appeals of right-wing extremism were the *afgantsy*, veterans of the lost Afghan war, and members of the armed forces generally.

High culture

Censorship

Intellectuals were hampered in their efforts to respond to these strivings by the tenacity of bureaucratic controls over cultural life, as well as by the social gulf that separated them, as it did the political establishment, from the masses. Beneath the mask of conformity there existed a broad range of opinions on a host of issues—philosophical, moral, political, and socio-economic. Informal discussions were vigorous, even though those who took part in them could not as yet form structured civic organizations (or at least, if they did so, such bodies had no genuine autonomy). In practice, however, there was a certain give-and-take between the authorities (the Party and especially the KGB) and those who, without being overt dissidents, sought to change some aspect of official policy.

With the Democratic movement reeling from the blows it suffered in 1971–3, an increasingly important role came to be played by academics and other professional people whose attitude to the regime, at least in public, was more ambivalent (see Chapter 6). They sought to preserve their moral integrity by making as few concessions as possible to the demands of Authority while ventilating their critical thoughts to friends in informal private circles. Some of their writings found their way into *samizdat* or *tamizdat* publications; others had to wait until the Gorbachev era or later before they appeared.

We may consider this 'cultural opposition' in so far as it was manifested in the world of learning and then sketch the dissidents' fortunes in the decade before Gorbachev acceded to power. But first let us take a glimpse at the machinery of repression.

As overseer of the vast censorship establishment, Andropov kept a close watch on the cultural scene. In a top secret report to the Party leadership (1975), since published, he warned his colleagues that young intellectuals were organizing dramatic performances in private homes and showing an unhealthy interest in the theatre of the absurd (Beckett, Ionesco, Pinter). He urged that aspiring artists and writers be found suitable jobs and accorded better publication prospects (*Ist.* 2/1993). These ideas do not seem to have been acted on. They were less imaginative than others which the formidable police chief managed to push through. As we shall see, he used the censorship mechanism 'creatively' in the struggle to maintain thought control, manipulating journal editors, and staging bogus controversies which engaged intellectuals' attention and sowed confusion among them.

The KGB and the military each had censorship agencies of their own, administratively independent of the better-known Glavlit. The latter body was responsible for controlling literature and journalism but did not have a free hand: the last word remained with the KGB and ideologists in the Party CC's Secretariat, i.e. with Andropov and Suslov. Whatever the two men's differences of temperament, they were at one in seeing the regime as threatened by 'the enemy's subversive efforts to pervert the minds of the creative intelligentsia' (as Andropov put it in the report mentioned above). There was a 400-page index of topics that might not be mentioned in public. Known familiarly to staff as the 'Talmud' (its proper title was *List of Information Banned from Appearing in the Open Press*), it was kept regularly up to date. Data on infant mortality and grain output, for instance, were added to such venerable 'non-facts' as accidents, natural disasters, or crime statistics (Vladimirov 1989).

The quasi-liberalism of the Khrushchev era was now definitely over. However, the very multiplicity of controlling organs occasionally led to lapses, and there were inconsistencies in the way the rules were applied. What one individual could not say in one place might be said by a less prominent figure elsewhere—for example, in some distant national republic. If a hitherto respected writer or scholar became associated with the Democratic movement or emigrated, as a rule his name became unmentionable and his works would be removed from public libraries. Even a reference to the Marxist-Leninist classics or to *Pravda* might be censored if the views expressed were no longer deemed 'correct'. On the other hand, a few copies of a banned film might be kept back and then quietly released years later for showing in the provinces. Few explanations were vouched for such vagaries. There were, however, shadowy figures who acted as informal intermediaries between newspaper editors or theatrical directors and their hidden controllers. Trusted by neither side yet useful to both, they could occasionally get a ban rescinded—and at other times might file a denunciation. Thus a journalist, Viktor Louis, was often used by the KGB as a conduit for information it wished to place in Western media. Scholars, journalists, and writers could sometimes bargain with the more approachable editors, but none of them could be sure that such deals would last—or even know who took the ultimate decision to ban or not to ban.

Historiography

For many years the supervisor of scholars and social scientists was a certain Trapeznikov. A historian as well as a senior Party official, he had earned his academic credentials with a voluminous work on Lenin's agrarian policy that showed scant regard for the sources and lacked all critical sense. As early as 1966 an end was put to efforts to portray truthfully the social and human costs of forced collectivization. Nekrich, who in a study of the outbreak of the Soviet–German war showed that Stalin was to blame for the initial disasters, was dismissed from his post in the Academy's Institute of History and expelled from the Party. The Party committee in the institute, which under his influence had taken a stand favourable to academic freedom, was purged. Later the institute was split in two to make it more manageable. Nekrich subsequently emigrated and his book, suppressed in the USSR, appeared abroad under a pseudonym.

Another 'scandal' erupted over a volume of historical essays published in Sverdlovsk in 1972. The contributors argued that on the eve of the Revolution Russia's socio-economic order had been characterized by great diversity—or, as they called it, 'multiformity' (*mnogoukladnost'*). This clumsy term had been used by Lenin, but to the historical-ideological establishment it seemed to challenge official doctrine that 'Great October' had been a 'law-governed' event—and so, by implication, the legitimacy of Party rule here and now. For the same reason in 1974 Volobuev, the Institute of History's director and a leading specialist on the revolutionary era, came to grief for over-emphasizing the 'spontaneous' character of the February 1917 uprising.

Historians who studied earlier periods encountered only slightly less difficulty. Academician Rybakov propounded a fanciful, myth-enshrouded view of medieval Rus' that his colleagues have since discredited as chauvinistic (Novosel'tsev 1993). The more professional scholars preferred archaeology or textual criticism. Respectable work was done, for instance, on unearthing documents written on birch-bark in medieval Novgorod, which could be used to support arguments for the richness of early Rus' culture. But even here one could run into trouble. Zimin was virtually ostracized for questioning the authenticity of the twelfth-century epic *The Lay of Igor's Host*, and his later books on Muscovite Russia came in for unjustifiably harsh criticism. Other historians produced notable studies of the peasantry, economic development, and the eighteenth-century Enlightenment. But every question studied, however remote in time, continued to be scrutinized for its hidden political message. In the early 1970s the authorities sanctioned an exchange of views in academic journals about the nature of Russian absolutism. The discussion was conducted in a highly scholastic form, for no one could contest the dubious orthodox doctrine, established in the 1930s, that Russia had been in a 'feudal' stage of development from the earliest times until 1861. Ever mindful of the ideological connotations of their remarks, some participants cautiously suggested that the topic ought to be studied in its contemporary European context. This was a way of hinting that the Soviet regime, too, required Westernization—or at least that it was less unique and worthy of emulation abroad than was officially believed. No such debate was held on any more recent subject, since this would have encouraged scepticism about Marxist-Leninist teaching.

In the late 1970s and early 1980s the chief threat to orthodoxy came less from potential 'Westernizers' in the historical profession—the 'new direction', as its protagonists called it—than from spokesmen for certain national minorities. Partly for linguistic reasons, Transcaucasian and Central Asian scholars enjoyed a leeway denied to Ukrainians or Balts. Many of them appraised positively their people's level of development prior to the Russian conquest and implied that colonial rule, whether tsarist or Soviet, had been a mixed blessing. But the ideologists in Moscow, alarmed by the rise of Islamic fundamentalism, reverted to the harsher, more chauvinistic line of the Stalin era, with its heavy emphasis on the 'progressive' aspects of the Russian connection. Some Central Asian writers dutifully fell into line, but the Kazakh Kalmyrzaev was one of those who did not. At a conference at Almaty (then Alma-Ata) in 1981, evidently with the tacit support of the republic's (Kazakh) first secretary, Kunaev, he challenged the current idealization of colonialism and called for a more truthful, objective approach (Weinerman 1993).

Military historians also succeeded in preserving a certain measure of autonomy, but their writings, especially on World War II, took an old-fashioned heroic-patriotic approach. The official multi-volume history of the war was so dry and schematic as to be unreadable. Even eminent commanders such as Marshal Zhukov had their memoirs arbitrarily cut and rewritten (Bonwetsch 1991). Worst treated of all were the wretched historians of the CPSU itself. As in earlier times they had to tailor their views—and, more importantly, their silences—to meet current political exigencies. This vice, termed 'conjuncturism' (*kon'iunkturnost'*), was often condemned but remained ineradicable. Khrushchev was now an 'unperson' and so the merits or demerits of Party policy under his leadership could not be examined. Bukharin and the other 'old Bolsheviks' exterminated in the Terror were likewise unmentionable, and so too were the deeds of Stalin himself and the nature of his system. Only occasional mildly derogatory references were now made to the 'cult of the individual'. It could not be discussed at length. This silence was indeed a 'law-governed phenomenon', for the regime of the great dictator's successors stood four-square on the foundations he had laid. Its claims had to be taken on trust. Significantly, Stalin made something of a comeback in the 1970s. His likeness, carved in stone, reappeared close to the Kremlin wall, where his mortal remains lay buried after their removal from Lenin's tomb. Among the older generation there were many who welcomed this stealthy rehabilitation, for they identified Stalin's rule with order and national grandeur and were blind to its human or moral costs.

Social sciences

Among the several branches of knowledge which Stalin had suppressed as subversive was sociology. In the 1960s its practitioners had cautiously begun to reassert the importance of their discipline. Social surveys appeared on various innocuous subjects, and in 1968 the Academy of Sciences was persuaded to sanction the establishment of an Institute for Concrete Sociological Research. Its director, Rumiantsev, attracted a number of capable scholars, but three years later he was sacked and the adjective 'concrete' disappeared from the institute's title. The work done became more ideological, the views expressed lacking in originality. Many sociologists swam with the tide, but even some middle-of-the-roaders found the neo-Stalinist current abhorrent and tried to resist it. Opposition was particularly strong among those who used mathematical techniques, for they were convinced that their studies were both well-grounded scientifically and had useful practical applications (Shlapentokh 1987). As with the historians, the struggle for academic freedom could be carried on most successfully away from Moscow. It assumed a particularly active form in Estonia, where sociologists took their cue from the West. Good work was also done in Sverdlovsk, Novosibirsk, and even Leningrad, for local Party chiefs often had practical reasons of their own for wanting to know how people lived and what they thought, and so were willing to sanction public opinion polls. Their scope had to be fairly narrow. One could not, of course, ask respondents for their views on the government, but resourceful pollsters found ways round this difficulty, e.g. by soliciting people's opinions on journals that pursued different approaches. Their findings could not always be published, and any evidence of disaffection was suppressed.

There was also a growing interest in political science. Some 'Party intellectuals' (Burlatsky, Shakhnazarov) helped to give such notions as 'political culture' and even pluralism a certain respectability. Butenko argued that Soviet society, too, suffered from contradictions. Kurashvili, of the Institute of State and Law, drew a distinction between 'command' and 'stimulatory' methods of economic management under socialism (1982) and called for more scope to be given to local initiative in the work of government (A. Brown 1984). These ideas were taken up and expanded by Zaslavskaia, from the Academy's Siberian branch at Novosibirsk, who stood for a humane brand of socialism. In a conference paper of 1982 she delivered swingeing criticisms of the economic system, demonstrating that middle-level functionaries were the most resistant to reform because they feared for their privileges. This confidential document, which became a source of inspiration for *perestroika*, was leaked to the West. It showed that courageous and thoughtful scholars could tackle delicate problems and outwit their controllers—or at least exploit the divergencies between them. 'Those who met in Novosibirsk', writes T. Shanin (1990), 'chose a path that could best be described by a saying originating in the Spanish colonial empire, "I obey, but I do not comply".'

The KGB maintained its own research network, as we know, which was well informed as to the real situation in academic life. It also had agents in practically all institutions and was not above recruiting students to inform on their teachers. Some of these *seksoty* were identical with the 'Party hacks' in the administration of university faculties and research institutes. Such functionaries did little genuine scholarly work but spent much time harassing staff

members who showed any independence of spirit. T
denied promotion or the 'privilege' of attending schol
ces (especially those held abroad). Their publicatio
delayed or prevented from appearing at all. The most
would be summoned before a meeting of their collea
condemnatory harangues and demands that they retract their
opinions. Those who refused to do so faced expulsion and relega-
tion to the provinces—where, as likely as not, they would join the
thinning ranks of the dissidents.

Dissent after 1972

Andrei Sakharov, awarded the Nobel Peace Prize in 1975 (but not
allowed to leave the country to accept it), increasingly became a
symbol of the Democratic movement. His courageous defence of
human rights, in conditions even more difficult than before the
police actions of 1971–2, inspired friends of liberty at home and
abroad. When his colleagues faced quasi-judicial proceedings he
would try to attend, despite all manner of obstruction, in order to
offer them moral support. In 1973 he held the first of several
informal press conferences in his apartment. On these occasions, as
well as in interviews with foreign correspondents and memoranda
to leading Soviet and international personages, he set forth the
argument that there was an essential link between world peace and
the observance of human rights by governments everywhere. He
backed those from the national minorities (Crimean Tatars, Jews,
Germans) who wished to return to their homelands or emigrate and
warned of the perils of pursuing détente without ensuring a duly
verified and mutually balanced reduction of nuclear arms. In 1974
he staged a hunger strike to draw attention to the plight of
dissidents confined in SPHs, which secured the advance release of
two prisoners. Some other activists, including Solzhenitsyn, thought
Sakharov naïvely idealistic but he was vindicated by the Helsinki
Final Act.[4]

This document internationalized the question of civil liberties in
the USSR and set up a mechanism to verify compliance with agreed
norms. Although it was too weak and cumbersome to stop continued repression of Soviet citizens who happened to think differently
from their government, it did at least bring cases of persecution to
the world community's attention. At the 'follow-up' conference in

elgrade (1978) delegates heard reports on abuses compiled by members of the 'Moscow Helsinki Group', a civic association set up by the physicist Yurii Orlov and others to monitor the authorities' observance of the agreement. (Sakharov did not join this committee but was 'represented' by his wife, Elena Bonner.) In its first six years the Group prepared no less than 195 reports on human rights issues and put out numerous statements and appeals. Many of these, unhappily, were on behalf of its own members, who one after another were arrested and sentenced to lengthy terms of imprisonment. Four died in captivity. Yet their places were taken by fresh volunteers and other Helsinki groups appeared in Ukraine, Transcaucasia, and Lithuania (IHFHR *Report* 1986).

On several occasions Sakharov and members of his family were threatened and harassed, but for some years the KGB did not dare to act too ruthlessly. They realized that, in view of the prestige attached to his name and the broad support he enjoyed among scientists and others abroad, his arrest and trial on trumped-up charges would undermine the USSR's credibility as an allegedly 'peace-loving' power. However, in 1979 Soviet policy at home and abroad lurched further to the right. When Brezhnev's Politburo[5] decided to send troops into Afghanistan the last restraints were removed from the KGB. A number of human-rights activists were arrested, some prisoners had their sentences arbitrarily extended, and it became more dangerous than before for lawyers to undertake the defence of political offenders. In an interview Sakharov denounced the invasion as 'a monstrous error' and called *inter alia* for an international boycott of the Olympic Games, which were due to be held in Moscow in 1980. This was the pretext the KGB had been waiting for. In flagrant disregard of all legal formalities, Andrei Dmitrievich was seized and shipped off to an undisclosed destination. This turned out to be Nizhnii Novgorod (Gor'ky), where he was kept under strict surveillance and in almost total isolation. He was even physically assaulted by police agents in plain clothes. He went on hunger strike in protest at his illegal detention and was forcibly fed. Despite all these humiliations his views remained as sagely moderate as ever. His ordeal continued until December 1986 when, freed by Gorbachev, he returned to Moscow in a blaze of glory. Public opinion polls showed him to be the individual for whom ordinary people had the greatest respect. He became an unofficial adviser to the government and a parliamentary deputy.

But three years later he died, aged 68, his demise expedited by years of suffering.

Sakharov's career had parallels with that of Leo Tolstoi. Both men abandoned the world of privilege to uphold their ideals; both became moral exemplars for their generation; both were feared by the political establishment of the day; and both regimes collapsed within a few years of their death. There were of course important differences: Tolstoi never suffered imprisonment, Sakharov's writing style was undistinguished. Another difference is even more important. Whereas Tolstoi had the respect and sympathy of the entire Russian educated class, Sakharov received less support than was his due from the world of learning during the pre-reform era. His approaches to his fellow academicians were usually rebuffed, although at least they did not expel him. In 1973 forty members of the Academy, including its president, Keldysh, signed a declaration expressing indignation at his views, and two years later the body censured him for accepting the Nobel Prize. The eminent scientist Kapitsa refused to join in the first of these campaigns but later declined Sakharov's appeal to intervene on behalf of his fellow-physicist Orlov. On the other hand, many prominent activists in the human rights movement (Turchin, Tverdokhlebov, Kovalev, Orlov) were members of the scientific community. Among the reasons for this reserve, in addition to those noted in Chapter 8, were gender— women in university faculties showed greater courage—and the fact that Soviet scientists, perhaps to an even greater degree than other intellectuals, were captivated by dreams of national grandeur. Thus there were limits to the resurgence of civil society during the Brezhnev years.

By the mid-1980s the KGB had managed to disorient and fragment the Democratic movement. But theirs was a hollow triumph which made it harder for Communist reformers to succeed when they took the helm.

14 The Russian National Movement

Origins

At the beginning of the twentieth century the Russian people lagged behind many others in the tsarist realm (Poles, Finns, even Balts and Ukrainians) in the development of a modern national consciousness. The social élite identified with the multi-national empire; in the terminology of the day, their thinking was *rossiiskii* rather than *russkii*. Ordinary folk either opted for a social (class) orientation or else had none at all, in that their horizons were limited to the local community. This helps to explain why Russia was defeated in World War I, why the Bolsheviks, with their utopian internationalist creed, won mass support in 1917, and why the Whites failed to worst the Reds in the ensuing civil war. Paradoxically, Russian national sentiment as a mass phenomenon first came to the fore under Stalin. It was fortified by his doctrine of 'socialism in a single country' and then by the all-out drive for economic development. Stalinism skewed the Revolution towards what would later scornfully be called 'national Communism'. From 1934 onward pseudo-patriotic motifs became ever more frequent in Soviet official discourse. They reached a high point during World War II, which was fought as much in pursuit of Russian national and state interests as of socialist revolution. The ideology of Stalin's last years, as we have seen, was a curious amalgam of elements from the Marxist–Bolshevik tradition, national chauvinism, pan-Slav imperialism and anti-Semitism: a potent brew. Even those sceptical about official claims on behalf of Russian priority in every field of endeavour took satisfaction in the honour and strength accruing to their nation, as the 'elder brother' in the Soviet family.

When Khrushchev swung the pendulum back towards neo-Leninist 'proletarian internationalism', this aggrieved neophyte

Russian patriots. They felt that their nation's interests were being sacrificed to those of the minorities or to the cause of 'national liberation' in the Third World. The surrender of the Crimea to Ukraine in 1954, for instance, was resented by the largely Russian population of that peninsula. Others claimed that the RSFSR was disadvantaged by the subsidies paid to help develop 'backward' union republics. Why did their republic not have its own capital city, Academy of Sciences, or even Communist Party, as the others did? Restlessness among the non-Russians suggested ingratitude for the efforts expended by Russians on their behalf. The fact that many minority intellectuals viewed matters in a very different light, and arraigned Moscow's policies as self-interested or exploitative, merely reinforced these prejudices—the emotional stuff of nationalism the world over.

In the view of one specialist, precisely because it developed under totalitarian conditions, (Great) Russian nationalism had an imperialistic flavour from the start (Goble 1990). This may be too harsh a judgement, but its protagonists certainly did find it difficult to define their identity clearly. Most of them had an 'imperial' rather than a national consciousness. Few of them viewed with equanimity the possibility of the Soviet Union breaking up and its peoples forming national states, with which a future independent Russia might live in harmony as one among equals. Such a prospect seemed likely to bring only chaos and mutual impoverishment. Surely at least the three Slavic peoples would have to hold together? Did not their common past prescribe a common destiny? On strategic and economic grounds alone, it seemed, a good case could be made out for keeping the entire Union firmly bonded to its Russian core, if (as then seemed unlikely) Communist rule should come to an end.

Cultural nationalism

The Russian national revival that took shape in the late 1960s was in part a response to the development of opposition in the minority regions, a topic discussed in Chapter 7. But it was much more than this. It was also a cultural phenomenon, an attempt to fill the spiritual void left by the collapse of faith in the official doctrine of 'proletarian internationalism' or world-wide revolution. One response was to return to religious values (see Chapter 8). This was not an option that appealed to everyone, yet many non-believers saw atheistic persecution as morally wrong and politically counter-productive. Most obviously the anti-religious campaign had led to the destruction and neglect of thousands of church buildings that had great architectural or historic merit. It had caused irreparable damage to the country's stock of cultural treasures, and betrayed a 'nihilistic' attitude to its rich traditions.

In making their case conservationists had to play down any sympathies they had for Orthodoxy *per se* and to stress aesthetic or material concerns: for instance, that a derelict church detracted from the beauty of the rural landscape or that foreign tourism to Russia's old cities would earn valuable hard currency. In this way the civic movement to salvage relics of the past won official approval for the establishment of an All-Russian Society for the Preservation of Historical and Cultural Monuments (VOOPIK, 1965). By 1972 the organization claimed seven million members; five years later the total exceeded twelve and by 1982 was approaching fifteen million. Similar bodies existed in the Baltic and Transcaucasian republics. The society's statute was framed in such a way as to ensure control by Party functionaries, and it was not allowed to publish a journal of its own. Lectures were, however, well attended and members displayed a good deal of enthusiasm for the cause, collecting funds to restore buildings and promoting educational projects.

Scholars compiled studies of early Russian art and architecture, some of which were published in large editions. Activists toured the countryside in search of venerable icons and manuscripts or specimens of peasant handicrafts. There was a certain nostalgic faddishness about all this—'Moscow and Leningrad youths . . . may be seen in all parts of northern Russia with their cameras and beards, searching for Russia's lost "soul" ', remarked one Western critic disparagingly (Haney 1973)—but it did have an underlying seriousness of purpose. Particularly influential was the example of the writer Vladimir Soloukhin, whose *Letters from the Russian Museum* appeared in 1966. He was himself an avid collector of, and expert on, early icon-painting. A veritable cult developed around Andrei Rublev, the gifted fourteenth-century artist-monk (who had the merit, rare in his day, of being a native rather than a Greek immigrant!). A museum of religious art, specializing in restoration work, opened in the former Moscow monastery where Rublev lay buried, and a brilliant film of his achievement, by Andrei Tarkovsky, earned international acclaim. Particularly important was the role played by D. S. Likhachev in the rediscovery of early Russian literature. A distinguished humanist, who did much behind the scenes to help colleagues in trouble for their ideas, he was backed by a pleiad of scholars, who were broad-minded enough to acknowledge, for example, the influences on early Rus' culture of Byzantium and the southern Slavs (Meyendorff 1977). The medieval town of Suzdal' was tastefully restored as a 'museum city' and became a landmark on the tourist circuit.

It must be acknowledged that VOOPIK's activities had only limited success in making good the spoils of progress. There was too little money available and too much bureaucratic obstruction. A great deal depended on the attitude of local authorities. In a few places they co-operated in forcing industrial enterprises to vacate church premises they had taken over, but elsewhere there were interminable disputes over the proper use of such buildings. None of those restored, so far as is known, was re-opened to worship: they remained 'monuments of culture' (their official designation, carved on a plaque at the entrance to each site). There could be no fundamental improvement until the state abandoned its atheistic ideology, allowed religious bodies to recover their property, and co-operated with them in their care and preservation. Unhappily, by the time this moment arrived the constraints on spending would be even tighter.

The national revival brought with it a renewed interest in Russian religious philosophy (Dostoevsky, Leont'ev, Berdiaev). Few of these writers' works were allowed to appear in print, but copies of old editions circulated surreptitiously. So, too, with the Slavophils, who underwent a partial rehabilitation in the 1970s. To circumvent the censor literary and cultural historians emphasized their contribution to the country's economic development and neglected the religious core of their beliefs. Notwithstanding this distortion some Russian intellectuals came to see themselves as neo-Slavophils,[1] and the animated discussions that took place—no longer in aristocratic salons but in modest apartment kitchens—had a remote affinity with those of the 'marvellous decade' (1838–48). The advocates of human rights were clearly in the 'Westernizer' camp, which—now as then—did not mean that they gave blanket endorsement to private property or commercialism. Some of them, for instance Roi

Medvedev, stood in the tradition of democratic socialism. Towards the other end of the spectrum—which quite naturally was more diverse than it had been in the early nineteenth century—were ranged those who attached supreme value to Russia's spiritual traditions. Common to all streams of thought was a concern with moral values and, perhaps, a certain vagueness or fluidity, a reluctance to be pinned down to hard-and-fast positions on specific issues. This facilitated the task of the political and security establishment, which up to a point could manipulate the debate—or suppress it altogether.

Political nationalism

In the late 1960s the censors permitted certain journals to develop an identifiable 'profile' and to conduct polemical exchanges. *Novyi mir*, until 1970 still under Tvardovsky's editorship, took a more Western or internationalist line, while Nikonov's *Molodaia gvardiia* ('Young Guard'), an organ of the Komsomol, was more 'nationalist'. Also in the patriotic camp were the literary magazines *Druzhba narodov* ('Friendship of Peoples') and *Nash sovremennik* ('Our Contemporary'), as well as the newspaper *Sovetskaia Rossiia*, originally published by the CC's Bureau for the RSFSR. In 1968 a certain Lobanov launched an attack in *Molodaia gvardiia* on the intelligentsia, whom he scorned as 'educated shopkeepers', susceptible to the lure of 'petty-bourgeois' mercantile values. Russian culture, he maintained, had to be based on the values of the common people. Another writer, the literary critic Viktor Chalmaev, developed the theme. In two articles, 'Great Strivings' and 'Inevitability', in the same journal he explored writers' quest through the ages for the essence of the Russian national character and lauded its enduring virtues. 'The feeling for social justice, patriotism, bravery, and also the search for truth' had enabled the people to resist infatuation with alien materialism.[2] Everything harmful had been brought in from the West. Seen in this light, Stalinism was the supreme embodiment of the 'Russian Idea'. The self-styled democrats were dismissed as demagogues who sought to seduce Russia's innocent youngsters with pseudo-progressive slogans. They were intellectuals, alienated from the masses, who would one day rise up against them, so bringing about 'a renaissance of the best of the people's traditions: this is the inevitablity of our time'.

Chalmaev's portentous philosophizing was criticized in *Novyi mir*, which branded its journalistic rival as a mouthpiece for Great Russian chauvinism. This in turn led eleven writers to publish an open letter in another periodical (July 1969). They fiercely attacked Dement'ev, author of one of these articles and an editor of *Novyi mir*, and defended Chalmaev's intentions, while grudgingly admitting that he had committed some factual errors. The irony was that each camp condemned the other in ideological terms as counter-revolutionary or anti-Soviet, and so virtually invited the Party to settle the score. It is said that officials in the CC's Cultural department backed *Molodaia gvardiia*, whereas those in Agitprop opposed it, and that in November 1970 the dispute came before the Politburo, which opted for the former. It decided to dismiss Nikonov from his editorial post—but to purge the *entire* board of *Novyi mir*.[3] Someone at top level (Poliansky, or even Suslov?) may have been protecting *Molodaia gvardiia*, and was now called to order (by Andropov?). Alternatively, the whole exchange may have been staged by Andropov to sow confusion amidst the intelligentsia. Even if this is so, it does not necessarily follow that the views expressed were not sincerely held—merely that in totalitarian conditions no intellectual discussion could be authentic. The KGB was clearly more sympathetic to the Russian nationalists than to the democrats, whom it treated more harshly. The affair is historically significant as marking the début of an 'unholy alliance' between extremists on the right and left, which would become a prominent feature of Russian political life in the late 1980s and 1990s.

In 1970 a manifesto entitled *A Nation Speaks* ('Slovo natsii'), signed by some unidentified 'Russian Patriots', took an overtly racist line. Civilization was allegedly under threat from the 'coloured' peoples. This was the fault of Western liberals, with their fallacious ideals of democracy and equality. Russia, however, could avoid 'biological degeneration' by ridding herself of Marxist internationalism and establishing 'a strong government based on national traditions'. 'For us the nation is primary and all else derivative.' The Soviet system, the writers continued, discriminated against Russians. Given the presence of so many Russian settlers in Ukraine, it would be better to allocate parts of it to Russia, so reducing it to a small non-viable territory cut off from the sea. The rights of Russian residents in Kazakhstan and Kyrgyzstan should also be upheld once Communism had been worsted in a peaceful 'ideological revolution'. The future lay with a 'united indivisible Russia', as the core of a League of Slavic States which, together with the Anglo-Saxon powers, would rule the world. The authors also struck an anti-Semitic note, alleging that Jews 'virtually mono-polized science and culture'.

This was a quasi-intellectual Fascism, which anticipated and complemented the 'street' variety noted above. It manifested itself most notoriously in a brochure entitled *Beware, Zionism!* (1969), written by Yu. S. Ivanov, a Party official subsequently transferred to the KGB (Reddaway 1972). In this publication, printed in no less than 75,000 copies, as in later Soviet propaganda, 'Zionism' served as a code-word to conceal hostility towards Jews generally. Much the same line was taken by the essayists Antonov, Semanov, and Shimanov. Antonov (who may have been a co-author of the manifesto mentioned above) looked forward to the unification of Orthodoxy and Leninism. Shimanov held that the sufferings which the Russians had undergone under Soviet rule had strengthened their spiritual resilience, so that the collapse of Communism would make possible the creation of a new Russian empire on Orthodox foundations. In the *samizdat* almanac *Many Years* (1980–1) Shima-nov warned of a 'Judaeo-masonic conspiracy' while simultaneous-ly—like anti-Semites elsewhere—claiming not to be prejudiced against Jews. Similar points were made by Semanov in his novel *Brusilov* (1980), where he wrote disparagingly of the 'cosmopolitan oligarchy' and 'those of other faiths' (*inovertsy*).

Extremist ideas of this kind, sometimes misleadingly referred to as 'national Bolshevism',[4] were too crude to win support among the intelligentsia, but the cause of the 'Russian right' was taken up by others whose opinions were more moderate. In 1971 Vladimir Osipov, a historian and former prisoner of conscience, founded an unofficial journal, *Veche*, named for the medieval Russian popular assembly. Ten issues appeared over the next three years. Dis-tributed through the mail (unlike the *Chronicle* or other *samizdat* publications), it contained articles on religious, historical, cultural, and environmental topics written from a perspective 'quite com-patible with democracy' (Alexeyeva 1985). The editorial standpoint was that, although Russia was menaced by enemies to the west and east (China), the path to true freedom lay through cultivating one's inner life in a spirit of Christian humility, rather than by adopting such 'external' devices as constitutionalism or the rule of law. *Veche* was 'a journal with many facets and extremely heterogeneous views' (Carter 1990) and its editor expressed reservations about some of the material he published. But the line taken towards the intelligentsia, past and present, was consistently antagonistic. This led to polemics that lowered its prestige and, together with police harassment, caused Osipov to suspend publication in March 1974. After producing two issues of a sequel, *Zemlia* ('The Land'), he was arrested and sentenced to eight years in a strict-regime camp. Sakharov nobly interceded on his behalf, while making it clear that he dissented from his ideas. Osipov returned the compliment by defending Sakharov from a vicious attack by the extremist Shimanov (Dunlop 1983).

By this time the liberals or 'Westernizers' had lost an influential patron in the Party *apparat*. Alexander Yakovlev, who after 1985 would become Gorbachev's right-hand man and the main intellectual force behind his cultural liberalization, was a professional historian and also acting head of Agitprop. In November 1972 he wrote an article in *Literaturnaia gazeta* highly critical of the nationalists. It brought a reply by Osipov in *Veche* charging him with 'national nihilism' and even Trotskyism. This was too much for his political masters, who ordered Yakovlev's dismissal. In May 1973 he was despatched as ambassador to Canada, where his views (in private at least) evolved towards liberal democracy.

Solzhenitsyn

All the writers discussed hitherto were essentially publicists with little pretension to literary renown. Far more significant were the views of Alexander Solzhenitsyn. He might be described as a cultural nationalist, although admittedly any label risks doing an injustice to modern Russia's greatest man of letters, the embodiment of her conscience. Awarded the Nobel Prize for Literature in 1970, Solzhenitsyn fought a lonely battle against Soviet officialdom until February 1974, when he was taken into custody and promptly deported to Germany. His many admirers in the West were taken aback by the strength of his patriotic sentiments, which challenged their own assumptions. Solzhenitsyn did not help his reputation abroad by making some provocative remarks about Western institutions and life-styles, and by the 1980s, when he produced what he considered his major work, *The Red Wheel*, it was all but ignored by the critics. He spent nearly twenty years in self-imposed isolation in Vermont before returning to his homeland in May 1994.

Solzhenitsyn should be judged as an artist, but here we are concerned merely with his role in the Russian national revival. His contribution was to lend it public respectability through the prestige of his name. Two points need to be borne in mind when considering his political views. First, they were rooted in a profound and sincere commitment to Christian values. Second, he himself did not claim that they were particularly original, or even consistent. They do not lend themselves to assessment by conventional criteria, precisely because they were not deduced from empirical observation of contemporary realities, or based on scientific study; they derived from a Romantic world-outlook and philosophy of history which he took over ready-made, as it were, from the Slavophils and *pochvenniki*, mediated through the celebrated miscellany *Vekhi* (1909). It was never Solzhenitsyn's purpose to devise a political credo. Drawn into politics against his will, he resented its claims on his time, which belonged rightfully to literature. Nevertheless from 1969 onward, when he wrote his open letter to the Fourth USW congress (see p. 176), he increasingly became the unofficial head of the literary opposition and his opinions carried weight.

Alexander Isaevich approved of Osipov's *Veche*, while declining an invitation to write for it, and even found some good in Chalmaev's article. His *Lenten Letter* to the Patriarch (1972) was followed in 1973 by another epistle addressed to the Soviet leaders (published in the West shortly after his arrival there) and then by several other statements and addresses, culminating in 'How Are We to Organize Russia?' (1990). Also relevant are his three articles in *From Under the Rubble* (1974), a miscellany conceived as a latter-day *Vekhi*, which he edited together with the mathematician Igor Shafarevich—who seems to have influenced his outlook, although later the two men parted company.

Solzhenitsyn's basic idea is that only a moral revolution can save humanity from catastrophe through its headlong descent into materialistic godlessness. Modern industrial civilization, based on false notions of progress, is doomed. The quest for unlimited freedom and equality has destroyed man's natural ties to the community and led to the triumph of expediency over principle. Western democracy, perverted by political partisanship and journalistic licence, cannot serve as a model for Russia, where the Communist system, based on violence and deceit, is likewise in decay. However, Russia does have a *chance* of survival, since her people have preserved something of the old communal spirit. The Orthodox Church, although corrupted by its compromise with the regime, can be revitalized from below and reorganized on the principle of *sobornost'* (collegiality). It could then become the focus of a nation-wide consensus and serve as a moral centre in reconstructing the ravaged country. This will be a long drawn-out process, involving a shift of authority from the centre to local councils. The economy should be privatized and small businesses and family farms take the place of giant industrial enterprises and *kolkhozy*. Conscription should be abolished, military expenditure reduced, and peaceful relations maintained with other states. The non-Russians should not be retained by force if free votes showed that their peoples wished to separate, but a federation of the Slav nations (to be called the Russian Union and to include northern Kazakhstan) is desirable.

As even this summary suggests, Alexander Isaevich is neither a monarchist nor an authoritarian, neither a chauvinist nor an advocate of Russian messianism—all of which have been alleged. The real trouble with his ideas is their imprecision. He is not interested in institutional details. He does not explain, for example, *how* the Church is to be renovated, given the legacy of the *Sergeevshchina*. In what ways can the national idea actually help to transform society? (Willerton 1993.) Solzhenitsyn is better at diagnosing the world's current ills than at proposing workable solutions. What he offers is essentially a myth, a prophetic vision—Russia reborn under divine guidance—which in less saintly hands can be given a most un-Christian twist. Already in the early 1970s his views led to friction within the dissident community. Later, in emigration, he remained an aloof and distant figure. Offended by the criticisms levelled against him, he withdrew into august silence. It was paradoxical that one who sought to reconcile his *narod* on the basis of Christian morality should have been so isolated from those best qualified to become his disciples. But then Solzhenitsyn had no wish to form a faction. Quite to the contrary, he seems to have exulted in his prophetic role, confident that in the long run his literary influence, not his impact as a public figure, would be decisive. In this he is probably correct, although it is still too early to judge, since his major works did not begin to appear in Russia until 1990 (and even then in relatively few copies).[5]

Nationalism in literature

In the shadow of Solzhenitsyn's genius there developed during the 1970s a whole pleiad of writers who employed cultural nationalist motifs in their work. They originated as members of the 'village prose' school, to which Solzhenitsyn's story 'Matriona's House' (1963: see Chapter 8) also belongs. After 1976 'village prose itself . . . began to wither away' (K. Clark 1990), partly under pressure from on high. Critics labelled it 'a literature of nostalgia', but this was to underestimate its enduring appeal to suppressed national sentiment, which could not be articulated freely. These writers saw 'urban man as lost, either shallow or alienated from himself, basing his life on false values or no values at all' (Hosking 1973). Counterposed to urban man is the peasant, rooted in his family and communal environment. Hard-working, tolerant, modest, warm-hearted, he senses instinctively that human solidarity is essential in order to survive deprivation and suffering. These heroes are not the youthful *kolkhozniki* beloved of socialist realist fiction, possessed of mechanical skills and upwardly mobile, but men and (especially) women who have paid the price of collectivization and its sequels.

Fedor Abramov's *Two Winters and Three Summers* (1968) is set, like much of his work, in the north Russian village of Pekashino. The period is the late 1940s, and the farmers are at the beck and call of an omnipotent district Party secretary. The boy hero Mikhail, his life stunted by this bondage, rebels and breaks free, but loses out to his rival Yegorsha, a youth who, having prospered in the city, returns to win the hand of Mikhail's sister. So far we are on familiar ground, but in another character we meet Yegorsha's opposite: Yevsei is an aged religious sectarian (Old Believer) who returns from Siberian exile, finds his property stolen, but refuses to seek retribution from his fellow-villagers, with whom he shares an intimate sense of community. Yevsei reprimands young Yegorsha for swearing by the Mother of God, but is rewarded for his piety by arrest on a trumped-up charge (Hosking 1973).

Old Believers also feature in the stories of Vasilii Belov, a younger and more sophisticated 'northern' writer. The hero of his novelette *That's How Things Are* (1966) is 'a kind of peasant Yurii Zhivago' who has the same preoccupation with ultimate questions such as human mortality and family responsibilities. The simple, good-natured Ivan Drynov, persuaded against his better judgement to go to town in search of a better life, gets back in time only to mourn his wife Katerina, mother of nine, who has collapsed and died from overwork. Knowing that he should have done the job that killed her, Ivan is overcome by inconsolable remorse. The ending is deliberately left open, but the message is clear: virtue is to be found only by keeping close to Nature and observing its laws. We have gone beyond a 1950s-style call on the Party to reform its ways: now it is the basic orientation of Soviet society that Belov calls in question. In another of his stories ('The Eve', 1972–6) Belov contests the ethical principles behind forced collectivization. His sympathies are clearly with a *kulak* victim and not with the atheistic outsiders, the men of violence. The morality in these tales is Christian (or pre-Christian) rather than Communist. Instead of rosy visions of a glorious future we find laments for a past that has largely been destroyed.

In the gifted Siberian writer Valentin Rasputin's most popular story, 'Farewell to Matiora' (1976), an ecological element enters into the narrative. Matiora—the name is linked etymologically to *mat'* (mother)—is an island in the Angara due to be flooded by the construction of a hydroelectric plant. The elderly heroine, Dar'ia, has lived all her life on the island and is wholly identified with it. She fights for its preservation against her grandson Andrei, who thoughtlessly leaves to join the building workers. The boy boasts that modern man has the power to achieve whatever he wishes. Dar'ia replies that 'people have forgotten their God-given place . . . We're no better than those who went before us . . . God sees how proud man has become . . . Watch out that this power of yours doesn't get the better of you.' She is invested with spiritual forces and enters into contact with the *genius loci*, the ancestral unconscious. Unwilling to be evacuated to a dismal new housing development, Dar'ia delays her departure until the last possible moment and prepares her ancient *izba* as if for a funeral before the demolition squad arrives to burn it down. The story ends in fire, fog, and flood, implying that catastrophe awaits man unless he ceases to worship the false god of material progress.

A similarly apocalyptic atmosphere pervades Rasputin's novelette 'The Fire' (1985, written 1965). Faced with his neighbours' unwillingness to acknowledge their responsibility for a conflagration, Ivan Petrovich tries to extinguish it, reflecting meanwhile on his unethical conduct in the past and the Last Judgement that awaits him. He comes to the conclusion that 'a man needs four supports in life: home, family, people to spend one's time with, and the land on which one's house stands.' These modest requirements Ivan Petrovich lacks, and the story closes with him wandering off to nowhere, 'a little man who had lost his way and despaired of finding a house of his own'. Clarifying his point later, the author explained that he had been speaking for 'the spiritual-moral world of millions': Russia herself has lost her way (Peters 1990; Porter 1989). 'O silent land of ours, how long will you remain silent?' By 1985 at least the patriots would not have to wait long for an answer.

In a brief sketch, 'Baikal' (1981), Rasputin movingly evokes the lake's natural glories. This 'jewel of Siberia' possessed 'a miraculous life-giving force, a spirit of timelessness' that led one to reflect that 'Nature in itself is always moral, only man can make it immoral.' He was not against development *per se*, but insisted that due attention be paid to the human and environmental costs.

The reader may at this point be wondering what these apparently unexceptionable sentiments have to do with Russian nationalism as a political concept. Neither Rasputin nor any other writer of his tendency could afford to confront directly such sensitive questions as, say, inter-ethnic relations, and so they emphasized the beauty of the Russian landscape, popular traditions, national character, and so forth. This was a kind of code. The implicit political message was a subversive one, although there were also points of contact with the official ideology. The censors' tolerance for the literary neo-russophiles was limited, and in 1982 the authorities tightened the screw. A Party CC resolution told writers to 'develop their creative ties with the practice of Communist construction', i.e. to go back to the production novel. But how was this objective to be achieved? This was a dead art form. Few readers found inspiration in, for instance, B. Galiazimov's account of the heroic construction workers who built a railway line around the town of Samotlor. 'Critical attention, and even literary prizes, were accorded to works written in a very different vein' (Clark 1990). Some writers found a way out in science fiction or detective stories, both of which genres enjoyed a considerable vogue, although this was not really what Authority wanted.

Only one author succeeded in combining a technological, futuristic theme with the conventions of village prose. This was the talented Chingiz Aitmatov, a Kyrgyz who writes in Russian as well as his native tongue. In *The Day Longer than a Hundred Years* (1980) he skilfully melds dramatic episodes on several planes, both realistic and fantastic. In the sub-plot astronauts discover a superior civilization in another galaxy—yet the cosmodrome from which they leave Earth 'represents . . . the intrusion of technological progress into the remote steppes of Central Asia, perpetrated without regard to . . . tradition or the will of the local people' (Shneidman 1989). There are many references to ancient Kazakh legends, such as that of the *mankurts*: native warriors who, if captured by the enemy, were subjected to cruel tortures and deprived of their memory. Aitmatov suggests here that indoctrination has led Soviet citizens, especially non-Russians, to forget their national traditions and 'live for the day, caring little about their people's past or their children's future'. This is much the same line of thought as Rasputin's, but Aitmatov takes it further, hinting at the regime's failure to fulfil its promises of 1956 and its readiness to tolerate abuses of power. 'He observes that anyone ready to sell his soul to the devil is a kind of *mankurt* and that every social system creates its own mental cripppples who serve its purpose.' That Aitmatov did indeed entertain such subversive ideas became clear from his later work, *The Execution Block* (1986), in which he developed his critique of the corruption and spiritual emptiness of Soviet society.

The fact that such notions could be ventilated at all shows that by the late Brezhnev era the system of literary controls had become more flexible. Although the censors continued to prevent the open articulation of dissenting views—the anti-Stalinist satires of Voinovich and Vladimov,[6] for instance, could appear only abroad—some other writers were permitted to express themselves in Aesopian language which initiated readers understood. To put the point a little differently, the boundaries of socialist realism were now redrawn less narrowly. It became a 'broad church' that could accommodate writing in many different moods, including sensitive explorations of human psychology and man's relationship to Nature and the divine. Few serious critics now even bothered to invoke the doctrine, for its meaning had become so diluted as to render it irrelevant and creative writers paid it no more than lip service.

As for the ageing conservatives ensconced in the USW establishment, their work was of little account except perhaps in regard to writing on World War II. Not surprisingly, it is here that one finds chauvinistic attitudes expressed most openly. The Belarusian writer Vasyl Bykov manages to treat the experiences of soldiers and partisans in a humanistic spirit. Yurii Bondarev adheres more closely to the heroic tradition, but his work (for example, *Hot Snow*, 1969, on the battle of Stalingrad) undeniably has literary quality. In his publicistic essays, where he gives vent to a fierce anti-Americanism, he redeems himself by a strong pro-environmental stance that brings him close to the neo-russophiles. Their school was definitely in the ascendant, whatever the cultural authorities might have wished.

The visual arts

Its influence also extended to the visual arts. Rasputin's *Farewell to Matiora* was adapted for the screen by Elem Klimov in 1983. A decade earlier Vasilii Shukshin had made a prize-winning film out of his story 'The Red Guelder Rose' (*Kalina krasnaia*, 1973). His death, at the age of 45, shortly after its phenomenal success was yet another occasion for a nation-wide outpouring of grief, which called forth over 160,000 letters of condolence. To Westerners the theme may sound sentimental, but at the time it broke several taboos. The hero, Yegor Produkin, is an amiable ex-convict who, on release from prison camp, returns to his native village and to Liuba, the girl with whom he has corresponded while 'inside'. There are scenes of a traditional 'Russian' steam bath and (inevitably!) of birch-trees, as well as allusions to the fate of the *kulaks*. Yegor secures a job on a farm and the couple go to see his aged mother, who lives in poverty, having been forsaken by her children. She does not recognize her son. Before he can summon up enough courage to introduce himself and start a new life, his past catches up with him. Mortally wounded by one-time fellow gangsters, he dies in Liuba's arms. 'There he lay, a Russian peasant, on his native steppe near his home, his cheek to the soil as if listening to a sound that he alone could hear.' In the background stands a derelict church, and the birch-trees are bespattered with blood.

Religious and mystical motifs are present also in Tarkovsky's *The Stalker* (1980), which depicts a terrifying journey through a landscape laid waste by a strange explosion. Widely seen as Russia's greatest post-war film director, Tarkovsky was in continual trouble with the authorities. In 1983 the Politburo refused to let him stay abroad to complete work on his last film, *Nostalgia*, and stripped him of his citizenship. (Official documents on this affair have since been published.) In general Goskino was hostile to all the most original, innovative directors. The Armenian film maker S. Parajanov, for instance, was arrested twice (1973, 1982).

The striking canvases of Il'ia Glazunov, notably 'The Mystery of the Twentieth Century' (first shown in 1978) and 'The Return of the Prodigal Son', drew on a repertoire of Christian symbols. In the latter a young Russian in jeans is depicted coming back repentantly to a home with icons on the walls. Another painting included the figure of the last tsar amidst other notabilities of the past. So closely is Orthodoxy bound up with the Russian historical tradition that it would be artificial to attempt to differentiate between religious and national themes in art. It is probably true that some painters jumped on the religious bandwagon for secular, indeed mundane, reasons. Glazunov's sincerity as an Orthodox convert has been called in question. Yet about a million people turned out to see an exhibition of his work in Leningrad which the authorities at first tried to ban. Entries in the visitors' book hailed his 'love for long-suffering Russia' or the 'new renaissance' of national values that his work heralded (Dunlop 1983). Brezhnev commissioned the artist to paint his portrait, as did some other leaders. This discreet patronage was a sign of the times. The cultural authorities tacitly acquiesced in privately organized exhibitions of unorthodox but national art, while meting out harsher treatment to avant-garde non-representational painters who followed Western models. In 1974 works displayed at one such exhibition in a Moscow park had been literally bulldozed into the ground on KGB orders. Thereafter a softer approach was generally taken. Among the intelligentsia there was a vogue for collecting ancient artefacts, and by the mid-1980s cultural nationalism may be said to have struck root in the Russian popular consciousness.

Religious life

Official 'liberalism' towards certain writers or artists was not accompanied by greater tolerance for the churches, although their atheist controllers seem to have been less successful than before in stemming the spread of religious belief. The KGB and its subordinate agency, the Council for Religious Affairs (CRA), probably reckoned that nationalist nonconformity would be far more dangerous if it was allowed to acquire an institutional base.

Statistics on the CRA's activities during the years 1980–4 have recently come to light (Krivov *et al.* 1993). In a secret report to the Party CC (May 1985) its chairman, Kharchev, claimed that there had been 'a decline in the number of religious organizations, clergy, baptisms . . . and breaches of regulations pertaining to [religious] cults', but his figures show that the record was uneven (see Table 14.1). For instance, the Russian Orthodox Church continued to face greater persecution than its Georgian or Armenian counterparts. A new atheist campaign launched in 1981 led to the demolition of over three hundred churches and chapels, most of them in Ukraine. Overall the Orthodox lost 246 congregations and gained only twenty-three over the five-year span. These figures include unregistered congregations and so may well be misleading, since not all of these will have come under CRA surveillance. The figures for baptisms are certainly understated, since this rite was often carried out in private to avoid repression. The highest rates were reported from Chuvashia, Moldova, and Gor'ky (Nizhnii Novgorod) province (respectively 49.7, 44.4, and 42.2 per cent of new-born children in 1984). Increases were particularly marked in the Baltic lands and in Georgia. (For marriages and funerals the rates were fairly stable.)

The increasing amount of money which congregations succeeded in collecting testifies to their vitality. By 1984 Russian Orthodox parishes are said to have had on average an end-of-year balance of 35,000 roubles at their disposition, an increase of 5,300 roubles on 1979. This was only a quarter as much as their Armenian co-religionists (135,000 roubles) and less than Muslim communities (40,200 roubles), but far more than the Baptists (2,600 roubles). From these sums the churches had *inter alia* to maintain clergy and buildings. There were thus wide variations in the amount available to parishes for this purpose: on average 2,490 roubles a year for Russian Orthodox but only fifty roubles for Baptists.[7]

Such statistical exercises can give little idea of what was really going on in the life of any of these denominations. A Western sociologist distinguishes between five forms of religious witness, ranging from worship in the privacy of one's home, the least 'activist', to efforts at public mobilization through petitions and the like; the most characteristic form was worship in a (registered) church (Biddulph 1979). The religious are said to have formed a 'deviant sub-culture' linked by strong internal ties of a 'communal' (self-regulating) type. Committed young Baptists might attend church up to three times a week and devote several more hours to charitable activities, informal study, or other social events. They enjoyed sympathy and support among non-believers, although less so among those with a higher education.

In so far as evidence of this kind is based on opinion research by (secular if not atheist) Soviet pollsters, care is needed in evaluating the results, since the questions asked were often loaded and respondents reluctant to answer them frankly. A leading student of Russian Orthodoxy points out that those categorized as 'believers' might well really be theists rather than Christians, in that they were ignorant of the Creed and did not adopt a Christian life-style (Ellis 1986). Yet the survival of popular piety in face of persecution she regards as 'one of the twentieth century's greatest miracles'. Not only was there a significant minority of young males in church congregations—I recall seeing a Soviet soldier in uniform at a Baptist service in Moscow—but the cohort of elderly worshippers was continually 'refreshed' by those who began to attend church on reaching pensionable age, when they would no longer risk penalties at their workplace for doing so.

Such discrimination was regularly practised against those in employment, and especially against the young, who were the chief target of atheist propaganda. Typically, in 1978 a biology student was expelled from Moscow State University because he was found to be in possession of religious writings. Children known to be believers would be barred from joining the Komsomol. This effectively prevented them from pursuing their education and obtaining a managerial or professional position. Teachers discovered to have religious views faced instant dismissal. In 1982 one woman teacher was threatened with incarceration in an SPH for this 'offence' and told that she could avoid it by renouncing her faith. She refused. Countless others withstood harassment in their everyday lives

TABLE 14.1. *CRA data on religious confessions, 1979/80–1984*

	Russian Orthodox	Georgian Orthodox	Armenian Orthodox[a]	Roman Catholic[b]	Evangelical Christian-Baptists	Other Protestants[c]	Jews	Muslims
Parishes (congregations):								
Registered closed	141	0		0	39	5	2	3
Unregistered closed	105	3	0	381	247	159	0	356
Registered opened	23	4	0	38	257	167	1	57
Net gain or loss	−223	1	0	−343	−29	3	−1	−302
Number of registered *plus* **unregistered (1984)**	6,806+63	51+4	33+0	1,068+29	2,294+268	1,000+239	91+22	392+419
Clergy:[d]								
1980	9,226	130	103	970	4,079	640	79	6,408
1984	9,748	148	133	907	4,379	706	64	4,657
Percentage change	+5.7	+13.8	+29.1	−6.5	+7.4	+10.3	−19.0	−27.3

Baptisms (ooo):							
1979	769.6	13.9	7.2	28.8	8.3	4.8	6.1
1984	711.2	14.5	7.9	29.5	7.0	6.7	8.7
Percentage change	−7.6	+4.3	+10.7	+2.4	+16.4	+38.1	—
Funds collected (millions of roubles)							
1979	180.7	2.9	2.3	2.8	4.4	1.6	1.3
1984	210.5	3.9	4.0	3.2	5.0	2.0	1.5
Percentage gain	16.5	35.6	72.5	15.9	13.5	26.2	42.1

[a] Armenian parishes and clergy: all confessions combined.
[b] Roman Catholic parishes: Uniates excluded.
[c] Lutherans, Methodists, Mennonites, Seventh Day Adventists; excludes Jehovah's Witnesses and some smaller sects.
[d] 'Servitors of the cult' (the official term); registered and unregistered communities.

ranging from simple mockery to loss of their apartment and physical assault by hooligans acting at the KGB's behest.

Security police penetration of the hierarchy seems to have intensified during the Brezhnev–Andropov era. In 1991 it was revealed that a KGB colonel, Milovanov, held the post of CRA deputy chairman, and a former chief of the agency stated that 'not a single bishop was confirmed in office without the Central Committee's and KGB's consent' (Albats 1992)—so substantiating charges that had been levelled at the hierarchy for years by critics at home and abroad. A KGB major and CRA functionary in Rostov province (1972–84) took no less than 142,000 roubles in bribes from various congregations, one of which (at Shakhty) even paid him a monthly stipend. Evidence also came to light about police repression of religious activists. In 1982 alone 229 such individuals were in prison and eighteen others exiled. That year, according to a KGB report to the Party CC, it conducted over 2,500 clandestine operations against 'hostile elements' in church circles (Reddaway 1993). These malpractices continued until the Soviet regime collapsed, despite half-hearted attempts by the Orthodox hierarchy to come to terms with its past and to remove from its ranks those most compromised by co-operation with the security police.

This penetration was not confined to the episcopate. At the lowest (parish) level it took the form of introducing vigilantes into the congregation during divine service. Priests were under constant surveillance. If they showed too much zeal, pressure would be brought to bear on the parish council to dismiss them. This might well cost them their residence permit, so that they would have to seek a menial job to avoid arrest on a charge of 'parasitism'. Several cases are known of clergy being sent to an SPH and maltreated there; others were sent to the Gulag. In 1983 Father A. Pivovarov, who had a parish in Siberia, received a sentence of three and a half years in a strict-regime prison camp for distributing unapproved religious literature. Fellow inmates were so impressed by his profound faith that they called him 'the light of Siberia' (Ellis 1986).

Similar persecution was endured by seminarians and monks. Among the two thousand or so students in ecclesiastical institutions, most of whom were training to become priests, were a number of secret informers—as a rule, genuine students who had been suborned into co-operating with the KGB. The monastic community at Pochaev, which had barely survived the onslaught during the 'black quinquennium', continued to suffer harassment. An atheist propaganda bureau was opened there (1978). The militia carried out raids on the premises. Monks were beaten, threatened, and expelled. Here, as in the historic monastery at Pskov, at least one archimandrite who had evidently been 'turned' by the police joined in the persecution.

Despite this repression, or because of it, there was a veritable flowering of religious dissent in the late 1970s. In June 1976 Christians of six denominations joined in appealing to the Soviet authorities and the World Council of Churches for an end to illegal state interference and discrimination. It was the first example of such ecumenical co-operation. Several well-known Orthodox activists signed the document. Among them were Father S. Zheludkov, who had been closely associated with the human rights movement, Igor Shafarevich, whom we have met as Solzhenitsyn's associate, and Gleb Yakunin. Perhaps the most outstanding figure was Father Dmitrii Dudko. A former prisoner of conscience, his popular evening sermons in a Moscow church, when he spoke frankly about topical issues, earned him the moral stature of a 'shadow Patriarch' (Dunlop 1983). He was ordered to stop preaching and transferred to a country parish, but his flock followed him there. An automobile accident was staged in an evident attempt to kill him, and as a result both his legs were broken. In 1978 Dudko began to put out a weekly bulletin in which he expressed his views and gave factual information about current events in the life of the Church. Further intimidation ensued, in which certain prelates co-operated with the security authorities.

Dudko was arrested in the wave of repression unleashed at the time of the Soviet invasion of Afghanistan. The authorities were particularly anxious to prevent contact between dissidents and foreigners expected to come to Moscow in 1980 for the Olympic Games. Under intense psychological pressure (and possibly after the administration of drugs), he publicly recanted his views. Yakunin, who in 1977 had set up an inter-denominational committee to defend believers' rights, was tried in August 1980 and put behind bars for ten years. Another victim of quasi-judicial repression was Alexander Ogorodnikov. In 1974 he had founded an informal religious-philosophical seminar in Moscow, reminiscent in some ways of those held before the 1905 revolution. Its proceedings attracted broad interest before it was forcibly broken up.

Ogorodnikov and his associates exemplified the best in the Russian national tradition. They avoided anti-Western polemics and endeavoured to promote understanding between the churches.

The KGB's apparent victory proved to be a Pyrrhic one since, by manipulating the Church hierarchy and repressing the most active Christian priests and laymen, it left the field open to nationalist zealots opposed to Gorbachev's reformist policies. But there was a cynical logic behind the KGB's actions. Liberal democracy was a far more potent threat to its power than Russian nationalism was. Police functionaries evidently calculated that, if Communism should become non-viable, nationalism could provide the *nomenklatura* with an alternative basis of support. In the 1960s the national movement had arisen independently of, and in opposition to, the political establishment. Yet the ties between them were never entirely sundered. Within a few years the 'unholy alliance' would bear dragon's teeth.

15 The Restless Empire

Nationality affairs under Brezhnev

The more perspicacious Soviet leaders recognized that the principal
threat the regime faced came from the national minorities. Census
data showed that overall they were growing more rapidly than
Russians. Efforts to promote the 'growing together' of all nations
of the Union on the basis of adherence to common Soviet values
were meeting with intermittent success at best. The ideal of their
eventual 'merger' was becoming a mirage, as remote as the achievement of a world-wide Communist order. For this reason during the
1970s it was rarely mentioned in public discourse and gave way to
the less menacing term 'complete unity'. A good deal of attention
was now devoted to concrete nationality problems by academics
(e.g. socio-linguists) and journalists. Scholars at the Institute of
Ethnography such as Bromlei and Starovoitova showed greater
understanding than their predecessors of the subjective, psychological dimension of nationalism (Lapidus 1992). Even so their writings
were disfigured by ideological bias. They could neither question the
formulas continually reiterated in official Party documents nor treat
frankly the practical problems that administrators faced. Instead
they had to tailor their arguments to show that Moscow's policies
were everywhere achieving excellent results and enjoying popular
acclaim. The general tone of these studies was one of expedient
optimism. Much of the work done was historical, or else inadequately based on statistical analysis. Partly for these reasons the
influence which these semi-official advisers exerted on decision-
making was limited.

Nationality policies were seldom clearly spelled out. On formal
occasions Party leaders would deliver oracular pronouncements
that concealed more than they revealed about their real intentions.
At the Twenty-third Party congress (1966) Brezhnev spoke of the
need to show 'solicitude for the interests and national peculiarities
of each people', which seemed to herald a more empirical approach

than that of Khrushchev. Five years later he chose to emphasize the regime's accomplishments: the creation in the USSR of 'a new historical community of peoples' united by ideology, socio-economic and cultural traits, and even a common destiny. However, in the next breath he singled out the Great Russians for their 'profound internationalism'. Discerning listeners concluded that this *narod* was 'more equal than the others'. When the fiftieth anniversary of the USSR's formation was celebrated in December 1972, a new concept came to the fore: 'the Soviet people'. The national question, it was now claimed, had been 'resolved completely and irrevocably'. Yet simultaneously Brezhnev warned that national prejudices were 'extremely tenacious phenomena, deeply embedded in the minds of insufficiently mature people'. In essence he took a 'centrist' line between the left-wing zealots, or 'fusionists', and the pragmatists who sought to avoid provoking the minorities by pressing forward too rapidly with the grand design. The former dreamed of redrawing administrative boundaries on economic lines and abolishing the Supreme Soviet's 'upper house', the Chamber of Nationalities, in which seats were allotted on a territorial basis. Neither idea was incorporated into the 1977 'Brezhnev' Constitution. Commenting on this, the Party leader declared that it would be 'untimely' to dissolve the federation or to deny the constituent republics the (formal) right to secede. This implied that ultimately a merger was still on the cards. According to one specialist the new Constitution actually *weakened* the legal force of the federal principle (Carrère d'Encausse 1982). Similarly, non-Russians were now granted only the 'possibility' of receiving instruction in their native tongue, whereas previously this had been a right (Connor 1992). There was, however, to be no artificial forcing of the process of 'growing together', and in general the line now taken seemed a little more benevolent than before. Official speakers gave the impression that the unity they sought to develop would not impoverish native cultures but rather lead to their mutual enrichment.

Such assurances would have been more credible to minority élites had they been backed up by tangible shifts of cultural policy in their favour. However, both Andropov and Chernenko reverted to earlier orthodoxy by using the politically loaded term 'merger'. Speaking on the sixtieth anniversary of the Union, Andropov hailed the 'unselfish fraternal aid' which the Russians had rendered the other peoples and claimed that their language 'has entered quite naturally into the lives of millions of people of all nationalities'. This was a provocative remark, given the minority leaders' fears of 'russification' through the fostering of the lingua franca by administrative measures and the continuing migration of large numbers of Russians to their republics, where they occupied prominent positions in many walks of life. How far the non-Russians' national identities were threatened by these policies will be considered shortly in the light of census data (with particular reference to two key regions, Central Asia and the Baltic). First let us look briefly at developments in the political and economic sphere.

Cadres policy

Under Brezhnev there was a tendency to appoint more natives to leading positions, especially those that were honorific, and to make the centre's control less obvious. The leaders appreciated that indirect rule was politically more advantageous. Now that the necessary native cadres had been built up a more flexible approach became practicable when making appointments. In the other Slav republics in particular there was no lack of apparently loyal functionaries from whom to choose. In Belarus there were actually proportionately more natives in the *apparat* than there were in the republic's population. This did not create any problems for the 'centre' since national consciousness was weaker here than in Ukraine. Shcherbitsky, a Brezhnev associate (and Ukrainian) who became the mercurial Shelest's successor as Ukrainian Party boss, turned out to be an enthusiastic russifier. He encouraged the 'exchange of cadres', i.e. the appointment of non-Ukrainians, and even referred to his compatriots as 'blood relatives' of the Russians. Nevertheless in 1979 88 per cent of the Ukrainian Party's Politburo and 92 per cent of provincial secretaries were Ukrainians, even though their share of the republic's population was smaller (73.6 per cent). Russians who rose to high office in Ukraine were less likely to be men 'parachuted in' from Moscow but rather local residents who had made their careers in the local Party machine. They did, however, tend to come from those regions of the republic that had a high concentration of Russians and, if appointed to posts in western Ukraine, where national sentiment was strongest, were perceived by their subjects as 'outsiders'. Whatever their national background, such men were selected for their readiness to obey orders as much as for their administrative ability. Careerists in the main, their loyalty to the 'centre' was bound to be brittle. To build up support, they naturally sought to cultivate local interests and to lobby behind the scenes on their behalf. The Ukrainian CP's very success in co-opting a significant section of the local élite created 'a growing potential for the politics of nationalism', noted one observer (L. K. Oliver) in 1981. This is why, just a few years later, a hard-line senior functionary like Leonid Kravchuk, secretary for ideological questions, could suddenly switch to the nationalist side when Moscow's power weakened and emerge as an effective leader of a sovereign Ukrainian state.

At the time such an outcome could not have been predicted. Yet it was under Brezhnev that the scene was set for the crumbling of the Soviet imperial structure. Unable to solve the national question, the 'centre' tacitly allowed local 'barons' to build up patronage networks which reinforced the sense of ethnic identity among those involved, even though their motive for bonding together might simply have been personal advantage. 'Brezhnev cut a deal with the republican élites which allowed them considerable autonomy, especially in personnel matters, but kept them out of federal decision-making, where Russians continued to dominate' (Gitelman 1992). In Transcaucasia and Central Asia such patronage links often smacked of corruption (see Chapter 10). The connection between the Uzbek gangster Adylov and his boss, Rashidov, was but the most spectacular of such 'affairs'. Rashidov himself owed his high office in part to the part he played in exposing the illicit activities of another clique of politicians (Kurbanov, Khojaev), who were brought to justice in 1976–7—whereupon their accusers surpassed them in wrongdoing. Rashidov's successor, Usmankhojaev, was later convicted on similar charges.

Andropov tried to tighten the screws even before he came to power in 1982. In all three Transcaucasian republics, as well as in Latvia and Lithuania, blue-collar workers were elected to the bureaux (executives) of the local Communist parties. Meetings were held in all union republics to underline the need for discipline in the face of 'imperialist subversion'. The example of the Polish ruling party's near-collapse when confronted by 'Solidarity' was fresh in everyone's mind. (At one such conference in Riga, Kravchuk came to warn Balts not to heed the siren voices from the Vatican under its newly elected Polish Pope!)

By this time the Baltic CPs had become sizeable organizations, measured in terms of absolute membership and ratio to population, and were also increasingly 'nativized', i.e. staffed by non-Russians. Taking the all-Union ratio of Party members to adults as 100, the figures for the Baltic are as shown in Table 15.1.

TABLE 15.1. *Ratio of party members to adults in Baltic states, 1970, 1982*

	1970	1982
Estonia	57	73
Latvia	54	66
Lithuania	49	63[1]

Many of these newcomers were, of course, Russians, as noted above. The native share of membership is not known for certain, but for Lithuania one estimate was 68.5 per cent in 1975, a rise of seven percentage points in ten years. It was lower in Estonia (52 per cent in 1965 and about the same in 1985) and especially in Latvia (39 per cent in 1965, 33 per cent in 1975).

More important was the native share of the republic parties' (and the CPSU's) leading bodies and other senior job-holders. In the Lithuanian Party CC natives comprised 77 per cent and in its bureau and secretariat 93 per cent (1976). In the Latvian Party the proportion was about 60 per cent of the CC (1981), while 84 per cent of the Politburo consisted of Russians or russified Latvians. The usual pattern, as we know, was for the republic Party's first secretary to be a native, largely to serve as 'front man', while more power was wielded by his deputy, the second secretary, who had charge of personnel matters. There had been some exceptions to this rule under Khrushchev, but 'in the 1970s this privilege was withdrawn' (Simon 1991). Even so some native first secretaries (Rashidov, Kunaev, Aliev) were in practice more powerful than their Russian deputies. Curiously, more locals were now appointed to head republic-level KGB organizations: in 1979 the ratio to Russians was 50 : 50. If the Kremlin trusted natives in such a sensitive post (no doubt because a Russian occupied the supervisory department in the Party organization!), it is not surprising to find them as Komsomol and trade-union chiefs or in most senior positions in the cultural field.

In government bodies, too, staff tended to be drawn from the local population. Thus it can be said that the union republics were administered on a day-to-day basis by natives, both at the top and especially at the lowest level, where officials came into daily contact with the population (Bialer 1986). Here, too, the pattern was far from uniform. Georgia and Armenia had the most 'nativized' administrations, Kazakhstan and the Baltic lands the least. In the Kazakh case this was mainly because the population was heavily Slavicized (47 per cent Russians and Ukrainians in 1979), and in the Baltic case because the territory was culturally so different and had been annexed by force (Rywkin 1977). In Central Asia many Russians objected to what they saw as preferential treatment of natives. Moscow took some account of this feeling but evidently reckoned that 'affirmative action' was better than the alternative of discriminating too overtly against non-Russians. 'The central Soviet authorities', one Western scholar remarks, 'were caught in a classic policy dilemma of being damned if they do and damned if they don't' (Karklins 1986).

Non-Russian, or at any rate non-Slavic, officials had limited upward career mobility—that is to say, there were few of them in key positions at the centre. 'In 1980 only three non-Slavs could be found among the 150 top functionaries in the CC apparatus' (Simon 1991). There were no more than three on the 97-member Council of Ministers, and the proportion was the same among military leaders. As for the Central Committee, between 1966 and 1981 Russians, and Slavs generally, increased their share of membership. By the latter date they accounted for 68.3 and 84.6 per cent respectively of full members,[2] as against 2.2 per cent for Balts and 4.4 per cent for Central Asians. The 22-man Politburo elected in December 1983 had 16 Russians and 3 other Slavs, 1 Azeri, 1 Georgian, and 1 Uzbek. The non-Slav members generally stayed in candidate rank. More significantly still, the all-powerful Secretariat had no non-Slavic members at all under Stalin's four immediate successors. But before crying 'discrimination' we have to remember that these bodies were executive, not representational, in character and that the Party's ethical code prevented its functionaries from promoting any special interest. Such personal influence as they could bring to bear had to be exerted surreptitiously.

Regional economic development

Decisions on investment priorities, resource allocation and production targets were, as we know, made in Moscow. From 1965 union-republic governments had the right to inspect plans relating to enterprises of all-Union subordination situated on their territory, but this conferred only an appearance of autonomy. They could not challenge such powerful institutions as Gosplan or the central economic ministries. From time to time at Party gatherings delegates from the non-Russian territories might cautiously advocate higher appropriations for some pet project, or for improvements to the local distribution system in regard to goods in short supply. In responding to these suggestions the leaders proceeded from their view of the interests of the Soviet economy as a whole. They thought in terms of regions, not nations.

Accordingly development continued to be concentrated in the RSFSR and the western republics. Lagging regions were subsidized by the repayment of a share of turnover tax. Between 1967 and 1979 the Central Asian republics retained 92 per cent of what they paid, whereas the figure for the RSFSR was only 45 per cent (and for the Union as a whole 53 per cent). But one cannot conclude from this that Moscow was committed, as a matter of priority, to equalizing inter-republican differences (Lubin 1984). Measuring regional inequalities is a complicated matter involving the use of variation coefficients, which may be weighted in innumerable different ways. Findings will differ according to the criterion taken: the extent of urbanization or industrialization, productivity, income levels, provision of services, and so forth (Bahry and Nechemias 1981). Most observers consider that the gap between the more and less advanced regions widened, particularly after the mid-1970s. This was mainly due to natural factors (e.g. differentials in the birth rate) rather than to deliberate policy, and had parallels elsewhere in the world.

In 1980 the RSFSR absorbed 62.4 per cent of total capital investment, much the same proportion as twenty years earlier, and 10 per cent more than its share of total population (52.4 per cent). The three Baltic republics had 2.8 per cent, the five Central Asian ones 12.5 per cent—a rise of 0.4 and 0.7 per cent for a population share of 2.8 and 15.3 per cent respectively (1979). Thus the latter, but not the former, were disadvantaged. Moreover, much of the Central Asian investment went to Russian-populated northern Kazakhstan. 'The planners did not acknowledge the [Central] Asian population's . . . demand for capital and jobs, let alone recover lost ground in industrialization' (Simon 1991). In fairness it should be added that Central Asians were notoriously loath to take up industrial jobs. One cannot fault the planners for failing to conjure up industries with heavy manpower requirements where the necessary raw materials did not exist (although certainly more could have been done to process Uzbek cotton on the spot). Had they tried to do so, they would have been rightly charged with wasting money and manpower.

Because of this regional differential in regard to investment, figures for industrial output per capita and labour productivity also varied significantly. According to G. Simon, in 1974 Turkmenistan, Tajikistan, and Uzbekistan, the three least developed republics industrially, produced only one quarter as much per head of population as the three most advanced ones (Estonia, Latvia, RSFSR). The overall rate of industrial growth between 1970 and 1985 was highest in the three Transcaucasian republics, followed by Uzbekistan, Kyrgyzstan, and Lithuania. The other two Baltic states and two other Central Asian ones grew more slowly than the RSFSR or the Union as a whole. Industrial productivity increased fastest in the Baltic region, with Estonia reaching twice the all-Union average; in Tajikistan, Uzbekistan, and Turkmenistan it was only just about half of this average. Agricultural productivity likewise grew more rapidly in the Baltic than in Central Asia. The two regions were at either end of the spectrum, the RSFSR in the middle. Central Asian farmers had less capital and machinery per head than those elsewhere; or, to put it differently, there was a superabundance of rural manpower in the region. During the Eleventh Five-Year Plan (1980–5) agricultural output was everywhere higher than it had been in the previous quinquennium. But in Kazakhstan this was barely so (0.1 per cent!), while the other four Central Asian republics were on average 3.5 percentage points ahead of the all-Union growth rate (6 per cent). The champions were in Transcaucasia: in Azerbaijan output grew by 32 per cent. In the latter cases the main reason was the greater degree of tolerance shown to private farming.

Living standards: the Baltic . . .

Income levels, too, rose everywhere during the period, but by and large those regions that stood low on the scale in the 1960s were still there twenty years later. Central Asia lost ground while the Baltic republics preserved their lead. Taking the all-Union rate of 'nominal per capita income'[3] as 100, the Slav republics ranged from 94 (Belarus) to 108 (RSFSR) in 1970, and from 96 (Ukraine) to 111 (RSFSR) in 1978. At the bottom of the scale was Tajikistan, which fell from 63 to 60 (1970-8). The other four Central Asian republics ranged from 72 to 87 (1970) and 70 to 88 (1978), with Kazakhstan at the top, as one would expect. In Transcaucasia Georgia stood highest and Azerbaijan lowest (94 and 63 respectively in 1978). The most favoured were the Baltic republics. All three did better than the RSFSR, although the gap narrowed over the eight-year span. In 1978 Estonia was 16 points ahead (127 : 111), as compared with 25 in 1970 (133 : 108). In 1981-4 the Baltic republics forged ahead again. According to Soviet figures Lithuania did best, with a national income 2.0 per cent greater than the all-Union average; Latvia was ahead by 0.8 per cent, Estonia by a mere 0.1 per cent. Lithuania also did much better than the other two Baltic republics as regards industrial and (especially) agricultural output, as well as agricultural productivity (Adirim 1990).

Another indicator of increasing well-being was the growth of savings deposits. By 1985 these were sixteen times greater in the Baltic than they had been in 1951, whereas the all-Union figure had risen ten times. Baltic residents were also better off than Russians and most others as regards housing[4] and food supply, although natives complained that Russians were allocated the choicest apartments and that too much food was exported to other parts of the Union. Nevertheless meat consumption was 'significantly higher than in the RSFSR' (87 kg. per head in Estonia, 66 kg. in the RSFSR in 1984), and the same was true of dairy products (Bohnet and Penkaitis 1990). Baltic residents owned far more cars per hundred households than Russians (Estonia 10.4, RSFSR 3.9 in 1984), as well as radios (183 : 101); the difference was less marked for television sets or refrigerators, but still appreciable. They went more frequently to the theatre—but read fewer newspapers, presumably because they found them biased.

Russians referred to the region as 'our (Soviet) West', and the general attractiveness of life there was one reason (although not the main one) for Slavic immigration. 'Russian tourists can be seen everywhere', noted one Western visitor to Tallinn. 'They come to buy up everything they find in the shops, which causes some local resentment.' Stores were better stocked, people more smartly dressed. 'Above all, things seem to work in Estonia. There is a greater sense of initiative and responsibility' (Binyon 1983). Local industries and state farms were managed with a lighter touch. The limits of the command economy were not overtly over-stepped, but this brought results. True, exporters were at a disadvantage because prices were set too low. The Baltic lands supplied neighbouring republics with electric power, chemicals, radios (one in five of all Soviet radios was produced in Latvia), machine tools, and fish, to mention only a few key products. Their industrial goods had a high reputation for quality and design. But this success did not reconcile the indigenous inhabitants to the *status quo*.

. . . and Central Asia

Though living standards in Central Asia were lower than elsewhere in the Union, this region, too, had its attractions for Russian settlers. They tended to concentrate in the larger cities, notably Tashkent, which had its separate 'European' and 'native' quarter. They did not mix a great deal with locals outside the work environment and saw no particular reason to learn the local language. In Tashkent only one-fifth of Russian residents claimed to have close friends among non-Russians, and not all of these were Uzbeks. In Uzbekistan the proportion of Russian urban residents who were bilingual in Uzbek rose in the 1970s but fell from 5.1 to 4.1 per cent between 1979 and 1989 (Arutunian 1992). In Kazakhstan the proportion was even slighter (0.4 to 0.6 per cent), as one would expect in view of the compact nature of Russian settlement in the north of that republic, and little better in Kyrgyzstan. Most Russian immigrants to Central Asia held managerial, technical, or industrial jobs (in Tashkent the proportion rose from 51 to 63 per cent between 1974 and 1988), while natives were mainly employed in agriculture and handicrafts. At Tashkent airport the director was an Uzbek but his five deputies were Russians, as were all but two of nineteen department heads (Lubin 1984). Thus social and economic relationships had a quasi-colonial character that contrasted with the authorities' proclaimed goals. M. I. Goldman points out that 'even if more has been taken out than has been put in, . . . the flow is not as one-sided as it is in the usual colonial relationships in the non-Communist world', but that was not the way non-Russians necessarily looked at the matter.

Uzbek intellectuals in particular resented the fact that their republican economy was so heavily geared to the production of cotton. In Central Asia as a whole the area sown to this crop rose by 15.4 per cent between 1965 and 1978, while the area sown to grain declined by 4.9 per cent (although this drop was offset by planting more irrigated land to rice, a local food staple). Overall the output of cotton more than doubled between 1960 and 1980; it grew less steeply over the next five years, but there was no change of basic policy on this sensitive matter, which made most of Central Asia heavily dependent on imported food. Their national élites, although to a large extent 'co-opted' by the regime and obliged to echo the official line in public, realized that their republics held second-class status. The lag was statistically evident in nearly all crucial sectors: production per capita, use of energy, life expectancy, provision of educational and health facilities.

In regard to consumer durables the picture was uneven. In 1984 collective farmers in Uzbekistan had four colour TV sets per 100 households (the same percentage as in the RSFSR), fewer refrigerators (61 : 77) or washing machines (41 : 77), but as many as 22 automobiles as against only one for collective farmers in the RSFSR! W. D. Connor (1991) points out that these figures give a better impression of social differences than data for per capita income, which do not take into account earnings from the second economy. Income differentials were not, it seems, the principal focus of Central Asian intellectuals' ill-feeling towards their masters. They did not want improvement at the cost of a forced industrialization drive that would bring in yet more Slavic immigrants and disrupt further their national cultures (as well as the ecological balance). For adherence to traditional values and life-styles was stronger among the USSR's Muslims than in any other part of the Union. Even the most fleeting visitor to the region appreciated that it was part of the Middle East, and that the Soviet way of life had made only a superficial impact. Nevertheless it was not the Muslim peoples, as some foreign observers expected at the time, that would take the lead in tearing the USSR apart when the opportunity arose. This was precisely because, although a process of 'national consolidation' was under way, their élites continued to draw inspiration from Islam, and only in part from modern Western concepts of nationalism, as did minority leaders in the European republics.

Islam and cultural opposition

The very nature of Islam—as much a way of life as a system of beliefs—enabled Soviet Muslims to resist sovietization better than Christians could. They had less need of clergy or places of worship. Islam was for them the principal 'marker' of identity, and external pressures served only to strengthen this natural bond. Muslim believers were required to observe the five 'pillars of faith',[5] which did not include, for example, regular attendance at a mosque. More important was adherence to certain rites and customs (circumcision, religious marriages, and funerals), which were kept to by almost every member of the community (*umma*). Although the intensity of religious commitment varied, atheism was unknown (Bennigsen 1975).

Accordingly, Soviet anti-Islamic propaganda had very little impact. In 1962, for example, the faithful simply ignored a decree (*fatwa*), put out by the state-controlled spiritual authorities,[6] condemning circumcision as harmful to health. As elsewhere in the Union, atheistic pressure diminished somewhat in the mid-1960s, partly for 'cosmetic' reasons connected with Soviet policy in the Middle East. However, the invasion of Afghanistan led to a new wave of persecution. Many mosques were closed. In Turkmenistan alone four thousand atheist lectures were held in the first six months of 1980. Efforts were made to popularize secular festivals (such as Shepherds' Day) as alternatives to traditional ones, and obstacles placed in the way of those wishing to undertake the pilgrimage to Mecca. The campaign was doomed to fail because, as one observer put it, 'the ideological base on which atheistic propaganda rests is totally alien in its philosophical orientation to that which the average Muslim imbibes with his mother's milk' (Ro'i 1984). Traditional habits were far stronger than external influences transmitted through school or Komsomol, so that young people 'tend to associate the attack on [their] belief system and entire life-style with the Russian, the alien'.

The upshot was an increase in inter-ethnic tension. Muslims and

Slavs each perceived the other as threatening cherished values. Russians condemned the (now largely symbolic) custom of exacting a bride-price (*kalym*) as a 'feudal relic', whereas Muslims considered it the height of indecency for a couple to kiss in public at a wedding banquet, as was the Russian custom, and strongly disapproved of premarital sex. R. Karklins (1986), who studied ethnic relations 'from below' at first hand, found 'a significant perceptual gap' between members of the two communities. Russians saw Soviet power as bringing 'progress' to 'backward' lands; Central Asians considered that advances towards modernity were *their own* achievement.

The Muslim peoples' most characteristic reaction to increased pressure from the centre was not to rebel but to adapt. They turned their political masters' strategy against them by 'penetrating' Communist parties and other agencies and 'corrupting' them from within. The local press abounded with indignant reports that apparently loyal, zealous Komsomol members were performing traditional Muslim rites. When arraigned for such apparently duplicitous behaviour, the 'offenders' protested that they saw nothing wrong in it: did not the Constitution guarantee freedom of belief? Numerous mosques and shrines throughout the USSR's Muslim lands (in Azerbaijan and the north Caucasus as well as Central Asia) were restored to their former glory—often with the use of public funds. The four mystic sects (*sufis*) underwent vigorous growth. These clandestine brotherhoods constituted a 'parallel Islam' with deeper roots in the population than the Muslim religious establishment. Founded centuries earlier, their primary purpose was to encourage private prayer and strengthen devotion to the faith, but in certain circumstances they might also assume a political role. Adherents (*murids*) avoided contact with non-Muslims and so were hard for the authorities to detect, especially since their creed allowed them to dissimulate their opinions where expedient. Thus they might outwardly behave as loyal Communists. Brotherhoods normally numbered several dozen members and would meet in private homes or, as their influence spread to the towns, in the native tea-houses that were a feature of the bazaar quarter. Their message could readily be transmitted by chain letters and then, thanks to modern technology, by transistor radio and tape-recorder. Women and young people were increasingly attracted to the *sufi* sects. In 1979 their following was estimated at half a million persons, of whom 300,000 were active in Central Asia (Bennigsen and Lemercier-Quelquejay 1986). Though decried by critics as 'reactionary', they had the hallmarks of an authentic resistance movement.

Opposition over secular issues was on a limited scale in the region, at least until the Afghan war broke out. In 1978, for instance, a brawl occurred in Almaty (Alma-Ata) over the university's admissions policy, which some Kazakhs claimed was biased against natives, and a few Uzbeks, notably B. Shakraev, were associated with the human-rights movement. More characteristic were expressions of cultural nationalism in the arts or scholarship. The Kazakh historians' role has been noted in Chapter 13. Also typical of this 'Islamic resurgence' was historical fiction such as Muhammad-Ali Mahmudov's *Eternal Heights* (1981) or Murad Aliev's *A Cuckoo in May*, 'a hymn to the Kyrgyz national past' (Taheri 1990). The practice of circulating forbidden texts in *samizdat*, nicknamed 'Islamizdat', began in 1981 and was most prevalent in Tajikistan. Some of them acquired an overtly political and fundamentalist slant. Certain local leaders, notably Kunaev in Kazakhstan, covertly tolerated these developments, or at least soft-pedalled repressive measures out of self-interest. Others, like Rashidov or his successor, used their political influence, as we know, in ways that smacked more of the mafia. Informal relationships of this kind within native élites laid the groundwork for the political nationalism that would gather force in the region from 1987 onward.

The Muslim leaders' (and peoples') achievement during the period under consideration here was a negative one: to avert the threat of assimilation. This they did by adhering stubbornly to their languages, limiting intermarriage with immigrants, refusing to leave their region for jobs elsewhere in the Union, and above all by maintaining fertility rates much higher than those of Slavs.

The language issue in Central Asia

Census data show that nearly all Central Asians continued to speak their own language 'first' and that the growth of bilingualism in Russian was less marked in the 1980s than it had been in the previous decade. Unfortunately the figures are none too reliable, since (especially in earlier censuses) respondents exaggerated their facility in Russian, which, as noted, was not independently checked.

Unless this were so, it would be hard to explain the variations in the Uzbeks' score (see Table 15.2). That more Kazakhs spoke Russian than other Muslim peoples did was due to their greater degree of exposure to Russian immigration. The strength of the bond to the native idiom is evident from the fact that in 1979 only 0.3 per cent fewer Uzbeks living outside their titular republic, as distinct from those within it, no longer spoke it 'first'.

The struggle against 'linguistic imperialism' (to use a pejorative term) was not so fierce in Central Asia as it was in Georgia, where in April 1978 thousands demonstrated in favour of keeping the constitutional formula that declared Georgian to be the state

TABLE 15.2. *Language use in Central Asia, 1970–1989*

Nationality[a]	Percentage regarding own language as native					Percentage claiming fluency in Russian				
	1970	1979	1970–9 change	1989	1979–89 change	1970	1979	1970–9 change	1989	1979–89 change
Uzbeks	98.6	98.5	−0.1	98.3	−0.2	14.5	49.3	+34.8	23.8	−25.5
Kazakhs	98.0	97.5	−0.5	97.0	−0.5	41.8	52.3	+10.5	60.4	+8.1
Kyrgyz	98.8	97.9	−0.9	97.8	−0.1	19.1	29.4	+10.3	35.2	+5.8
Tajiks	98.5	97.8	−0.7	97.7	−0.1	15.4	29.6	+14.2	27.7	−1.9
Turkmen	98.9	98.7	−0.2	98.5	−0.2	15.4	25.4	+10.0	27.7	+2.3

[a] Includes those residing in the titular republic and in other republics of the Union.

Note: those not regarding their own language as native may have opted for another non-Russian language rather than Russian.

Sources: Rakowska-Harmstone 1977; Simon 1991, 1993.

language—and forced Moscow to give in. The Muslims took a gentler approach. Philologists toiled to replace Russian loan-words with terms of Oriental (Arabic or Persian) derivation, such as *darilfunun* for *universitet* (Critchlow 1977). Kyrgyz campaigned (with eventual success) for their capital to revert to its native name, Bishkek, in lieu of the 'unpronounceable' Frunze (Wixman 1986).[7] Both Uzbeks and Kazakhs won concessions in the field of press and publishing. By 1978 73 per cent of all copies of newspapers printed in the former republic were in the local idiom, as against 60 per cent in 1965 (Fierman 1985)—although in the Union as a whole the tendency was the other way. (The Ukrainians suffered most from this.) The central authorities' response was sluggish, or so it seems in retrospect. Social pressure was brought to bear on leading functionaries to speak in Russian on formal public occasions. The number of Russian-language teachers was increased (in Tajik native schools it doubled from 1967 to 1974/5, to 4,648: Shorish 1976). Thereafter several high-level conferences were held in Tashkent and elsewhere to improve the quality of instruction. It was made an obligatory subject at school even for first-grade pupils. This could of course only be a long-term measure. It seems to have been implemented more dilatorily in Central Asia than in Ukraine or Belarus, presumably because native officials were cool towards it.

Demographic issues

Likewise they dragged their feet over schemes to relocate surplus local labour to areas in the north where there was a shortage. Rashidov, the Uzbek Party boss, managed to send a 'brigade' of his compatriots to do construction work in Novgorod (1980), but efforts to recruit vast numbers for melioration projects in central Russia never got off the ground (Agursky 1982). Uzbeks even resisted industrial employment in their own republic, as we have noted. Asked about this by a Western visitor, they would reply 'we are traders', or even 'we are poets' (Lubin 1984). Educated natives preferred to take jobs in science or culture— where, incidentally, the Slav presence was less intrusive. Many were glad that Russian immigrants would do jobs which they themselves despised as inferior.

Deep-rooted cultural attitudes, rather than any deliberate policy, also account for the Muslim peoples' high birth rate, which more than offset the influx of Slavic or other 'European'[8] immigrants. There had been one and a half million of these between 1959 and 1970 (mainly to the 'virgin lands' of Kazakhstan). In the latter year non-Muslims accounted for 59 per cent of the total population of this republic; in Kyrgyzstan the figure was 40 per cent, in the other republics from 17 to 19 per cent (Rywkin 1982). These were high figures, but already their share was starting to decline. There- after the demographic shift became much more marked, as the figures in Table 15.3 show. Between 1970 and 1979 the USSR's *total* Muslim population grew by 8.7 million to 43.8 million, of whom 26 million lived in Central Asia, where the Russian population was then 9.3 million (6.0 million of them in Kazakh- stan). By 1989 Central Asia's Russian population had grown by a mere 200,000 or so to 9.5 million, over two-thirds of whom were

TABLE 15.3. *Population changes in Central Asia, 1970–1989* (000s)

	Uzbekistan		Kazakhstan		Kyrgyzstan		Tajikistan		Turkmenistan	
	Total	%	Total	%	Total	%	Total	%	Total	%
All nationalities:										
1970	11,799		13,009		2,934		2,900		2,159	
1979	15,391		14,684		3,529		3,801		2,759	
1989	19,808		16,536		4,290		5,109		3,534	
'European' population:										
1970	1,714	14.3	6,620	51.6	976	33.3	376	13.0	348	16.1
1979	1,879	12.2	7,971	54.3	1,122	31.9	484	12.7	386	14.0
1989	–	–	–	–	–	–	–	–	–	–
Russian element of 'European' population:										
1970	1,496	12.5	5,509	42.4	856	29.2	344	11.9	313	14.5
1979	1,666	10.8	5,991	40.8	912	25.9	395	10.4	349	12.6
1989	1,644	8.3	6,223	37.8	915	21.5	386	7.6	334	9.5
Titular nationality:										
1970	7,734	64.7	4,161	32.6	1,285	43.8	1,630	56.2	1,417	65.6
1979	10,866	68.7	5,289	36.0	1,687	47.9	2,237	58.8	1,892	68.4
1989*	14,123	71.3	6,536	39.7	2,227	52.3	3,166	62.2	2,525	71.9

*1989 figures extrapolated from percentage totals.

Note: All percentages are of total republic populations. Slightly different figures for these are given in Simon 1993.

Sources: 1970: *Itogi* 1972; 1979: *Chislennost' i sostav* 1984; 1989: [TsSU], *Sotsial'noe razvitie*, 1991; Simon 1993.

concentrated in outlying areas, whereas the USSR's total Muslim population was now 58.4 million, or 20.3 per cent as against 16.5 per cent ten years earlier (Ra'anan 1990).[9] As the Union began to disintegrate, Europeans left the region in droves, tilting the ethnic balance further in favour of the natives, who were now asserting their claims to independence. This development had been foreseen by Western observers, although they were surprised by its head-long pace. At the time scholarly attention was focused rather on the effects that the ethnic imbalance would have on economic growth (labour shortages in the north) or on the armed forces (command problems). But these concerns were soon overtaken by events.

The Baltic

Languages and cultures

In the Baltic the indigenous nations had a harder struggle to preserve their languages—the basis of their identity—and cultures from Sovietization. They laboured under the disadvantage that their populations were small, but this was offset by their greater cohesiveness. Local élites and peoples were at one in having a well-developed national consciousness, fortified by memories of independence and the aggression by which it had been so cruelly ended. If Central Asian nationalism was still largely in its 'cultural' phase, its Baltic counterpart was definitely political. This is not to deny the very important role of the churches—as well as writers and other cultural leaders—in keeping the national spirit alive. Active resistance, to be sure, was confined to a very small segment of the populace. But with hindsight one can appreciate why in 1988 it was the Baltic republics, and specifically Lithuania, that took the lead in forming civic organizations that swiftly developed broad political aims. The foundations of this activism were laid during the so-called 'years of dependence'.

The degree of retention of the native language, although not as high as in Central Asia, was very marked, as the census data show, and there was little change over two decades (see Table 15.4). In

TABLE 15.4. *Language use among the Baltic peoples, 1970–1989*

Nationality[a]	Percentage regarding own language as native					Percentage claiming fluency in Russian				
	1970	1979	1970–9 change	1989	1979–89 change	1970	1979	1970–9 change	1989	1980–9 change
Estonians	95.5	95.3	−0.2	95.5	0.2	29.0	24.2	−4.8	33.9	9.7
Latvians	95.2	95.0	−0.2	94.8	−0.2	45.2	56.7	11.5	64.4	7.7
Lithuanians	97.9	97.9	0	97.7	−0.2	35.9	52.1	16.0	37.9	−14.2

[a] Includes residents of titular republic and those living outside it.

Sources: Simon 1991; 1993.

Lithuania bilingualism in Russian grew rapidly (and incredibly!) in the 1970s, only to fall almost as steeply in the 1980s. (The figure may have been inflated by a much higher number of Russian-speakers among Lithuanians in the diaspora.) In Latvia it rose more steadily, no doubt due to the much stronger Russian presence in that republic. There was more contact with Slavic immigrants here than in Estonia, where the communities lived apart. If Estonians learned any neighbour's tongue, it was most likely to be Finnish. Curiously, the highly localized and old established Russian colony in eastern Estonia showed a tendency to become 'Estonianized'

(Taagepera 1990). In both Estonia and Lithuania there was a two-way pattern among those few (1 per cent of the population or less) who reported that they 'mainly' spoke a language different from that of their nationality. In Lithuania in 1979 slightly *more* Russians adopted Lithuanian than the reverse. If we consider people in this category as linguistically (and culturally) assimilated, it follows that this process worked both ways too. Over 2 per cent of Latvians spoke Russian as their main language (1979), but the rate of increase was so slow that 'fusionist' zealots would have had to wait until AD 4800 before the last Latvian had been absorbed! (Taagepera 1990). People who changed their linguistic affiliation generally did so for family reasons (e.g. mixed marriages). Such decisions had little to do with political preferences or official fostering of the lingua franca.

As one specialist on Latvian nationalism has pointed out, 'linguistic identity is by itself a rather insensitive tool for predicting changes in cultural values or political attitudes' (Penikis 1977). Much depends on how vital the national culture is. In Latvia traditional song festivals not only generated hundreds of musical compositions but also led to extensive ethnographic research.

TABLE 15.5. *Population changes in the Baltic republics, 1970–1989* (000s)

	Estonia		Latvia		Lithuania	
	Total	%	Total	%	Total	%
All nationalities:						
1970	1,356		2,366		3,116	
1979	1,466		2,503		3,461	
1989	1,568		2,668		3,670	
Russians:						
1970	335	24.7	705	29.8	268	8.6
1979	409	27.9	821	32.8	303	8.9
1989	475	30.3	907	34.0	345	9.4
Titular nationality:						
1970	925	68.2	1,342	56.8	2,507	80.1
1979	948	64.7	1,344	53.7	2,712	80.0
1989	963	61.5	1,387	52.0	2,924	79.6

Note: Total eastern Slavic population (1979–89) was as follows: Estonia 31.9 and 35.1%; Latvia 39.9 and 42.1%; Lithuania 11.6 and 12.3%

Sources: Dellenbrant 1990; Parming 1980; Clemens Jr. 1990; Simon 1991; TsSU 1984.

Volumes of poetry or essays were quickly sold out. *Literature and Art*, the leading cultural journal, had a remarkably high circulation. Pupils who spoke Baltic languages actually had *more* texts in them per capita than Russian-speaking children did (1972: Pool 1978). In Estonia 75 per cent of all publications were in the native idiom and that republic ranked first in the Union as regards the ratio of copies of books published in the titular language to speakers (1970, 1979: Raun 1985). When the screw was tightened the number of copies of magazines printed in Estonian fell by 21 percentage points (99 to 78) and of books by 10 (83 to 73: 1965–80). But the proportion of *belles-lettres* published in Russian (16 per cent) did *not* grow over the two decades. Most television programmes were of Russian origin, but Estonians could compensate for this by watching Finnish ones or by switching to radio, where 88 per cent of offerings were in Estonian (1980). Even so the situation was admittedly fraught with danger. In 1980–1 Western opinion researchers carried out a systematic survey among recent emigrés (the 'Soviet Interview Project'). The highest proportion of respondents correctly identified relations between Balts and Russians as those that were most conflict-prone.[10]

Demography

The prime cause of this tension was, of course, continued Slavic immigration. In 1975–9 the average annual increase (after allowing for outmigration) was 20,200 (4,900 to Estonia, 9,100 to Latvia and 6,200 to Lithuania), as against 29,000 in 1965–9 and almost as many in 1970–4 (Misiunas and Taagepera 1983). The influx was declining, and the proportion of immigrants who left again was rising: by 1980 it had reached 90 per cent. The threat of 'swamping' was much slighter in Lithuania than it was in the other Baltic republics, as Table 15.5 shows. But in Latvia the native share of population fell by 4.8 per cent, and in Estonia by 6.7 per cent, over the nineteen years between the 1970 and 1989 censuses. In the former case natives were barely in a majority in their titular republic in 1989. Moreover, the 14 per cent of the Latvian population in the 'others' category consisted mainly of (Slavic) Belarusians and Ukrainians. In the Baltic region the flow of migrants was inward over the twenty-year span 1965–85; although the general trend was one of decline, during the quinquennium 1981–5 it swelled markedly.[11]

Particularly alarming, in the eyes of nationally conscious Balts, was the fact that the immigrants were urbanized and comprised so many well-educated specialists. In Estonia and Latvia the native birth rate remained low. In 1974 Latvia had 'the world's lowest birth rate' and in rural areas it fell below the death rate (Küng 1981): this was the nadir in that nation's demographic crisis. Over the decade 1979–89 Estonians increased by only 0.7 per cent, and by 1989 numbered just over one million (1,027,000, including those living outside their titular republic). This was the lowest rate of any indigenous national group in the Union. For Latvians the equivalent figures were 1.4 per cent (1,459,000), and for Lithuanians a healthy 7.6 per cent (3,067,000). In regard to fertility Lithuanians were actually *ahead* of Slavs (Russians 5.6 per cent, Ukrainians 4.3 per cent), but of course far below Central Asians (Tajiks 45.5 per cent!). The fact that they were less 'modernized' than other Balts had much to do with this: so too did their Catholicism.

Political opposition

These reasons also help to explain why Lithuania was also ahead of the other Baltic lands in organizing resistance to the Soviet regime. The Catholics' *samizdat Chronicle* (see Chapter 8) had put out sixty-seven issues by late 1985. At times it contained a good deal of secular material. The same mixed content characterized *Dawn* (Aušra), which ran to forty-two issues by 1984. Its title evoked a famous nineteenth-century forerunner. Over a dozen other *samizdat* journals came out from 1975 onward, more than in any other region of the country. Some of them, e.g. *The Nation's Path* (1980), took a radical nationalist line. Several activists were arrested and sentenced to heavy prison terms, especially during the 'third wave' of repression in 1980–1; others, including the celebrated poet T. Venclova, were allowed to emigrate and then deprived of their citizenship; three priests met suspicious deaths in 'road accidents' (Alexeyeva 1985). The local Party chief, Griskevičius, was a loyal functionary who had less leeway than his forerunner, Snieckus, and seems to have given the KGB their head. Yet it could not stamp out opposition entirely. The example of Polish 'Solidarity' was infectious.

Of particular significance were joint actions by resistance groups in all three Baltic republics, which got under way in 1975. Twenty-one individuals, most of them Lithuanians, signed a statement protesting against the invasion of Afghanistan (January 1980). A larger number (forty-five) signed a protest to mark the fortieth anniversary of the 1939 Nazi–Soviet pact, which had cost the Baltic states their independence. This was potentially a devastating issue for the regime, as the future would show.

In Latvia and Estonia opposition activity was less intense than in Lithuania. This was due to differences of temperament, the confessional divide, the lure of prosperity, and a natural caution owing to the presence of so many Russian settlers—and troops. Nevertheless in Latvia several clandestine organizations were formed in the late 1970s which lasted for some time before being detected. They included a Social-Democratic group which managed to maintain contact with emigrés in Sweden for several years before its two leaders were arrested (November 1980) and jailed. There were also Christian Democratic and Baptist groups. The ultimate objective of all of them was independence. In Estonia the National Front and Democratic Movement shared this aim. The latter organization published four journals, two of them in Russian. Four of its leaders, one a Russian (S. Soldatov) and another a Ukrainian (A. Yuskevich), were put on trial in 1975. In the following years *samizdat* literature proliferated in Estonia. The most successful clandestine journal was the *Saturday Gazette*, edited by students at the university of Tartu. Young people were to the fore among patriotic activists. They went on to stage rallies at which national symbols were proudly displayed. One of these gatherings, held in the autumn of 1980, attracted five thousand participants. Simultaneously one thousand workers came out on strike. It was the first such industrial action in decades. Here, too, Polish 'Solidarity' was the catalyst (Kukk 1993).

For all this few Balts thought in 1985 that their countries would achieve independence within a few years, or that popular pressure would play such a role. The political will certainly existed, the opportunity did not. Before freedom could come the regime had to crack at the centre—and this, contrary to everyone's expectations, it obligingly did.

PART IV

The Empire Cracks Up

16 Revolution from Above

Why the collapse?

Not every regime that faces a crisis necessarily collapses. Yet in the USSR the accession to power of Mikhail Sergeevich Gorbachev in March 1985 unleashed a chain reaction. Within less than seven years it led to the extinction of the world's number two superpower. Historians are naturally tempted to see such an astonishing development as foreordained, and to try to explain it by the working out of long-term processes. Yet clearly an element of chance was involved as well. How much importance should be attached to the character of the man in charge, and to his 'errors' or miscalculations, as against impersonal, structural factors?

Perhaps the end of Soviet Communism, like its beginnings, can best be explained by weighing up probabilities at successive historical moments. In the earlier case the road led to an increasingly violent catastrophe, as various alternative courses of development were successively ruled out; after 1985 efforts to reform the system progressively multiplied the options available and led to an emancipation that, however painful, at least cost relatively little bloodshed. Neither outcome was predictable or even expected by the main actors involved. On the other hand, their decisions were certainly shaped by social and political forces not of their making. In retrospect it is clear that during the Brezhnev era a new generation of Soviet citizens came to the fore who could not be satisfied by the simple certainties of the official ideology. Better educated than their parents or grandparents, and accustomed to a modest level of prosperity, the members of this urban élite sought greater individual autonomy and material well-being. These yearnings evoked a response among writers and other intellectuals whose views became widely known, despite the censorship. In this way an informal 'second culture' took shape that was potentially as subversive of collectivist values as the 'second economy' was of the state-socialist order. By the mid-1980s there were many pointers to impending crisis: falling growth rates, major ecological disasters, and the army's inability to defeat the Afghan *mujaheddin*—to mention only three of the most obvious.

All this made systemic change likely, but not inevitable. Other options were still open. The most plausible scenario was that by embarking on a programme of reform the Party would restore its shaken credibility and maintain its rule, perhaps in slightly amended form. This required both a peaceful international environment and an unusual degree of skill on the part of the reformist leaders. They needed to know just where they were heading and to take the people into their confidence. In the event Gorbachev did permit a fair measure of freedom of expression (*glasnost'*), but failed to answer clearly the question what *perestroika* (restructuring) really involved or how it was to be achieved. This vagueness was partly deliberate, partly the fruit of his general approach to politics. He was basically a pragmatist, but could not shake off a residual Marxist-Leninist dogmatism. It was hard for him to state his objectives unambiguously, since they were constantly changing. As has been well said, he tried to be both Luther and the Pope.

Tactical considerations, too, led him to obfuscate. In the face of emerging conservative and radical lobbies he had to take a 'centrist' line, advancing or retreating as the constellation of power changed. But each successive tactical shift reduced his area of manœuvre and added to the ranks of the disaffected. They seized on the new opportunities to make their views known. The greater the amount of liberty conceded, the more difficult it became to check its unwelcome consequences without resorting to coercive methods that had supposedly been abandoned. From 1989 onwards the regime began to lose control.

There was, therefore, an inner logic at work: vacillation was, so to speak, written into the reformers' script in advance. Their 'text' was shaped by the nature of the regime they inherited: a rigid authoritarianism that had persisted for more than half a century. The *nomenklatura* constituted a carapace on society that could not easily be budged. Its members had a myriad hidden channels of influence through which they could obstruct implementation of measures that threatened their vital interests. The force of inertia was strong also among the common people, for whom socialism was a cushion against insecurity. Few saw any advantage to themselves in abandoning it for a free-market system, with all its risks and dangers, as some of their leaders now proposed. Certainly, the modern Western life-style had its attractions for urban youth, but this seldom extended to adopting the self-reliant, competitive spirit (supposedly) characteristic of 'capitalism'. Many would gladly have settled for some blend of the two systems, but 'market socialism' was soon shown up as a non-viable option, and no one was certain just what it entailed. Consequently an intellectual void formed at the heart of Russian society. The vacuum would readily be filled by radical nationalist ideas mixed with nostalgia for the recent past. Soon the 'era of stagnation' under Brezhnev began to take on a radiant hue as the economy broke down and incomes plummeted. The popular constituency for democracy or liberalism, never very broad, began to evaporate. Among the non-Russian minorities the situation was different. As Moscow's power waned, local leaders could seek to mobilize mass support for national objectives—first for cultural autonomy and then for full sovereignty and independence. In this way Gorbachev's 'revolution from above', at first largely a matter of rhetoric, was complemented by a very real 'revolution from below'.

Rise of Gorbachev

None of this, to repeat, was on the cards in March 1985. It was by no means a foregone conclusion even that Gorbachev would succeed to power. Had such a run-of-the-mill functionary as Grishin or Romanov been chosen in his stead, events would have taken a very different course. This is not to say that Gorbachev was at that time identified with reform. On the contrary, after his election he assured fellow Politburo members that 'we have no need to change our policy. It is correct and truly Leninist. We have to pick up speed and move forward [to] . . . our radiant future' (*Ist.* 0/1993).

Gorbachev owed his appointment in part to his personal qualities—his relative youth (54), intelligence, charm, and determination: it was no accident that Gromyko, when presenting him to the CC for endorsement, referred to his 'iron teeth'—and in part to the backing he received from the KGB, which expected him to pursue Andropov's policy of tightening social discipline (which indeed he initially did). Gorbachev was of course an *apparatchik*, but an unusual one, who had thirty years' experience as a Party official. He was unusual in that he held two academic degrees (in law and agricultural economics). On the other hand, there was nothing very remarkable about his ascent up the hierarchical ladder in Stavropol' province, where he had occupied senior Party positions since 1962.

In 1978 he moved to Moscow, becoming a CC secretary and soon afterwards (1980) a full member of the Politburo. This was indeed a meteoric rise. It owed much to the patronage of Andropov (and before him Kulakov). Among Gorbachev's duties was supervision of agricultural policy, where, however, his modest innovations were not conspicuously successful. An official then engaged in drafting the new Party programme recalls in his memoirs that when Gorbachev intervened in the discussion it was to urge closer attention to Lenin's ideas, although his attitude was more realistic than that of his fellow secretaries; already then he was a 'centrist' (Pechenev 1991). The story that Andropov wanted Gorbachev to succeed him is uncorroborated and probably false. In any case in February 1984, when one ailing veteran General Secretary gave way to another, Chernenko, Gorbachev's career did not suffer. He had taken care to secure the new chief's goodwill.

Chernenko made him in effect his deputy, with the task of chairing sessions of the Politburo and Secretariat on his behalf. In this capacity Gorbachev gained valuable top-level political experience. He was attentive to others' opinions and manœuvred skilfully between competing political forces. Romanov was a particularly dangerous rival, since he was the only other 'young' Politburo member with a seat on the Secretariat. The death of the elderly Defence minister, Ustinov, at the end of 1984 'noticeably strengthened Gorbachev's chances', writes Pechenev. Shortly afterwards he made a major speech which the Party faithful saw as marking him out as their next leader. In it he spoke of *perestroika, glasnost'*, and democratization—terms that would become watchwords of the reform drive. Abroad, too, he won Margaret Thatcher's endorsement as 'a man one can do business with'. Within three months lung disease had taken Chernenko to his grave—state funerals had become a regular feature of the Moscow scene—and Gorbachev was poised for his decisive battle.

Just how real the challenge was is not yet clear—according to one account there was a tie vote of four to four—but certainly 'a last-ditch effort to stop Gorbachev' was made by men who feared for their positions if he won. In his favour were his 'credentials as a disciplinarian' and a stature that Grishin and Romanov lacked. Furthermore there was a general feeling that it would be dangerous to choose another old-timer. A natural 'bandwagon effect' led some older colleagues to back the most likely victor. Finally, Gorbachev's opponents knew that the KGB chief, Chebrikov, had at his disposal damaging evidence (*kompromat*) about their misuse of power that could be brought into play if they resisted (Breslauer 1989).

Gorbachev in power

That the Gorbachev of 1985 was cast in conservative mould is evident from the steps he took to consolidate his power. In April Chebrikov was promoted to full membership of the Politburo, as were two other 'Andropov men' on the Secretariat, Ligachev and Ryzhkov, who were allowed to skip the preliminary candidate stage. Ryzhkov, who had managed a large engineering plant before joining Gosplan, later succeeded the eighty-year-old Tikhonov as prime minister. In July Romanov lost his posts in the top Party bodies and disappeared from view amidst rumours of scandal. (He was said *inter alia* to have 'borrowed' precious tsarist silverware for a private drinking party.) Two other old-timers, Grishin and Rusakov, followed him into limbo early in 1986. The new faces included Eduard Shevardnadze, who replaced Gromyko as foreign minister (the latter became head of state), and Boris Yeltsin, who took over from Grishin as Party chief in Moscow and was appointed a CC secretary. The newcomers were former Gorbachev associates and currently his allies, but the coalition soon crumbled, the puritanical Ligachev emerging as leader of a conservative faction and Yeltsin, a quick-tempered politician with populist leanings, heading a radical one. When the Politburo and Secretariat were re-elected at the Twenty-seventh Party congress in March 1986, half of their members had not served on either body before Gorbachev's takeover.

Lower down the hierarchy the central Party apparatus lost fifty-seven senior functionaries during the new leader's first year in office, and 40 per cent of the CC members elected in 1986 were fresh to the job. The turnover was the second highest on that body since Stalin's death. Brezhnev's policy of maintaining 'stability of cadres' had allowed the average age of members of the leading organs to climb to embarrassing heights. There was now a modest rejuvenation (to age 60 on the CC). In the government some two-thirds of ministers were replaced by June 1987, and their inflated staffs reduced. At provincial level one-quarter of the powerful Party secretaries (*obkomsecs*) were dismissed within a year, and by mid-1987 the proportion had reached 55 per cent. The purge was particularly thorough in the Central Asian republics. In Uzbekistan, for instance, 80 per cent of the local Party CC members were ousted. In the militia no less than 25,000 policemen had lost their jobs by 1988, of whom 1,500 were convicted of offences. Even the KGB felt the winds of change, although as in the 1950s it successfully weathered the storm.

The reshuffle at the top gave Gorbachev a phalanx of supporters. 'Not only did the newly appointed men feel indebted to [him]; so too did those who were allowed to keep their jobs' (Voslensky 1989). However, the rules of the political game were changing. Not all his clients looked on their patron with the old dog-like subservience. Indeed, this was one major aim of the shake-up: to replace the unthinkingly loyal *apparatchiki* of earlier administrations with men capable of seizing the initiative and exercising power in more responsible fashion. Gorbachev set an example by adopting a refreshingly open and forthright leadership style. Like Khrushchev before him, he toured the country, meeting local officials and members of the public. His tone was, however, less hectoring. Instead he exhorted his listeners to join in the work of renovating Soviet society and accelerating economic growth. His approach was down to earth, often emotional, and his rhetoric relatively jargon-free, especially whenever he spoke without notes, or had his remarks televised direct, as in Leningrad in May 1985. This speech 'captivated people who had long since lost interest in the appearance of Party leaders' (Zh. A. Medvedev 1986). When the text was published some passages were omitted, evidently because officials thought his criticisms went too close to the bone. Gorbachev attacked his forerunners for closing their eyes to abuses and encouraging inertia. Theirs had been 'an era of stagnation'.

This was of course a familiar technique, used by successive authoritarian leaders to give a false impression that a new age had dawned with their accession. But more was involved than window-dressing. Gorbachev actually *meant* what he said when he called for more criticism and self-criticism, although there were limits to his tolerance. More to the point, he had a dynamism and ruthless will to succeed that had no parallel in recent Soviet history. One had to go back to Lenin, with whom the new chief was fond of comparing himself. His ideal was the later Lenin, the reflective leader of 1922, who realized that things had gone badly wrong and was willing to use unconventional methods to set them right, but without forsaking basic objectives. 'Gravely ill, Lenin was deeply concerned for the future of socialism. He perceived the dangers lurking . . . This was why he used methods that did not seem to be intrinsic to socialism, or at least diverged in some respects from generally accepted notions . . .' he wrote, in an effort to allay misgivings among left-conservatives in the Party (Gorbachev 1987).

Gorbachev's aim, as he never tired of repeating, was to reinvigorate socialism by returning to its roots. He was not (then, at least) either a liberal or a democrat in the accepted sense. While condemning Stalinist 'deformations' of the true gospel, he praised the collectivization of agriculture, although (as he later revealed) his own father, a farmer, had been among its victims. 'If we learn to work better, be more honest and decent, then we shall create a truly socialist way of life.' This homely philosophy rested on a superficial view of human nature: if ordinary folk were treated properly and their interests advanced by those in power, they would respond sympathetically with a general revival of morality and civic sense. This shallow optimism overlooked the point that 'utmost respect for the individual and consideration for personal dignity' were incompatible with maintenance of collectivism. Once given scope to think and act for themselves, Soviet citizens were bound to ask awkward questions, claim their basic rights, and set up autonomous organizations with this end in view. Inevitably, this would challenge the existing power structure. Why did Gorbachev, an experienced politician, fail to see this and hold to the illusion that 'more democracy' was compatible with 'more socialism'? One reason may have been a faith in the miracle-working power of the written and spoken word, an integral part of Leninist political culture. Mikhail Sergeevich was by no means the first leader to become a captive of his own propaganda and verbal skills.

Early economic measures

The first two years of Gorbachev's rule were a wordy era. There was no end to the devising of future-oriented statements and resolutions. They included a new Party statute and programme, along with national economic plans covering the next five and fifteen years. These documents were formally adopted at the Twenty-seventh Party congress (February–March 1986), which was held on schedule and not postponed, as some more cautious leaders wished. When one looks at the reforms actually accomplished, their scope appears relatively modest. The measures taken were very much in the spirit of Andropov, designed to improve efficiency and strengthen discipline without making structural changes. Some of them even deserve to be called counter-reforms. In November 1985, without any previous discussion, five ministries and a state committee were merged to form a 'bureaucratic leviathan' (Hosking), the State Agro-Industrial Committee, under a hitherto little-known official, Murakhovsky, a Gorbachev associate who had spent his entire career in the Stavropol' region. He was appointed a first deputy prime minister, which on paper gave him enormous power as agricultural supremo. Yet little was heard of him thereafter and within four years the unwieldy organization had been broken up. According to *Pravda*, it had not done much more than 'flood the farms with instructions and regulations' in time-honoured fashion. The episode was reminiscent of Khrushchev's ill-fated bureaucratic manipulations, although Gorbachev was better able than his predecessor to learn from his mistakes.

Another new institution, the State Acceptance Committee (Gospriemka), was scarcely more successful. Its purpose was to improve control over the quality of industrial products, so that civilian goods might attain the same standard as military ones, which had always been vetted more rigorously. Instead of inspectors being drawn from employees of the enterprise concerned, which made them reluctant to offend management or their fellow-workers, they were to be outsiders. In some factories zealous Gospriemka officials rejected up to 10 per cent of output. In Uzbekistan the rejection rate was said to have reached 74 per cent, and by late 1987 a total of 6 milliard roubles worth of goods had been written off as scrap. The practice led to disaffection among men who found their pay docked for poor workmanship, and even to occasional strikes. 'Workers rightly complained that quality problems were often not their fault but the result of defective materials or managerial errors' (Rutland 1990). The innovation had more critics than supporters among economists, who saw it as another 'top-down, administrative answer to a problem whose long-run solution must lie in managers being dependent on customers', i.e. on the introduction of market relations.

But this was not what the General Secretary had in mind. He hailed quality control as a 'litmus test' that had allegedly shown 'total working-class support for *perestroika*'. This was self-delusion. 'We do not want to weaken the role of the centre', he went on, 'because otherwise we would lose the advantages of the planned economy.' This was to co-exist with a 'socialist market', whose size and shape was left unclear. The same point was made still more forcefully by Prime Minister Ryzhkov and the conservative Ligachev: economic reform was to be carried out 'in the framework of scientific socialism, without any deviations towards a market economy'. So what followed were half-measures that, instead of improving the situation, made it worse, since they undermined the old system of economic management before the foundations of a new one had been laid. In 1985 industrial output rose by 3.9 per cent, less than in the last year of 'stagnation' (4.2 per cent). Over the next two years it picked up to 4.9 per cent, but then dropped back to 3.8 per cent.[1] In 1987 the increase in labour productivity stood at only 2.4 per cent as against a planned 4.0 per cent, but in 1985-9 grew twice as fast as it had in the previous quinquennium (1.7 per cent per annum).

'Acceleration' at first meant introducing new technologies, such as computerization, and shifting investment into modernizing the engineering industry. According to the Twelfth Five-Year Plan, a document that soon became embarrassingly outdated, by 1990 one-third of the industry's capital stock was to be replaced, so that 90 per cent of its products would meet world standards. At the same time output was to double. This drive, 'pursued with sound and fury in the early years, . . . was a classic case of trying to do too much too fast' (Schroeder 1991). It was a mistake to try to make plants introduce new equipment and at the same time increase the quantity and quality of the goods they produced, as well as change their composition. Much of the money invested was wasted.

Matters were not helped by the policy of decentralizing decision-making to individual regions, which was reminiscent of Khrushchev's 1958 reform but extended it to enterprises as well. They were allowed greater latitude to dispose of the funds they generated and to enter into contracts with other firms. Instead of allocating this money to investment, many managers preferred to put it into the wage fund, in order to compensate their workpeople for current hardships and buy social peace—at the cost of accelerating the inflationary spiral. Since the construction industry was also decentralized at this time, enterprises trying to modernize had to make new arrangements with local concerns. Shortages of materials and finance meant that building projects took twice as long to complete as they were supposed to. A larger proportion had to be left unfinished. In 1984 the volume of these abandoned schemes had been equivalent to 78 per cent of the funds invested; five years later the figure was 94 per cent.

'Acceleration' was intended to bring an improvement in living standards, but this prospect turned out to be something of a mirage. Over the five years 1985-9 consumption grew annually by an average of 0.7 per cent, compared with 1.2 per cent during the previous quinquennium (Schroeder 1991). Food supply per head increased: for meat, for example, the figure rose from 39 kg. to 46 kg. in 1989, and for dairy products[2] from 131 to 146 kg. The output of consumer durables also increased. The number of washing machines produced, for instance, rose by 32 per cent (from 5.1 to 6.7 million) and of tape-recorders by 22 per cent (from 4.7 to 5.7 million); that of television sets grew by 6 per cent whereas that of radio receivers fell by 3 per cent. If queues got longer, this was partly because people now had more money to spend. Savings bank deposits took a further upward leap (from 20.1 milliard roubles in 1985 to 45.2 milliard in 1984: Åslund 1991). The massive excess of purchasing power ('rouble overhang') fuelled inflationary pressures. Domestic industry could not make up for goods that were no longer imported in order to save precious foreign currency. Shopping was as frustrating an activity as it had always been, goods more expensive—and consumers less inhibited about expressing dissatisfaction.

The rising inflation rate—some 7 to 10 per cent per annum by 1989—was of concern to the authorities, as was the increased budget deficit. By 1989 this had reached almost 10 per cent of GNP (92 milliard roubles as against an estimated average of 2.4 per cent in 1981-5). The Chernobyl disaster and the 1988 Armenian earthquake added vastly to the government's bills at a time when world oil prices were falling sharply. This was particularly unfortunate for the reformers, since fuel exports had traditionally provided such a large share of revenue. Receipts also declined from the profits tax, since enterprises could use more of their gains for purposes of their own, and from turnover tax. Finally, state revenue from the sale of vodka was reduced as a result of Gorbachev's assault on the old demon of alcohol abuse.

The temperance campaign

This campaign, which began in May 1985, was an expression of the new leader's 'ascetic-disciplinary bent' (Tarschys 1993), inherited from Andropov. It combined temperance propaganda with a reduction in output of state-produced liquor and stricter enforcement of the ban on *samogon*. Within a year a new civic organization, known officially as the All-Union Voluntary Society for Sobriety, claimed 12 million members. The number of outlets for the sale of spirits was halved: in all of Moscow there were only seventy-nine. Habitual drunkards faced fines or dismissal. Some towns enthusiastically declared themselves 'dry'. By the end of 1987 sales of spirits had fallen to 46 per cent of their 1980 level. Alcohol-related diseases, crime, and accidents declined. Over the three years 627,000 distillers of home brew are said to have been prosecuted. Nevertheless their product was still cheaper than its officially sanctioned competitor. Its contribution to total liquor intake is thought to have risen from 3.4 litres per capita in 1984 to 5.2 litres in 1987 (Treml 1991). The quality probably deteriorated, since many customers turned to industrial products (methylated spirits, anti-freeze, etc.).

Despite this alcohol consumption *did* drop (from 14.6 to 9.7 litres per head, and in the RSFSR from 13.4 to 5.6 litres, 1984–8), so that in the short term the campaign may be adjudged a success. It was one reason why life expectancy rates improved. However, not enough resources were allotted to counselling and therapy; by and large the approach taken was a heavy-handed administrative one. The campaign cost the state an estimated 28 milliard roubles in lost revenue. Although this aspect was not publicized, it explains why the drive ran out of steam in 1988. The CC eased restrictions on liquor sales and opted for a 'more balanced' approach. Alcoholism was after all a long-term problem, which could be overcome only by raising the social and cultural level of those groups worst afflicted. Gorbachev's traditional-style measures generated a good deal of social tension and—their most serious failing from the reformers' viewpoint—'the expected boost in economic efficiency failed to materialize' (Rutland 1990).

Towards freedom of expression

It took some time for the inadequacies of these policies to sink in. Nevertheless in 1986 there were signs that Gorbachev was moving to the left. It was now that he developed the concept of *glasnost'*. Its meaning changed. At first it had signified greater 'openness' in handling information from official sources and more lively self-criticism. Gradually it came to imply a limited freedom of expression in the media. In terms of the power struggle, *glasnost'* was a device for enlisting the intelligentsia's aid against elements in the *nomenklatura* opposed to reform. It originated in a desire to improve the quality of information received by the leadership, since traditional channels were biased and ineffective (Tolz 1993). The shock of the explosion at Chernobyl showed the high cost of official secretiveness. At first the accident was treated in the time-honoured way, by imposing a news black-out and spreading erroneous or misleading information. But as the scale of the tragedy became known internationally the leaders realized that a more sophisticated approach was required.

It would have been too much to expect an explicit statement favouring tolerance of all dissenting opinions subject only to legal safeguards (i.e. genuine pluralism of opinion), or outright abolition of censorship. For Gorbachev's attitude to *glasnost'* was ambiguous and instrumental. He saw it, not as a concession to Western-style liberalism, but as a means of strengthening Party rule in new conditions. 'We need *glasnost'* as we need air', he intoned, adding that 'criticism can be an effective instrument of *perestroika* only if it is based on absolute truth and scrupulous concern for justice.' But these fine sentiments were followed by a warning: 'if anyone else tries to fit their suit on us, let them beware! *Glasnost'* is aimed at strengthening our [socialist] society.' In other words, Authority was still to decide what was acceptable, and inconvenient opinions could be barred on the grounds that they expressed personal prejudice, not the views of any 'responsible' segment of society.

Despite these limitations a veritable 'information explosion' occurred, especially from 1988 onward. The credit for this should go to Gorbachev, even though he got more of a bang than he had expected. There had been nothing comparable since the NEP era. Thousands of people who had hitherto kept silent rushed into print. New journals mushroomed. Books and films that had been banned or left 'in the drawer' were published or screened. Countless ordinary folk wrote letters to the newspapers or their leaders. This had always been a popular practice, since the expression of unorthodox views in this form went unpunished, but now letter-writers forsook their customary restraint. Particularly important were the visual media. It is no exaggeration to say that as a result of *glasnost'* the way people thought and acted was transformed. One after another taboos were broken and apparently impregnable dogmas called in question. So rapid was the pace of change that what seemed unconventional one month might be a commonplace by the next.

The process of intellectual emancipation was at first under Party control. It was set in motion by informal hints to editors or cultural officials. When *Pravda* censured television journalists for their sterile way of presenting the news, this was meant—and immediately recognized—as a signal to the media to become bolder in treating sensitive issues. In August 1986 the accidental sinking of a cruise ship in the Black Sea was covered promptly. The 1986 annual statistical handbook 'contained a wealth of information that had not been available for some time: figures for infant mortality, for instance, were again reported' (White 1991). There were revelations, as we know, about the sad state of the health services. Crime, drugs, and prostitution were among other social ills aired in the press, evidently because they were no longer listed in the 'Talmud'. (When a censor was interviewed for the first time in November 1988, he stated that its size had been reduced by a third.) Those periodicals (notably *Moscow News* and *Arguments and Facts*) which approached current problems frankly were rewarded by phenomenal increases in circulation. That of *Novyi mir* more than doubled in two years. Now, unlike the 1960s, it no longer stood alone. From 1987 onward public opinion polls could be organized with a fair amount of freedom, and in March 1988, after five years of pressure behind the scenes, Zaslavskaia became head of a major sociological research centre under the acronym VTsIOM.[3]

The literary intelligentsia

Perhaps the most sensitive topic with which this institute had to deal was the privileges enjoyed by members of the *nomenklatura*.

Oddly, this question was broached as early as December 1985, in a speech by Yevtushenko to the RSFSR writers' union. 'It is morally impermissible', he said, 'that there should be any kind of restricted distribution of food and consumer goods, including the . . . special identity cards enabling the holder to buy things in special shops in this hall.' His speech was published, but in a 'drastically sanitized' version (Walker 1987). The Union of Soviet Writers, a conservative bastion, held its Eighth congress in June 1987. The debates were fierce. Liberal-leaning authors criticized interference in cultural matters by incompetent officials and warned of ecological threats such as the Siberian rivers diversion scheme. The delegates appealed for this project to be halted, and for once were listened to. The 'village prose' writer Sergei Zalygin, the new (1986) editor of *Novyi mir* and a hydraulic engineer by training, hailed the decision as the first victory scored by public opinion over officialdom (Hosking 1990). There was also much controversy over the ambiguous role played by the union's ageing leadership. The chairman, G. Markov, who was seriously compromised by his collaboration with the security authorities, had to resign. One-third of the union's secretariat were newcomers, among them Yevtushenko (who had taken the lead privately in pressing for relaxation of censorship), Voznesensky, and Okudzhava. However, left-conservatives managed to hang on to several key posts.

More successful than the writers were members of the cinematographers' union, who in May 1987 elected a new board without seeking the Party authorities' prior consent and under E. Klimov's leadership set to work on changing the whole system of film-making. They benefited from the fact that the head of Goskino had meanwhile (December 1986) been replaced. Later in the year people in the theatre went further by setting up a new organization altogether. Two famous creative artists who had been exiled abroad, Tarkovsky and Liubimov, were invited to return. For Tarkovsky the invitation came too late—he died later that year of cancer in Paris—but his works were at least widely shown. So, too, was Tengiz Abuladze's *Repentance*, despite efforts by officials to have it banned or cut. This film, completed in 1984, dealt allegorically with the Stalin terror and caused a sensation, although its message was conveyed obliquely. The story focuses less on the figure of Varlam, a sinister Georgian dictator and Beria look-alike, than on his son, a respectable comfort-loving bourgeois, and his grandson, who revolts against the latter's hypocritical complacency. The tone was anything but denunciatory—but this may explain the film's extraordinary appeal to members of the 'third generation', who were only starting to come to terms with the moral legacy of Stalinism. In 1988 it was followed by Alexander Prokshin's *Cold Summer of '53*, which dealt unsentimentally with the problems of *zeks* released after Stalin's death.

It was only to be expected that historical themes would feature prominently in the literature of this era. Among works belatedly released by the censor was Anatolii Rybakov's *Children of the Arbat* (1987), written two decades earlier. It describes the darkening Soviet scene in the early 1930s through the eyes of a child and contains a remarkable effort to reconstruct the mental world of Stalin himself. (Solzhenitsyn had done so earlier, in *First Circle*, but his novel had yet to appear in the USSR.) Later Rybakov continued his narrative in *1935 and Other Years* (1988). Dudintsev, the pace-maker of the earlier 'thaw' (see Chapter 6), resurfaced with *White Coats* (1987), which dealt with Lysenkoism in the late 1940s. So, too, did Daniil Granin's *The Aurochs*, a 'documentary novella' that exalted the famous geneticist Timofeev-Resovsky, who had been punished under Stalin for pursuing research into the harmful effects of radiation. The 'aurochs' in the title suggested that its hero was 'the last of a noble breed, . . . untameable and completely unconcerned with conforming to the regnant conventions' (K. Clark 1990).

Particularly important was the rehabilitation extended to emigré writers and others who had been regularly execrated during their lifetime. In 1987 Pasternak was posthumously restored to USW membership and later his house at Peredelkino was turned into a museum; by 1988 *Dr Zhivago* was appearing in *Novyi mir*. Its effect on Soviet readers was fairly muted, for in the meantime they had become used to stronger fare, such as Vasilii Grossman's World War II novel *Life and Fate*, Yevgeniia Ginzburg's graphic account of Terror and Gulag, *Into the Whirlwind*, and Nadezhda Mandelshtam's two-volume memoir on the persecution of her poet husband (and the intelligentsia generally) in the 1930s (*Hope against Hope, Hope Abandoned*). Early anti-utopian satires by Zamiatin, Platonov, Bulgakov, and Orwell came out, and countless readers found that their message had lost none of its freshness. Among emigré authors whose writings appeared in literary journals were (besides Zamiatin) Vladimir Nabokov, Josef Brodsky, Vladimir Voinovich, and Viktor Nekrasov. Until now 'Russia abroad' had been either passed over in silence or depicted as consisting of 'renegades' in the 'enemy camp'. Now people suddenly realized what a heavy price the revolution had exacted by depriving Russians — and others, too — of the best of their cultural tradition.

History rediscovered

It was as though the skein of time were being unravelled from the bottom up. Academic historians were slow to react to the new opportunities, for they had been so thoroughly tamed. Instead the initiative was taken by journalists, dramatists and others. Even the visual record of the past was 'revised', for photographs appeared in which 'unpersons' such as Trotsky, who had hitherto been 'brushed out' by the censor, were restored to their rightful place. In *The Brest-Litovsk Peace* (1987) the playwright Mikhail Shatrov broke a taboo by taking as his subject the controversies in the Party early in 1918. Trotsky, Bukharin, and the Menshevik leader Martov were depicted with relative objectivity, and Lenin himself as a real-life creature, beset by doubts and vacillations. In *Further, Further . . .* (1988) Lenin was shown as accepting blame for having appointed Stalin as General Secretary.

All this was not to the taste of conservatives for whom the Bolshevik leader was an iconic figure, or even of Gorbachev, who was keen to invoke Lenin's authority for his own *perestroika*. Until 1989 historians trod gingerly here, realizing that if they knocked down this central pillar of the faith the Party would lose its last shred of legitimacy. Accordingly they focused attention on 'deformations of socialism' in the Stalin era, although many of them knew well that the source of evil lay further back in time. This half-heartedness fitted in with Gorbachev's instrumental approach. 'If today we sometimes approach history critically', he declared in November 1987, marking the revolution's seventieth anniversary, 'this is only because we want to get a better and fuller picture of the way to the future.' His keynote speech articulated a political compromise within the leadership, where Ligachev and other conservatives were on the rebound. A few months later Gorbachev felt strong enough to take a more robust stand. He now declared that 'there must be no forgotten names or blank spots' in the historical record. In February 1988 Bukharin and others who had been shot just fifty years earlier were at long last rehabilitated. So too were various other 'oppositionists' from the 1920s onwards. It now became possible, not just to 'correct' the injustices done to members of the Soviet élite during the Terror, but to question the merits of collectivization and the 'great turn' of 1929. It was only a question of time before Trotsky, too, received due appreciation. Thereafter the spotlight turned on the non-Bolshevik socialists of the revolutionary era and then on non-socialist alternatives to 'Great October'. Late in 1988 the philosopher Alexander Tsipko began to grapple with Marx himself, taking him to task for having taught that the class struggle was an inevitable and progressive phenomenon.

By now thoroughly disoriented by the toppling of so many idols, a number of Communists, anxious to find a new father figure with whom to identify, joined Russian patriots in bringing out of the cupboard portraits of Stolypin and even Nicholas II. Sometimes their images were carried by demonstrators in the street, where they incongruously jostled those of Lenin or Stalin! Hitherto people had been led to believe that all problems were soluble and that socialism was incomparably superior to other systems. Now a veritable Pandora's box had been opened. It was no longer evident that man could transform society by the exercise of his will. This 'dealt a major blow to [people's] mental hygiene and emotional well-being' (Hollander citing P. L. Berger 1991).

Exposure of past crimes and falsehoods was more than just a matter for scholarly debate. At Kuropaty near Minsk excavators gradually uncovered the remains of some 30,000 victims of the Terror. Other graves came to light in Ukraine (Vinnitsa, Donetsk, Bykovnya), outside Leningrad, near Cheliabinsk in the Urals, on an island in the Caspian Sea, and in Siberia. Even so the authorities stubbornly refused to acknowledge the painful truth that the massacre of Polish officers and other prisoners at Katyn in 1940 had been carried out by the NKVD on the Politburo's orders. (The relevant documents, which were kept in a specially secure place, were finally published in 1993.) Writers and artists helped to sponsor a civic association, Memorial, which in November 1988 held a 'conscience week' to draw attention to the plight of Gulag veterans. Dmitrii Yurasov compiled a card index of Stalin's known victims, whose sacrifice Memorial sought to commemorate by setting up monuments at their one-time places of confinement and in central Moscow.

The churches

The churches, weakened as they had been by decades of repression, were hard pressed to satisfy the welling-up of moral and religious sentiment. Even so all confessions benefited from the atheists' discomfiture. Gorbachev, it was later revealed, had been baptized into the Orthodox Church, but this is no reason to consider him a covert believer. Nor did he mean Muslims only when, speaking in Tashkent in November 1986, he called for 'a decisive and uncompromising struggle against religious phenomena'. Nevertheless this conventional attitude did not blind him to the advantages of utilizing churchpeople's goodwill in order to further *perestroika*. To this end he was prepared to sanction the transfer of certain religious buildings to ecclesiastical control. Among them was the Danilov monastery in Moscow[4] and the famous shrine of Optina *pustyn'* near Kaluga. Another monastery near Yaroslavl' that had been in State hands became a home for the aged. The secular authorities hoped that, by allowing the religious to engage in charitable activities, they could divert popular disaffection away from themselves. Baptists as well as Orthodox Christians did indeed begin to minister to the sick and aged, but the need was great and their resources minuscule.

In the view of one stern critic, 'Gorbachev wanted a transition from a crude anti-religious approach which alienated millions of believers to a more subtle one which turned believers into atheists without their being aware of it' (Dunlop 1990). If this was indeed so, the strategy may be said to have backfired. Late in 1984 the CRA acquired a new chairman, Kharchev, who took a more lenient line.[5] Leading churchmen were allowed to publish in learned journals, to participate in public debates with laymen, and even to appear on television. This was clearly done with an eye to foreign opinion. In June 1988 the Russian Orthodox Church was due to celebrate its millennium and the regime was anxious to extract the maximum propaganda value from the event. State officials attended part of the celebrations. The Synod adopted a new statute which relaxed many of the restrictions imposed in 1961, notably on the clergy's activities. Previously, in April 1988, Gorbachev had received Patriarch Pimen' (soon to be succeeded on his death by Alexi) and other senior ecclesiastics in the first such meeting since 1943. He promised a new approach to Church–State relations that would uphold believers' rights, and specifically a new law ensuring freedom of conscience. This concession was in part a response to renewed demands for a reform of the law on religious cults. A priest in Krasnoiarsk was one of many who wanted the Constitution to allow all citizens equal rights to propagate religious or anti-religious views. Writers, jurists and, most remarkably of all, even CRA officials joined in the call for new legal arrangements. Freedom of conscience was eventually enshrined in a law (albeit an imperfect one) passed on 1 October 1990, and that same year the CRA was abolished. Parish life slowly revived. In 1988 alone the authorities registered 1,610 new religious communities, 1,244 of which were Russian Orthodox. (In June of that year the latter had 6,893 parishes, over 4,000 of them in Ukraine.)

Civic groups

Organizations with religious or charitable aims were prominent among the host of civic groups that sprang up once police controls were relaxed. By December 1987 *Pravda* estimated at 30,000 the total number of such 'informals' (*neformaly*), as they came to be called; a year or so later the number had doubled. They were particularly popular among the young: a poll conducted in five urban centres showed that 60 per cent of youngsters belonged to one (Riordan 1988). Many of these groups were, however, ephemeral and of little or no political consequence. They included sports clubs, choral societies, associations for protecting the environment or historical monuments, and so forth. (In Leningrad there was a 'Gulliver Club' for tall people which ran its own café and marriage bureau!)

It was only a question of time before the more serious civic bodies came together in order to advance their aims and began to devise political programmes ('platforms'). As early as August 1987 a 'Club for Social Initiatives' in Moscow held a conference attended by some six hundred representatives of forty-eight civic bodies, including Memorial. They were mostly moderates who were willing to co-operate with the Party leadership in achieving social regeneration. True to form, a minority faction broke away to protest the socialist orientation of the main body. Two federations were set up. In mid-1988 the larger group joined with several other associations in trying to set up 'popular fronts in support of *perestroika*' in various localities.

These fronts acted as an extra-parliamentary opposition to the Party apparatus where conservatives were blocking reform. This sometimes led to direct confrontations, for example in Yaroslavl', where the front held weekly meetings in a football stadium. Resolutions were passed calling for action on a wide range of issues, culminating in a demand for open election to leading public posts and abolition of shops to which functionaries alone had access (Hosking 1990). Elsewhere coalitions of civic groups held demonstrations and put out their own newspapers, such as *Herald of the Urals* in Yeltsin's bastion of Sverdlovsk. Two of the most successful informal press organs were *Glasnost'* and *Ekspress-Khronika*, edited respectively by Sergei Grigoriants and Alexander Podrabinek. The latter had previously compiled a successful clandestine bulletin on psychiatric abuse (see Chapter 9). By the spring of 1988 copies were being distributed in fifty-three different towns. However, the legal status of these journals was still shaky. Officials frequently put obstacles in the editors' way, by denying them premises or paper, or refusing registration on specious grounds—for instance, that there was now so much freedom of information in the regular media that they were superfluous.

The central Party leadership, too, was worried at the growth of opposition tendencies. The horse having bolted, it tried to close the stable door—with predictable results. In June 1987 the Supreme Soviet adopted a law on 'nation-wide discussion of important matters of state life' which sought to regulate the way in which citizens might propose changes to the law. *Pravda* warned journalists not to treat matters sensationally and to balance critical comments with favourable mention of the measures being taken to remedy defects. In February 1988 the government banned independent publishing houses and printing co-operatives. Three months later Grigoriants was briefly arrested and much of his printing equipment confiscated. This was an effort to stop him and several associates from forming the Democratic Union, a political group committed to a multi-party system and trade-union independence. On the other hand, in Moscow at least the police seem to have been told to deal gently with those who attended unauthorized demonstrations. This ambiguity reflected growing divisions within the leadership.

The leadership divided

Gorbachev's new thrust toward reform 'led him into uncharted territories' and so 'awaken[ed] suspicion and resentment among some of those who had helped him come to power' (Hosking 1990). Party and government functionaries who had lost their jobs, or who feared for their future, naturally enough made their views known informally to their superiors. In the Politburo Gorbachev could rely on the backing of Shevardnadze and Alexander Yakovlev (who joined it in January 1987, becoming a full member five months later). Yakovlev emerged as the most articulate and consistent advocate of *perestroika*. He saw it as primarily a moral issue: people had to be encouraged to act as creative, responsible individuals. A very different viewpoint was taken by Ligachev and the KGB chairman, Chebrikov. When Gorbachev temporarily faded from public view in August–September 1987 (he was writing his book, *Perestroika*), both men came out with statements reasserting orthodox Leninist ideas. Ligachev acclaimed Soviet achievements in the 1930s. Chebrikov warned that 'imperialists' were subverting Soviet youngsters and declared that 'socialist democracy' had to go hand in hand with discipline. He was particularly scathing about the civic groups, which he saw as penetrated by 'extremists'. Another hardliner (and Brezhnev hold-over), Aliev, was dropped from the Politburo in October 1987, after a stormy CC plenum that saw the temporary humiliation of the fiery Boris Yeltsin.

As Party boss in Moscow Yeltsin had purged so many clients of his long-serving predecessor, Grishin, that this evoked Gorbachev's displeasure. In one year some eight hundred individuals were charged with corruption, often on the basis of anonymous denunciations.[6] Yeltsin cultivated the common touch. He travelled around the city by public transport, visited shops to express sympathy with customers in the queues, and convoked citizens' assemblies at which he responded to questions with unusual frankness. Once he tackled the privileged facilities that existed for Party cadres, he ran into opposition in the CC and Politburo—from Gorbachev but more especially from Ligachev (and Solomentsev).

As the conflicts became ever more bitter, Yeltsin revolted inwardly against the whole institutional set-up. In his view the country had a leadership unworthy of it. Politburo sessions he deemed purposeless, since his colleagues simply mouthed phrases like 'democratization' in which they did not believe. The Central Committee apparatus (where he himself served as a secretary!) 'produced nothing but paper'. The Council of Ministers was so disorganized that he ceased to attend its sessions. In the summer of 1987 Yeltsin went to see Gorbachev privately. He called for a radicalization of *perestroika* and listed no less than twenty points of disagreement. The leader, furious, responded by criticizing Yeltsin's conduct of affairs in Moscow. Boris Nikolaevich submitted his resignation but Gorbachev asked him to hold on until the next CC plenum. Yeltsin agreed—evidently because he had decided that this assembly would make a fine forum for an open showdown.

This was to breach the long-standing unwritten convention that Party leaders, however deep their differences, should preserve a façade of unanimity before the Party's 'parliament'. Perhaps this aspect of the 'Yeltsin affair' shocked the delegates more than what Yeltsin actually *said* on 21 October 1987 (Breslauer 1989). He suggested that two years of *perestroika* had achieved nothing concrete; despite all efforts to curb it, bureaucracy was thriving; Politburo members were glorifying the leader in time-honoured fashion, and Ligachev was especially to blame for obstructing democratic reforms. As might be expected, succeeding speakers vied with each other in denouncing the errant Boris Nikolaevich. On 11 November he was fired as Moscow chief and in February 1988 he lost his Politburo seat as well. He stood publicly condemned for 'political adventurism' and placing his own ambitions ahead of the Party's interests. An element of personal vindictiveness was indeed involved. Yeltsin himself acknowledged in public that ambition had clouded his judgement. He suffered only a minor demotion and within a few months staged a political comeback. But after this incident the CPSU would never be the same again. It was as if a spell had been broken. Another consequence was to create an unbridgeable rift between the two leaders that did much to weaken the political establishment over the years to come.

Despite the split in the 'reformist' camp, when Yeltsin left the Politburo Gorbachev managed to strengthen his own position. Two of his supporters, Masliukov and Razumovsky, were appointed candidate members. The main report, on education, was unremarkable. It was delivered by Ligachev, who still wielded considerable power as (unofficial) chairman of the Secretariat, where he was responsible *inter alia* for ideological matters. His hand has been detected behind the celebrated 'Andreeva letter'.[7] This letter was published in the left-conservative organ *Sovetskaia Rossiia* on 13 March 1988, during Gorbachev's absence abroad, and was made obligatory reading at Party meetings. Nina Andreeva was a hitherto unknown chemistry teacher in Leningrad, the wife of an instructor in Marxism-Leninism. In her letter (which was actually written by a team of professionals under the supervision of the newspaper's editor) she deplored attacks on Stalin and tolerance of Western mass culture under *glasnost'*. The advocates of reform, she suggested, were rootless intellectuals, liberals in disguise who wanted to revert to capitalism. The content of the letter mattered less than the fact of its publication. It was 'a manifesto of the forces opposed to *perestroika*', as Yakovlev put in a *Pravda* editorial on 5 April— after a three-week delay that caused near-panic among friends of reform.

Not for the last time, it looked as if Gorbachev were about to be unseated. Once again he regained the inititative. The journal's editor acknowledged his error in publishing the letter. Ligachev's influence was reduced by making chairmanship of the Secretariat rotate. The battle at the top spread downwards to Party organizations across the land. Preparations were now under way for the convocation of an extraordinary Party conference.[8] In the electoral campaign reformist candidates frequently encountered obstruction by provincial and regional Party officials, who substituted their own nominees. There was nothing very unusual about this—except that now the 'centre' intervened in these disputes on the 'wrong' side! In several cities (notably L'viv, Samara, Yaroslavl', and Omsk) reformers staged protest demonstrations against these abuses. Some officials were dismissed.

At the conference (28 June–1 July) the debates were unusually candid and lively. Some questions were left to be decided by the delegates on a majority vote, instead of the decision being handed down from above. In another break with tradition the public was told much of what was going on while the conference was in session. They heard a delegate call for the resignation of leading right-wingers, including Gromyko (now head of state). Ligachev and Yeltsin engaged in another heated exchange—the first time rival Party leaders had confronted one another in full view of the media-watching public. But the key development was Gorbachev's far-reaching scheme for a thorough reform of Soviet institutions in order to 'democratize' the political system. Approved after stormy discussions, it went beyond what had previously been endorsed by the CC. It was designed to make *perestroika* 'irreversible' by taking a big step towards a constitutional order. Whether Gorbachev realized it or not, it spelled the end of the Party's monopoly of power—and thus of the USSR that Lenin and Stalin had built. Hitherto, when Gorbachev had termed *perestroika* 'revolutionary', the epithet had smacked of loose rhetoric. But this was indeed 'revolution from above'.

Towards constitutional government

'Democratization' was the third plank, along with *perestroika* and *glasnost'*, in Gorbachev's intellectual armoury. Little was heard of it during his first year or so in office, when the emphasis was on economic, not political, reform. At the Twenty-seventh Party congress the General Secretary spoke of 'developing socialist democracy' and reinvigorating the soviets, but these were stock phrases in Party jargon. Few of his listeners heeded a passing reference to the need for 'correctives' to the electoral system in order to make sure that the most qualified people were voted into office. It was not until the CC plenum of January 1987 that 'electoral and political reform . . . became an explicit objective . . . as part of a much larger programme of "democratizing" all areas of Soviet life' (White, Gill, and Slider 1993). Its purpose, Gorbachev made clear, was to undermine his adversaries in the establishment.

The spring-cleaning was to begin at home, in the CPSU itself. To overcome inertia, intolerance of criticism and other familiar deficiencies, he declared, basic structural changes were needed. Above all, Party committees, when electing their executive officers, were no longer to endorse mechanically a single nominee of the centre but to have a real choice between several competing candidates. The first instance of such an election, in a district of Kemerovo province the next month, was widely publicized. The example caught on, but only at the lowest (district) level. Senior appointments continued to be filled in the traditional way. But even this was seen as a threat by left-conservatives in the Party *apparat* and elsewhere. They were already unnerved by the reformist leaders' encouragement of permissiveness in the media, which seemed to endanger the Party's 'leading role' in public life. While not opposed to reforms as such, they wanted them to be introduced gradually. Foot-dragging had been effective in the early 1960s, when Khrushchev had sought to limit officials' tenure of their posts. Might not the same techniques work against Gorbachev?

This was why the *nomenklatura* offered stubborn resistance to the new procedures when electing delegates to the Nineteenth Party conference. Many viewed the gathering with apprehension, for its purpose had been defined as 'to take measures to democratize further the life of the Party and society'. Articles in the press made it clear that this meant changing the relationship *between* the Party and society. The CPSU was to withdraw from direct management of economic affairs, and government business generally, and leave this to the soviets, as state organs, in accordance with Lenin's original intentions. In June 1987 an experiment had been carried out when soviets were re-elected. In about 5 per cent of constituencies there had been more than a single candidate. Voters took these contests more seriously than the others and several deputies lost their seats to 'outsiders'. This came as a shock. 'The experiment introduced a small measure of unpredictability into local political recruitment . . . It was an important step in dismantling the *nomenklatura* as a system and destroying [its] powers as a group' (Hill and Loewenhardt 1991).

Yet this had not been the aim of the exercise; nor did Gorbachev in 1988 set out to wreck the Soviet bureaucracy. He wanted to improve officials' performance, make them behave responsibly and open up government to fresh talent. The scheme for constitutional reform endorsed at the Party conference did *not* mean abandonment of Party control! On the contrary, the chairman of a soviet executive (*ispolkom*) was 'normally' to be the first secretary of the local Party committee. But his candidacy was to be properly discussed and, if someone better were available, rejected. One might well call this 'guided democracy'. The calculation in Gorbachev's mind was that only in exceptional cases would the Party's nominee fail to be approved; where this happened, the machine could live with it. He tacitly assumed that under a 'democratized' Soviet system all contending groups or individuals would have much ground in common and so would accept Communist pre-eminence. Local politics would be characterized by consensus, not polarization. As in the 'people's democracies' of Eastern Europe, multi-party government would serve as a façade for Communist rule, maintained by manipulation as much as by coercion.

Such a view seems amazingly naïve in retrospect. It underestimated the tensions generated by decades of abuse by an omnipotent *apparat* and the political dynamism which *perestroika* inevitably unleashed—particularly in the non-Russian areas, where a wide spectrum of political opinions was emerging. Even leaving nationalism out of account, it was inevitable that local leaders, tired of centralism and dictatorship, would seek to assert their independence. There could not be a half-way house on the road to democracy and pluralism—or, to put it differently, once the Party loosened its iron grip its power would evaporate. 'Quasi-parliamentarianism' was bound to generate demands for 'a comprehensive multiparty system that would gobble up the CPSU' (Simon 1993).

These considerations applied with even greater force to the new arrangements envisaged at the apex of the pyramid. Characteristically, the principle of separation of powers was not to be adhered to rigorously but covertly subverted, although less crudely than under the existing dispensation. Gorbachev's scheme provided for a two-tier legislature, whose purpose was to act as a check on the executive arm of government. A Congress of People's Deputies, with 2,250 members, meeting annually, was to wield supreme legislative power; but of these representatives one-third were to be chosen by 'social organizations' such as trade unions and (last but not least!) the CPSU. From this throng the Congress was to elect a Supreme Soviet of 542 deputies, in two chambers as before, that would, however, meet twice a year for several months—not just a few days. Sessions were to last five years, double the previous term, one-fifth of the deputies standing down annually. In this way the Supreme Soviet would, it was hoped, become an effective parliamentary body, instead of simply a rubber stamp. It had the power to amend the Constitution and to determine the main lines of policy. It elected its Chairman, a new office clearly tailored to Gorbachev's requirements. He was to exercise 'general guidance' over the work of state institutions, nominate people to leading positions, and issue 'directives'. It was understood that this post would 'normally' be held by the General Secretary of the CPSU—which, according to the Constitution in force (Article 6), was still 'the nucleus of [the] political system and of all state and public organizations'.

Thus pluralism was an aspiration, not a fact. This ambiguity shaped the outcome of the elections to the Congress, held on 26 March 1989. As in the *Party* elections of the previous year, these were fiercely contested, with ample use of underhand methods. The system of 'reserved' seats for official candidates meant that some citizens had more than one vote. The electoral law did not make it mandatory for there to be more than one candidate. Any social organization could nominate candidates, but in each constituency a 'selection conference' decided which candidates should be registered. These gatherings gave Party officials ample opportunity to manipulate the results. Of all candidates nominated only 2,884 (38 per cent) leaped this hurdle. The Party set a poor example by nominating, for the 100 'reserved' seats it was allotted, just 100 candidates—among them, predictably, all current members of its Politburo. There was rather more debate in the trade unions, which produced 114 candidates for 100 seats, and in the Union of Soviet Writers several rounds of voting were required before it chose its twelve allotted candidates, prominent conservatives (Bondarev) and liberals (Yevtushenko) both failing to secure nomination. The Academy of Sciences' first list of twenty-three candidates excluded Sakharov, but after vigorous campaigning by his supporters he was eventually successful.

In the general constituencies behaviour varied widely. In some places (including all seventeen constituencies in Kazakhstan!) selection conferences were so thoroughly packed that the local Party boss was elected unopposed. Alternative candidates were frequently harassed or discriminated against. But there was also a fair number of genuine contests between individuals who, despite their common background, advanced distinctive programmes. There were cases of local people forcing selection conferences to yield and register popular candidates. In 384 out of 1,500 constituencies only a single name appeared on the ballot-paper. Turn-out was high (89.8 per cent). In many places run-off elections had to be held as no candidate secured half the vote. Several prominent officials went down to defeat, among them the Party leaders in Moscow, Leningrad, Kiev, and Minsk. In Ukraine the first secretary was returned but five provincial ones were repudiated by their electors; nation-wide this fate befell thirty-eight local bosses. Particularly distressing for the establishment were the results in the Baltic republics, where candidates backed by national Popular Fronts all but swept the board.[9] A strong effort was made to spoil Yeltsin's campaign in Moscow, but he received a triumphant 89.4 per cent of the vote. Despite these victories committed reformers had no hope of controlling the assembly. Not only was there a solid conservative majority, but it was more elitist in composition than previous pseudo-legislatures had been.

One can readily understand why Yurii Solov'ev, the defeated Leningrad leader, complained that the CPSU had turned into a 'debating society'. In the meantime the reformers had forced through important changes to the Party's structure. The powers of the Secretariat were greatly reduced by the formation of six[10] high-powered commissions for ideology, cadres policy, law, agriculture, and so on. The CC apparatus was thinned by nearly a third and the number of its departments reduced from twenty to nine; outside Moscow the cuts went even deeper. In April 1989 Gorbachev rid the CC of 110 'dead souls' (whose average age was 68.6). Most of them had lost their jobs since the last congress. This was effectively a *coup* which weakened that body's ability to resist his policies. There was a flood of information about the Party's activities, past and present, in a new journal, the *Izvestiia* (News) of the CC. Among the topics treated were the Party's finances, hitherto a closely guarded secret. Its income was put at 1.3 milliard roubles (81 per cent from membership dues) and expenditure at 1.7 milliard roubles; the CC apparatus alone cost 50 million roubles a year. Membership was said to be holding steady at 19.5 million (October 1988), but soon began to dwindle drastically, for with Gorbachev's constitutional reform the Party lost relevance.

Among Party officials frustration was naturally intense. At a conference of regional secretaries in June 1989 and at the next CC plenum in July, there were loud complaints at the course *perestroika* was taking. However, the conservative members of the Politburo—Ligachev (now demoted to responsibility for agriculture), Shcherbitsky, Chebrikov, Zaikov—could not agree on a realistic alternative policy. Gorbachev brusquely told them not to panic and hinted at a further purge. Possibly he wanted to force his opponents to come into the open so that he could remove them.

Chebrikov and Shcherbitsky were indeed sacked soon afterwards, but the new KGB chief, Kriuchkov, was predictably no friend of reform. The Party leader faced vocal opponents on both flanks. His ability to manœuvre was diminishing, for his power was precariously balanced between the two main institutional hierarchies. The new 'democratized' governmental structure was no substitute for the Party and KGB apparatuses. Yet writing in *Pravda* (31 July 1989) Mikhail Sergeevich lectured those nostalgic for the 'good old days' that they had gone for ever.

The first Congress of People's Deputies (25 May–9 June 1989) duly elected Gorbachev Chairman of the Supreme Soviet, but by a less than unanimous vote (2,213 : 87). He had to field some embarrassing questions: did he have a *dacha* in the Crimea? Was he not under the influence of his wife, Raisa? The deputies soon broadened the scope of their criticism to include all aspects of policy. One of them asked for more 'openness' about the KGB. Another took Ligachev to task for his dismal record on agriculture. Sakharov wanted the CPSU to relinquish its monopoly of power. Yevtushenko proposed that all trials of dissidents be legally voided. Another writer called for Solzhenitsyn's citizenship to be restored and Lenin's body to be removed from the Mausoleum. All this was explosive stuff. The nation watched the proceedings on television in a state of incredulous excitement. Every day brought fresh revelations: about ecological disasters, for instance, or the Nazi–Soviet pact, a topic that lay most heavily on the hearts of deputies from the Baltic.

Meanwhile the Congress had given birth to a reformed Supreme Soviet. It proved as rumbustious an assembly as the parent body. At its first session (7 June–4 August 1989) it set up several committees and standing commissions which scrutinized the government's programme and conduct. Ten of Prime Minister Ryzhkov's original nominees for ministerial posts were rejected. Others were subjected to a humiliating inquisition. Late in July the radical deputies, meeting in a Moscow cinema, set up a parliamentary 'fraction'[11] which took the non-committal name Inter-regional Deputies Group. It published a newspaper of its own but was unable to enforce discipline on its members, which was a source of weakness. The leading lights were Yeltsin, Sakharov, the historian Yurii Afanas'ev, and G. Popov, the mayor of Moscow. Yeltsin set the tone by telling a foreign reporter that Ligachev was 'ripe for retirement' and followed this up by calling for a special session of Congress to reform electoral procedures.

The radicals' campaign was not unsuccessful. On 24 October, during its second session (25 September–28 November 1989) the Supreme Soviet did indeed vote to eliminate the unpopular provision for the separate indirect election of deputies through 'social organizations'.[12] In doing so it overruled its chairman, Gorbachev, who had wanted to extend the practice throughout the legislative system. The assembly also rejected his request for a general ban on strikes, which were wreaking havoc in the coal industry. It approved the government's programme of economic recovery, but many delegates on the left and right made it abundantly clear that they had little faith in it. The USSR's quasi-parliamentary system did not function well. Deputies wasted time discussing current political issues or scandals instead of engaging in solid legislative work. Frequently the assembly infringed its standing orders, e.g. by allowing deputies to vote for absentees, and it was easily manipulated by its eighteen-man presidium or twenty-nine-member secretariat (Mann 1990). The 'fractions' that took shape represented special interests. There was no regular party-political give-and-take, as in a truly democratic body. All in all, the new supreme legislature set a poor example to those formed in its likeness in the several union republics.

As routine set in, debates in the two chambers no longer commanded as much public interest as they had initially enjoyed. The focus of political life moved away from the 'White House' (as its fine modern building came to be called) to the press and even to the street. A draft law on the media aroused a great deal of commotion. Radicals found it too restrictive. Gorbachev tried to dismiss V. Starkov, editor of *Arguments and Facts*, which had achieved a record circulation of 22 million copies. He criticized the Inter-regional Group as 'a clique striving to achieve power'—as though, in a pluralist system, this was not what political forces normally tried to do! *Pravda*, whose circulation dropped by over 40 per cent in ten months, published an article, probably inspired by the KGB, critical of Yeltsin's personal behaviour. The radical leader claimed that he had been slandered. The Party organ apologized. Later its editor was dismissed and his successor promised that in future it would hew to a more open, truthful line. Addressing a large crowd in Moscow on 15 October, Yeltsin provocatively called for Ligachev to be dropped from the Politburo. Two weeks later, at another big gathering, he charged Gorbachev with being the country's 'leading conservative'. This was unfair, for the Party leader held to his 'centrist' line, which meant that he tacked to and fro. On 15 November he dropped a hint that a shift to the left was impending. To a student forum he stated that, although all political changes had to take place within a socialist framework, 'any article in the Constitution can be discussed, amended or even eliminated, and this applies even to Article 6'.

This was to concede one of the radicals' chief demands, which he had hitherto stoutly resisted. Characteristically, Gorbachev seized the initiative himself. On 5 February 1990 he told the Party CC that in future Communists would have to earn their 'leading role' in Soviet society on their merits, instead of having this status constitutionally guaranteed. The dropping of Article 6 was duly endorsed by the Congress one month later. This was a further move in the dance of institutions. The purpose was to strengthen the state organs *vis-à-vis* those of the Party, and more particularly to make the former a stronger 'pillar' of the leadership. For Gorbachev aspired to be nothing less than *President* of the USSR, on the American or French (Fifth Republic) model, an office invested with 'the requisite plenipotentiary powers', so that he might carry through *perestroika* without let or hindrance. He was already head of state (chairman of the Presidium of the Supreme Soviet), an office inherited from Gromyko on 1 October 1988. But that was a largely honorific post. Now the Presidency was to become the main locus of power.

As in the earlier stage of constitutional reform, the discussion revolved chiefly around the question whether it was wise to concentrate so much executive power in a single individual, particularly one who was simultaneously Party General Secretary. Would this not simply recreate a personal dictatorship, which in other hands might be akin to Stalin's, and side-track the new legislative organs? Moreover, how could the extensive powers he sought be reconciled with the new rights being accorded to the union republics?

These were serious questions. Deputies were not alone in arguing that, if the new system were to function effectively, there had to be a proper balance between the several arms of government. Their fears were not allayed by assurances that the *next* President (but not the incumbent!) would be elected by a universal, secret ballot, that the chief executive could not serve for more than two terms, or that the Congress could recall him should he violate the Constitution. Gorbachev got only 1,329 votes (out of about 2,000 cast) when sworn in as President on 15 March 1990. No less than 1,303 deputies, a simple majority, voted in favour of a resolution that the President should hold no other political or government post. But Gorbachev cleverly got this classed as a constitutional amendment, which needed a two-thirds majority, and the motion was therefore lost.

This was a serious error which cast a shadow over the new Presidency. The man who held this high office was king in all but name. He commanded the armed forces, could appoint and dismiss ministers, declare states of emergency or 'temporary presidential rule', and issue decrees that had 'binding force'. Yet in the last resort this vast accumulation of power depended on his *authority* as an independent lofty arbiter between competing interests—and this authority was, alas, fatally compromised. For Gorbachev had not stood for popular election. Instead he owed his eminence to his leadership role in the CPSU. This undermined his legitimacy and became a major handicap, not least in his struggle with Yeltsin. Gorbachev's 'reign'—and indeed the Presidency itself—would last for less than two years, and most of this time would be taken up with efforts to stop the country from falling apart.

In 1987, when the constitutional changes had first been mooted, Gorbachev had been in a relatively strong position. By 1990, when they were in force, he was an embattled figure. He had lit a fire that would consume the Soviet regime. At first the flames had been under control. By 1988 they were attacking the basement. By 1990 the houses next door were ablaze.

17   Revolution from Below

Effervescence among the nationalities

The process of imperial disintegration was, in retrospect, remarkably non-violent. Most of the hostilities occurred in Transcaucasia, in the course of inter-ethnic feuding rather than an onslaught by minorities on the central power. In Central Asia local political élites slipped unobtrusively into the driving seat and appeased the citizenry by turning the wheel a little to the left. Serious fighting would break out here too—in Tajikistan—but only after the USSR had collapsed. The region that took the lead, as close students of nationality affairs predicted, was the Baltic, with first Estonia and then Lithuania to the forefront. From the north-west, and from Moldova in the south-west, disaffection spread to the Slav republics: Ukraine, Belarus—and Russia herself, where a nationalist resurgence was stimulated by events in the 'borderlands' that seemed to threaten Russian residents there. The smaller peoples, notably Crimean Tatars but also Ossetians, Chechens, Ingush, Abkhazians, and even Yakuts, added their contribution to the imbroglio. All the protagonists had in mind the precedents in Eastern Europe, where in 1989 Moscow gave up control over one after another of the former 'satellite' states that it had dominated since the 1940s.

The collapse of Communist power along the empire's outer perimeter gave a fillip to minority activists throughout the USSR. The amount of popular support they could garner varied greatly. Some ethnic groups in the Caucasus achieved near-total mobilization. Elsewhere agitation might be confined to the intelligentsia, and the local *nomenklatura* manage to keep control of the 'popular fronts' that emerged. These fronts were coalitions of activist groups that often called themselves parties, although until democratic structures had been built the term was inappropriate. Republican parliaments (Supreme Soviets) achieved authenticity by fresh elections on democratic lines and came into their own as means of legitimating new centres of regional power.

Moscow did its best to contain the ferment, sometimes resorting to violent measures of repression—as in Tbilisi in April 1989, Baku in January 1990, and Vilnius in January 1991—but also by engaging in dialogue. Policy often had to be improvised 'on the hoof'. Gorbachev, who had made his career in a region where ethnic tensions were not particularly marked, underestimated their explosive potential—as he later implicitly acknowledged. A rationalist, he assumed too readily that national animosities could be defused by socio-economic progress. As late as November 1987, when it was 'already clear that the national question was a volcano that might erupt at any time', he was uttering soothing statements to the effect that the problem had essentially been solved but needed review by experts (Friedgut 1992). In P. A. Goble's view (1990) he suffered from 'ethnic blindness', as evidenced by the policy of appointing Russians to replace errant native leaders in the union-republic parties.

It was one such 'exchange of cadres' in Kazakhstan—of Kunaev, a Kazakh, by Kolbin, a Russian, in December 1986—that prompted the first serious trouble. Kazakh students marched in protest. They destroyed, among other 'imperial' symbols, a bust of the late Brezhnev. Nine demonstrators were killed, five hundred arrested. Crowds demanded the latter's release, cars were set on fire, and seventeen more people met their death, including three policemen; several dozen were injured. Protests were staged in sympathy in several other places (Taheri 1990). A commission of inquiry was set up but its report was not made public. Despite this ominous warning the proportion of non-Russians in leading Party bodies tended to decline during the early years of *perestroika*. It is difficult to avoid the conclusion that the new leader, preoccupied with what he saw as far more substantial issues, displayed a remarkable degree of complacency.

Armenia versus Azerbaijan

Gorbachev was not alone in this. Western experts, too, had to consult their reference books when disorders broke out in the Nagornyi Karabakh autonomous region (NKAO). Of the 200,000 inhabitants of this 4,400 square kilometre mountainous area 90 per cent were Armenians, but Stalin had placed it under Azerbaijani control. It was in practice administered from Baku, treated as a colony, and neglected in the provision of electric power, roads, and social services. Azerbaijani nationalists and Islamic extremists looked with suspicion on the Christian Armenians living in their republic, who were half a million strong. These feelings were reciprocated across the border. There were far fewer Azeris in Armenia, but their birth rate was twice as high as that of the titular nationality. Patriotic activists kept alive memories of outrages suffered long ago at Moslem hands. *Glasnost'* allowed the Armenian Unified National party to emerge from the shadows and build up a flexible organization with considerable popular support. Its propaganda focused on the return of the NKAO to the 'motherland'. In January 1988 violence broke out in its capital, Stepanakert. Azeri mobs responded by staging a *pogrom* of Armenian residents in Sumgait, near Baku. According to official figures 90 people were killed and 1,500 injured. Armenians put the toll much higher. Hundreds of thousands fled. Azeris in Armenia, no longer feeling secure, followed their example. By February 1990 the total number of refugees was estimated at half a million.

In both republics rallies drew vast crowds and political organizations proliferated. The dispute ranged the Party and government leaderships of the two republics against each other. Moscow attempted to bring about a negotiated settlement, but neither protagonist was in a mood to listen. Extra troops were introduced, above all to guard communications, but often the soldiers lost or surrendered their weapons to irregular militia bands. Armenian guerillas established armed camps in the NKAO and exchanged sporadic gunfire with Azerbaijani and Russian soldiers. The disputed region was placed under a 'special administrative regime', but this proved ineffective. After it was done away with in November 1989 violence escalated, and soon both sides were using heavy weapons and aircraft. Azerbaijan set up its own internal security force and imposed a blockade on Armenia which caused much suffering, especially as it came on the heels of a disastrous earthquake. One in six of the population was rendered homeless.

In September 1989 the Azerbaijani government, putting national interests ahead of Party loyalty,[1] passed a law declaring the disputed region an inviolable part of its own territory and threatened to exercise its constitutional right to secede from the Union if it were forced to surrender control. The Communists were under strong pressure from a popular front which made the achievement of national sovereignty its prime objective. To demonstrate their determination patriotic activists seized control of the city of Lenkoran (January 1990) and there were further *pogroms*. But when Soviet armed forces tried to restore order in Baku they encountered stiff opposition. Fighting broke out in which 125 people were killed. The funeral of the victims attracted a crowd of more than one million. A new Party leader, Mutalibov, took over. Lacking authentic popular support, he had to play along with the nationalists. By the end of the year Azerbaijan was to all intents and purposes independent. In symbolic recognition of this fact, its parliament voted to drop the terms 'Soviet' and 'socialist' from the republic's title and to adopt a new flag and anthem.

A local *ayatollah*, Pasha-Zadeh, preached 'holy war' against the infidels, but few listened. Azerbaijani nationalism was pre-eminently a secular phenomenon. So, too, was that of its principal antagonist. Armenian patriots enjoyed the active support of the national Church and, even more important, of the diaspora, which provided funds and (presumably) arms. At first the initiative lay with a 'Karabakh committee' under L. Ter-Petrosian. Since Moscow (and Baku) clung to the principle that inter-republic frontiers were inviolable, it proposed that the NKAO's status should be elevated to that of a union-republic. But the idea of '*two* Armenias' was even less acceptable to the Azeris or the Russians. The latter summarily arrested and deported the committee's leaders, so giving them martyrs' auras. Vast crowds demanded their return—and full national sovereignty to boot. In December 1989 Armenia followed Azerbaijan's example by declaring the NKAO part of its territory.

Mutual intransigence doomed an effort by the USSR Supreme Soviet, at a closed session four months later, to engineer a political compromise. Each side to the dispute suspected Moscow of showing partiality to the other. On this point the Armenians may have had a slightly better case, since the central authorities' position on border changes was indeed legalistic. But this had good grounds: if they conceded the principle that a territory's administrative status should be determined solely by its ethnic make-up, scarcely any border in the Union would remain unchallenged. In August 1990 Ter-Petrosian, now released, was elected chairman of the Armenian parliament and *de facto* national leader. He had much greater support than the (non-elected) local Party chief. The main political force was now the Armenian Pan-National Movement (as it styled itself). As parliament debated the sovereignty issue a national army took shape. Antagonism mounted towards Moscow, which was blamed for the continuing hostilities with Azerbaijan. In March 1991 Armenia refused to join in holding an all-Union referendum to approve 'federalization' of the USSR. Instead it decided to hold a referendum of its own to endorse secession. Hitherto the constitutional right to secede from the USSR had been a mere fiction. But a law of April 1990 laid down a complicated and time-consuming procedure whereby this right could be exercised. Armenians reckoned that their republic, being ethnically the most homogeneous, could afford to be the first to put it to the test. In the event, however, this proved unnecessary, since the *coup* of August 1991 (see below, p. 400) created a totally new situation in which Armenia could simply declare itself independent without fear of the consequences (September 1991).

Alas, few of its citizens had cause to celebrate. By this time the battles in the NKAO had escalated to the level of all-out war—a war which Armenia then looked like losing. Coupled with economic breakdown and social distress, this created a mood of frustration and fractured the tenuous political consensus that had hitherto prevailed.

Georgia

Equally unstable, as it turned out, was unity among Georgians, although for a different reason. Many outside observers had thought that with modernization local ethnic particularisms had been subsumed in common allegiance to a single Georgian nation. However, this view was shown to be too sanguine. At first, to be sure, Georgians stood united in opposition to the imperial power. Patriotic societies were set up, named for historic national figures such as Il'ia Chavchavadze (1987) and Shota Rustaveli (1988), which pursued both cultural and political goals. The former body was more active and soon generated a splinter group, the National Democratic party, which openly called for secession. During 1988 many noisy meetings, demonstrations, and strikes were staged in the capital, Tbilisi, and other towns to protest proposed amendments to the Constitution which seemed to threaten greater centralization. Demands for independence featured prominently on the banners carried by participants. In February 1989, on the anniversary of the republic's forcible annexation in 1921, there were further massive protests. Yet two months later the ambiguous character of Georgian nationalism manifested itself. The 100,000 demonstrators who gathered in front of Party and government headquarters demanded not just independence for Georgia but the full integration into their state of Abkhazia, a region in the north-west that had autonomous republic status. Sauce for the goose was clearly not sauce for the gander.

The point here was the ethnic 'mix'. A majority (46 per cent) of the population in the Abkhazian ASSR consisted of Georgians. Russians and Armenians each comprised 14–15 per cent, whereas the titular nationality accounted for a mere 18 per cent. As seen from Tbilisi, Abkhazian autonomy was therefore 'artificial', a privilege conferred illegitimately by the 'Centre', with which the Abkhazians were suspected of colluding to the detriment of Georgia's interests, and for which they were rewarded *inter alia* by over-representation in well-paid jobs (S. F. Jones 1992). This raised the whole problem of the relative rights of smaller peoples *vis-à-vis* more powerful neighbours in ethnically stratified regions. Successive Soviet constitutions had 'solved' it by setting up an intricate hierarchy of administrative units while simultaneously reserving real power to the centralized Party. In a democratic system there was no place for such a subtle (or nefarious, according to one's viewpoint) device. In default of an agreed objective criterion to measure qualifications for statehood, answers were likely to be arrived at by the gun.

It was, however, not Abkhazians but Georgians who were the victims when, on 9 April 1989, Interior ministry troops opened fire on a crowd of peaceful (largely female) demonstrators in Tbilisi, killing nineteen and injuring between three and four thousand, five hundred of whom were taken to hospital. Of 290 people 'traumatized', twenty-one individuals (including some women) were struck by soldiers wielding shovels—as an unofficial video recording showed—and others by truncheons. Some three hundred of the injured were asphyxiated by poison gas.[2] There had been nothing like this since Novocherkassk in 1962. The massacre caused an uproar, not confined to Georgia. Many believed that the shootings had been ordered by conservatives in the Politburo, or even by

Gorbachev (who was abroad at the time and protested his innocence). The Georgian Party's first secretary, Patiashvili, resigned and was replaced by an ex-head of the local KGB, Gumbaridze. The appointment was hardly calculated to appease the indignant local population, whose emotions were kept at fever pitch by inspired leaks and mutual accusations of incompetence.

Worse violence was yet to come. In July twenty-two people, two-thirds of them Georgian, were killed in raids on police stations in Abkhazia, which the public in Tbilisi suspected of having been staged with official (i.e. Russo-Abkhaz) connivance. Georgian writers demanded national sovereignty (within a reformed USSR), which *inter alia* meant that union-republic law should have precedence over all-Union legislation. Georgia was to have an army of its own, to be deployed exclusively within the republic's borders. The latter demand was naturally enough popular with conscripts. As in other parts of the Union, they refused to report for duty when called up. These proposals were endorsed by the principal political groups and then, in November, by the Georgian parliament. Here, too, symbols were important. That winter statues of Lenin—there were few left of Stalin!—came tumbling down all over the republic. A 'national forum' in May 1990, attended by 6,200 delegates, voted to set up a coalition government and to initiate talks with Moscow on secession.

Some of the moderates present argued that the first task should be to set up a functioning democracy, with a clear popular mandate, before seeking to realize ultimate national goals. The radical nationalist majority, however, had a different agenda. Under the leadership of Zviad Gamsakhurdia, a former dissident who had been victimized under Brezhnev, Georgia's political élite drifted into confrontation with another ethnic group, the (southern) Ossetians. The leaders of this 60,000-strong community on the southern flank of the Caucasus wanted to join their more numerous co-nationals in the North Ossetian autonomous republic, which was part of the RSFSR. As a first step they declared their republic sovereign, i.e. independent of Georgia (August 1990). To zealots in Tbilisi this was further proof that Georgia's minorities were being manipulated by Moscow. The declaration was promptly annulled by the Georgian Supreme Soviet. South Ossetia's autonomous status was revoked, a state of emergency declared, and Georgian troops sent in. Fighting broke out in which Soviet (Russian) units, sent there to keep the peace, sometimes became embroiled. Thousands more fled their homes, swelling the hordes of refugees. This conflict, like that in Abkhazia, would simmer on for years.

No less than thirty-four parties put up candidates for Georgia's first free elections, held early in October 1990. The victor was Gamsakhurdia's 'Round Table/Free Georgia', an unstable coalition which, after several run-off contests, ended up with 54 per cent of the seats in the new legislature. This body promptly called for the full restoration of national sovereignty. In an ensuing referendum 98.9 per cent of those polling favoured independence, which was formally declared on 9 April 1991—two years to the day since the Tbilisi massacre. Unfortunately the new regime failed to justify its democratic supporters' hopes. It took an intransigently chauvinistic line, declaring Georgian the sole official language, threatening awkward journalists, and arbitrarily dismissing local officials. Before long not just Abkhazians or Ossetians but Georgians, too, were venting dissatisfaction. J. Ioseliani, the head of the national militia (Mkhedroni)—little better than bandits, as some thought—denounced the country's new regime as 'Fascist'. This was a polemical exaggeration, to be sure, but it expressed the popular mood, which was one of latent violence. In August 1991 25,000 militiamen raised the standard of revolt and the country sank into chaos. In many cases the only distinction between the contending groups was ethnic or clan affiliation, much as it had been centuries earlier. Tragically, although Georgia had enjoyed three years of precarious independence between 1918 and 1921, its experiences under Soviet rule had not favoured the development of a modern political culture.

Central Asia

This was less true of Central Asia, where modernization had created viable national élites, even though here, too, old clan allegiances were still in evidence. They accounted for mafia-like behaviour and the favouring of kinsmen when appointments were made. However, it would be just as misleading to exaggerate the strength of these bonds as it would be to overstress religious ones. The Islamic renascence was a fact, but it did not lead, as some feared (or hoped), to a fundamentalist triumph. Tajikistan, close to Iran geographically and ethnically, was the only republic where a politicized Islam became a major factor. Late in 1989 young zealots in the Kulab district who had embraced the Wahhabi sect clashed with older believers. There was also some infiltration by *mujaheddin* from nearby Afghanistan, where the unfortunate Soviet intervention ended in February 1989 with the withdrawal of the last troops. After Tajikistan gained its independence in 1991, this conflict would remain a serious problem, but the Islamic victory proved ephemeral.

Elsewhere in Central Asia it was even easier for the secularized élite to retain power, adapting smoothly to new conditions. One reason for this moderation was economic. All these republics were dependent on subsidies from the centre. Their leaders wanted them to continue, however much they might object to specific investment decisions, the scarcity of consumer goods, or restrictions on private activity. Another reason was psychological. High birth rates and the tenacity of native culture gave local élites a sense of security *vis-à-vis* the imperial power. Thus they were able to press ahead with measures to increase the proportion of natives in the administration, 'indigenize' cultural offerings, and promote use of the local idiom in schools. In Uzbekistan newspapers printed lists of recommended non-Slavic words and told readers how to write in Arabic script, which until recently had been banned (Critchlow 1990). Many Russian residents were alienated by these policies and decided to leave. In the first nine months of 1990 177,000 quit Uzbekistan alone. Soon the trickle of emigrants became a flood. In Turkmenistan, for example, measures were taken to stem it lest the republic suffer the loss of too many qualified personnel.

Making Uzbek the official language was one of the principal demands advanced in Uzbekistan by 'Unity' (*Birlik*), a civic body formed towards the end of 1988. As elsewhere, cultural and economic concerns at first loomed large, along with ecological ones. Kazakhs demanded an end to nuclear weapon tests in their republic and made contact with Green activists elsewhere with the same problem, notably in the Arctic (Novaia Zemlia, a major proving-ground, experienced environmental destruction on an even more catastrophic scale)—and Nevada. (This movement took the name 'Nevada-Semipalatinsk'.) In February 1990 *Birlik* gave birth to the more expressly political movement 'Independence' (*Erk*). It sought to achieve its ends through the existing institutional structure rather than by mobilizing public opinion (Ro'i 1992). In each of the Central Asian republics opposition parties were relatively weak.

Their support seldom extended far beyond the intelligentsia. Frequently their activities were harassed by the establishment, which controlled the local legislature (and, of course, the police).

Acts of violence were much rarer than in Transcaucasia. They were chiefly directed against 'outsiders', which suggests that at the grass-roots level political culture was still fairly primitive. One Western scholar characterizes these outbreaks as 'anomic [or] quasi-organized, often with an economic as well as a nationality component' (Connor 1992). That is to say, simple people were often jealous of what they perceived as privileges enjoyed by alien neighbours. As in many other poor communities, rumours spread quickly and mobs acted on impulse. There were two major clashes. In June 1989 Uzbeks in the over-populated Fergana valley attacked Meskhetians whom they blamed for charging excessively high prices for fruit.[3] The death toll was officially put at 105, the number of injured at 1,011, but higher figures circulated. Over 60,000 Meskhetians had to be hastily evacuated. (Shortly afterwards, evidently in emulation, Kazakhs at Novyi Uzen' attacked Chechens and others of Caucasian origin.) The second major incident, just one year later, occurred in the Osh region of Kyrgyzstan, in another part of the Fergana valley. It ranged Kyrgyz against members of the local Uzbek minority and had its origin in local rivalries over land rights and jobs. The toll was given as 230 killed, 400 missing, and 4,000 injured.

By this time many local Party chiefs, emulating Gorbachev, had managed to have themselves chosen as President by the local legislature. The first to do so was I. A. Karimov in Uzbekistan (March 1990). He advocated close links with Russia in a USSR reconstituted as a confederation of sovereign republics. He was less of a centralist than Gorbachev—each member-state was to have veto rights—but was seen as an appeaser by some nationally conscious Uzbeks (Critchlow 1991). In April V. Nazarbaev, Kazakh Party chief since 1989, was elected President of that republic. As was only natural in view of the large Slav element in the population, he likewise took a moderate line. Yet he was much more than a Moscow puppet. The Kazakhs held several trump cards: their republic's vast size, its rich agricultural and mineral resources, and its strategic location between Russia and China. By October 1990 the legislature had adopted a sovereignty declaration with the usual provision on legal precedence. This step had previously been taken by Kyrgyzstan, Tajikistan, and Turkmenistan. It was a logical move on the road towards independence. This came more rapidly than anyone expected just one year later, after the failed *putsch*.

The case of Kyrgyzstan is special in that its President, A. Akaev, was a respected physicist (indeed, the head of the local Academy of Sciences), rather than the local Party boss. The latter, Masaliev, had a well-earned reputation as a pro-Russian conservative which cost him his job (April 1991). In its so-called 'silk revolution' (B. Brown 1991) Kyrgyzstan purged its official title of the terms 'Soviet' and 'socialist' and successfully steered an intermediate course between the Scylla of submissiveness to the 'Centre' and the Charybdis of provoking it. As in Kazakhstan, restraint was dictated by consideration for the interests of the republic's sizeable cohort of Russian residents, while the republic's economic resources and strategic situation made forward moves possible. Once independence had been won, these two republics would take the lead in opening up Central Asia to Western trade and investment and privatizing (or quasi-privatizing) the economy. Their policies might not satisfy advocates of democracy and civil rights (or Islamic zealots either), but did at least bring a modicum of stability. Judged by the criterion of *Realpolitik*, they made good sense.

The Baltic states

Patriotic activists throughout the USSR drew inspiration from the three Baltic republics, where conditions were most favourable for an assertion of national claims. In each of them the native population was united and aware of its historic traditions (which included, of course, over twenty years of independence). They generated several statesmanlike leaders (A. Rüütel and V. Landsbergis, to name but two)—convinced democrats and capable negotiators who combined flexibility with firmness. The best proof of their sagacity was their success in winning over to their cause large segments of the Russian minorities in their republics as well as elements within the communist establishment. In 1989–90 all three ruling parties split off from the CPSU, leaving loyalist rumps whose support was confined to extremists among the resident Slavic population. There were some extremists in the nationalist camp, too, but they had relatively little influence within the popular fronts—broad

coalitions which brought together people of the most varied backgrounds in the common cause. The most impressive demonstration
of their strength was on 23 August 1989, the fiftieth anniversary of
the Hitler–Stalin pact that had led to the republics' annexation.
Over one million Balts linked hands in a human chain that extended
from Tallinn through Riga to Vilnius. The three nations had
previously set up a Baltic Council to co-ordinate their activities. It
acquired solid support among parliamentary deputies of all three
countries.

The Baltic renascence began in Liepaja (Latvia) in the autumn of
1986 when a group of workers set up a human rights organization,
'Helsinki-86', which demanded *inter alia* the restoration of cultural
rights (notably use of the native language), an end to russification—
and the holding of a referendum on secession. Although not
repressed at once, the initiators were harassed and defamed in the
media. This had the effect of bringing their ideas to public attention, so that the group 'played an important role in catalysing
national political consciousness among the Latvian population'
(Levits 1990). So, too, did ecological concerns. The poet Arvids
Ulme headed a civic club for environmental protection which soon
began to put forward demands for political changes, since its
members realized that nothing useful could be done so long as all
important decisions were taken in Moscow.

The most powerful stimulus to action came from history. The
first major public demonstration in the entire Union since the 1960s
took place in Riga on 14 June 1987, when thousands gathered to
mark the anniversary of the mass deportation of Latvian citizens in
1941. Other rallies followed on 23 August and 18 November (the
date when independence had been declared in 1918). On the last
occasion there were street clashes, and sympathy demonstrations
were staged elsewhere in the Baltic. Estonian students at Tartu
university had taken up the environmentalist cause and also demanded greater economic autonomy.[4] Both these issues were connected with Russian immigration and so had political overtones.
The protesters went on to demand the resignation of K. Vaino, the
Party's first secretary, i.e. its 'Estonianization'. Remarkably, the
same line was taken by the editors of the local Party newspaper,
Edasi. The Party CC and government even issued a decree obliging
new immigrants to pay a sizeable fee (up to 16,000 roubles). Few
did so, but this showed the degree to which the political

establishment was willing to go along with the patriots' agenda. In the Baltic Communism was a more brittle phenomenon than it was in other minority republics.

Meanwhile in Lithuania the long-serving Griskevičius had died (November 1987). He was succeeded by an ineffective middle-of-the-roader, R. Songaila, who tried but failed to ban Lithuanian citizens from demonstrating on *their* Independence Day (16 February 1988). The 'national awakening' started later here, but in 1988 Lithuania rapidly moved to the vanguard. This was partly because patriots had less need to worry about Slavs in their midst. There was also a strong native element among the local Party cadres. These officials at first took a conciliatory stance, e.g. over the display of national symbols or the rewriting of history, reckoning that thereby they could channel the movement in an acceptable direction. Accordingly they joined with non-Communists in setting up a 'General Popular Front for *Perestroika*' (in Lithuanian: *Sajūdis*: 3 June 1988). Of its founding members nearly half belonged to the Lithuanian CP. *Sajūdis* organized mass rallies and quickly became the most influential political force. Such a body had previously been formed in Estonia (*Rahvarinne*, April); a Latvian one emerged in October. At the inaugural congress of *Sajūdis* in October 1988 no less than one thousand civic organizations were represented. At first it called only for greater autonomy, civil rights and so on; but under pressure from below its leaders, among them the musicologist Landsbergis, began to strike a more radical note. They were, however, careful not to press too openly for independence.

A competition developed between nationalists and Communists for control over the front. The former had the wind of popular favour in their sails. Their rivals were hamstrung by their past—and by contradictory signals emanating from Moscow. Reformers in the Soviet capital wanted the Lithuanian Party to seize the initiative by making timely concessions, while conservatives urged them to deal severely with manifestations of 'bourgeois' tendencies. Confusion was made worse by frequent changes in the local leadership. Songaila's successor in Lithuania, A. Brazauskas, showed greater skill in handling the democrats, with whom he had more in common than with the pro-Muscovites in his own party. In October 1989, at a plenum of the local CC, 97 members out of 111 effectively decided that their party should secede from the CPSU. Despite appeals and threats from Moscow, two months later their decision was upheld at an extraordinary congress by a large margin (855 : 160). The minority group took the title 'Lithuanian Representative Organization of the CPSU'; the majority adopted a new democratic programme and chose a fresh string of leaders under Brazauskas. In the Latvian party, by contrast, where the apparatus was more russified, the pro-independence faction found itself in a minority when the schism occurred (April 1990).

Sovereignty and confrontation

Meanwhile the republics' Supreme Soviets had been re-elected by democratic procedures and turned into authentic legislatures. They passed laws giving the local language official status (Latvia, October 1988; Estonia and Lithuania, January 1989) and restoring pre–Soviet national flags, anthems, and public holidays. The next step was the restoration of national sovereignty. The first to act was Estonia, which on 16 November 1988 unilaterally amended the republic's (Soviet) Constitution in a democratic sense. In doing so it made use of powers that had hitherto existed only on paper. This bold step was taken, amidst scenes of great popular enthusiasm, by leaders who were convinced that if Moscow implemented its own draft proposals, which had been published three weeks earlier, this would actually *curtail* the rights of the Union's member states. Accordingly the parliament in Tallinn proclaimed that henceforth Estonian legislation had precedence over Union law on its territory. The human-rights provisions contained in United Nations documents were written into the Estonian Constitution. Public organizations like the Popular Front were accorded constitutional rights, e.g. to nominate candidates for election. Last but not least, ownership of the republic's land, mineral resources, waterways, banks, state industries, etc. was vested in the Estonian state. This created the legal basis for later acts transferring ownership of state enterprises to co-operative or private firms, so facilitating transition to a market economy, as well as other laws on immigration, environmental protection, and so forth.

The Estonian legislature's action was promptly annulled by Moscow, but the republic's leaders refused to bend the knee. They knew that right was on their side, since the Soviet regime had been imposed by force and lacked legitimacy. The ensuing constitutional crisis took the form of a 'war of laws' that soon extended to other rebellious republics as well. In the Baltic region several months passed before Estonia's example was followed by Lithuania (18 May 1989)[5] and then by Latvia (28 July 1989). Thereafter the governments of both states, backed by legislatures in which popular fronts called the tune, pushed ahead with measures to liberalize cultural life and assert control over their respective economies. In the agrarian domain they worked towards a mixed system in which private homesteads would co-exist alongside collective and state farms.

The main obstacle to economic autonomy was the republics' dependence on energy imports from other parts of the Soviet Union (i.e. from Russia). This enabled the 'Centre' to exert pressure. It had another instrument to hand in the local associations set up in the winter of 1988–9 by Russians and other opponents of self-determination in the Baltic: an 'International Movement' (*Interdvizhenie*) in Estonia, an 'International Front' (*Interfront*) in Latvia, and a (much weaker) 'Unity' group in Lithuania. In the summer of 1989 40,000 workers in Estonia, mainly Slavic immigrants, came out on strike, with the active support of management, to protest alleged discrimination in the republic's new electoral law. The government compromised, freeing voters (but not candidates) from a residency requirement, but this failed to satisfy the incorrigibles. The local 'internationalists' had close ties with the military authorities, who were alarmed that so many conscript soldiers from the Baltic were refusing to report for duty. This issue led to friction with the local authorities, who gave the deserters covert backing. Some men joined militia bands; others were rounded up and often harshly treated. The climate grew more violent. By 1990 the Soviet authorities were resorting to acts of terrorism. These were carried out mainly by the KGB and military, aided by pro-Moscow Communists and fronts—as well as by some elements in the CPSU's central *apparat*, while its reformist leadership temporized.

On 11 March 1990 Lithuania unilaterally declared itself independent. Soviet tanks entered Vilnius, troops occupied government buildings and arrested alleged deserters—some of them hospital patients. But Gorbachev would not give the military their head. Concerned that outright repression in the Baltic would discredit *perestroika*, he declared that force would be used only if civilian lives were in danger (26 March). Instead Moscow applied pressure indirectly. In April deliveries of oil and gas were reduced. Lithuania had to ration food. Its leaders turned for support to the Western powers, but they were above all anxious not to jeopardize détente and urged a negotiated settlement. Reluctantly Vilnius agreed to suspend implementation of its independence declaration and entered into 'talks about talks' with Moscow on resuming co-operation. By late June tension had eased both in Lithuania and in Estonia, where in May *Interdvizhenie* activists had attempted what the premier, E. Savisaar, termed an 'armed *putsch*'. The Baltic states were fortunate in that they could exploit the 'dual power' that now existed in Moscow, where Boris Yeltsin, as elected Russian leader, had emerged as a more dangerous rival than ever to Gorbachev. Yeltsin gave the Balts verbal support, as did several Russian municipalities, including Leningrad. Friendly ties were established with neighbouring Belarus and other dissident republics.

The hard-liners were not to be assuaged. On 29 August 1990 the CC Secretariat secretly resolved on a *coup* to instal a pro-Moscow regime in Latvia, where the situation seemed most propitious to such a design. The functionary chiefly responsible, O. Shenin, apparently calculated that the war looming in the Persian Gulf would distract Western opinion. While the talks in Moscow continued, largely as diplomatic cover, the proponents of tough measures reviewed their strike force. On 17 November Colonel V. Alksnis, an officer of 'Russian Latvian' extraction, *Interfront* member and leader of the conservative 'Union' (*Soiuz*) faction in the all-Union legislature, secretly gave Gorbachev an ultimatum to 'restore order' in the country within one month. The President was now leaning heavily to the right (see below, p. 396). He seems to have given the plotters the impression either that he approved of their plans or that he would back them if the *coup* were successful. In December several bombs exploded mysteriously in Riga. In the event not Latvia but Lithuania was chosen as the principal target.

On 13 January 1991, two days before the Allied deadline in the Gulf expired, Soviet troops stormed a media centre in Vilnius, killing fourteen and injuring over 150 persons. A 'national salvation committee' announced that it was taking over. A similar committee was formed in Latvia, where on 20 January troops occupied the Interior ministry. Here there were six fatal casualties. Television watchers around the world saw civilian defenders of democracy being crushed to death beneath the tracks of Soviet tanks.

International outrage was not, however, the main reason why the *coup* failed. What doomed it was rather (i) the unexpectedly stiff resistance offered by the population—tens of thousands of Lithuanians were willing to risk their lives to protect their parliamentary institutions, and Yeltsin came to Estonia to denounce the attack in Russia's name; and (ii) Gorbachev's hesitations. He cancelled preparations for a similar *putsch* in Tallinn and then half-heartedly distanced himself from the violence in Vilnius and Riga. A characteristically ambiguous Politburo statement (16 January) expressed regret for the casualties—but blamed them on the Lithuanians!

Alksnis publicly blamed Gorbachev for 'losing his nerve' and claimed—plausibly—that his men had been betrayed. Liberal Russian opinion turned further against the President. Other republics became less willing to accept a new Union treaty. In March the Baltic states boycotted the Union-wide referendum on its underlying principle—and did not stand alone.[6] Instead the three nations voted massively in favour of independence. Russian residents joined in, too: in Riga, where only one-third of the city's population was Latvian, the affirmative vote was 60.7 per cent.[7]

Moldova

Developments in Moldova (as Moldavia became known in May 1990) resembled those in the Baltic, although there were analogies with the situation in Transcaucasia. To take the former first, opposition began over cultural, and especially linguistic, issues. To justify their annexation of the region in 1940, the Soviet authorities had insisted that the 'Moldavians' were a nationality distinct from the Romanians, with their own language, and to widen the differences between them had changed the alphabet from Latin to Cyrillic. These moves had always been unpopular. In 1989 the republic had 4.3 million inhabitants, 64.4 per cent of whom were 'Moldavians'; over one-quarter were Slavs (Ukrainians 13.8 per cent, Russians 12.9 per cent). The latter were mostly resident in the towns, but also in the industrialized district of Tiraspol' east of the Dniester.

The protest movement started in 1988 among intellectuals, whose main demands were that 'Moldavian' be recognized as the republic's official language and the Latin alphabet restored. A subsidiary motif at the time was historical. Kishinev students called for correction of the 'historical aberrations of Stalinism', i.e. for the truth to be told about the annexation. This logically entailed its formal repudiation and raised the prospect of possible merger with Romania. So long as that country groaned under Ceausescu's dictatorship, this option had very limited appeal. Even after that regime came to a sanguinary end (December 1989) most Moldovan leaders soft-pedalled this emotional issue, realizing that it would antagonize not just Moscow but local Russians as well. As in the Baltic, there were calls for a ban on (Slav) immigration. National symbols were displayed at mass rallies. Eighty thousand people are said to have attended one such gathering (25 June 1989) held to mark the annexation, which speakers described as 'the source of all our people's misfortunes'. Again as in the Baltic, Russian residents set up 'internationalist' organizations, went on strike, and staged counter-demonstrations which likewise attracted considerable popular support. But they could not match their opponents, who on 27 August assembled no less than a quarter of a million followers to ensure that the republic's legislature passed a language law in the sense they desired. On paper at least they were more successful in this than nationalists anywhere else in the Union, for both 'Moldovan' and Russian were declared 'languages of inter-ethnic communication'.

Thereafter developments in the republic began to emulate the Transcaucasian pattern. The multi-tiered ethnic stratification encouraged activists to resort to violence. In November 1989 Moldovans clashed with Russian residents. Troops were rushed in but themselves came under attack. Over two hundred were injured. Two areas of the republic where Moldovans were in a minority claimed autonomous status. During 1990 Russians in 'Trans-Dniestria' and also Turkic-speaking Gagauz in the south set up their own administrations backed by militia bands. Pitched battles broke out with Moldovans. General Lebed''s Fourteenth (Soviet) army, ostensibly present to keep the peace, gave the 'internationa-lists' covert support. M. Snegur, the (ex-)Communist chairman of the Moldovan legislature, and eventually President, manœuvred skilfully between the nationalists, who formed a popular front, and the Communists, who split. Under pressure by the former the government refused to take part in negotiations for a new Union treaty and instead forged direct links with other republics.

But internally Moldova was weak. Neither the self-styled democrats nor the Communists could assure the government solid support in the legislature. Party-political life became very confused, with individual functionaries wielding much power behind the scenes. Meanwhile the economy disintegrated. Privatization measures expanded the scope of the black market. In May 1991 parliament voted out the Popular Front government of M. Druc for alleged corruption, but characteristically his successor, V. Muravschi, drew support from the same political formation. In a state of latent civil war one could not expect an alternation of parties according to Westminster rules.

Belarus and Ukraine

The same picture obtained, *mutatis mutandis*, in the Slav republics, although the level of violence here was lower. The strength of Belarus nationalism came as something of a surprise, given the extent of russification. Its radicalization was in large part a response to Chernobyl, whose devastating effect on this republic gradually became clear—as did the extent of Stalinist terror in the region, once the mass graves at Kuropaty and elsewhere were dug up. 'Renewal' (*Adradzhenie*), a popular front-type association of civic bodies, was founded in June 1989, at a congress that had to be held in Vilnius because of obstruction by the local *nomenklatura*. The elections the next spring brought gains for the democrats, but they did not control the legislature. A resolution legalizing 'Renewal' failed by a single vote (May 1990). Two months later the balance of power had shifted in their favour. Parliament proclaimed Belarus a sovereign state, which was to have its own currency and armed forces. This was not, however, meant as a secessionist move. Unlike the Baltic states or Moldova, the republic's leaders wanted to remain within a reconstituted USSR. So, too, did 83 per cent of its population, to judge by the March 1991 referendum results—the highest proportion anywhere except in Central Asia. Given the republic's location, limited resources and general sorry state, this made much sense.

Ukrainians were deeply split on this issue. In the 1991 referendum 70.5 per cent of those voting endorsed the 'Centre' 's formula, but simultaneously 80.2 per cent backed a statement that the republic's future status should conform to the terms of the sovereignty declaration proclaimed the previous 16 July (one day before that of Belarus). This ambiguity, or 'centrism', had its roots in Ukraine's ethnic geography. As we know, the nationally conscious elements were concentrated in the west, while the east (Donbas) and south (Crimea) had large Russian populations, and it was politic not to offend them. As yet there was no marked tension between the two groups, and many Russian residents were willing to give the cause of Ukrainian sovereignty their support, on the understanding that difficulties would be resolved by peaceful dialogue. The Ukrainian national movement was more anti-Soviet (or anti-centralist) than anti-Russian—a state of affairs that reflected the two peoples' common cultural heritage. In 1988–9 it was expressed chiefly in a successful campaign to legalize the Uniate Church—a development eyed askance in Moscow ecclesiastical circles.

At this time the climate in Kiev was too chilly for the patriots to articulate far-reaching political demands. There was conspicuously less *glasnost'* in Ukraine than in Russia. A 'popular front to promote *perestroika*' had been formed as early as June 1987, and there were mass rallies in L'viv and other towns, but not until September 1989 could Ukraine's popular front, known simply as 'the Movement' (*Rukh*), hold its founding congress. Shcherbitsky's ouster later that month removed a major obstacle, but even so the front did not achieve legal status until the following February. The delay hindered it from scoring as well as its Baltic counterparts in the ensuing elections. *Rukh* took all 24 seats in L'viv and won a landslide victory in the western part of the republic. It also did well in Kiev (eighteen seats out of twenty-two), but in Khar'kov secured only one-third. Nevertheless, the front demonstrated an impressive ability to mobilize crowds. It emulated an earlier achievement of the Balts by forming a human chain from L'viv to Kiev, a distance of over five hundred kilometres.

The breakthrough came in the summer of 1990, when the Ukrainian CP, at its Twenty-eighth congress, reversed itself on the national issue and adopted a line close to that of *Rukh*. As in the Baltic, the *volte-face* can be seen as a tactic to outbid the nationalists, but in Ukraine it had greater success. For *Rukh* essentially took a middle-of-the-road line. This continued to be the case even after its second congress (October 1990), when it came out in favour of full independence. Its leadership was split. The moderate wing was represented by Leonid Kravchuk, who until recently, as a leading Party official in Kiev, had been a bitter foe of the nationalists. More radical were the veteran dissidents Ivan

Drach and Viacheslav Chornovil, whose political base lay in the west. Characteristic of Kravchuk's policy was a search for accommodation with the 'Centre', e.g. over the Union treaty or the potentially explosive issue of the Crimea, to which he (and the legislature) were willing to grant autonomous status. To fervent nationalists this smacked of appeasement at the expense of Ukraine's territorial integrity.

Nevertheless the situation was evolving rapidly, and contrary to all earlier expectations it was Ukraine, of all the rebellious republics, that would deal the final knife-thrust to the tottering USSR (see Chapter 18). From mid-1990 onwards there was a fatal weakness at the heart of the empire, symbolized by the Yeltsin–Gorbachev dyarchy. The conservative *coup* of August 1991 made it infinitely more difficult to keep the Union together. It was less the cause of the empire's disintegration than a symptom of the cancer that was eating it away. This had its origin in the inability of Communism, whether of the orthodox or the reformist variety, to contain centrifugal pressures that had been building up for decades.

18 Nemesis

Russian nationalism under Gorbachev

In Russia the national movement was bound to take a different form than it did in other union republics, where élites had a more readily identifiable common foe, usually although not invariably the 'imperial' power, against which they could rally popular support. Many Russians, too, felt that their nation's interests had been neglected under the existing dispensation, but for this they blamed not just the 'Centre' but also those minorities which, they believed, had derived an unfair advantage from the Soviet system. To this sense of grudge was added concern for the fate of their co-nationals in minority areas. Many of these expatriates—over 25 million, according to some calculations—had gone there unwillingly. Did they deserve to be seen as colonialist *pieds-noirs?* Whether employed as cadres or as simple workers and farmers (in Kazakhstan, for example), they had laboured for the common good. If abuses had been committed, surely the blame for them should be placed on the makers of imperial policy, not its executants? There should be no question of collective guilt.

This defensive psychology helps to explain the success of right-wing Russian nationalist groups in the late 1980s. This development needs to be seen in proportion. Democrats attracted far larger crowds than did patriotic 'extremists' (not all of whom were necessarily extreme). On the other hand, the political mood at the popular level was fluid and party affiliations unstable. Few self-styled democrats advocated free-market 'capitalism', although logically economic liberalism should have gone hand in hand with its political counterpart. As social conditions deteriorated, many who considered themselves to be on the left would drift rightward (to use conventional labels that were no longer very appropriate). Where democratic and national values clashed, the latter might well prove stronger in the long run. But during the years 1989–91, which are our concern here, the former prevailed. Given the relative weakness of Russia's democratic traditions, it was remarkable that so many people should have endorsed the ideals of self-government, the rule of law, and respect for human rights. This was largely an achievement of the dissent movement. Sakharov's funeral in December 1989 was an occasion for a nation-wide display of genuine grief, mingled with fear lest the precarious liberties so recently won might be equally speedily snuffed out.

The political scene in Russia (RSFSR) had four main distinguishing characteristics. First, the various groups and parties did not combine into a single umbrella organization analogous to *Sajūdis* or *Rukh*. They did form local alliances, as well as coalitions ('blocs') for electoral purposes, and these scored significant successes, but they proved to be ephemeral. Second, the 'fractions' that emerged in the several parliamentary chambers were not well matched to equivalent formations active among the population at large. Third, parties (or 'proto-parties', to be more precise) tended to coalesce around prominent individuals, whose shifting personal relationships led to frequent realignments and splits, rather than around specific ideas or programmes. The public mood was much less ideological than it had been in, say, 1917–22. Fourth, some political groupings did not arise spontaneously but owed their origins to covert machinations within the Party and/or KGB establishment, which have yet to be satisfactorily clarified. These four features were by no means exclusive to Russia, but in combination they acquire considerable weight.

The Right

At the right end of the political spectrum an important role was played by *Pamiat'* (Memory)—not to be confused with Memorial (see Chapter 16). 'It originated . . . as an action group of those concerned about protection of the environment and historical monuments' (Hosking 1990), and from 1986 onward became increasingly chauvinistic, even anti-Semitic. Its leaders were better at identifying negative targets than at defining positive aims. Activists (sometimes called 'warriors') sent threatening letters to prominent reformers such as Yakovlev, Zaslavskaia, or Vitalii Korotich, editor of *Ogonek*, whom they accused of promoting 'cosmopolitan' ideas, and spread propaganda by *samizdat* methods. Nationalists strongly supported the temperance movement, both on principle and because it gave them a chance to establish a mass base. So too, did the societies united under VOOPIK, which came under *Pamiat'*'s control in April 1987.

Soon its influence extended beyond the Moscow and Leningrad metropolitan areas. Groups appeared in Novosibirsk, Sverdlovsk and other provincial towns, as well as in some minority regions. *Pamiat'* was the first political group to hold a public demonstration on Moscow's Red Square (December 1989). Shortly afterwards a gang of anti-Semites under K. Smirnov-Ostashvili achieved notoriety by breaking up a meeting in the Central House of Writers, which earned their leader a sentence of two years in a camp on a charge of inciting racial hatred.

The price of success was fragmentation. *Pamiat'* split into no less than nine factions, loosely grouped into two 'streams'—yet, according to a KGB spokesman, had only about a thousand members (Dunlop 1990). It did not, however, stand alone. A Slavic Literary Fund headed by Rasputin and Bondarev claimed eighty associated organizations, the United Council of Russia three hundred. This was the body that most strongly backed 'internationalist' organizations in the Baltic, Moldova and elsewhere. More moderate were the 'Christian Renaissance' group led by V. Osipov, which comprised only (!) two factions—presumably because it was so small—and A. Ogorodnikov's Christian Democratic Union. Cossacks and monarchists added an exotic touch to the Russian right.

All these groups were opposed to market economics, democracy, and the West in general. As regards the merits of Soviet-style socialism, they were ambivalent. Veniamin Yavin set up a United Russian Workers' Front in Leningrad that appealed to (ex-)Communists. Yurii Prokushev, of the 'Unity' group, pointed proudly to the achievements of the Soviet 1930s, as a counterbalance to current denunciations of Stalinism, and many others hailed Russia's pre- and post-revolutionary military traditions. Alexander Rutskoi, a twice-wounded Afghan War veteran, was among several senior officers represented in the 'Fatherland' (*Otechestvo*) society, formed in March 1989. He would soon achieve prominence as Russia's Vice-president, first an ally and then a bitter foe of Yeltsin. In the March 1990 elections the left-conservatives performed poorly, but they had weight in the all-Union parliament, where *Soiuz* was the fastest growing fraction, as well as in the army, KGB, and the higher reaches of industrial management. For tactical reasons senior officials in large firms, which depended on state subsidies, often preferred to adopt a 'centrist' label.

The democratic Left

On the left (in the Western sense) or liberal side the first major grouping was the Democratic Union, formed in May 1988. It had a loose structure and initially at least rejected any co-operation with the CPSU. It refused to take part in the 1989 or 1990 elections and instead was active in organizing popular demonstrations. (An estimated 6.4 million people took part in rallies in the first two months of 1990 alone: Karklins 1994.) These demonstrations were sometimes broken up by the police and those responsible for them arrested. Less radical was the Democratic Party of Russia (DPR), founded in May 1990. It was headed by Nikolai Travkin, an engineer and 'a power-conscious politician who ran a tight ship' (Simon 1993), assisted by the chess champion Kasparov and Yeltsin's future aide Burbulis. By the summer of 1991 it had some 35,000 members and commanded roughly 30 per cent of the votes. Although its leaders were former Communists, they 'supported a market economy based on private property and the convocation of a Constituent Assembly which would make a clean break with the Soviet past' (White, Gill, and Slider 1993).

Presumably in order to confuse the electorate, unidentified members of the establishment (no doubt KGB officers) set up a Liberal Democratic party which had no claim whatever to such a title (Wishnevsky 1990). It formed a 'Centrist Bloc' with other mysterious parties hitherto unknown to the public. Early in 1991 this bloc gave its blessing to the 'national salvation committees' in the Baltic and evidently was working towards a similar *coup* in Moscow as well. Soon thereafter the bloc faded from the scene, but the LDP would survive the USSR's collapse and achieve world-wide notoriety at the end of 1993.

Genuine democratic parties included Christian, Constitutional, and Social Democrats. The first of these was split between a 'union' and a 'movement', neither of which, however, enjoyed broad support. The second, the liberal CDs, explicitly identified themselves with their pre-revolutionary Kadet forerunners, whereas the SDs avoided too close an association with Menshevism, which they saw as too Marxist in ideology (and perhaps as one of history's lost causes). Most of these parties joined the DPR and others in forming the 'Democratic Russia' electoral bloc, which did quite well in the 1990 elections, although they did not control any of the new parliamentary bodies, even at the level of the RSFSR. Indeed, how could they hope to do so unless they united into a single powerful opposition party? Electoral blocs were essentially city- or province-wide coalitions, such as Moscow's 'Elections-90'. Parliamentary politics in the RSFSR had an unreal character, for the party that mattered most in the legislature, and in public life generally, was that strange animal, the *Russian* CP.

The Russian CP

In theory this was as 'independent' of the CPSU as the Communist parties in other union republics, which of course could look back on a longer history. The RCP seems to have been the brainchild of a leading left-conservative functionary in Leningrad, B. V. Gidaspov, and was, so to speak, an extension of the anti-reform faction within the CPSU. Another sponsor was the Leningrad United Russian Workers' Front. At its initial conference in April 1990 there were calls on Gorbachev, Yakovlev (and even Ligachev!) to resign. Gorbachev tried to delay its inaugural congress (June), but then took the chair at it. He had to listen to bitter attacks for having allowed the initiative to pass to 'revisionists' and other foes. '*Perestroika* is counter-revolution', declared one delegate roundly. Yeltsin came to Gorbachev's defence, but his nominee for the post of first secretary was defeated in the ballot by the conservative candidate, Polozkov of Krasnodar, who later succeeded Ligachev as leader of the reactionaries in the parent party. A resolution was passed pledging loyalty to 'time-tested Marxist-Leninist ideas', but another one called for a 'regulated market economy'. The contradiction was suggestive. The new party had to give at least an appearance of willingness to move with the times. It was more of a nuisance factor than a serious menace, strong enough to obstruct reform bills in the new Russian legislature[1] but not to unseat either Yeltsin or Gorbachev.

Yeltsin versus Gorbachev

At its first session (16 May–22 June 1990) the RSFSR Congress of People's Deputies voted in favour of national sovereignty, i.e.

Russian law was to have precedence over that of the Union. This was the heart of Yeltsin's programme. On 29 May he narrowly (535 : 467) defeated his main conservative rival, A. Vlasov, in the third ballot in a race for chairmanship of the Supreme Soviet. This was effectively the most important post in the republic. The prime minister, Silaev, was not Yeltsin's choice but by and large the government reflected his preferences. Parliament, too, reluctantly followed his lead. It served as backdrop to a 'clash of titans' (Rahr) in which Yeltsin and Gorbachev confronted one another over a whole range of issues.

An element of personal vendetta was involved, although this was not the most essential point. The two men were divided by temperament and style as well as ideology. Gorbachev, though intellectually superior to his rival, remained a Communist at heart. 'The socialist option', he averred, was irreversible. Yeltsin was pledged to the introduction of parliamentary democracy and a market economy. Gorbachev wanted to strengthen the USSR by recasting it on federal (but not confederal) lines. This meant that the central government would continue to wield considerable power, as would the planning agencies; private property was to be permitted, but was not to become dominant. Non-Communist parties should be allowed to operate, but the tone of political discourse would be set by a (reunited) CPSU. For Yeltsin this was to perpetuate the rule of the *apparat*. Angry and combative, he sought to *split* the all-Union Party, to win over the reformists to the democratic camp, and to nationalize (i.e. confiscate) the Party's property. On 12 July he shocked fellow delegates to the CPSU's Twenty-eighth Congress by demonstratively announcing his resignation. He invited Gorbachev to do the same so that they might both concentrate on their government jobs. Yeltsin was willing to tolerate the Party's continued existence, but only if it democratized itself (changing its name in the process) and gave up its behind-the-scenes role in government. 'Primary Party organizations in the army, the security organs and state agencies must be abolished, while in industry their fate should be determined by workers' collectives . . . ' (cited from Dobrokhotov 1992).

The future Union, in Yeltsin's view, was to be a loose confederation of independent sovereign states. The 'Centre' would have only minimal power to co-ordinate defence and foreign policy, so that it would in effect exist at the republics' sufferance. The KGB was to be recast as an organization to protect human rights: 'only in that way can one destroy this monster, which has terrorized and crushed everyone in our country for more than seventy years.' This was said to the Latvians on 3 August; by the year's end he would be speaking of the need to set up a Russian army. This was rank heresy in the eyes of Gorbachev, for whom united armed forces were essential to defend the future Union's security (15 November), and whose dwindling power depended increasingly on the support of loyalists in the KGB. Yeltsin was willing to discuss a new Union treaty, but refused to sign any such document until the 'Centre' explicitly recognized Russia's sovereignty and agreed to devolve power to the republics along the lines he had suggested.

In the meantime the RSFSR sought to strengthen its relations with other members of the emerging community of post-Soviet states. It was party to a plethora of 'horizontal' treaties. Gorbachev refused to yield on devolution and responded to Yeltsin's 'offensive'—or so his rival alleged—by stirring up Russia's own minority peoples (Yakuts, Chechens, Bashkirs, etc.), which began to demand the same degree of sovereignty at Russia's expense that she was demanding from the Union. To be sure, these national aspirations did not need much external stimulation. They developed spontaneously. However, the declarations of sovereignty passed by the soviets of these autonomous republics (and even by some *Russian* towns and provinces!) weakened Yeltsin's position. To parry the threat, he toured the country trying to persuade local leaders to accept his viewpoint, but met with only intermittent success: *l'appetit vient en mangeant*.

In the economic sphere the two leaders were not as far apart as they seemed to be from their rhetorical exchanges. At issue was less the direction of reform than its pace. Yeltsin did not disdain to stoop to demagogy, as when he criticized the central government for authorizing price rises that were an integral part of the 'marketization' that he himself supposedly favoured, or threatened to reduce drastically revenue payments to the all-Union budget. He complained of accelerating inflation, yet this stemmed in part from costly measures to protect the socially disadvantaged, or to maintain industrial subsidies, that his own government had passed. By the autumn Yeltsin was blaming his rival for the crisis: had he not first agreed to 'stabilization' plans worked out by leading economists and then reneged on them under pressure from

Ryzhkov and other conservatives? The charge was not groundless, as we shall see in a moment, but it obscured Yeltsin's own lukewarmness towards privatization and other radical 'shock therapy' measures. The harsh truth was that *neither* Gorbachev's advisers *nor* Yeltsin's could offer practical solutions to the problems created by the breakdown of the command economy.

Politically, the dyarchy in Moscow weakened both protagonists. Public opinion surveys showed that Yeltsin had a higher approval rating than Gorbachev (whose score fell from 52 per cent in December 1989 to 21 per cent in October 1990). However, such polls did not register the disillusionment that was rapidly spreading among the populace. Ordinary folk resented the fact that their leaders were engrossed in a partisan struggle of no apparent relevance to the masses' worsening plight. This mood could only benefit extremists. In the short term it led Gorbachev to make a tactical shift to the right—with fatal consequences for his Presidency. The effects were not felt at once, since he continued to manœuvre with his customary adroitness, but he had forfeited his natural constituency and his power was poised dangerously over a void.

Economic crisis

The economic catastrophe was both a cause and a consequence of the empire's disintegration. National minority leaders objected that the 'Centre' was inhibiting them from taking remedial measures of their own, and ignored orders or instructions they received from Moscow. But by asserting claims to control local resources and industries they destroyed old-established relationships between suppliers and consumers within what had hitherto been an all-Union market of sorts, however unfree in its workings. The planners' old policy of concentrating the production of particular items (ball-bearings, light-bulbs) in one or two industrial centres, in order to promote regional interdependence, had nefarious consequences once those regions began to claim autonomy. Contracts between firms in different 'sovereign' republics could not be kept to. The same applied to agreements between authorities at various levels. In October 1990, for example, Kazakhstan ran short of forty types of consumer goods and banned their export to other republics. Some months earlier trade barriers had gone up even between Moscow and three neighbouring provinces. Residents from the latter were prohibited from buying up goods in the capital, and so their own local officials took counter-measures.

However, the main reason for the economic crisis lay much deeper. It had its roots in decisions taken (or not taken) during the early phases of *perestroika*, when the money supply was allowed to get out of hand. Enterprises, subject to 'soft budgetary constraints', were allowed to pay their workpeople more, while prices remained more or less stable. Social benefits rose even faster. Since there was little or nothing to buy in the shops, inflationary pressures built up. The amount of currency put into circulation rose by around 4 per cent per annum in 1985–6, reached 5.9 per cent in 1987, and doubled in 1988 (11.8 per cent); over the next two years the figure leaped to 18.4 and 28.0 per cent (Åslund 1991). By the end of 1990 the excess purchasing power ('rouble overhang') was estimated by the IMF at 250 milliard roubles. Most of these funds were held by enterprises. Total individual savings (including money kept *outside* banks!) accounted for an estimated 80.5 milliard roubles—3.3 times as much as in 1985 (24.3 milliard roubles)—whereas total purchases had risen only 1.4 times (from 347 to 493 milliard roubles).[2] Western economists took the view that the government should have forced through a currency reform to mop up excess funds. But such a move was evidently not considered—and anyway may not have been politically possible: this was not 1947! Instead of government expenditure being drastically curbed, it rose from 49.7 per cent of GNP in 1985 to an average of 52.4 per cent over the years 1987–9.

Where did the money go? Much went on defence, of course, since it took years before Gorbachev's bold cuts to the military budget took effect.[3] Investment rose from 9.0 per cent of GNP in 1985 to 10 and 9.7 per cent respectively over the next two years—this was the era of the engineering modernization drive—but then tapered off. On the other hand, expenditure on consumer subsidies continued to rise: from 7.5 per cent of GNP in 1985 to 10.9 per cent in 1989. So, too, did expenditure on social insurance and health care (from 10.7 to 11.4 per cent of GNP). In terms of current roubles subsidies nearly doubled between 1985 and 1990 (from 58 to 110.5 milliard roubles). Meanwhile revenue grew only slightly in absolute terms and actually declined when calculated as a share of GNP (from 48 to 43.5 per cent, 1985–9). Although the budget deficit did not look very large by Western standards, according to Åslund 'it was financed by highly liquid assets: bank accounts and enterprise accounts. The domestic state debt rose from 18.2 per cent of GNP at the end of 1985 to 42.8 per cent of GNP at the end of 1989.'

Towards the market?

Preoccupied with political problems, the leadership did not realize the gravity of the crisis until mid-1989, when a 'reform commission' was set up under the liberal economist Leonid Abalkin. His team apparently convinced Gorbachev that it was essential to move towards a market economy. But at what pace? The commission's programme, announced in October 1989, envisaged a relatively leisurely six-year term. In other respects, though, it was a radical document. It provided for the introduction of stock exchanges, commercial companies, and household farms (although these were to lease, not own, the land). These 'capitalist' notions met with stiff opposition. The more cautious senior officials, among them Prime Minister Ryzhkov and Gosplan chief Masliukov, worked out an alternative programme (December 1989). This focused on 'stabilization' and postponed for three years introduction of any major move to the market. Until then retail prices were not to be increased. In this way Gorbachev managed to keep his options open while the clock ticked remorselessly on.

In March 1990 Abalkin sent Gorbachev a memorandum (as yet unpublished) warning him that radical reforms could be delayed no longer. Thereupon a special commission of twenty-four leading economists was set up with Gorbachev in the chair. Its task was to prepare a new reform package within a month. This was duly presented to the Supreme Soviet (24 May). It proposed *inter alia* a massive (up to 50 per cent) jump in retail prices in the near future, with limited compensation for the hardest hit. The news led to panic among consumers, who withdrew their savings and bought up whatever they could still find in the shops. Ultimately the price rise did not go through. At the ensuing Twenty-eighth Party congress the reformists came in for heavy criticism, but the resolutions which it adopted on economic policy were vague and contradictory. The 'parade of programmes' was set to continue.

Meanwhile the radical economists had responded to Gorbachev's tergiversations by elaborating a plan for a rapid move to the market, with extensive privatization (February 1990). Its principal author, Grigorii Yavlinsky, was a young (aged 38) member of the Abalkin commission who thought that its chairman was too ready to compromise with the conservatives. His programme envisaged 'shock therapy' on the Polish model and was to be carried through within four hundred days. This term (later extended to five hundred days) was featured in the plan's title. The ever-vacillating Gorbachev endorsed the scheme, but in April it was turned down by his chief advisory agency, the Presidential Council. The radicals did the obvious: they turned to Boris Yeltsin, who was himself now assembling a team of reform-minded economists. Yavlinsky joined it, as did an even younger (aged 32) colleague, Boris Fedorov. Both men became senior ministers in the RSFSR government.

But this was a government that spoke louder than it acted. There was no way it could introduce a market economy on its own so long as the USSR still existed: the 'Centre', after all, controlled monetary policy and much else. Yeltsin, who had begun his 'reign' so tempestuously, was obliged to offer Gorbachev an olive branch two weeks later (12 June). At the end of July the two leaders agreed to set up a *joint* working group under Stanislav Shatalin. It comprised men from both teams, as well as representatives from all republics except Estonia. These men toiled around the clock to produce a blueprint for fundamental reform. By 1 September two hefty volumes were ready, which included the drafts of no less than twenty-one legal acts. 'The USSR had never seen a reform programme that was as concrete, comprehensive or radical. The word socialism was not even used.' Moreover, times were such that there seemed every likelihood of it being adopted by the legislature.

But once again Gorbachev drew back—and once again the conservatives, meeting separately, came up with a rival programme. Its aim was not free enterprise but a *'regulated* market economy'—with the 'Centre', of course, doing the regulating. Instead of choosing between the two drafts, the Supreme Soviet temporized and then, at Gorbachev's behest, decided to give *him* three weeks to produce a compromise version. These 'guidelines' turned out to be just milk-and-water platitudes. A great opportunity had been missed—not only by Gorbachev but by Yeltsin too. Leading reformers resigned or were dismissed from *both* governments. The mood in Moscow turned ugly. Responding to popular agitation, the central legislature passed a law specifying severe penalties for 'speculators'. The KGB was instructed to combat 'economic sabotage' more energetically. In one of his many little-regarded Presidential edicts, Gorbachev reverted to the old revolutionary nostrum of 'workers' control'. Vigilante groups were to inspect the books of all enterprises they suspected of wrongdoing and force them to close down.

The mafia

Indeed there was a mafia at work—but was this the best way of dealing with it? Criminal activity, after all, had been endemic under the old dispensation. It received a fillip during *perestroika*, especially with the creation of producers' co-operatives, which were legalized in May 1988. These were designed to help satisfy consumer demand that could not be met through the state retail network, and to invigorate the socialist sector by providing competition. By mid-1990 five million people were employed in co-operatives; they produced goods worth 30 milliard roubles, equivalent to about 3 per cent of GNP (Tedstrom 1990). They were particularly active in the service sector (catering, repair work, etc.) and performed many jobs previously done by people 'on the side' (*nalevo*) (see Chapter 10). Much the same applies to the individual (family) enterprises sanctioned by a law that had come into force in May 1987. The main problem was that no provision was made to ensure that private or co-operative business men (*biznesmeny*, a pejorative term) could obtain sufficient supplies of material legally. They were virtually obliged to turn to unauthorized sources. Some found ways of getting rich quick—members of one co-operative making costume jewellery earned half a million roubles in four months—but they ran the risk of being taxed at arbitrary rates, or otherwise harassed, by local officials unsympathetic to the very notion of private enterprise.

The public, too, looked askance at the 'profiteers', especially if they happened to be foreigners. Chechens and others from the Caucasus, who took to such work with natural aplomb, were frequently targets of popular wrath. In Ashkhabad rioters wrecked a co-operative they blamed for monopolizing certain commodities and driving up prices in state stores (Connor 1991). Elderly people and blue-collar workers objected vociferously to the high earnings of some entrepreneurs, whom they compared invidiously to the 'Nepmen' and 'bourgeois' of popular mythology. The prospect of transition to a free market awakened deep-rooted egalitarian sentiments. Envy of those who 'made good' had been the foundation of mass support for Stalinism. As living conditions became harsher, many were eager to seek out culprits whom they could hold responsible for their misfortunes. They were in no mood to consider the argument that gross inequalities of income, exploitation and economic crime might be a result of the *under*-development of market relations. Instead they hearkened to those who decried individualism and threatened confiscation of 'illicit' wealth. In this way a psychological climate was formed in which neo-Communist and right-wing nationalist ideas could merge and prosper.

Gorbachev moves right

On 7 November 1990 the anniversary of the revolution was marked in an unconventional manner. Instead of the usual parade a specially invited crowd assembled on Red Square. Two shots were fired at Gorbachev. Apparently the gunman, an unemployed worker, acted alone, but there were many others who thought that the crisis could be solved by violence. In an interview with the left-conservative paper *Sovetskaia Rossiia* (21 November) the *Soiuz* leader Alksnis warned that 'a veritable civil war' was getting under way. He was well placed to know, for a few days earlier he had called on the Supreme Soviet to get rid of Gorbachev and had helped set up a National Salvation Committee to rule the country in his stead. Gorbachev apparently yielded to pressure by conservatives in the two (all-Union and Russian) Communist parties. The precise terms of his surrender are unclear, but presumably involved a public apology—on the 29th he admitted to the Moscow *gorkom* that 'we stand guilty before the working class' for (unspecified) errors in economic and nationality policy—and, more to the point, agreement to *coups* in the Baltic and the appointment of 'reliable' men to certain key posts.

The first beneficiary was Boris Pugo, who on 2 December became Interior minister. A 'Russian Latvian', he was a client of Pel'she, the long-serving boss of the Latvian Party, and had taken over its leadership in 1984 after serving for six years as republic KGB chief. Alksnis welcomed his appointment, predicting that other reformists' heads would soon roll (Bungs 1990), but his fellow-deputies disowned him. G. Yanaev, who as former chairman of the body that supervised youth organizations had close KGB ties, was chosen for the new post of Vice-President. This move was designed to counterbalance Gorbachev, who had been granted additional powers by parliament and had reshuffled the top executive agencies in the hope of strengthening the Presidency.[4] Last but not least, Prime Minister Ryzhkov suffered a heart attack and was replaced by Valentin Pavlov, hitherto Finance minister.

In the Congress a deputy, V. Cherniak, spoke of a 'creeping reactionary *coup d'état*'. A still more eloquent warning came from the Foreign minister, Shevardnadze. On 20 December he unexpectedly resigned. No one, he complained (meaning Gorbachev), had come to his aid when conservatives attacked him for allegedly betraying Soviet interests abroad; a dictatorship was impending. Gorbachev called the statement 'unforgivable'. Reformers were dismayed, reactionaries jubilant. But the key question was: who was going to be the dictator, Gorbachev himself or one of his foes on the right? The latter were led to believe that the President was on their side and would use his new powers to rule more decisively. But he, it seems, wanted above all to avoid shedding blood. In this he differed from the KGB chief, Kriuchkov, who said that 'the possibility of bloodshed' had to be taken into account if order were to be restored, or a major-general and editor of a leading military journal, who opined that what the country needed was 'another Beria'.

This uncertainty at the top saved the cause of liberty in the Baltic for, as we know, at some point in the operation Gorbachev drew back. He also vacillated over measures to limit press freedom in Russia, first proposing that legal guarantees be suspended but then, after his proposal had been turned down by Parliament, stating that he would not insist on the measure (16 January 1991). Yeltsin strongly backed the Balts. So, too, did deputies in the Inter-regional group and other prominent reformers. In the depths of a Moscow winter one hundred thousand people turned out to demand the resignation of Gorbachev, Pugo, and Defence minister Dmitrii Yazov (20 January). Few voices were raised in the President's defence, but a resolution condemning him for resorting to violence was blocked by conservative deputies. Citizens in Leningrad set up a committee to defend the city's elected institutions from possible attack. Joint patrols of soldiers and police were set up in several places by a Presidential decree whose legality was promptly challenged by the left.

Were the liberals unduly alarmist? Rumour abounded. Eaves-dropping equipment was discovered in Yeltsin's office. Had the KGB acted alone or at Gorbachev's bidding? The tension between the two men reached unparalleled heights, and they rarely met. Instead the struggle was carried into the streets. On 22 February 1991 'Democratic Russia' marked Army Day with a rally praising Yeltsin's government and indicting its rival. The next day the armed forces' supporters (including some soldiers in civilian clothes) demonstrated in favour of the forces. Journalists estimated the size of the first crowd at 400,000 and the second at 300,000. But this was scarcely an accurate guide to the state of public opinion.

Nor was the turnout (75 per cent) or the vote at the referendums held on 17 March. Gorbachev had set great store by this device. He hoped for a clear verdict throughout the land on turning the USSR into a 'union of sovereign equal states' with a strong central power. The question had been framed in the broadest possible terms,[5] and so the overwhelming support it received in the RSFSR was none too surprising. Few people were concerned about constitutional niceties, and there was little point in voting 'No' in the absence of any alternative proposal. But the significance of the vote was undermined chiefly by Yeltsin's clever ruse of tabling a *second* question: should Russia have its own President? The job would obviously go to him. It seemed likely to strengthen Russia's weight *vis-à-vis* other republics and the 'Centre'. This made it palatable to people of most political colours, and 70 per cent of those voting favoured the idea.

Not so to Parliament, where conservatives called an extraordinary session of Congress (28 March), with Gorbachev's tacit blessing, and tabled a resolution of non-confidence in Yeltsin. Amidst popular uproar outside the chamber this failed. Instead the deputies gave their chairman special powers pending the Presidential election. Boris Nikolaevich owed his survival mainly to a split in the Russian CP. Led by Rutskoi, a reformist group broke away to form a separate pro-Yeltsin 'fraction' in the assembly, known as 'Communists for Democracy'. Thus the Party schisms in the Baltic states were replicated in the RSFSR, too. On 12 June, after a fractious campaign during which a bomb exploded at Democratic Russia's headquarters, Yeltsin was duly chosen as Russia's first President.

The 'job description' was a carbon copy of Gorbachev's, but the way the two leaders had reached high office was different. For Yeltsin won power in an authentic popular contest, securing (in round figures) 57 per cent of the votes cast to 17 per cent for Ryzhkov, and 8 per cent for the 'dark horse' Vladimir Zhirinovsky, soon to stand revealed as an ex-KGB officer and nationalist fanatic. At the time optimists could be forgiven for believing that Russia was at last heading for democracy. Alas, this prospect was imperilled by the rapidly deteriorating economic situation.

The economy in free fall

During the first six months of 1991 Soviet GNP fell by 10 per cent, gross industrial output by 6.2 per cent, and labour productivity by 11 per cent. Inflation was rising at the rate of 2 to 3 per cent a *week*. The budget deficit, originally set at 26.6 milliard roubles for the entire year, was growing by nearly that amount (21 to 22 milliard roubles) each month. Prices zoomed, while promised wage increases could not always be paid. There were not enough banknotes, even though the printing presses worked overtime. Pavlov, the new Soviet premier, was no friend of the market. He made a bad start by accusing Western bankers of trying to sabotage the Soviet economy. Yet he did seek to mop up surplus purchasing power by ordering fifty- and one-hundred-rouble banknotes to be withdrawn from circulation (22 January). The measure was also designed to confiscate dubiously acquired fortunes. However, it dealt a grievous blow to thousands of legitimate small savers. Equally unpopular was an 'anti-crisis programme' introduced on 2 April by Presidential decree, but swiftly countermanded. It provided for increases in retail prices of about 60 per cent, to be partially (85 per cent) offset by higher wages. Not only was there insufficient cash to pay these supplements, but the goods famine worsened. The extra commodities needed to absorb the flow of paper roubles simply did not exist (Bush 1991).

In this situation it was unrealistic to expect lavish foreign investment and aid, although Western governments and international agencies did try to help where they could. But should such funds go to the 'Centre', with its lukewarm attitude to the market, or to those individual republics that were making greater progress towards liberal economic principles? To create at least a semblance of stability, it was essential for the republics to adopt agreed policies, but the nationalist upsurge made this extremely difficult. Their governments were under intense pressure from below to consolidate economic sovereignty and so feared to make concessions. Nevertheless on 17 June nine states did reach an agreement with the 'Centre' whereby each of them was to have the right to conduct its own commercial and monetary policy. The Union's currency and gold reserves—as well as its external debt—were to be divided up between them according to an agreed formula. This of course still left a great deal unsaid, but the picture was not all gloom. In several fields there was progress towards introducing market relations. Laws were passed on the restriction of monopolies, bankruptcies, and contractual relations between enterprises. The tax system was reformed and measures taken to attract and protect foreign firms which engaged in joint ventures.

This was mere 'pie in the sky' for the average hard-pressed citizen, faced with what seemed to be a prospect of ever-increasing misery. Some workers resorted to strike action, although it was clear that it would be counter-productive. Until now labour had by and large been remarkably docile. As early as 1989 coal-miners, the most active group, had set up independent trade unions and works committees in several coalfields, which bargained on their behalf with government representatives. Their leaders' political outlook varied. The most radically minded were miners in the Kuznetsk basin in Siberia. Since these pits were relatively modern and productive, they hoped that they might do better under private enterprise. In March 1991 Donets basin coal-miners inaugurated a two-month-long strike which soon spread to other fields and assumed an overtly political character. The miners trusted Yeltsin, who placed the Kuznetsk pits under the RSFSR's control (27 April), more than they did Gorbachev.

The August 1991 *coup*

It has been argued (Ashwin 1991) that it was this factor that pushed Gorbachev back towards the left. He realized that labour militancy was so strong that a repressive policy was impracticable. Apart from this the President, fortified by his success in the referendum, could afford to wriggle free of the conservative embrace that had limited his freedom of action in recent months. On 23 April the talks at Novo-Ogarevo, a *dacha* outside Moscow, eventuated in an agreement between nine states and the 'Centre' on the main provisions of a new Union treaty. It involved a number of concessions on Gorbachev's part to the states' aspirations which it would be superfluous to examine here, not least because the accord was fated never to be implemented. 'Nine plus one', as it came to be called, aroused bitterness and anger in the left-conservative camp. Even the initial draft, it was held there, had violated the Soviet Constitution. Now it could be argued that the President had sanctioned the breakup of the USSR. For extremists this was a *casus belli*. The formal signing of the treaty, they held, had to be prevented at all costs. Yeltsin's latest victory at the polls made the prospect of an alliance between him and Gorbachev most alarming. Moreover, ten days after he had been sworn in as President (10 July), in the presence of the Orthodox Patriarch, Yeltsin issued a decree prohibiting all Party activities in government agencies and instructing the Russian legislature to extend the decree's scope to cover the armed forces, security organs, and judiciary. Offenders faced heavy fines. By the time the decree came into force (4 August) one-third of enterprise managers in Leningrad had requested Party cells to vacate the premises. For the CPSU the writing was on the wall.

It is curious that the conservatives should have repeated their earlier strategic error. Once again they could not make up their minds whether Gorbachev was with them or against them. Might not suitable inducements bring him back into the fold? Their first move was therefore a 'soft' one. Pavlov asked the Supreme Soviet for additional powers, on the grounds that Gorbachev was 'too busy' to oversee the work of Cabinet. *Izvestiia* accused Pavlov of seeking to usurp power. But Gorbachev played the matter down: journalists should not over-dramatize conflicts at the top, and there was 'no crisis' between him and Pavlov; as for the right-wingers who were agitating for an extraordinary Party congress at which to unseat him, 'they do not worry me' (Mann 1991). This sounded like over-confidence, but Gorbachev knew that the Party was split three ways. The rightists were themselves fragmented (into a 'Marxist Platform', 'Bolshevik Platform', 'Communist Initiative', etc.) and did not seem likely to prevail. On 25–6 July, at what would prove to be its last plenum, the Central Committee met to discuss the General Secretary's draft of a new Party programme. This was a highly un-Leninist document which purported to reconcile socialism with the market. Even so it received preliminary approval at the gathering. Thus Gorbachev evidently still commanded a majority—although when it reconvened on 5 August, the CC expelled Rutskoi and another prominent reform Communist, Lipitsky, for 'factionalism'. The Party's mood was brittle and uncertain. It was losing members fast (4.2 million over eighteen months) and the rapid pace of events left the survivors disoriented. Many would gladly have seen a firmer hand on the tiller.

This was precisely what the 'August plotters' were about to offer. The leading conspirators were Pavlov, Yanaev, Kriuchkov, and Yazov, respectively Prime Minister, Vice-President and ministers of State Security and Defence. To this core group were added Pugo, the Interior minister, Baklanov, first vice-chairman of the Defence Council, and two other men 'representing' industry and agriculture, Tiziakov and Starodubtsev. (The position of the Supreme Soviet chairman, Luk'ianov, was somewhat equivocal.) None of the eight were Politburo or Secretariat members (for these bodies had been effectively purged by Gorbachev); otherwise, in terms of offices held, it was a powerful grouping.

Just when and where the conspirators first came together is still unclear, for at the time of writing (May 1994) they have yet to be brought to justice. As plots go—and Russian history offers many intriguing precedents—it seems to have been organized rather casually. As in 1917, a 'dress rehearsal' preceded the 'first night' (July/October 1917, January/August 1991). But the latter-day Bolsheviks had neither a Lenin to lead them nor a proletariat to follow them. The movement's revolutionary *élan* had long since evaporated. They lacked a clear concept of their goals or a well-formulated action plan. (Yazov would say later, 'We had no real plan.') Apparently they viewed Yeltsin and the radicals as the real enemy and hoped to win over Gorbachev; his fate was to be decided later.[6] They knew what they disliked—the Union treaty, the new Party programme, market economics—but were less sure of what they wanted. How far was the clock to be put back: to 1988, to 1984, or to 1953? The second date is the most plausible. They were left-conservatives rather than out-and-out Stalinists. 'The plotters tried to present their actions as being in conformity with the Constitution', remarks R. Sakwa (1993). 'There was only one problem . . ., and that was that Gorbachev refused to step down, even temporarily, and thus they were in fact subverting the Constitution.'

The Union treaty was due to be signed on 20 August. Early in the morning of 19 August tanks rolled into the centre of Moscow. The media announced the formation of a State Emergency Committee consisting of the eight men first named above, which was said to have assumed power. A six-month state of emergency was imposed on Moscow, Leningrad, and certain other places. Press freedom was suspended. Gorbachev was said to be ill—a transparent subterfuge. On the previous day the plotters had sent a delegation to the Crimea, where the President was on holiday, to seek his agreement to the state of emergency. He refused to take part in the plot, and so KGB agents from Sevastopol' placed him and his family under house arrest. But their isolation was not total. Guards erected a radio antenna. Gorbachev could hear foreign broadcasts but was unable to communicate himself.

Already on 19 August opposition to the *putsch* began to mobilize. In an 'Appeal to Citizens of Russia' Yeltsin and Silaev condemned it as unconstitutional and branded the Emergency Committee illegal. There was a call for a general strike. Tank crews were heckled by civilians. Large crowds, which included many young people, assembled outside the 'White House'. Some were prepared to defend it if necessary against assault, as earlier in Vilnius, and barricades went up. In his finest hour Yeltsin climbed on to an armoured vehicle to encourage the defenders. Reinforcements arrived, but the troops did not attack. Apparently orders were given to storm the building, but some units (including even the KGB's élite 'Alpha' force) refused to obey (Karpukhin 1992).

Yeltsin's courageous gesture was, strictly speaking, superfluous, for in Gorbachev's absence the plot was running out of steam. When Pavlov appeared on television, viewers noticed that his hands were shaking nervously. Yazov resigned. Journalists defied the restrictions, which were enforced irresolutely. Communications with the provinces and foreign countries were not entirely cut off. Abroad the *coup* was roundly condemned. Reaction in the union republics varied, but nowhere did the plotters receive enthusiastic support. Those inclined to sit on the fence swiftly regained courage once it became clear that the attempt had failed.

A delegation went to rescue Gorbachev and his family. Unlike Khrushchev in 1964, who had returned under duress to a hostile capital, Gorbachev had been 'liberated'—but in a sense he too was no longer free. He was in Yeltsin's power. Clearly he bore some responsibility for what had occurred, since the plotters were his appointees, and he had done nothing to avert the *coup*. Yeltsin humiliated Gorbachev in public by obliging him to read out before the television cameras the Cabinet minutes of 19 August, which showed that of twenty ministers eighteen had either approved the *coup* or had failed to oppose it—implying that he was himself to blame. Gorbachev's position had been fatally weakened. He had to acknowledge his rival's pre-eminence: 'first of all I must note the outstanding role of Boris Nikolaevich Yeltsin, President of Russia, who was at the centre of resistance to the plot', he declared on 22 August. The *putsch* had been 'a big lesson for all of us'.

Russia after the *coup*

The August *coup* not only undermined Gorbachev but also discredited the Soviet system. The centre of power moved from Moscow to the republics. One after another they declared their independence, the Baltic states once again taking the lead. For a time at least the old command structures were put out of action. Gorbachev resigned as General Secretary of the CPSU (24 August) and followed Yeltsin's precedent by ordering its property (reputedly worth about 5 milliard roubles) 'nationalized' and banning Party cells in the armed forces and KGB. He recommended that the Central Committee disband, and the Secretariat, disclaiming any foreknowledge of the *coup*, concurred. The Party's headquarters in Moscow and Leningrad were sealed. Its archives passed under the RSFSR's control. On 29 August the USSR Supreme Soviet formally suspended the Party's activities throughout the Union until its role in the plot had been clarified. *Pravda* and five other Party organs had been suspended already on the 23rd, but the ban was later rescinded. At the end of September the Komsomol held an extraordinary congress and likewise decided to disband.

A month later Yeltsin converted the earlier suspension of the CPSU and its Russian counterpart into a permanent ban (6 November). The argument was that they were not authentic parties but anti-constitutional bodies that had subverted society and the State. The wisdom of this move was questioned by some democrats. In any case the prohibition was not effective. Several Communist organizations continued to exist with a minimum of · concealment. Rutskoi's dissident group turned itself into a 'People's

Party of Free Russia' and laid claim to all the banned parties' property in the RSFSR (26 October). The very next day there appeared a rival 'Socialist Party of Working People'. Other local Communist groups appeared in St Petersburg,[7] Yekaterinburg (the former Sverdlovsk) and elsewhere. At Eastertide in 1992 the Russian CP itself rose from the dead as the 'United Communist Party of Russia'. Similar developments occurred in other union republics, where Party stalwarts could exploit the fears and discontents of the Russian diaspora. More important still, members of the old *nomenklatura* remained prominent in government and economic management all over the former Soviet Union. They adapted themselves to unfamiliar conditions with such skill as they could muster. Communism might have suffered defeat with the collapse of the *coup*, but it had not been routed.

An even harder nut to crack was the KGB. It, too, lost formal control of its archives as well as of the border troops (but not all its paramilitary formations). However, it managed to preserve its central core institutions. For it was too useful to be dispensed with in the new Russia. Yeltsin had previously (5 May) set up a *Russian KGB* under Major-General Ivanenko, a senior officer of the parent body, so that continuity was assured. On 5 October he issued a Presidential decree making this organization, now called the Federal Security Agency (AFB), the legal heir of the all-Union one, which had become the Inter-republican Security Service. Not for the first time the Cheka had changed its spots.

To be sure, its new head, Bakatin, was an ex-MVD man, the organization's effectives were greatly reduced, and its structure decentralized. But old traditions die hard. By December recentralization was already under way. The ex-KGB was merged with the two (Russian and all-Union) Interior ministries into an RSFSR Security and Internal Affairs ministry. Yeltsin had recreated the 'monster' he had criticized the year before. Even some 'democratic' security officials objected to this, as did Russia's new Constitutional Court. Ostensibly now under parliamentary control, the AFB had little difficulty infiltrating its controllers (Yasmann 1993). An all-Union law of 16 May 1991, which gave the security services a legal status they had previously lacked, permitted spying on the mail and electronic eavesdropping. Did the new bodies make less use of these devices? Did they concentrate on repressing crime instead of performing political tasks? It would be easier to answer such questions with assurance if Kriuchkov and the other officers who had helped to plan the *putsch* had been tried and punished.[8] In the view of some observers, with the Party now in eclipse the KGB's role had actually increased.

On the other side of the political equation were the liberals and radicals. The defeat of the *coup* owed much to Democratic Russia, which played a role analogous to that of the popular fronts in the Baltic. But it was less well equipped than they were for regular legislative work in Parliament. Its relatively inexperienced leaders could not decide whether it should be a party or a movement.[9] The democratic politicians were not at one as to the future shape of the RSFSR. Some of them reacted towards the Volga Tatars, who wanted to establish a sovereign Tatarstan, with the same arrogance that Gorbachev had shown towards the Lithuanians (Hosking 1991). Party realignments were continuous. The most successful in building a mass base was Travkin's group, which by the autumn is said to have had 45,000 members in 549 branches. The Christian Democrats claimed 15,000, the Republicans 7,000, the Social Democrats a mere 5,000. The political landscape was equally fragmented in Ukraine, where the Republicans were in the lead with only 10,000 members (Schneider 1991).

At government level the picture was also dispiriting. Yeltsin soon began to squander the popular credit he had acquired from his heroic stand against the plotters, although he remained far ahead of Gorbachev in the polls. It was excusable that, in the heat of the moment, three innocent individuals accidentally killed in the *mêlée* should be elevated to the rank of national martyrs and buried with pomp: every regime, after all, needs its myths. More serious was the fact that Russia's President emulated his rival in building up a powerful executive *apparat* largely independent of legislative control. As so often in the past, there were two competing bureaucracies—that of the government ministries and of the Presidential bodies—which got in each other's way. Critics complained of a lack of professional competence.

Moreover, Yeltsin was less accessible than Gorbachev. Rutskoi was soon to complain that he had tried twelve times without success to telephone him (Yeltsin) when he was holidaying in the Crimea. His manner tended towards the imperious. In an age of electronic media a leader's 'image' may sometimes matter more than his actual character or performance. Yeltsin's treatment of the press was likewise heavy-handed. The editor of the respected *Nezavisi-maia gazeta* ('Independent Newspaper'), Tret'iakov, was officially reprimanded for publishing an article about the danger of a nuclear confrontation between Russia and Ukraine. The real reason, he thought, was *lèse-majesté*. To be sure, some journalistic comment was malevolent or irresponsible. The conservative *Sovetskaia Rossiia* published attacks on both Yeltsin and Gorbachev. The Press and Information ministry ordered its closure, but was over-ruled by the judiciary. These straws in the wind pointed to poten-tially dangerous authoritarian tendencies in the 'democratic' camp.

In Yeltsin's defence it should be made clear that he stood some way to the left of his Parliament, where deputies were instinctively suspicious of the executive power. It was thus another victory for the President when, on 1 November, the Russian Congress agreed that he might rule by decree for a year in order to force through economic reforms. Never one to shun responsibility, he took on the job of Prime Minister as well. His speech on this occasion was statesmanlike. In the manner of a latter-day Stolypin he reviewed the grim state of the nation and outlined two main objectives. The first was to stabilize the economy by exercising a strict monetary policy, reforming the tax system, supporting the rouble and lib-eralizing prices. 'Without this all talk of . . . the market is empty chatter.' The second was 'the creation of a healthy mixed economy with a powerful private sector [and] speeding up land reform'.

The goals were sound, but did the political will to achieve them exist? And could Russia live amicably with her neighbours if she proceeded from her 'national state interests', which *inter alia* meant charging them world prices for exports of fuel and other essentials? By the time these questions were posed with full force Russia stood on her own. The Soviet Union had collapsed.

The USSR collapses

Keeping the empire together was Gorbachev's main preoccupation in the post-*coup* period. But with the Party now in abeyance he had only his moral authority to rely on, and that had suffered greatly. Wisely he placed economic agreements ahead of political ones. On 4 September an Inter-regional Economic Council was set up. It complemented a Council of Republics, which became the upper house in a reformed Supreme Soviet. These institutions were designed to run the Union for a 'transitional period' of undefined duration. But the 'Centre' no longer called the tune.

After the *putsch* those union republics that had yet to declare themselves independent proceeded to do so. Ukraine took this step already on 24 August, Belarus the next day. Moldova, Uzbekistan, and Kyrgyzstan swiftly followed suit, as did Tajikistan (9 September); Kazakhstan, ever the moderate, waited until mid-December. The Baltic states' independence was recognized without delay by Russia as well as by Western states. The Baltic governments took prompt action to close down Party and KGB branches. It was harder to get rid of Soviet troops, which the central military authorities sought to use as a bargaining chip in return for concessions in favour of the Russian minorities in these states. They objected to alleged discrimination in the citizenship laws which Baltic governments and parliaments were elaborating. Latvia, for example, wanted to impose a qualification of sixteen years' residence in that republic, along with a loyalty oath and proof of adequate knowledge of the country's language and laws. Spokesmen for the Russian community called this 'apartheid'. The immigrants' political organizations were treated, not without reason, as potentially subversive. Many Russians left, but countless others had nowhere else to go. The seeds were being sown of future conflict.

If there was less tension in Central Asia, this was because several republican leaders had reacted ambiguously to the *coup*. In Uzbekistan, Tajikistan, and Turkmenistan they hedged their bets. This was not the case in Kyrgyzstan, where the local KGB, with Party backing, had tried to unseat Akaev. He reacted vigorously, dismissing the head of the security police and suspending the Party's activities for six months. He then stood for re-election—unopposed—and won with no less than 95 per cent of the votes cast (12 October). Akaev expressed 'distress' at the lack of competition, but one may doubt whether his discomfiture lasted long. In Kazakhstan the Party first secretary, Nazarbaev, resigned after the *coup* and, like Akaev, re-emerged triumphantly as President with a 90 per cent vote in his favour; he, too, was sole candidate. The democratic and Islamic opposition put up a better showing in Tajikistan, where seven candidates ran for the Presidency. The former Party leader, Nabiev, won, securing only a modest 58 per cent of the votes (24 November).

It was in Central Asia, in the Kazakh capital Almaty (Alma-Ata), that on 1 October the twelve remaining Soviet republics (i.e. all but the Baltic states) declared their intention to form an economic community. Several signatories stated that they wanted certain supplementary points cleared up first, and in the event only eight republics signed the treaty (18 October). The absentees were Georgia, Azerbaijan, Moldova—and, last but not least, Ukraine. Until the last moment there was some doubt as to whether the RSFSR would be among their number but Gorbachev yielded on the points under dispute. He hailed the accord as 'a tremendous event'. In reality it conceded so much power to the republics as to make it unworkable, given the scale of the problems that beset them. There were too many divergent interests, for example, over pricing goods in inter-republic trade, deciding contributions to the central budget, and sharing out the Union's debts.

The extent of the divergences became clear in the talks in the Council of Republics and at Novo-Ogarevo on the new Union treaty. In a sense the negotiating parties were being asked to reconcile diametrically opposed objectives: to consolidate their independence and to relinquish it in the common interest. One could hardly expect a process that in Western Europe was taking decades to be rushed through in a matter of months by states at such varied stages of development and with a dubious imperial legacy behind them. On 4 November Gorbachev upbraided his interlocutors for abusing the political capital they had gained from the *coup*. But he was asking the impossible. Ten days later he seemed to have lined up seven signatory states: Russia, Belarus, and the five Central Asian republics. But when they met on 25 November Yeltsin, to general surprise, raised new objections. He found the draft too centralist. Russia wanted confederation, not federation. Again Gorbachev yielded: he had no choice. The new Union was to have no Constitution other than those of its members. The autonomous republics were not to join it as independent entities, for this would spell the breakup of Russia—who clearly expected to play first fiddle, despite her formal commitment to recognize her partners' sovereign equality.

At this point Ukraine stepped in. Public opinion in the 'second Soviet republic' had been upset by an incautious remark by a Yeltsin spokesman, on 26 August, that the RSFSR reserved the right to raise frontier issues with its (independent) neighbours. *Rukh* called this 'an attempt to divide our Fatherland'. Kravchuk, who after a moment's vacillation on 19 August had recovered his balance and was about to quit his Party, pointed out that 'territorial claims are very dangerous'. There could be no question of Ukraine signing the Union treaty until the republic's declaration of independence had been confirmed by a popular referendum, due to be held on 1 December. The 'frontier affair' blew over, but there was no lack of other points of friction. Not the least of these had to do with military matters, especially the fate of the thousands of nuclear missiles stationed on Ukrainian soil. Ukrainian nationalists, who were strongest in the west, took the view that sovereignty was of little account without armed forces, and formed the nucleus of an officer corps. On 7 November the government approved provisions that the republic should have a 450,000-strong army, 'purely for defence'. It had previously assumed jurisdiction over Soviet military units and government communications in Ukraine, first *de facto* and then (17 October) *de jure*. The service chiefs objected, but made no impression on Ukraine's Defence minister (who, curiously, was a Russian, Morozov). On 30 November Morozov announced that Ukraine was determined to have a navy as well, so threatening the integrity of the Black Sea fleet. The possibility of an armed conflict loomed.

In this febrile atmosphere there was no point in asking the Ukrainian legislature to ratify the Union treaty. Even the 'centrist' Kravchuk remained cool to the idea and pronounced the proposed economic community 'still-born' (23 November). In a massive poll—turn-out was 84.1 per cent—90.3 per cent of those voting endorsed the sovereignty declaration. Most remarkably, large numbers of Russians and other minority groups came out in favour of it: in Khar'kov the affirmative vote was 86 per cent, and even in the Crimea, where Russians comprised 67 per cent of the population, 54 per cent went along with the idea. Simultaneously the electors made Kravchuk their President. Many saw the former Party chief as a stabilizing factor. He secured 61.5 per cent of the vote, as against 23 and 4 per cent respectively for the former dissidents Chornovil and Luk'ianenko. There were several other candidates and the election campaign was fairly fought. Some thirty million people had delivered a resoundingly negative verdict on all that 'Moscow' stood for. This, more than any other factor, spelled the end of the USSR.

It remained to draw up its obituary notice. On 7–8 December the leaders of the three Slav republics—Kravchuk, Yeltsin, and Shush-kevich for Belarus—met on an estate near Brest-Litovsk. Once again, as in an earlier Russian revolution (1918), this border town was fated to play a historic role. Precisely because of its negative associations, the agreement was named for the Belarus capital, Minsk. Formally the parties to it declared that the Soviet Union 'is ceasing to exist as a subject of international law and a geopolitical reality'. They reiterated their allegiance to democratic values, privatization and the creation of a 'unified economic space'—although the rouble was to be retained only temporarily, pending the introduction of national currencies. There was no need to issue any stirring call for civil disobedience to the old organs of power, whose decisions were flatly stated to have lost validity. Within days the 'Minsk' agreement had been ratified by the three legislatures. The treaties of 1922 were invalidated. The leaders of some non-Slav republics were unhappy that they had not been invited to the meeting, but in Almaty on 21 December eight of them[10] joined the new Commonwealth of Independent States. All affirmed their respect for current borders.

Gorbachev played his part with dignity. He did all he could to ensure a smooth transition to the new order, without concealing his misgivings that it would not survive unless there were adequate co-ordinating institutions at the centre. This need was most urgent in the foreign policy and defence fields, since a disintegration of the nuclear deterrent, as he put it, threatened 'mischief on a world-wide scale'. On 25 December he delivered a moving valedictory address. The date officially set for the USSR's demise was fixed—conveniently for the historian—for 31 December 1991. The all-Union ministries, diplomatic embassies abroad, and central television came under Russian control. At midnight the Red flag over the Kremlin gave way to the Russian tricolour. There were few on-lookers and no euphoric applause. The Soviet legacy was too heavy, the future too uncertain, for celebration.

Afterword

This legacy cannot be assessed comprehensively here: the task would take another book. We lack sufficient historical distance from the subject. An appreciation would need to set the Soviet experience against that of other empires in the East and West. The following remarks are therefore necessarily subjective.

Russia and the other CIS states approached the millennium with more disadvantages than most countries. On the positive side, as a result of the forced industrialization drive that had been the Soviet regime's chief preoccupation since 1929, they had populations that were in the majority urbanized, 'broken-in' to the routines of factory or office life, and 'modern' in their tastes and aspirations. Educational levels were generally high, and there was an ample supply of engineers, agronomists, and other specialists with respectable technical qualifications. Of every thousand persons in employment in 1989, sixty-eight men and sixty-two women had received a higher education. Those who had completed secondary schooling numbered 259 and 294 per thousand respectively. Moreover, educated 'cadres' were widely distributed across the land. Uzbekistan and Georgia, for instance, were (apparently) above the all-Union average.[1] The former Soviet Union's vast population was complemented by a wealth of natural resources unequalled anywhere in the world, ranging from precious minerals through oil and gas deposits, timber stands, and fish stocks off its coasts, to the famed belt of rich 'black earth' (*chernozem*) soil.

But it was the negative side of the balance-sheet that loomed larger in the eyes of contemporaries. Among these liabilities were:

(a) environmental damage on a catastrophic scale, with consequent adverse effects on human health;

(b) the imbalance in industrial development, which bequeathed to the new states a large number of giant plants geared principally to the needs of the military–industrial complex, not those of consumers;

(c) a managerial élite used to receiving and giving orders, rather than to thinking independently and taking decisions promptly;

(d) an over-bureaucratized agricultural system with low productivity levels and a rural population deprived of its natural sense of property and entrepreneurial spirit;

(e) the persistence of ethnic animosities. 'All the new republics are burdened with potentially dangerous national conflicts, . . . yet they lack the legal and other institutional devices to mediate them and to guarantee minorities' cultural rights' (Geyer 1993);

(f) *homo sovieticus.*

The 'new Soviet man' might be a figment of the propagandists' imagination, but seven decades of tutelage by an omnipotent Party-state certainly left its mark on people's psychology—and not only in Russia, although it was more evident there than in, say, Transcaucasia. Stalin crushed his subjects' civic sense along with the autonomous organizations that are the life-blood of any society. To be sure, as we have seen in Part III, civil society re-emerged in the Brezhnev years. But it was an uphill struggle in which anyone who thought or acted independently soon came up against the might of the repressive apparatus. Citizens had to adapt their conduct to the prevailing norms. This meant splitting one's personality, saying one thing in public while thinking another in private, a habit that fostered ambiguity and deviousness. Informal pressures did succeed in eroding the Party's ideological credibility, and this was no mean feat. But the struggle cost the opposition dear, too—not just physically but also morally. Deeds of heroism there were aplenty, and even more feats of passive resistance. But they were no adequate substitute for the stable network of social linkages, patiently elaborated over generations, that is the fabric of civilization. During the half-century that preceded World War I, Russia had woven such a fabric, but in the ensuing 'iron age' it had been all but eaten away. War and famine took their toll, and they were followed by Stalin's all-encompassing totalitarian order. The only institution that survived as an alternative nucleus of social relationships was the family (and countless families, of course, were torn apart or destroyed). Informal groupings of friends were important, too. They saved many lives and helped to keep people sane. They were also the basis of client–patron networks. The role of these circles (*kruzhki*) has yet to be studied. It would be a hard job for historians to tackle, since the evidence is almost exclusively oral.

Generalizations about national psychology are hazardous. Opinion polls can tell us something, but their interpretation is delicate. Towards the end of 1990 respondents were asked which individual would make the greatest difference to the Soviet Union by the year 2000. 'Jesus Christ came first with 58 per cent and Andrei Sakharov second with 48 per cent, but Lenin was a creditable third with 36 per cent' (White, Gill, and Slider 1993). Does this mean that corresponding values were attached to Christianity, human rights, and Communism? Probably not. In another (all-Union) survey, taken after the August 1991 *coup*, 62 per cent of respondents considered it an illegal act. Gorbachev himself put support for the *coup* at 40 per cent, and in a later (1992) poll 46 per cent regarded the plotters as 'victims of circumstances' rather than as guilty men. Clearly, public opinion was very volatile. As people's material situation worsened in the post-Soviet period, the old regime's standing improved.

If analysis of *vox populi* invites speculation, so too does the historical record. Were Gorbachev's reforms intrinsically at fault, or could *perestroika* have worked if it had been attempted earlier? Those who answer the latter question in the affirmative blame the Brezhnev 'era of stagnation' for greatly augmenting the scale of the problems needing solution, and so heightening people's aspirations for change. On the other hand, it can be argued that in October 1964 the 'constituency' for any substantial reform effort was much weaker than it had become by 1985. Others consider that the (post-) Stalin system was inherently so faulty that at no time could any fundamental reform from above have been successful. The latter view is probably correct. For Stalinism was essentially *ideocratic*, i.e. it derived its legitimacy from the claim to be fulfilling a Supreme Purpose. History knows no other example of such a regime turning peacefully into a democratic *Rechtsstaat*. (Franco's Spain, for instance, is not in the same league as Stalin's USSR.) The Communist regimes in Eastern Europe, Stalinist 'clones', without exception tumbled as soon as Moscow withdrew its military and political backing. Cambodia and Cuba demonstrate the difficulties.

Another view sometimes expressed is that *perestroika* might have succeeded if it had been confined to economic liberalization and there had been no *glasnost'* or democratization. But Gorbachev did not have a 'Chinese option'. It was impossible to encourage popular initiative in the economic sphere without letting the truth be told about the defects of the existing system. One revelation led inevitably to another, because there was such an immense pent-up desire for access to the treasury of long-forbidden knowledge. To a large extent the regime's power rested on its monopoly of information and its control of all media of communication. Once this secrecy was breached, it was bound to fall: the facts were simply too incriminating. 'In the final account', writes V. Kontorovich, 'the regime's delegitimation was the main reason for the collapse of the whole system . . . All the coercive institutions were still in place, but with ideology destroyed [their personnel] were unsure what to do and the people saw no reason to obey them' (cited by Ellman 1993).

One may take the view that the failure of Gorbachev's reforms was 'pre-programmed' by the gravity and interdependence of the problems he inherited, yet still hold that (*a*) the situation in 1985, though critical, was not desperate, and (*b*) avoidable errors of judgement by the reformist leadership contributed to the system's demise.

On the first point, it was quite feasible that the Politburo might have chosen someone far more conservative than Gorbachev. In that case the system might well have gone on much as it was, propelled by inertia, for many more years. One Russian economist reckons that a positive rate of economic growth could have been maintained up to the year 2000 (Ellman 1993, citing S. Dubrovsky 1991). He presumably reached this reckoning on the basis of fallible Soviet statistical measurements. Moreover, such a prognosis leaves out of account non-economic factors, notably the institutional and international environment. An unreconstructed Soviet Union, committed to the arms race and to expanding its influence abroad by every available means, would sooner or later have come into conflict with the Western alliance and/or China. In 1985 the nuclear clock was approaching midnight. The USSR's international relations have been left out of consideration in these pages, but the omission distorts the picture. Let it be said that Gorbachev's principal achievements, his claim to a secure niche in history, lie in the field of foreign affairs. Specifically, he sought to end the 'cold war' by accepting arms limitation agreements based on an unequal reduction of the balance of forces. In doing so he took a calculated risk for the sake of peace—and found a ready response. This spared the world a nuclear holocaust—but changed the global power ratio to the USSR's disadvantage.[2]

As for Gorbachev's miscalculations, these have been discussed severally above. They were so grandiose that some contemporary observers thought they might be 'deliberate mistakes', i.e. that he was following a secret agenda and working to bring down the regime. Others believed that he was really in full control of his critics and that the evidence of impending catastrophe was illusory or exaggerated. Neither of these interpretations holds up.

Some of the most striking errors were:

(a) authorizing the 'spending spree' of 1985–6, which undermined the country's financial stability—already more seriously threatened than he realized, since under his predecessors budgetary matters had been treated as top secret;

(b) underestimating the gravity of ethnic tensions, which did not lend themselves to resolution by the rational, common-sense methods he applied;

(c) believing that the 'socialist option' was irreversible while weakening the Party machinery that embodied it;

(d) refusing to endorse the 1990 Shatalin programme for transition to a free market.

All these miscalculations were rooted in a failure to appreciate the true nature of the Soviet political system, which, being totalitarian, was held together ultimately by coercion and mendacious propaganda. 'The crux of Gorbachev's fatal misconception . . .', writes R. Karklins (1994), 'was that he did not see it [the system] . . . as being mutually exclusive with democracy.' By trying to liberalize some elements of it he undermined its internal coherence. In particular, the furtherance of *glasnost'* 'destroyed the underpinnings of the single official ideology'. It may seem churlish so to criticize a statesman who, after all, emancipated several hundred million people from thraldom. It is only fair to add that the oppressive and inefficient features of the Soviet system that he endeavoured to cure were the result of far graver errors of diagnosis by Stalin, Lenin, and Marx—all of whom might be assigned to the company of Molière's Drs Fleurant and Purgon. Since they had nearly killed the patient, should we blame Dr Gorbachev for being unable to resuscitate him?

The collapse of the USSR was an event of world-historical proportions. To assess it we need to adopt a perspective longer than that of the years immediately preceding its demise, and to consider what kind of 'empire' it was. It had both traditional and non-traditional features. To take the former first, there is nothing unusual about governments catering for the interests of élites or violently repressing dissenting groups, including whole ethnic minorities. The *nomenklatura* system of appointments would have been readily understood by the Pharaohs. Soviet Russia was the 'last of the empires' in the sense that it inherited a mantle of oriental despotism (Wittfogel) that was of great antiquity. Its lineage can be traced back through Imperial Russia to Muscovy, Byzantium, and beyond. Centralized, secretive bureaucratic government, a subservient priesthood, militarization, servitude for the tillers of the soil—these were some of its key features (not all of them necessarily present throughout). Historical precedents can be found even for such apparently unique Soviet practices as Party control of the government and multiple organs of verification. Contemporaries of Stalin liked to compare him with the tyrannical Ivan Groznyi, and the parallel seems to have struck the fancy of Iosif Vissarionovich himself (Tucker 1990).

But to concentrate exclusively on Eurasian despotic traditions is to misunderstand the nature of Soviet rule, indeed to abuse history. It can lead all too easily to national and racist stereotyping. The non-traditional element in the Soviet empire was far more important. *The USSR was not just the last of the Eurasian empires but also the first modern ideocratic-technocratic one.* Its *raison d'être* was to build a world-wide Communist order. The maximization of Russian/Soviet power was a means to this end, not an end in itself. It is of course true that this teleological ultimate goal mattered little to the average functionary, or even to some Party leaders. They were preoccupied with the here and now, with immediate practical problems—or, as some would say, with furthering their own power and interests. But this does not detract from the importance of ideology. It was, so to speak, the 'guiding star' or compass of the imperial system, the element that gave coherence to policies and decisions that otherwise would have been adjudged counterproductive. Solzhenitsyn was among those who saw this clearly. Soviet citizens who no longer believed in Marxism-Leninism had to act as if they did: this was all that the regime required of them.

(Under Stalin, of course, even sincere belief was not enough for survival.) The official doctrine never existed in pure form. It was always manipulated by the leader(s) of the day. They and their ideologues were often cynical, but this did not prevent them from insisting on public observance of the doctrine, and they maintained a large army of propagandists and controllers to this end—until Gorbachev, with his naïve belief in a 'return to the roots', exposed it as a fraud.

The impending collapse of the official belief structure had been foreseen by some perspicacious commentators. Ten years or so before Gorbachev Alain Besançon (1976) suggested that the Soviet regime was evolving from an ideocracy into a logocracy. 'Ideas are emptied of their content and retain only a verbal substance . . . The ideology rests upon a void. Its surface calm conceals its precariousness. Each shock causes damage that is harder to make good . . . The fabric is still intact and carefully maintained, but it has become thinned, worn down.'

In its early years the Soviet system was genuinely fideistic. Its appeal to the faithful was quasi-religious. Belief in the doctrine went hand in hand with emotional commitment, a sense of moral righteousness that could be exploited by those in power in order to rationalize and justify the revolutionary order, even when under Stalin this involved mass murder and the extension of Party controls to all domains of thought. But as the movement matured it became secularized. By the 1960s, if not earlier, 'the true believer is supplanted by the personal ambition of the careerist and the jurisdictional jealousies of the bureaucrat' (Daniels 1962). What bound the Party and its subjects was no longer zeal in the cause but material interest. Privilege and corruption took hold, Utopia receded. The ideology ceased to be credible—and ultimately self-destructed.

It is sometimes said that the Soviet Union 'imploded'. Strictly speaking, this is not true. The revolution of the nationalities was a reaction to the breakdown of authority at the centre. So too were protests by other sectional groups (intellectuals, miners). If one must seek a metaphor in the realm of fission, then it would be more accurate to speak of 'a chain of explosions'.

The USSR was the world's first ideocratic empire, but it was not the only one. It had parallels in the right-wing dictatorships of the inter-war era. These parallels should not be overworked, for the differences were as important as the similarities. Stalinists and Nazis did not learn much from each other, because the Soviet dictator had already perfected his techniques of rule before his German counterpart took power, and Hitler was too contemptuous of his rival in the East to study his achievements. Their partnership (1939–41) was tempestuous and brief. To be sure, the two regimes shared a cynical cult of power and disregarded all civilized norms of behaviour. Their crimes against humanity are on an equally appalling scale. But with half a century's historical hindsight what strikes one, surely, is less any *equivalence* in their conduct than their common *origin*.

Europe's attempted suicide in 1914–18 bred mass hatreds and frustrations that could be assuaged only by further blood-letting. Human values were eclipsed, the divine law trampled underfoot, old élites discredited or eliminated. In the social chaos and dislocation caused by the Great War, plebeian elements rose to the surface all over the continent. Many of their leaders were demagogues, easily attracted to grandiose schemes for a total remaking of mankind. Their designs could be rendered plausible to segments of the populace by the credit generally attached to modern science and technology, whose marvellous advances could so easily be abused.

Fortunately for humanity, the 'totalitarian temptation' proved to be of relatively short duration in terms of man's history. In 1943–5 the Fascist powers went down to defeat. Paradoxically, the Allied victory helped to consolidate Stalinism in the USSR and made possible its extension to Eastern and Central Europe. Yet Iosif Jugashvili had a mortal frame. His system could not survive his demise without modification. It adapted to new circumstances but in doing so became subtly transmuted. Society took heart. A handful of active dissenters emerged. They had the tacit support of millions. Doubt spread within the ruling *apparat*. Brezhnev's rule, with its neo-Stalinist features, was a poor copy of the original. Fifty years after the end of World War II, the great Soviet tyrant was not much more than a grey blur in the folk memory. His empire had given way to a host of independent modern nations. With varying degrees of success they were learning to live in peace with one another, to satisfy the requirements of democracy, and to cope with the ecological and psychological damage, poverty, and social distress that was the legacy of their common Soviet past. Their efforts merited aid as well as goodwill from the international community.

Notes

Chapter 1 (pages 9–38)

1. Another 105,000 of them were returned between Mar. 1946 and Jan. 1952, mainly from east European countries. The number of Soviet citizens who managed to stay abroad, most of them as 'displaced persons', was estimated by the repatriation agency at 452,000. Of these over half belonged to the three Baltic peoples and another third were Ukrainians or Belarusians (Zemskov 1990; Bonwetsch 1993).

2. Prior to Peter I's reign a legal distinction had existed between full and debt-contract slaves (*kholopy*)—and between both these categories and serfs (*krepostnye*). Similarly, in Stalin's Russia the *zeks* (prisoners) were principally divided between inmates of corrective-labour camps (ITK) and colonies (ITL) and 'special settlers' or exiles; others were held in ordinary jails and transit prisons. There are some intriguing legal parallels: for example, the principle that a free woman marrying a special settler acquired her husband's status had been recognized in ancient Russian law (Zemskov 1994). The *kholopy* were, of course, not incarcerated and did not owe their fate to action by the state, but the latter enforced their private owners' rights. The parallels should not, however, be pressed too far. A comparison with the status of various 'non-Aryan' peoples according to Nazi racial theories would be equally instructive.

3. In January 1945 there were still 631,000 survivors of the so-called *kulaks*, peasants deported for allegedly resisting collectivization during the First Five-Year Plan era. Mostly Russians or other Slavs, as distinct from members of non-Slavic minorities, they were gradually released from twenty-eight areas of settlement during the next few years: by Jan. 1952 they numbered 42,000 (Zemskov 1994).

4. In a later study (1993) Zemskov provided more complete police data on Baltic prisoners, 1951/3 as shown in tables 1.4—1.6 Baltic emigré sources estimate the total number of those deported at *c*.330,000 (Misiunas and Taagepera 1983). The difference can be explained in part by the death of many in captivity or by execution. According to B. Starkov (1993), on two days alone, 22 and 23 May 1948, no less than 11,345 'relatives of nationalists' and 39,766 *kulaks* were deported from the western territories. He refers to an

MVD report of 1953 which mentions a figure of '270,000 re-pressed', which presumably applies to all the Baltic peoples, not just to Lithuania as the context would suggest.

TABLE 1.4. *Balts in camps and colonies, January 1951*[a]

	Camps	Colonies	Total
Estonians	18,185	6,433	24,618
Latvians	21,689	6,831	28,520
Lithuanians	35,773	7,243	43,016
Totals	75,647	20,507	96,154[b]

[a] No figures are offered for a later date.

[b] 44,036 prisoners were confined in 'special' camps and prisons for 'particularly dangerous state criminals'. Zemskov does not make it clear whether they are included in the above figure.

TABLE 1.5. *Balts in exile ('special settlements'), January 1953*

'Special category exiles'[a]		'Special settlers'
Estonians	1,389	
Latvians	2,847	
Lithuanians	1,956	
Total	6,192	172,362[b]

[a] *Ssyl'no-pereselentsy* (sentenced to permanent exile), *ssyl'nye*, and *vyslannye*.

[b] 'On strength'; actually present 170,495; fugitives 162; under arrest 1,458.

TABLE 1.6. *Composition of 'special settlers', January 1953*[a]

Survivors of:	
1940–1 deportations[b]	14,301
1945–9 deportations	139,957
Peasants from Lithuania	18,104
Total	172,362

[a] 'on strength' figure.

[b] original figure 25,586.

[c] Of this total, 29 per cent were men, 47 per cent women, and 24 per cent children.

5. Zoshchenko was the author of a comic story about a monkey that escaped from a zoo, spent a day observing life in a Soviet city, but found the experience so distasteful that it returned with relief to captivity (Hosking 1985). This and other satires were not to the taste of humourless Party bureaucrats.

6. The common appellation 'affair' rests on a mistranslation of the Russian *delo*, in the sense of a (criminal) case or dossier of indictment. Malenkov's son has recently claimed that his father's role was innocuous (Malenkov 1992), but there is as yet no documentary evidence to support his claim.

7. Zhdanov had taken the leading role in founding the Cominform, so that Tito's defection, on top of other foreign policy reverses, weakened his position at home.

8. According to one theory, this was Poskrebyshev, Stalin's personal secretary, but he, too, had fallen foul of his master and been dismissed in December 1952; he then disappeared from view and retired in 1954. Stalin also had his bodyguard, Vlasik, arrested.

9. Recent accounts differ as to the details. The discovery may have been made as late as the morning of 2 March, but this story conflicts with other evidence.

Chapter 2 (pages 41–63)

1. Voroshilov, whom Khrushchev referred to rudely in the unexpurgated version of his memoirs as 'the biggest heap of s∗∗∗ ever to wear uniform', was not dropped from the Presidium until July 1960; he had then for four years been head of the Soviet state!

Chapter 3 (pages 64–83)

1. These trials were attended by a select audience which apparently included some ex-prisoners, but only the verdicts were reported in the press. The information given above was revealed only in 1989. According to another recent (KGB) source some 1,500 investigators were convicted of infringing 'socialist legality', but this figure has yet to be verified. Many escaped by virtue of the March 1953 amnesty law, which covered abuse of office, or else invoked the rule of negative prescription, a ten-year lapse of time since the offence (Albats 1992).

Chapter 4 (pages 84–102)

1. This revaluation did not affect domestic prices, but signified a depreciation of the rouble *vis-à-vis* foreign currencies. The official exchange rate to the dollar was raised from a farcical 1r. = 25 cents, to 1r. = $1.11, which at least was good for Soviet citizens' morale.

Chapter 5 (pages 103–19)

1. They disappeared after two years, their place being taken by local agencies of a new central body for machinery supply, Selkhoztekhnika.

2. Wädekin (1975) argues that it did not, citing 1972 Soviet data that show collective farmers' earnings rising by 41 per cent while industrial workers' earnings increased by 43 per cent between 1962 and 1969. He puts collective farmers' total household income at 1,223 roubles in 1960, and 1,870 roubles in 1965, with 42.9 per cent and 36.5 per cent of this coming from the private sector—less than McAuley's estimate which we have quoted above. The latter (1979) puts collective farmers' total income in 1960 and 1965 at 379 and 551 roubles respectively. This works out at 66.4 per cent and 76.4 per cent of state employees' income, suggesting that the gap was closing quite fast.

Chapter 6 (*pages 120–40*)

1. A pun. The word can be translated as 'district capital' or 'paradise city'.
2. Among them were several that later appeared in the West, notably Yevgeniia Ginzburg's memoir *Into the Whirlwind* and Varlam Shalamov's *Kolyma Tales*. Lydia Chukovskaia's novel about the Terror, *The Deserted House*, written in 1939–40, was approved for publication in 1963 but permission was then rescinded; it came out abroad in 1966. Also suppressed was Vasilii Grossman's great war novel *Life and Fate*, the manuscript of which was handed over to the KGB by the very journal editor to whom it was submitted, and did not appear abroad until 1980. Suslov told the author that his work would not be published in the Soviet Union for two hundred years. On *samizdat* and *tamizdat*, see Chapter 8.
3. A possible change in Bukharin's status as 'unperson' was discussed at top level on several occasions, but without result.
4. These were renamed 'general-educational evening and shift secondary schools', presumably to improve their image. They expanded from 2.3 million pupils in 1958/9 to 4.0 million in 1962/3.

Chapter 7 (*pages 141–62*)

1. The limitations of the theory are shown by the fact that the most active and articulate minorities in the USSR at this time, the Crimean Tatars, Chechens, and Ingush, were among the least 'mobilized' groups in terms of industrialization, urbanization, development of an intelligentsia, and other commonly applied sociological criteria—except, notably, mobility: for it was precisely their deportation *en bloc* to Central Asia by Stalin's henchmen in 1944, and the refusal of his successors to repudiate fully this barbarous act, that explains the all-encompassing vehemence of their campaign to be allowed to return to their ancestral territories. Early

modernization theorists were in any case not sure whether in-creased inter-ethnic contact among 'mobilized' peoples led to as-similation or to conflict. Empirical observation shows the latter outcome to be more likely, as is now generally recognized; but it occurs for varied reasons that need analysis in each particular case. Modernization theory, though very influential and certainly su-perior to its Marxist-Leninist counterpart, likewise suffers from sociological determinism and is best regarded by historians as a stimulating concept rather than as a 'model'.

2. Also revealing are the figures for Party members as a share of the total adult population of each republic in 1959 and 1970 (January), although these do *not* distinguish them by ethnic allegiance. Taking the all-Union figure as 100, the RSFSR's ratio shrank slightly (from 117 to 115), while that of Ukraine grew slightly (from 76 to 78); massive increases were registered in Belarus (61 to 80) and Estonia (60 to 79), and significant ones in Latvia (67 to 78), Lithuania (47 to 62), and Moldova (49 to 57). In Transcaucasia and Central Asia the ratio fell, because the population here was growing faster than elsewhere. All republics registered a higher percentage of adults who were Party members (Katz *et al.* 1975).

3. Other figures for Ukraine suggest that pupils receiving instruction in Ukrainian declined from 75 per cent in 1953/4 to 62 per cent in 1967/8 (Solchanyk 1985).

4. The other reasons had to do with foreign policy. Shelest took a 'hawkish' line towards the Prague spring and receiving President Nixon in Moscow for a summit meeting at the height of the Vietnam war. It is possible that he did so to camouflage his unorthodoxy on the national question; on the other hand, the Ukrainian leadership had grounds for fearing that Dubček's ideas might prove popular among Ukrainians.

Chapter 8 (pages 165–82)

1. Contemporary Western writers often gave figures of 22,000 and 10,000 churches. The former, which derives from the untrustworthy Metropolitan Nikodim, seems to have included 'non-functioning' churches and chapels.

2. This body, formed in January 1966 and headed by Kuroedov, amalgamated the two previously existing agencies that controlled Orthodox and non-Orthodox Christian churches.

3. Levitin was allowed to emigrate in 1974 and died in 1991. Talantov died in jail in 1971.

4. One of these evenings is movingly described by Mihajlov (1964), who quotes extensively from the camp songs.

5. On the expiry of his term Siniavsky was allowed to emigrate and took up a professorial appointment at the Sorbonne.

6. Penalties could amount to three years' jail (or one year of 'corrective labour') for the latter offence and seven years behind bars for the former.

7. The first were N. Gorbanevskaia, I. Gabai, and A. Yakobson. Later editors included S. Kovalev, T. Velikanova, T. Khodorovich, and Yu. Shikhanovich.

8. In 1973 Amalrik's sentence was extended but later he was allowed to go abroad, where he met an accidental death in 1980.

9. Grigorenko was sentenced to indefinite confinement in one of the worst such 'hospitals' but secured release in 1974, partly through the intervention of Solzhenitsyn and international diplomatic pressure. In 1977 he emigrated to the United States, where he died in 1987.

Chapter 9 (pages 183–202)

1. The total number of prosecutions for EDCS in 1967–74 was 4,879, of which about two-thirds were political, but this figure excludes prosecutions under Article 190–1.

2. This estimate is based on KGB information (1991) that at that date there were 1,053 labour camps with 760,000 inmates and 230 'settlement colonies'; 200 of the former are said to have been closed since 1985 (Ahlberg 1992).

3. Among them were Drs Snezhnevsky, director of the Psychiatric Institute of the Academy of Medical Sciences, Morozov and Lunts, of the Serbsky Institute for Forensic Psychiatry, and Vartanian of the All-Union Scientific Centre for Mental Health.

4. The Presidium had reverted to its old name by a decision of the Twenty-third Party congress (1966).

5. In 1986 no less than 2.7 million copies of Brezhnev's works (166 titles, including translations) remained unsold and were ordered to be pulped (*Ist*. 2/1994).

6. According to some sources this was Alzheimer's disease, although this is not stated by Chazov, head of the Health ministry's Fourth main directorate, whose account is otherwise informative. The historical parallel is closest in that relatives of 'Nurse N' received official favours: her undistinguished husband was rapidly promoted from captain to general. Of course before the Revolution it was not the tsar but his heir who was the invalid.

7. The commission was established in 1962 with Khrushchev as chairman. Originally it had several quasi-independent lawyer mem-

bers, but as reconstituted under Brezhnev in 1966 these individuals were replaced by Supreme Soviet deputies, i.e. in effect Party officials. The body appears to have remained dormant for years. In spring 1977 it was joined by twenty-one new members, making seventy-five in all. The secretary was Ponomarev, a leading ideological functionary.

Chapter 10 (pages 203–20)

1. This convoluted phrasing is necessary to include officials in the trade unions, Komsomol, and cultural agencies which were not formally part of the state administration.

2. In the first indigenous study of the *nomenklatura* (Korzhikhina and Fignater 1993), the authors, using Party records, put the number of Party officials in 1985 at 447,720. But not all of these will necessarily have been engaged full-time in Party or government work.

3. M. Matthews (1978) offers the following estimates:

TABLE 10.3.   *Monthly earnings of selected groups (1970–1973)* (roubles)

Government minister[a][b]	625
Party secretary, province	810
Manager, large enterprise:	
Coal	656
Oil/gas	483
Light industry	352
Director, research institute[c]	500–700
Newspaper editor, republic level	500–600
Shop manager (1975)	160–215[d]
Secondary schoolteacher, taxi-driver	140
Doctor	100–130
Skilled worker	80–140
Minimum wage[e]	60

[a] Includes 13th month, certificate-rouble allowance.
[b] Higher in defence sector.
[c] Plus 100 roubles for teaching.
[d] Source: Lane 1985.
[e] 1968.

These data need adjustment to include other personal income and transfer payments (pensions and allowances). According to A. McAuley, an industrial worker's annual disposable income in 1974 was 1,016 roubles. It had risen at a rate of 2.0 per cent per annum (1970–4), but if all state employees are included the increase was 2.9 per cent. This suggests that non-industrial workers were the prime beneficiaries. If one takes wages and salaries only, however, managerial and technical staff were relatively *worse* off *vis-à-vis* workers, falling from 100 : 136 in 1970 to 100 : 124 in 1975—and to 100 : 113 in 1981 (Lane 1985).

4. A pun on the 'little land', the Taman peninsula, where Brezhnev performed his much-acclaimed heroic exploits during World War II.

5. The Central Statistical Administration estimated that in 1972 the population paid 800 million roubles for goods sold above the official price (Kazantsev 1993), but this is probably too low.

Chapter 11 (pages 221–43)

1. For selected sectors of the economy the figures are as follows:

TABLE 11.6. *Capital and labour productivity: Selected sectors of economy, 1966–1979*

	Capital productivity			Labour productivity		
	1966–70	1971–5	1976–9	1966–70	1971–5	1976–9
Industry	2.2	−2.8	−3.3	3.2	4.1	1.6
Mining and manufacturing	−2.0	−3.2	−3.6	3.2	4.0	1.5
Construction	−6.3	−5.5	−6.1	1.1	2.4	0.8
Agriculture	−4.3	−8.0	−5.2	3.2	1.5	0.7

Source: Bialer 1986, citing US Congress, Joint Economic Committee 1982. For more recent estimates, calculated on a different basis, see Pitzer and Bankol 1991.

2. This accords with an earlier (1982) estimate by one Western specialist (Wiles) which was twice that of the CIA. P. Hanson (1984) puts the price increase for consumer durables in the 1970s at 3 to 4 per cent, while T. Buck and J. Cole (1987) suggest 2 per cent or less for all goods, but point out that if unofficial trade is included the inflation rate would be much higher.

3. These data are unreliable in that the figures for household income overstate the amount received as transfer payments (Bater 1989). On the other hand, a careful survey of emigrés, which excludes the value of social services but includes earnings from private work, arrives at a figure for 'actual' gross income (400 roubles a month) which is almost identical with the official figure (Vinokur and Ofer 1987).

4. The relevant figures are as follows:

TABLE 11.7. *Housing construction, 1971–1985*

Plan	Co-operative (%)	'By the population' (%)	Total (million sq. m.)	Percentage change compared to previous quinquennium
Ninth, 1971–5	6.0	22.1	544.8	5.1
Tenth, 1976–80	5.2	17.3	527.3	−3.2
Eleventh, 1981–5	6.0	14.5	552.2	4.7

5. 'The All-State System for Collection and Processing of Information for Reporting, Planning and Management of the National Economy.' This title must surely have broken some record for bureaucratic clumsiness, hence the convenient acronym.

6. This involved time-and-motion studies, setting norms for individual machines, and payment by piece-rates.

7. 20 to 22 per cent 'unplanned and spontaneous' (*tekuchii*), as distinct from 'normal' replacement of retirees or invalids.

Chapter 12 (pages 244–62)

1. Of 'land units', a synthetic measure.

2. Procurement prices remained stable from 1965 to 1978 but were raised three times over the next five years (Wegren 1992).

3. Figures for 1 January of the succeeding year.

4. According to budgetary data: TsSU 1991. Bater 1989 puts rural incomes at nine-tenths of urban ones in 1985, but presumably includes *sovkhoz* workers. Table 12.3 gives some basic data on the two types of farm during the Brezhnev era.

TABLE 12.3. *Collective and state farms, 1965–1985*

	1965	1975	1985
Kolkhozy:			
Number	36,300	28,500	26,200
Households (millions)	15.4	13.5	12.6
Sown area (million ha.)	105.1	98.2	91.3
Cattle (million)	38.3	47.6	50.6
Sovkhozy:			
Number	11,700	18,100	22,700
Employees (millions)	8.2	10.3	11.9
Sown area (million ha.)	89.1	107.3	108.2
Cattle (million)	24.5	35.6	42.0

5. This unofficial estimate was, however, challenged by Moscow scientists, who adhered to the figure of thirty deaths and 145 sufferers from acute radiation. Further evacuations from the 30-kilometre zone followed in and after 1990. In 1993 a Belarusian minister stated that 800,000 children had been directly affected by the Chernobyl explosion and that the frequency of cancer among them was fifty times the norm. Congenital birth defects were 40 per cent up on 1985 and the leading cause of infant mortality. One-quarter of the republic's territory was still contaminated (and 40 per cent affected to some degree); 18 per cent of the arable land could not be cultivated. In April 1994 it was officially stated that Belarusian children had the world's highest rate of cancer of the thyroid gland (38 cases per million). They also suffered changes of the immune system that made them susceptible to many other ailments.

Chapter 13 (pages 263–83)

1. The coefficient of natural increase per thousand inhabitants in selected union republics (*not* ethnic groups!) was as follows:

TABLE 13.2. *Coefficient of natural increase (per 000 inhabitants)*

	1980	1985	1989
USSR	8.0	8.8	7.6
RSFSR	4.9	5.3	3.9
Ukraine	3.5	2.9	1.7
Estonia	2.8	2.8	3.7
Latvia	1.4	2.1	2.4
Lithuania	4.6	5.4	4.8
Armenia	17.4	18.9	15.6
Uzbekistan	26.4	30.2	27.0
Tajikistan	40.0	40.2	32.2

2. 'Women's consultations' remained stable at 10 to 12 million per annum (1975–85), which works out at roughly twice for every child born.

3. According to one Soviet source, in the late 1980s the number of women who worked manually, without any mechanical aids, was 4.2 million, of whom 300,000 had to lift loads of over 10 kg., which could mean a total of 7 tons a day; 3.5 million were employed on jobs harmful to their health (Lemeshev 1991).

4. This agreement (1 August 1975) was not a formal treaty and so was binding on the USSR in a moral rather than a strictly legal sense. The human rights provisions contained in so-called 'Basket 2' were

a *quid pro quo* for Western agreement to recognize the legality of existing boundaries in Europe, which enhanced the USSR's international security.

5. The decision was actually taken by Brezhnev with a few of his cronies (Andropov, Gromyko, Ustinov) and then approved by the other members (A. S. Grossman 1993). Chazov (1992) puts Tikhonov in the inner group. Cherniaev (1993) places prime responsibility on Gromyko, Ustinov, Andropov, and Ponomarev (in that order).

Chapter 14 (pages 284–306)

1. Or, more properly, neo-*pochvenniki*, i.e. adherents of the 'native soil' movement of the 1850s.

2. He used the term *chuzhebesie*, borrowed from the 'forefather of pan-Slavism', Juraj Križanić, the seventeenth-century Croat traveller to Muscovy.

3. Tvardovsky resigned in February 1970, after the dismissal of several trusted lieutenants; he died of cancer in December 1971.

4. By analogy with an influential current of thought in the emigration of the 1920s (*Smenovekhovtsy*), which saw the Bolsheviks as misguided patriots who expressed the Russian national spirit. Stalinism cruelly exposed the irreality of such ideas.

5. In April 1990 *Novyi mir* put out a seven-volume edition of his *Collected Works*, three of which contained the text of *The Gulag Archipelago*, one-third of which had appeared in the journal in 1989. His epic chronicle of Russian history from 1914 to April 1917, *The Red Wheel*, appeared in Paris from 1985 onwards. It had four 'knots', the first of which was a reworking of *August 1914* (1978–83). Part of the second 'knot' was previously published in 1976 as *Lenin in Zurich*. In 1993 details emerged of the Politburo's decision to exile Solzhenitsyn abroad, as advocated by Andropov. Several leaders (Podgorny, Shelepin, Gromyko) would have preferred to keep him in a Soviet jail (*Ist.* 3/1993).

6. Vladimir Voinovich, author of the brilliant *Life and Strange Adventures of the Soldier Private Chonkin* (Paris, 1975; written 1963–70), emigrated in 1980. He was followed three years later by Georgii Vladimov, whose *Faithful Ruslan* (Frankfurt, 1975; written 1963–5) depicted with grim humour the breakup of the Gulag as seen through the eyes of a police dog.

7. These are not *actual* payments, which in 1984 totalled 68 million roubles for all churches. From the data given on the breakdown of expenditure and the number of clergy, average expenditure per (registered) clergyman works out at 855 roubles for Orthodox and 362 roubles for Baptists—but from these figures one would have to

deduct unknown amounts for non-clerical employees and building up a reserve.

Chapter 15 (pages 307–28)

1. Such data need adjustment for age differentials, but the following table indicates the general trend.

TABLE 15.6. *National composition of the CPSU, 1982* (number of members and candidates per 10,000 inhabitants)

All-Union:	678		
Slavs:		*Central Asians*:	
Russians	774	Uzbeks	525
Ukrainians	672	Kazakhs	525
Belarusians	706	Kyrgyz	348
		Turkmen	320
		Tajiks	268
Balts:		*Transcaucasians*:	
Estonians	561	Georgians	826
Latvians	508	Armenians	645
Lithuanians	459	Azeris	534

Source: Simon 1991.

The non-Russian Slavs reached or exceeded the all-Union ratio. The Party was stronger in Transcaucasia (especially Georgia, still in the lead) than in the Baltic or Central Asia, where three republics lagged by a considerable margin.

2. Apart from 20 whose nationality is unknown. See table in Simon 1991: 418, where however columns 5 and 6 are not strictly comparable, since the former includes candidate members.

3. As defined by A. McAuley, i.e. wages, earnings from private plots, social security payments, and interest from savings accounts, but excluding state expenditure on education and health as well as income from the second economy.

4. TABLE 15.7. *Provision of housing, RSFSR and Baltic republics, 1970—1985* (sq. m. per urban inhabitant)

	All-Union average	RSFSR	Estonia	Latvia	Lithuania
1970	11.1	11.2	13.4	13.8	12.0
1980	13.0	13.2	16.0	15.7	14.4
1985	14.1	14.1*	17.6	16.5	15.8

* 1984.

5. These were: monetary contributions (*sadaqa*), pilgrimages (*hajj*), fasting during Ramadan (*sawn*), five daily prayers (*salat*), and private profession of the faith (*shahada*).

6. The 'Spiritual Directorate' in Tashkent, which had responsibility for Muslims in Central Asia (including Kazakhstan), was the most important of four administrative bodies set up in 1942–4; the others were at Ufa, Makhachkala, and Baku. They came under the CRA and played much the same role as it did in controlling (and restricting) religious practices.

7. They may also have objected to the name's historical associations. M. V. Frunze (1885–1925), the Bolshevik military leader, had *inter alia* been active in Turkestan in 1919–20.

8. By 'Europeans' is meant here (and in Table 15.3) eastern Slavs, Germans, and Jews—the only groups large enough to be listed separately in the census data for the region. The figures for 'total European' are thus slightly understated. In considering ethnic relations it is better to take *all* European-origin immigrants than just Russians, as is usually done.

9. Recently published data on the flow of migrants to and from Central Asia (irrespective of nationality) show that 'the transition from net migration inflow to outflow took place in the mid-1970s, when there were no marked ethnic contradictions', and therefore had other (socio-economic) causes (Perevedentsev 1993).

10. In replying to another question, 92 per cent identified Estonians and Russians as the pair of nations whose relations were worst. On the methodology of the SIP, see Millar 1988. Although these 'third-wave' emigrés were 77 per cent Jewish, ethnic bias was deemed to be insignificant when questions of a general nature were answered. The total number of respondents was 2,793.

11. The figures (irrespective of nationality) are as follows (thousands): 1966–70: +151.9; 1971–5: +130.1; 1975–80: +101.4; 1981–5: +120.9; 1986–90: +99.1. For Estonia the peak years (over 6,000 per annum) were 1971–3, 1976, 1981, and 1985–6 (Park 1994).

Chapter 16 (*pages 331–62*)

1. Medvedev 1986, RFE/RL *Reports*. According to CIA figures, the average annual rate of industrial growth in 1985–9 was 2.2 per cent, as against 1.9 per cent in 1980–4; GNP rose from 1.7 to 1.9 per cent over the same time-span (Schroeder 1991).

2. Including fats of vegetable origin and margarine.

3. All-Union Centre for the Study of Public Opinion.

4. This decision had been taken before his accession. Used as an electrical factory and then as a home for juvenile delinquents, it

became the seat of the Orthodox Patriarch in lieu of Zagorsk. The foundations were blessed in 1985 'at a moving ceremony which had all the building workers crossing themselves and joining in hymns they still knew by heart' (Walker 1987). In Ukraine the Kiev monastery of the Caves was likewise restored to the Church.

5. He evidently went too far for his KGB superiors, as well as some members of the hierarchy, and in June 1989 lost his job to a hard-liner, Khristoradnov.

6. Such denunciations were not banned until February 1988, by an amendment to a law of April 1968. According to an Interior ministry report (1984), three-quarters of the delations received were found to be unsubstantiated.

7. Responsibility was later claimed by V. Nikonov (Wishnevsky 1991). Cherniaev (1993) identifies Ligachev as the principal source of high-level support for publication of the article. He was backed by Gromyko, Solomentsev, and Luk'ianov at a fierce debate in the Politburo on the affair. Gorbachev was furious but treated Ligachev with calculated moderation.

8. The Party statutes allowed conferences to be called between congresses. None had been held since 1941, the Eighteenth. Formally, a conference differed from a congress in that it had no power to re-elect the CC. The real significance of the gathering was that it gave the leadership a means of mobilizing grass-roots support for its policies without waiting until the five-year term between congresses had expired.

9. In Lithuania the popular front won 31 seats out of 42, in Latvia 25 seats out of 29, and in Estonia 15 seats out of 21.

10. Actually seven commissions, for there was another unpublicized one under Gorbachev himself which master-minded the entire operation (Lukes 1990).

11. As in pre-revolutionary Russia, this term was preferred to (parliamentary) party. The distinction expressed a subtle difference in the way deputies viewed their role.

12. In practice this became optional. The RSFSR, Kazakhstan, and Belarus retained this form of indirect representation but Ukraine did not. Republics were also left free to decide whether to retain conferences for the selection of deputies.

Chapter 17 (pages 363–83)

1. The Party's first secretary, Vezirov, had succeeded Bagirov in May 1988. Both men belonged to the 'machine' established during his long tenure of power by Aliev (1969–82), a mafia boss who was a veritable symbol of Brezhnevian 'stagnation'.

2. These details became known in 1993 with publication of a report submitted in December 1989 by an investigating commission chaired by A. Sobchak, sent by the Congress of People's Deputies. This exposed the fallacies in previous accounts and divided the blame between central and republic-level officials, who had over-reacted and irresponsibly opted for illegal and unnecessarily harsh repressive measures. Troops and police numbering 2,550 had confronted a crowd of 8,000 to 10,000. Four gas grenades of non-regulation type were fired at the crowd on the orders of a junior officer, Lieutenant-Colonel Baklanov, but this fact was covered up by the military authorities (*IA* 3/1993).

3. The Meskhetians were Georgian Muslims who had been deported to Central Asia on Stalin's orders in 1944.

4. Gorbachev's scheme for decentralizing economic management, first tested in Estonia, contributed to civic activism.

5. The Estonian parliament's declaration actually *followed* one in the same sense passed on 20 October 1988 by Lithuania's *Sajudis*, which the local Party had prevented the Lithuania Supreme Soviet from endorsing—much to the ire of a crowd of citizens assembled outside the building (Vardys 1991).

6. Georgia and Armenia likewise abstained, and in Moldova the native population stayed away from the poll. In Ukraine other questions were added which undermined its force. In Russia, Belarus, and Central Asia, however, the response was overwhelmingly positive.

7. By republics the figures are as follows:

TABLE 17.1. *Results of referendum in Baltic states, March 1991* (per cent)

	Estonia	Latvia	Lithuania*
Turn-out	83.0	87.6	84.4
Affirmative vote	77.7	73.7	90.5

*Held on 9 February 1991.

Chapter 18 (pages 384–411)

1. The RSFSR copied the all-Union arrangements and had both a Congress of People's Deputies and a Supreme Soviet. Party-political alignments were very fluid.

2. Purchases include commodities and services from the state and co-operative sectors. Savings are total monetary income less purchases, direct taxes, and social fees (Åslund 1991). K. Bush (1991)

puts the 'rouble overhang' at 500 milliard roubles (individual), plus 800 milliard roubles in enterprise deposits.

3. Ministry of Defence expenditure (pay etc.) was officially put at 20 milliard roubles per annum under Gorbachev (to 1989). This excludes military production, which is estimated to have risen (in current producers' prices) from 95 milliard roubles in 1985 to 120 milliard roubles in 1989; some of this was recouped by exports. After correction for 'value added', domestic military production rose from 109 to 141 milliard roubles or, on another reckoning, from 86 to 133 milliard roubles (1985–9: Kushnirsky 1993).

4. The Presidential Council was dissolved; the Federal Council, hitherto a consultative body, became a policy-making one, and a new Security Council was established. The government became a *Cabinet* of ministers.

5. 'Do you consider necessary the preservation of the USSR as a renewed federation of equal sovereign republics, in which the rights and freedom of the individual of any nationality will be fully guaranteed?'

6. In this there is a curious historical parallel with the Kornilov movement in July 1917. The conservative General saw the left-wing soviets as the principal foe and Kerensky's Provisional Government as their auxiliaries. He hoped to compromise with Kerensky, suppress the left and deal with him later. Kerensky, however, refused and by turning against Kornilov doomed his enterprise. Both the right and the centre were discredited and then destroyed by the extreme left. In 1991 Gorbachev acted likewise and also lost authority. Fortunately for Russia, Yeltsin was neither a Lenin nor a Kornilov.

7. Leningrad reverted to its pre-1914 name, St Petersburg, on 1 October 1991.

8. Rumours circulated that warrants had been issued for the arrest of 300,000 people and steps taken to reactivate the Gulag (Albats 1992).

9. By mid-December the latter tendency won out with the constitution of a Movement for Democratic Reforms headed by Yakovlev, Rutskoi, and St Petersburg's vigorous mayor, Sobchak; it did not, however, survive for long.

10. The five Central Asian republics, plus Azerbaijan, Armenia, and Moldova.

Afterword (*pages 412–20*)

1. Respectively 948 and 942; the average was 921 (employed persons). These figures include those with *incomplete* secondary education, hence the caveat.

2. Some Western writers hold that the USSR's collapse was a result of the United States' military and technological lead. The link is probably at best an indirect one, but there is as yet not enough evidence to answer the question definitively. One would need access to the Soviet general staff's situation analyses at the time.

Bibliography

For reasons of economy this list is restricted to works referred to in the text. Anonymous items are entered under the name of the compiler or contributor where known. Journal titles are abbreviated as follows:

IA *Istoricheskii arkhiv. Nauchno-publikatorskii zhurnal* (Moscow).
ICC *Izvestiia Tsentral'nogo komiteta KPSS* (Moscow).
Ist. *Istochnik. Dokumenty russkoi istorii. Prilozhenie k zhurnalu 'Rodina'* (Moscow).
OA *Otechestvennye arkhivy* (Moscow).
OI *Otechestvennaia istoriia* (Moscow).
SR *Slavic Review* (Columbus, Ohio, now Philadelphia).
SS *Soviet Studies* now *Europe–Asia Studies* (Glasgow).

ADAM, J. (1980), 'The Present Soviet Incentive System', *SS* 32: 349–65.

ADAMS, J. S. (1978), 'Institutional Change in the 1970s: The Case of the USSR People's Control Committee', *SR* 37: 457–72.

ADIRIM, I. (1990), 'Realities of Economic Growth and Distribution in the Baltic States', in D. A. Loeber *et al.* (eds.), *Regional identity*, 287–98.

AGURSKY, M. (1982), 'Der Einfluss des Nationalitätenproblems auf die Aussenpolitik der UdSSR', in G. Brunner and H. G. Herlemann (eds.), *Politische Kultur*, 65–84.

AHLBERG, R. (1992), 'Stalinistische Vergangenheitsbewältigung. Auseinandersetzung über die Zahl der GULAG-Opfer', *Osteuropa*, 11: 921–37.

AJUBEI, A. I. (1989), *Te desiat' let*, Moscow.

AKSIUTIN, Yu. V. (1989) (compilation), *N. S. Khrushchev: Materialy k biograwi,* Moscow.

ALBATS (ALBAZ), Ye. (J.) (1992), *Geheimimperium KGB: Totengräber der Sowjetunion,* trans. V. and S. Danilov, Munich.

ALEXEYEVA, L. (1985), *Soviet Dissent: Contemporary Movements for National, Religious and Human Rights,* trans. C. Pearce and J. Glad, Middletown, Conn.

ALLILUEVA, S. (1967), *Twenty Letters to a Friend,* trans. P. Johnson, London.

ALLWORTH, E. (1990), *The Modern Uzbeks: From the Fourteenth Century to the Present: A Cultural History,* Stanford, Calif.

AMALRIK, A. (1969), 'Will the Soviet Union Survive until 1984?' *Survey*, 73: 47–79 (also New York, 1970).

—— (1970), *Involuntary Journey to Siberia*, trans. M. Harari and M. Hayward, New York.

ANDERSON, B. (1987), 'The Life Course of Soviet Women...', in J. R. Millar (ed.), *Politics, Work and Daily Life*, 203–40.

ARUTUNIAN, YU. V. *et al.*, (1992), *Russkie: Etno-sotsiologicheskie ocherki*, Moscow.

ÅSLUND, A. (1991), *Gorbachev's Struggle for Economic Reform*, London.

ATKINSON, D., DALLIN, D. J., LAPIDUS, G. W. (1977) (eds.), *Women in Russia*, Stanford, Calif.

AVZEGER, L. (1991), 'Ispoved' byvshego tsenzora', *Gorizont*: 23–30 (first pub. in *Chernyi kabinet*, Tel Aviv, n.d.; Eng. trans., *Russian Politics and Law*, 31 (1992–3), 46–66.)

AZRAEL, J. R. (1978) (ed.), *Soviet Nationality Policies and Practices*, New York and London.

BAHRY, D. and NECHEMIAS, C. (1981), 'Half Full or Half Empty? The Debate over Soviet Regional Equality', *SR* 40: 366–83.

BALZER, H. D. (1991) (ed.), *Five Years that Shook the World: Gorbachev's Unfinished Revolution*, Boulder, Colo.

BARKER, E. (1973), *Die Rolle der Parteiorgane in der sowjetischen Wirtschaftslenkung 1957–1965*, Wiesbaden.

BARSUKOV, N. A. (1992), (introd.), 'Khrushchevskie vremena: Neprinuzhdennye besedy s politicheskimi deiateliami "velikogo desiatiletiia"', *Neizvestnaia Rossiia, XX vek*, fasc. i, Moscow, 279–305.

—— (1994), 'Na perelome', *Svobodnaia mysl'* 6: 95–106.

BATER, J. H. (1989), *The Soviet Scene: A Geographical Perspective*, London and New York.

BEISSINGER, M. R. (1983), 'The Political Élite', in J. Cracraft (ed.), *Soviet Union Today*, 35–51.

BEN-BARAK, S. (1990), 'The Impact of Socio-economic, Socio-cultural and Socio-political Factors on Demographic Trends: The Soviet Model' in Z. Gitelman (ed.), *Politics of Nationality*, 141–75.

BENNIGSEN, A. (1975), 'Islam in the Soviet Union: The Religious Factor and the Nationality Problem', in B. R. Bockiurkiw and J. W. Strong (eds.), *Religion and Atheism in the USSR and Eastern Europe*, London and New York, 91–100.

—— and LEMERCIER-QUELQUEJAY, C. (1986), *Le soufi et le commissaire: Les confrères musulmanes en URSS*, Paris.

BERNER, W. *et al.* (1975), *The Soviet Union 1973*. London.

BERRY, M. J. (1987), 'Science, Technology', in M. McCauley (ed.), *Khrushchev and Khrushchevism*, 71–94.

BESANÇON, A. (1976), 'Court traité de soviétologie à l'usage des autorités civiles, militaires et religieuses', repr. in idem (ed.), *Présent soviétique et passé russe*, Paris, 1980, 177–287.

BESEMERES, J. F. (1980), *Socialist Population Politics. The Political Implications of Demographic Trends in the USSR and Eastern Europe*, White Plains, NY.

BIALER, S. (1980), *Stalin's Successors: Leadership, Stability and Change in the Soviet Union*, Cambridge.

—— (1986), *The Soviet Paradox: External Expansion, Internal Decline*, New York.

—— (1989) (ed.), *Politics, Society and Nationality inside Gorbachev's Russia*, Boulder, Colo. and London.

BIDDULPH, H. L. (1979), 'Religious Participation of Youth in the USSR', *SS* 31: 417–33.

BINYON, M. (1983), *Life in Russia*, London.

BLOCH, S. and REDDAWAY, P. (1984), *Soviet Psychiatric Abuse: The Shadow over World Psychiatry*, London.

BOHNET, A. and PENKAITIS, N. (1990), 'Comparative Living Standards', in D. A. Loeber *et al.* (eds.), *Regional Identity*, 299–314.

BONWETSCH, B. (1991), 'Der "Grosse Vaterländische Krieg" und seine Geschichte', in D. Geyer (ed.), *Die Umwertung der sowjetischen Geschichte*, Göttingen, 167–87.

—— (1993), 'Sowjetische Zwangsarbeiter vor und nach 1945: Ein doppelter Leidensweg', *Jahrbücher für Geschichte Osteuropas* 41: 532–46.

BRADA, J. C. and WÄDEKIN, K.-E. (1988) (eds.), *Socialist Agriculture in Transition: Organizational Response to Failing Performance*, Boulder, Colo. and London.

BRESLAUER, G. W. (1982), *Khrushchev and Brezhnev as Leaders: Building Authority in Soviet Politics*, London.

—— (1989), 'From Brezhnev to Gorbachev: Ends and Means of Soviet Leadership Selection', in R. Taras (ed.), *Leadership Change in Communist States*, Boston and London, 24–72.

BROWN, A. (1980), 'The Power of the General Secretary of the CPSU', in T. H. Rigby, A. Brown, and P. Reddaway (eds.), *Authority, Power and Policy*, 135–57.

—— (1984), 'Political Science in the Soviet Union', *SS* 36: 317–44.

—— and KASER, M. (1975) (eds.), *The Soviet Union Since the Fall of Khrushchev*, London and New York.

BROWN, D. (1978), *Soviet Russian Literature Since Stalin*, New York and London.

BRUMBERG, A. (1962), *Russia under Khrushchev: An Anthology from 'Problems of Communism'*, New York.

BRUNNER, G. and HERLEMANN, H. G. (1980), (eds.), *Politische Kultur,*

Nationalitäten und Dissidenten in der Sowjetunion: ausgewählte Beiträge zum II. Weltkongress für sowjetische und osteuropäische Studien, Berlin.

BUCK, T. and COLE, J. (1987), *Modern Soviet Economic Performance*, Oxford.

BUGAI, N. F. (1991), ' "Pogruzheny v eshelony i otpravleny k mestam poselenii . . ." L. Beriia—I. Stalinu', *Istoriia SSSR* 1: 143–60.

—— (1992), '20—40-e gody: Deportatsiia naseleniia s territorii Yevropeiskoi Rossii', *OI*, 4: 37–49.

BURLATSKY, F. (1990), *Chrushchov: Ein politisches Porträt*, trans. V. Jovanovska, Düsseldorf.

BUSH, K. (1981), 'Retail Prices in Moscow and Four Western Cities in March 1979', in L. B. Schapiro and J. Godson (eds.), *Soviet Worker*, 251–85.

CAMPBELL, R. W. (1967), *Soviet Economic Power: Its Organization, Growth and Challenge*, 2nd edn., London.

CARRÈRE D'ENCAUSSE, H. (1978), *L'empire éclaté: La révolte des nations en URSS*, Paris.

—— (1981), *Stalin: Order Through Terror. (A History of the Soviet Union, 1917–1953)* ii, trans. V. Ionescu, London and New York.

—— (1982), 'Die Nationalitätenfrage auf der Tagesordnung des Kreml', in G. Brunner and H. G. Herlemann (eds.), *Politische Kultur*, 85–96.

CARTER, S. K. (1990), *Russian Nationalism: Yesterday, Today, Tomorrow*, London.

CHAPMAN, J. G. (1977), 'Equal Pay for Equal Work?', in D. Atkinson, D. J. Dallin, and G. W. Lapidus (eds.), *Women in Russia*, 225–39.

CHAZOV, Ye. (1992), *Zdorov'e i vlast': Vospominaniia 'kremlevskogo vracha'*, Moscow.

CHERNEV, A. D. (1992), 'Vlast' i istoricheskaia nauka', *OA* 3: 62–88, 4: 43–64, 5: 31–55.

CHERNIAEV, A. S. (1993), *Shest' let s Gorbachevym: po dnevnikovym zapisiam*, Moscow.

CHOLDIN, M. T. and FRIEDBERG, M. (1989), *The Red Pencil: Scholars and Censors in the USSR*, Cambridge.

CHRISTIAN, D. (1982), 'The Supervisory Function in Russian and Soviet History', *SR* 41: 73–90.

CHUEV, F. (1991), *Sto sorok besed s Molotovym: Iz dnevnika*, Moscow.

CLARK K. (1981), *The Soviet Novel: History as Ritual*, Chicago and London.

—— (1990), 'The Changing Image of Science and Technology in Soviet Literature', in L. R. Graham (ed.), *Science and the Soviet Social Order*, Cambridge, Mass., 259–98.

CLARK, W. A. (1993), 'Crime and Punishment in Soviet Officialdom, 1965–1990', *Europe–Asia Studies* 45: 259–80.

CLARKE, R. A. (1972), *Soviet Economic Facts, 1917–1970*, London and Basingstoke.

CLEMENS, W. C., Jr. (1990), 'Baltic Communism and Nationalism', in U. Ra'anan (ed.), *Soviet Empire*, 95–121.

COHEN, S. F., RABINOWITCH, A., and SHARLET, R. (1980) (eds.). *The Soviet Union Since Stalin*, Bloomington, Ind. and London.

COLTON, T. J. (1977), 'The Zhukov Affair Reconsidered', *SS* 29: 185–213.

CONNOR, W. D. (1971), 'Alcohol and Soviet Society', *SR* 30: 570–88.

—— (1991), 'Class, Social Structure, Nationality,' in A. J. Motyl (ed.), *Post-Soviet Nations*, 272–301.

—— (1991), 'Soviet Policies Towards Non-Russian Peoples in Theoretic and Historic Perspective', ibid., 30–49.

CONYNGHAM, W. J. (1982), *The Modernization of Soviet Industrial Management: Socio-economic Development and the Search for Viability*, Cambridge.

CONQUEST, R. (1967), *Power and Policy in the USSR: The Struggle for Stalin's Succession, 1945–1960*, New York and Evanston, Ill. (1st edn., 1961).

CRACRAFT, J. (1983) (ed.), *The Soviet Union Today: An Interpretive Guide*, Chicago.

CRITCHLOW, J. (1977), 'Nationalism in Uzbekistan in the Brezhnev Era', in G. W. Simmonds (ed.), *Nationalism*, 306–15.

—— (1990), 'Islam in Soviet Central Asia: Renaissance or Revolution?', in *Religion in Communist Lands*, 18: 196–210.

DANIELS, R. V. (1962), *The Nature of Communism*, New York.

DAVIS, N. (1991), 'The Number of Churches Before and After the Khrushchev Anti-Religious Drive', *SR* 50: 612–20.

DE JONGE, A. (1986), *Stalin and the Shaping of the Soviet Union*, London.

DELLENBRANT, J. (1990), 'The Integration of the Baltic Republics into the Soviet Union', in D. A. Loeber *et al.* (eds.), *Regional Identity*, 101–20.

DE PAUW, J. W. (1969), 'The Private Sector in Soviet Agriculture', *SR* 28: 63–71.

DOBROKHOTOV, L. N. (1992), *Gorbachev—Yeltsin: 1500 dnei politicheskogo protivostoianiia* (compilation), Moscow.

DODGE, N. T. (1977), 'Women in the Professions', in D. Atkinson, D. J. Dallin, and G. W. Lapidus (eds.), *Women in Russia*, 205–24.

DOVRING, F. (1966), 'Soviet Farm Mechanization in Perspective', *SR* 25: 287–302.

DUGIN, A. N. (1990), 'Stalinizm: Legendy i fakty', *Slovo*, 7.

DUNLOP, J. B. (1983), *Faces of Contemporary Russian Nationalism*, Princeton, NJ.

—— (1985), *The New Russian Nationalism* (foreword R. Byrnes), New York.

—— (1990), 'The Russian Orthodox Church and Nationalism after 1988', *Religion in Communist Lands*, 18: 292–306.

DUNN, E. (1977), 'Russian Rural Women', in D. Atkinson, D. J. Dallin, and G. W. Lapidus (eds.), *Women in Russia*, 167–88.

DYKER, D. A. (1981), 'Planning and the Worker', in L. B. Schapiro and J. Godson (eds.), *Soviet Worker*, 39–75.

EKMANIS, R. (1975), 'Latvian Literature', in G. S. N. Luckyj (ed.), *Discordant Voices*, 47–88.

ELLIS, J. (1986), *The Russian Orthodox Church: A Contemporary History*, Beckenham and Sydney.

ELLMAN, M. (1986), 'The Macro-economic Situation in the USSR', *SS* 38: 530–42.

—— (1993), 'Multiple Causes of the Collapse', *Radio Liberty Report*, 4 June, 55–8.

ERICSON, R. E. (1992), 'Soviet Economic Structure and the National Question', in A. J. Motyl (ed.), *Post-Soviet Nations*, 240–71.

FAINSOD, M. (1963), *How Russia is Ruled* (rev. edn.), Cambridge, Mass. and London.

FAIRBANKS, C. H., Jr. (1978), 'National Cadres as a Force in the Soviet System: The Evidence of Beria's Career', in J. R. Azrael (ed.), *Soviet Nationality Policies*, 144–86.

FELDBRUGGE, F. J. M. (1977), 'Soviet Corrective Labour Law', in D. D. Barry, *et al.* (eds.), *Soviet Law After Stalin*, Leiden, i. 33–69.

—— (1984), 'Government and Shadow Economy in the Soviet Union', *SS* 36: 528–43.

—— (1987) (ed.), *The Distinctiveness of Soviet Law*, Dordrecht.

FIELD, M. G. (1987), 'Medical Care in the Soviet Union: Promises and Realities', in H. G. Herlemann (ed.), *Quality of Life*, 65–82.

—— (1991), 'Soviet Health Problems . . .', in A. Jones, W. D. Connor, and D. E. Powell (eds.), *Soviet Social Problems*, 78–93.

FIERMAN, W. (1985), 'Language Development in Uzbekistan', in I. T. Kreindler (ed.), *Sociolinguistic Perspectives*, 205–33.

FILTZER, D. A. (1987), 'Labour', in M. McCauley (ed.), *Khrushchev and Khrushchevism*, 118–37.

—— (1989), 'The Soviet Wage Reform of 1956–1962', *SS* 41: 88–110.

FISCHER, M. E. (1983), 'Women', in J. Cracraft (ed.), *Soviet Union Today*, 305–16.

FISHER, W. A. (1977), 'Ethnic Consciousness and Intermarriage:

Correlates of Endogamy among Major Soviet Nationalities', *SS* 29: 395–408.

FLETCHER, W. C. (1971), 'Religious Dissent in the USSR in the 1960s', *SR* 30: 298–316.

FRANKEL, E. R. (1981), *'Novyi mir': A Case Study in the Politics of Literature*, Cambridge.

FRIEDGUT, T. H. (1979), *Political Participation in the USSR*, Princeton, NJ.

—— (1992), 'Nations of the USSR . . .', in A. J. Motyl (ed.), *Post-Soviet Nations*, 190–219.

GAGNON, V. P., Jr. (1987), 'Gorbachev and the Collective Contract Brigade', *SS* 39: 1–23.

GEYER, D. (1993), 'Der Zerfall des Sowjetimperiums und die Renaissance der Nationalismen', in H. A. Winkler and H. Kaelble (eds.), *Nationalismus—Nationalitäten—Supranationalität*, Stuttgart 156–86.

GITELMAN, Z. (1983), 'Are Nations Merging in the USSR?', *Problems of Communism*, 32, Sept.–Oct., 35–47.

—— (1990), 'The Nationalities', in S. White, A. Pravda, and Z. Gitelman (eds.), *Developments in Soviet Politics*, 137–58.

—— (1992), *The Politics of Nationality and the Erosion of the USSR: Selected Papers from the IVth World Congress for Soviet and East European Studies, Harrogate, 1990*, Basingstoke.

GOBLE, P. A. (1990), 'Sowjetstaat und russischer Nationalismus', in A. Kappeler (ed.), *Die Russen*, Cologne, 91–102.

GODSON, J. (1981), 'The Role of the Trade Unions', in L. B. Schapiro and J. Godson (eds.), *Soviet Worker*, 106–29.

GOLDBERG, J. (1990), 'Socialist Realism as Institutional Practice', in H. Günther (ed.), *The Culture of the Stalin Period*, 149–77.

GOLDMAN, M. I. (1972), *Spoils of Progress: Environmental Pollution in the Soviet Union*, Cambridge, Mass. and London.

—— (1983), *USSR in Crisis: The Failure of an Economic System*, New York and London.

—— (1992), 'Environmentalism and Nationalism: An Unlikely Twist in an Unlikely Direction', in J. Massey Stewart (ed.), *Soviet Environment*, 1–10.

GOLOMSTOCK, I. (1990), 'Problems in the Study of Stalinist Culture', in H. Günther (ed.), *The Culture of the Stalin Period*, 110–21.

GORBACHEV, M. S. (1987), *Perestroika: New Thinking for our Country and the World*, New York and London.

GORLIN, A. (1974), 'The Soviet Economic Associations', *SS* 26: 3–27.

GRAZIOSI, I. (1992), 'The Great Strikes of 1953 in Soviet Labour Camps in Accounts of Their Participants: A Review', *Cahiers du monde russe et soviétique*, 33: 419–46.

GRIGORENKO, P. (1980), *Erinnerungen*, Munich.

GROSSMAN, A. S. (1993) (contrib.), 'Sekretnye dokumenty iz osobykh papok', *Voprosy istorii*, 3: 3–33.

GROSSMAN, G. (1956), 'Soviet Agriculture since Stalin', *Annals of the American Academy of Political and Social Science*, Jan.

—— (1963), 'The Soviet Economy in the Post-Stalin Decade', in W. Petersen (ed.), *The Realities of World Communism*, Englewood Cliffs, NJ.

GROYS, B. (1990), 'The Birth of Socialist Realism from the Spirit of the Russian Avant-garde', in H. Günther (ed.), *The Culture of the Stalin Period*, 122–48.

GÜNTHER, H. (1990) (ed.), *The Culture of the Stalin Period*, London.

HAHN, W. G. (1982), *Postwar Soviet Politics: The Fall of Zhdanov and the Defeat of Moderation, 1946–1953*, Ithaca, NY and London.

HAJDA, L. (1980), 'Nationality and Age in Soviet Population Change', *SS* 32: 475–99.

HANEY, J. V. (1973), 'The Revival of Interest in the Russian Past in the Soviet Union', *SR* 32: 1–16.

HANSON, P. (1968), *The Consumer in the Soviet Economy*, London and Toronto.

—— (1983), 'Success Indicators Revisited', *SS* 35: 1–13.

HARRISON, M. (1993), 'Soviet Economic Growth since 1928: The Alternative Statistics of G. I. Khanin', *Europe–Asia Studies*, 45: 141–67.

HAUSLOHNER, P. (1990), 'Politics Before Gorbachev: Destalinization and the Roots of Reform', in S. Bialer (ed.), *Politics, Society and Nationality*, 41–90.

HAZARD, J. N. (1971), 'Soviet Law and Justice', in J. W. Strong (ed.), *The Soviet Union under Brezhnev and Kosygin: The Transition Years*, New York, Toronto, and Melbourne, 93–114.

HEDLUND, S. (1984), *Crisis in Soviet Agriculture*, Beckenham and Sydney.

HEGAARD, S. E. (1977), 'Nationalism in Azerbaijan in the Era of Brezhnev', in G. W. Simmonds, *Nationalism*, 188–99.

HELLER, M. (1975), *Stacheldraht der Revolution: Die Welt der KZ-Lager in der sowjetischen Literatur*, Stuttgart.

HERLEMANN, H. G. (1987) (ed.), *The Quality of Life in the Soviet Union*, Boulder, Colo. and London.

HILL, R. J. (1990), 'The Party', in S. White, A. Pravda, and Z. Gitelman (eds.), *Developments in Soviet Politics*, 67–86.

—— and LÖWENHARDT, J. (1991), '*Nomenklatura* and *perestroika*', *Government and Opposition*, 26: 229–43.

HINGLEY, R. (1983), *Pasternak: A Biography*, New York.

HOFFMANN, E. P. (1980), 'Changing Soviet Perspectives on Leadership and Administration', in S. F. Cohen, A. Rabinowitch, and R. Sharlet (eds.), *Soviet Union since Stalin*, 71–92.

HOLLANDER, P. (1991), 'Politics and Social Problems', in A. Jones, W. D. Connor and D. E. Powell (eds.), *Soviet Social Problems*, 9–23.

HOSKING, G. (1973), 'The Russian Peasant Rediscovered: "Village Prose" of the 1960s', *SR* 32: 705–24.

—— (1980), *Beyond Socialist Realism: Soviet Fiction Since Ivan Denisovich*, London and New York.

—— (1985), *A History of the Soviet Union*, London.

—— (1990), *The Awakening of the Soviet Union*, Cambridge, Mass.

IGRITSKY, YU. I. (1993), 'Snova o totalitarizme', *OI* 1: 3–17.

International Helsinki Federation for Human Rights (1986), *The Moscow Helsinki Group: Ten Years: Their Vision, Their Achievements, The Price they Paid: A Report, 1976–1986*, Vienna.

IOFFE, O. S. (1985), *Soviet Law and Soviet Reality*, Dordrecht, Boston, and Lancaster.

JOHNSON, D. GALE (1983), 'Agriculture', in J. Cracraft, *Soviet Union Today*, 195–207.

JONES, A., CONNOR, W. D., and POWELL, D. E. (1991) (eds.), *Soviet Social Problems*, Boulder, Colo., San Francisco, and Oxford.

JONES, D. and SMOGORZEWSKA, J. (1982), 'Dairy Farming in the USSR: Policy and Reality', *SS* 34: 254–69.

JONES, S. F. (1990), 'Revolutions within Revolutions: Minorities in the Georgian Republic', in Z. Gitelman (ed.), *Politics of Nationality*, 77–101.

JOWITT, K. (1983), 'Soviet Neo-traditionalism: The Political Corruption of a Leninist Regime', *SS* 35: 275–97.

JUVILER, P. H. (1991), '... Perestroika for the Family?', in A. Jones, W. D. Connor, and D. E. Powell (eds.), *Soviet Social Problems*, 194–212.

KAMENETSKY, I. (1977) (ed.), *Nationalism and Human Rights: Processes of Modernization in the USSR*, Littleton, Colo.

KAMINSKAYA, D. (1982), *Final Judgement: My Life as a Soviet Defense Attorney*, New York.

KAPPELER, A. (1990) (ed.), *Die Russen: ihr Nationalbewusstsein in Geschichte und Gegenwart*, Cologne.

KARCZ, J. F. (1970), 'Some Major Persisting Problems in Soviet Agriculture', *SR* 29: 417–28.

KARKLINS, R. (1986), *Ethnic Relations in the USSR: The Perspective from Below*, Boston and London.

—— (1989), 'The Organization of Power in Soviet Labour Camps', *SS* 41: 276–97.

—— (1994), 'Explaining Regime Change in the Soviet Union', *Europe-Asia Studies*, 46: 29–45.

KARPUKHIN, V. (1992), 'They Refused to Storm the White House. Interview with KGB Major-General V. Karpukhin and Subordinate Officers', *Russian Politics and Law*, 31:/1: 8–15

KASER, M. (1970), *Wirtschaftspolitik der Sowjetunion: Ideologie und Praxis*, Munich.

—— (1975), 'The Economy: A General Assessement', in A. Brown and M. Kaser (eds.), *Soviet Union*, 196–217.

KATSENELINBOIGEN, A. (1977), 'Coloured Markets in the Soviet Union', *SS*, 29: 62–85.

KATZ, Z., ROGERS, R., and HARNED, F. (1975) (eds.), *Handbook of Major Soviet Nationalities*, New York and London.

KAZANTSEV, B. N. (1993), ' "Chastnik" v sfere bytovogo obsluzhivaniia', *Sotsiologicheskie issledovaniia* 11: 50–8.

KHRUSHCHEV, N. S. (1971), *Khrushchev Remembers*, trans., S. Talbott, Boston and London.

—— (1991), *Khrushchev Remembers: The Glasnost' Tapes*, Boston and London.

KIRBY, D. (forthcoming), *The Baltic World, 1762–1993*, London and New York.

KNIGHT, A. W. (1988), *The KGB: Police and Politics in the Soviet Union*, Boston and London.

—— (1993), *Beria: Stalin's First Lieutenant*, Princeton, NJ.

KOKURIN, A. I. (1994) (comp.) 'Vosstanie v Steplage, mai—illun' 1954 g.', *OA* 4: 33–81.

KOMAROV, B. (pseud.: Z. Vol'fson) (1980), *The Destruction of Nature in the Soviet Union*, London.

KONDRATEV, F. (1994), 'Sovetskaia psikhiatriia: Sekrety perevernutoi stranitsy istorii', *Rossiiskaia iustitsiia*, 1: 24–38.

KORZHIKHINA, T. P. AND FIGNATER, YU. YU. (1993), 'Sovetskaia nomenklatura: Stanovlenie, mekhanizm, deistviia', *Voprosy istorii*, 7: 25–38.

KRAIUSHKIN, A. and TEPTSOV, N. (1992), 'Kak snizhali tseny v kontse 40-kh—nachale 50-kh gg. i chto ob etom govoril narod', *Neizvestnaia Rossiia: XX vek*, fasc. ii, Moscow, 282–96.

KOZYREV, A. (1989), 'Bud'te velikodushny!', in Yu. V. Aksiutin (ed.), *Khrushchev*, 131–3.

KRAMER, J. M. (1983), 'Environmental Problems', in J. Cracraft (ed.), *Soviet Union Today*, 153–61.

KREINDLER, I. T. (1985) (ed.), *Sociolinguistic Perspectives on Soviet National Languages: Their Past, Present and Future*, Berlin, New York, and Amsterdam.

KRIVOV, N. A., SIGACHEV, YU. V., and CHERNOBAEV, A. A. (1993) (comps.), 'Religii i tserkvi v SSSR: Statisticheskii otchet Soveta po delam religii pri Sovete ministrov za 1984 g.', *IA* 1: 137–44, 2: 90–126.

KUKK, M. (1993), 'Political Opposition in Soviet Estonia, 1940–1987', *Journal of Baltic Studies*, 24: 369–84.

KÜNG, A. (1981), *A Dream of Freedom: Four Decades of National Survival versus Russian Imperialism in Estonia, Latvia and Lithuania, 1940–1980*, Cardiff and Toronto.

KUSHNIRSKY, F. I. (1993), 'Lessons from Estimating Military Production of the Former Soviet Union', *Europe–Asia Studies*, 45: 483–503.

KUTUZOV, V. A. (1989), 'Tak nazyvaemoe "Leningradskoe delo" ', *Voprosy istorii KPSS* 3: 53–67.

LANE, D. (1985), *Soviet Economy and Society*, New York.

LAPIDUS, G. W. (1992), 'New Thinking and the National Question', in A. Brown (ed.), *New Thinking in Soviet Politics*, Basingstoke, 39–70.

LAZAREV, V. (1992) (contrib.), 'Posledniaia bolezn' Stalina: Iz otchetov MVD SSSR o nastroeniiakh v armii vesnoi 1953 g', *Neizvestnaia Rossiia: XX vek*, fasc. ii, Moscow, 253–8.

LEBEDEV, V. A. (1992) (contrib.), ' "Ob'ediniates' vokrug Khrista— bol'sheviki povysili tseny." Otnoshenie naseleniia SSSR k povysheniiu tsen na produkty pitaniia v 1962 g.', *Neizvestnaia Rossiia: XX vek*, fasc. ii, Moscow, 145–76.

LEMESHEV, M. YA. (1991), *Désastre écologique en URSS: Les ravages de la bureaucratie*, Paris.

LESAGE, M. (1978), *La constitution de l'URSS, 7 octobre 1977: Texte et commentaires*, Paris.

LEVADA, YU. (1989), 'Stalinskie al'ternativy', in Kh. Kobo (ed.), *Osmyslit' kul't Stalina*, Moscow, 448–59.

LEVITS, E. (1990), 'Lettland unter sowjetischen Herrschaft', in B. Meissner (ed.), *Die baltischen Staaten*, 131–70.

LOEBER, D. A., VARDYS, V. S., and KITCHING, L. P. A. (1990) (eds.), *Regional Identity under Soviet Rule: The Case of the Baltic States*, Hackettstown, NJ.

LÖWENTHAL, R. (1970), 'Development versus Utopia in Communist Policy', in C. Johnson (ed.), *Change in Communist Systems*, Stanford, Calif., 33–116.

LUBIN, N. (1984), *Labour and Nationality in Soviet Central Asia: An Uneasy Compromise*, London and Basingstoke.

LUCKYJ, G. S. N. (1975), 'Ukrainian Literature,' in idem (ed.), *Discordant Voices*, 127–38.

—— (1975), *Discordant Voices: The Non-Russian Soviet Literatures, 1953–1973*, Oakville, Ont.

LUKES, I. (1990), 'Will the CPSU Survive Gorbachev's Reform?', in U. Ra'anan (ed.), *Soviet Empire*, 3–21.

McAULEY, A. (1979), *Economic Welfare in the Soviet Union: Poverty, Living Standards and Inequality*, Madison, Wis.

McCAULEY, M. (1976), *Khrushchev and the Development of Soviet Agriculture: The Virgin Lands Programme, 1953–1964*, London and Basingstoke.

—— (1981), *The Soviet Union Since 1917*, London and New York.

—— (1987) (ed.), *Khrushchev and Khrushchevism*, Bloomington, Ind.

—— (1991), *Nikita Khrushchev*, London.

MADISON, B. (1977), 'Social Services for Women: Problems and Priorities', in D. Atkinson, D. J. Dallin, G. W. Lapidus (eds.), *Women in Russia*, 307–32.

MALENKOV, A. (1992), *O moem ottse Georgii Malenkove*, Moscow.

MARCHENKO, A. T. (1969), *My Testimony*, trans. A. Scammell, London.

MARIE-SCHWARTZENBERG, N. (1993), *Le KGB: Des origines à nos jours*, Paris.

MARPLES, D. R. (1986), *Chernobyl and Nuclear Power in the USSR*, Basingstoke.

—— (1991), 'Chernobyl: Observations on the Fifth Anniversary', *Soviet Economy*, 7: 175–88.

MASSEY STEWART, J. (1992) (ed.), *The Soviet Environment: Problems, Policies and Politics*, Cambridge.

'Materialy plenuma TsK KPSS: oktiabr' 1964', *IA* 1/1993, 3–19.

MATTHEWS, M. (1972), *Class and Society in Soviet Russia*, London.

—— (1978), *Privilege in the Soviet Union: A Study of Élite Life-styles under Communism*, London.

MEDVEDEV, R. A. (1984), *Khruschchev*. trans. B. Pearce, Garden City, NY.

—— (1989), *Let History Judge: The Origins and Consequences of Stalinism*, rev. edn., trans. G. Shriver, New York.

MEDVEDEV, ZH. A. (1969), *The Rise and Fall of T. D. Lysenko*, trans. I. J. Lerner, New York.

—— (1979), *Nuclear Disaster in the Urals*, London.

—— (1986), *Gorbachev*, New York and London.

—— (1990), *The Legacy of Chernobyl*, New York.

MEHNERT, K. (1962), *Soviet Man and His World*, trans. M. Rosenbaum, New York.

MEISSNER, B. (1990) (ed.), *Die baltischen Staaten: Estland, Lettland, Litauen*, Cologne.

MEYENDORFF, J. (1977), 'The Byzantine Impact on Russian Civilization', in S. H. Baron and N. Heer (eds.), *Windows on the Russian Past: Essays on Soviet Historiography Since Stalin*, Columbus, Ohio, 45–56.

MICKIEWICZ, E. P. (1971), 'The Modernization of Party Propaganda in the USSR', *SR* 30: 257–76.

—— (1981), *Media and the Russian Public*, New York.

MICKLIN, P. P. (1992), 'Water Management in Soviet Central Asia: Problems and Prospects', in J. Massey Stewart (ed.), *Soviet Environment*, 88–114.

MIHAJLOV, M. (1964), *Moskauer Sommer 1964*, Bern.

MILLAR, J. R. (1973), 'Financial Innovation in Contemporary Soviet Agricultural Policy', *SR* 32: 91–114.

—— (1985), 'The Little Deal: Brezhnev's Contribution to Acquisitive Socialism', *SR* 44: 694–706.

—— (1988), 'History, Method and the Problem of Bias', in idem (ed.), *Politics, Work and Daily Life*, 3–30.

—— (1988), (ed.), *Politics, Work and Daily Life in the USSR: A Survey of Former Soviet Citizens*, Cambridge.

MILLER, R. F. and FÉHER, F. (1984) (eds.), *Khrushchev and the Communist World*, London and Toyota, NJ.

MISIUNAS, R. J. and TAAGEPERA, R. (1983), *The Baltic States: Years of Dependence, 1940–1980*, London.

MOTE, V. L. (1992), 'BAM after the Fanfare', in J. Massey Stewart (ed.), *Soviet Environment*, 40–56.

MOTYL, A. J. (1992), 'The End of Sovietology', in idem (ed.), *Post-Soviet Nations*, 302–15.

—— (1992) (ed.), *The Post-Soviet Nations: Perspectives on the Demise of the USSR*, New York.

Neizvestnaia Rossiia: XX vek, Moscow, 1992–.

NEKRICH, A. M. (1979), *Otreshis' ot strakha: Vospominaniia istorika*, London.

NIKIFOROV, E. I. (1993) (comp.), 'Novoe o vystavke v Manezhe 1962 g.', *OA* 2: 38–45.

NOSOV, E. (1989), 'Kostroma ne Aiova (1988)', in Yu. V. Aksiutin (ed.), *Khrushchev*, 97–105.

NOVAK, M. (1990), *Du Printemps de Prague au Printemps de Moscou*, Geneva.

NOVE, A. (1970), 'Soviet Agriculture under Brezhnev', *SR* 29: 379–410.

—— (1979), *Political Economy and Soviet Socialism*, London.

—— (1984), 'Soviet Agriculture: The Search for Solutions' (lecture).

—— (1988), 'Rosefielde on Birman: A Comment', *SS* 40: 640–3.

—— (1989*a*), *Glasnost' in Action: Cultural Renaissance in Russia*, London and Boston.

—— (1989*b*), *Stalinism and After: The Road to Gorbachev*, 3rd edn., London and Boston.

—— (1990), *An Economic History of the USSR*, 3rd edn., London.

NOVOSEL'TSEV, A. P. (1993), ' "Mir istorii" ili mif istorii', *Voprosy istorii* 1: 23–31.

ODINTSOV, M. I. (1994), 'Pis'ma i dialogi "Khrushchevskoi ottepeli"', *OA* 5: 55–64.

O'HEARN, D. (1980), 'The Consumer Second Economy: Size and Effects', *SS* 32: 218–34.

OLCOTT, M. B. (1985), 'Politics of Language Reform in Kazakhstan', in I. T. Kreindler (ed.), *Sociolinguistic Perspectives*, 183–204.

OLIVER, J. H. (1973), 'Turnover and "Family Circles" in Soviet Administration', *SR*, 32: 527–45.

OLIVER, L. K. (1981), 'Ukrainian Nationalism in the 1970s', dissertation, Indiana University.

ORR, R. (1973), 'Reflections on Totalitarianism . . .', *Political Studies* 21: 481–9.

PARK, A. (1994), 'Ethnicity and Independence: The Case of Estonia in Comparative Perspective', *Europe–Asia Studies*, 46: 69–87.

PARMING, T. (1977), 'Nationalism in Soviet Estonia since 1964', in G. W. Simmonds (ed.), *Nationalism*, 116–34.

—— (1980), 'Population Processes and the Nationality Issue in the Soviet Baltic', *SS* 32: 398–414.

PASTERNAK, B. (1958), *Doctor Zhivago*, trans. M. Hayward and M. Harari, London.

PECHENEV, V. (1991), *Gorbachev: k vershinam vlasti. Iz teoretiko-memuarnykh razmyshlenii*, Moscow.

PENIKIS, J. J. (1977), 'Latvian Nationalism: Preface to a Dissenting View', in G. W. Simmonds (ed.), *Nationalism*, 157–63.

PEREVEDENTSEV, V. (1993), *Migration in the Soviet Union before and after 1991* (Russia and the Successor States Briefing Service, 4, Aug.).

PESKOV, YU. A. (1992–3), 'Privileges in Party Organs' [1990], *Russian Politics and Law*, 31/1: 79–89.

PETERS, J.-U. (1990), 'Nationalistische Tendenzen innerhalb der Literatur der Perestroika,' in A. Kappeler (ed.), *Die Russen*, Cologne, 129–44.

PIETSCH, A.-J. (1987), 'Self-fulfilment through Work: Working Conditions in Soviet Factories', in H. G. Herlemann (ed.), *Quality of Life*, 117–31.

PITZER, J. S. and BANKOL, A. P. (1991), 'Recent GNP and Productivity Trends', *Soviet Economy* 7: 46–82.

PLIUSHCH, L. (1977), *Dans le carnaval de l'histoire: Mémoires.* trans. S. Vincent, Paris.

PONOMAREV, A. N. (1993), 'Nikita Khrushchev: Nachalo kar'ery: Dokumental'nyi ocherk', *Neizvestnaia Rossiia: XX vek*, fasc. iii, Moscow, 119–42.

POOL, J. (1978), 'Soviet Language Planning: Goals, Results, Options', in J. R. Azrael (ed.), *Soviet Nationality Policies*, 223–49.

POPOV, A. (1988), 'Kogda vybora net', *Ogonek*, 33: 18–19.

POPOV, V. P. (1992), 'Gosudarstvennyi terror v Sovetskoi Rossii', 1923–1953 gg.: istochniki i ikh interpretatsiia', *OA* 2: 20–31.
—— (1993), 'Neizvestnaia initsiativa Khrushcheva (o podgotovke ukaza 1948 g. o vyselenii krest'ian)', *OA* 2: 31–7.
PORTER, R. (1989), *Four Contemporary Russian Writers*, Oxford, New York, and Munich.
'Posledniaia "antipartiinaia" gruppa: Stenograficheskii otchet iun'skogo (1957 g.) plenuma TsK KPSS', *IA* 3/1993–.
POWELL, D. E. (1983), 'A Troubled Society', in J. Cracraft (ed.), *Soviet Union Today*, 317–29.
—— (1991), 'Aging and the Elderly,' in A. Jones, W. D. Connor, and D. E. Powell (eds.), *Soviet Social Problems*, 172–93.
RA'ANAN, U. (1990), 'The Russian Problem', in idem (ed.), *Soviet Empire*, 63–74.
—— (1990), (ed.), *The Soviet Empire: The Challenge of National and Democratic Movements*, Lexington, Mass. and Toronto.
RAKOWSKA-HARMSTONE, T. (1974), 'The Dialectics of Nationalism in the USSR', *Problems of Communism* 23/3: 1–22.
—— (1977), 'Nationalism in Central Asia since 1964', in G. W. Simmonds (ed.), *Nationalism*, 272–94.
RAPOPORT, YA. L. (1991), *The Doctors' Plot of 1953*, Cambridge, Mass.
RASPUTIN, V. (1990), *Izbrannye proizvedeniia v 2 tt.* ii, *Povesti. Ocherki*, Moscow.
RAUN, T. U. (1985), 'Language Development and Policy in Estonia', in I. T. Kreindler (ed.), *Sociolinguistic Perspectives*, 13–36.
REDDAWAY, P. (1972), (ed. and trans.), *Uncensored Russia: Protest and Dissent in the Soviet Union*, New York and Toronto.
—— (1975), 'The Development of Dissent and Opposition', in A. Brown and M. Kaser, *Soviet Union*, 121–56.
—— (1980), 'Policy Towards Dissent Since Khrushchev', in T. H. Rigby, A. Brown, and P. Reddaway (eds.), *Authority, Power and Policy*, 158–92.
—— (1993), 'Sovietology and Dissent: New Sources on Protest', *Radio Liberty Report*, 5: 12–16.
REMEIKIS, T. (1977), 'Political Developments in Lithuania During the Brezhnev Era', in G. W. Simmonds (ed.), *Nationalism*, 164–80.
—— (1980), *Opposition to Soviet Rule in Lithuania, 1945–1980*, Chicago.
RIGBY, T. H. (1968), *Communist Party Membership in the USSR, 1917–1967*, Princeton, NJ.
—— (1976), 'Politics in the Mono-organizational Society', in A. Janos (ed.) *Authoritarian Politics in Communist Europe*, Berkeley, Calif., 31–80.

RIGBY, T. H., BROWN, A., and REDDAWAY, P. (1980) (eds.), *Authority, Power and Policy in the USSR: Essays Dedicated to Leonard Schapiro*, London and Basingstoke.

RIORDAN, J. (1988), 'Soviet Youth: Pioneers of Change', *SS* 40: 556–72.

RO'I, YA (1984), 'The Task of Creating the New Soviet Man: Atheistic Propaganda in the Soviet Muslim Areas', *SS* 36: 26–44.

—— (1992), 'Nationalism in Central Asia in the Context of *glasnost'* and *perestroika*', in Z. Gitelman (ed.), *Politics of Nationality*, 50–76.

ROSSIANOV, K. O. (1994), 'Stalin as Lysenko's Editor: Reshaping Political Discourse in Soviet Science', *Russian history/Histoire russe*, 21: 49–64.

RUMER, B. (1989), 'Soviet Estimates of the Rate of Inflation', *SS* 41: 298–317.

RUTLAND, P. (1984), 'The Shchekino Method and the Struggle to Raise Labour Productivity in Soviet Industry', *SS* 36: 345–65.

—— (1990), 'Economic Management and Reform', in S. White, A. Pravda, and Z. Gitelman (eds.), *Developments in Soviet Politics*, 160–84.

RYWKIN, M. (1977), 'Religion, Modern Nationalism and Political Power in Soviet Central Asia', in I. Kamenetsky (ed.), *Nationalism and Human Rights*, 189–201.

—— (1982), *Moscow's Muslim Challenge: Soviet Central Asia*, Armonk, NY and London.

SAKHAROV, A. D. (1990) *Memoirs*, trans. R. Lourie, London.

SAKWA, R. (1993) (ed.) *Russian Politics and Society*, London and New York.

[SAVITSKY, V. M.] (1991–2), 'Fear: Confessions of a Well-known Legal Expert who has Criticized the Draft Law on the KGB', in *Soviet Law and Government* 30/2: 88–96.

SCAMMELL, M. (1984), *Solzhenitsyn: A Biography*, London.

SCHAPIRO, L. B. and GODSON, J. (1981) (eds.), *The Soviet Worker: Illusions and Realities*, London and Basingstoke.

SCHROEDER, G. E. (1991), 'The Soviet Economy on a Treadmill of *perestroika*', in H. D. Balzer (ed.), *Five Years*, 34–48.

SCHWARTZ, H. (1965), *The Soviet Economy since Stalin*, London.

SEEGER, M. (1981), 'Eye-witness to Failure', in L. B. Schapiro and J. Godson (eds.), *Soviet Worker*, 76–105.

SHANIN, T. (1990), foreword to T. Zaslavskaya, *The Second Socialist Revolution: An Alternative Soviet Strategy*, trans. S. M. Davies and I. Warren, London.

SHATZ, M. S. (1980), *Soviet Dissent in Historical Perspective*, New York.

SHLAPENTOKH, V. (1987), *Politics of Sociology in the Soviet Union*, Boulder, Colo. and London.

SHNEIDMAN, N. N. (1979), *Soviet Literature in the 1970s: Artistic Diversity and Ideological Conformity*, Toronto, Buffalo, NY, and London.

—— (1989), *Soviet Literature in the 1980s: Decade of Transition*, Toronto, Buffalo, NY, and London.

SHORISH, M. M. (1976), 'The Pedagogical, Linguistic and Logistical Problems of Teaching Russian to Soviet Central Asians', *SR* 35: 443–62.

SIEGL, E. (1991), 'Sowjetische Planer haben den Aralsee getötet', *Tages-Anzeiger* 9 Apr., Zurich.

SIMIS, K. M. (1982), *USSR: The Corrupt Society: The Secret World of Soviet Capitalism*, New York.

SIMMONDS, G. W. (1977) (ed.) *Nationalism in the USSR and Eastern Europe in the Era of Brezhnev and Kosygin*, Detroit.

SIMON, G. (1991) *Nationalism and Policy Toward the Nationalities in the Soviet Union: From Totalitarian Dictatorship to post-Stalinist Society*, trans. K. and O. Forster, Boulder, Colo. and Oxford.

—— (1993) and SIMON, N. (1993), *Verfall und Untergang des sowjetischen Imperiums*, Munich.

SMIRNOV, G. L. (1993), 'Malen'kie sekrety Bol'shogo doma. Vospominaniia o rabote v apparate TsK KPSS', *Neizvestnaia Rossiia: XX vek*, fasc. iii, Moscow, 361–82.

SMITH, G. A. E. (1987), 'Agriculture', in M. McCauley (ed.), *Khrushchev and Khrushchevism*, 95–117.

SOLCHANYK, R. (1985) 'Language Politics in the Ukraine', in I. T. Kreindler (ed.), *Sociolinguistic Perspectives*, 57–105.

SOLZHENITSYN, A. I. (1963), *One Day in the Life of Ivan Denisovich*, trans. M. Hayward and R. Hingley, New York.

—— (1973–5), *The Gulag Archipelago, 1918–1956: An Experiment in Literary Investigation*, trans. T. P. Whitney, 3 vols., New York.

—— *et al.* (1974) (eds.), *From Under the Rubble*, Boston.

SORLIN, P. (1964), *La société soviétique, 1917–1964*, Paris.

STARKOV, B. (1993), 'Sto dnei "Lubianskogo marshala" ', *Ist.* 4: 82–90.

STITES, R. (1992), *Russian Popular Culture: Entertainment and Society since 1900*, Cambridge.

STUART, R.C. (1979) 'Women in Soviet Rural Management', *SR* 38: 603–13.

TAAGEPERA, R. (1990), 'Who Assimilates Whom?', in D. A. Loeber *et al.* (eds.), *Regional Identity*, 137–50.

TAHERI, A. (1990), *Islam/URSS: La révolte de l'Islam en URSS*, trans. J. Lahena, Paris.

TARSCHYS, D. (1993), 'The Success of a Failure: Gorbachev's Alcohol Policy, 1985–1988', *Europe–Asia Studies*, 45: 7–25.

TATU, M. (1969), *Power in the Kremlin: From Khrushchev's Decline to Collective Leadership*, London.

TOLZ, V. (1993), 'The New Role of the Media and Public Opinion under Mikhail Gorbachev', *Journal of Communist Studies*, 9/1: 192–209.

TREML, V. G. (1982), 'Death from Alcohol Poisoning in the USSR', *SS* 34: 487–505.

—— (1985), *Alcohol in the Soviet Underground Economy* (Berkeley-Duke Occasional Papers on the Second Economy in the USSR, no. 5), Berkeley, Calif.

—— (1987), 'Alcohol Abuse and Quality of Life in the Soviet Union', in H. G. Herlemann (ed.), *Quality of Life*, 151–62.

—— (1991), 'Drinking and Alcohol Abuse in the USSR in the 1980s', in A. Jones, W. D. Connor, and D. E. Powell (eds.), *Soviet Social Problems*, 119–36.

TRUBIN, N. (1991), 'How it Was: Novocherkassk 1962', in *Soviet Law and Government*, 30/4: 21–7.

TsSU (Tsentral'noe statisticheskoe upravlenie SSSR), *Chislennost' i sostav naseleniia SSSR: po dannym Vsesoiuznoi perepisi naseleniia 1979 g.*, Moscow, 1984.

TsSU (Gosudarstvennyi komitet SSSR po statistike. Informatsionno-izdatel'skii tsentr), *Sotsial'noe razvitie SSSR 1989: statisticheskii sbornik*, Moscow, 1991.

TsSU, *Vsesoiuznaia perepis' naseleniia* [1970 g.] Moscow, 1973.

TUCKER, R. C. (1990), *Stalin in Power: The Revolution from Above, 1928–1941*, New York and London.

VAKSER, A. Z. (1992), 'Personal'nye dela chlenov KPSS kak istoricheskii istochnik', *OI* 5: 91–104.

VALOVOI, D. (1989), 'N. Khrushchev: "podvernut'sia litsom k ekonomike" ' repr. in Yu. V. Aksiutin (ed.), *Khrushchev*, 93–7.

VAN DEN BERG, G. R. (1983), 'The Soviet Union and the Death Penalty', *SS* 35: 154–74.

——(1987), 'Quantitative Aspects of the Stalinist System of Justice and Terror in the Soviet Union', in F. J. M. Feldbrugge (ed.), *Distinctiveness*, 97–141.

VAN GOUDOEVER, A. P. (1986), *The Limits of Destalinization in the Soviet Union*, trans. F. Hijkoop, London and Sydney.

VARDYS, V. S. (1991), *Sajūdis*: National Revolution in Lithuania', in J. A. Trapans (ed.), *Toward Independence: The Baltic Popular Movements*, Boulder, Colo., San Francisco, and Oxford, 11–23.

VERBITSKAIA, O. M. (1992), *Rossiiskoe krest'ianstvo ot Stalina k Khrushchevu*, Moscow.

VINOKUR, A. and OFER, G. (1987) 'Inequality of Earnings, Household

Income and Wealth in the 1970s', in J. R. Millar (ed.), *Politics, Work and Daily Life*, 171–202.

VLADIMIROV, L. (1989) (discussion remarks) in M. Tax Choldin and M. Friedberg (eds.), *The Red Pencil: Artists, Scholars and Censors in the USSR*, Boston and London, 15–20.

VLADIMOV, G. N. (pseud.: G. N. Volosevich) (1979), *Faithful Ruslan: The Story of a Guard Dog*, trans. M. Glenny, Harmondsworth.

VOINOVICH, V. N. (1976), *Zhizn' i neobychainye prikliucheniia soldata Ivana Chonkina*, 3rd edn., Paris.

VOLIN, L. (1970), *A Century of Russian Agriculture: From Alexander II to Khrushchev*, Cambridge, Mass.

VOLKOV, I. M. (1991), 'Zasukha, golod 1946–1947 gg.', *Istoriia SSSR*, 4: 3–19

VOLOBUEV, O. and KULESHOV, S. (1989), 'Tak i ne "prorvalsia" k narodu', in Yu. V. Aksiutin (ed.), *Khrushchev*, 161–70.

VORONKOV, V. (1993), 'Die Protestbewegung der "Sechziger"–Generation: der Widerstand gegen das sowjetische Regime 1956–1985', *Osteuropa*, 10: 939–48.

VOSKRESENSKY, L. (1989), 'Boltovnia—dama opasnaia' in Yu. V. Aksiutin (ed.), *Khrushchev*, 113–4.

VOSLENSKY, M. (1980), *La nomenklatura: Les privilégiés en URSS*, trans. C. Nugue. Paris.

—— (1989), *Sterbliche Götter: Die Lehrmeister der Nomenklatura*, Erlangen, Bonn, and Vienna.

WÄDEKIN, K.-E. (1973), *The Private Sector in Soviet Agriculture*, trans. K. Bush, ed. J. Karcz, Berkeley and London.

—— (1975), 'Income Distribution in Soviet Agriculture', *SS* 27: 3–26.

—— (1988), 'Agrarian Structures and Policies . . . ', in J. C. Brada and K.-E. Wädekin (eds.), *Socialist Agriculture*, 55–74.

WALKER, M. (1987), *The Waking Giant: The Soviet Union Under Gorbachev*, London and New York.

WEGREN, S. K. (1992), 'Dilemmas of Agrarian Reform in the Soviet Union', *SS* 44: 3–36.

WEINERMAN, E. (1993), 'The Polemics between Moscow and Central Asians on the Decline of Central Asia and Tsarist Russia's Role in the History of the Region', *Slavonic & East European Review*, 71: 428–81.

WHEATCROFT, S. G. (1990), 'More Light on the Scale of Repression and Excess Mortality in the Soviet Union in the 1930s', *SS* 42: 355–67.

WHITE, S. (1979), 'The USSR: Patterns of Autocracy and Industrialism', in A. Brown and J. Gray (eds.), *Political Culture and Political Change in Communist States*, 2nd edn., London and Basingstoke, 25–58.

WHITE, S. (1991), *Gorbachev and after*, 3rd edn., Cambridge.

—— and KRYSHTANOVSKAYA, O. (1993), 'Public Attitudes to the KGB: A Research Note', *Europe–Asia Studies* 45: 169–75.

—— GILL, G. and SLIDER, D. (1993), *The Politics of Transition: Shaping a Post-Soviet Future*, Cambridge and New York.

—— PRAVDA, A. and GITELMAN, Z. (eds.) (1990), *Developments in Soviet Politics*, London.

WILES, P. (J. D.) (1981), 'Wage and Income Policies', in L. B. Schapiro and J. Godson (eds.), *Soviet Worker*, 15–38.

—— (1982), 'Soviet Consumption and Investment Prices...' *SS* 34: 289–95.

WILLERTON, J. P. (1992), *Patronage and Politics in the USSR*, Cambridge.

—— (1993), 'Solzhenitsyn's Challenge to Russia and the West', *International Journal of Social Economics*, 20/5–7: 181–97.

WIXMAN, R. (1986), 'Applied Soviet Nationality Policy: A Suggested Rationale', in C. Lemercier-Quelquejay, G. Veinstein, and S. E. Wimbush (eds.), *Passé turco-tatar, présent soviétique: Études offerts à A. Bennigsen*, Louvain and Paris, 449–68.

WRIGHT, A. W. (1980), 'Soviet Economic Planning and Performance', in S. F. Cohen, A. Rabinowitch, and R. Sharlet (eds.), *Soviet Union Since Stalin*, 113–34.

YANOWITCH, M. (1963), 'The Soviet Income Revolution', *SR* 22: 683–97.

YESAKOV, V., IVANOVA, S., and LEVINA, E. (1991), 'Iz istorii bor'by s lysenkovshchinoi', *ICC* 4: 125–41, 7: 109–21.

ZEMSKOV, V. N. (1989), ' "Arkhipelag GULAG": Glazami pisatelia i statistika', *Argumenty i fakty*, 45: 6–7 (also replies to readers' enquiries in 39: 8; 40: 8).

—— (1990*a*), 'K voprosu o repatriatsii sovetskikh grazhdan, 1945–1951 gg', *Istoriia SSSR* 4: 26–41.

—— (1990*b*), 'Spetsposelentsy: Po dokumentatsii NKVD-MGB SSSR,' *Sotsiologicheskie issledovaniia*, 11: 3–17.

—— (1991*a*), 'Massovoe osvobozhdenie spetsposelentsev i ssyl'nykh', *Sotsiologicheskie issledovaniia*, 1: 5–26.

—— (1991*b*), 'Gulag: Istoriko-sotsiologicheskii aspekt', *Sotsiologicheskie issledovaniia*, 6: 10–27, 7: 3–16.

—— (1993), 'Prinuditel'nye migratsii iz Pribaltiki v 1940–1950-kh gg', *OA* 1: 4–19.

—— (1994), 'Sud'ba "kulatskoi ssylki" 1930–1954', *OI* 1: 118–47.

ZIMMERMAN, W. (1987), 'Mobilized Participation and the Nature of Soviet Dictatorship', in J. R. Millar (ed.), *Politics, Work and Daily Life*, 332–53.

Not included above are the following contributors of articles to *Radio Liberty Report*:

Ashwin, S. 33/1990; Brown, B. 16/1991; Bungs, D. 50/1990; Bush, K. 5, 15/1991; Critchlow, J. 9/1991; Golitsyn, G. S. 2/1993; Hosking, G. A. 41/1991; Mann, D. 3/1990; Marples, D. R. 7, 22/1991, 5/1993; Schneider, E. 50/1991; Tedstrom, J. 37/1990; Wishnevsky, J. 47/1990, 5/1991; Yasmann, V. 2/1993.

Glossary

Agitprop Agitation and Propaganda department (of CC of CPSU)

agrogorod 'agro-town', an urbanized settlement for country folk

apparatchik (pl.: *-iki*) member of the apparatus (*apparat*), Party functionary

apparatus senior officials of CPSU and/or government

artel' traditional co-operative work group

CC Central Committee (of CPSU)

'Centre', the all-Union Party and government organs, as opposed to those at provincial and especially union-republic level

CMEA Council for Mutual Economic Assistance ('Comecon')

CP Communist Party

CPSU Communist Party of the Soviet Union (to 1952: All-Union Communist Party (bolshevik))

CRA Council for Religious Affairs

dacha suburban cottage or hut, sometimes with vegetable allotment

delator 'denouncer', one who informs on others to the authorities

EDCS especially dangerous crimes against the state

General Secretary (of CPSU) the chief officer; from 1953 to 1966 known as 'First Secretary'

glasnost' 'openness', 'publicity' (falling short of Western concept of freedom of information)

glavk (pl.: *-ki*) chief department (of an economic ministry)

gorkom city committee (of CPSU)

Gosplan State Planning Commission (Committee)

Gulag more properly, GULag, Chief Administration of Corrective-Labour Camps, a department of the NKVD; loosely, the Soviet penal system under Stalin

ITK corrective-labour colony(ies)

ITL corrective-labour camp(s)

KGB Committee for State Security (*Komitet gosudarstvennoi bezopasnosti*), 1954–91; successor to Cheka, GPU, OGPU, NKVD, MVD, and MGB.

kolkhoz (pl.: *-zy*) collective farm

kolkhoznik, *-itsa* member of a *kolkhoz*

kompromat compromising materials

Komsomol Young Communist League (*Kommunisticheskii soiuz molodezhi*) *kulak* derogatory term for a well-to-do peasant

left-conservatives orthodox or hard-line communists (in Anglo-American usage, generally 'conservatives')

Lubianka popularly, secret police headquarters on Dzerzhinsky Square, Moscow

mestnichestvo localism; pursuit of local or regional interests at the expense of all-Union ones

militia regular (as distinct from state security) police

MTS machine-tractor station (to 1958)

nalevo on the side (literally, 'on the left')

NEP New Economic Policy (1921–8)

NKVD People's Commissariat of Internal Affairs (to 1946)

nomenklatura list of official positions to which holders are appointed by a Party organization at a certain level; more generally, persons in authority or enjoying privileges

obkom provincial committee (of CPSU)

oblast' province (chief administrative division of a republic)

perestroika 'restructuring'; a reform of the institutional order initiated from above

plenum full assembly (esp. of members of CC of CPSU)

Politburo Political Bureau of CC of CPSU, the Party's supreme decision-making body; from 1952 to 1966 known as Presidium

primary organization 'cell'; basic unit in organization of CPSU, generally operating at members' place of work

raikom district committee (of CPSU)

raion district (administrative division of a province or large city)

RSFSR Russian Soviet Federative Socialist Republic

samizdat literally, 'self-publishing'; writings produced and circulated without submission to the censorship

seksot secret collaborator (with security police)

SMERSH literally, 'death to spies'; Soviet counter-intelligence organization during World War II

sovkhoz (pl.: -zy) state farm

sovnarkhoz (SNKh) regional or republican council of national economy

SPH special psychiatric hospital (run by or on behalf of security police)

ssylka, vysylka forms of administrative exile

Supreme Soviet legislature at all-Union level, comprising two chambers, the Council of the Union and the Council of Nationalities; or its counterparts at union-republic level

tamizdat literally, 'published there', i.e. abroad

troika group of three; specifically, three-member board with special powers to sentence accused without following regular procedure

trudoden' (pl.: ***-dni***) work-day, a unit of account for calculating remuneration of ***kolkhozniki*** for their labour in the farm's 'socialist' sector

ukaz decree

union republic constituent state within the (federal) USSR

USW Union of Soviet Writers

VOOPIK All-Russian Society for the Preservation of Historical and Cultural Monuments

VUZ (pl.: VUZy) higher educational institution (***vysshee uchebnoe zavedenie***)

zek prison slang for prisoner (***zakliuchennyi***)

Index

OXFORD

MORE OXFORD PAPERBACKS

This book is just one of nearly 1000 Oxford Paperbacks currently in print. If you would like details of other Oxford Paperbacks, including titles in the World's Classics, Oxford Reference, Oxford Books, OPUS, Past Masters, Oxford Authors, and Oxford Shakespeare series, please write to:

UK and Europe: Oxford Paperbacks Publicity Manager, Arts and Reference Publicity Department, Oxford University Press, Walton Street, Oxford OX2 6DP.

Customers in UK and Europe will find Oxford Paperbacks available in all good bookshops. But in case of difficulty please send orders to the Cash-with-Order Department, Oxford University Press Distribution Services, Saxon Way West, Corby, Northants NN18 9ES. Tel: 01536 741519; Fax: 01536 746337. Please send a cheque for the total cost of the books, plus £1.75 postage and packing for orders under £20; £2.75 for orders over £20. Customers outside the UK should add 10% of the cost of the books for postage and packing.

USA: Oxford Paperbacks Marketing Manager, Oxford University Press, Inc., 200 Madison Avenue, New York, N.Y. 10016.

Canada: Trade Department, Oxford University Press, 70 Wynford Drive, Don Mills, Ontario M3C 1J9.

Australia: Trade Marketing Manager, Oxford University Press, G.P.O. Box 2784Y, Melbourne 3001, Victoria.

South Africa: Oxford University Press, P.O. Box 1141, Cape Town 8000.

HISTORY IN OXFORD PAPERBACKS
TUDOR ENGLAND
John Guy

Tudor England is a compelling account of political and religious developments from the advent of the Tudors in the 1460s to the death of Elizabeth I in 1603.

Following Henry VII's capture of the Crown at Bosworth in 1485, Tudor England witnessed far-reaching changes in government and the Reformation of the Church under Henry VIII, Edward VI, Mary, and Elizabeth; that story is enriched here with character studies of the monarchs and politicians that bring to life their personalities as well as their policies.

Authoritative, clearly argued, and crisply written, this comprehensive book will be indispensable to anyone interested in the Tudor Age.

'lucid, scholarly, remarkably accomplished . . . an excellent overview' *Sunday Times*

'the first comprehensive history of Tudor England for more than thirty years' Patrick Collinson, *Observer*

OPUS

General Editors: Walter Bodmer
Christopher Butler, Robert Evans,
John Skorupski

METROPOLIS

Emrys Jones

Past civilizations have always expressed themselves in great cities, immense in size, wealth, and in their contribution to human progress. We are still enthralled by ancient cities like Babylon, Rome, and Constantinople. Today, giant cities abound, but some are pre-eminent. As always, they represent the greatest achievements of different cultures. But increasingly, they have also been drawn into a world economic system as communications have improved.

Metropolis explores the idea of a class of supercities in the past and in the present, and in the western and developing worlds. It analyses the characteristics they share as well as those that make them unique; the effect of technology on their form and function; and the problems that come with size—congestion, poverty and inequality, squalor—that are sobering contrasts to the inherent glamour and attraction of great cities throughout time.

PHILOSOPHY IN OXFORD PAPERBACKS
THE GREAT PHILOSOPHERS
Bryan Magee

Beginning with the death of Socrates in 399, and following the story through the centuries to recent figures such as Bertrand Russell and Wittgenstein, Bryan Magee and fifteen contemporary writers and philosophers provide an accessible and exciting introduction to Western philosophy and its greatest thinkers.

Bryan Magee in conversation with:

A. J. Ayer	John Passmore
Michael Ayers	Anthony Quinton
Miles Burnyeat	John Searle
Frederick Copleston	Peter Singer
Hubert Dreyfus	J. P. Stern
Anthony Kenny	Geoffrey Warnock
Sidney Morgenbesser	Bernard Williams
Martha Nussbaum	

'Magee is to be congratulated . . . anyone who sees the programmes or reads the book will be left in no danger of believing philosophical thinking is unpractical and uninteresting.' Ronald Hayman, *Times Educational Supplement*

'one of the liveliest, fast-paced introductions to philosophy, ancient and modern that one could wish for' *Universe*